Wordsworth Crossword Companion

Wordsworth Crossword Companion

STEPHEN CURTIS

MARTIN MANSER

Wordsworth Reference

This edition published 2001 by Wordsworth Editions Limited
8B East Street, Ware, Hertfordshire SG12 9HJ

ISBN 1 84022 305 7

Typeset by Antony Gray

Printed and bound in Great Britain by
Mackays of Chatham plc, Chatham, Kent

INTRODUCTION

The solving of crossword puzzles is a kind of aerobics for the little grey cells. It puts one's mental suppleness to the test, it taxes the staying power of one's vocabulary, it usually produces no immediate reward, but completing the exercise gives a satisfying feeling of achievement. A fascination with words (their multiplicity, variety, oddity, their slippery ambiguity and their often chameleon-like ability to change) lurks within many people even if they have no reason to use words other than straightforwardly in their ordinary lives. In the same way, in the course of a lifetime, the average person accumulates a stock of miscellaneous knowledge that, while it may contribute to ensuring the continuity of culture, often has very little practical application in the everyday world. Who vitally needs to know who Daedalus was, which battles Napoleon won and lost, or what the chemical symbol is for tin? Yet both the word-fascination and the knowledge seem valuable to those who have them, and they need an outlet for them. Crosswords provide one, along with quizzes and other word games. The purpose of this book is to make crossword solving easier for people who are already hooked on this particular form of intellectual exercise and pastime, to try and stop them, perhaps, from getting stuck after filling in three or four answers. It also aims to provide an introduction for those who would like to try their hands at the game.

It would seem that almost as soon as language became at all sophisticated its users began to play about with it. Riddles are part of the folklore of most peoples; the earliest riddles in English are found in the earliest form of the language, Anglo-Saxon: 'Bold singers, they go in companies, call out loudly; they tread the timbered cliff and at times the eaves of men's houses. How do they call themselves?'[1] The Greek and Roman oracles were experts in exploiting ambiguity in language and sentence construction and in spreading disinformation: 'I say that you, O Pyrrhus, the Romans can defeat.' It is obvious too how much Shakespeare and the other Elizabethans enjoyed playing with words. The poet George Herbert, for example, is quite happy to use the pun or the 'sounds like' for religious purposes:

> . . . instantly I . . . perceived
> That to my broken heart He was I EASE YOU
> And to my whole is JESU.

---

1 The answer is rooks or jackdaws (from Anglo-Saxon riddles translated by Michael Alexander in *Voices*, vol. 1, edited by Geoffrey Summerfield, Penguin).

The modern cryptic crossword clue is the descendant, it might be said, of these ancient riddles, oracular utterances and puns, but, historically speaking, crosswords themselves are a very recent invention.

Though based on a British nineteenth-century children's game and introduced by a British-born emigrant, the modern crossword actually began in the United States. The first published crossword puzzle was included in a Sunday supplement to the *New York World* in December 1913; the first British crossword was printed in the *Sunday Express* in 1924. And, despite what has been said about their complex ancestry, the early crosswords were comparatively simple affairs. They, obviously, filled a need, however, growing rapidly in popularity and complexity on both sides of the Atlantic and in languages other than English. It is perhaps an indicator of how far crosswords had developed by the outbreak of the Second World War that one way in which the British government recruited code breakers for the top-secret Ultra project at Bletchley was to advertise for people interested in solving crossword puzzles.

Crosswords nowadays appear in almost every daily and weekly newspaper and magazine. There is considerable variety in format, in the way the basic box is arranged – crosswords in many countries, for example, do not use the black squares to blank out parts of the grid that we are familiar with in Britain, using a heavy line instead to mark divisions. Likewise, specialist publications contain specialist crosswords relating to the particular subject matter that their readers are interested in. The starting points for this book, however, are the standard types of crossword found in British newspapers, the quick crossword and the cryptic. A brief word about both these types is now in order.

Quick crosswords

The quick crossword is really a straightforward crossword. It does not usually play tricks on you. It asks you a straight question and, always assuming you know the answer, it is comparatively quick to solve. It requires some factual knowledge – the *Daily Telegraph* quick crossword for 27 April 1999, for example, asked for the name of the capital of Denmark and an old stringed instrument. Its stock in trade, however, is the synonym, a synonym being a word with the same meaning as another. That same *Daily Telegraph* quick crossword's first down clues are 'Sprightly (4)' and 'Loafer (5)' – the answers being 'spry' and 'idler' respectively, words with the same meaning as those in the clue, if we may be forgiven for stating the obvious. The fact that the same or a similar meaning is shared by more than one word is the basis of a very large percentage of crossword clues, including most cryptic ones. And since English, as a language, is particularly rich in synonyms, it is by no means always easy to find the right one.

Of course, that is not quite the end of the story. Even a one-word clue in a quick crossword can possess a certain degree of complexity owing to the fact that two or more words with very different meanings can be spelt in the same way and that the same word can function in two or more different parts of speech. A basic knowledge of grammar, or at least a basic awareness of grammatical possibilities, is useful to a crossword solver at any level. The same *Daily Telegraph* crossword referred to in the previous paragraph has a clue 'Mesh (3)'. The answer is the fairly obvious 'net' – 'mesh' here is a noun. But if 'net' had not fitted it would at least have been worth considering the possibility that the setter might have intended 'mesh' to be understood as a verb. It also has a clue 'Row (3)', however, and here the possibilities are much more extensive. Does the setter mean 'row – *noun* a file or series', 'row – *noun* a noise or quarrel' or 'row – *verb* propel a boat with oars'?

A considerable portion of this book is given over to providing help with clues of this kind. It gives the synonyms for common words, especially for common words that exist in more than one part of speech or have several different meanings (*see* **How to use this book** *below*). If, by mischance, you cannot find a synonym here that fits your requirements, then a thesaurus is your best bet. It also contains many lists of useful names – the names, for instance, of capital cities and musical instruments. For an overview of the lists it has on offer, please see pp. 16–18.

Cryptic crosswords

A cryptic crossword is one that is not straightforward. The clue is presented in the form of a code that the solver first has to crack before proceeding to find an answer. Where the setter of a quick crossword is asking simply 'what is the name of the capital of Denmark?' or 'what is another word for "sprightly"?', the setter of a cryptic crossword is asking you, the solver, to find out first what question he or she is asking and then work out a suitable response. So, for instance, if that *Daily Telegraph* clue 'Loafer (5)' had appeared in a cryptic crossword, instead of looking for a five-letter word meaning 'somebody who loafs about', one might be better employed in a bit of lateral thinking. Perhaps one should imagine the setter asking 'what might the word loafer mean if it didn't mean an idler (or a type of shoe)?' And a fruitful response might then be that it could refer to somebody who makes things into loaves, or somebody who simply makes loaves. Hence the cryptic answer to 'Loafer' (5) could be 'baker'.

If you can extend that type of lateral and punning thinking from single words to whole phrases and sentences, then you are well on the way to being able to cope with cryptic crossword clues. Here is a nice example from the *Bath Chronicle* crossword (8 July 2000) that illustrates how rereading an apparently straightforward statement leads you to the correct answer. 'Wine left on the boat (4)'. Don't think about tourists forgetting their duty-frees, break down the phrase in a different way and try and get the parts of it to relate to one another: 'wine = left on the boat' or 'wine left = on the boat'. Ask yourself whether 'left' means 'left behind' or 'left-hand' (in which case it might easily be abbreviated as L). Ask yourself too whether 'on the boat' is to be taken specifically or in a more general way as pointing you towards a nautical term. In this instance, there is a four-letter word with two meanings that cover everything in the clue: 'port' – a type of wine, and the left-hand side of a boat. But you have to free yourself from the ordinary flow and the ordinary grammar of the sentence to be able to realise that.

It has often been said that the basic principle for solving cryptic clues is to distrust the setter totally. This is sound advice, but the situation is slightly more complicated than that. The solver must be able to trust the setter to have provided within the clue all the elements necessary to arrive at a solution. A good crossword compiler, like a good detective novelist, provides all the necessary pointers to the right answer, but does not necessarily make them easy to spot and often throws in a few red herrings at the same time. So, after making that first act of faith, the solver has then to assume that a battle of wits is on. Though all the elements are there, they will not be presented in the right order or in accordance with normal logic, and the compiler will probably have been at pains to disguise his or her drift.

Compiling crossword clues is, if you like, a minor art form. A good cryptic clue should look like a piece of ordinary language, a statement, a question or, perhaps, a dictionary definition – though often a slightly comical one. It will usually be somewhat compressed – again like many dictionary definitions, ordinary telegraphese rather than ordinary prose – because the good compiler will not waste space and, more importantly, will not include anything that does not contribute to the final solution. It will, however, make reasonable sense as it stands. Take the clue 'Throw one's weight about on the sports field' (3,3,4).[2] To 'throw one's weight about' is a common English figurative phrase and it would be perfectly possible for a bossy person to throw his or her weight about anywhere. The reference to 'the sports field', however, suggests a context in which someone might 'throw their weight' literally rather than figuratively. Once one has taken that cue, once one has deciphered the clue as a coded reference to an athletic event ('on the sports field') that involves throwing a weight, it is quite easy to come up with the answer: 'put the shot'.

Clues and cues

The fact is that, as often as not, a clue of the cryptic kind contains a clue of the straightforward kind concealed within itself. It also frequently contains a cue to direct solvers as to how to use the rest of the coded message to arrive at the right answer. To take a fairly simple example, the *Daily Telegraph* compiler mentioned earlier asked straight out for the capital of Denmark. *Aquila*, a compiler for the *Independent* (5 May 1999), asks for another capital

2 Quoted in 'Linguistic Aspects of the Cryptic Crossword' by Steve Coffey, *English Today*, Vol. 14, No. 1, January 1998.

city in a more roundabout way: 'African capital, also known as Latin America initially' (6). The solver might toy with the idea that 'African capital' has something to do with money, but is likely to come back fairly quickly to the more likely assumption that 'African capital city' is the clue. He or she then has to endeavour to construct the name of one from the material *Aquila* provides. In this case 'initially' is the cue, the key word that tells the solver how to work with the material. As a cue 'initially' can have a double function (*see entry for* initial). In this instance, however, it prompts to place a decoded version of 'Latin America' (not straightforward LA, but L for Latin and US for America) *initially* (in the front position) and follow it with the usual abbreviation of 'also known as' to produce 'Lusaka', the capital of Zambia.

Here is another reasonably simple example from a *Radio Times* prize crossword (no. 28, July 2000): 'Il Duce replaced man of numbers (6)', which allows itself to be dissected systematically. If one were doing a sentence analysis on this clue, one would say that it consisted of three basic parts 'Il Duce' (subject), 'replaced' (verb) and 'man of numbers' (object). For crossword purposes, the corresponding three parts of the clue are the clue proper, the cue and the raw material, it is merely a question of deciding which is which. In this instance, the experienced crossword solver would know and even the inexperienced one might guess that 'replaced' is the cue. Verbs often, though by no means always, have that function. 'Replaced' is, in fact, a common anagram clue (*for* anagram *and* anagram cue *see below*). Since the answer has 6 letters, it is then not too difficult to decide that 'Il Duce' provides the raw material for the anagram. The clue proper then is 'man of numbers'. 'Man of numbers' could be interpreted in various ways, but if it is taken to mean a mathematician, the letters of 'Il Duce' will provide us with a highly plausible (and indeed the correct) answer: 'Euclid'.

The clue, cue and raw material principle will work for many clues. But nobody wants crossword solving to be too simple or formulaic. Here, for contrast, is a rather clever example of a red herring from *The Times* (30 April 1999): 'Suspect drops of water caused corrosion' (8). Like 'replace', 'suspect' is a common anagram cue. The setter perhaps hoped to send the solver off on a wild-goose chase after an anagram. In this case, however, though 'suspect' looks like an adjective describing drops of water, it is in fact a verb and the clue proper. If 'drops of water' are understood as a 'mist' and 'corrosion' as 'rust', when the two are put together we arrive at a straightforward synonym for 'suspect' (verb), namely 'mistrust'.

Anagrams

Anagrams occur in crosswords of all kinds. An anagram is a word whose letters can be rearranged to make another word. The five letters of 'teach' can be rearranged to make 'cheat', and the seven letters of 'gyrated' reorganised into 'tragedy'. More complicatedly, 'main ploy' is an anagram for 'Olympian', 'pound grew' for 'gunpowder' and 'World Cup team' for 'talcum powder'.[3]

In quick crosswords an anagram is usually labelled as such. The *Daily Telegraph* crossword which we have extensively quarried already contains the clue 'La Paz (anag.) (5)' (the answer is 'plaza'). Cryptic compilers are seldom so helpful and generally use the clue, cue and material procedure. One then has to locate precisely those words which are to be rearranged, and solving the anagram may only provide a part of the answer. The *Daily Telegraph*'s main crossword for the same day contains the clue 'Succeed, KO team maybe you, say, had been included'. The answer 'make out' (= succeed) is mainly an anagram of 'KO team' – but it needs an additional 'u' (signalled by 'you, say,') to complete it.

Anagram cues

The word in the clue just quoted which tells the solver to look out for an anagram is 'maybe'. 'Maybe', therefore, is an anagram cue. Similarly words such as 'perhaps' or 'possibly' – words that suggest there is a doubt about something – frequently have this function. But the same job can be done by many other words that can be fitted even more naturally and inconspicuously into the phraseology of the clue. Verbs that denote changing, breaking, making and remaking, or reordering ('alter', 'arrange', 'order', 'shatter', 'smash', 'upset', etc.), or adverbs and adverbial phrases suggesting that things are out of order ('crazily', 'madly', 'in a mess', 'untidily' and, especially, 'out', etc.) are very often used for this purpose. In the clue 'Pupils grouped together and tortured master' (6) (*The Times*, 26 April 1999), the anagram cue is 'tortured' and the answer is an anagram of 'master', namely 'stream'. The Everyman crossword in *The Observer* of 18 April 1999 contained the clue 'The Bovril's drunk eating a biscuit' – a particularly clever one in which the main clue is 'biscuit', the anagram cue is 'drunk' and the answer is an anagram of 'The Bovril' incorporating the additional letter A ('eating a') – Bath Oliver. The *Radio Times* prize crossword no. 28 (July 2000) contains an even less conspicuous cue in the word 'made': 'The train seats are made fireproof (4-9)' – answer 'heat-resistant'.

There are too many words that signal anagrams for them all to be listed here individually (and compilers are continually discovering new ones!), but a great many are listed in the body of the book. They are indicated by the formula '*cryptic* anagram cue'. When you find a word marked in this way in a clue, there is a better than even chance that an anagram is part of the solution.

---

3   Also in Coffey, *English Today*.

Other cryptic devices

Five other techniques are used so commonly by crossword compilers as to merit mentioning here. One is word reversal. The letters of a word in the clue may appear in the answer in reverse order, as perhaps in 'Mad dog swears back' (6), answer 'goddam'. Just as there are anagram cues, there are reversal cues: adverbs such as 'back' in across clues and 'up' in down clues, and verbs that denote backward ('return', 'revert') or upward movement ('raise', 'rise'). Clue 10 across in the *Guardian* crossword of 8 May 1999 was 'A tramp returning from Oklahoma' – answer 'Tulsa'.

Another is the placing of a word or a set of letters inside another word. The cues for this are often either verbs of going or putting inside, verbs of containing, verbs of surrounding, or verbs of eating (see the 'Bath Oliver' clue above). *The Times* crossword of 27 April 1999 had the clue 'Missile soldiers installed in new depot (7)', which contains two different cues – 'new', an anagram cue, and 'installed', an insertion cue. Placing an abbreviation for soldiers (OR = other ranks) inside anagram of 'depot', produces the correct answer 'torpedo'.

A third is to direct the solver to a particular letter or letters in a word in the clue – usually the first, last or middle letter or letters. The cues for this are the words you might expect: 'first', 'initial', 'start', 'last', 'end', 'middle', 'centre' or 'heart'. *The Times* crossword of 13 May 1999 provides a fairly standard example: 'Labourer, having lost heart, is blue'. A labourer is a 'navvy' in this instance. Take away the central letter of 'navvy' ('lost heart') and the answer is 'navy' (blue).

A fourth is to make use of the fact that although some words in English may be spelt differently they are actually pronounced the same. You need a word that sounds the same as another either to understand the clue or to construct the answer. The cues for this procedure are words like 'we hear', 'say', 'sound' or, as in this clue from the *Independent* (5 May 1999), 'report', 'reported' or 'reportedly': 'Colonel's reported cases' (9). Here the cue 'reported' prompts you to look for a word that sounds like 'colonel's', in this case 'kernels' and the answer is 'nutshells'.

Finally, there are clues which already contain the answer, lurking unobtrusively in their midst. These 'hidden word' clues are generally signalled by words such as 'hide', 'conceal', 'hold' or 'contain' or, as in this instance from the *Guardian* (29 January 2000) simply 'from': 'Architectural style from Greenlan*d or Ic*eland (5)' = 'doric'.

Where words have a cueing function of the kind referred to in this section, that function is indicated in a separate section of the entry labelled *cryptic* and an explanation and example are often given.

How to use this book

This book is intended to provide basic assistance to anyone who needs help in solving a crossword clue. In the first instance it offers a range of words of equivalent meaning, synonyms, for many common terms. Since almost all crossword clues come with an indication of the number of the letters forming the answer, the basic principle of organisation in the book is based on the number of letters in any given word. This applies not only to all lists of synonyms, but to the majority of longer lists of things. For greater clarity, where words have several different functions and different meanings, the synonyms are divided up in accordance with the different senses, so that a typical entry looks like this:

> **game** I *n* 1 (4) play; (5) sport; (7) pastime; (9) amusement; (10) recreation; 2 (5) event, match, round; (6) partie; (7) contest; 3 animals hunted for sport; II *adj* 1 (5) eager, ready; (6) willing; (5) **brave**, plucky; (8) spirited.

'Game' is used as both a noun and an adjective. Roman numerals in bold type (**I**, **II**, etc.) separate off the different parts of speech. Arabic numerals in bold (**1**, **2**, **3**) separate off the various senses in which a word may be used in a particular part of speech. This subdivision is not too hard and fast, for, as noted above, crosswords depend on the ability of words to possess different meanings and operate as different parts of speech. For reasons of space, it is not always possible to give all the possible synonyms at every entry. When a term is printed in bold (like **brave** above), the intention is to cross-refer to another entry where further synonyms or further information may be found. If the word 'game' is used as or in a clue, the answer will quite often be the name of a particular game. The main entry only contains synonyms for the generic term 'game'. The names of specific games are given in a list following the main entry.

The book also notes words that are frequently used as cryptic 'cues'. Where a word is often used cryptically, its cryptic function is indicated in a separate subsection headed by a Roman numeral at the end of the main entry. Where the reader encounters the notes *cryptic* anagram cue or *cryptic* hidden word cue, he or she is directed to the relevant section of the Introduction (**Anagram cues** or **Other cryptic devices**).

Further, the book contains notes and lists featuring general-knowledge information. The name of, for instance, a Greek or Roman god or a Shakespearean character may be asked for or alluded to in a clue. What counts as general cultural property that a solver can reasonably be expected to possess changes as time goes on, and we may be felt to err on the conservative side in what we offer here, but it reflects what we have found one is usually expected to know about when tackling mainstream crosswords.

Example clues

Other than those specifically labelled as having been taken from published crosswords, all the example clues have been made up by the compilers. Any coincidence with other published clues is purely coincidental. The compilers apologize in advance for any deficiencies in the clues or in any other aspect of this book.

Final warning

It is perhaps worth noting that the English language never stands still. Not only are new words being added all the time, but the form and use of existing ones may undergo subtle alteration. Such things as spelling and hyphenation are not entirely standard. The same term may be spelt as one solid word, two separate words or two elements joined by a hyphen. This may occasionally have a bearing on the letter-count given for cues. Likewise, most modern British dictionaries show words such as 'realize' or 'recognize' spelt with a 'z', giving the more traditional 's' spelling only as a variant. For obvious reasons the 's' spelling predominates in crosswords and is shown in the entries in this book, but the reader is warned of the possible appearance of a 'z'.

Acknowledgements

The compilers would like to thank Tom Curtis and Sally Collins for assistance in the preparation of the lists given in this book. They would also like, in a general way, to show their appreciation for the efforts of crossword compilers everywhere without whose deviousness, fiendish ingenuity, terrible sense of humour, and, last but not least, extraordinary skill with words, this book would not be necessary.

STEPHEN CURTIS
MARTIN MANSER

BOOKS REFERRED TO IN COMPILING THIS VOLUME

Brewer's Dictionary of Phrase and Fable (Cassell)
Chambers Biographical Dictionary
Chambers Combined Dictionary Thesaurus
Chambers Word File (Prebble & Griffiths)
Chambers Word Lists (Prebble)
Collins Crossword Companion (Howard-Williams)
Collins English Dictionary
New Oxford Dictionary of English
Oxford Crossword Dictionary
Random House Word Menu (Glazier)
Sunday Express Wordmaster Dictionary (Coleman: Dobbs)

ABBREVIATIONS

A	Austria, Austrian	Jap.	Japan, Japanese
abbrev	abbreviation	*lit.*	literature
adj	adjective	Med.	Mediterranean
adv	adverb	Mex.	Mexico, Mexican
Afr.	Africa, African	*myth*	mythology
Arg.	Argentina, Argentinian	*n*	noun
astrol.	astrology	NL	Netherlands (Dutch, Flemish)
astron.	astronomy		
Aus.	Australia, Australian	Pak.	Pakistan, Pakistani
Belg.	Belgian, Belgium	Pers.	Persian
Braz.	Brazil, Brazilian	Pol.	Poland, Polish
Can.	Canada, Canadian	Port.	Portugal, Portuguese
Ch.	China, Chinese	*prep*	preposition
Cz.	Czech (Republic)	*rel.*	religion, religious
Dan.	Danish	Rom.	Roman
Eng.	England, English	Roma.	Romania, Romanian
esp.	especially	Russ.	Russia, Russian
Eur.	Europe	SA	South Africa, South African
fict.	fiction, fictional		
Finn.	Finnish, Finland	Scot.	Scotland, Scottish
Fr.	France, French	UK	United Kingdom (English, Scottish, Welsh, or Northern Irish)
geog.	geography, geographic		
Ger.	Germany, German		
Gk	Greek		
hist.	history, historical	Ukr.	Ukraine
Hung.	Hungary, Hungarian	US	United States, American
Ind.	India, Indian	*v*	verb

LISTS

A

Abbeys
Accents
Actors
Actresses
Admirals
Aircraft
Airlines
Airports
Alloys
Alphabet (Greek)
Alphabet (Hebrew)
Alphabet (Phonetic)
American Indians
Andersen stories
Angels
Animals
Anniversaries
Antelopes
Apes
Apocrypha
Apostles
Architects
Armour
Art forms
Assemblies (animals)
Austen novels
Awards

B

Ballets
Ballet dancers
Ballet movements
Ball games
Baseball teams
Bats
Battles
Bears
Bible (Books of)
Birds
Birthstones
Board games
Boats
Bones
Bottle sizes
Boxers
Boys' names
Brontë novels
Butterflies

C

Canterbury Tales
Cantons (Swiss)
Capitals
Cars (makes)
Card games
Carriages
Carroll characters
Cases (grammar)
Cats
Cathedrals
Cattle
Cheeses
Choreographers
Church architecture
Clergy
Clouds
Clubs (golf)
Coins
Colleges
Colours
Comics (children's)
Composers
Constellations
Cosmetics
Counties
Currencies

D

Dances
Deer
Deserts
Detectives
Diamonds
Diarists
Dickens (novels)
Dickens (characters)
Dinosaurs
Diseases (humans)
Diseases (animals)
Dishes
Doctors
Dogs
Drinks
Drugs (medical)
Drugs (narcotic)
Ducks
Dwarfs (the Seven)

E

Ear (parts)
Elements (chemical)
Emperors (Roman)
Emperors (other)
Empresses
Entertainers
Entertainments
Essayists
Explorers (land)
Explorers (sea)
Explosives
Eye (parts)
Eye (conditions)

F

Fabrics
Fabulous creatures

Female animals
Fielding positions
Fish
Flowers
Football positions
Football teams (UK)
Football teams
  (Europe)
Football teams
  (USA)
Fortifications
Fruit
Fuels
Fur (types)
Furniture

G

Galleries (art)
Games
Game animals
Gangsters
Gases
Geese (*at* **goose**)
Gems
Generals
Geological eras
Ghosts
Giants
Gilbert and Sullivan
  operas
Gilbert and Sullivan
  characters
Girls' names
Gods (Greek, Roman,
  etc)
Goddesses (Greek,
  Roman, etc)
Golf courses
Golfers
Grasses
Gulfs
Guns

H

Hardy novels
Harness (parts)
Headgear
Heraldic colours
Heraldic terms
Herbs
Hills
Historians
Homes of animals
Horses

I J K L

Impressionist painters
Insects
Inventors
Islands (British)
Islands (world)
Jewellery
Kings (Bible)
Kings of England
Kings of Scotland
Knighthood (orders
  of)
Knots
Lakes (Britain &
  Ireland)
Lakes (world)
Languages
Liqueurs
Lizards
Lochs
Lovers

M N

Machines
Magazines
Male animals
Markets of London
Marsupials
Martial arts
Measures
Meats

Medals
Metals
Metres
Minerals
Monastic orders
Monkeys
Moons
Mountains
Mountain ranges
Musicals
Musical instruments
Musical terms
Musical works
Noble titles
Novelists
Nuts

O P

Oratorios
Paints
Painters
Parasites
Parliaments
Patron saints
Paul's Epistles
Philosophers
Plagues of Egypt (10)
Planets
Plants
Playwrights
Poets
Poisons
Pop groups
Popes
Ports
Potter (Beatrix) books
Presidents of the USA
Prime ministers
Prophets
Provinces of Canada
Public schools
Punctuation marks

R

Racecourses
Racing circuits
Ranks (Army)
Ranks (Royal Navy)
Ranks (RAF)
Reference works
Regions of Scotland
Relations
Religions
Reptiles
Rivers
Rocks
Rodents
Rooms
Round Table
    (Knights of)
Royal dynasties
Royal titles

S

Sails

Sailing ships
Sailors
Sauces
Sculptors
Seas
Shakespeare plays
Shakespeare characters
Shapes
Shaw plays
Shellfish
Ships
Shrubs
Singers (classical)
Singers (popular)
Snakes
Spices
Spirits
Sports

T

Teas
Tempi

Test match venues
Theatres
Tools
Trees

U V W Z

Underwear
Unions
Universities
Vegetables
Vehicles
Vestments
Volcanoes
Waterfalls
Weapons
Weather
Weights
Winds
Wines
Wodehouse characters
Writers
Zodiac

A

A *abbrev* advanced, alto, America, ampere, answer, argon, atomic, Austria (international vehicle registration), key (music), note (music).

a *cryptic* **French** un, une; **German** ein, eine, einer; **Italian** un, una, uno

Aaron *Bible* the brother of **Moses**, and the first high priest of the Israelites, said to have had a particularly long beard and a rod that on one occasion turned into a serpent and, on another, flowered.

Aaron's beard *and* **Aaron's rod** types of plant.

AB *abbrev* able seaman.

aback I take aback (7) stagger; (8) surprise; (10) disconcert; **II** *cryptic* reverse the order of the letters in the word referred to, as in: 'Electric current flows when mother taken aback by French father' (6) = ampere.

abandon I *v* **1** (4) drop, dump, jilt, quit; (5) ditch, leave, scrap; (6) desert, maroon, strand; (7) forsake; **2** (5) waive, yield; (6) forego, recant, resign; (8) renounce; (10) relinquish; (2 words) give up; **II** *n* (6) excess; (7) licence; (10) debauchery, indulgence; (11) dissipation.

abbey *n* (6) church, friary, priory; (7) minster; (9) monastery.

> ### FAMOUS ABBEYS IN BRITAIN
> Bath, Battle, Buckfast, Fountains, Furness, Glastonbury, Kirkstall, Melrose, Netley, Romsey, Rievaulx, Tewkesbury, Tintern, Westminster

abbreviate *v* (3) cut; (4) clip, trim; (6) digest, précis, lessen, reduce; (7) abridge, curtail, shorten; (8) abstract, compress, condense, truncate.

Abel *Bible* Adam's second son, 'a keeper of sheep', victim of the first murder at the hands of his brother **Cain**.

abet *v* **I** (3) aid; (4) back, help; (5) serve; (6) assist, foster, hasten; (7) advance, forward, further, promote, support; (9) encourage; (10) facilitate; **II** *cryptic* punning reference to 'a bet'.

able *adj* (4) good; (5) adept, handy; (6) adroit, clever, expert, gifted; (7) capable, skilful, skilled; (8) talented; (9) competent, effective, efficient; (10) proficient; (12) accomplished.

abnormal *adj* (3) odd, rum; (4) rare; (5) eerie, queer, weird; (6) chance, creepy; (7) bizarre, deviant, erratic, offbeat, uncanny, unusual; (8) aberrant, atypical, freakish, peculiar, uncommon; (9) anomalous, eccentric, irregular, unnatural; (10) outlandish; (12) supernatural; (13) extraordinary.

aboard *cryptic* place the letters S . . . S (as in: SS = steamship) around another word to create the answer, as in: 'Ship goes ahead when eleven come aboard' (6) = steams (eleven = team).

abolish *v* (3) end; (4) stop; (5) annul; (6) cancel, repeal, revoke; (7) destroy, nullify, rescind; (8) overturn; (9) eliminate, eradicate, overthrow, terminate; (2+ words) do away with, get rid of, put an end to, stamp out.

abominable *adj* (3) bad; (4) foul, mean, ugly, vile; (5) dirty, nasty; (6) filthy, odious; (7) obscene, vicious; (8) horrible; (9) loathsome, obnoxious, offensive, repellent, repugnant, repulsive, revolting; (10) disgusting, nauseating, unpleasant; (12) disagreeable; (13) objectionable.

abominable snowman *n* (4) yeti; (7) bigfoot.

about I *prep* (2) on, re; (9) regarding; (10) concerning, respecting; **II** *adv & prep* (4) near; (5) close; (6) almost, around, beside, nearly; (7) roughly; (11) surrounding; (13) approximately; **III** *cryptic* **1** use letters C or CA (= circa), or RE (re = with respect to); **2** reverse the order of the letters of a word in the clue or answer, as in: 'Thousand policemen going about to find one famous alien' (5) = Spock (thousand = K); **3** place the letters of one part of the answer around those of another, as in: 'Midday? It's about time I had an idea' (6) = notion (time = T).

Abraham *Bible* the patriarch who was the founder of the Jewish nation, originally from the city of Ur (of the Chaldees), husband of Sarah and father of **Isaac** (whom he was willing to sacrifice at God's command).

Absalom *Bible* a son of King **David** who rebelled against his father, was defeated in battle, and, escaping on a mule, got his head or his hair entangled in the boughs of an oak tree, where he was killed, against David's orders, by Joab.

absolute *adj* **1** (4) full; (5) sheer, total, utter, whole; (6) entire; (7) perfect; (8) complete, outright, thorough; (9) downright; (10) consummate; (11) unqualified; (13) unconditional; **2** (7) supreme; (8) despotic; (9) unlimited; (10) tyrannical; (12) totalitarian, unrestricted.

absorb *v* **1** (4) blot, hold, soak; (6) devour, engulf, imbibe, ingest, retain; (10) assimilate, understand; (2 words) drink in, take in, soak up; **2** (4) fill, grip; (5) rivet; (6) occupy; (7) engross, enthral; (8)intrigue; (9) fascinate, preoccupy, spellbind.

abstract **I** *adj* (7) complex, general; (8) abstruse; (10) conceptual, idealistic; (11) theoretical; (12) hypothetical, metaphysical; **II** *n* (6) digest, précis, résumé; (7) epitome, outline, summary; (8) synopsis; **III** *v* **1** (6) detach, remove; (7) extract; (8) separate, withdraw; (10) dissociate; **2** (6) précis; (7) outline; (8) condense; (9) summarise (*or* summarize).

abuse **I** *v & n* **1** (4) harm, hurt; (5) waste, wrong; (6) damage, misuse; (8) travesty; **2** (5) libel, smear; (6) insult; (7) slander; **II** *v* **1** (5) wrong; (6) ill-use, molest; (7) corrupt, distort, exploit, pervert, oppress; (8) ill-treat, misapply, maltreat, mistreat,

squander; (14) misappropriate; **2** (5) scold, swear; (6) defame, malign, revile, vilify; (7) upbraid; (8) badmouth; (9) disparage; (2 words) slag off; **III** *n* **1** (11) molestation; (12) maltreatment, mistreatment; **2** (6) tirade; (7) cursing, offence; (8) swearing; (10) defamation; (13) disparagement; **IV** **abuse, abused,** etc *cryptic* ANAGRAM CUE.

abusive *adj* **1** (4) rude (5) cruel; (7) hurtful; (8) scathing; (9) injurious, insulting, offensive; (10) defamatory, derogatory, pejorative; **2** (5) wrong; (7) harmful; (12) exploitative; (13) inappropriate.

abyss *n* (3) pit; (4) gulf, hole, void; (5) chasm, gorge; (6) crater, depths.

AC *abbrev* account (bill), across, actinium, alternating current.

accent *n* (4) tone; (5) twang; (6) brogue, stress; (8) emphasis; (10) inflection; (11) enunciation; (13) pronunciation.

ACCENTS ON LETTERS

(5) acute (´), breve (˘), grave (`), tilde
(~); (6) macron (¯), umlaut (¨);
(7) cedilla (ç); (9) diaeresis (¨);
(10) circumflex (^).

---

accept **I** *v* **1** (4) gain, take; (5) adopt; (7) acquire, receive, welcome; (9) undertake; **2** (5) admit, allow, agree; (7) approve, consent; (9) recognise (*or* recognize); (11) acknowledge; **3** (4) bear; (5) stand; (8) tolerate; (2+ words) put up with; **II** *cryptic* one word has a letter, letters, or another word inserted into it, as in: 'Typist, having deleted letter, accepts criticism and vows total silence' (8) = trappist (criticism = rap).

acceptable *adj* (2) OK; (4) fine, so-so; (7) correct, welcome; (8) adequate, passable, pleasant, suitable; (9) tolerable; (10) admissible, gratifying; (12) satisfactory.

account **I** *n* **1** (3) tab; (4) bill; (5) score, tally; (7) invoice; (9) reckoning, statement; **2** (4) tale; (5) **story**; (6) report; (7) write-up; (9) narrative; (11) description; **II** *v* (4) deem; (5) think; (6) regard; (8) consider; **III** **account for 1** (6) answer; (7)

explain, justify; **2** (4) kill; (7) destroy; (2+ words) put paid to; **IV** *cryptic* letters AC.

Acheron *Gk myth* one of the rivers of the **Underworld** across which **Charon** ferried the souls of the dead.

achieve *v* (2) do; (3) win; (4) earn, gain; (5) reach; (6) attain, effect, finish, fulfil, obtain; (7) acquire, execute, perform, realise (*or* realize), succeed; (8) complete, dispatch, finalise (*or* finalize); (9) discharge, implement; (10) accomplish; (2 words) bring about, carry out.

achievement *n* (4) deed, feat; (8) dispatch; (9) discharge, execution; (10) attainment, completion, fulfilment; (11) performance; (14) accomplishment.

Achilles *Gk myth & lit.* the Greeks' great hero and chief warrior in the war against Troy. The son of Thetis, he was said to have been made invulnerable by being dipped in the waters of the river Styx by his mother. As she held him by his heel to do this, he remained vulnerable in that part. His followers were the Myrmidons, his friend/lover was Patroclus, he killed the Trojan hero **Hector**, and was in turn killed by Hector's brother **Paris** with an arrow in the heel.

act I *n* **1** (4) deed, feat, move, step; (5) doing; (6) action, stroke; (7) exploit; (9) execution, manoeuvre; (10) enterprise, operation; (11) undertaking; **2** (4) sham, show; (5) front; (8) feigning, pretence; (13) dissimulation; **3** (4) item, turn; (6) shtick; (7) routine; (11) performance; **4** (3) law; (4) bill; (5) edict, order; (6) decree; (7) measure, statute; **II** *v* **1** (2) do; (4) work; (6) behave; (7) operate, perform; (8) function; **2** (4) play; (5) enact, stage; (7) portray; (9) represent; **3** (4) sham; (5) feign; (7) pretend.

Actaeon *Gk myth* a huntsman who happened upon the goddess Artemis (Diana) bathing in a river. He spied on her, and for his temerity was changed into a stag and hunted to death by his own hounds.

action *n* **1** *see* **act I 1**; **2** (4) life, work; (6) energy, vigour; (8) activity, exertion; (10) excitement; **3** (5) fight, clash; (6) battle,

combat; (7) warfare; (8) conflict, fighting, skirmish; **4** (4) case, suit; (7) lawsuit; (10) litigation; **5** (5) works; (8) workings; (9) mechanism.

active *adj* **1** (4) busy; (5) agile; (6) lively, nimble; (7) running, working; (8) animated, diligent, vigorous; (9)energetic; (11) industrious; **2** (7) devoted, engaged; (8) involved, militant; (9) committed; (12) enthusiastic.2

activity *n* **1** (6) action, bustle, hustle, motion; (8) industry, movement; (9) commotion; (10) liveliness; **2** (3) job; (4) task, work; (5) hobby; (6) scheme; (7) pastime, project, venture; (8) interest; (10) occupation; (11) undertaking.

actor *n* (3) ham; (4) lead; (5) extra; (6) mummer, player; (7) artiste; (8) thespian; (9) principal; (2 words) leading lady, leading man.

FAMOUS ACTORS

see also **actress**

(3) Eve (Trevor), Fox (Edward/James/Michael J.), Hay (Will), Lee (Bruce/Christopher), Lom (Herbert), Mix (Tom), Ray (Aldo), Rix (Brian), Sim (Alastair).

(4) Alda (Alan), Caan (James), Cobb (Lee J.), Cole (George), Dean (James),Dunn (Clive), Ford (Glenn/Harrison), Holm (Ian), Hope (Bob), Hurt (John), Kaye (Danny), Keel (Howard), Ladd (Alan), Lowe (Arthur), Marx (Chico/Groucho/Harpo), More (Kenneth), Muni (Paul), Peck (Gregory), Penn (Sean), Raft (George), Reed (Oliver), Sher (Antony), Soul (David), Thaw (John), Todd (Richard), Torn (Rip), Tree (Herbert Beerbohm), West (Sam/Timothy).

(5) Baker (Colin/Stanley/Tom), Bates (Alan), Bolam (James), Caine (Michael), Clift (Montgomery), Conti (Tom), Cosby (Bill), Cross (Ben), Dance (Charles), Donat (Robert), Finch (Peter), Flynn

list continued over

(Errol), Fonda (Henry/Peter), Grant (Cary), Hardy (Robert), Irons (Jeremy), Kline (Kevin), Lorre (Peter), Mason (James), Mills (John), Moore (Roger), Nimoy (Leonard), Nolte (Nick), Power (Tyrone), Quinn (Anthony), Segal (George), Stamp (Terence), Topol, Wayne (John).

(6) Bannen (Ian), Beatty (Warren), Bogart (Humphrey), Brando (Marlon), Briers (Richard), Burton (Richard), Cagney (James), Callow (Simon), Chaney (Lon), Cleese (John), Coburn (James), Cotton (Joseph), Cruise (Tom), Curtis (Tony), De Niro (Robert), De Vito (Danny), Fields (W.C.), Gambon (Michael), Harris (Richard), Havers (Nigel), Heston (Charlton), Hudson (Rock), Hunter (Tab), Irving (Henry), Jacobi (Derek), Keaton (Buster), Laurel (Stan), Lemmon (Jack), Lugosi (Bela), MacNee (Patrick), Malden (Karl), Mature (Victor), Newman (Paul), O'Toole (Peter), Pacino (Al), Quayle (Anthony), Reagan (Ronald), Rogers (Roy/Will), Rooney (Mickey), Sallis (Peter), Sharif (Omar), Sinden (Donald), Suchet (David), Swayze (Patrick), Voight (John), Welles (Orson), Wolfit (Donald).

(7) Ackland (Joss), Astaire (Fred), Blakely (Colin), Blessed (Brian), Bogarde (Dirk), Branagh (Kenneth), Bridges (Beau/Jeff/Lloyd), Bronson (Charles), Brynner (Yul), Burbage (Richard), Chaplin (Charlie), Connery (Sean), Cushing (Peter), Douglas (Kirk/Michael), Garrick (David), Gielgud (John), Gleason (Jackie), Granger (Stewart), Hawkins (Jack), Hopkins (Anthony), Hoffman (Dustin), Hordern (Michael), Hoskins (Bob), McCowen (Alec), McQueen (Steve), Milland (Ray), Nettles (John), Olivier (Laurence), Perkins (Anthony), Pertwee (Bill/John), Poitier (Sidney), Redford (Robert), Robards (Jason), Sellers

(Peter), Shatner (William), Steiger (Rod), Stewart (James), Ustinov (Peter).

(8) Basehart (Richard), Dreyfuss (Richard), Eastwood (Clint), Guinness (Alec), Harrison (Rex), Laughton (Charles), Redgrave (Corin/Michael), Stallone (Sylvester), Woodward (Edward).

(9) Barrymore (John/Lionel), Fairbanks (Douglas), Lancaster (Burt), Nicholson (Jack), Pleasence (Donald), Troughton (Michael/Patrick), Valentino (Rudolph), Waterston (Sam).

(10) Carmichael (Ian), Le Mesurier (John), Richardson (Ralph).

(12) Attenborough (Richard).

actress *n see* **actor**.

FAMOUS ACTRESSES

(3) Bow (Clara), Day (Doris), Loy (Myrna), Roc (Patricia).

(4) Ball (Lucille), Bara (Theda), Cher, Dors (Diana), Faye (Alice), Gish (Lillian), Hawn (Goldie), Hird (Thora), Kerr (Deborah), Lake (Veronica), Laye (Evelyn), Lisi (Virna), Page (Geraldine), Reid (Beryl), Rigg (Diana), Syms (Sylvia), West (Mae), Wray (Faye), York (Susannah).

(5) Annis (Francesca), Bloom (Claire), Caron (Leslie), Close (Glenn), Davis (Bette), Dench (Judi), Derek (Bo), Evans (Edith), Fonda (Jane), Gabor (Zsa Zsa), Garbo (Greta), Hodge (Patricia), Imrie (Celia), Lange (Jessica), Leigh (Janet/Vivien), Loren (Sophia), Miles (Sarah), Moore (Demi), Novak (Kim), O'Neal (Tatum), Quick (Diana), Smith (Maggie), Tandy (Jessica), Terry (Ellen), Tutin (Dorothy), Welch (Raquel).

(6) Atkins (Eileen), Bacall (Lauren), Bardot (Brigitte), Bergen (Candice),

list continued over

Bisset (Jacqueline), Cooper (Gladys), Curtis (Jamie Lee), Durbin (Deanna), Ekberg (Anita), Ekland (Britt), Farrow (Mia), Foster (Jodie), Gaynor (Mitzi), Grable (Betty), Hedren (Tippi), Hiller (Wendy), Keaton (Diane), Lamarr (Hedy), Lamour (Dorothy), Lipman (Maureen), Lumley (Joanna), Merman (Ethel), Midler (Bette), Mirren (Helen), Monroe (Marilyn), Moreau (Jeanne), Neagle (Anna), Oberon (Merle), Rogers (Ginger), Scales (Prunella), Sommer (Elke), Spacek (Sissy), Streep (Meryl), Suzman (Janet), Taylor (Elizabeth), Temple (Shirley), Turner (Kathleen), Weaver (Sigourney), Whitty (May), Winger (Debra).

(7) Agutter (Jenny), Andrews (Julie), Bergman (Ingrid), Calvert (Phyllis), Colbert (Claudette), Collins (Joan), Fricker (Brenda), Gardner (Ava), Garland (Judy), Gingold (Hermione), Goddard (Paulette), Hayward (Susan), Hepburn (Audrey/Katharine), Jackson (Glenda), Jacques (Hattie), Johnson (Celia), Kendall (Kay), Lombard (Carole), Siddons (Mrs Sarah), Simmons (Jean), Swanson (Gloria), Ullmann (Liv), Winters (Shelley), Walters (Julie), Windsor (Barbara), Withers (Googie).

(8) Bancroft (Anne), Bankhead (Tallulah), Basinger (Kim), Blackman (Honor), Crawford (Joan), Fielding (Fenella), Fontaine (Joan), Hayworth (Rita), Lansbury (Angela), Lockwood (Margaret), MacLaine (Shirley), Minnelli (Liza), Phillips (Sian), Pickford (Mary), Redgrave (Jemma/Lynn/Vanessa), Reynolds (Debbie), Stanwyck (Barbara).

(9) Bernhardt (Sarah), Greenwood (Joan), Hampshire (Susan), Lapotaire (Jane), Mansfield (Jayne), Plowright (Joan), Stevenson (Juliet), Wanamaker (Zoe).

(10) Lanchester (Elsa), Tushingham (Rita), Zetterling (Mai).

Adam *Bible* the first man, according to Genesis, created by God from the dust and placed in the Garden of Eden. His wife, Eve, was fashioned from one of his ribs. Adam and Eve committed the original sin by eating the fruit of the tree of knowledge of good and evil and were banished from paradise. With Eve he had three sons, Cain, Abel, and Seth.

addict *n* **1** (4) user; (6) junkie; (7) tripper; (9) mainliner; **2** (3) fan; (4) buff; (5) fiend, freak; (7) devotee; (10) enthusiast.

addition I *n* **1** (5) bonus, extra; (7) adjunct; (8) addendum, additive, appendix, increase; (9) extension, increment; (10) supplement; (11) enlargement; **2** (8) counting; (9) totalling; (11) combination; **II add, added, addition, *or* additionally** *cryptic* attach an extra letter or letters to the main part of the answer to complete it, as in: 'Additional greens cause fashionable upsets' (7) = inverts (fashionable = in, vert = green in heraldry).

adjust I *v* (3) fix, set; (4) tune; (5) adapt, alter; (6) change; (7) arrange, balance, convert, rectify, remodel, reshape; (8) accustom, fine-tune, regulate; (9) harmonise (*or* harmonize), reconcile; (11) acclimatise (*or* acclimatize), accommodate; **II** *cryptic* ANAGRAM CUE.

admiral *n*

FAMOUS ADMIRALS

(4) Byng (UK), Howe (UK), Spee (Ger.), Togo (Jap.).

(5) Anson (UK), Blake (UK), Hawke (UK), Rooke (UK), Tromp (NL).

(6) Beatty (UK), Benbow (UK), Dönitz (Ger.), Fisher (UK), Nelson (UK), Nimitz (US), Rodney (UK), Ruyter (NL), Scheer (Ger.).

(7) Canaris (Ger.), Decatur (US), Doenitz (Ger.), Tirpitz (Ger.).

(8) Boscawen (UK), Jellicoe (UK), Yamamoto (Jap.).

(9) St Vincent (UK).

(10) Villeneuve (Fr.)

(11) Collingwood (UK), Mountbatten (UK).

admit v 1 (6) accept; (7) receive; (2 words) let in, take in; 2 (3) own; (5) allow, grant; (7) concede, confess; (9) recognise (or recognize); (11) acknowledge.

Adonis Gk myth a handsome young man, loved by Aphrodite (Venus), killed by a boar when hunting.

adorn v (4) deck, trim; (6) colour, enrich; (8) beautify, decorate, ornament, prettify, renovate; (9) embellish, refurbish; (2 words) do up, tart up.

adrift cryptic ANAGRAM CUE, as in: 'Greek character cast adrift in middle eastern post' (6) = Muscat (mu = 12th letter of the Greek alphabet).

advance I v 1 (6) thrive; (7) develop, improve, proceed, prosper; (8) flourish, increase, progress; (2 words) go ahead, go forward, move ahead, move on; 2 (5) speed; (6) assist, foster, hasten; (7) benefit, promote, support; (10) accelerate facilitate; 3 (3) pay; (4) give, lend, loan; II n 1 (4) step; (7) headway; (8) progress; (11) development; (12) breakthrough; 2 (4) loan; (6) credit; (7) deposit; (10) prepayment.

advantage n (3) aid, use; (4) edge, gain, good, help, lead; (5) asset, avail, point, start, value, worth; (6) object, profit; (7) benefit, purpose, service, utility; (8) blessing; (10) usefulness.

Aeneas Gk & Rom. myth a Trojan prince, the son of Anchises and **Aphrodite**, who escaped the sack of Troy and, after many wanderings and a love affair with **Dido**, Queen of Carthage, landed in Italy and became the ultimate founder of the Roman state.

Aeneid lit. the epic poem by **Virgil** that recounts the story of **Aeneas** in twelve books.

Aeolus Gk myth the god of winds, who lived on an island in the Aegean and kept the winds penned up in a cave.

affect v 1 (5) alter; (6) change, modify, regard; (7) concern, involve; (9) transform, influence; (2 words) act on, apply to, bear on, relate to; 2 (4) grab, move,

stir; (5) touch, upset; (6) excite, strike; (7) impress, inspire, disturb, perturb.

affected adj (5) false; (6) forced, pseudo; (7) feigned, stilted; (8) laboured, mannered, strained; (9) insincere, unnatural; (10) artificial.

afraid adj (5) timid; (6) scared, yellow; (7) alarmed, anxious, fearful, nervous; (8) timorous; (9) petrified, terrified; (10) frightened; (12) apprehensive, fainthearted.

Agamemnon Gk myth & lit. the commander of the Greek forces during the Trojan war, brother of **Menelaus**, who sacrificed his daughter Iphigenia to ensure a favourable wind for the fleet sailing to Troy. On his return from the war he was murdered by his wife Clytemnestra and her lover Aegisthus. His other children, Orestes and Electra, avenged him.

age I n 1 (6) dotage; (8) maturity, senility; (9) seniority; 2 (3) day, era; (4) time; (6) period; (7) century; (10) generation; II v (5) ripen; (6) mature, mellow, season.

agent n 1 (3) rep; (6) broker, deputy, factor; (9) go-between; (10) substitute; (12) intermediary; (14) representative; 2 (5) cause, means; (6) medium; (7) channel, vehicle; 3 (3) spy; (4) mole.

agree v 1 (5) grant; (6) accede, assent, comply, concur; (7) consent; 2 (3) fit; (4) suit; (5) match, tally; (6) accord; (7) conform; (10) correspond.

agreeable 1 (4) nice; (7) affable; (8) friendly, likeable, pleasant; (9) congenial, enjoyable; (10) attractive, delightful, gratifying; 2 (7) willing.

agreement n 1 (4) deal, pact; (6) accord, treaty; (7) bargain, compact; (8) contract, covenant; (10) settlement; (11) arrangement; (13) understanding; 2 (6) assent; (7) consent; (8) approval; 3 (7) concord, harmony; (8) affinity, sympathy; (9) unanimity; (10) similarity; (11) concurrence; (13) compatibility; (14) correspondence.

Ahab I Bible a king of Israel, the husband of Jezebel, who had Naboth killed to obtain his vineyard and was rebuked by Elijah; ‖ *lit.* the captain of the *Pequod* and hunter of Moby Dick in Herman Melville's novel.

aid I *v* (4) abet, back, help; (5) boost, serve; (6) assist, favour, foster, hasten; (7) advance, forward, further, promote, succour, support; (8) mitigate; (9) alleviate, encourage, subsidise (*or* subsidize); (10) facilitate; ‖ *n* I (4) help, prop; (6) advice, helper; (7) service, support; (8) guidance; (10) assistance; (11) co-operation; (13) collaboration; 2 (5) grant; (6) relief; (7) benefit, funding, subsidy, welfare; (8) donation; (9) patronage; (11) sponsorship; (12) contribution.

ailment *n see* **disease**.

aim I *n & v* (4) hope, plan; (5) dream, point; (6) design, desire, target; (7) attempt, purpose; (9) endeavour; ‖ *n* (3) end; (4) butt, goal; (6) intent, motive, object, reason; (8) ambition; (9) intention, objective; (10) aspiration; ‖‖ *v* I (5) level, train; (6) direct; 2 (4) mean, seek, want, wish; (6) aspire, intend, strive; (7) propose, resolve.

air I *n* I (4) puff, wind; (6) breath, breeze; (7) draught; (10) atmosphere; 2 (4) look, mien; (6) manner; (7) bearing; (9) demeanour; (10) appearance; 3 (4) **song**, tune; ‖ *v* I (6) aerate; (9) ventilate; 2 (5) utter, voiᶜᵉe; (6) reveal; (7) declare, discuss, publish; (8) announce, disclose; (11) communicate.

aircraft *n* (3) jet, UFO; (4) kite; (5) plane; (8) airliner, airplane; (9) aeroplane.

TYPES AND MAKES OF AIRCRAFT

(3) Mig.

(4) Avro, Spad, VTOL, Zero.

(5) blimp, Camel, Comet, jumbo, scout, Stuka, Taube.

(6) Airbus, Boeing, bomber, Cessna, Dakota, fan-jet, Fokker, glider, Hawker, Hunter, Meteor, Mirage, Nimrod, pusher, rocket, Sukhoi, tanker, Tomcat, Victor, Vulcan.

(7) airship, Antonov, balloon, biplane, chopper, Dornier, Douglas, fighter, Gloster, Grumman, Harrier, Javelin, jump-jet, Junkers, Mustang, Phantom, Sopwith, Tempest, Tornado, trainer, Trident, Tristar, Tupolev, Typhoon, Valiant, Vampire, Vickers.

(8) autogyro, Brabazon, Catalina, Chipmunk, Comanche, Concorde, Hercules, Ilyushin, jetplane, Lysander, Lockheed, Mosquito, seaplane, Spitfire, Stirling, triplane, turbofan, Vanguard, Viscount, Zeppelin.

(9) Buccaneer, dirigible, Focke-Wolf, Gladiator, Hurricane, Lancaster, Liberator, Lightning, monoplane, spaceship, swing-wing, Swordfish, turboprop; (2 words) Tiger Moth.

(10) divebomber, gyrocopter, hang-glider, helicopter, hovercraft, Hindenburg, microlight, Shackleton, spacecraft, Sunderland, Wellington; (2 words) flying boat, flying wing.

(11) Beaufighter, interceptor, Thunderbolt.

(12) single-seater; (2 words) Space Shuttle.

(13) Messerschmitt.

(14) (2 words) Flying Fortress.

---

airline *n*

AIRLINES

(2) BA (UK).

(3) BEA (UK), CSA (Czech), JAL (Jap.), JAT (Yugoslavia), KLM (Holland), LAN (Chile), LAP (Paraguay), LOT (Pol.), PIA (Pakistan), SAA (SA), SAS (Scandinavia), SIA (Singapore), TAP (Port.), THY (Turkey), TWA (US), UAL (US), UTA (Fr.).

(4) BOAC (UK); (2 words) El Al (Israel).

(5) Delta (US), Varig (Brazil), Viasa (Venezuela); (2 words) Pan Am (US).

list continued over

---

(6) Brymon (UK), Iberia (Sp.), Qantas (Aus.), Sabena (Belgium), Virgin (UK).

(7) Braniff (US), Finnair (Finland), Olympic (Greece), Ryanair (Ire.).

(8) Aeroflot (Russ.), Alitalia (It.), Swissair (Switzerland).

(9) Britannia (UK), Lufthansa (Ger.); (2 words) Aer Lingus (Ire.).

airman I *n* (5) flier, pilot; (7) aviator; (10) balloonist; II *cryptic* **composer, musician.**

airport *n*

AIRPORTS

(4) Dyce (Aberdeen), Hurn (Bournemouth), Luqa (Malta), Lydd (Kent), Orly (Paris), Riem (Munich), Seeb (Oman).

(5) Logan (Boston), Lungi (Freetown), Luton, Luzon (Manila), Mahon (Minorca), O'Hare (Chicago), Palam (Delhi), Palma (Majorca), Speke (Liverpool), Tegel (Berlin).

(6) Changi (Singapore), Deurne (Antwerp), Dorval (Montreal), Dulles (Washington), Dum Dum (Calcutta), Elmdon (Birmingham), Ezeiza (Buenos Aires), Filton (Bristol), Gander (Newfoundland), Haneda (Tokyo), Kloten (Zürich), Narita (Tokyo), Newark (New Jersey), Okecie (Warsaw), Saddam (Baghdad), Subang (Kuala Lumpur), Vantaa (Helsinki).

(7) Arlanda (Stockholm), Athinai (Athens), Barajas (Madrid), Fornebu (Oslo), Gatwick, Kastrup (Copenhagen), Larnaca (Cyprus), Lyneham (Wilts), Manston (Kent), Mirabel (Montreal), Ringway (Manchester).

(8) Cointrin (Geneva), Heathrow (London), Idlewild (NY), Jan Smuts (Johannesburg), Leuchars (St Andrews), Lulsgate (Bristol), Malpensa (Milan),

Mehrabad (Teheran), Rongotai (Wellington), Schiphol (Amsterdam), Stansted (Essex), Thruxton (Andover).

(9) Cranfield (Beds), Downsview (Toronto), Eastleigh (Southampton), Fiumicino (Rome), Hung-Chaio (Shanghai), Prestwick (Ayrshire), Schwechat (Vienna), Templehof (Verlin), Yeovilton; (2 words) Ben Gurion (Tel Aviv), J F Kennedy (NY), La Guardia (NY), Le Bourget (Paris), Le Touquet (Paris), Marco Polo (Venice).

(10) Aldergrove (Belfast), Biggin Hill (Kent), Hartsfield (Atlanta), Hellenikon (Athens), Ronaldsway (Isle of Man), Schonefeld (Berlin), Tullmarine (Melbourne).

(11) Brize Norton (Oxford), Fühlsbüttel (Hamburg).

(12) Benito Juárez (Buenos Aires), Echterdingen (Stuttgart), Metropolitan (Detroit), Sheremetyevo (Moscow).

alert *adj* (4) wary; (5) awake, chary; (7) heedful; (8) cautious, vigilant, watchful; (9) attentive, observant.

Alexander *hist.* king of Macedon who conquered Greece and then led a combined Greek force to conquer the Persian empire and reach as far as India. He was the son of Philip and Olympias, his horse was named Bucephalus, his wives were Roxana and Barsine.

Alice *lit.* the heroine of *Alice in Wonderland* and *Through the Looking Glass* by Lewis Carroll, *see also* **Carroll**.

allocate I *v* (5) allot; (6) assign, devote; (7) earmark; (8) dedicate; (9) apportion, designate; (10) distribute; II **allocate** *or* **allocated** *cryptic* ANAGRAM CUE.

allow *v* (3) let; (6) enable, permit; (7) certify, charter, empower, entitle, license, warrant; (8) sanction; (9) authorise (*or* authorize), franchise.

alloy I *n* (5) blend; (7) amalgam; (8) compound, mixture; (9) composite; (11) combination; II *v* (3) mix; (6) debase; (10)

adulterate; **III** **alloy** *or* **alloyed** *cryptic* ANAGRAM CUE.

ALLOYS

(5) brass, steel; (6) bronze, ormolu, pewter, tombac; (9) pinchbeck.

alone *adv & adj* (4) solo; (5) apart; (6) single; (7) unaided; (13) unaccompanied.

alphabet *n*

GREEK ALPHABET

alpha, beta, gamma, delta, epsilon, zeta, eta, theta, iota, kappa, lambda, mu, nu, xi, omicron, pi, rho, sigma, tao, upsilon, phi, chi, psi, omega.

HEBREW ALPHABET

aleph, beth, gimel, daleth, he, vav (waw), zayin, heth, teth, yod (yodh), kaph, lamedh, mem, nun, samekh, 'ayin, pe, sadhe (sade), qoph, resh, sin, shin, tav (taw).

PHONETIC ALPHABET

Communications Code Words

A = Alpha, B = Bravo, C = Charlie, D = Delta, E = Echo, F = Foxtrot, G = Golf, H = Hotel, I = India, J = Juliet, K = Kilo, L = Lima, M = Mike, N = November, O = Oscar, P = Papa, Q = Quebec, R = Romeo, S = Sierra, T = Tango, U = Uniform, V = Victor, W = Whisky, X = X-ray, Y = Yankee, Z = Zulu.

alter *v & * **alteration** *n see* **change**.

alternate **I** *v* (6) change, rotate; (7) replace; (10) substitute; (11) intersperse; **II** *adj* (2 words) every other, every second; **III** *cryptic* ANAGRAM CUE.

alternative **I** *adj & n* (5) other; (6) second; (7) another; (10) substitute; (11) replacement; **II** *n* (6) choice, option; (10) preference; **III** *adj* (6) fringe; (9) different; (10) unorthodox; (14) unconventional; **IV** *cryptic* ANAGRAM CUE

aluminium *cryptic* abbreviated as AL

always *cryptic* letters EER or EVER.

amalgamate *v* (4) ally, fuse, join, link, pool; (5) marry, merge, unify, unite; (6) couple; (7) combine; (8) coalesce, federate; (9) associate, co-operate; (11) collaborate, confederate, consolidate.

Amazon **I** *Gk myth* a race of women warriors supposed to have lived in Syria. The best-known Queens of the Amazons were Hippolyta and Penthesilea; **II** *geog.* the great river of South America, rising in Peru and flowing mainly through Brazil.

American *cryptic* letters US.

American Indian *n*

AMERICAN INDIAN PEOPLES

(3) Fox, Ute, Wea.

(4) Cree, Crow, Erie, Hopi, Inca, Kogi, Maya, Tupi, Zuni.

(5) Adena, Aztec, Creek, Haida, Huron, Miami, Moati, Nazca, Olmec, Omaha, Osage, Ponca, Sioux, Yaqui.

(6) Apache, Apinai, Atoara, Cayuga, Dakota, Kayopo, Lenape, Micmac, Mohave, Mohawk, Mojave, Muisca, Nootka, Oneida, Ottawa, Panare, Pawnee, Seneca, Siwash, Toltec, Tupian.

(7) Arapaho, Araucan, Catawba, Chibcha, Choctaw, Fuegian, Mohican, Ojibway, Quechua, Shawnee, Tairona, Tlingit, Waimiri, Wyandot, Zapotec.

(8) Arikaree, Cherokee, Cheyenne, Chibchan, Chippewa, Comanche, Delaware, Iroquois, Mesquito, Nez Percé, Onondaga, Puebloan, Quechuan, Seminole, Shoshone, Sihasapa, Silksika.

(9) Blackfoot, Chamacoco, Chickasaw, Guaranian, Hoochinoo, Puelchean, Sac and Fox, Tuscarora.

(10) Alacalufan, Algonquian, Athabascan, Miccosukee, Patagonian.

amiss **I** *adv* (4) awry; (5) wrong; **II** *cryptic* **1** ANAGRAM CUE; **2** understand as A MISS = girl, woman *see* **girl**.

Andersen, Hans Christian *lit.*

ANDERSEN STORIES

The Emperor's New Clothes, The
Tinderbox, The Little Mermaid, The
(Steadfast) Tin Soldier, The Princess
and the Pea, The Ugly Duckling,
The Red Shoes, Thumbelina, The
Snow Queen

Andromeda *Gk myth* the beautiful
daughter of Cepheus and Cassiopeia who
was chained to a rock to be devoured by a
sea monster but was rescued by **Perseus**.

angel *n* (7) darling, paragon; (8) treasure.

TYPES OF ANGEL

(5) power; (6) cherub, seraph, throne,
virtue; (8) dominion; (9) archangel;
(12) principality.

anger I *n* (3) ire; (4) fury, rage; (5) pique,
wrath; (6) frenzy, temper; (7) madness,
passion; (8) ferocity, violence; (11) displeasure; **II** *v* (3) irk, vex; (4) miff, rile; (5)
annoy, upset; (6) bother, enrage, harass,
needle, nettle, ruffle; (7) afflict, agitate,
disturb, incense, provoke; (8) irritate; (9)
aggravate, infuriate; (10) exasperate.

angle I *n* **1** (5) acute; (6) obtuse, reflex;
2 (4) bend, knee, nook; (5) elbow; (6)
corner; (7) flexure; **3** (5) facet, slant; (6)
aspect; (8) approach, position; (10) standpoint; (11) perspective; **II** *v* fish with a rod
and line.

angry *adj* **1** (3) mad; (5) cross, irate,
upset; (6) miffed, raging; (7) annoyed,
enraged, furious; (8) agitated, incensed;
(9) irritated; (10) infuriated; (11) exasper-
ated; **2** (3) red; (4) sore; (7) painful; (8)
inflamed.

animal I *n* **1** (4) bird; (5) beast; (6)
mammal, rodent; (7) reptile; (8) creature;
(9) amphibian; **2** (5) brute; (6) savage; (7)
monster; **II** *adj* (4) wild; (6) carnal; (7)
bestial, brutish, fleshly, sensual; (8)
physical; (11) instinctive.

ANIMALS

see also **bird, fish, insect, reptile**.

(3) ape, bat, cat, cow, doe, dog, elk,
ewe, fox, gnu, hog, kid, pig, ram, rat,
sow, yak, zho.

(4) anoa, bear, boar, buck, bull, calf,
coon, deer, euro, eyra, gaur, goat,
hare, ibex, joey, lamb, lion, lynx,
mink, mole, neat, puma, seal, tahr,
wolf, zebu.

(5) bison, camel, civet, coati, fitch,
fossa, gayal, genet, hippo, horse,
hyena, izard, koala, lemur, liger,
llama, manis, manul, moose, mouse,
okapi, otter, ounce, panda, pekan,
rasse, ratel, rhino, sable, sheep, shoat,
shrew, skunk, sloth, stirk, stoat,
swine, takin, tapir, tayra, tiger, tigon,
urial, whale, zebra.

(6) alpaca, angora, aoudad, argali,
badger, bharal, bobcat, cougar,
coyote, cuscus, desman, ermine,
fennec, ferret, fox-bat, gerbil, gibbon,
grison, heifer, impala, jaguar, kalong,
margay, marten, monkey, musk-ox,
ocelot, ovibos, possum, rabbit,
racoon, serval, teledu, tenrec, vicuña,
walrus, weasel, wombat.

(7) ant-bear, banteng, bearcat,
bighorn, buffalo, bullock, bushcat,
caracal, cheetah, dolphin, echidna,
fitchet, foumart, giraffe, glutton,
grizzly, guanaco, hamster, leopard,
linsang, lioness, markhor, meerkat,
miniver, muskrat, opossum, palm-cat,
panther, peccary, polecat, sun-bear,
tigress, wallaby, wart-hog, zorilla; (2
words) blue fox, sea lion, wild cat.

(8) aardvark, aardwolf, anteater,
bactrian, babirusa, bushbaby,
bushbuck, cacomixl, carcajou,
duckbill, elephant, fruit-bat,
hedgehog, kangaroo, kinkajou,
mongoose, pangolin, platypus,
reindeer, ringtail, seladang, serotine,
squirrel, suricate, tamandua, tiger-
cat, toddy-cat, wallaroo; (2 words)
grey wolf, wild boar.

list continued over

(9) armadillo, binturong, catamount, dromedary, flying-fox, ground-hog, hawksbill, honey-bear, ichneumon, musk-shrew, musteline, pademelon, palm-civet, phalanger, rearmouse, silver-fox, sloth-bear, thylacine, tree-shrew, wolverine, woodchuck; (2 words) brown bear, koala bear, polar bear.

(10) cacomistle, cameleopard, chimpanzee, coati-mundi, honey-mouse, jaguarundi, leopard-cat, leopardess, otter-shrew, pantheress, pinemartin, rhinoceros, shrew-mouse, timber-wolf, vampire-bat;. (2 words) giant panda, golden mole, Mexican hog.

(11) barbastelle, beech-marten, grizzly bear, honey-badger, mountain-cat, pipistrelle, prairie-wolf, snow-leopard, stone-marten.

(12) bush kangaroo, catamountain, cinnamon-bear, flittermouse, hippopotamus, mountain-goat, mountain-lion, water-buffalo.

(13) mountain-sheep, squirrel-shrew, star-nosed mole, Tasmanian wolf.

anniversary *n* (4) date; (11) celebration; (13) commemoration.

ANNIVERSARIES

(1) paper, (2) cotton, (3) feather, (4) flower, (5) wood, (6) candy, (7) wool or copper, (8) bronze, (9) pottery, (10) tin, (11) steel, (12) silk, (13) lace, (14) ivory, (15) crystal, (20) china, (25) silver, (30) pearl, (35) coral, (40) ruby, (45) sapphire, (50) gold, (55) emerald, (60) diamond, (65) blue sapphire, (70) platinum, (75) diamond.

---

annoy *v* (3) vex; (4) rile; (5) anger, upset, worry; (6) bother, harass, pester, ruffle; (7) afflict, agitate, disturb, perplex, torment, trouble; (8) distress, irritate; (9) aggravate, displease, infuriate; (10) disconcert; (13) inconvenience

annoying *adj* (6) trying; (7) galling; (8) tiresome; (9) vexatious, wearisome; (10) irritating; (11) aggravating, troublesome; (12) exasperating.

annul *v* (5) quash, upset; (6) cancel, offset; (7) nullify, reverse, subvert; (8) overturn; (9) undermine; (10) invalidate, neutralise (*or* neutralize).

antelope *n* (4) buck, deer; (7) gazelle.

ANTELOPES

(3) gnu, goa, kob.

(4) dama, kudu, oryx, puku, tahr, thar, topi.

(5) addax, beira, beisa, bongo, bubal, chiru, eland, goral, izard, kaama, nagor, nyala, okapi, oribi, saiga, sasin, serow, takin, wanto, yakin.

(6) chital, dik-dik, duiker, dzeren, dzeron, impala, nilgai, pallah, reebok.

(7) blesbok, bubalis, chamois, gemsbok, grysbok, sassaby.

(8) bontebok, bushbuck, chinkara, reedbuck, steinbok.

(9) blackbuck, pronghorn, springbok.

(10) hartebeest, wildebeest

(12) klipspringer.

---

anticipate I *v* **1** (5) await, guess, think, trust; (6) assume, demand, expect, reckon; (7) believe, foresee, imagine, predict, presume, project, require, suppose, surmise; (8) envisage, envision, forecast; (11) contemplate; (2+ words) bank on, bargain on, count on, hope for, look for, look forward to, rely on; **2** (7) pre-empt, prevent; (9) forestall; **II** *cryptic* place the letters or word referred to in front of another word to complete the answer, as in: 'Police report initially anticipates trouble at the art gallery' (5) = Prado (*see* **initial**).

Antony *see* **Mark Antony**.

Antony and Cleopatra *lit.* a tragedy by Shakespeare.
Plot outline: In the midst of a passionate affair with Cleopatra, Queen of Egypt, which is generally disapproved of by his

comrades and soldiers, Mark Antony is summoned to return to Rome by his fellow rulers Octavius Caesar and Lepidus to deal with a revolt. He departs, leaving Cleopatra bored and doleful at home. Though Rome is officially ruled by a group of three, it is obvious that only two of the three, Octavius and Antony, really count, that their characters are very different, and that Antony's luxurious Egyptian lifestyle is deeply offensive to Octavius's rather puritanical Romanness. So when the revolt is settled peacefully Antony attempts to patch up his frayed relationship with Octavius, by marrying his sister, Octavia. However, as his chief follower and friend Enobarbus had previously prophesied, Antony cannot long remain away from Egypt – where Cleopatra waits enraged by news of his marriage. Antony goes back to her. The insult to his family provides a pretext for Octavius to declare war on Antony. He defeats Antony's forces at sea, at the Battle of Actium, where Antony disgraces himself in his own eyes by fleeing from the action when he sees Cleopatra's galley turn and flee. On land, Antony recovers enough to rally his troops, but his allies begin to desert him, including eventually Enobarbus. Octavius wins the land battle, Antony stabs himself, but lives to be taken to the monument where Cleopatra has taken refuge with her women and die in her arms. Octavius attempts to take Cleopatra alive, but she has an asp smuggled in to her and kills herself by applying it to her bosom.

anyway *cryptic* ANAGRAM CUE.

ape l *n* 1 (6) monkey, pongid; (7) primate (10) anthropoid; ll *v* (5) mimic; (6) follow, mirror, parody, parrot, repeat; (7) emulate, imitate; (8) simulate; (9) duplicate, reproduce; (10) caricature; (11) impersonate (2 words) send up, take off.

APES

(5) chimp, jocko, pongo; (6) gibbon; (7) gorilla, siamang; (9) orang-utan; (10) chimpanzee.

Aphrodite *Gk myth* the goddess of love, mother of **Eros**, wife of **Hephaestus** – Roman equivalent **Venus**.

Apocrypha *Bible* books on biblical subjects but omitted from the canonical version of the Bible itself.

BOOKS OF THE APOCRYPHA

Baruch, Bel and the Dragon, Ecclesiasticus, Epistle of Jeremiah, Esdras (I & II), Esther (additions), History of Susanna, Judith, Maccabees (I & II), Prayer of Manasses, Song of the Three Holy Children, Tobit, Wisdom of Solomon.

Apollo *Gk & Rom. myth* the god of the arts in general, medicine, music, prophecy and the sun.

apostle *n* (5) envoy; (7) teacher; (8) advocate, disciple, follower; (9) supporter.

THE TWELVE APOSTLES

Andrew, John, Philip, Bartholomew, Judas Iscariot, Simon the Canaanite, James, Matthew, Thaddeus, James the Less, Peter (Simon Peter), Thomas

also named as Apostles

Jude, Matthias, Paul.

---

apostrophe *cryptic* for clues containing words that begin with an apostrophe, see **cockney**.

apparatus *n* (3) rig; (4) gear; (5) tools; (6) device, gadget, tackle; (7) machine; (9) equipment, machinery; (11) contraption; (13) paraphernalia.

appeal l *v* 1 (3) ask, beg, sue; (4) call, pray; (5) apply, plead; (6) invoke; (7) beseech, entreat, implore, request; (10) supplicate; 2 (4) lure; (5) charm, tempt; (6) allure, please; (7) attract; (8) interest; (9) fascinate; ll *n* 1 (4) plea, suit; (6) prayer; (7) request; (8) entreaty, petition; (10) invocation; (12) supplication; 2 (5) charm (6) allure, beauty; (8) charisma, interest; (10) attraction; (11) enchantment, fascination.

apply *v* **1** (7) request, solicit; (2 words) ask for, put in for, try for; **2** (3) lay, put, rub; (5) paint, smear; (6) spread; **3** (5) refer; (6) relate; (7) concern, pertain; **4** (3) use; (5) wield; (6) employ; (7) utilise (*or* utilize); (8) exercise; (2+ words) bring to bear.

appoint *v* **1** (4) hire, name; (5) elect; (6) assign, choose, detail, employ, engage, select; (7) install; (8) nominate; (9) designate; **2** (3) fix, set; (6) decide; (6) decree, ordain, settle; (7) arrange; (9) determine, establish.

appointment *n* **1** (4) date; (5) tryst; (7) meeting; (9) interview; (10) engagement, rendezvous; (11) assignation; (12) consultation; **2** (3) job; (4) post; (5) place; (6) office; (7) posting; (8) position; (9) situation; **3** (6) choice; (8) election; (10) nomination.

appropriate I *adj* (3) apt; (5) right; (6) proper, timely; (7) fitting, germane, related; (8) apposite, becoming, material, relevant, spot-on, suitable; (9) opportune, pertinent; (10) admissible, applicable, seasonable; **II** *v* (4) take; (5) seize, steal, usurp; (8) impound; (10) commandeer, confiscate; (11) requisition.

April *n* the four month, whose name derives from the Latin verb *aperire* to open.

apt *adj* **1** *see* **appropriate**; **2** (5) given, prone; (6) liable, likely; (8) disposed, inclined; **3** (5) quick; (6) clever, gifted.

Aquarius *astrol. & astron.* the constellation that is the eleventh sign of the zodiac, also known as the Water Carrier.

Archer *see* **Sagittarius**.

architect *n* (5) maker; (7) builder, creator, founder, planner; (8) designer, engineer; (10) originator; (11) constructor.

FAMOUS ARCHITECTS

(4) Adam (Robert), Kent (William), Nash (John), Shaw (Norman), Wood (John), Wren (Christopher).

(5) Barry (Charles), Dance (George), Gibbs (James), Gaudi (Antonio), Levau (Louis), Pugin (Arthur Welby), Scott (George Gilbert *and* Giles Gilbert), Soane (John).

(6) Foster (Norman), Paxton (Joseph), Rogers (Richard), Smirke (Robert), Spence (Basil), Street (George), Wright (Frank Lloyd).

(7) Bernini (Lorenzo), Gropius (Walter), Latrobe (Benjamin), Lutyens (Edwin), Mansard (Francois), Neumann (Balthazar), Telford (William).

(8) Bramante (Donato), Palladio (Andrea), Sullivan (Louis), Vanbrugh (John).

(9) Borromini (Carlo), Hawksmoor (Nicholas).

(10) Mackintosh (Charles Rennie).

(11) Le Corbusier. (12) Michelangelo.

---

area *n* **1** (4) part, ward, zone; (5) manor, patch; (6) domain, region, sector, sphere; (7) quarter; (8) district, division, locality, province; (9) territory; (10) department; (13) neighbourhood; **2** (3) are; (4) acre, rood; (7) hectare; (2 words) square inch square foot, square mile; **3** (4) size; (5) range, scope, width; (6) extent; (7) breadth, compass.

Ares *Gk myth* the god of war, equivalent to the Roman god **Mars**.

argent *heraldry* silver.

argon *cryptic* abbreviated as A.

Argonauts *Gk myth* the crew of the ship Argo who accompanied **Jason** in his quest for the Golden Fleece.

argue *v* **1** (3) row; (4) feud; (5) brawl, clash, fight, scrap; (6) bicker; (7) dispute, quibble, wrangle; (8) conflict, disagree, squabble; **2** (4) show; (5) claim, imply; (6) reason; (7) contend, suggest; (8) indicate, maintain; (11) demonstrate.

argument *n* 1 (3) row; (4) feud, rift, spat, tiff; (5) brawl, clash, fight, scrap; (7) discord, dispute, quibble, wrangle; (8) conflict, squabble; (9) complaint, grievance; (10) difference, dissension; (11) controversy; (12) disagreement; (16) misunderstanding; 2 (4) case, plea; (5) claim; (6) thesis; (9) assertion, reasoning; (10) contention.

Argus *Gk myth* a monster with a hundred eyes, set by **Hera** to watch over Io to prevent Zeus from mating with her. Argus's eyes were eventually set in the tail of Hera's bird, the peacock.

Ariadne *Gk myth* the daughter of King **Minos** who gave **Theseus** the 'clue' (ball of thread) that enabled him to find his way through the labyrinth to kill the **Minotaur** and escape alive. She escaped with Theseus, but was later abandoned by him on the island of Naxos where she was found by the god **Dionysus**, who subsequently married her.

Aries *astrol. & astron.* the constellation that is the first sign of the zodiac, also known as the Ram.

arm I *n* 1 (4) limb; (6) branch; (7) section; (8) division, offshoot; (9) extension; (10) projection; 2 *see* **weapon**; II *v* (5) equip; (6) supply; (7) fortify, provide.

armour *n* (4) mail; (7) panoply.

PARTS OF A SUIT OF ARMOUR

(4) helm (head); (5) visor (face); (6) beaver (face), cuisse (thigh), gorget (neck), greave (leg), helmet, tasset (hip); (7) cuirass (breast), hauberk (body), sabaton (foot); (8) corselet (body), gauntlet (hand), pauldron (shoulder), vambrace (forearm); (9) habergeon (body); (11) breastplate.

---

army I *n* (4) host; (5) corps, force, horde; (6) troops; (8) military; *for army ranks see* **rank**; II *cryptic* letters SA (Salvation Army) or TA (Territorial Army).

around *adv, prep see* **about**.

arrange I *v* 1 (4) sort, tidy; (5) align, array, group, order, range; (6) deploy; (7) dispose, marshal; (8) classify, organise (*or* organize); (9) catalogue; 2 (3) set; (5) adapt, score; (10) instrument; (11) orchestrate; II **arrange** *or* **arranged** *cryptic* ANAGRAM CUE.

arrangement I *n* 1 (4) plan; (5) array, order; (6) layout, line-up, method, scheme, system; (7) display; (8) grouping, sequence; (9) structure; (11) disposition; (12) organisation (*or* organization); (14) classification; 2 (5) terms; (8) contract; (9) agreement; (13) understanding; II *cryptic* ANAGRAM CUE.

arrogant *adj* (4) smug, vain; (5) cocky, proud; (6) snooty; (7) haughty; (8) boastful, snobbish; (9) big-headed, conceited; (11) egotistical; (12) supercilious.

arsenic *cryptic* abbreviated as AS.

art *n* (5) craft, knack, skill; (6) method; (9) technique.

ART FORMS

(4) film; (5) music; (6) poetry; (7) carving, drawing; (8) painting; (9) sculpture; (10) literature.

Artemis *Gk myth* the goddess of the moon, chastity, and hunting, the equivalent of the Roman goddess **Diana**.

artist I *n* (4) poet; (6) writer; (7) painter; (8) composer, musician, novelist, sculptor; *see also* **painter**, **poet** *etc*; II *cryptic* letters RA (Royal Academician).

artiste *n* (5) actor; (6) dancer, player, singer; (7) actress; (9) performer; (11) entertainer.

ascend I *v* (4) rise, soar; (5) climb, mount, scale; (2 words) go up, lift off, take off; II **ascend, ascending, ascent** *cryptic in down clues* reverse the order of the letters of a word in the clue or of part of the answer, as in: 'Following the French ascended stair with ropes' (7) = lariats (the French = la).

ask *v* (3) beg, sue; (4) call, pray; (5) apply, plead; (6) appeal; (7) beseech, entreat, implore, request; (10) supplicate.

assemble *v* 1 (5) amass, group, rally; (6) gather, muster; (7) collect; (10)

accumulate; **2** (4) make; (5) build; (7) compose; (9) construct, fabricate; (2 words) put together.

assembly *n* **1** (5) crowd, group, rally; (7) meeting; (9) concourse, gathering; (10) collection; (12) congregation; **2** (7) council; (8) congress; (11) convocation; **3** (6) making; (12) construction.

ASSEMBLIES OF ANIMALS AND BIRDS

ants – army, colony, nest; *apes* – shrewdness; *asses* – drove, herd, pace; *badgers* – cete, colony; *bears* – sloth; *bees* – hive, swarm; *bitterns* – sedge; *boars* – herd, singular, sounder; *cats* – clowder, cluster; *cattle* – drove, herd; *choughs* – chattering; *colts* – rag, rake; *coots* – covert, raft; *cranes* – herd, siege; *crows* – hover, murder; *deer* – herd, leash; *dogs* – kennel, pack; *donkeys* – drove, herd, pace; *doves* – dole, dule, flight; *ducks* – flush, pump, team, smeath; *eagles* – convocation; *elephants* – herd; *elks* – gang; *falcons* – cast; *ferrets* – business, cast, fesnying; *finches* – charm, trembling; *fish* – shoal; *foxes* – lead, skulk; *frogs* – army, colony; *goats* – flock, herd, tribe; *grouse* – covey; *gulls* – colony; *hares* – down, drove, leash; *hens* – brood; *herrings* – cran; *herons* – sedge; *hinds* – parcel; *horses* – harras(e), herd, remuda, stable, team, troop; *hounds* – kennel, pack; *jays* – band, party; *kangaroos* – herd, mob, troop; *kittens* – kindle, litter; *lapwings* – deceit, desert; *larks* – exaltation; *leopards* – leap, lepe; *lions* – pride, troop; *magpies* – tiding, tittering; *mares* – stud; *martens* – richesse; *moles* – company, labour; *monkeys* – cartload, tribe, troop; *mules* – barren, pack, rake, span; *nightingales* – watch; *otters* – bevy, family; *owls* – parliament, stare; *oxen* – span, team, yoke; *partridges* – covey; *penguins* – colony, rookery; *pheasants* – bouquet, nye; *pigs* – herd, sounder; *piglets* – farrow, litter; *plovers* – congregation, leash, wing; *polecats* – chine; *porpoises* – school; *puppies* – litter; *rabbits* – bury, colony; *rats* – colony; *ravens* – unkindness; *rhinoceroses* – crash; *rooks* – building, parliament; *seals* – bob, colony, crash; *sheep* – drove, flock, fold, trip; *snakes* – den, nest, pit; *swans* – bank, bevy, game, head, squadron, wedge, whiteness; *swine* – droylt, sounder; *teal* – coil, knob, raft, spring; *thrushes* – mutation; *tigers* – ambush; *turtles* – dule; *wagtails* – walk; *walruses* – herd, pod; *whales* – gam, herd, pod, school; *widgeons* – bunch, coil, company, knob; *wolves* – herd, pack, rout; *zebras* – herd.

---

assess *v* (3) try; (4) cost; (5) count, gauge, guess, value; (6) reckon; (7) compute, examine, measure; (8) appraise, estimate, evaluate; (9) arbitrate, ascertain, calculate, determine; (10) adjudicate.

assist *v* **1** (3) aid; (4) abet, back, help; (5) boost, serve; (6) assist, favour, foster, hasten; (7) advance, forward, further, promote, succour, support; (8) mitigate; (9) alleviate, encourage, subsidise (*or* subsidize); (10) facilitate; **2** (6) attend; (2 words) be present, take part.

assistance *n* **1** (3) aid; (4) help, prop; (6) advice, helper; (7) service, support; (8) guidance; (11) co-operation; (13) collaboration; **2** (5) grant; (6) relief; (7) benefit, funding, subsidy, welfare; (8) donation; (9) patronage; (11) sponsorship; (12) contribution.

assistant *n* (4) aide; (6) helper; (7) abettor, partner; (9) accessory, ancillary, auxiliary; (10) accomplice; (11) subordinate; (12) collaborator.

As You Like It *lit.*
A comedy by Shakespeare.
Plot outline: Rosalind, the heroine of *As You Like It*, is the daughter of a duke, Duke Senior, who has been overthrown and banished by younger brother, Duke Frederick. Rosalind is soon banished for treachery in her turn and, disguised as a boy (Ganymede) and accompanied by her

best friend Celia (Duke Frederick's daughter) and Touchstone, a clown, sets out to find her father in the Forest of Arden. Meanwhile the hero, Orlando, whom Rosalind first encounters and falls in love with when he wins a wrestling match, has also become the victim of his elder brother Oliver's jealousy and is forced to flee to the forest for his life. In the forest Duke Senior is living a simple life in the company of some faithful followers, amongst them Jaques (the melancholy Jaques) who is far more cynical about the delights and virtues of country living than his fellows. All the main characters meet at various times in the forest. The main motor of the plot is the confusion caused by Rosalind's being disguised as a boy. Instead of revealing herself to Orlando when they meet, she persuades him to practise wooing his Rosalind by pretend-courting her in her male disguise. Likewise she catches the eye of a love-shy shepherdess, Phoebe, who has consistently rejected the advances of a love-sick shepherd Silvius. Eventually, the complications are resolved, and at the end of the play Rosalind marries Orlando, Celia marries his reformed brother Oliver, Phoebe finally accepts Silvius and even the fool, Touchstone, finds a country wench, Audrey, to marry. Duke Senior is restored to his dukedom while his brother comes to do penance as a hermit and the whole cast returns to court – with the exception of Jaques who decides to remain. Jaques also has the most famous speech in the play – the 'seven ages of man' speech (*see* **seven ages**).

Athene *Gk myth* the goddess of wisdom, patroness of Athens, the equivalent of the Roman goddess **Minerva**.

athletic *adj* (3) fit; (5) agile; (6) active, sporty, strong, supple; (8) muscular; *for* athletic events *see* **sport**.

attach *v* (3) fix, pin, tie; (4) bind, glue, join, nail; (5) rivet, stick, unite; (6) anchor, cement, couple, fasten, secure.

attempt I *n & v* (3) try; (7) venture; (9) endeavour; II *v* (4) seek; (6) strive; (9) undertake; III *n* (2) go; (4) bash, shot, stab; (5) crack; (6) effort.

attend *v* 1 (5) visit; (8) frequent; (2 words) be present, take part; 2 (4) help, mind, tend; (5) serve; (6) escort; (7) control; (8) minister; (9) accompany, chaperone, supervise; (2 words) deal with, look after, wait on; 3 (4) heed, list, mark; (6) listen, notice, regard; (11) concentrate.

attendant I *n* (4) aide, page; (6) escort, helper, second; (7) servant; (8) follower, retainer; II *adj* (7) related; (9) resultant; (10) associated, consequent, subsequent; (11) concomitant.

attention *n* (4) care, heed; (6) notice, regard; (7) concern; (9) alertness, awareness, treatment, vigilance; (11) observation; (13) consideration, concentration.

attentive *adj* (4) wary; (5) alert, awake, chary; (7) heedful, mindful; (8) cautious, vigilant, watchful; (9) observant.

attitude *n* 1 (4) idea, mind, view; (6) belief, theory; (7) feeling, opinion; (8) judgment, position; (9) judgement, sentiment; (11) disposition; (2+ words) point of view, way of thinking; 2 (4) pose; (6) stance; (7) posture; (8) position.

attract *v* (4) draw, lure, pull; (5) charm, tempt; (6) allure, appeal, arouse, entice, excite, invite, please; (7) bewitch, enchant; (8) interest; (9) captivate, fascinate.

attraction *n* 1 (4) draw, lure, pull; (5) charm (6) allure, appeal, beauty; (8) charisma, interest; (9) magnetism; (11) enchantment, fascination; 2 (4) bait; (10) enticement, inducement, temptation; 3 (4) ride; (5) sight; (8) sideshow; (9) amusement; (13) entertainment.

attractive *adj* 1 (8) charming, enticing, exciting, inviting, pleasant, pleasing; (9) agreeable, appealing, seductive; (10) bewitching, enchanting; (11) captivating, fascinating, interesting; 2 (6) lovely, pretty; (8) gorgeous, handsome, stunning; (9) beautiful, glamorous; (11) good-looking.

August *n* the eighth month, named after the first Roman emperor, Augustus.

Austen, Jane *lit.* English novelist.

> ### NOVELS OF JANE AUSTEN
>
> Emma, Persuasion, Sense and Sensibility, Mansfield Park, Pride and Prejudice, The Watsons (unfinished), Northanger Abbey, Sanditon (unfinished).

Austria *cryptic* abbreviated as A.

author *n* 1 (6) **writer;** 2 (5) maker; (7) creator, founder, planner; (8) designer, inventor; (10) originator; (11) constructor.

authority *n* 1 (4) rule, sway; (5) power; (8) dominion; (9) influence, supremacy; (10) government; (11) sovereignty; 2 (6) permit; (7) warrant; (8) sanction; (10) permission; (11) prerogative; 3 (6) expert, pundit; (7) scholar; (10) specialist.

aver *v* (3) say; (5) state; (7) contend, declare; (8) maintain.

average I *n & adj* (3) par; (4) mean; (6) median, medium, middle; (8) standard; II *n* (4) norm, rule; III *adj* (4) fair, so-so; (5) usual; (6) common, normal; (7) regular, routine, typical; (8) mediocre, middling, passable; (9) tolerable; (11) indifferent; (12) satisfactory; (13) unexceptional; (15) undistinguished.

averse *adj* (4) anti; (5) loath; (7) hostile, opposed; (9) reluctant, unwilling.

aversion *n* (4) fear; (6) hatred, horror, phobia; (7) disgust, dislike; (8) distaste, loathing; (9) antipathy; (10) abhorrence, reluctance, repugnance; (11) detestation.

award I *v* (4) give; (5) endow, grant; (6) bestow, confer; (7) present; (8) dispense; II *n* (4) gift; (5) grant, medal, prize; (6) trophy; (7) bursary; (10) exhibition; (11) scholarship.

> ### AWARDS
>
> (4) Brit (UK, music), Emmy (US, TV), Tony (US, stage); (5) Bafta (UK, film), Oscar (US, film); (6) Grammy (US, music); (7) Olivier (UK, stage); (2 words) Golden Bear (Berlin, film), Golden Globe (Hollywood), Golden Palm (Cannes, film), Golden Rose (Montreux, TV).

aware *adj* (5) alert, awake, sharp; (7) heedful, mindful; (8) familiar; (9) attentive, cognisant (*or* cognizant), conscious; (10) acquainted, conversant; (13) knowledgeable.

awful I *adj* 1 (3) bad; (4) foul, vile; (6) horrid, rotten; (7) ghastly, hateful, hideous; (8) dreadful, gruesome, horrible, horrific, shocking; (9) appalling, frightful, obnoxious, offensive, repugnant, repulsive, revolting; (10) disgusting, outrageous, unpleasant; 2 (5) grave; (7) extreme, serious; (9) desperate, harrowing; (11) distressing; II *cryptic* ANAGRAM CUE.

awkward I *adj* 1 (5) inept; (6) clumsy, gauche; (8) bungling, inexpert, ungainly, unwieldy; (9) inelegant, unskilful; (10) cumbersome; (13) uncoordinated; 2 (4) hard; (6) knotty, thorny, tricky; (8) ticklish; (9) difficult; (11) complicated, problematic; 3 (11) embarrassed; (13) uncomfortable; (2+ words) ill at ease; II **awkward** *or* **awkwardly** *cryptic* ANAGRAM CUE.

B

B *abbrev* bachelor, bass, Belgium (international vehicle registration), bishop, black, boron, key (music), note (music).

b *abbrev* born, bowled.

Baal *rel.*, *Bible* a fertility god of the Phoenicians and the Canaanites. For some of the prophets of the Old Testament, Baal became the archetypal false god of the heathen (bow the knee to Baal).

Bacchus *Rom. myth* god of wine, equivalent of the Greek god **Dionysius**.

back I *n* (4) rear, rump, tail; (5) stern; (6) behind; (7) reverse; (9) posterior; **II** *v* **1** (6) assist, favour, second; (7) bolster, endorse, finance, promote, sponsor, support, sustain; (8) advocate, champion, sanction; (9) encourage, subsidise (*or* subsidize); (10) underwrite; **2** (7) retreat, reverse; (8) withdraw; **III back, backed, backing** *cryptic* reverse the order of the letters in a word or words in the clue or answer as in: 'Brigitte Bardot takes arsenic after backing horse for biblical malefactor' (8) = Barabbas (horse = arab, arsenic = As).

background *n* **1** (7) context, milieu, scenery, setting; (11) environment; (13) circumstances; **2** (6) record; (7) history; (10) experience, upbringing; (11) credentials.

backward I *adv* (6) astern, behind; (8) rearward; **II** *adj* **1** (4) late, slow; (6) stupid; (8) immature, retarded; (9) subnormal; (14) underdeveloped; **2** (3) **shy**; (7) bashful; **III** *cryptic* reverse the order of the letters in a word or words in the clue or answer as in: 'On bus going backward fifteen fall down' (7) = subside (fifteen or 15 = [Rugby] side).

bad I *adj* **1** (4) foul, evil, vile; (5) wrong; (6) impure, sinful, wicked; (7) corrupt, harmful, heinous, immoral, ungodly; vicious; (8) depraved, indecent, shameful, spiteful; (9) dissolute, malicious, unethical; (10) abominable, degenerate, iniquitous; (11) mischievous; (12) unprincipled, unscrupulous; **2** (4) poor, weak; (5) sorry; (6) faulty, feeble; (7) average; (8) inferior, mediocre, pathetic; (9) third-rate, worthless; (10) second-rate, uninspired; (11) incompetent, ineffective, inefficient; substandard; (14) unsatisfactory; (15) undistinguished; **3** (3) off; (4) sour; (6) mouldy, putrid, rancid, rotten, spoilt; (7) decayed, tainted; **4** (5) nasty; (10) unpleasant; (12) disagreeable; **5** (5) sorry, upset; (6) guilty; (7) ashamed; (8) contrite; (9) regretful; (10) remorseful; (11) embarrassed; **6** *see* **ill**; **7** *see* **serious**; **II bad** *or* **badly** *cryptic* = ANAGRAM CUE.

bag I *n* (4) case, grip, pack, sack; (5) scrip; (7) carrier, holdall, satchel; (8) reticule, rucksack, suitcase; (9) briefcase, container, portfolio; **II** *v* **1** (4) kill, trap; (5) catch, shoot; **2** (4) book, grab, take; (6) corner, obtain; (7) acquire, reserve; (10) commandeer; (11) appropriate; **III bags** (5) pants; (8) trousers.

baggage *n* **1** (3) kit; (4) gear; (5) cases, traps; (6) things; (7) luggage; (9) equipment; **2** (4) jade, minx; (5) hussy.

bail I *n* (4) bond; (6) pledge, surety; (8) security; (9) guarantee; **II bail (out)** *v* **1** (3) aid; (4) free, help; (6) assist, rescue; (7) finance; (8) liberate; **2** (4) pump; (5) empty, scoop; **3** (4) jump, quit; (6) escape.

Balder *Norse myth* the god of light, son of Odin and Frigg, vulnerable only to mistletoe. **Loki** tricked the blind god Hodhr into killing him with a sprig of it.

bale I *n & v* (4) pack, wrap; (5) truss; (6) bundle; **II** *n* (3) ill, woe; (4) evil; (6) misery; (11) destruction; **III bale out** *v see* **bail out**.

ball *n* **1** (3) orb; (4) pill, shot; (5) globe; (6) bullet, pellet, sphere; (7) globule; **2** (5) dance; (6) soirée; (10) masquerade; *see below for* **ball game**.

ballet *n* (5) dance; *see also* **choreographer**.

FAMOUS BALLETS

Coppelia, La fille mal gardée, Romeo and Juliet, Daphnis and Chloë, Les Sylphides, Sleeping Beauty, Firebird (The), Nutcracker (The), Swan Lake, Giselle, Petrushka, La Bayadère, Rite of Spring (The)

BALLET DANCERS

(7) danseur; (8) coryphée, figurant; (9) ballerina, figurante; (2+ words) corps de ballet.

(4) Grey (Beryl)

(5) Dolin (Anton), Gable (Christopher).

(6) Ashton (Frederick), Dowell (Anthony), Sibley (Antoinette)

(7) Bussell (Darcy), Fonteyn (Margot), Markova (Alicia), Nureyev (Rudolf), Pavlova (Anna), Rambert (Marie), Seymour (Lynn), Ulanova (Galina).

(8) Helpman (Robert), Nijinsky (Vaslav), (2 words) de Valois (Ninette).

BALLET MOVEMENTS

(3) pas; (4) jeté, plié; (5) brisé, coupé, fondu, passé, piqué, tendu; (6) ballon, chaîné, croisé, écarté, effacé, frappé, pointe, relevé, royale; (7) allongé, bourrée, échappé, fouetté, sissone, soutenu; (8) batterie, cabriole, glissade, , stulchak; (9) arabesque, battement, entrechat, pirouette, promenade; (10) soubresant.

---

ball game *n*

BALL GAMES

(4) golf, polo, pool; (5) fives, rugby; (6) hockey, pelota, shinty, squash, tennis; (7) cricket, croquet, hurling, netball, rackets, snooker; (8) baseball, football, handball, hardball, lacrosse, rounders, softball; (9) billiards; (10) basketball, volleyball.

Balthazar I *rel.* one of the three **Magi; II** *see* **bottle**.

ban I *v & n* (3) bar; (4) veto; (5) block; (7) boycott, embargo; **II** *v* (4) stop; (6) censor, forbid, oppose, outlaw, refuse, reject; (7) exclude, prevent; (8) disallow, preclude, prohibit; (9) interdict, proscribe; (2 words) rule out; **III** *n* (5) curse, taboo; (8) anathema; (11) prohibition, restriction; (12) interdiction.

band I *n* 1 (3) bar, tie; (4) belt, sash, tape; (5) strip; (6) ribbon, streak, stripe; 2 (3) lot, mob, set; (4) club, crew, gang, pack, ring, team; (5) batch, bunch, class, crowd, group, squad; (6) circle, clique; (7) cluster, coterie; (8) category; (9) gathering; 3 (5) combo; (7) players; (8) ensemble; (9) orchestra; **II** *v* (4) ally, join; (5) group, merge, unite; (6) gather.

bank I *n & v* 1 (4) heap, mass, pile; (5) drift, mound, stack; 2 (4) tilt; (5) slant, slope; **II** *n* 1 (5) ridge; (7) rampart; (10) embankment; 2 (4) edge; (5) beach, shore; (6) strand; 3 (4) fund, pool; (5) cache, hoard, lodge, stock, store; (7) deposit, reserve; (10) depository, re-pository; **III** *v* (4) keep, save; (7) deposit; (9) stockpile; (10) accumulate; (2 words) pay in; **IV bank on** (4) rely; (5) count, trust; (6) depend.

bar I *v & n* (3) ban; (4) stop, veto; (5) block; (9) barricade; **II** *n* 1 (3) rod; (4) pole, rail; (5) shaft, stake, stick; (6) batten, paling; (7) railing; (9) stanchion; 2 (4) lump, slab; (5) chunk, ingot, wedge; 3 (8) obstacle; (9) deterrent, hindrance; (10) impediment; 4 (3) inn, pub; (4) snug; (6) bistro, lounge, public, saloon, tavern; (7) counter; 5 (8) sandbank; **III** *v* 1 (4) bolt, lock, shut; 2 (6) forbid, oppose, outlaw, refuse, reject; (7) exclude, prevent; (8) disallow, preclude, prohibit, proscribe; (9) interdict; (2 words) rule out.

Barabbas *Bible* a robber released by Pontius Pilate in place of Jesus on the wishes of the mob.

bare I *adj* 1 (4) nude; (5) naked; (8) stripped; (9) uncovered; 2 (4) arid, open; (5) bleak, empty, waste; (6) barren, lonely, vacant; (8) deserted, desolate, for-

---

saken, isolated, solitary; (9) windswept; (10) unoccupied; (11) uninhabited, unpopulated, unprotected, unsheltered; 3 (5) plain, stark; (6) simple; II *v* (5) strip; (6) denude, divest, expose; (7) uncover; (8) unclothe.

barium *cryptic* abbreviated as BA.

base I *n* 1 (4) foot, rest; (5) stand; (6) bottom, plinth; (7) support; (8) pedestal; (10) foundation; 2 (4) camp, post; (5) depot; (6) centre; (12) headquarters; 3 *see* **basis**; II *v* 1 (5) build, found; (6) derive, ground; (9) construct, establish; 2 (6) locate; (7) install, station; III *adj* 1 (3) low; (4) mean; (6) humble; 2 (6) wicked; (7) corrupt, ignoble, immoral; (11) treacherous; (13) dishonourable.

baseball *n*

BASEBALL TEAMS

Atlanta Braves, New York Mets / Yankees, Baltimore Orioles, Philadelphia Phillies, Boston Red Sox, Pittsburgh Pirates, Chicago Cubs / White Sox, St Louis Cardinals, Cleveland Indians, San Francisco Giants, Detroit Tigers, Seattle Mariners, Houston Astros, Texas Rangers, Los Angeles Dodgers, Toronto Blue Jays, Minnesota Twins

basic *adj* 1 (3) key; (5) vital; (7) crucial; (8) critical, decisive; (9) essential, important, necessary, requisite; (11) fundamental, life-or-death, significant; (13) indispensable; 2 (5) plain, stark; (6) simple; (7) spartan; (9) primitive; (10) elementary; (11) rudimentary.

basis *n* (4) core, root; (5) heart; (6) origin, source; (7) essence, premise; (9) principle; (10) foundation, groundwork.

bat *n* 1 (4) club; (6) racket; 2 (9) rearmouse (*or* reremouse).

TYPES OF BAT

(7) noctule, vampire; (8) serotine; (9) horseshoe; (11) barbastelle, pipistrelle; (2 words) flying fox.

battle I *n & v* (3) war; (4) feud; (5) clash, **fight**; (6) combat; (7) contest; (8) campaign, conflict, skirmish, struggle; II *n* (4) fray; (6) action; (8) argument; (10) engagement.

BATTLES

(3) Goa, Ulm.

(4) Acre, Alma, Caen, Mons, Nile, Oran, Rome, Vimy.

(5) Aduwa, Alamo, Anzio, Arras, Boyne, Cadiz, Crecy, Douro, Eylau, Lagos, Lewes, Ligny, Marne, Sedan, Sluys, Somme, Texel, Valmy, Ypres.

(6) Actium, Arnhem, Barnet, Cannae, Dieppe, Dunbar, Majuba, Maldon, Midway, Minden, Naseby, Sadowa, Saigon, Shiloh, Tobruk, Towton, Verdun, Wagram.

(7) Aboukir, Cassino, Corunna, Dunkirk, Evesham, Flodden, Iwo Jima, Jutland, Leipzig, Lepanto, Magenta, Marengo, Matapan, Newbury, Okinawa, Plassey, Poltava, Preston, Salamis, Salerno, Taranto, Vitoria; (2 words) Bull Run.

(8) Antietam, Blenheim, Borodino, Bosworth, Culloden, Edgehill, Fontenoy, Hastings, Marathon, Omdurman, Philippi, Quiberon, Saratoga, Talavera, Waterloo; (2 words) Spion Kop, St Albans.

(9) Agincourt, Balaclava, Caporetto, Dettingen, Falklands, Gallipoli, Lansdowne, Oudenarde, Ramillies, Solferino, Steenkirk Trafalgar, Worcester; (2 words) El Alamein, St Vincent.

(10) Austerlitz, Brandywine, Camperdown, Copenhagen, Gettysburg, Malplaquet, Paardeberg, Sevastopol, Stalingrad, Tannenberg, Tewkesbury (2 words) Aboukir Bay, Bunker Hill, Quatre Bras, River Plate.

(11) Bannockburn, Guadalcanal, Hohenlinden, Isandhlwana, Prestonpans, Sheriffmuir,

list continued over

Thermopylae; (2 words) Marston Moor, Pearl Harbor, Quiberon Bay, Rorke's Drift; (2+ words) Dien Bien Phu.

(12) Roncesvalles, Seringapatam.

(13) Killiecrankie, Magersfontein, Passchendaele; (2+ words) Little Big Horn.

beam l *n* 1 (4) pole, spar; (5) board, joist, plank; (6) girder, rafter, summer, timber; 2 (3) ray; (5) gleam, shaft; 3 (5) width; (7) breadth; ll *v* 1 (4) grin; (5) smile; 2 (4) emit, send; (5) relay; (8) transmit; (9) broadcast.

bear[1] *v* 1 (4) take; (5) bring, carry; (6) convey; (9) transport; 2 (4) hold; (6) uphold; (7) support, sustain; (8) shoulder; 3 (4) face; (5) brave, stand, stick; (6) endure, suffer; (7) stomach, undergo, weather; (8) tolerate; (9) withstand; (2+ words) go through, put up with; 4 (5) breed, yield; (6) foster; (7) harbour, nourish, nurture, produce; (8) generate; (2+ words) bring forth, give birth to; 5 (2) go; (4) bend, turn; (5) curve; (6) swerve; (7) deviate.

bear[2] *n* (4) ursa; (5) bruin.

TYPES OF BEAR

(5) black, brown, koala, panda, polar; (6) kodiak; (7) grizzly; (9) Himalayan.

---

bearing l *n* 1 (3) air; (4) mien; (6) manner; (7) posture; (8) carriage; (9) behaviour, demeanour; (11) comportment; 2 (3) aim, way; (5) track; (6) course; (9) direction; (11) orientation; ll *cryptic* letter N, E, S, W, *etc see* **compass points**.

beat l *v* 1 (3) hit, tan; (4) bash, cane, flog, lick, wham, whip; (5) birch, knock, pound, thump, whack; (6) batter, hammer, lather, thrash, strike, wallop; 2 (4) best, foil, rout, ruin; (5) cream, worst; (6) defeat; (7) conquer, trounce; (8) confound, overcome, vanquish; (9) checkmate, frustrate, overpower, overthrow, overwhelm, slaughter, subjugate; 3 (5) stump; (6) baffle, puzzle; (7) flummox, perplex; (8) confound; (9) bamboozle; 4 (5) pulse, throb; (6) quiver;

(7) flutter, pulsate, vibrate; (9) palpitate; ll *n* 1 (4) time; (5) metre, tempo; (6) accent, rhythm, stress; 2 (3) way; (4) path; (5) round, route; (6) course; (7) circuit.

beautiful *adj* (4) fair; (6) lovely; (7) radiant; (8) alluring, charming, gorgeous, handsome, stunning; (9) appealing, exquisite, ravishing; (10) attractive (11) good-looking.

beer *n* (3) ale; (4) mild, pint; (5) brown, lager, stout; (6) bitter, porter.

beetle l *n* 1 (3) bug; (6) chafer, insect, scarab; (8) glow-worm; (9) cockroach; (10) cockchafer; (2+ words) death watch beetle, dung beetle; 2 (4) maul; (6) hammer, sledge; ll *v* (2) go; (3) run; (4) move; (7) scamper, scuttle.

begin *v* (4) form, open; (5) cause, found, plant, start; (6) create, launch, prompt; (7) trigger; (8) activate, commence, initiate; (9) establish, institute, introduce, originate; (10) inaugurate; (2 words) set up.

beginner l *n* (3) deb; (4) tyro; (6) novice; (7) learner; (9) fledgling; (10) apprentice; ll *cryptic* 1 use the first letter of the relevant word, as in: 'Calls because hesitant beginner is taken sick' (5) = hails; 2 use the letter L in the answer, as in: 'Firm, having taken on beginner, falsifies accounts and goes to the dogs' (7) = collies (firm = CO).

beginning l *n* (3) off; (4) dawn; (5) birth, break, onset, start; (6) launch, origin, outset; (7) opening; (9) inception; (10) foundation; (11) institution; (12) commencement, inauguration; ll *cryptic* use the first letter of the relevant word.

behaviour *n* (4) ways; (6) doings, habits, manner; (7) actions, bearing, conduct, manners; (8) attitude, dealings; (11) comportment.

behead *cryptic* remove the first letter or letters from a word in the clue, as in: 'King George beheading a thistle finds stuff that's tough and chewy' (7) = gristle (King George = GR (Georgius Rex)).

Belgium *cryptic* abbreviated as B.

belief *n* 1 (4) idea, view; (5) creed, dogma, faith, tenet; (6) notion, theory; (7) opinion; (8) attitude, judgment, position; (9) judgement, principle, sentiment; (10) conviction, impression, persuasion; (11) presumption; (2+ words) point of view, way of thinking; 2 (5) trust; (8) reliance; (9) assurance, certainty; (10) confidence.

believe *v* (4) deem, hold, wear; (5) guess, judge, think, trust; (6) accept, assume, credit, gather, reckon; (7) presume, suppose, swallow; (8) consider.

Bellerophon *Gk myth* a hero who rode the winged horse Pegasus and slew the **Chimaera**.

Belshazzar *Bible* a king of Babylon, son of Nebuchadnezzar. He held a feast at which he used gold and silver vessels taken by his father from the temple in Jerusalem and 'the writing on the wall' mysteriously appeared. It said: 'Mene, mene tekel upharsin.' The prophet Daniel interpreted this as, 'God hath numbered thy kingdom and finished it. Thou art weighed in the balances, and art found wanting. Thy kingdom is divided and given to the Medes and the Persians.'

bend I *n & v* (3) arc, bow; (4) coil, hook, loop, roll, turn, veer, wrap; (5) angle, curve, twine, twist; (6) corner, spiral, zigzag; (7) meander; II *n* (5) crook, elbow; (7) turning; (9) curvature; III *v* (4) flex, lean; (5) stoop; (6) buckle, crouch; (7) contort, deviate, deflect, incline; IV *cryptic* 1 use letter S or U; 2 ANAGRAM CUE.

beneficial *adj* (6) useful; (7) helpful; (8) edifying, fruitful, valuable; (9) effective, practical, rewarding; (10) favourable, productive, profitable, worthwhile; (12) advantageous.

benefit I *n & v* (3) aid; (4) gain, help; (5) avail; (6) favour, profit; (9) advantage; II *n* (3) use; (4) boon, good; (5) asset, point, value, worth; (6) object; (7) purpose, service, welfare; (8) blessing; (10) usefulness; III *v* (5) serve; (6) assist, better; (7) advance, further, improve, promote.

bent I *adj* 1 (5) bowed; (6) angled, arched, curved; (7) crooked, hunched, stooped, twisted; 2 (7) corrupt, illegal; (8) criminal; (9) dishonest; 3 (3) set; (5) fixed; (6) intent; (10) determined; II *n* (4) gift, hang; (5) flair, forte, skill, trick; (6) talent; (7) ability, faculty; (8) aptitude, facility, tendency; (9) expertise; (10) propensity; (11) inclination; III *cryptic* ANAGRAM CUE.

best I *adj* (3) top; (5) first, prime; (6) choice, finest; (7) leading, optimum; II *n* (4) pick; (5) cream, elite; (6) flower; III *v* (4) beat; (6) defeat; IV *cryptic* letters A or AI.

bet I *n & v* (3) bid; (4) punt, risk; (5) stake, wager; (6) gamble; II *n* (4) ante; (6) double, treble, yankee; (7) flutter; (11) accumulator, speculation.

betray *v* 1 (3) rat; (4) sell, shop; (5) grass; (6) desert; (7) abandon, forsake; (11) double-cross; (2 words) inform on, let down, sell out; 2 (4) show, tell; (6) expose, reveal; (7) divulge; (8) disclose, manifest.

biased *adj* (6) angled, loaded, unfair, warped; (7) bigoted, partial, slanted; (8) one-sided; (9) blinkered, distorted, jaundiced; (10) prejudiced.

Bible I *n* (4) book; (6) manual; (9) Scripture, testament; (10) Scriptures; (2 words) good book; II *cryptic* AV (Authorised Version), CEV (Contemporary English Version), NEB (New English Bible), NIV (New International Version), NT (New Testament), OT (Old Testament), RV (Revised Version).

BOOKS OF THE BIBLE

Acts, Amos, Chronicles (I & II), Colossians, Corinthians (I & II), Daniel, Deuteronomy, Ecclesiastes, Ephesians, Esther, Exodus, Ezekiel, Ezra, Galatians, Genesis, Habakkuk, Haggai, Hebrews, Hosea, Isaiah, James, Jeremiah, Job, Joel, John, John (Epistles I, II, & III), Jonah, Joshua, Jude, Judges, Kings (I & II), Lamentations, Leviticus, Luke, Malachi, Mark, Matthew, Micah, Nahum, Nehemiah, Numbers, Obadiah, Peter (I & II), Philemon,

list continued over

Philippians, Proverbs, Psalms, Revelation, Romans, Ruth, Samuel (I & II), Song of Songs (or Song of Solomon), Thessalonians (I & II), Timothy (I & II), Titus, Zechariah, Zephaniah.

big I *adj* (4) huge, vast, wide; (5) ample, broad, bulky, giant, great, jumbo, large, roomy; (7) immense, mammoth, monster, outsize, titanic; (8) colossal, enormous, gigantic, king-size, sizeable, spacious; (9) extensive; II *cryptic* letter L (large) or letters OS (outsize), XL (extra large) etc.

bill I *n* 1 (3) tab; (5) check; (7) account, charges, invoice; (9) reckoning, statement; 2 (3) act; (7) measure; (8) proposal; (11) legislation; 3 (6) notice, poster; (7) handout, leaflet, placard; (13) advertisement; 4 (6) line-up; (9) programme; 5 (4) beak; 6 (4) pike; (7) halberd; II *v* 1 (5) debit; (6) charge; (7) invoice; 2 (4) hype, list; (8) announce, proclaim; (9) advertise; III *cryptic* letters AC (account).

bind I *v* 1 (3) tie; (4) join, knot, lash, link, moor, rope; (6) attach, fasten, secure, tether; (7) connect; 2 (5) limit; (6) hamper, hinder; (8) restrain, restrict; II *n* (3) fix, jam; (6) plight; (11) predicament.

bird *n* 1 (4) fowl; (9) fledgling; (2 words) dicky bird, feathered friend; 2 (4) girl; (5) woman.

TYPES OF BIRD

(2) o-o (*or* oo).

(3) auk, cob, daw, emu, hen, jay, kea, mew, moa (*extinct*), nun, owl, pen, pie, roc (*myth*), tit, tui.

(4) cirl, cock, coot, crow, dodo (*extinct*), dove, duck, erne, eyas, guan, gull, hawk, hern, huia (*extinct*), ibis, jack, kaka, kite, kiwi, knot, koel, lark, loon, lory, mina, monk, myna, nene, pern, poll, rail, rhea, rook, ruff, rype, shag, skua, smee, smew, sora, swan, taha, teal, tern, tody, wawa, weka, wren, yite.

(5) biddy, booby, capon, chick, colin,

crake, crane, diver, drake, eagle, egret, eider, finch, galah, glede, goose, grebe, herne, hobby, homer, jäger, junco, macaw, madge, mavis, merle, murre, mynah, nandu, nelly, noddy, ousel, ouzel, owlet, piper, pipit, polly, poult, quail, raven, reeve, robin, saker, scaup, serin, snipe, solan, squab, stare, stint, stork, swift, terek, twite, urubu, veery, wader, wavey.

(6) amazon, ancona, argala, auklet, avocet, bantam, barbet, bishop, bonxie, brahma, budgie, bulbul, canary, chough, chukar, cochin, condor, corbie, coucal, cuckoo, culver, curlew, cygnet, darter, dipper, drongo, duiker, dunlin, eaglet, falcon, fulmar, gambet, gander, gannet, gentle, gentoo, godwit, gooney, goslet, grouse, guinea, hermit, hoopoe, houdan, jabiru, jacana, kakapo, lanner, linnet, loriot, magpie, martin, merlin, missel, monaul, mopoke, motmot, oriole, osprey, ox-bird, parrot, pastor, pea-hen, peewit, petrel, pigeon, plover, pouter, puffin, pullet, red-cap, roller, rumkin, runner, scoter, sea-mew, shrike, siskin, sultan, surrey, tercel, thrush, tomtit, toucan, towhee, trogon, turbit, turkey, willet, yaffle, yucker.

(7) ant-bird, apteryx, babbler, bee-kite, bittern, bluecap, blue-eye, blue-tit, boobook, bullbat, bunting, bush-tit, bustard, buzzard, catbird, chicken, coal-tit, cob-swan, colibri, corella, cotinga, courlan, courser, cowbird, creeper, cropper, dorking, dovekie, dunnock, emu-wren, fantail, fern-owl, flicker, gadwall, gobbler, gorcock, gorcrow, goshawk, gosling, grackle, greyhen, greylag, halcyon, harrier, hoatzin, ice-bird, jacamar, jackdaw, jacobin, kestrel, lapwing, leghorn, mallard, manakin, marabou, martlet, minivet, minorca, moorhen, noctule, oil-bird, ortolan, ostrich, oven-tit, peacock, pea-fowl,

list continued over

pelican, penguin, pinnock, pintado, pochard, poulard, quetzal, redpoll, redwing, rooster, rosella, ruddock, sakeret, saw-bill, scooper, sea-bird, sea-crow, sea-dove, sea-duck, sea-fowl, seagull, sea-hawk, sea-lark, seriema, skimmer, sparrow, squacco, sun-bird, swallow, tanager, tattler, tiercel, tinamou, titlark, touraco, tumbler, vulture, wagtail, warbler, wax-bill, wax-wing, whooper, widgeon, woodhen, wood-owl, wren-tit, wrybill, wryneck.(2 words) barn owl, blue jay, grey owl.

(8) accentor, adjutant, alcatras, amadavat, baldpate, barnacle, bateleur, bee-eater, bell-bird, berghaan, blackcap, bluebird, bluewing, boatbill, boat-tail, bobolink, capuchin, caracara, cardinal, cargoose, churn-owl, cockatoo, cockerel, curassow, dabchick, didapper, dotterel, duckling, dundiver, eagle-owl, falconet, fireback, firebird, flamingo, game-bird, game-cock, garganey, greenlet, grosbeak, guacharo, hackbolt, hangbird, hawfinch, heath-hen, hernshaw, hornbill, king-bird, kingcrow, landrail, lanneret, lorikeet, lovebird, lyre-bird, man-of-war, megapode, moorcock, moorfowl, more-pork, murrelet, musk-duck, nestling, nightjar, night-owl, nuthatch, oven-bird, ox-pecker, parakeet, pea-chick, pheasant, poorwill, popinjay, puff-bird, rain-bird, redshank, redstart, reed-bird, reedling, reed-wren, rice-bird, ring-dove, screamer, sea-eagle, shelduck, shoebill, silktail, snowbird, songbird, starling, surfbird, tawny-owl, thrasher, throstle, titmouse, tragopan, troupial, wheatear, whimbrel, whinchat, whitecap, woodchat, woodcock, wood-ibis, woodlark, zopilote; (2 words) brown owl, hazel hen, maori hen, mute swan, old squaw, rock dove, water hen, wild duck.

(9) albatross, ant-thrush, baltimore, beccafico, blackbird, blackcock, blackhead, bowerbird, brambling, bullfinch, campanero, cassowary, chaffinch, chickadee, cockatiel, cock-robin, cormorant, corncrake, crossbill, dandy-cock, eagle-hawk, eider-duck, fieldfare, fig-pecker, firecrest, flute-bird, frairbird, frogmouth, gallinule, gerfalcon, goldcrest, golden-eye, goldfinch, goosander, grey-goose, guillemot, guinea-hen, gyrfalcon, heathcock, heathfowl, honey-bird, jack-snipe, jenny-wren, kittiwake, malle-hen, mallemuck, merganser, mound-bird, nighthawk, orpington, ossifrage, partridge, peregrine, phalarope, pine-finch, ptarmigan, razor-bill, riflebird, rock-pipit, sandpiper, sapsucker, scald-crow, sheldrake, shoveller, snakebird, snow-goose, solitaire, spoonbill, stock-dove, stonechat, stone-hawk, storm-bird, storm-cock, swordbill, thickhead, thick-knee, trochilus, trumpeter, turkey-hen, turnstone, waterbird, watercock, waterfowl, windhover, wyandotte; (2 words) bald eagle, black swan, field lark, horned owl, ring ouzel, scrub bird, widow bird, wild goose.

(10) aberdevine, australorp, bluebreast, bluethroat, budgerigar, bufflehead, butterball, canvasback, chiffchaff, demoiselle, flycatcher, four-o-clock, goatsucker, gooney-bird, greenfinch, greenshank, ground-dove, hen-harrier, honey-eater, honey-guide, kingfisher, kookaburra, meadowlark, nutcracker, pratincole, regent-bird, ring-plover, roadrunner, rockhopper, runner-duck, saddleback, sanderling, sandgrouse, screech-owl, shearwater, sicklebill, tailorbird, tropicbird, turtledove, wattlebird, weaverbird, wonga-wonga, woodgrouse, woodpecker, woodpigeon, woodthrush, yellowbird; (2 words)

list continued over

brent goose, bush shrike, cape pigeon, ember goose, grey parrot, guinea fowl, indigo bird, jungle fowl, mallee bird, mallee fowl, mutton bird, night heron, parson bird, piping crow, prairie hen, rock pigeon, sage grouse, sand martin, scoter duck, sea swallow, solan goose, song thrush, sun bittern, turkey cock, tyrant bird, velvet duck, water ouzel, whydah bird, zebra finch.

(11) butcherbird, cock-sparrow, honeysucker, hummingbird, lammergeyer, leatherhead, mockingbird, nightingale, scissorbill, sparrowhawk, whitethroat, woodswallow; (2 words) black grouse, brush turkey, carrion crow, frigate bird, golden eagle, green linnet, hazel grouse, herring gull, java sparrow, king penguin, king vulture, meadow pipit, muscovy duck, purple finch, reed bunting, reed warbler, royston crow, scrub turkey, snow bunting, song sparrow, spanish fowl, storm petrel, tree creeper, wood warbler.

(12) capercaillie, falcon-gentle, whippoorwill, yellowhammer; (2 words) cardinal bird, drongo shrike, golden plover, hedge sparrow, homing pigeon, honey buzzard, Indian runner, mandarin duck, man-of-war bird, marsh harrier, missel thrush, painted snipe, Plymouth rock, rifleman bird, sedge warbler, stormy petrel, umbrella bird, velvet scoter, water wagtail, willow grouse.

(13) (2 words) barnacle goose, buff orpington, carrier pigeon, oyster catcher, secretary bird, willow warbler.

(14) (2+ words) bird of paradise, emperor penguin, golden pheasant, griffon vulture, prairie chicken, Rhode Island red.

(15) (2 words) Baltimore oriole, Dartford warbler, laughing jackass, peregrine falcon.

birthstone *n*

BIRTHSTONES
January – garnet
February – amethyst
March – bloodstone
April – diamond
May – emerald
June – agate
July – cornelian (*or* carnelian)
August – sardonyx
September – chrysolite
October – opal
November – topaz
December – turquoise

bishop *cryptic* letters B or RR (right reverend).

bit *n* 1 (4) bite, lump, part, some; (5) chunk, piece, scrap, share, slice; (6) morsel; (7) element, portion, section, segment; (8) division, fraction, fragment; (9) component; (11) constituent; 2 (4) bore, head; (5) drill; 3 unit of information for a computer.

bitter *adj* 1 (4) acid, sour, tart; (5) acrid, sharp; (8) vinegary; 2 (7) acerbic, cynical; (8) sardonic; (9) jaundiced, rancorous, resentful; (11) acrimonious; 2 (4) deep; (5) acute, cruel, harsh; (6) savage, severe; (7) intense, painful; 3 (3) raw; (4) cold; (6) biting.

bizarre I *adj* (3) odd; (5) alien, queer; (6) exotic; (7) curious, strange, unusual; (8) imported; (9) different; (10) introduced, outlandish, unfamiliar; (13) extra-ordinary; **II** *cryptic* ANAGRAM CUE.

blank *adj* 1 (4) free, void; (5) empty; (6) vacant, unused; (8) unfilled; (9) available; (10) unoccupied; 2 (5) inane; (6) absent; (7) vacuous; (14) expressionless.

bleak *adj* 1 (4) arid, bare, wild; (5) empty, waste; (6) barren, lonely, vacant; (8) derelict, deserted, desolate, forsaken, isolated, solitary; (9) abandoned, cheerless, neglected; (10) unoccupied; (11) comfortless, godforsaken, uninhabited, unpopulated; (12) unfrequented; 2 (3) sad; (6) dismal, gloomy; (7) forlorn; (9) miserable; (10) depressing, melancholy.

blemish I *n & v* (4) blot, flaw, mark, spot; (5) speck, stain, taint; (6) blotch, damage; (7) tarnish; (8) disgrace; (9) dishonour; II *v* (3) mar; (5) abase, lower, sully; (6) debase, deface, defile, demean, reduce; (7) corrupt, degrade, devalue, pollute; (9) disfigure; III *n* (5) fault; (6) defect, naevus; (9) birthmark, deformity; (12) imperfection.

blend I *v* (3) mix; (4) fuse, join, link; (5) marry, merge, unite; (6) mingle; (7) combine; (8) coalesce; (9) harmonise (*or* harmonize); (10) amalgamate; II *n* (5) union; (7) amalgam, mixture; (8) compound, marriage; (9) composite; (11) combination; III *cryptic* ANAGRAM CUE.

block I *n* 1 (4) cube, lump, mass; (5) brick, chunk; (6) square; 2 (7) barrier; (8) blockage, obstacle, stoppage; (10) resistance; (11) obstruction; II *v* 1 (3) bar, dam, jam; (4) clog, halt, plug, stop; (5) choke, close; (6) hinder, impede, retard, thwart; (7) inhibit, prevent; (8) obstruct, restrict; (9) interfere, interrupt; 2 (5) avert, avoid, parry, repel; (2 words) fend off, stave off, turn aside.

bloom I *n & v* (3) bud; (6) flower; (7) blossom; II *n* (4) glow; (5) blush, flush, prime; (6) beauty, health, heyday, lustre, vigour; (8) radiance; III *v* (3) wax; (4) blow, grow, open; (6) sprout, thrive; (7) develop, prosper; (8) flourish.

bloomer I *n* (4) boob; (5) gaffe; (7) **blunder**, clanger, mistake; II *cryptic* = flower.

blossom *n & v see* **bloom**.

blow I *n* 1 (3) hit, rap; (4) bang, bash, biff, clip, cuff, slap; (5) clout, crack, knock, punch, smack, swipe, thump, whack; (6) buffet, stroke, wallop; 2 (4) jolt; (5) shock, upset; (7) reverse, setback; (8) calamity, disaster; (9) bombshell; (10) affliction, misfortune; (11) catastrophe; (14) disappointment; 3 (4) gale, gust, wind; (5) blast, storm; II *v* 1 (4) gasp, gust, pant, puff, sigh, waft; (7) breathe; 2 (4) flap, sway, toss; (5) whirl, whisk; (6) ripple, ruffle; (7) flutter; 3 (5) spend, waste; (8) squander.

blue *n & adj* 1 (4) cyan, navy; (5) azure; (6) cobalt, indigo; (8) sapphire; (9) turquoise; (10) aquamarine; (11) ultramarine; 2 (3) sad; (4) down; (9) depressed; 3 (5) bawdy, dirty; (6) risqué, smutty; (7) obscene; (12) pornographic.

blunder I *n* (4) boob, slip; (5) error, fluff, gaffe; (6) cock-up, howler, slip-up; (7) balls-up, bloomer, clanger, mistake; (9) oversight; (2 words) faux pas; II *v* 1 (3) err; (5) botch; (6) bungle; (8) misjudge; (12) miscalculate; (2 words) cock up, slip up; 2 (5) barge; (6) bumble; (7) stagger, stumble; (8) flounder; III *cryptic* ANAGRAM CUE.

blunt I *adj* 1 (4) dull, worn; (5) round; (7) rounded, stubbed; (11) unsharpened; 2 (4) curt, open, rude; (5) frank, overt, plain; (6) abrupt, candid, direct, honest; (7) brusque, uncivil; (8) explicit, straight, truthful; (9) downright, outspoken; (10) forthright; (13) unceremonious; II *v* (4) dull, numb; (5) abate, allay; (6) deaden, lessen, reduce, soften, weaken.

Boadicea *hist.* Queen of the Iceni, an ancient British tribe, who rebelled again the occupying Roman forces and defeated them near Colchester and sacked London and Verulamium before being defeated herself. Also, and more correctly, called Boudicca.

board I *n* 1 (4) slab, slat; (5) panel, plank, sheet, strip; (6) timber; 2 (4) food, keep; (5) meals, table; (7) rations; 3 (5) group; (7) council; (9) committee, directors, governors; (10) commission, management; II *v* (5) enter, mount; (6) embark; (2 words) get on; III *cryptic* 1 *see entry at* on board; 2 reference to a board game, see below.

BOARD GAMES

(2) Go; (4) Ludo; (5) Chess, Halma; (6) Cluedo®; (7) Othello, Pachisi; (8) Checkers, Cribbage, Draughts, Mahjongg, Monopoly®; (9) Bagatelle, Diplomacy®; (10) Backgammon; (2+ words) Snakes and Ladders, Trivial Pursuit®.

---

boat I *n* (5) craft; (6) vessel; II *v* (3) row; (4) punt, sail; (6) cruise.

BOATS

for larger vessels see also **ship**.

(3) gig.

(4) dory, four, pink, pram, prau, proa, punt, raft, scow, yawl.

(5) balsa, barge, canoe, coble, eight, ferry, kayak, ketch, praam, scull, shell, skiff, smack, xebec, yacht, zebec.

(6) curagh, cutter, dinghy, dogger, dugout, galley, hooker, launch, lugger, randan, sampan, tartan, whaler, wherry.

(7) coracle, currach, curragh, felucca, gondola, pirogue, sculler, shallop, zebeck.

(8) cockboat, lifeboat, longboat, trimaran.

(9) catamaran, jollyboat, motor-boat, outrigger, speedboat.

(10) rowing-boat.

body *n* **1** (5) build, torso, trunk; (6) figure; (7) anatomy; (8) physique; **2** (5) stiff; (6) corpse; (7) cadaver, carcass; **3** (4) band, mass; (5) crowd, group; (6) throng; (7) company, society; (11) association, corporation; (12) organisation (*or* organization); **4** (4) bulk; (7) density; (8) firmness, fullness, richness, solidity; (9) substance.

boil I *v* **1** (4) foam, stew; (5) froth, steam; (6) bubble, seethe, simmer; **2** (4) bake; (5) roast; (6) sizzle; (7) swelter; II *cryptic* ANAGRAM CUE.

bold *adj* **1** (5) **brave**; (6) daring; (8) intrepid; (9) audacious, confident; (11) adventurous; **2** (5) brash; (6) brazen, cheeky; (7) forward; (8) impudent, insolent; (9) shameless; **3** (4) loud; (5) showy, vivid; (6) bright, flashy, marked; (8) striking; (9) colourful, prominent; (10) pronounced; (11) conspicuous, eye-catching.

bond I *n* **1** (3) tie; (4) link; (7) kinship; (10) connection; (11) affiliation, correlation; (12) relationship; **2** (4) band, cord, rope; (5) chain; (6) fetter, string; (7)

manacle, shackle; **3** (4) word; (6) pledge; (8) contract, covenant; II *v* (3) tie; (4) bind, fuse, glue; (5) paste, stick, unite; (6) fasten; (7) connect.

bone *n*

HUMAN BONES

(3) jaw, rib; (4) axis, ulna; (5) femur, ilium, incus, pubis, skull, spine, talus, tibia; (6) carpus, coccyx, fibula, pelvis, radius, sacrum, stapes, tarsus; (7) cranium, humerus, ischium, malleus, maxilla, patella, phalanx, scapula, sternum; (8) clavicle, temporal, vertebra; (9) calcaneum, trapezium; (10) metacarpus.

book I *n* **1** (4) tome, work; (5) bible, novel; (6) annual, manual, volume; (7) edition; (11) publication; **2** (4) part; (5) canto; *for books of the Bible, see* **Bible**; II *v* **1** (3) bag; (5) order; (6) engage; (7) charter, reserve; **2** (3) log; (4) list; (5) enter; III **book** *or* **booklet** *cryptic* letters BK, ED, NT, OT, VOL.

border I *n* (3) lip, rim; (4) brim, side; (5) brink, limit, verge; (6) border, bounds, fringe, margin; (8) boundary, frontier; (9) perimeter, periphery, threshold; II *v* **1** (3) hem; (4) edge; **2** (4) abut; (5) touch; (6) adjoin.

bore I *v* **1** (4) mine, sink; (5) drill; (6) burrow, pierce, tunnel; (9) penetrate; **2** (4) tire; (5) weary; (6) bother; II *n* (4) bind, drag, pain; (8) nuisance.

bored *adj* (5) jaded, tired, weary; (8) listless, restless; (2 words) fed up.

boring *adj* (4) drab, dull; (5) banal; (6) dreary; (7) humdrum, tedious; (8) tiresome; (9) laborious, wearisome; (10) long-winded, monotonous, unexciting; (13) uninteresting.

born *cryptic* letter B or letters NE or NEE (née).

boron *cryptic* abbreviated as B.

borrow *v* (4) crib, copy, lift, take; (5) adopt, cadge, mimic; (6) sponge; (7) imitate; (8) scrounge; (10) plagiarise (*or* plagiarize).

bother I *n & v* (5) upset, worry; (7) trouble; (8) distress; (13) inconvenience; **II** *n* **1** (3) ado; (4) fuss; (5) grief, trial; (7) anxiety, problem; (8) nuisance; (9) agitation, annoyance; (10) affliction, irritation, misfortune; (11) aggravation, tribulation; **2** (4) care; (5) pains; (6) effort; (7) thought; (9) attention; **3** (6) strife, tumult, unrest; (8) conflict, disorder, upheaval; (9) commotion; (11) disturbance; **4** (7) ailment, disease, illness; **III** *v* (3) nag, vex; (5) annoy; (6) harass, ruffle; (7) afflict, agitate, disturb, perplex; (8) irritate; (10) disconcert; **IV bother** *or* **bothered** *cryptic* ANAGRAM CUE.

bottle *n* **1** (5) flask, phial; (6) carafe, carboy, flagon; (8) decanter, demijohn; **2** (5) nerve; (7) courage.

LARGE BOTTLES

magnum (2 bottles), jeroboam (4 bottles), rehoboam (6 bottles), methuselah (8 bottles), salmanazar (12 bottles), balthazar (16 bottles), nebuchadnezzar (20 bottles)

---

bottom I *n* **1** (3) bed; (4) base, foot, sole; (5) nadir; (6) ground, seabed; (9) underside; (10) underneath; **2** (3) ass, bum; (4) arse, butt, rear, rump, seat, tail; (6) behind; (8) backside, buttocks; (9) posterior; **II** *adj* (4) last; (5) basic, least; (6) lowest; (11) fundamental; **III Bottom** *lit.* chief comic character in Shakespeare's **A Midsummer Night's Dream.**

Boudicca *hist. see* **Boadicea.**

bound I *v & n* **1** (3) hop; (4) jump, leap, skip; (5) caper, frisk, vault; (6) bounce, frolic, spring; **2** (5) limit; (6) border; **II** *v* (7) contain; (8) restrict; (12) circumscribe; **III** *n see* **boundary.**

boundary *n* (3) end, rim; (4) brim, edge, line; (5) brink, limit, verge; (6) border, bounds, fringe, margin, utmost; (7) ceiling, extreme, maximum, minimum, outline; (8) confines, frontier, terminus; (9) extremity, perimeter, precincts, threshold.

bow I *n & v* (3) bob, nod; (4) bend; (6) curtsy, kowtow, salaam, salute; (7) incline;

II *n* **1** (9) obeisance; **2** (4) stem; (5) front; **3** (6) weapon; (7) longbow; (8) crossbow.

box I *n* (4) case, pack; (5) chest, crate, trunk; (6) carton, coffer, coffin, packet; (9) container; (10) receptacle; **II** *v* **1** (4) pack, wrap; (6) encase; (7) confine, enclose; **2** (4) spar; (5) fight, punch.

boxer *n* (3) dog; (7) fighter; (8) pugilist; (9) flyweight; (11) heavyweight, lightweight; (12) bantamweight, middleweight, welterweight; (13) cruiserweight, featherweight.

FAMOUS BOXERS

Ali (Muhammad), Baer (Max), Bruno (Frank), Bugner (Joe), Clay (Cassius = Ali), Conteh (John), Cooper (Henry), Dempsey (Jack), Foreman (George), Frazier (Joe), La Motta (Jake), Lewis (Lennox), Liston (Sonny), Louis (Joe), Marciano (Rocky), Patterson (Floyd), Robinson (Sugar Ray), Schmeling (Max), Spinks (Leon), Tunney (Gene), Turpin (Randolph), Tyson (Mike).

---

boy I *n* (3) kid, lad, son; (5) youth; (6) nipper; (9) youngster; **II** *cryptic* frequently the word 'boy' or 'man' prompts for a boy's name - *see below*.

BOYS' NAMES

(3) Abe, Aby, Alf, Ali, Art, Asa, Ben, Bob, Bud, Col, Dai, Dan, Dec, Dee, Del, Den, Dod, Don, Eli, Ern, Gil, Gus, Guy, Hal, Hew, Huw, Ian, Ike, Ira, Ivo, Jan, Jay, Jed, Jem, Jim, Job, Joe, Jon, Ken, Kev, Kim, Kit, Lee, Len, Leo, Lev, Lew, Lou, Mat, Max, Mel, Nat, Ned, Nye, Odo, Pat, Pip, Ray, Red, Reg, Rex, Rod, Rog, Roy, Sam, Seb, Sid, Sly, Tam, Ted, Tim, Tom, Val, Van, Vic, Viv, Wat, Wes, Wyn.

(4) Abel, Adam, Alan, Alec, Aled, Algy, Alun, Alva, Alyn, Amos, Andy, Axel, Bart, Bert, Bill, Boyd, Bram, Bryn, Buck, Burt, Cain, Carl, Cary, Chad, Chas, Chay, Chip, Clem,

list continued over

Dale, Dave, Davy, Dean, Dick, Dirk, Dion, Drew, Duff, Duke, Earl, Eddy, Egon, Emil, Eric, Erle, Eryl, Esau, Evan, Ewan, Ezra, Fats, Finn, Fred, Fulk, Gary, Gene, Glen, Glyn, Greg, Hank, Hans, Hope, Huey, Hugh, Hugo, Iain, Igor, Ivan, Jack, Jake, Jean, Jeff, Jess, Jock, Jody, Joel, Joey, John, Josh, Joss, Juan, Jude, Karl, Keir, Kent, King, Kirk, Kurt, Kyle, Lars, Leon, Liam, Luke, Marc, Mark, Matt, Mick, Mort, Muir, Neil, Nero, Nick, Niki, Noah, Noël, Olaf, Olav, Omar, Otho, Otis, Otto, Owen, Paul, Pepe, Pete, Phil, René, Rhys, Rick, Rolf, Rory, Ross, Russ, Ryan, Saul, Sean, Seth, Stan, Sven, Theo, Thor, Toby, Todd, Tony, Trev, Vere, Walt, Wilf, Will, Wynn, Yves, Zeke.

(5) Aaron, Abdul, Abner, Abram, Adolf, Aidan, Airey, Alain, Alban, Alfie, Alick, Allan, Allen, Alvin, Alywin, Alwyn, Amyan, André, Angel, Angus, Anton, Archy, Artie, Aubyn, Barry, Basil, Benny, Bevis, Billy, Blake, Bobby, Booth, Boris, Brett, Brain, Bruce, Bruno, Bryan, Buddy, Bunny, Busby, Caius, Caleb, Carew, Carol, Cecil, Chris, Chuck, Claud, Cliff, Clint, Clive, Clyde, Colin, Conan, Cosmo, Craig, Cyril, Cyrus, Dacre, Damon, Danny, Darcy, Daryl, David, Davie, Denis, Denny, Denys, Derek, Dicky, Donal, Duane, Dwane, Dylan, Eamon, Earle, Eddie, Edgar, Edwin, Eldon, Elias, Ellis, Elmer, Elton, Elvis, Elwyn, Emery, Emile, Emlyn, Emrys, Enoch, Ernie, Ernst, Errol, Ewart, Felix, Ferdy, Flann, Floyd, Frank, Frans, Franz, Fritz, Garry, Garth, Gavin, Geoff, Gerry, Giles, Glenn, Grant, Griff, Guido, Gyles, Harry, Heinz, Henri, Henry, Hiram, Homer, Horst, Humph, Hyram, Hywel, Inigo, Innes, Isaac, Izaak, Jabez, Jacky, Jacob, Jaime, James, Jamie, Jared, Jason, Jerry, Jesse, Jimmy, Jonah, Jonas, Jules, Keith, Kelly, Kenny, Kevin, Lance, Larry,

Leigh, Lenny, Leroy, Lewin, Lewis, Lloyd, Louie, Louis, Lucas, Luigi, Major, Micah, Micky, Miles, Monty, Moses, Mungo, Murdo, Nahum, Neddy, Nevil, Niall, Nigel, Nolan, Oscar, Osman, Osric, Oswin, Paddy, Pedro, Percy, Perry, Peter, Piers, Ralph, Ramon, Raoul, Rhett, Ricky, Rider, Roald, Robin, Roddy, Roger, Rollo, Romeo, Rowan, Rubin, Rufus, Sacha, Sandy, Scott, Serge, Shane, Silas, Simon, Solly, Sonny, Spiro, Steve, Taffy, Teddy, Terry, Tibor, Titus, Tommy, Ulick, Ulric, Ultan, Urban, Uriah, Vince, Wahab, Wally, Wayne, Willy, Wolfe, Woody, Wyatt.

(6) Adolph, Adrian, Aeneas, Alaric, Albert, Aldred, Alexis, Alfred, Andrew, Angelo, Anselm, Antony, Archie, Armand, Arnold, Arthur, Ashley, Ashoka, Aubrey, Austin, Aylmer, Aylwin, Barney, Benito, Benjie, Bennie, Bernie, Bertie, Brutus, Bulwer, Buster, Caesar, Calvin, Carlos, Caspar, Cedric, Claude, Colley, Connor, Conrad, Cuddie, Damian, Daniel, Darren, Darryl, Declan, Delroy, Dennis, Denzil, Dermot, Deryck, Dickie, Donald, Donnie, Dougal, Dugald, Duggie, Duncan, Dundas, Dwight, Eamonn, Edmond, Edmund, Eduard, Edward, Egbert, Eldred, Elliot, Ernest, Esmond, Eugene, Evelyn, Fabian, Fergus, Finlay, Forbes, Gareth, Gaston, Gawain, George, Gerald, Gerard, Gideon, Godwin, Gordon, Graeme, Graham, Grogan, Gunter, Gwilym, Hamish, Hamlet, Hansel, Harold, Harris, Harvey, Haydon, Hector, Hedley, Helmut, Herman, Hilary, Hilton, Horace, Howard, Howell, Hubert, Hughie, Ignace, Ingram, Irvine, Isaiah, Isodor, Israel, Jackie, Jarvis, Jasper, Jeremy, Jerome, Jervis, Jethro, Johann, Johnny, Joseph, Joshua, Josiah, Julian, Julius, Justin, Justus,

list continued over

Kieran, Konrad, Laurie, Lawrie, Lemuel, Leslie, Lester, Lionel, Lorcan, Lucius, Ludwig, Luther, Magnus, Manuel, Marcel, Marcus, Martin, Martyn, Melvin, Melvyn, Merlin, Mickie, Milton, Morgan, Morris, Mostyn, Murphy, Murray, Nathan, Neddie, Nelson, Nichol, Ninian, Norman, Norris, Oliver, Onslow, Osbert, Osmond, Osmund, Oswald, Pascal, Pascoe, Paulus, Pearce, Pelham, Perkin, Philip, Pierce, Pierre, Ramsay, Randal, Rastus, Rayner, Reggie, Rhodes, Richie, Robbie, Robert, Rodger, Rodney, Roland, Ronald, Rowley, Rudolf, Rupert, Samson, Samuel, Sancho, Seamas, Seamus, Sefton, Selwyn, Sexton, Sidney, Simeon, Simkin, Soames, Stefan, Steven, Stevie, Stuart, Sydney, Thomas, Tobias, Trevor, Tybalt, Tyrone, Vernon, Victor, Virgil, Vivian, Vyvian, Wallis, Walter, Warren, Wesley, Wilbur, Willie, Xavier, Yehudi.

(7) Abraham, Absalom, Ainsley, Alfonso, Alister, Almeric, Amadeus, Ambrose, Anatole, Aneurin, Anthony, Antoine, Antonio, Artemus, Auberon, Auguste, Baldwin, Baptist, Barclay, Barnaby, Bernard, Bertram, Brandon, Brendan, Brynmor, Cameron, Caradoc, Casimir, Charles, Charley, Charlie, Chester, Clayton, Clement, Clinton, Compton, Connell, Crispin, Cyprian, Delbert, Derrick, Desmond, Diggory, Dominic, Donovan, Douglas, Edouard, Eleazer, Ephraim, Erasmus, Eustace, Everard, Ezekiel, Feargal, Findlay, Francis, Frankie, Freddie, Gabriel, Georgie, Geraint, Gervase, Gilbert, Gloster, Godfrey, Gregory, Gustave, Hadrian, Halbert, Hartley, Herbert, Hermann, Hilaire, Horatio, Humbert, Humphrey, Ingleby, Isidore, Jackson, Jacques, Jeffrey, Joachim, Jocelyn, Johnnie, Kenneth, Kimball, Lachlan,

Lambert, Lazarus, Leonard, Leopold, Lindsay, Lorenzo, Ludovic, Malachi, Malcolm, Matthew, Maurice, Maxwell, Maynard, Merrick, Michael, Montagu, Myrddin, Neville, Nicolas, Obadiah, Octavus, Orlando, Orpheus, Orville, Osborne, Patrick, Perseus, Phineas, Quentin, Quintin, Ranulph, Raphael, Raymond, Raymund, Redvers, Reynard, Reynold, Richard, Royston, Rudolph, Rudyard, Russell, Sampson, Seymour, Sheldon, Shelley, Sigmund, Solomon, Spencer, Stanley, Stavros, Stephen, Steuart, Stewart, Tarquin, Terence, Timothy, Torquil, Tristan, Ulysses, Umberto, Vaughan, Vincent, Wallace, Wilfred, Wilfrid, Wilhelm, William, Winston, Wyndham, Wynford, Zachary, Zebedee.

(8) Achilles, Adolphus, Alasdair, Alastair, Algernon, Alistair, Aloysius, Alphonso, Antonius, Augustus, Aurelius, Bardolph, Barnabas, Bartlemy, Benedict, Benjamin, Bertrand, Beverley, Campbell, Christie, Clarence, Claudius, Clifford, Constant, Courtney, Crawford, Crispian, Cuthbert, Dinsdale, Dominick, Ebenezer, Emmanuel, Ethelred, Eusebius, Farquhar, Francois, Franklin, Frederic, Geoffrey, Giovanni, Giuseppe, Greville, Griffith, Gustavus, Hamilton, Harrison, Havelock, Hercules, Hereward, Hezekiah, Horatius, Humphrey, Ignatius, Immanuel, Jedediah, Jeremiah, Jonathon, Kimberly, Kingsley, Lancelot, Laurence, Lawrence, Leonidas, Llewelyn, Ludovick, Lutwidge, Meredith, Montague, Mortimer, Nehemiah, Nicholas, Octavius, Oliphant, Oughtred, Paulinus, Perceval, Percival, Peterkin, Philemon, Randolph, Reginald, Robinson, Roderick, Ruairidh, Salvador, Secundus, Septimus,

list continued over

Sherlock, Siegmund, Sinclair, Stafford, Sylvanus, Terrance, Thaddeus, Theobald, Theodore, Tristram, Vladimir.

(9) Alexander, Alphonsus, Archibald, Aristotle, Athelstan, Augustine, Balthazar, Bartimeus, Christian, Cornelius, Demetrius, Dionysius, Engelbert, Ethelbert, Ferdinand, Frederick, Gillespie, Granville, Grenville, Justinian, Kimberley, Launcelot, Llewellyn, Lucretius, Mackenzie, Marmaduke, Nathaniel, Nicodemus, Peregrine, Rodriguez, Rupprecht, Sebastian, Siegfried, Sigismund, Stanislas, Sylvester, Thaddaeus, Theodoric, Valentine, Zachariah, Zechariah.

(10) Athanasius, Athelstane, Barrington, Desederius, Hildebrand, Maximilian, Pierrepont, Stanislaus, Theodosius, Theophilus, Washington, Willoughby.

(11) Bartholomew, Christopher, Constantine, Desideratus, Sacheverell.

branch I *n* 1 (4) limb; (5) bough, shoot, sprig; (8) offshoot; 2 (3) arm; (4) part; (6) office; (7) section; (8) division; (10) department; II *v* (4) fork; (6) divide; (7) diverge; (8) separate.

brand I *n & v* (3) tag; (4) mark; (5) label, stamp; II *n* 1 (4) kind, make, **sort**, type; 2 (4) logo, mark, sign; (6) emblem, symbol; (8) hallmark; (9) trademark; II *v* (4) burn, scar, sear; (7) censure; (10) stigmatise (*or* stigmatize).

brave I *adj* (4) **bold**; (5) gutsy; (6) feisty, heroic, plucky; (7) gallant, valiant; (8) fearless, unafraid; (9) dauntless, undaunted; (10) courageous; II *v* (4) dare, defy, face; (8) confront; (9) challenge.

bravery *n* (4) grit, guts; (5) nerve, pluck; (6) bottle, daring, mettle, spirit, valour; (7) courage, heroism; (8) audacity, boldness; (9) fortitude, gallantry, hardihood.

break I *v & n* (4) gash; (5) crack, split; (8) fracture; II *v* 1 (4) bust, harm, hurt, ruin,

snap; (5) smash, spoil, wreck (6) deface, impair, injure, weaken; (7) despoil, shatter; (8) demolish, mutilate, sabotage; (9) devastate; 2 (3) end; (4) halt; (5) pause; III *n* 1 (3) gap; (4) hole; (5) cleft; (6) breach; (7) fissure, opening, rupture; 2 (3) nap; (4) halt, lull, rest; (5) space, spell; (6) recess, siesta, snooze; (7) holiday, respite; (8) breather, interval, vacation; (9) entr'acte, interlude; (12) intermission, interruption; 3 (6) chance; (7) opening; (8) occasion; (11) opportunity; IV **break, breaking, broke** etc *cryptic* 1 ANAGRAM CUE; 2 insert a letter, letters, or word into another to complete the answer, as in: 'Woman, not politically correct, breaks bank and leaves it on its last legs' (8) = moribund (bank = mound).

breed I *n* (4) line, race, type; (5) stock; (6) family, strain; (7) lineage, species, variety; (8) pedigree; II *v* 1 (8) multiply; (9) procreate, propagate, reproduce; 2 (4) rear; (5) cause, raise; (6) arouse, create; (7) develop, nourish, produce; (8) engender, generate, occasion.

brew *cryptic* ANAGRAM CUE.

bridge I *n & v* (3) tie; (4) link, span; II *n* (4) arch; (7) flyover, pontoon, viaduct; (8) aqueduct, causeway, crossing, overpass; III *v* (5) cross; (7) connect; (8) traverse.

bridge player *cryptic* letter N, E, S, or W (from the fact that the four players in a game of bridge are usually designated north, south, east and west).

brief I *adj* 1 (4) fast; (5) hasty, short, swift; (7) cursory, hurried, passing; (8) fleeting; (9) ephemeral, momentary, temporary, transient; (10) transitory; 2 (4) curt; (5) crisp, pithy, terse; (7) concise, laconic; (8) abridged, succinct; (9) curtailed, thumbnail; (10) compressed; 3 (4) mini; (5) small; (6) skimpy; II *n* 1 (4) case; (5) remit; (6) orders; (7) defence, dossier, mandate; (9) directive; (10) commission; (12) instructions; 2 *slang* (6) lawyer; (9) barrister, solicitor; III *v* (5) guide, prime; (6) advise, direct, inform, notify; (8) instruct; (2+ words) bring up to date, bring up to speed, fill in, gen up; IV **briefs** (5) pants; (6) shorts; (7) panties.

bright *adj* 1 (4) bold, loud; (5) clear, light, vivid; (6) flashy, glossy, marked, strong; (7) glaring, glowing, intense, shining, vibrant; (8) dazzling, gleaming, luminous; (9) brilliant, colourful, prominent, sparkling; (10) glistening, glittering; (11) conspicuous, eye-catching; 2 (5) acute, quick, sharp, smart; (6) astute, brainy, clever; (10) perceptive; (11) intelligent, quick-witted; 3 (4) fine, rosy; (5) sunny; (7) hopeful; (9) cloudless, promising; (10) auspicious, propitious; 4 (5) happy, jolly, merry; (6) lively; (9) vivacious.

brilliant *adj* 1 *see* **bright** 1 2 (6) adept, bright, **clever**, expert, gifted; (7) skilful; (8) masterly, talented, virtuoso; (11) exceptional, outstanding; (12) accomplished; 3 (3) fab; (5) brill, great, super; (6) superb; (7) amazing, awesome; (8) fabulous, smashing, terrific; (9) fantastic, wonderful; (10) incredible, marvellous, phenomenal, stupendous, tremendous; (11) magnificent, outstanding, sensational; (12) unbelievable.

broad l *adj* 1 (4) full, vast, wide; (5) baggy, loose, roomy; (7) dilated, immense; (8) expanded, spacious; (9) extensive; (10) widespread; 2 (4) full; (7) general; (8) catholic, eclectic; (9) inclusive, universal; (11) far-reaching; (13) comprehensive; 3 *see* **broad-minded**; ll *n* 1 (4) lake; (5) river; 2 *US slang* (5) woman.

broadcast l *v* 1 (3) air; (4) beam, send; (5) relay; (8) televise, transmit; 2 (6) report; (7) publish; (8) announce; (9) advertise, circulate, publicise (*or* publicize); (10) promulgate; (11) disseminate; 3 (3) sow; (6) spread; ll *n* (4) show; (9) programme; (12) transmission.

broad-minded *adj* (7) lenient, liberal; (8) tolerant; (10) charitable, permissive; (11) enlightened; (14) latitudinarian.

broke l *adj* (4) bust; (5) skint, stony; (6) ruined; (8) bankrupt; (9) destitute, insolvent, penniless; (12) impoverished; ll *see* **break**.

broken l *adj* 1 (4) bust; (5) kaput; (7) smashed; (9) defective, fractured, shattered; (13) unserviceable; (2+ words) on the blink, out of order; 2 (7) halting; (8) hesitant; (9) spasmodic; (10) disjointed; (11) interrupted; (12) disconnected, intermittent; (13) discontinuous; 3 (4) down, weak; (5) tamed; (6) beaten; (7) crushed; (8) defeated; ll *cryptic* ANAGRAM CUE.

Brontë *lit.* a Yorkshire family, based in Haworth, of four gifted siblings. The three sisters all wrote successful novels; their brother, Bramwell, however, achieved little success as a painter.

> ### NOVELS BY THE BRONTË SISTERS
> *Anne* (pseudonym, Acton Bell): Agnes Grey, The Tenant of Wildfell Hall. *Charlotte* (pseudonym, Currer Bell) Jane Eyre, The Professor, Shirley, Villette. *Emily* (pseudonym, Ellis Bell) Wuthering Heights.

brook l *n* (4) beck, burn, rill; (5) creek, river; (6) stream; (7) channel, rivulet; ll *v* (4) bear; (5) stand; (8) tolerate.

brown *adj & n* (3) bay, tan; (4) rust; (5) khaki, sepia, tawny, umber; (6) coffee; (8) brunette, chestnut, mahogany; (9) chocolate.

Bucephalus *hist.* the horse ridden by Alexander the Great.

bug l *n* 1 (4) germ; (5) virus; (7) disease, microbe; (9) bacterium, infection; 2 (5) aphid; (6) beetle, insect; (8) parasite; 3 (4) flaw; (5) fault; (6) defect, glitch; (7) gremlin; 4 listening device; ll *v* (3) irk, vex; (5) annoy; (6) bother; (7) disturb; (8) irritate.

build l *v* 1 (4) form, make; (5) erect, raise; (8) assemble; (9) construct, fabricate; 2 (6) extend; (7) develop, enlarge; (8) increase; (9) intensify; ll *n* (4) body; (5) frame, shape; (6) figure; (8) physique; lll *cryptic* ANAGRAM CUE.

Bull *astrol & astron see* **Taurus**.

burden l *n & v* (4) load; (6) weight; ll *n* 1 (4) care, duty, onus; (5) cargo; (6) strain, stress; (7) freight; (10) obligation; 2 (5) theme; (6) chorus, repeat; (7) refrain; lll *v* (3) tax; (7) oppress; (8) encumber, handicap.

burn I *v* 1 (3) tan; (4) char, sear; (5) blaze, flame, flare, parch, scald, singe; (6) ignite, kindle, scorch; (7) consume, cremate, flicker; (8) smoulder; (10) incinerate; 2 (4) hurt; (5) smart, sting; (6) tingle; II *n* (5) brook; (6) stream.

burrow I *n* (3) den, set; (4) hole, lair; (5) earth; (6) warren; II *v* (3) dig; (4) mine; (5) delve; (6) tunnel; (8) excavate.

burst I *n & v* (4) tear; (5) break, crack, split; (6) breach; (7) rupture; (8) puncture; II *v* (6) shiver; (7) explode, shatter; (8) fragment; (12) disintegrate; III *n* 1 (4) bang; (5) blast; (9) explosion; 2 (3) fit; (4) rush; (5) spate, spurt, surge; (8) outbreak; (9) discharge; IV *cryptic* ANAGRAM CUE.

bury *v* (4) sink; (5) cover, embed, inter, plant; (6) engulf, entomb, shroud; (7) conceal, immerse; (8) submerge.

bush *n* 1 (5) hedge, shrub; (7) thicket; 2 (5) brush, scrub, wilds; (9) backwoods, boondocks; 3 (6) lining, sleeve.

business *n* 1 (5) trade; (8) commerce, industry; 2 (4) firm; (7) company, concern, venture; (10) enterprise; (11) corporation; (12) organisation (*or* organization); (13) establishment; 3 (3) job; (4) line, work; (6) career; (7) calling; (8) vocation; (10) employment, profession; 4 (5) issue, point, topic; (6) affair, matter; (7) problem, subject; (8) question.

bust I *v* 1 (5) **break, burst;** 2 (6) arrest; II *n* 1 (5) bosom, chest; (6) breast; (7) breasts; 2 (5) torso; (6) statue; (9) sculpture; 3 (4) raid; (6) search; III *adj* 1 (6) **broken;** 2 (5) **broke**.

busy *adj* 1 (7) engaged, working; (8) diligent, occupied; (11) industrious; (2+ words) hard at it, on the job, tied up; 2 (4) full; (6) active, hectic, lively; (7) crowded, teeming; (8) bustling, swarming.

butterfly *n* (6) psyche; (7) vanessa.

TYPES OF BUTTERFLY

(5) argus, comma; (7) peacock, ringlet, skipper; (8) grayling; (9) brimstone; (10) fritillary, hairstreak; (11) swallowtail; (13) tortoiseshell; (2+ words) cabbage white, Camberwell beauty, common blue, large blue, red admiral.

---

buy *v* 1 (3) get; (4) gain; (6) obtain, secure; (7) acquire; (8) purchase; 2 (4) wear; (6) accept; (7) **believe,** swallow.

C

C *abbrev* carbon, Celsius, centigrade, century, Cuba (international vehicle registration), key (music), note (music), 100 (Roman numeral).

c *abbrev* caught, cent, century, *circa* (around), cubic.

cadmium *cryptic* abbreviated as Cd.

Caesar *see* **Julius Caesar**.

cage I *n* (3) pen; (4) coop; (5) hutch, pound; (9) enclosure; II *v* (5) fence, limit; (7) confine, impound; (8) imprison, restrict; (11) incarcerate.

Cain *Bible* the first son of Adam and Eve, 'a tiller of the ground' and the first murderer. He killed his brother **Abel** and was banished by God. God set His mark on Cain to prevent anyone from slaying him in revenge, and Cain 'dwelt in the land of Nod'.

cake *n* I (3) bun; (4) baba; (5) fancy, lardy, scone, torte; (6) éclair, gateau, muffin, parkin, sponge; (7) bannock, brownie, madeira, savarin; (8) doughnut, macaroon, meringue, vacherin; (9) madeleine; (10) battenburg, florentine; (11) gingerbread; (2+ words) angel cake, birthday cake, Christmas cake, cream horn, cream puff, Danish pastry, devil's food cake, Sally Lunn, Victoria sponge, wedding cake; 2 (3) bar; (4) loaf, lump, mass, slab; (5) block.

calamity *n see* **catastrophe**.

calcium *cryptic* abbreviated as Ca.

calculate *v* (4) rate; (5) count, gauge, judge, value, weigh; (6) figure, reckon; (7) compute; (8) estimate; (9) determine, enumerate.

calculating *adj* (3) sly; (6) crafty, shrewd; (7) cunning, devious; (8) scheming; (9) designing; (10) contriving.

call I *n & v* (3) cry; (4) bawl, hail, howl, roar, yell; (5) cheer, chirp, shout; (6) bellow, scream, shriek; II *v* I (3) bid; (5) rally; (6) beckon, gather, invite, muster, summon; (7) collect, convene; (8) assemble; 2 (4) ring; (5) phone; (9) telephone; 3 (3) dub; (4) name; (5) label, title; (7) baptise (*or* baptize), entitle; (8) christen; (9) designate; III *n* I (4) plea; (5) order; (6) appeal, demand; (7) bidding, command, request, summons; (8) vocation; (10) invitation; 2 (4) bell, buzz, ring; (6) tinkle; 3 (4) need; (5) cause; (6) excuse, reason; (7) grounds; (8) occasion.

calm I *adj* I (4) still; (5) quiet; (6) gentle, placid, serene, smooth; (7) pacific, restful; (8) peaceful, relaxing, tranquil, windless; (10) uneventful; 2 (4) cool; (6) placid, sedate; (7) relaxed, unmoved; (8) composed; (9) collected, impassive, unruffled; (10) untroubled; (11) undisturbed, unemotional, unflappable, unperturbed; (13) dispassionate, imperturbable, self-possessed; II *n* (4) hush; (5) peace, quiet; (8) serenity; (9) stillness; (12) tranquillity; III *v* (4) hush; (5) abate, allay, quell, relax, still; (6) pacify, sedate, soothe, subdue; (7) assuage, placate, quieten; (12) tranquillise (*or* tranquillize).

cancel *v* I (4) drop; (5) quash; (6) repeal, revoke; (7) abandon, rescind, reverse; (8) override, overrule, overturn; (10) invalidate, neutralise (*or* neutralize); (11) countermand; (2 words) call off; 2 (5) erase; (6) delete; (10) obliterate.

Cancer *astrol. & astron.* the constellation that is the fourth sign of the zodiac, also known as the Crab.

cant I *v* (3) tip; (4) lean, slew, tilt; (5) slope; (7) incline; II *n* I (5) slang; (6) jargon; 2 (9) hypocrisy.

Canterbury Tales *lit.* the best-known literary work of **Geoffrey Chaucer** comprising a selection of verse stories supposedly told by the members of a group of pilgrims journeying from

Southwark to Canterbury. Apart from Chaucer himself and the landlord (Harry Bailey) of the Tabard Inn in Southwark, the pilgrims and tale-tellers include: Canon's Yeoman, Clerk, Cook, Franklin, Friar, Knight, Manciple, Man of Law, Merchant, Miller, Monk, Nun's Priest, Parson, Physician, Prioress, Reeve, Shipman, Squire, Summoner, Wife of Bath.

canton *n* (6) region; (8) division.

CANTONS OF SWITZERLAND

Aargau, Appenzell, Basel-land, Berne, Fribourg, Geneva, Graubunden, Glarus, Jura, Lucerne, Neuchâtel, Nidwalden, Obwalden, St Gallen, Schaffhausen, Schwyz, Solothurn, Thurgau, Ticino, Unterwalden, Uri, Valais, Vaud, Zug, Zurich.

---

capable *adj* (4) able; (5) adept; (6) clever, gifted; (7) skilful; (8) talented; (9) competent, efficient, qualified; (10) proficient; (11) experienced, intelligent; (12) accomplished.

cape *n* 1 (4) coat, robe, wrap; (5) cloak, shawl; (6) poncho, tippet; 2 (4) head, ness; (5) point; (8) headland; (10) promontory.

capital I *n* 1 (4) city; 2 (6) letter; 3 (4) cash; (5) funds, means, money, stock; (6) assets, wealth; (7) finance; (9) principal; (11) wherewithal; II *adj* 1 (4) main; (5) chief, first, prime; (7) leading, primary; (9) principal; 2 (5) super; (8) splendid; (9) first-rate; III *cryptic* letters AI (A1) or UC (upper case).

WORLD CAPITALS

Afghanistan – Kabul, *Albania* – Tirana, *Algeria* – El Djezair (was Algiers), *Andorra* – La Vieja, *Angola* – Luanda, *Antigua Is.* – St. John's, *Argentina* – Buenos Aires, *Ascension Is.* – Georgetown, *Australia* – Canberra, *Austria* – Vienna, *Bahamas* – Nassau, *Bahrain* – Manama, *Balearic Is.* – Palma, *Bangladesh* – Dhaka (was Dacca), *Barbados* – Bridgetown, *Belgium* – Brussels, *Bermuda* – Hamilton, *Bhutan* – Thimphu, *Bolivia* – La Paz, *Bosnia* – Sarajevo, *Botswana* – Gaborone, *Burkina Faso* – Ouagadougou, *Brazil* – Brasilia (was Rio de Janeiro), *Bulgaria* – Sofia, *Burma* (now Myanmar) – Rangoon, *Burundi* – Bujumbura, *Cambodia* – Phnom Penh, *Cameroon* – Yaoundé, *Canada* – Ottawa, *Canary Is.* – Las Palmas, *Cape Verde Is.* – Praia, *Central Africa Republic* – Bangui, *Chad* – Ndjamena (was Fort Lamy), *Chile* – Santiago, *China* – Beijing (formerly Peking), *Colombia* – Bogota, *Congo, Democratic Republic of* – Kinshasa, *Corsica* – Ajaccio, *Costa Rica* – San Jose, *Côte d'Ivoire* – Yamoussoukro, *Crete* – Canea, *Croatia* – Zagreb, *Cuba* – Havana, *Cyclades Is.* – Hermoupolis, *Cyprus* – Nicosia, *Czech Republic* – Prague, *Denmark* – Copenhagen, *Djibouti* – Djibouti, *Dominica Is.* – Roseau, *Dominican Republic* – Santo Domingo, *Ecuador* – Quito, *Egypt* – Cairo, *Eire* – Dublin, *Elba Is.* – Porto Ferraio, *El Salvador* – San Salvador, *England* – London, *Equatorial Guinea* – Malabo (was Santa Isabel), *Eritrea* – Asmara, *Estonia* – Tallinn, *Ethiopia* – Addis Ababa, *Faeroe Is.* – Thorshavn, *Falkland Is.* – Stanley, *Fiji Is.* – Suva, *Finland* – Helsinki, *France* – Paris, *Gabon* – Libreville, *The Gambia* – Banjul (was Bathurst), *Germany* – Berlin (Bonn), *Ghana* – Accra, *Greece* – Athens, *Greenland* – Godthab, *Grenada Is.* – St George's, *Guadeloupe* – Basse-Terre, *Guam* – Agana, *Guatemala* – Guatemala City, *Guinea* – Conakry, *Guinea Bissau* – Bissau, *Guyana* – Georgetown, *Haiti* – Port au Prince, *Honduras* – Tegucigalpa, *Hungary* – Budapest, *Iceland* – Reykjavik, *India* – Delhi, *Indonesia* – Jakarta, *Iran* – Teh(e)ran, *Iraq* – Baghdad, *Ireland, Rep. of* – Dublin, *Israel* – Jerusalem (unrecognised –

list continued over

was Tel Aviv), *Italy* – Rome, *Ivory Coast* (now Côte d'Ivoire) – Yamoussoukro (was Abidjan), *Jamaica* – Kingston, *Japan* – Tokyo, *Jordan* – Amman, *Kenya* – Nairobi, *Kiribati* – Jarawa, *Korea (North)* – Pyongyang, *Korea (South)* – Seoul, *Kuwait* – Kuwait, *Laos* – Vientiane, *Latvia* – Riga, *Lebanon* – Beirut, *Leeward Is.* – St John, *Lesotho* – Maseru, *Liberia* – Monrovia, *Libya* – Tripoli, *Liechtenstein* – Vaduz, *Lithuania* – Vilnius, *Luxembourg* – Luxembourg, *Macau* – Macau, *Macedonia* – Skopje, *Malagasy Rep.* – Tananarive, *Malawi* – Lilongwe, *Malaysia* – Kuala Lumpur, *Maldives* – Male, *Mali* – Bamako, *Malta* – Val(l)etta, *Martinique Is.* – Fort de France, *Mauritania* – Nouakchott, *Mauritius* – Port Louis, *Mexico* – Mexico City, *Micronesia* – Kolonia, *Mozambique* – Maputo, *Monaco* – Monaco, *Mongolia* – Ulan Bator, *Morocco* – Rabat, *Myanmar* (was Burma) – Rangoon, *Namibia* – Windhoek, *Naura* – Yoren, *Nepal* – Katmandu, *Netherlands* – The Hague, *New Zealand* – Wellington, *Nicaragua* – Managua, *Niger* – Niamey, *Northern Ireland* – Belfast, *Norway* – Oslo, *Oman* – Muscat, *Pakistan* – Islamabad (was Karachi), *Panama* – Panama, *Papua New Guinea* – Port Moresby, *Paraguay* – Asuncion, *Peru* – Lima, *Philippines* – Manila, *Poland* – Warsaw, *Portugal* – Lisbon, *Puerto Rico* – San Juan, *Qatar* – Doha, *Romania* – Bucharest, *Russia* – Moscow, *Rwanda* – Kigali, *Sabah* – Kota Kinabalu, *St Helena Is.* – Jamestown, *St Kitts-Nevis Is.* – Basseterre, *St Lucia Is.* – Castries, *St Vincent Is.* – Kingstown, *San Marino* – San Marino, *Sarawak* – Kuching, *Sardinia* – Cagliari, *Saudi Arabia* – Riyadh, *Scotland* – Edinburgh, *Senegal* – Dakar, *Serbia* – Belgrade, *Seychelles* – Victoria, *Sicily* – Palermo, *Sierra Leone* – Freetown, *Singapore Is.* – Singapore, *Slovakia* – Bratislava, *Solomon Is.* – Honiara, *Somali* – Mogadishu, *South Africa* – Pretoria, *Spain* – Madrid, *Sri Lanka* – Colombo, *Sudan* – Khartoum, *Surinam* – Paramaribo, *Swaziland* – Mbabane, *Sweden* – Stockholm, *Switzerland* – Berne, *Syria* – Damascus, *Taiwan* – Taipei, *Tanzania* – Dodoma, *Thailand* – Bangkok, *Tibet* – Lhasa, *Togo* – Lomé, *Tonga (Friendly Is.)* – Nukualofa, *Trinidad & Tobago* – Port of Spain, *Tristan da Cunha* – Edinburgh, *Tunisia* – Tunis, *Turkey* – Ankara, *Tuvalu* – Funafuti, *Uganda* – Kampala, *United Arab Emirates* – Abu Dhabi, *Uruguay* – Montevideo, *USA* – Washington, *Vanuatu* – Vila, *Venezuela* – Caracas, *Vietnam* – Hanoi, *Virgin Is, Br* – Roadtown, *Virgin Is, US* – Charlotte Amalie, *Wales* – Cardiff, *Western Sahara* – Aaiun, *Western Samoa* – Apia, *Windward Is.* – St George, *Yugoslavia* – Belgrade, *Zambia* – Lusaka, *Zimbabwe* – Harare.

Capricorn *astrol. & astron.* the constellation that is the tenth sign of the zodiac, also known as the Goat.

car *n* (4) auto, jeep, limo, mini; (5) coupé, sedan; (6) banger, estate, roller, saloon, wheels; (8) fastback; (9) cabriolet, hatchback, limousine; (10) automobile; (11) convertible; (2 words) beach buggy, estate car, people carrier, station wagon.

MAKES OF CAR

Alfa Romeo, Aston Martin, Audi, Austin, Bentley, BMW, Bugatti, Buick, Cadillac, Chevrolet, Chrysler, Citroën, Daewoo, Daimler, Dodge, Ferrari, Fiat, Ford, General Motors, Honda, Isuzu, Jaguar, Lada, Lamborghini, Land-Rover, Maserati, Mazda, Mercedes, MG, Mitsubishi, Nissan, Opel, Packard, Peugeot, Pontiac, Porsche, Proton, Renault, Rolls Royce, Rover, Saab, Seat, Skoda, Subaru, Toyota, Vauxhall, Volkswagen, Volvo.

---

card *n* **1** (3) ace; (4) club, jack, king; (5) deuce, heart, joker, queen, spade; (7) diamond; **2** (3) wag; (7) caution; (9) character.

card game *n*

CARD GAMES

(3) gin, loo, maw, nap, pit.

(4) brag, crib, faro, grab, skat, snap, solo, stop.

(5) bunko, demon, monte, ombre, pitch, poker, rummy, spoof, vingt, whist.

(6) boston, bridge, casino, ecarte, euchre, fantan, hearts, piquet, spider.

(7) bezique, canasta, cassino, carlton, pontoon, primero, streets.

(8) baccarat, canfield, cribbage, klondyke, napoleon, patience, pinochle.

(9) blackjack, newmarket, solitaire, twenty-one.

(2+ words) all fours, auction bridge, beggar-my-neighbour, chase the ace, contract bridge, happy families, knockout whist, old maid, racing demons, solo whist.

---

care I *n* **1** (4) heed; (6) regard; (7) caution; (8) prudence; (9) attention, vigilance; (12) thoroughness; (13) consideration; **2** (6) charge; (7) control, custody, keeping; (10) protection; (11) supervision; (14) responsibility; **3** (5) worry; (6) strain, stress; (7) anxiety, concern, trouble; (8) distress, pressure; (10) affliction; II *v* (4) mind; (5) worry; (6) bother; III **care for 1** (4) mind, tend (5) nurse, watch; (7) protect; (2 words) attend to, look after, minister to; **2** (4) like, love; (5) enjoy.

career I *n* (3) job; (4) line, work; (5) trade; (7) calling; (8) business, vocation; (10) employment, livelihood, occupation, profession; II *v* (4) dash, race, rush, tear; (5) shoot, speed; (6) gallop, hurtle.

careful *adj* **1** (4) wary; (5) alert, chary; (7) mindful, prudent; (8) cautious, vigilant, watchful; (9) attentive, judicious; (10) thoughtful; (11) circumspect; **2** (7) precise; (8) thorough; (10) meticulous, particular; (11) painstaking, punctilious; (13) conscientious.

careless *adj* **1** (5) hasty, messy; (6) casual, sloppy, untidy; (7) offhand; (8) slapdash, slipshod; (9) negligent; (10) disorderly; **2** (6) remiss; (8) heedless; (9) forgetful; (10) unthinking; (11) inattentive, thoughtless; (13) irresponsible.

carriage *n* **1** (3) car; (5) coach, wagon; (7) vehicle; **2** (7) freight, postage; (8) delivery; (9) transport; (10) conveyance; **3** (3) air; (7) bearing, posture; (10) deportment.

HORSE-DRAWN CARRIAGES

(3) fly, gig.

(4) dray, trap.

(5) buggy, coach, stage, sulky, tonga, wagon.

(6) berlin, calash, chaise, fiacre, gharri, hansom, landau, surrey, troika.

(7) britzka (*or* britska), cariole, caroche, chariot, dog-cart, droshky, fourgon, growler, hackney, phaeton, tilbury, tumbrel.

(8) barouche, brougham, carriole, clarence, curricle, stanhope, victoria.

(9) cabriolet, dandy-cart, diligence, landaulet, wagonette.

(10) four-in-hand, post-chaise, shandrydan, spring-cart, stagecoach.

(11) jaunting-car, three-in-hand.

Carroll, **Lewis** *lit.* pseudonym of Charles Lutwidge Dodgson, author of *Alice in Wonderland* and *Through the Looking Glass* (including the nonsense poem *Jabberwocky*) and *The Hunting of the Snark*.

CARROLL CHARACTERS

include: Alice, Caterpillar, Cheshire Cat, Dormouse, Duchess, Gryphon, Humpty Dumpty, Mad Hatter,

list continued over

March Hare, Mock Turtle, Queen of Hearts, Red Queen, Tweedledum and Tweedledee, Walrus and the Carpenter, White Knight, White Rabbit

carry *v* 1 (4) bear, take; (5) bring, fetch, relay; (6) convey; (9) transport; 2 (4) hold; (6) uphold; (7) support, sustain; (8) maintain, shoulder, underpin; 3 (5) print; (6) report; (7) contain; (9) broadcast; 4 (4) sell; (5) stock; (6) retail.

case I *n* 1 (3) bag, box; (4) grip, pack; (5) chest, cover, crate, shell, trunk; (6) carton, casket, coffer, holder, jacket, packet, sheath; (7) hold-all, wrapper; (8) suitcase; (9) container; (10) receptacle; 2 (5) event, point; (7) example; (8) instance, occasion; (9) situation; (10) occurrence; (12) circumstance; 3 (4) suit; (5) trial; (6) action; (7) lawsuit; (11) proceedings; II *cryptic* **in case (of)** place one part of the answer inside another part, as in: 'Formal headgear expected for work in that case' (3, 3) = top hat (work = op, inside 'that') OR 'Guarantee that one has rights in case of need' (7) = warrant (need = want, one = A, rights = RR).

GRAMMATICAL CASES
(6) dative; (8) ablative, genitive, vocative; (10) accusative, nominative, possessive.

cast I *v & n* 1 (3) lob; (4) hurl, toss; (5) chuck, fling, heave, pitch, sling, throw; (6) launch; 2 (4) form; (5) model, mould, shape; II *v* 1 (4) emit, send, shed; (6) direct; (7) diffuse, project, radiate, scatter; 2 (4) shed; (6) slough; (7) discard; (8) jettison; (2+ words) get rid of, throw away, throw off; III *n* (6) actors, troupe; (7) company; (2 words) dramatis personae.

Castor *Gk myth* one of the heavenly twins, brother of **Pollux** (*see also* **Gemini**).

cat *n* 1 (*male* tom, *female* queen, *young* kitten, *group* cluster – *of kittens*, kindle) (4) puss; (5) kitty, moggy, pussy, tabby; (6) moggie; (9) marmalade; (13) tortoise-shell; 2 (4) lash, whip; (7) scourge.

BREEDS OF CAT
(4) Manx; (7) Burmese, Persian, Siamese; (10) Abyssinian (2 words) Maine coon, Russian blue.

ANIMALS OF THE CAT FAMILY
(4) eyra, lion, lynx, puma; (5) civet, genet, ounce, rasse, tiger, tigon; (6) bobcat, cougar, jaguar, margay, ocelot, serval; (7) caracal, cheetah, leopard; (10) jaguarundi.

catastrophe *n* (4) ruin; (5) trial; (6) fiasco, mishap; (7) debacle, failure, reverse, tragedy; (8) calamity, disaster, distress; (9) adversity, cataclysm, mischance; (10) affliction, misfortune; (11) tribulation; (12) misadventure.

catch I *v* 1 (4) grab, grip, hold, take; (5) grasp, seize; (6) clutch; (7) capture; 2 (3) net; (4) hook, trap; (5) ravel, snare; (6) enmesh, entrap, muddle, tangle; (7) confuse, embroil, ensnare, involve; (8) entangle; (9) implicate; 3 (6) arrest, detect, expose, unmask; 4 (3) get; (4) hear; (5) grasp; (10) understand; 5 (5) light; (6) ignite; II *n* 1 (4) bolt, clip, hasp, hook, lock; (5) clasp, latch; (8) fastener; 2 (4) snag; (5) hitch; (7) problem; (8) drawback, obstacle; 3 (3) air; (4) song; (5) ditty.

cathedral *n* (5) church.

BRITISH CATHEDRALS
Aberdeen, Bangor, Bristol, Canterbury, Chester, Chichester, Coventry, Durham, Edinburgh, Ely, Exeter, Glasgow, Gloucester, Guildford, Lichfield, Lincoln, Liverpool, Llandaff, Manchester, Norwich, Oxford, Peterborough, Ripon, Rochester, St Albans, St David's, St Paul's, Salisbury, Truro, Wells, Winchester, Worcester, York Minster.

cattle *n* (*male* bull, steer, *female* cow, heifer, *young* calf, *group* herd, drove) (4) kine, oxen; (5) stock; (6) beasts; (9) livestock.

BREEDS OF CATTLE

(5) Devon, Kyloe, Luing; (6) Ankole, dexter, Durham, Jersey; (7) Brahman, cattabu, cattalo; (8) Alderney, Ayrshire, Friesian, Galloway, Guernsey, Hereford, Highland, Holstein, Limousin, longhorn; (9) Charolais, Romagnola, shorthorn; (10) Africander; (2 words) Aberdeen Angus, Red Poll, Welsh Black.

caught *cryptic* abbreviated as C or CT.

cause I *n* **1** (5) basis; (6) excuse, ground, motive, reason; (7) grounds, impulse, purpose, warrant; (8) stimulus; (9) incentive, intention, rationale; (10) inducement; (13) justification; **2** (4) root; (5) agent; (6) origin, source, spring; **3** (3) aim, end; (5) ideal; (6) object; (9) movement, principle; (10) conviction; **II** *v* (6) create, effect, incite, induce, prompt; (7) produce, provoke; (8) generate, motivate, occasion; (9) stimulate; (11) precipitate; (2+ words) bring about, give rise, to lead to.

celebrate *v* **1** (4) keep, mark; (5) extol; (6) honour, praise; (7) glorify, observe; (11) commemorate; **2** (5) exult, feast, party, revel; (7) rejoice.

celebrated *adj* (5) famed; (6) famous; (7) eminent, notable, popular; (8) renowned; (9) acclaimed, prominent, well-known; (11) illustrious, outstanding, prestigious; (13) distinguished.

celebration *n* (2) do; (4) gala, rave; (5) feast, party; (7) knees-up, revelry; (8) festival; (9) festivity; (11) merrymaking; (13) jollification.

celebrity *n* **1** (3) VIP; (4) lion, name, star; (8) luminary; (9) dignitary, personage, superstar; (11) personality; **2** (4) fame; (5) glory; (6) renown; (8) eminence; (10) prominence.

centaur *Gk myth* a creature with the head and trunk of a man growing from the body of a horse. The centaurs were supposed to be natives of Thessaly and were eventually driven out by the Lapiths.

centre I *n* (3) hub; (4) axis, core, crux; (5) focus, heart, pivot; (6) middle; (7) nucleus; **II** *v* **1** (5) focus; (6) adjust; (11) concentrate; **2** (2 words) hinge on, pivot on, revolve around; **III centre** *or* **central** use the middle letter or letters of the word referred to, as in: 'In the centre of London two fifths are in poverty' (4) = need (fifth = fifth letter of alphabet).

Ceres *Rom. myth* goddess of nature, corn, crops, and vegetation. Greek equivalent **Demeter** – *see also* **Proserpina, Persephone.**

certain *adj* **1** (3) set; (4) firm, sure; (5) clear, exact, fixed; (6) marked, proven; (7) assured, decided, obvious, precise, settled; (8) clear-cut, definite, explicit, positive, specific; (9) confident; (10) determined, guaranteed, undeniable; (11) indubitable, irrefutable; (14) unquestionable; **2** (8) specific; (10) individual, particular.

chair *n see* **seat.**

champion I *n* **1** (3) ace; (6) victor, winner; (11) titleholder; **2** (6) backer, patron; (8) advocate, defender, upholder; (9) supporter; **II** *v* (4) back; (6) defend, uphold; (7) espouse, promote, support; (8) advocate, maintain.

change I *v* **1** (4) turn, vary; (5) adapt, alter, amend; (6) adjust, modify, mutate, reform, revise; (7) convert, remodel, reshape; (9) transform; (11) transfigure; (12) metamorphose; **2** (4) swap; (5) trade; (6) switch; (7) replace; (8) exchange; (9) alternate; (10) substitute; **II** *n* **1** (8) revision; (9) variation; (10) adjustment, alteration, conversion; (12) modification; (14) transformation; **2** (7) novelty, variety; (10) difference, innovation; **3** (5) coins, money; (6) copper, silver; **III** *cryptic* ANAGRAM CUE.

changeable *adj* (6) fitful; (7) mutable, varying; (8) flexible, shifting, unstable, unsteady, variable, wavering; (10) inconstant; (11) fluctuating; (13) unpredictable.

character *n* **1** (6) make-up, nature, temper; (11) disposition, personality, temperament; (12) constitution; **2** (4) card, case; (5) crank; (7) oddball; (9) eccentric; (10) individual; **3** (4) mark, sign; (6) cipher, figure, letter, number, symbol.

characteristic I *adj* 1 (3) own; (6) proper, single, unique; (7) special; (8) discrete, distinct, peculiar, personal, separate, singular, specific; (10) individual, particular; (11) distinctive; (13) idiosyncratic; 2 (5) stock, usual; (6) common, normal; (7) average, routine, typical; (8) orthodox, standard; (14) representative; II *n* (4) mark; (5) trait; (7) feature, quality, symptom; (8) hallmark, property; (9) attribute; (11) peculiarity; (12) idiosyncrasy.

charge I *n & v* (5) order; (6) decree, demand; (7) command, request; (10) commission; II *n* 1 (5) edict; (6) diktat; (7) precept; (9) direction, directive; (10) injunction; (11) instruction; 2 (3) fee; (4) cost, bill; (5) price; (6) amount; 3 (4) care; (7) control, custody, keeping; (14) responsibility; 4 (5) count; (10) accusation, allegation, indictment; 5 (6) attack, onrush; (7) assault; (9) onslaught; 6 (4) arms; (5) badge; (6) device, shield; (7) bearing III *v* 1 (3) ask; (4) levy; (5) exact; (6) demand; 2 (5) blame; (6) accuse, indict; (7) impeach; 3 (4) dash, race, rush; (5) storm; (6) assail, attack; (8) stampede; 4 (4) fill, load; (5) boost.

charm I *n* 1 (6) allure, appeal; (9) magnetism; (10) attraction; (11) enchantment, fascination; 2 (5) magic, spell; (6) amulet, fetish; (7) trinket; (8) talisman; II *v* (6) cajole; (7) attract, beguile, bewitch, delight; (9) captivate, enrapture, fascinate, mesmerise (*or* mesmerize).

Charon *Gk myth* the ferryman who conveyed the souls of the dead across the River Styx (or Acheron) to the Underworld.

chat I *v & n* (4) talk; (6) gossip, natter; (7) chatter; II *v* (7) discuss; (8) converse; (11) communicate; III *n* (7) chinwag; (10) discussion; (12) consultation, conversation.

chatter *n & v* (4) chat, talk, yack; (6) babble, gossip, rabbit, tattle; (7) prattle.

Chaucer, Geoffrey *lit.* the greatest poet who wrote in Middle English. His major works are *The Canterbury Tales*, *Troilus and Criseyde*, *The House of Fame*, *The Legend of Good Women*, and *The Parlement of Fowles*. See also **Canterbury Tales**.

cheap *adj* 1 (6) budget; (7) bargain, economy, reduced; (8) cut-price; (9) knockdown; (10) reasonable; (11) inexpensive; 2 (4) poor; (5) tacky, tatty; (6) common, shoddy, tawdry; (8) inferior; 3 (3) low; (4) mean; (6) unfair; (9) underhand; (10) despicable; (12) contemptible.

cheat I *v* (2) do; (3) con; (4) dupe, fool; (5) trick; (6) diddle, fleece; (7) deceive, defraud, mislead, swindle; (8) hoodwink; (11) double-cross; II *n* 1 (5) fraud, rogue, shark, sharp; (6) con-man; (7) sharper; (8) deceiver, impostor, swindler; (9) fraudster; 2 (4) hoax, scam; (5) sting; (9) deception.

check I *v & n* (4) curb; (5) block, bound, limit; (7) control; (8) handicap; II *v* 1 (3) try, vet; (5) prove; (6) assess, screen, verify; (7) analyse, examine; (8) evaluate; (11) investigate; 2 (6) hamper, hinder, impede, retard, thwart; (7) confine, control, delimit; (8) encumber, obstruct, restrain, restrict; (9) frustrate, hamstring; III *n* 1 (5) audit; (8) once-over, scrutiny; (11) examination; (13) investigation; 2 (4) blow; (6) damper; (7) reverse, setback; (9) hindrance; (10) impediment.

cheese *n*

TYPES OF CHEESE

(4) blue, Brie, curd, Edam, Feta, sage.

(5) cream, Derby, Gouda, Swiss.

(6) Dunlop, paneer.

(7) Boursin, Cheddar, cottage, Crowdie, Gruyère, ricotta, Stilton.

(8) Cheshire, Cotswold, Emmental, Parmesan, Pecorino, Tilsiter.

(9) Camembert, Gambozola, Jarlsberg, Leicester, Limburger, Lymeswold, mouse-trap, Mozarella, Provolone, Roquefort.

(10) Caerphilly, Dolcelatte, Emmentaler, Gorgonzola, Lancashire, Mascarpone.

(11) Wensleydale.

(2 words) Bel Paese, Double Gloucester, Pont-l'Éveque, Port Salut.

---

chemical element *see* **element**.

chessman, chesspiece *n* (4) king, pawn, rook; (5) queen; (6) bishop, castle, knight.

chief I *adj* (3) key; (4) head, main; (5) first, major, prime; (6) ruling, senior; (7) central, highest, leading, primary, supreme; (8) cardinal, dominant, foremost; (9) essential, principal, sovereign; **II** *n* (4) boss, head, lord; (5) ruler; (6) leader; (8) director, governor; (9) chieftain, commander; (10) ringleader.

child *n* (3) boy, kid, son, tot; (4) baby, brat, girl; (5) scion, sprog, youth; (6) infant, nipper; (7) toddler; (8) daughter, juvenile, teenager; (9) youngster.

children *n pl* (5) brood, issue, young; (6) babies, family, litter; (7) progeny; (9) offspring.

Chimaera *or* **Chimera** *Gk myth* a fire-breathing monster with the head of a lion, the body of a goat and the tail of a dragon, slain by **Bellerophon**.

Chiron *Gk myth* a wise **centaur** who was the tutor of many Greek heroes, especially Achilles.

choice I *n* **1** (4) pick; (6) option; (8) decision, election; (9) selection; (10) preference; **2** (5) range; (7) mixture, variety; (10) assortment; **II** *adj* (3) top; (4) best, plum; (5) elite, prime, prize; (6) select; (7) special; (9) exclusive, first-rate; (10) first-class, hand-picked.

choose *v* (4) pick; (5) elect; (5) adopt; (6) decide, select; (7) appoint; (9) designate; (2 words) decide on, opt for, plump for, settle on, single out, vote for.

chop *v* **1** (3) cut, hew, lop; (4) hack; (5) sever, slice, split; (6) cleave, divide; (8) truncate; **2** (3) axe; (4) sack, trim; (5) slash; (6) cancel; (8) decrease.

choreographer *n*

FAMOUS CHOREOGRAPHERS

(6) Ashton (Frederick), Cranko (Johnny), Fokine (Michel), Graham (Martha), Petipa (Marcel); (7) Massine (Léonide); (9) Diaghilev (Sergei); (10) Balanchine (George).

chromium *cryptic* abbreviated as CR.

church I *n* (5) abbey, temple; (6) chapel; (7) minster; (8) basilica; (9) cathedral; **II** *cryptic* letters CE, CH, or RC, as in: 'Upbraid for being concealed in church' (5) = chide.

PARTS OF A CHURCH BUILDING

(4) apse, font, jube, nave.

(5) aisle, altar, choir, crypt, spire, tower.

(6) adytum, belfry, chapel, fleche, pulpit, vestry.

(7) chancel, galilee, lectern, narthex, reredos, steeple.

(8) cloister, crossing, sacristy, transept.

(9) campanile, sanctuary, triforium.

(10) clerestory, rood-screen, tabernacle.

(12) chapterhouse.

(2 words) Lady chapel, organ loft.

for priests etc see **clergy**; *for religious clothing see* **vestments**.

churchman *see* **clergy**.

circa *prep* (1) C; (2) CA; (5) about, (6) around; (7) roughly.

circle I *n* **1** (3) orb; (4) coil, disc, hoop, loop, ring, turn; (5) globe, orbit, round; (6) spiral; (7) circuit; (9) perimeter; (10) revolution; (13) circumference; **2** (3) set; (4) band, club; (5) group; (6) clique; (7) coterie, society; (10) fellowship; **II** *v* (4) gird, loop, ring; (7) embrace; (8) encircle, surround; (9) encompass; **III** *cryptic* place the letters of one word in the clue or answer around those of another.

city I *n* (4) town; (10) metropolis; (11) conurbation; (12) municipality; **II** *cryptic* letters EC (postal code for the City of London) or sometimes LA (Los Angeles) or NY (New York) or UR (Biblical city, birthplace of Abraham).

clasp I *v & n* (3) hug; (4) grip, hold; (5) grasp; (6) clinch, clutch, cuddle; (7) embrace, squeeze; **II** *v* (5) press; (6) attach, enfold, fasten, secure; III *n* (3) pin; (4) clip, hasp, hook; (5) catch; (6) buckle; (8) fastener.

clean I *v & n* (4) bath, dust, wash, wipe; (5) purge, rinse, scrub, sweep; (6) douche, shower, sponge, vacuum; (7) shampoo; II *v* (3) mop; (4) swab; (5) bathe; (6) purify; (7) cleanse, launder; (9) disinfect; (13) decontaminate; III *adj* 1 (4) pure; (5) fresh; (6) washed; (7) aseptic, sterile; (8) hygienic, pristine, sanitary, spotless; (9) unsullied; (10) unpolluted; 2 (4) good; (5) moral; (6) chaste, decent, honest; (7) upright; (8) innocent, virtuous.

clergy I *n* (7) clerics; (8) ministry; (9) churchmen; (10) priesthood; II **clergy-man, churchman** etc *cryptic* letters DD (doctor of divinity) or RR (right reverend) or REV.

CLERGY AND RELIGIOUS OFFICEHOLDERS

(3) nun.

(4) abbé, curé, dean, guru, imam, lama, monk, pope, yogi.

(5) abbot, bonze, canon, druid, elder, fakir, friar, hadji, mufti, padre, prior, rabbi, vicar.

(6) abbess, bishop, curate, deacon, mullah, nuncio, parson, pastor, rector, sexton, sister, verger.

(7) acolyte, brahmin, brother, muezzin, pontiff, prelate, primate.

(8) cardinal, chaplain, minister, ordinand, prioress, sidesman.

(9) ayatollah, deaconess, moderator, monsignor, patriarch, presbyter, sacristan, suffragan.

(10) archbishop, archdeacon, missionary, prebendary.

(12) churchwarden, ecclesiastic, metropolitan.

---

clever *adj* (3) apt; (4) able, wise; (5) acute, canny, quick, sharp, smart; (6) astute, brainy, bright, gifted, shrewd; (7) clued-up, cunning, erudite, knowing, learned, prudent, skilful; (8) rational, sensible,

talented; (9) brilliant, ingenious, inventive, judicious; (10) perceptive, reasonable; (11) intelligent, quick-witted; (13) knowledgeable.

climb I *v* 1 (4) rise, soar, shin; (5) mount, scale; (6) ascend; (7) clamber; 2 (6) spiral; (8) escalate, increase; II *cryptic* reverse the order of the letters of a word in a down clue, as in: 'Disprove theory of climbing root' (5) = rebut.

cloth I *n* (5) stuff; (6) fabric; (7) textile; (8) material; *for types of cloth see* **fabric**; II **the cloth** *see* **clergy**.

clothes *or* **clothing** *n* (3) rig; (4) duds, garb, gear, togs, wear; (5) dress, get-up; (6) attire, outfit; (8) garments, wardrobe.

cloud I *n & v* (3) fog; (4) blur, mist, rack, scud; II *n* (4) haze; (6) vapour; III *v* (3) dim; (4) dull, veil; (6) shadow, shroud; (7) confuse, obscure; (9) obfuscate.

TYPES OF CLOUD

(6) cirrus, nimbus; (7) cumulus, stratus; (12) cirrocumulus, cirrostratus, cumulonimbus.

---

club I *n* 1 (3) bat; (4) cosh, mace; (6) cudgel; (8) bludgeon; (9) truncheon; 2 (5) group, guild, order, union; (6) league; (7) company, society; (10) fraternity; (11) association; II *v* (3) hit; (4) beat; (5) clout; (6) batter, strike.

GOLF CLUBS

(4) iron, wood; (5) cleek, spoon, wedge; (6) driver, mashie, putter; (7) brassie, niblick; (9) sandwedge.

---

clumsy I *adj* (5) inept; (6) gauche; (7) awkward; (8) bungling, inexpert, ungainly, unwieldy; (9) inelegant, unskilful; (10) cumbersome; (13) uncoordinated; II **clumsy** *or* **clumsily** *cryptic* ANAGRAM CUE.

coach I *n* 1 *see* **carriage**; 2 (5) tutor; (7) teacher, trainer; (10) instructor; II *v* (5) drill, prime, teach, train, tutor; (7) prepare; (8) instruct.

coarse *adj* 1 (5) lumpy, rough; (6) uneven; (7) bristly; (8) scratchy; 2 (4) rude; (5) bawdy, crude; (6) common, earthy, ribald, risqué, vulgar; (7) boorish, ill-bred, uncouth; (8) impolite, indecent, plebeian; (9) offensive, tasteless, unrefined.

Cockney *cryptic* Usually indicates that an 'h' should be omitted in the answer, as in: 'Cockney gardener's tool for trimming border' (5) (*Times Crossword no 21,335*) = edger ((h)edger). Alternatively, a Cockney term or spelling may be required, as in: 'Short-term secretary to Cockney devil' (7) (*Daily Telegraph Crossword / 22,859*) = tempter (temp + ter = to). Often an 'h' is omitted in the clue, usually indicating that the 'h' should also be omitted from a word in the answer, as in: ' 'Enry bottom? – Must be a record!' (5) = album (Henry = (H)al).

coin I *n* (3) bit; (4) cash; (5) money, piece; II *v* (5) forge; (6) create, devise, invent; (2 words) make up.

COINS

(2) as (Rom.).

(3) bob (UK), écu (Fr.), sou (Fr.).

(5) crown (Eng, Scand), daric (Pers), ducat (Eur), franc (Fr.), frank (Eur), groat (Eng.), obang (Jap), penny (UK), pound (UK), royal (Eng).

(6) aureus (Rom), bezant/byzant (Turk), dollar (US et al), florin (UK), guinea (UK), nickel (US), obolus (Gk), peseta (Sp.), rouble (Russ.), shekel (Israel), stater (Gk), stiver (sl), talent (Bible), tanner (UK), tester (UK), zechin (Hebr.).

(7) carolin (Ger.), prindle (Sc.), quarter (US), solidus (Rom.).

(8) denarius (Rom.), doubloon (Sp.), farthing (UK), maravedi (Sp.), shilling (UK).

(9) dandiprat (OE), half-crown (UK), halfpenny (UK), sovereign (UK).

(10) krugerrand (SA).

(2+ words) Maria Theresa dollar (A), piece of eight (Sp).

---

cold I *adj* **1** (3) icy, raw; (4) cool; (5) chill, nippy, parky, polar; (6) arctic, biting, bitter, chilly, frosty, frozen, wintry; (7) glacial; (8) freezing; **2** (5) aloof, stony; (6) frigid; (7) distant, hostile; (8) reserved; (9) apathetic, unfeeling; (10) unfriendly; (11) half-hearted, indifferent, standoffish, unwelcoming; (12) uninterested, unresponsive; (13) unsympathetic; (14) unenthusiastic; II *cryptic* letter C.

college

OXFORD AND CAMBRIDGE COLLEGES

(3) New (O).

(5) Caius (C), Clare (C), Jesus (C, O), Keble (O), Kings (C), Oriel (O).

(6) Darwin (C), Exeter (O), Girton (C), Merton (O), Queens' (C), Queen's (O), Selwyn (C), Wadham (O).

(7) Balliol (O), Christ's (C), Downing (C), Lincoln (O), Newnham (C), Trinity (C, O).

(8) Emmanuel (C), Gonville (C), Hertford (O), Homerton (C), Magdalen (O), Pembroke (C, O), Robinson (C).

(9) Brasenose (O), Churchill (C), Magdalene (C), Worcester (O).

(10) Peterhouse (C), Somerville (O), University (O).

(11) Fitzwilliam (C).

(12) Christchurch (O).

(2+ words) St Anne's (O), St Hugh's (O), St John's (O), All Souls (O), St Hilda's (O), St Peter's (O), Corpus Christi (C, O), St Catherine's (C, O), Sidney Sussex (C), Trinity Hall (C), Lady Margaret Hall (O), St Edmund Hall (O).

---

colour I *n & v* (3) dye, hue; (4) tint, tone; (5) paint, shade, stain; (6) crayon, pastel; (7) pigment; (8) tincture; II *v* **1** (4) bias; (6) affect; (7) distort, falsify; (9) influence, prejudice; **2** (5) blush, flush; (6) redden.

A RIOT OF COLOURS

(3) bay, dun, jet, red, tan.

(4) anil, blue, buff, cyan, dove, drab, ecru, fawn, gold, grey, lake, lime, navy, opal, pink, plum, puce, roan, rose, ruby, rust, sage, saxe.

(5) amber, azure, beige, black, blush, brown, coral, cream, ebony, green, hazel, ivory, khaki, lemon, lilac, lovat, mauve, mouse, ochre, olive, pansy, peach, sable, sepia, slate, straw, taupe, tawny, topaz, umber, white.

(6) auburn, bistre, bronze, canary, cerise, cherry, chrome, claret, cobalt, copper, fallow, indigo, madder, maroon, orange, purple, russet, salmon, sienna, silver, sorrel, Titian, violet, yellow.

(7) apricot, avocado, biscuit, caramel, carmine, celadon, crimson, emerald, grizzle, jacinth, magenta, mustard, saffron, scarlet, sky-blue.

(8) amethyst, blood-red, brick-red, burgundy, charcoal, chestnut, cinnamon, dove-grey, eau-de-nil, gunmetal, hyacinth, lavender, magnolia, mahogany, navy-blue, pea-green, primrose, sapphire, viridian.

(9) aubergine, carnation, champagne, chocolate, pearl-grey, sage-green, slate-grey, tangerine, turquoise, vermilion.

(10) aquamarine, salmon-pink.

(11) bottle-green, ultramarine.

(2 words) Cambridge blue, old gold, Oxford blue

combat I *n* 1 (3) war; (6) action, battle, strife; (7) warfare; (8) conflict, fighting; (11) hostilities; (12) belligerence; 2 (4) bout, duel; (5) fight; (8) struggle; II *v* (4) defy; (5) fight; (6) oppose, resist; (9) withstand.

combine I *v* (3) mix; (4) ally, bind, bond, fuse, join, link, pool; (5) blend, marry, merge, unify, unite; (6) couple; (7) connect; (8) coalesce, federate; (9) associate, co-operate, integrate; (10) amalgamate;

(11) collaborate, confederate, consolidate, incorporate; II *n* (5) group, union; (6) cartel, league; (8) alliance; (9) syndicate; (10) consortium; (11) association.

comfort I *n* 1 (4) ease; (6) luxury; (8) cosiness, snugness; 2 (3) aid; (4) help; (5) cheer; (6) relief; (7) support; (11) consolation, reassurance; (12) satisfaction; (13) encouragement; II *v* (4) ease; (5) cheer; (7) console, gladden, hearten, relieve; (8) reassure; (9) encourage.

comfortable *adj* 1 (4) cosy, easy, snug; (7) relaxed, restful; (8) pleasant, relaxing; (9) contented; (2 words) at ease; 2 (7) well-off; (8) affluent, well-to-do; (10) prosperous; 3 (4) good; (5) large; (8) sizeable.

comic I *adj* (5) droll, funny, light, witty; (6) absurd; (7) amusing; (8) farcical, humorous; (9) facetious, hilarious; (10) ridiculous; II *n* (3) wag, wit; (5) clown, joker; (6) jester; (7) buffoon; (8) comedian.

COMICS

Children's papers

(3) BOP (Boy's Own Paper), Gem; (4) Girl, Lion; (5) Beano, Dandy, Eagle, Robin, Rover, Swift; (6) Beezer, Magnet, Wizard; (7) Hotspur; (8) Bullseye, Champion; (2 words) Children's Newspaper.

command I *n & v* (5) order; (6) charge, decree, demand; (7) mandate; II *n* (5) edict; (6) diktat; (7) precept; (9) direction, directive; (10) injunction; (11) instruction; II *v* 1 (3) bid; (6) compel, direct, enjoin; (7) require; (8) instruct; 2 (4) head, lead, rule; (6) govern; (7) captain, control

common *adj* 1 (5) stock, usual; (6) normal; (7) average, general, routine, typical; (8) everyday, expected, familiar, frequent, habitual, ordinary, orthodox, standard; (9) customary; (10) accustomed, widespread; (11) predictable; (14) characteristic, representative; 2 (5) crude; (6) coarse, vulgar; (8) plebeian; 3 (5) joint; (6) mutual, shared; (8) communal; (10) collective.

communicate *v* (4) talk; (5) phone; (6) convey, impart, report, reveal, spread; (7) declare, publish; (8) acquaint, converse, disclose, proclaim, transmit; (10) correspond.

communications code words *see* PHONETIC ALPHABET *at* **alphabet**.

compact I *adj* (4) firm, neat; (5) close, dense, short, small, solid; (9) condensed; (10) compressed; II *n* (4) deal, pact; (6) accord, treaty; (7) bargain; (8) contract, covenant; (9) agreement; (10) settlement; (11) arrangement; (13) understanding.

company I *n* 1 (4) firm; (5) house; (7) concern, venture; (8) business; (10) enterprise; (11) association, corporation; (12) organisation (*or* organization); (13) establishment; 2 (6) guests; (7) callers, society; (8) presence, visitors; (10) fellowship; II *cryptic* letters CO.

compass *n* (5) gamut, range, scope.

compass points *cryptic* the names of the various points of the compass, or the adjectives associated with them (*northern, eastern etc*), often occur in clues and usually require the relevant abbreviation (N = north, E = east, S = south, W = west, NE = northeast *etc*), as in: 'Parliamentary corruption in southern fields, we hear' (6) = sleaze (fields = leas) *or* 'Southwest admits birds' (8) = swallows.

compel *v* (4) make, urge; (5) drive, force, press; (6) coerce, impose, oblige; (7) dragoon; (8) browbeat, bulldoze; (9) constrain, pressgang; (10) pressurise (*or* pressurize); (11) necessitate.

competent *adj* (3) fit; (4) able; (5) adept; (6) clever, expert; (7) capable, skilful, trained; (8) talented; (9) efficient, qualified; (10) proficient; (11) experienced, intelligent; (12) accomplished.

compiler *cryptic* letters I or ME (referring to the setter of the puzzle).

complain *v* (4) moan; (5) argue, groan; (6) object; (7) protest; (8) disagree; (10) disapprove.

complaint *n* 1 (4) moan; (6) outcry; (7) dissent, protest; (9) grievance, objection;

(10) opposition; 2 (7) ailment, illness; *see* **disease**.

complete I *adj* (4) done, full; (5) sheer, total, utter, uncut, whole; (6) entire, intact; (7) perfect; (8) absolute, finished, outright, thorough; (9) downright, out-and-out; (10) unabridged; (11) unqualified; (12) unexpurgated; (13) unconditional; II *v* (3) end; (5) close; (6) finish, fulfil; (7) achieve, realise (*or* realize); (8) conclude, finalise (*or* finalize); (9) terminate; (10) accomplish, consummate.

compose I *v* (4) form, make; (5) build, frame, write; (6) create; (7) arrange; (9) construct; II **compose** *or* **composed** *cryptic* ANAGRAM CUE.

composer *n* (6) writer; (8) musician.

COMPOSERS

(3) Bax (Arnold, UK), Maw (Nicholas, UK).

(4) Abel (Karl, Ger.), Adam (Adolphe, Fr.), Arne (Thomas, UK), Bach (Johann Sebastian, Ger. *and his sons* Carl Philipp Emmanuel, Johann Christian, Johann Christoph and Wilhelm Friedemann), Bart (Lionel, UK), Berg (Alban, A.), Blow (John, UK), Byrd (William, UK), Cage (John, US), Ives (Charles, US), Kern (Jerome, US), Lalo (Edouard, Fr.), Nono (Luigi, It.), Orff (Carl, Ger.), Wolf (Hugo, A.).

(5) Auber (Daniel, Fr.), Berio (Luciano, It.), Bizet (Georges, Fr.), Bliss (Arthur, UK), Dufay (Guillaume, Fr.), Dukas (Paul, Fr.), Elgar (Edward, UK), Falla (Manuel de, Sp.), Fauré (Gabriel, Fr.), Finzi (Gerald, UK), Gluck (Christoph, Ger.), Grieg (Edvard Hagerup, Nor.), Haydn (Josef, A.), Henze (Hans Werner, Ger.), Holst (Gustav, UK), Ibert (Jacques, Fr.), Lehar (Franz, A.), Liszt (Franz, Hung.), Loewe (Karl, Ger.), Lully (Giovanni, It./Fr.), Parry (Hubert, UK), Ravel (Maurice, Fr.), Reger (Max, Ger.),

list continued over

Satie (Eric, Fr.), Sousa (John Philip, USA), Spohr (Ludwig, Ger.), Suppé (Franz von A.), Verdi (Guiseppe, It.), Weber (Carl von, Ger.), Weill (Kurt, Ger.), Widor (Charles, Fr.).

(6) Arnold (Malcolm, UK), Barber (Samuel, US), Bartok (Bela, Hung.), Berlin (Irving, US), Brahms (Johannes, Ger.), Bridge (Frank, UK), Busoni (Ferrucio, It.), Chopin (Frédéric, Pol.), Coates (Eric, UK), Czerny (Karl, A.), Delius (Frederick, UK), Dvorak (Antonin, Cz.), Eisler (Hans, Ger.), Enesco (Georges, Roma.), Foster (Stephen, US), Franck (César, Fr.), German (Edward, UK), Glinka (Mikhail, Russ.), Gounod (Charles, Fr.), Handel (George Frederick Ger./UK), Hummel (Johann, Nepomuk, A.), Kodaly (Zoltan, Hung.), Mahler (Gustav, A.), Mozart (Wolfgang Amadeus, A.), Porter (Cole, US), Rameau (Jean-Philippe, Fr.), Rubbra (Edmund, UK), Schütz (Heinrich, Ger.), Tallis (Thomas, UK), Varese (Edgar, US), Wagner (Richard, Ger.), Walton (William, UK), Webern (Anton, A.), Wesley (Samuel Sebastian, UK).

(7) Albéniz (Isaac, Sp.), Bellini (Vincenzo, It.), Berlioz (Hector, Fr.), Borodin (Alexander, Russ.), Britten (Benjamin, UK), Copland (Aaron, US), Corelli (Arcangelo, It.), Debussy (Claude, Fr.), Delibes (Léo, Fr.), Gibbons (Orlando, UK), Howells (Herbert, UK), Ireland (John, UK), Janacek (Leos, Cz.), Martinu (Bohuslav, Cz.), Menotti (Carlo, US), Milhaud (Darius, Fr.), Novello (Ivor, UK), Poulenc (François, Fr.), Puccini (Giacomo, It.), Purcell (Henry, UK), Rodgers (Richard, US), Romberg (Sigmund, US), Rossini (Gioacchino, It.), Smetana (Bedrich, Cz.), Stainer (John, UK), Strauss (Johann, A.; Richard, Ger.), Tippett (Michael, UK), Vivaldi (Antonio, It.), Weelkes (Thomas, UK).

(8) Albinoni (Tomasso, It.), Bruckner (Anton, A.), Chabrier (Emmanuel, Fr.), Clementi (Musio, It.) Couperin (François, Fr.), Dohnanyi (Ernst, Hung.), Gershwin (George, US), Glazunov (Aleksandr, Russ.), Grainger (Percy, Aus.), Granados (Enrique, Sp.), Honegger (Arthur, Fr.), Ketelbey (Albert, UK), Kreisler (Fritz, A.), Mascagni (Pietro, It.), Massenet (Jules, Fr.), Messiaen (Olivier, Fr.), Paganini (Niccolo, It.), Respighi (Ottorino, It.), Schubert (Franz, A.), Schumann (Robert, Ger.), Scriabin (Alexandr, Russ.), Sibelius (Jean, Finn.), Sondheim (Stephen, US), Stanford (Charles, UK), Sullivan (Arthur, UK), Taverner (John, UK), Telemann (George Philipp, Ger.),Victoria (Tom(s, Sp.).

(9) Addinsell (Richard, UK), Balakirev (Mili, Russ.), Beethoven (Ludwig van, Ger.), Bernstein (Leonard, US), Buxtehude (Diderich, Dan.), Cherubini (Luigi, It.), Donizetti (Gaetano, It.), Dunstable (John, UK), Hindemith (Paul, Ger.), Meyerbeer (Giacomo, Ger.), Offenbach (Jacques, Fr.), Pergolesi (Giovanni, It.), Prokofiev (Sergei, Russ.), Scarlatti (Domenico/Alessandro, It.).

(10) Boccherini (Luigi, It.), Ferrabosco (Alfonso, UK), Monteverdi (Claudio, It.), Mussorgsky (Modest, Russ.), Palestrina (Giovanni, It.), Penderecki (Krzysztof, Pol.), Ponchielli (Amilcare, It.), Saint-Saens (Camille, Fr.), Schoenberg (Arnold, A.), Stravinsky (Igor, Russ.), Villa-Lobos (Heitor, Braz.), Waldteufel (Emile, Fr.).

(11) Charpentier (Gustave, Fr.), Dittersdorf (Karl, A.), Humperdinck (Engelbert, Ger.), Leoncavallo (Ruggiero, It.), Lloyd-Webber (Andrew, UK), Mendelssohn (Felix, Ger.), Rachmaninov (Sergei, Russ.),

list continued over

Stockhausen (Karl-Heinz, Ger.), Tchaikovsky (Peter, Russ.), Wolf-Ferrari (Ermanno, It.).

(12) Dallapiccola (Luigi, It.), Shostakovich (Dimitri, Russ.).

(13) Khatchaturian (Aram, Russ.).

(14) Rimsky-Korsakov (Nikolai, Russ.).

(15) Vaughan Williams (Ralph, UK).

conceal I *v see* hide I; II *cryptic* HIDDEN WORD CUE.

concern I *v & n* (5) upset, worry; (6) bother; (7) trouble; (8) disquiet, distress; II *v* (5) touch; (6) affect, regard; (7) involve; (8) interest; (2 words) refer to, relate; III *n* 1 (4) care; (6) sorrow, unease; (7) anxiety; 2 (4) heed; (7) thought; (9) attention; (13) consideration; 3 (3) job; (4) duty, task; (6) affair, matter; (8) interest; 4 (4) firm; (7) company, venture; (8) business; (10) enterprise; (11) corporation; (12) organisation (*or* organization); (13) establishment.

concise *adj* (5) pithy, short, terse; (7) compact, summary; (8) abridged, succinct; (9) condensed, curtailed; (10) compressed.

conclude I *v* 1 (3) end; (5) close; (6) clinch, finish; (8) **complete**; (9) culminate, terminate; 2 (5) infer; (6) assume, decide, deduce; (7) surmise; (9) determine, establish; II **conclude, concluding, conclusion** *etc* use the final letter of the word in question.

condition I *n* 1 (4) case, form, nick; (5) shape, state; (6) fettle, health; (8) position; (9) situation; (13) circumstances; 2 (7) ailment, illness; *see* **disease**; 3 (4) must; (5) terms; (7) proviso; (10) limitation; (11) requirement, reservation; (13) qualification; II *v* (5) mould, prime, train; (6) affect; (7) educate, prepare; (8) accustom; (9) brainwash, influence; (12) indoctrinate; III **conditioned** *or* **conditioning** *cryptic* ANAGRAM CUE.

conduct I *n* 1 (4) ways; (6) doings, habits, manner; (7) actions, bearing, manners; (8) attitude, dealings; (9) behaviour; (11)

comportment; 2 (7) running; (8) guidance; (9) direction; (10) leadership, management; (11) supervision; II *v* 1 (4) lead, take; (5) bring, carry, ferry, guide, usher; (6) convey, escort; (9) accompany, transport; 2 (3) run; (4) wage; (6) handle, manage, pursue; (7) oversee; (8) practise, regulate; (9) undertake; (10) administer; (2 words) carry on, carry out, engage in.

confine I *v* (4) cage; (5) bound, cramp, limit; (7) enclose; (8) imprison, restrict; (9) constrain; (11) incarcerate; (12) circumscribe; II *cryptic* insert the letters forming one part of the answer inside those of another part.

conflict I *n & v* (3) row, war; (4) feud, spat, tiff; (5) brawl, clash, fight, scrap; (7) dispute, quibble, wrangle; (8) squabble; II *n* 1 (3) war; (6) battle, combat, enmity, strife; (7) warfare; (8) campaign, struggle; (9) fighting; (11) belligerence, hostilities; 2 (4) rift, tiff; (6) breach, schism; (7) discord, rupture; (8) argument, vendetta; (9) complaint, grievance; (10) difference, dissension; (11) controversy; (12) disagreement; (16) misunderstanding; III *v* (6) differ; (8) disagree.

confuse I *v* 1 (6) jumble, muddle, tangle; (8) disorder; (10) complicate, disarrange; (2 words) mix up; 2 (6) baffle, puzzle; (7) mystify, perplex; (8) bewilder, confound; (10) discompose, disconcert; II **confuse, confused** *cryptic* ANAGRAM CUE.

connect I *v* (3) tie; (4) bind, join, knot, lash, link, moor, rope, yoke; (5) hitch, unite; (6) attach, couple, fasten, secure, tether; (7) bracket, harness; (9) associate; II **connect, connected, connection** *cryptic* join two (or more) words together to make the answer, as in: 'Traitor wants connection with lady preferably' (6) = rather (lady = her).

conscious *adj* (5) alert, awake, aware; (7) heedful, mindful; (8) familiar; (9) attentive, cognisant (*or* cognizant); (10) acquainted, conversant; (13) knowledgeable.

consequence *n* 1 (5) fruit; (6) effect, issue, sequel, upshot, result; (7) outcome, product; (8) reaction; (10) end-product;

(12) repercussion; **2** (4) note; (5) value; (6) weight; (7) concern; (10) importance; (12) significance.

consequent *adj* (7) related; (9) attendant, resultant; (10) associated, subsequent; (11) concomitant.

consider *v* **1** (4) muse; (5) think; (6) ponder, reason; (7) reflect; (8) cogitate, meditate, ruminate; (10) deliberate; (11) contemplate; **2** (4) deem, hold; (5) judge; (6) esteem, reckon, regard; (7) believe; (8) conclude, estimate; **3** (4) plan; (6) expect, intend; (7) imagine, suppose, surmise; (8) conceive, envisage.

constant *adj* **1** (7) abiding, endless, eternal, non-stop; (8) unbroken; (9) continual, permanent, perpetual, unceasing; (10) continuous, persistent, relentless; (11) everlasting, never-ending, unremitting; (13) uninterrupted; **2** (4) true; (5) loyal; (6) trusty; (7) devoted, staunch; (8) faithful, reliable; (9) steadfast; (10) dependable.

constellation *n* (5) group, stars; (13) configuration.

CONSTELLATIONS

(3) Ara (altar), Leo (lion).

(4) Argo (ship), Crux (southern cross), Grus (crane), Lyra (lyre).

(5) Aries (ram), Cetus (sea monster), Draco (dragon), Hydra (water snake), Indus, Lepus (hare), Libra (scales), Lupus (wolf), Musca (fly), Orion (hunter), Virgo (virgin).

(6) Aquila (eagle), Auriga (charioteer), Bootes (herdsman), Cancer (crab), Carina (keel), Corvus (crow), Crater, Cygnus (swan), Dorado (gilded), Fornax (kiln), Gemini (twins), Hydrus (water serpent), Pisces (fishes), Plough, Puppis (poop - of *Argo*), Taurus (bull), Tucana (toucan).

(7) Cepheus (myth king), Columba (dove), Pegasus (winged horse), Perseus, Phoenix, Scorpio (scorpion), Serpens (serpent).

(8) Aquarius (water carrier), Eridanus (River Po), Hercules.

(9) Andromeda, Centaurus (centaur), Delphinus (dolphin), Ophiuchus (serpent bearer).

(10) Triangulum (triangle).

(11) Capricornus (sea goat), Cassiopoeia (myth queen), Sagittarius (archer).

(2 words) Canes Venatici (hunting dogs), Canis Major (great dog), Canis Minor (little dog), Corona Borealis (northern crown), Piscis Austrinus (southern fish), Triangulum Australe, Ursa Major (great bear), Ursa Minor (little bear).

---

construct I *v* (4) form, make; (5) build, erect, model, raise, shape; (7) compose; (8) assemble; (9) fabricate, formulate; (11) manufacture; **II construct, constructed** *cryptic* ANAGRAM CUE.

contain I *v* **1** (4) hold, seat; (5) carry; (7) embrace, enclose, include, support, sustain; (8) comprise, surround; (11) accommodate, incorporate; **2** (5) limit; (7) control **II** *cryptic* **1** one word is placed around another word, letter, or letters, as in: 'Large barrel contains the French servant' (5) = valet; **2** HIDDEN WORD CUE, as in: 'French armoury holds wherewithal to mount offensive' (5) = charm.

continual *adj* (7) abiding, endless, eternal, non-stop; (8) constant, unbroken; (9) permanent, perpetual, unceasing; (10) continuous, persistent, relentless; (11) everlasting, never-ending, unremitting; (13) uninterrupted.

continuous I *adj see* **continual**; **II continuous** *or* **continuously** *cryptic* join two words in the clue together to form the answer (or the clue to the answer), as in: 'Practitioners of old religion roast fowl continuously' (8) = heathens.

contract I *n* (4) deal, pact; (6) accord, treaty; (7) bargain, compact; (8) covenant; (9) agreement; (10) commitment, settlement; (11) arrangement; (13) understanding; **II** *v* (6) lessen, reduce, shrink; (7) curtail, shorten, tighten; (8) diminish.

convention *n* (4) form, rule; (5) habit, usage; (6) custom; (7) routine; (8) practice; (9) etiquette, procedure, tradition.

conversation *n* (4) chat, talk; (6) gossip, natter; (7) chatter, chinwag; (8) dialogue, exchange; (9) discourse; (10) discussion; (12) consultation; (13) communication.

converse I *adj & n* (7) counter, reverse; (8) contrary, opposite; II *v* (4) chat, talk; (6) confer, gossip, natter; (7) chatter, discuss; III **converse** *or* **conversely** *cryptic* reverse the order of the letters in a word.

convey *v* 1 (4) lead, take; (5) bring, carry, ferry, guide, usher; (6) escort; (7) conduct; (9) transport; 2 (4) tell; (6) impart, relate, reveal; (7) express, signify; (11) communicate.

cool *adj* 1 (4) mild; (5) fresh, nippy; (6) breezy, chilly; (8) lukewarm; (10) refreshing; 2 (4) calm; (6) casual; (7) relaxed, unmoved; (8) composed, laid-back; (9) collected, impassive, unruffled; (10) nonchalant, untroubled; (11) undisturbed, unemotional, unflappable, unperturbed; (13) dispassionate, imperturbable; 3 (4) cold; (5) aloof; (6) frigid; (7) distant, hostile; (8) reserved; (9) apathetic; (10) unfriendly; (11) half-hearted, standoffish, unwelcoming; (12) uninterested; (14) unenthusiastic; II *v* 1 (3) fan; (5) chill; (6) freeze; (11) refrigerate; 2 (4) calm, hush; (5) abate, allay, quell, relax, still; (6) dampen, lessen, pacify, sedate, soothe, subdue, temper; (7) assuage, placate, quieten; (8) moderate; (12) tranquillise (*or* tranquillize).

copper *cryptic* letters CU or PC.

copy I *n & v* (4) crib, echo, twin; (5) clone, match, Xerox®; (6) repeat; (9) duplicate, Photostat®; II *n* (4) mate, pair; (5) image; (6) double, fellow; (7) forgery, replica, tracing; (9) imitation, lookalike; (10) plagiarism; (11) counterfeit, counterpart; (12) reproduction; III *v* (3) ape; (5) mimic, trace; (6) mirror, parrot; (7) emulate, imitate; (8) simulate; (9) reproduce; (10) transcribe; (11) impersonate.

core *n see* **centre, heart**.

corner I *n* (4) bend, nook; (5) angle, crook, joint, niche; (6) recess; II *v* (3) bag; (4) grab, take; (6) obtain; (7) acquire, reserve; (10) commandeer; (11) appropriate.

correct I *adj* 1 (4) true; (5) exact, right; (7) precise; (8) accurate, faithful, flawless, unerring; (9) faultless; (11) word-perfect; 2 (3) apt, fit; (4) meet; (5) right; (6) proper, seemly, suited; (7) fitting; (8) suitable; (11) appropriate; 3 (10) scrupulous; (11) painstaking, punctilious; II *v* (5) amend; (6) better, reform; (7) improve, rectify, redress.

cosmetic I *n* (6) makeup; (11) greasepaint; II *adj* (7) surface; (10) decorative; (11) superficial.

TYPES OF COSMETIC

(4) kohl, talc; (5) liner, rouge;
(6) powder; (7) blusher, cologne,
lanolin, mascara, pancake;
(8) eyeliner, lipstick; (9) eyeshadow,
sunscreen; (10) foundation;
(11) conditioner, highlighter,
moisturiser (*or* moisturizer).

---

cost I *n* 1 (4) rate; (5) price, value, worth; (6) amount, charge, figure, outlay; (7) expense, payment; 2 (4) loss, toll; (7) penalty; (9) sacrifice; II *v* (4) rate; (5) price; (6) assess; (8) appraise, estimate, evaluate;

country I *n* (4) area, land, zone; (5) state; (6) domain, nation, region, sector; (7) kingdom, terrain; (8) district, province, republic; (9) territory; (10) dependency; II *adj* (5) rural; (6) rustic; (8) agrarian, regional.

county *n* (4) area; (5) shire; (6) region.

COUNTIES OF ENGLAND

Avon (ex), Bedfordshire (Beds),
Berkshire (Berks), Buckinghamshire
(Bucks), Cambridgeshire (Cambs),
Cheshire (Ches), Cleveland (ex),
Cornwall, Cumberland (ex),
Cumbria, Derbyshire (Derbys),
Devonshire (Devon), Dorset,
Durham, Essex, Gloucestershire
(Glos), Hampshire (Hants),

list continued over

Herefordshire, Hertfordshire (Herts), Huntingdonshire (ex), Isle of Wight (IOW), Kent, Lancashire (Lancs), Leicestershire (Leics), Lincolnshire (Lincs), Middlesex (ex) (Middx), Norfolk, Northamptonshire (Northants), Northumberland, Nottinghamshire (Notts), Oxfordshire (Oxon), Rutland, Shropshire (Salop), Somerset (Som), Staffordshire (Staffs), Suffolk, Surrey, Sussex, Tyne & Wear, Warwickshire, West Midlands, Westmorland (ex), Wiltshire (Wilts), Worcestershire (Worcs), Yorkshire (Yorks).

COUNTIES OF IRELAND

Carlow, Cavan, Clare, Connaught, Cork, Donegal, Dublin, Galway, Kerry, Kildare, Kilkenny, Laois, Leinster, Leitrim, Limerick, Longford, Louth, Mayo, Meath, Monaghan, Offaly, Roscommon, Sligo, Tipperary, Waterford, Westmeath, Wexford, Wicklow.

COUNTIES OF NORTHERN IRELAND

Antrim, Armagh, Down, Fermanagh, Londonderry, Tyrone.

FORMER COUNTIES OF SCOTLAND

for Scottish regions see **region**.

Aberdeenshire, Angus, Argyllshire, Banffshire, Berwickshire, Caithness, Clackmannanshire, Dumfriesshire, Dunbartonshire, East Lothian, Fife, Inverness-shire, Kincardineshire, Kinross-shire, Kirkcudbrightshire, Lanarkshire, Midlothian, Morayshire, Nairn, Peeblesshire, Perth, Renfrewshire, Ross & Cromarty, Roxburghshire, Selkirkshire, Stirlingshire, Sutherland, West Lothian, Wigtownshire.

COUNTIES OF WALES

Brecknockshire (ex), Caernarvonshire, Caerphilly, Cardiganshire (ex), Carmarthenshire, Ceredigion, Clwyd (ex), Conwy, Denbighshire, Dyfed (ex), Flintshire, Glamorgan (ex), Gwent (ex), Gwynedd, Isle of Anglesey, Merioneth (ex), Monmouthshire, Montgomeryshire (ex), Pembrokeshire, Powys, Radnorshire (ex).

couple I *n* (3) duo, two; (4) pair; (5) brace, twins; (7) twosome; **II** *v* (3) tie; (4) join, link, pair, yoke; (5) hitch, unite; (7) bracket, connect, harness; (9) associate.

courage *n* (4) grit, guts; (5) nerve, pluck; (6) bottle, daring, mettle, spirit, valour; (7) bravery, heroism; (8) audacity, boldness; (9) fortitude, gallantry, hardihood.

courageous *adj* (4) bold; (5) brave, gutsy; (6) feisty, heroic, plucky; (7) gallant, valiant; (8) fearless, intrepid, unafraid; (9) dauntless, undaunted.

cover I *n & v* (3) cap, lid, top; (4) case, coat, hide, mask, veil, wrap; (5) cloak, front, guard; (6) screen, shield, shroud; (8) disguise; (10) camouflage; **II** *n* **1** (6) jacket; (7) wrapper; (8) envelope; **2** (6) façade, refuge; (7) defence, pretext, shelter; (8) pretence; (10) protection; **III** *v* **1** (5) spray, strew; (6) spread; (7) spatter; (8) sprinkle; **2** (7) conceal, obscure; **3** (5) treat; (7) contain, embrace, examine, include; (8) comprise, consider; (9) encompass; (11) incorporate.

Crab *see* **Cancer**.

crack I *n & v* (3) pop; (4) snap; (5) break, burst, split; (8) fracture; **II** *v* **1** (3) **hit**; (5) knock; **2** (5) **solve**; (8) decipher; **III** *n* **1** (3) gap; (4) flaw, rift; (5) chink; (7) crevice, fissure; **2** (3) dig, gag; (4) jibe, joke, quip; (9) witticism; **IV** *adj* (3) ace, top; (6) expert; (8) top-notch; (9) first-rate; (10) first-class; **V** crack, cracked, *etc cryptic* ANAGRAM CUE.

crazy I *adj* **1** (3) mad; (4) bats, nuts, wild; (6) absurd, insane; (7) frantic, idiotic, lunatic; (8) demented, deranged; (9) psychotic; (10) irrational, unbalanced; **2** (5) angry, cross; (7) annoyed, furious; **3** (6) hectic; (7) chaotic; (8) confused; **II** crazy *or* crazily *cryptic* ANAGRAM CUE.

create *v* (4) coin, form, make; (5) build, cause, hatch, raise; (6) arouse, devise, invent; (7) compose, develop, produce; (8) engender, generate, occasion.

credit I *n* **1** (5) faith, trust; (8) reliance; **2** (5) glory; (6) esteem, honour, praise, thanks; (8) approval; (11) recognition; (12) commendation; **II** *v* **1** (5) trust; (6) accept; (7) believe, swallow; **2** (6) assign; (7) ascribe; (9) attribute; **III** *cryptic* letters CR.

cricket *n for fielding position in cricket, see* **fielder**.

crime *n* (3) sin; (4) foul; (5) wrong; (6) felony; (7) misdeed, offence; (8) trespass; (9) violation; (10) wrongdoing; (12) infringement, misdemeanour; (13) transgression.

criminal I *n* (4) hood, thug; (5) crook, felon, heavy, rough, tough; (6) sinner; (7) culprit, hoodlum, mobster, ruffian; (8) evildoer, gangster, offender; (9) miscreant, racketeer, wrongdoer; (10) delinquent, law-breaker, trespasser; (12) transgressor; **II** *adj* (3) bad; (4) evil; (5) wrong; (6) sinful, unfair, unjust, wicked; (7) crooked, illegal, illicit, immoral; (8) unlawful; (9) dishonest, unethical; (11) blameworthy.

cripple I *v* (4) lame, maim; (6) **damage**, impair, injure; (7) disable; (8) handicap, paralyse; **II** *cryptic* ANAGRAM CUE.

critical *adj* **1** (8) negative; **2** (3) key; (5) basic, vital; (7) crucial; (8) decisive; (9) essential, important, necessary, requisite; (10) imperative; (11) fundamental, life-or-death, significant; (13) indispensable.

Cronos *or* **Cronus** (*also* **Kronos**) *Gk myth* The second chief god, son of Uranus and Gaea (*or* Gaia), a Titan who devoured his own children to prevent them dethroning him, but was eventually overcome by **Zeus** – equivalent of Roman **Saturn**.

crook *n see* **criminal I**.

crooked I *adj* **1** (4) bent; (5) bowed; (6) angled, arched, curved; (7) crooked, hunched, stooped, twisted; **2** (5) false,

lying, shady; (6) crafty, dubious, sneaky; (7) corrupt, illegal; (8) cheating, criminal, two-faced; (9) deceitful, deceiving, deceptive, dishonest, swindling, underhand; (10) fraudulent, misleading, unreliable, untruthful; (11) duplicitous; treacherous; (12) disreputable, hypocritical, unprincipled; (13) double-dealing, untrustworthy; **II** *cryptic* ANAGRAM CUE.

crucial *adj* (3) key; (5) basic, vital; (8) critical, decisive; (9) essential, important, necessary, requisite; (10) imperative; (11) fundamental, life-or-death, significant; (13) indispensable.

cruel *adj* (4) mean; (5) harsh, nasty; (6) unkind; (7) callous, inhuman; (8) inhumane, sadistic, spiteful, uncaring; (9) malicious, unfeeling; (10) malevolent, unfriendly; (11) hard-hearted, insensitive, thoughtless; (13) unsympathetic.

crustacean *n see* **shellfish**.

cry I *n & v* (4) bawl, call, hail, howl, roar, wail, yell; (5) cheer, shout; (6) bellow, scream, shriek; (7) screech; **II** *v* (3) sob; (4) blub, weep; (6) snivel; (7) blubber, whimper.

cure I *v* (3) fix; (4) ease, heal, help, mend; (5) solve, treat; (6) remedy, repair; (7) correct, rectify, redress, relieve; (10) counteract; **II** *n* (6) answer, remedy; (7) panacea, therapy; (8) antidote, medicine, solution; (9) treatment; (10) corrective; (14) countermeasure; **III** *cryptic* ANAGRAM CUE.

currency *n* (5) money; (6) tender; (7) coinage.

CURRENCIES

Country	Currency	Small units	Country	Currency	Small units
Albania	lek	qintars	Kenya	shillings	cents
Algeria	dinar	centimes	Korea	whan	jun
Argentina	austral	centavos	Laos	kip	at
Armenia	dram		Lebanon	pound	piastres
Austria	schilling	groschen	Liberia	dollar	cents
Bangladesh	taka	paisa	Libya	dinar	dirhams
Belarus	rubel	zaichik	Luxembourg	franc	centimes
Belgium	franc	centimes	Malawi	kwacha	tambala
Bolivia	boliviano	centavos	Malta	pound	cents
Brazil	crucado	centavos	Mexico	peso	centavos
Bulgaria	lev	stotinki	Moldova	leu	
Burma	kyat	pyas	Morocco	dirham	francs
Cambodia	riel	sen	Netherlands	guilder	cents
Canada	dollar	cents	New Zealand	dollar	cents
Chile	peso	centesimos	Nicaragua	cordoba	centavos
China	yuan	chiao/fen	Nigeria	naira	kobos
Colombia	peso	centavos	Norway	krone	ore
Costa Rica	colon	centimos	Pakistan	rupee	paisas
Cuba	peso	centavos	Panama	balboa	centismos
Cyprus	pound	mils	Paraguay	guarani	centismos
Czech Republic	koruna	honers	Peru	sol	centavos
Denmark	krone	ore	Philippines	peso	centavos
Ecuador	sucre	centavos	Poland	zloty	groszy
Egypt	pound	piastres	Portugal	escudo	centavos
El Salvador	colon	centavos	Romania	leu	bani
Ethiopia	dollar	cents	Russia	rouble	kopeks
Finland	markka	pennia	Saudi Arabia	rial	qursh
France	franc	centimes	Spain	peseta	centimos
Germany	mark	pfennigs	Sri Lanka	rupee	cents
Greece	drachma	lepton	Sweden	krona	ore
Guatemala	quetzal	centavos	Switzerland	franc	centimes
Guinea	sily	gauris	Syria	pound	piastres
Haiti	gourde	centimes	Thailand	baht	satangs
Honduras	lempira	centavos	Tunisia	dinar	millimes
Hungary	forint	fillers	Turkey	lira	kurus
Iceland	krona	aurar	UK	pound	pennies/pence
India	rupee	paisis			
Indonesia	rupiah	sen	USA	dollar	cents
Iran	rial	dinars	Uruguay	peso	centesimos
Iraq	dinar	fils	Uzbekistan	som	
Ireland	punt	pennies	Venezuela	bolivar	centimos
Israel	shekel	agorots	Vietnam	dong	xu
Italy	lira	centesimi	Yemen	riyal	bugshas
Japan	yen	sen	Yugoslavia	dinar	paras
Jordan	dinar	fils			

current I *adj* **1** (6) actual, modern, trendy; (7) ongoing, popular, present; (8) existing, up-to-date; (12) contemporary; **2** (6) common; (7) general; (9) prevalent; (10) widespread; II *n* (3) jet; (4) flow, tide; (5) trend; (6) course, stream; (7) draught; (8) tendency.

curve *n & v* (3) arc, bow; (4) bend, coil, loop, roll, wrap; (5) bulge, twine, twist; (6) ramble, spiral, wreath, zigzag; (7) meander.

custom *n* (4) form, rule, wont; (5) habit, usage; (6) praxis; (7) routine; (8) practice; (9) etiquette, procedure, tradition; (10) convention.

cut I *n & v* (4) nick, gash, slit, stab; (5) slash, slice, wound; II *v* **1** (3) hew, lop; (4) chop, clip, crop, hack, pare, trim; (5) carve, prune, sever, shave; (6) cleave, divide; **2** (4) edit; (6) digest, précis, lessen, reduce; (7) abridge, curtail, shorten; (8) abstract, compress, condense, truncate; (10) abbreviate; **3** (3) axe; (4) sack; (5) erase, scrub; (6) cancel, delete, efface, remove, strike; (2 words) cross out, edit out, rub out, strike out; **4** (4) snub; (6) ignore; III *n* **1** (8) incision; (10) laceration; **2** (6) saving; (7) economy; (8) decrease; (9) reduction; **3** (5) quota, share, whack; (6) ration; IV **cut** *or* **cut out** *cryptic* used as a cue to omit certain letters or syllables from part of a word, as in: 'Cut scene, insert an element of spectacle, turn critic into an admirer' (9) = respecter (critic = reviewer, scene = view, and *see* **element**).

Cyclops *Gk myth* a member of a race of giants with a single eye in the middle of their foreheads. The most famous of them was **Polyphemus**.

D

D *abbrev* Democrat (US political party), deuterium, diamonds (card suit), Germany (international vehicle registration), key (music), note (music), 500 (Roman numeral).

d *abbrev* daughter, diameter, died, down, pence *or* penny (from Latin *denarius*).

dab I *v* (3) pat, tap; (4) daub, swab, wipe; (5) touch; (6) dabble, stroke; **II** *n* (3) pat, tap; (4) drop, spot; (5) fleck, smear, speck, touch, trace; (6) dollop, smudge; **III** *n* freshwater fish; **IV dabs** *pl n* fingerprints.

dabble *v* **1** (3) dab, dip, wet; (5) (6) paddle, splash; (7) moisten; (8) sprinkle; **2** (3) toy; (5) dally; (6) fiddle, potter, tinker, trifle.

dabbler *n* (7) amateur, trifler; (10) dilettante.

da capo *adv* musical instruction to go back to the beginning of a piece or section.

dace *n* fish.

dacha *n* Russian country cottage or retreat.

dacoit *n* Indian bandit.

dactyl *n* type of poetic foot consisting of two short or unstressed syllables followed by a long or stressed one.

dad *n* (2) pa; (3) pop; (4) papa, *père*, pops, sire; (5) daddy, pater; (6) father; (2 words) old man.

daddy *n see* **dad**.

daddy-long-legs *n* popular name for the insect, the cranefly. Its grubs are known as leather-jackets.

Daedalus *Gk myth* an engineer, inventor and sculptor, who built the labyrinth for King **Minos** of Crete to house the **Minotaur**, was imprisoned by Minos and escaped by constructing wings for himself and his son **Icarus** (Icarus flew too near the sun and fell to his death during the escape).

daffodil I *n* yellow spring flower of narcissus family; **II** *cryptic* famous poems about daffodils were written by William **Wordsworth** and Robert **Herrick.**

daft *adj* (3) mad; (4) bats, nuts, wild; (5) barmy, crazy, dotty, inane, loopy, nutty, potty, screwy, silly; (6) absurd, crazed, insane, mental, simple, stupid, unwise; (7) barking, bonkers, foolish, idiotic, lunatic; (9) fanatical, imprudent, ludicrous, senseless (10) infatuated, ridiculous; (11) impractical, unrealistic; (12) enthusiastic, irresponsible.

dagger *n see* **knife**.

daguerreotype *n* early type of photograph or photographic process invented by Louis Daguerre.

Dáil *or* **Dáil Éireann** the lower house of the Irish parliament.

daily I *adj* (6) common; (7) diurnal, regular, routine (8) everyday, ordinary; (9) customary, quotidian; (11) commonplace; **II** *n* **1** *see* **newspaper**; **2** (4) char; (7) cleaner; (8) charlady.

Daily Planet *fict.* the newspaper for which Clark Kent (**Superman**) worked as a reporter.

Daily Worker *hist.* former British newspaper representing Communist viewpoint, subsequently renamed *Morning Star*.

dainty *adj* **1** (4) fine, neat, thin, tiny; (5) frail, light, small; (6) flimsy, petite, pretty, slight; (7) elegant, fragile, refined, slender; (8) delicate, graceful; (9) exquisite; **2** (5) **fussy**; (6) choosy; (7) finicky; (10) fastidious, particular, scrupulous.

dais *n see* **platform**.

Daleks *TV* mechanised adversaries of Dr Who in long-running television science-fiction series – catchphrase 'Exterminate!'

daltonism *n* colour blindness – from the scientist John Dalton who suffered from it and described the condition in 1794.

dam I *n* (7) barrage, barrier; (8) blockage; (9) barricade; (10) embankment; (11) obstruction; **II** *v* (4) stem; (5) block, check; (6) staunch; (7) confine; (8) obstruct, restrict; (9) barricade; **III** *cryptic* the mother of an animal such as a horse, sheep, etc. or an archaic word for a person's mother - *see* **mother.**

damage I *n & v* (4) dent, gash, harm, hole, hurt, ruin; (5) break, crack, split, wreck; **II** *n* (4) harm, loss; (5) havoc; (6) cracks, injury; (8) wreckage; (9) detriment, suffering; (10) mutilation; (11) destruc- tion, devastation; **III** *v* (3) mar; (5) crush, smash, spoil; (6) deface, impair, injure, ravage, weaken; (7) despoil, shatter; (8) mutilate, sabotage; (9) devastate; (12) incapacitate; **IV damages** (9) indemnity; (11) restitution; (12) compensation; (13) reimbursement; **V damage** *or* **damaged** ANAGRAM CUE.

Dam Busters *n pl* the airmen of 617 squadron of the RAF who carried out raids against the Möhne, Eder and Sorpe dams in Germany in 1943 using bouncing bombs.

damn *v* (4) slam, doom; (5) curse, slate; (7) censure, condemn; (8) denounce; (9) castigate, criticise (*or* criticize), imprecate.

Damon and Pythias *Gk myth* legendary examples of true friendship. When Pythias was condemned to death by Dionysus, the tyrant of Syracuse, Damon stood bail for him so that he could go home and put his affairs in order, agreeing to be executed in his place if Pythias did not return. Just before the execution was due to be carried out, Pythias did return, which so impressed Dionysus that he pardoned him.

damp I *adj* (3) wet; (4) dank, dewy; (5) humid, moist, misty, muggy, rainy, soggy; (6) clammy; (7) drizzly, showery; **II** *n* (3) dew, fog, wet; (4) mist; (5) spray; (6) vapour; (7) drizzle; (8) dampness, dankness, humidity, moisture; (9) moistness; (10) clamminess, **III** *v* **1** (3) wet; (5) spray, water; (6) dampen; (7) moisten (8) irrigate, sprinkle; **2** (4) calm, dash, dull; (5) abate, allay, check, deter; (6) absorb, deaden, lessen, muffle, reduce, stifle, subdue; (8) decrease, diminish, moderate.

dampen *see* **damp** *v*.

Danae *Gk myth* the daughter of King Acrisius who became the mother of **Perseus** by **Zeus**, who came to her in the form of a shower of gold.

dance I *v* (3) bob, bop, hop, jig, tap; (4) frug, jive, trip; (5) caper, disco, frisk, waltz; (6) cavort, frolic, prance, shimmy; (7) rollick, shuffle; (2 words) foot it, trip it; (3 words) strip the willow; (4 words) trip the light fantastic; **II** *n* (3) hop; (4) ball, prom (US), rave; (5) disco; (6) ballet; (7) ceilidh, hoe-down, knees-up, shindig; (8) hunt-ball, tea-dance; *see also* **ballet**; **III dances, danced** *or* **dancing** ANAGRAM CUE.

NAMES OF DANCES, STEPS ETC

(3) hay, hey, jig, pas, set, tap.

(4) frug, go-go, haka, jeté, hula, jive, reel, shag.

(5) bebop, conga, fling, galop, glide, gopak, limbo, loure, mambo, pavan, polka, round, rumba, salsa, samba, stomp, tango, twist, valse, volta, waltz.

(6) bolero, Boston, cha-cha, dosi-do, minuet, morris, nautch, pavane, pointe, shimmy, veleta (*or* valeta).

(7) beguine, carioca, courant, csardas (*or* czardas), fouetté, foxtrot, gavotte, lancers, Ländler, mazurka, one-step, ragtime, roundel, shuffle, two-step.

(8) ballroom, bunny-hug, cachucha, cakewalk, chaconne, cotillon, fandango, flamenco, flip-flop, galliard, habanera, hornpipe, hulahula, rigadoon, saraband, snowball.

(9) allemande, arabesque, bossanova, cha-cha-cha, ecossaise, entrechat,

list continued over

---

farandole, formation, jitterbug, passepied, pirouette, polonaise, promenade, quadrille, quick-step, sand-dance

(10) carmagnole, charleston, hokey-cokey, Scottische, strathspey, tarantella, turkey-trot.

(11) choreograph, discothèque.

(12) break-dancing, choreography.

(2 words) (9) clog dance, paso doble, Paul Jones; (10) belly dance, Gay Gordons, thé dansant, square dance; (11) black bottom, Lambeth walk, morris dance, (12) country dance, foursome reel; (13) Boston two-step, eightsome reel, Highland fling, morris dancing, Viennese waltz; (14) country dancing; (15) ballroom dancing, hesitation waltz, invitation waltz, military two-step, soft-shoe shuffle; (16) Circassian circle.

(3+ words) (9) pas de deux; (13) palais de danse; (15) Roger de Coverley; (18) Sir Roger de Coverley.

danger *n* (4) risk; (5) peril; (6) hazard, menace, threat; (8) jeopardy; (9) liability (10) insecurity; (14) precariousness.

dangerous *adj* (5) dicey, grave, hairy, nasty, risky; (6) chancy, unsafe; (7) exposed, serious; (8) alarming, critical, insecure, menacing, perilous, reckless; (9) breakneck, hazardous; (10) precarious, vulnerable; (11) threatening, treacherous

Daniel *Bible* 1 a Hebrew prophet who interpreted the dreams of the Babylonian king **Nebuchadnezzar**, was thrown into the lions' den, and is presented in the apocryphal Book of Susanna as a wise judge; 2 a book of the Old Testament.

Dante *lit.* an Italian poet, full name Dante Alighieri, author of *The Divine Comedy* and the *Vita Nuova*, inspired by his love for Beatrice (Portinari).

Danton *hist.* a leader of the French Revolution.

Danube *geog.* a river in southern Europe flowing through Germany, Austria, Hungary, Yugoslavia, and Romania. Three capitals are on the Danube: Vienna, Budapest and Belgrade.

Daphne *Gk myth* a nymph who was changed into a laurel tree to save her from Apollo.

Daphnis 1 *Gk myth* a Sicilian shepherd who invented pastoral poetry; 2 *lit.* **Daphnis and Chloë** the lovers in an idyllic pastoral story.

dappled *adj* (7) flecked, mottled, piebald, specked, spotted; (8) freckled, speckled, stippled; (9) chequered (*or* checkered); (10) bespeckled, variegated.

darbies *pl n* handcuffs.

Darby and Joan *trad.* the archetypal old couple who have enjoyed a long and happy marriage.

Dardanelles *geog.* a strait connecting the Sea of Marmara to the Aegean Sea, formerly known as the Hellespont, scene of the attack on Gallipoli by the Allies during World War I.

dare *v* 1 (4) risk; (7) presume, venture; 2 (4) defy, goad; (5) brave, taunt; (7) provoke; (8) confront; (9) challenge; (2+ words) egg on; throw down the gauntlet.

daring I *adj* 1 (4) bold, rash; (5) brave; (6) heroic, plucky; (7) defiant, gallant, valiant; (8) fearless, intrepid, reckless; (9) audacious, dauntless, impetuous, impulsive; (10) courageous, headstrong; (11) adventurous; 2 (6) low-cut, risqué; (7) naughty; II *n* (4) dash, gall, grit, guts; (5) nerve, pluck; (6) spirit; (7) bravery, courage, prowess; (8) audacity, boldness, defiance, rashness; (11) impetuosity, intrepidity; (12) fearlessness.

dark I *adj* 1 (3) dim, sad; (4) grim; (5) black, dusky, murky, sooty. unlit; (6) cloudy, dismal, gloomy, sombre, twilit; (7) obscure, shadowy, swarthy; (8) mournful, overcast, starless; (9) cheerless, lightless; (13) unilluminated; 2 (4) evil; (6) hidden, secret, wicked (7) cryptic, unknown; (8)

abstruse, sinister; (9) enigmatic; (10) mysterious; **II in the dark** *phr* (7) unaware; (8) ignorant; (9) oblivious, unknowing, unwitting; (10) uninformed; (11) unconscious, uninitiated; (13) unenlightened.

Darling I *hist.* **Grace Darling**, the daughter of a Northumberland lighthouse-keeper who, together with her father, rescued survivors from the wreck of the *Forfarshire* in 1838; II *lit.* surname of the family visited by Peter Pan in the novel by J. M. Barrie – the children's names were Wendy, John and Michael; III *geog.* a river in southeastern Australia.

darling I *n* (3) pet; (4) dear, love; (5) honey, sweet; (7) acushla (Irish), beloved, dearest; (8) precious; (9) favourite; (10) sweetheart; (2+ words) blue-eyed boy, ewe lamb; II *adj* (4) cute, dear, (5) sweet; (6) adored, lovely; (7) beloved, dearest; (8) adorable, precious; (9) cherished, favourite; (10) delightful.

Dart *geog.* a river in Devon.

dart I *v* 1 (3) fly, run; (4) bolt, dash, flit, leap, race, rush, tear; (5) bound, flash, hurry, speed (6) spring, sprint; (7) scuttle; 2 (4) cast, hurl; (5) fling, shoot, sling, throw; II *n* 1 (4) barb, bolt; (5) arrow, shaft; 2 (4) fold, seam, tuck; (5) pleat; (6) gusset; III **darts** *sport* (4) game; (6) arrows.

dash I *v* 1 (3) fly, run; (4) bolt, dart, flit, leap, race, rush, tear; (5) bound, flash, hurry, speed (6) hasten, sprint; (7) scuttle; 2 (4) cast, hurl; (5) fling, knock, shoot, sling, throw; 3 (4) ruin; (5) daunt, smash, spoil; (6) blight, dampen; (7) destroy, shatter; (8) confound; (9) frustrate; (10) disappoint, discourage; II *n* 1 (3) bit; (4) drop, hint, spot; (5) patch, pinch, touch; (6) little, splash; (7) flavour, soupçon; (10) suggestion; 2 (4) elan; (5) style, verve; (6) vigour; (7) panache; (10) confidence; 3 (6) hyphen; III 1 *cryptic* letter M or N or letters EM or EN (from em and en dashes used in printing); 2 associated with dots in Morse code.

data *n* (3) gen; (4) info; (5) facts, input; (7) details, figures; (11) information.

date *n* 1 (3) age, day, era; (4) ides (Roman), time; (5) epoch, nones (Roman), stage; (6) period; (7) calends (*or* kalends (Roman)); 2 (5) tryst; (6) escort, friend; (7) meeting, partner; (9) boyfriend, (10) engagement, girlfriend, rendezvous; (11) appointment, assignation; 3 (4) palm, tree; (5) fruit.

dated *adj* (5) passé; (8) obsolete, outdated, outmoded; (10) antiquated; (12) old-fashioned; (13) unfashionable; (3 words) behind the times, out of date.

daub I *v* (3) dab; (5) slosh; (6) splash, splosh, spread; (7) plaster, spatter, splodge; II *n* 1 (3) dab; (4) drop, spot; (5) fleck, smear, speck, touch, trace; (6) dollop, smudge; (7) splodge; 2 a bad painting.

dauber *n* a bad painter.

daughter *cryptic* letter D (abbreviation).

daunt *v* (3) awe; (5) alarm, deter, scare; (6) dampen, dismay; (7) overawe, unnerve; (8) dispirit, frighten; (10) discourage, dishearten, intimidate.

dauntless *adj* (4) bold; (5) brave, (6) daring, heroic, plucky; (7) defiant, gallant, valiant; (8) fearless, intrepid, resolute; (9) undaunted; (10) courageous, unyielding; (11) indomitable, lionhearted.

dauphin *n* the title held by the eldest sons of the kings of France.

dauphine *n* the title of the wife of the dauphin.

David I *Bible* the youngest son of **Jesse**, who killed the Philistine giant **Goliath** with a stone from his slingshot. He became a favourite of King **Saul** and formed a legendary friendship with Saul's son Jonathan. The prophet **Samuel** anointed him as Saul's successor. After eventually defeating Saul in battle he became King of Israel. While king he desired Bathsheba, the wife of Uriah the Hittite, and arranged for Uriah to be killed in battle so that he could marry her. David is traditionally credited with the authorship of the Book of Psalms. His wives were Michal, Abigail, Eglah,

Bathsheba and Abishag. His sons were Amnon, Chileab, **Absalom**, Adonijah, Shepatiah, Ithream and **Solomon**. He had a daughter Tamar. Absalom rebelled against him, but was killed. David was succeeded as king by Solomon. **II St David** a missionary saint, the patron saint of Wales (feast day March 1); **III Jacques Louis David** French portrait painter at the time of the French revolution and court painter to the Emperor Napoleon I. **IV** the name of two kings of Scotland. David II was the son of Robert the Bruce.

Davidson *cryptic* any of the sons of the biblical David, especially Absalom or Solomon.

dawn I *n* (5) birth, onset, start; (6) advent, origin; (7) glimmer, morning, sunrise; (8) daybreak, daylight; (9) beginning, emergence; (11) glimmerings; (two words) first light; **II** *v* (4) open, rise; (5) arise, begin, break, start; (6) appear, emerge; (7) develop, glimmer, lighten; (8) brighten; (9) originate.

day I *n* 1 (4) dawn; (6) Friday, Monday, Sunday; (7) morning, Tuesday; (8) daybreak, daylight, Thursday, Saturday; (9) Wednesday; **2** (3) age, day, era; (4) time; (5) epoch, stage; (6) period; **II** *cryptic* letter D.

dB (*or* **DB**) *abbrev* decibel.

DC *abbrev* 1 da capo; 2 direct current *see also* **AC**; 3 District Commissioner; 4 District of Columbia (US).

dead I *adj* 1 (4) dull, late, gone, numb, over; (5) inert, kaput, tired; (6) barren, boring, desert, dreary, frozen; (7) defunct, extinct; (8) deceased, departed, finished, lifeless, obsolete; (9) apathetic, exhausted, inanimate, inorganic, unfeeling; (10) insensible; (11) uninhabited, unpopulated; (12) unresponsive; (13) anaesthetised (*or* anaesthetized); (two words) done in, passed away, passed over, worn out; **2** (5) exact, total, utter; (6) entire; (7) perfect, precise; (8) absolute, complete, outright; (9) downright; (11) unqualified; **II** *adv* (4) very; (5) right; (6) really; (7) exactly, totally, utterly; (8)

entirely; (9) extremely, perfectly, precisely; (10) absolutely, completely. (2+ words) on the nose, right on, spot on.

deadly *adj* 1 (5) fatal; (6) lethal, mortal; (7) telling; (8) accurate, unerring, venomous; (9) malignant, murdering, murderous, poisonous; (10) pernicious; (11) destructive; **2** (4) dull, (6) boring, dreary; (7) tedious; (8) tiresome; (10) monotonous, unexciting; (13) uninteresting.

deal I *n* 1 (4) pact; (5) trade; (6) treaty; (7) bargain; (8) contract; (9) agreement; (11) arrangement, transaction; (13) understanding; **2** (4) hand; (5) round; (12) distribution **3** (4) pine, wood; **II** *v* (5) trade; (6) handle; (7) traffic; **III deal** *or* **deal out** (4) dole, give, hand, mete; (5) allot, share; (6) assign, bestow, divide; (8) dispense; (9) apportion; (10) distribute (2 words) dole out, give out, hand out, mete out, share out; **IV deal with** (5) treat; (6) handle, manage, tackle; (7) concern; (8) consider; (2 words) attend to, cope with, refer to, relate to, see to.

dear I *adj* 1 (5) close, loved, sweet; (6) adored, lovely, valued; (7) beloved, darling; (8) adorable, esteemed, intimate, precious; (9) appealing, cherished, favourite, treasured; **2** (4) high; (5) steep; (6) costly, pricey; (9) expensive; (10) exorbitant, high-priced, overpriced; (12) extortionate; **II** *n* (3) luv, pet; (4) duck, lamb, love; (5) honey, sweet; (7) beloved, darling; (8) precious; (9) favourite; (10) sweetheart; (2+ words) blue-eyed boy, ewe lamb; **III** *sounds like* **deer**.

Dear John letter *n* a letter from a woman to a man ending a romantic relationship.

dearth *n* (4) lack, need, want; (6) famine; (7) absence, paucity, poverty; (8) scarcity, shortage, sparsity; (10) deficiency, inadequacy, scantiness; (13) insufficiency.

death I *n* (3) end (4) loss; (6) demise, finish, murder; (7) decease, killing, passing, slaying (8) casualty, fatality; (9) cessation, departure; (10) eradication, expiration, extinction; (11) destruction, dissolution; (12) annihilation, obliteration; (13) extermination; ‖ *personification* the (Grim) Reaper.

deb ‖ *n* (4) tyro; (6) novice; (7) learner; (8) beginner; (9) debutante; ‖ *cryptic* the letter L (learner).

debase *v* (5) abase, lower, stain, taint; (6) defile, demean, reduce (7) corrupt, degrade, devalue, pollute; (8) disgrace; (9) dishonour; (10) adulterate; (11) contaminate.

debatable *adj* (4) moot; (7) dubious, unclear; (8) arguable, doubtful; (9) ambiguous, uncertain, undecided, unsettled; (10) disputable; (11) contentious, contestable, problematic; (12) questionable; (13) controversial, problematical; (2+ words) at issue, in dispute, open to question.

debate ‖ *n* (5) forum; (7) dispute, meeting; (8) argument; (9); symposium; (10) conference, contention, discussion, reflection; (11) controversy, disputation; (12) conversation, deliberation; (13) consideration ‖ *v* (4) talk; (5) argue; (6) ponder; (7) contend, discuss, dispute, reflect; (8) meditate; (10) deliberate.

debt ‖ *n* (3) due, IOU; (5) claim, debit, score; (6) marker; (7) arrears; (9) liability; (10) obligation; ‖ *cryptic* letters IOU (debts – IOUs); ‖‖ in debt ‖ *phrase* (5) owing; (8) indebted, overdrawn; (3 words) in the red; 2 *cryptic* insert letter or word into DEBT or RED.

dec *abbrev* ‖ deceased; 2 December; 3 declared (*cricket*).

decamp *v see* **depart**.

decay ‖ *v* (3) rot; (4) fade, fail, sink; (5) erode, spoil; (6) fester, perish, wither, (7) corrode, crumble, putrefy, shrivel; (9) decompose; (10) degenerate; (11) deteriorate; (12) disintegrate; (2 words) break down, break up, go off, waste away, wear away ‖ *n* (3) rot; (6) fading; (7) erosion, failure, rotting, wasting; (8) collapse, spoilage, spoiling; (9) corrosion, crumbling, decadence, perishing; (12) degeneration, dilapidation, putrefaction; (13) decomposition, deterioration; (14) disintegration; ‖‖ *cryptic* ANAGRAM CUE.

deceased *adj see* **dead**.

deceit *n* (4) ruse; (5) craft, feint, fraud, guile; (7) cunning, slyness, swindle; (8) artifice, cheating, pretence, trickery; (9) deception, duplicity, hypocrisy, treachery; (10) craftiness, subterfuge; (11) fraudulence; (13) double-dealing; (15) underhandedness; (17) misrepresentation.

deceitful *adj* (3) sly; (4) sham; (5) false; (6) crafty, sneaky; (8) guileful, illusive, two-faced; (9) deceiving, deceptive, dishonest, insincere, underhand; (10) fraudulent, misleading, unreliable; (11) duplicitous; treacherous; (12) hypocritical; (13) double-dealing, untrustworthy.

deceive *v* (2) do; (3) con, kid; (4) dupe, fool, gull, have, hoax; (5) abuse, cheat, trick; (6) betray, delude; (7) beguile, defraud, ensnare, swindle, two-time; (8) hoodwink; (9) bamboozle; (11) double-cross; (2+ words) have on, pull sb's leg, take for a ride, take in.

December *n* (3) Dec; (5) month. In the Roman calendar, December was the tenth month (*decem* Latin for ten).

decent *adj* ‖ (3) fit; (4) clad, nice, pure; (5) moral; (6) chaste, modest, proper, seemly; (7) clothed, fitting; (8) becoming, decorous, suitable; (9) befitting (11) appropriate, presentable, respectable; 2 (4) kind, nice; (6) polite; (7) helpful; (8) friendly, generous, gracious, obliging, tolerant; (9) courteous; 3 (2) OK; (4) good; (8) adequate; (9) competent, tolerable; (10) acceptable, reasonable, sufficient; (12) satisfactory.

deception *n* (3) con, lie; (4) hoax, ploy, ruse, wile; (5) bluff, cheat, craft, feint, fraud, guile, snare, trick; (6) deceit; (7) cunning, leg-pull, slyness, swindle; (8) artifice, cheating, pretence, trickery; (9) duplicity, hypocrisy, imposture, stratagem, treachery; (10) craftiness, subterfuge; (11) dissembling, fraudulence, insincerity; (13) deceptiveness, double-dealing; (15) underhandedness; (17) misrepresentation.

deceptive *adj* (4) fake, mock, sham; (5) false; (8) illusive, illusory, spurious; (9)

deceiving; (10) fallacious, misleading, unreliable.

deck I *n* 1 of ship; 2 (4) pack; (5) cards; 3 (5) floor; (6) ground; **II** *v* 1 *see* **decorate**; 2 (5) floor; (2 words) knock down.

declare *v* 1 (3) say; (4) aver, show; (5) claim, state, swear; (6) affirm, assert, reveal; (7) confess, confirm, profess, testify, witness; (8) announce, maintain, proclaim; (9) broadcast, pronounce; 2 *cricket* (3) end; (5) close; (6) finish.

decline I *v* 1 (3) dip; (4) drop, fade, fail, fall, sink, wane; (5) decay, erode; (6) lessen, reduce, wither, worsen; (7) corrode, crumble, dwindle, shrivel; (8) decrease; (10) degenerate; (11) deteriorate; 2 (4) deny; (5) avoid, evade, spurn; (6) rebuff, refuse, reject, forego; (2 words) turn down; **II** *n* (3) ebb; (4) drop, fall; (5) decay, slump; (7) erosion; (8) collapse, decrease, downturn; (9) abatement, decadence, dwindling, recession, reduction, weakening, worsening; (10) diminution, falling-off; (12) degeneration; (13) decomposition, deterioration; (14) disintegration

decompose I *v* (3) rot; (4) fade, fail, sink; (5) decay, erode, spoil; (6) fester, perish, wither; (7) corrode, crumble, putrefy, shrivel; (8) dissolve, separate; (10) degenerate; (11) deteriorate; (12) disintegrate; (2 words) break down, break up, go off, waste away, wear away; **II** *cryptic* ANAGRAM CUE.

decorate *v* 1 (4) deck, trim; (5) adorn, paint, paper; (6) colour, enrich; (8) beautify, ornament, prettify, renovate; (9) embellish, refurbish; (2 words) do up, tart up; 2 *give medal* (4) cite; (5) award, crown; (6) honour.

decoration *n* 1 (4) trim; (5) frill; (6) frills, scroll; (7) garnish; (8) flourish, ornament, trimming; (9) adornment; (13) embellishment, ornamentation; (14) beautification; 2 *see* **medal**.

decrease I *v* (3) cut, dip, ebb; (4) drop, ease, fade, fail, fall, sink, slim, wane; (5) abate, allay, check, lower, taper; (6) absorb, deaden, lessen, muffle, reduce, shrink, stifle, subdue; (7) decline, lighten,

slacken; (8) contract, diminish, moderate; (9) alleviate; **II** *n* (3) cut; (4) drop, fall, loss; (5) decay, slump; (7) erosion; (8) collapse, decrease, downturn, lowering, step-down; (9) abatement, dwindling, lessening, recession, reduction, shrinkage; (10) diminution, falling-off, moderation; (11) contraction; (12) degeneration; (13) deterioration; **III** *cryptic* = **de-crease** (4) iron; (5) press.

decree I *n* (3) law; (5) edict, order; (6) ruling; (7) command, dictate, mandate, precept, statute; (9) enactment, ordinance; (10) injunction, regulation; (12) proclamation; **II** *v* (4) rule; (5) enact, order; (6) decide, enjoin, ordain; (7) command, dictate; (8) proclaim; (9) determine; prescribe; (2 words) lay down.

deed *n* 1 (3) act; (4) fact, feat; (6) action; (7) exploit; (11) achievement, performance; (14) accomplishment; 2 (5) title; (6) record; (8) contract, document; (10) instrument; (3 words) proof of title.

deep I *adj* 1 (3) low; (4) bass, wise; (5) acute, grave; (6) severe, strange; (7) booming, earnest, extreme, intense, learned, obscure, serious, sincere; (8) abstruse, esoteric, profound, resonant; (9) difficult, enigmatic, heartfelt, unplumbed, recondite, secretive; (10) bottomless, discerning, fathomless, mysterious, perceptive; 2 **deep in** (8) absorbed; (9) engrossed; (12) preoccupied; **II the deep** *n* (3) sea; (5) ocean.

deer *n* I (3) doe; (4) buck, fawn, hart, herd hind, stag; (5) Bambi, royal; *see also* **antelope**; **II** *sounds like* **dear**;

TYPES OF DEER

(3) elk, nur, red, roe.

(4) axis, musk, rusa, sika.

(5) izard, moose.

(6) chital, fallow, sambur.

(7) barking, caribou, chamois, muntjac (*or* muntjak).

(8) reindeer.

(10) chevrotain.

(2 words) fallow deer, red deer, roe deer.

---

deface *see* **disfigure**.

defeat I *v* (4) balk, beat, best, foil, rout, ruin; (5) cream, quell, repel, stump, thump, worst; (6) baffle, hammer, subdue, thrash; (7) flummox, trounce, conquer; (8) confound, overcome, vanquish; (9) checkmate, frustrate, overpower, overthrow, overwhelm, slaughter, subjugate; II *n* (4) rout; (7) beating, failure, reverse, setback; (8) conquest; (9) checkmate, overthrow.

defect I *n* (3) bug; (4) flaw, lack, spot; (5) error, fault, taint; (7) absence, blemish, failing, frailty, mistake; (8) weakness; (10) deficiency, inadequacy; (11) shortcoming; II *v* (3) rat; (5) rebel; (6) desert, renege, revolt; (7) renegue; (10) apostatise (*or* apostatize); (2 words) break faith, change sides, go over.

defence *n* I (5) cover, guard; (6) screen, shield; (7) bastion, bulwark, rampart, shelter; (8) buttress, immunity, security; (9) barricade, earthwork, safeguard; (10) deterrence, earthworks, protection, resistance; (14) fortifications; 2 (4) case, plea; (5) alibi; (6) excuse; (7) apology; (8) apologia; (11) exoneration, explanation, vindication; (13) justification; 3 (7) counsel; 4 (5) backs; (9) defenders; (2 words) back four.

defend *v* I (5) cover, guard; (6) screen, secure, shield; (7) fortify, shelter; (9) barricade, safeguard; 2 (6) uphold; (7) endorse, explain, justify, support, sustain; (8) champion; (9) vindicate; (11) rationalise (*or* rationalize); (2+ words) argue for, plead for, speak for, stand by, stand up for.

defile I *v* I (5) abase, lower, stain, taint; (6) befoul, debase, demean, reduce (7) corrupt, degrade, devalue, pollute, profane; (8) disgrace; (9) desecrate, dishonour; (10) adulterate; (11) contaminate; 2 (4) pass; (5) march (*in file*); II *n* (3) col; (4) pass; (5) gorge; (6) valley.

define *v* (5) bound, limit; (7) clarify, delimit, explain, specify; (8) describe; (9) demarcate, designate, determine, interpret; (12) characterise (*or* characterize); (2 words) make clear, mark out, spell out.

definite *adj* (3) set; (4) firm, sure; (5) clear, exact, fixed; (6) marked; (7) assured, certain, decided, obvious, precise, settled; (8) clear-cut, explicit, positive, specific; (10) determined, guaranteed, particular.

definite article *n see* **the**.

definitive *adj* (5) exact, final; (7) perfect; (8) absolute, decisive, reliable, standard, ultimate; (10) conclusive, exhaustive.

deformed I *adj* (4) bent; (6) maimed, warped; (7) buckled, crooked, defaced, mangled, twisted; (8) crippled; (9) contorted, distorted, misshapen, mutilated, perverted; (10) disfigured; II *cryptic* ANAGRAM CUE.

degrade *v* (5) abase, lower, stain, taint; (6) debase, defile, demean, reduce (7) corrupt, devalue, pollute; (8) disgrace; (9) dishonour; (10) adulterate; (11) contaminate.

degree I *n* (4) mark, pass, rank, step, unit; (5) class, first, grade, level, order, range, stage, third; (6) amount, extent, second, status; (7) ranking; (8) position, standard, standing; (9) intensity; II *cryptic* the letters BA, MA or any other combination used to indicate a university degree.

deity *n see* **god**.

dejected *adj see* **depressed** 1.

Delaware *cryptic* abbreviated as Del or DE.

delay I *v* (3) lag; (4) halt, stay, stop, wait; (5) check, defer, stall, tarry; (6) shelve, dawdle, detain, hinder, impede, linger, loiter; (7) suspend; (8) postpone; (10) dilly dally; (2 words) hold back, hold over, hold up, put back, set back. II *n* (4) lull, stay, wait; (5) check; (6) hold-up; (7) setback; (8) dawdling, stoppage; (9) deferment, hindrance; (10) impediment, suspension; (11) obstruction; (12) postponement; (2 words) time lag.

delete I *v* (3) cut; (4) edit; (5) erase, scrub; (6) cancel, efface, remove, strike; (2 words) cross out, edit out, rub out, strike out; II *cryptic* used as a cue to omit certain letters or syllables from part of a word, as in: 'In Cromer (capital deleted), on a donkey, looking foolish' (5) = crass (capital = Rome).

deliberate I *adj* (4) slow; (6) willed; (7) careful, express, planned, studied; (8) cautious; (9) conscious, unhurried; (10) calculated, methodical, thoughtful; (11) intentional, prearranged; (12) premeditated; II *v* (4) talk; (5) think; (6) confer, debate, ponder; (7) consult, discuss, reflect; (8) cogitate, converse, meditate; (2 words) talk about, talk over, think about, think over.

delicate *adj* 1 (4) fine, thin, tiny; (5) frail, light, small; (6) dainty, flimsy, petite, pretty, slight; (7) fragile, refined, slender; (8) graceful; (9) exquisite; 2 (3) ill; (4) sick; (6) unwell.

Delilah *Bible* the woman who was the lover of **Samson** and betrayed him to the Philistines after she had wormed out of him the fact that the secret of his strength was in his long hair.

deliver *v* 1 (4) bowl, give, send; (5) bring, carry, grant, yield; (6) commit, convey, direct, supply; (7) inflict, transfer; (9) surrender; (10) relinquish; (2 words) give up, hand over; 2 (3) say; (5) speak, utter; (8) proclaim; (9) pronounce; 3 (4) free; (6) ransom, redeem; (7) release; (8) liberate; (10) emancipate. 4 (2) do; (7) achieve, perform, succeed.

delivery *n* 1 (4) load, post; (5) batch; (6) parcel; (7) freight; (8) carriage, dispatch, shipment; (10) conveyance; (11) consignment; (12) transmission; 2 (4) ball; 3 (6) rescue; (7) release; (10) liberation; (12) emancipation; 4 (6) speech; (9) elocution, utterance; (10) intonation; (11) enunciation; (12) articulation; 5 (5) birth; (6) labour; (10) childbirth; (11) confinement.

deliveryman I *n* (7) milkman; (9) roundsman, tradesman; II *cryptic* (6) bowler, doctor; (7) pitcher; (2 words) male nurse.

Delphi *hist.* site of a famous oracle in ancient Greece: *see* **oracle**.

delphic *adj* (7) obscure; (8) oracular; (9) confusing, ambiguous.

delta *n* 1 the fourth letter of Greek alphabet, equivalent to D, the capital letter being in the shape of a triangle; 2 a triangular area of silt at the mouth of a large river.

demand I *v* (3) ask; (4) call, need; (5) claim, order; (6) desire, entail, insist; (7) command, involve, request, require, solicit; (11) necessitate, requisition; (2 words) ask for, call for, insist on, wish for; II *v* (4) call, need, wish; (5) claim, order; (7) command.

Demeter *Gk myth* goddess of nature, corn, crops, and vegetation. Roman equivalent **Ceres** – *see also* **Persephone**.

Democrat I *n cryptic* abbreviated as Dem. II the symbol of the US Democratic Party is an elephant.

demolish I *v* (3) mar; (4) dent, harm, hole, hurt, ruin, snap; (5) break, crack, crush, smash, split, spoil, wreck; (6) deface, impair, injure, ravage, weaken; (7) despoil, shatter; (8) mutilate, sabotage; (9) devastate; (12) incapacitate; II **demolish** *or* **demolished** *cryptic* ANAGRAM CUE.

demon *n see* **devil**.

demonstrate *v* 1 (4) show; (5) prove, teach; (7) display, exhibit, explain, testify; (8) indicate, manifest; (9) establish; (10) illustrate; (12) substantiate; 2 (5) march, rally; (6) parade, picket; (7) protest; (2 words) sit in.

demonstration *n* 1 (4) test; (5) proof, trial; (7) display; (8) evidence; (10) exhibition, exposition, expression; (11) description, explanation; (12) illustration, presentation; (13) manifestation; 2 (4) demo; (5) march, rally, sit-in; (6) parade, picket; (7) protest.

denarius *n* penny (pl **denarii** pence), orig. a Roman silver coin worth ten asses; abbreviation d.

deny *v* 1 (4) veto; (6) disown, forbid, oppose, rebuff, recant, refuse, refute, reject; (8) disclaim, disprove, renounce, withhold; (9) disaffirm, repudiate; (10)

contradict; (2 words) turn down; **2 deny oneself** (6) forego; (7) abstain, forbear, refrain; (8) renounce; (2 words) do without, go without.

depart I *v* **1** (2) go; (4) exit, quit; (5) leave, split; (6) decamp, escape, remove, retire, vanish; (7) migrate, retreat; (8) withdraw; (9) disappear; (2+ words) absent oneself, go away, move away, set off, take off, take one's leave; **2** (4) veer; (6) differ, swerve; (7) deviate, digress, diverge; II *cryptic* omit a letter or letters, as in (*Guardian, 1 May 1999*): 'Bed unoccupied by departing rough' = unkempt (bunk empty – with by omitted).

departed *adj see* **dead**.

department *n* (4) area, line, unit; (5) field, realm; (6) branch, domain, office, region, sector, sphere; (7) concern, section; (8) district, division; (10) speciality; (11) subdivision; (14) responsibility.

depict *v see* **describe** I.

depressed *adj* **1** (3) low, sad; (4) blue, down, glum; (5) moody; (6) bereft, dismal, gloomy, gutted, morose; (7) forlorn, unhappy; (8) dejected, downcast, wretched; (9) miserable; (10) despondent, distressed, melancholy; (11) crestfallen, downhearted; (12) disheartened; **2** (6) dented, hollow, sunken; (7) concave; (8) indented, recessed; **3** (4) poor; (8) deprived; (9) destitute; (13) disadvantaged; (15) poverty-stricken.

depressing *adj* (3) sad; (4) grey; (5) bleak; (6) dismal, dreary, gloomy, sombre; (8) mournful; (9) cheerless, saddening; (11) distressing.

depression *n* **1** (5) blues, dumps, gloom; (7) despair, sadness; (8) doldrums; (10) gloominess, melancholy; (11) despondency, unhappiness; (12) hopelessness; **2** (3) col, dip; (4) bowl, dent, dint, glen, vale; (6) cavity, dimple, valley; (10) impression; (11) indentation; **3** (5) slump; (9) recession; (10) stagnation; (2 words) hard times; **4** (3) low; (7) cyclone.

deranged I *adj see* **crazy, mad**; II *cryptic* ANAGRAM CUE.

Derby *n* **1** (4) game, race; (7) classic, contest; **2** (3) hat; (6) bowler.

descend *v* **1** (3) dip; (4) dive, drop, fall, sink; (5) slope; (6) plunge, tumble; (7) plummet; (2 words) go down, move down *etc*; **2 descend on** (4) raid; (6) attack, invade, waylay; (2+ words) fall on, force oneself on, impose on.

describe I *v* **1** (4) call, draw, tell; (5) paint, trace; (6) define, depict, detail, relate, report, sketch; (7) explain, express, narrate, outline, present, recount, specify; (9) delineate; (10) illustrate; (12) characterise (*or* characterize); **2** (6) circle; (8) encircle, surround; II *cryptic* can indicate that a word is to be split and placed around another word, as in: 'Sally describes it backwards in a spicy fashion' = saltily.

desert I *v* (3) rat; (4) deny, flit, jilt, quit; (5) leave; (6) decamp, maroon, recant, strand; (7) abandon, abscond, forsake; (2 words) give up, rat on, turn tail; II *adj* (3) dry; (4) arid, bare, wild; (5) waste; (6) barren; (7) sterile; (8) desolate, solitary; (9) infertile; (11) uninhabited, unpopulated; III *n* (5) waste, wilds; (9) wasteland; (10) wilderness; IV *cryptic* **1** sounds like **dessert**; **2** may indicate that particular letters or a word are to be removed, as in: 'Rats desert S.S. Starlight – and the cargo's gone too!' (5) = light (in the sense of not carrying a load).

DESERTS

Arabian (Africa), Anatolian (Turkey), Arunta (Australia), Atacama (Chile), Colorado (US), Death Valley (US), Empty Quarter (Arabia), Gibson (Australia), Gila (US), Gobi (China), Great Sandy (Australia), Kalahari (Africa), Kara (Kum) (Russia), Libyan (N Africa), Mohave (US), Namib (Africa), Negev (Israel), Nubian (Africa), Nullarbor Plain (Australia), Patagonian (S America), Qara Qum (*see* Kara Kum), Sahara (N Africa), Sechura (Peru), Sinai (Egypt), Takla Makan (China), Thar (India).

deserted *adj* (5) empty; (6) lonely, vacant; (7) forlorn; (8) derelict, desolate, forsaken, isolated; (9) abandoned, neglected; (10) unoccupied; (11) godforsaken, uninhabited, unpopulated.

deserts *pl n* (3) due; (6) return, reward, rights; (7) nemesis, payment; (10) punishment; (11) comeuppance, retribution.

design I *v* (4) draw, plan; (5) draft, shape; (6) create, devise, intend, invent, sketch, tailor; (7) develop, fashion outline; (8) conceive; (9) blueprint, construct, fabricate, originate; II *n* 1 (4) plan; (5) draft, guide, model; (6) sketch; (7) drawing, outline, pattern; (9) blueprint, construct; 2 (4) form; (5) motif, shape, style; (7) pattern; (8) ornament; (9) structure; (11) arrangement, composition; (12) organisation (*or* organization); (13) ornamentation. 3 (3) aim, end; (4) goal, plot; (6) object, scheme; (7) project, purpose; (9) intention, objective.

desire I *n & v* (4) lust, need, wish; (5) fancy; (6) hunger; II *n* (3) yen; (5) mania; (6) ardour; (7) craving, longing, passion; (8) appetite, yearning; (10) aspiration; (13) concupiscence; II *v* (3) ask; (4) long, want; (5) crave, yearn; (7) request, solicit; (2 words) crave for, hanker after, hunger for, long for, yearn for.

desolate I *adj* 1 (4) arid, bare, wild; (5) bleak, empty, waste; (6) barren, lonely, vacant; (8) derelict, deserted, forsaken, isolated, solitary; (9) abandoned, cheerless, neglected; (10) unoccupied; (11) comfortless, godforsaken, uninhabited, unpopulated; (12) unfrequented; 2 (3) sad; (6) bereft, dismal, gloomy; (7) forlorn; (8) dejected, downcast, wretched; (9) depressed, miserable; (10) despondent, distressed, melancholy; (12) disheartened; II *v* (4) ruin; (5) spoil, wreck; (6) denude; ravage; (7) despoil, destroy; (9) devastate; (2 words) lay waste.

despondent *adj see* **depressed** 1.

dessert *n* I (5) sweet; (6) afters; (7) pudding; II sounds like **desert**.

destroy I *v* (3) gut, mar; (4) dent, harm, hole, hurt, raze (*or* rase), rout, ruin, snap, undo; (5) break, crack, crush, level, smash, split, spoil, waste, wreck; (6) deface, impair, injure, ravage, thrash, uproot; (7) despoil, nullify, shatter, torpedo; (8) decimate, demolish, mutilate, sabotage; (9) devastate, dismantle, eliminate, eradicate; (10) extinguish; (12) incapacitate; II *cryptic* ANAGRAM CUE.

destruction *n* (4) loss, ruin; (5) havoc; (6) damage, defeat, injury; (8) wreckage; (9) overthrow, ruination; (10) demolition, extinction, mutilation; (11) devastation, elimination, eradication, liquidation.

detect *v* (3) see, spy; (4) espy, find, note, spot; (5) sight, trace; (6) expose, notice, reveal, unmask; (7) discern, observe, uncover; (8) discover, identify, perceive; (9) ascertain, recognise (*or* recognize); (11) distinguish.

detach I *v* (4) free, undo; (5) loose, sever, unfix; (6) divide, remove; (7) disjoin, unhitch; (8) estrange, separate, uncouple, unfasten; (9) disengage, segregate; (10) disconnect, dissociate; (11) disentangle; II **detach** *or* **detached** *cryptic* remove a letter, letters or word from another word in the clue, as in: 'Goes crazy detaching trailer from locomotive' (4) = loco ('trailer' being the latter part of the word).

detached I *adj* 1 (4) free; (5) loose; (7) unfixed; (8) separate; (9) separated, uncoupled; (12) disconnected; 2 (5) aloof; (10) impersonal; (11) independent, unconcerned; (13) disinterested, dispassionate; II *cryptic see* **detach**.

detail I *n* 1 (4) fact, item; (5) point; (6) aspect, factor, nicety, trifle; (7) element, feature; (10) triviality; (12) technicality; 2 **details** (8) minutiae; (9) specifics; (11) intricacies, particulars; (2 words) fine print, small print; 3 (4) unit; (5) squad; (10) commission, detachment; II *v* 1 (4) list; (6) relate; (7) itemise (*or* itemize), recount, specify; (9) catalogue; 2 (5) order; (6) assign, charge; (7) appoint; (8) delegate; (10) commission; III *cryptic* remove the last letter or letters from a words, as in: 'Edison, perhaps, made a detailed inventory' = inventor.

detective I *n* (3) tec; (4) dick, G-man; (6) sleuth; (7) gumshoe; (8) Sherlock; (9) policeman; (12) investigator; (15) plain-clothes man; (2 words) private eye; **II detectives** *cryptic* CID, FBI.

FAMOUS (LITERARY) DETECTIVES

Bergerac, Jim (TV), Blake, Sexton, Bucket, Inspector (Dickens), Cannon, Frank (TV), Carter, Nick (Hammett), Chan, Charlie (films), Colombo (films), Dalgleish, Adam (P. D. James), Dalziel and Pascoe (TV), Dupin, Auguste (E. A. Poe), Father Brown (Chesterton), French, Inspector (Allingham), Frost, Jack (TV), Ghote, Inspector, Hammer, Mike (Spillane), Hart and Hart (TV), Holmes, Sherlock (Conan Doyle), Kojak (TV), Lestrade, (Conan Doyle), Maigret (Simenon), Marlowe, Philip (Chandler), Marple, Miss (Christie, TV), Mason, Perry (Gardner), Morse, Inspector (Dexter, TV), Poirot, Hercule (Christie, TV), Shoestring, Eddie (TV), Spade, Sam (Hammett), Trent (Bentley), van der Valk (TV), Warshawski, V. I., Wexford, Inspector (Rendell), Wimsey, Lord Peter (Sayers).

---

determine *v* 1 (3) fix; (5) check; (6) decide, define, detect; settle, verify; (7) resolve; (8) conclude, discover, identify; (9) ascertain, establish; **2** (5) guide; (6) affect, direct, govern, ordain; (7) dictate; (8) regulate; (2 words) lay down.

determined *adj* (4) firm; (5) fixed; (6) dogged, intent; (7) decided; (8) resolute, resolved; (9) convinced, insistent, stead-fast, tenacious; (10) purposeful; (12) strong-minded, strong-willed; single-minded; (2 word) bent on, intent on, set on.

Deucalion *Gk myth* a Noah figure in Greek mythology. A son of Prometheus, he built a boat to survive the Great Flood, landing on Mt **Parnassus**, where he and his wife Pyrrha created a new race by throwing stones over their shoulders.

deuce *n* 1 a card, throw of a dice *etc* with a value of two; **2** a score of 40 points each in tennis; **3** (5) devil; (7) dickens.

deuterium *symbol* D.

devastate *v* 1 (4) raze (*or* rase), ruin, sack; (5) spoil, waste, wreck; (6) denude; ravage; (7) despoil, destroy, pillage, plunder, ransack; (8) demolish, desolate; (2 words) lay waste; **2** (5) shock, upset; (6) dismay; (7) shatter; (8) distress; (10) disconcert.

devastated I *adj* (5) upset; (6) gutted; (7) shocked; (8) dismayed; (9) shattered; (10) distressed; (12) disconcerted; (13) grief-stricken; **II** *cryptic* ANAGRAM CUE.

devil I *n* 1 (3) Dis, imp; (5) demon, deuce, fiend, Hades, Satan; (6) Belial, spirit; (7) Lucifer, tempter; (8) Apollyon; (9) Beelzebub; (14) Mephistopheles; **2** (6) helper, junior; (9) assistant; **II devil for** (4) help; (6) assist.

diamond *n* 1 (3) gem, ice; (4) rock; (7) adamant, lozenge; (10) rhinestone; **2** the playing area for baseball; **3** 60th anniversary.

FAMOUS DIAMONDS

Cullinan, Koh-i-noor, Great Mogul Shah, Hope, Star of India

Diana I *Rom myth* the goddess of the moon, hunting and fertility, equivalent to the Greek goddess Artemis, frequently referred to as Diana the huntress. Actaeon was torn to pieces by his own hounds for having accidentally seen her bathing. The temple of Diana at Ephesus was one of the **Seven Wonders of the World**; **II** *cryptic* abbreviated as Di.

diarist

FAMOUS DIARISTS

Burney, Fanny (18th cent.), Clark, Allan (Conservative Party politics and sexual adventures, late 20th cent.), Crossman, Richard (Labour Party politics, mid 20th cent.), Evelyn, Sir John (17th cent.),

list continued over

Frank, Anne (Jewish girl in hiding
from the Nazis in Holland during
World War II), Kilvert, Rev. Francis
(late 19th cent.), Mole, Adrian *fict.*
(fictional teenage schoolboy diarist
created by Sue Townsend), Pepys,
Samuel (17th cent. includes account of
Great Fire of London and various
sexual adventures), Pooter, Mr *fict.*
(hero of 'Diary of a Nobody' by
George and Weedon Grossmith – late
19th cent.), Robinson, Henry Crabb
(early 19th cent.), Wesley, John (late
18th cent. – the actual and spiritual
journeys of the founder of
Methodism).

Dickens, Charles – pseudonyms Boz,
Quiz.

NOVELS OF DICKENS

Barnaby Rudge (BR), Bleak House
(BH), A Christmas Carol (CC),
David Copperfield (DC), Dombey
and Son (Dom), Great Expectations
(GE), Hard Times (HT), Little
Dorrit (LD), Martin Chuzzlewit
(MC), Nicholas Nickleby (NN), The
Old Curiosity Shop (OCS), Oliver
Twist (OT), Our Mutual Friend
(OMF), Pickwick Papers (PP), A
Tale of Two Cities (TC).

WELL-KNOWN DICKENS CHARACTERS

abbreviations of novel titles as above

Artful Dodger (OT) *pickpocket*,
Bardell, Mrs (PP) *sues Pickwick for
breach of promise*, Barkis (DC) *carrier
who 'is willin'' to marry Peggotty*,
Blackpool, Stephen (HT) *non-
unionised tragic worker hero*, Boffin,
Nicodemus (OMF) *inherits dustheap*,
Bounderby, Mr (HT) *mill owner*,
Brownlow, Mr (OT) *Oliver Twist's
benefactor*, Bucket (BH) *detective*,
Bumble, Mr (OT) *beadle*, Carker,
James (Dom) *office manager*, Carton,
Sydney (TC) *drunken lawyer, takes
friend's place and is guillotined: 'It is a*

far, far better thing …', Cheeryble
Bros (NN) *Nicholas Nickleby's
benefactors*, Clenham, John (LD)
marries Little Dorrit, Copperfield,
David (DC) *twice-married writer*,
Cratchit, Bob (CC) *Scrooge's clerk,
father of Tiny Tim*, Crummles,
Vincent (NN) *manager of travelling
theatre company*, Darnay, Charles
(TC) *saved by Sydney Carton*, Dick,
Mr (DC) *Betsy Trotwood's simple
companion*, Defarge, Madame (TC)
fanatical revolutionary and tricoteuse,
Dodson and Fogg (PP) *lawyers*,
Estella (GE) *Miss Havisham's ward
and Pip's idol*, Fagin (OT) *Jewish fence
and tutor to pickpockets*, Gamp, Sarah
(MC) *drunken nurse with umbrella and
imaginary friend Mrs Harris*, Gargery,
Joe (GE) *blacksmith, Pip's brother-in-
law and foster-father*, Gradgrind, Mr
(HT) *schoolmaster with devotion to
facts*, Grimwig, Mr (OT) *sceptical
friend of Mr Brownlow*, Havisham,
Miss (GE) *jilted recluse, who Pip
believes to be his benefactor*, Heep,
Uriah (DC) *' 'umble' clerk to Mr
Whitfield, revealed as swindler*, Jaggers,
Mr (GE) *lawyer managing Pip's
affairs*, Jingle, Alfred (PP) *scrounging
actor, talks telegraphese*, La Creevy,
Miss (NN) *talkative painter*, Little
Dorrit (LD) *the 'child of the
Marshalsea'*, Little Em'ly (DC)
Peggotty's niece, betrayed by Steerforth,
Little Nell (OCS) *unfortunate heroine*,
Magwitch, Abel (GE) *convict, Pip's
actual benefactor*, Manette, Dr (TC)
prisoner in Bastille, who cobbled shoes,
Manette, Lucy (TC) *his daughter, who
marries Charles Darnay*, Micawber,
Wilkins, Mr (DC) *optimist ('something
will turn up') in perpetual financial
difficulty*, Nancy (OT) *Bill Sikes'
woman – murdered by him*, Noggs,
Newman (NN) *honest clerk*,
Pecksniff, Seth (MC) *architect,
hypocrite and cheat, with two daughters,
Charity and Mercy*,

list continued over

Peggotty, Clara (DC) *faithful servant who marries Barkis*, Pickwick, Samuel (PP), Pinch, Tom (MC) *Pecksniff's virtuous drudge*, Pip (GE) *snobbish hero*, Pirrip, Philip (GE) *Pip's full name*, Pocket, Herbert (GE) *Pip's friend in London*, Pross, Miss (TC) *Lucy Manette's governess*, Quilp, Daniel (OCS) *villainous dwarf*, Scrooge, Ebenezer (CC) *miser 'Christmas, humbug!'*, Sikes, Bill (OT) *burglar and murderer*, Smike (NN) *boy saved from Squeers' school by Nicholas Nickleby*, Snodgrass, Augustus (PP) *member of Pickwick's travelling party*, Spenlow, Dora (DC) *David Copperfield's first 'child' wife*, Squeers, Wackford (NN) *appalling headmaster of Dotheboys Hall*, Steerforth, James (DC) *hero-worshipped by David but seduces Little Em'ly*, Swiveller, Dick (OCS) *cheerful but in debt*, Tapley, Mark (MC) *Martin Chuzzlewit's cheerful servant and companion*, Tiny Tim (CC) *Bob Cratchit's lame youngest child – 'God bless us every one'*, Trotter, Job (PP) *Jingle's servant*, Trotwood, Betsy (DC) *David Copperfield's benevolent though abrasive and donkey-hating aunt*, Tupman, Tracy (PP) *Pickwick companion with eye for ladies*, Twist, Oliver (OT) *workhouse boy who asks for more*, Varden, Dolly (BR) *locksmith's daughter*, Weller, Sam (PP) *Pickwick's servant – pronounces 'v' as 'w'*, Wemmick, Mr (GE) *Jaggers' clerk, lives in castle and looks after his 'aged P'*, Wickfield, Agnes (DC) *David Copperfield's second wife*, Winkle, Nathaniel (PP) *member of Pickwick's travelling party*, Wren, Jenny (OMF) *crippled seamstress*.

Dido *hist., lit.* founder and queen of Carthage – according to Virgil's *Aeneid* she fell in love with **Aeneas** and killed herself when he deserted her.

die *v* (2) go; (3) end; (6) depart, expire; (7) decease; (2+ words) breathe one's last, give up the ghost, go to glory, meet one's maker, pass away, pass over.

SLANG EXPRESSIONS FOR 'TO DIE'

(2 words) conk out, peg out, snuff it.

(3 words) bite the dust, have had it, kick the bucket, pop one's clogs.

(4 words) cash in one's chips, go for a burton, have had one's chips, hop (*or* fall) off the twig.

---

differently *adv* ANAGRAM CUE.

diminish *v* (4) calm, dash, dull; (5) abate, allay, check, deter; (6) absorb, deaden, lessen, muffle, reduce, stifle, subdue; (8) decrease, diminish, moderate.

dinosaur *n* 1 a prehistoric reptile; 2 a person or institution whose ways are thought to be completely out of date.

DINOSAURS

allosaurus, ankylosaurus, bronto-saurus, cetiosaurus, diplodocus, iguanodon, megalosaurus, ptero-dactyl, stegosaurus, triceratops, tyrannosaurus, velociraptor.

Diogenes *hist.* a Greek cynic philosopher who, according to legend, lived in a tub.

Dionysus *Gk myth* the god of wine, equivalent to Roman **Bacchus**.

direct I *adj* 1 (7) non-stop, through; (8) straight; (11) undeviating; (13) uninterrupted; 2 (5) blunt, frank; (6) candid, honest; (8) explicit; (9) outspoken; (10) forthright; (15) straightforward; 3 (5) exact; (8) absolute, complete; (9) diametric; (11) diametrical; II *v* 1 (3) aim; (4) lead, turn; (5) guide, focus, point; (7) conduct; 2 (3) run; (4) tell; (5) order; (6) govern, manage, ordain; (7) command, control, dictate; (8) instruct, organise (*or* organize), regulate; (9) supervise; (10) administer; (11) superintend; (2 words) lay down.

direction I *n* 1 (4) east, west; (5) north, south etc *see also* **compass points**; 2 (3) way; (4) road; (5) drift, route, trend; (6) course; (7) bearing, heading; (8) tendency; 3 (3) tip; (4) hint; (5) guide; (7) control, pointer; (8) guidance; (9) guideline; (10) indication, leadership, management; (11) instruction, supervision; (14) administration; **‖** *cryptic* use an abbreviation for a compass point (E, N, S, W *etc*) in the answer, as in: 'Skeletons in the cupboard disturb rest following directions to Cuba' (7) = secrets (directions S & E, Cuba abbreviated as C).

Dis *Rom. myth* a name for the god of the **Underworld** (Pluto) or the **Underworld** itself (*Gk* Hades).

discharge ‖ *v* **1** *see* dismiss 1; **2** (4) fire; (5) shoot; (6) unload; (2 words) let off; **3** (2) do; (6) fulfil; (7) execute, perform; (2 words) carry out; **4** (3) pay; (5) clear; (6) settle; (9) liquidate; (2 words) pay off; **5** (4) free; (5) clear; (6) acquit, pardon; (7) absolve, release; (9) exonerate; **‖** *n* (3) pus; (8) emission; (9) secretion.

discover *v* (3) fix. see; (4) find, spot; (5) learn; (6) decide, define, detect, locate, notice, verify; (7) realise (*or* realize), uncover, unearth; (8) conclude, identify, perceive; (9) ascertain, determine, establish, recognise (*or* recognize); (2 words) come (up)on, dig up, find out, happen (up)on, light (up)on, stumble (up)on, work out.

discuss *v* (4) talk; (5) argue; (6) confer, debate, ponder; (7) consult, contend, dispute, examine, reflect; (8) converse, (9) negotiate (10) deliberate; (2 words) talk about, talk over.

discussion *n* (5) forum; (6) debate, review; (7) dispute, meeting, seminar; (8) analysis, argument, exchange; (9); symposium; (10) conference, contention, reflection; (11) controversy, disputation, examination, negotiation; (12) consultation, conversation, deliberation; (13) consideration.

disease *n* (3) ill; (6) malady; (7) ailment, illness; (8) disorder, sickness; (9) complaint, condition, infection; (10) affliction.

DISEASES AND SIMILAR CONDITIONS AFFECTING HUMANS

(3) bug, fit, flu, gyp, mal, pip, pox, tic, wen.

(4) ache, acne, ague, AIDS, clap, gout, itch, rash, stye, yaws.

(5) bends, chill, colic, cough, croup, fever, hives, lupus, mania, mumps, palsy, piles, polio, ulcer, worms.

(6) angina, anuria, apnoea, asthma, ataxia, autism, callus, cancer, caries, chorea, dengue, dropsy, eczema, gravel, grippe, hernia, herpes, jet-lag, megrim, myopia, nausea, oedema, otalgy, otitis, plague, quinsy, rabies, scurvy, sepsis, stress, stroke, thrush, tumour, typhus.

(7) allergy, amnesia, anaemia, anthrax, aphasia, bulimia, catarrh, cholera, colitis, dysuria, earache, gumboil, leprosy, lockjaw, lumbago, malaria, measles, otalgia, pink-eye, podagra, pyrexia, rickets, roseola, rubella, rupture, scabies, tetanus, typhoid, uraemia, variola, verruca, whitlow.

(8) agraphia, alopecia, aneurysm, anorexia, apoplexy, backache, beriberi, botulism, bursitis, cachexia, club-foot, coronary, cystitis, diabetes, dyslexia, embolism, enuresis, epilepsy, ergotism, erythema, fibrosis, gangrene, glaucoma, headache, hydropsy, hook-worm, impetigo, insomnia, jaundice, mastitis, migraine, pellagra, pleurisy, pruritis, ringworm, sciatica, scrofula, shingles, smallpox, syphilis, tinnitus, trachoma.

(9) arthritis, bilharzia, carcinoma, catalepsy, chilblain, cirrhosis, daltonism, diarrhoea, dysentery, dyspepsia, dystrophy, eclampsia, emphysema, enteritis, frostbite, gastritis, halitosis, heartburn, hepatitis, influenza, leukaemia, neuralgia, nystagmus, phlebitis, pneumonia, porphyria, psoriasis, sclerosis, sunstroke, toothache, vaginitis. *list continued over*

(10) asbestosis, bronchitis, chicken-pox, concussion, depression, dermatitis, diphtheria, dipsomania, erysipelas, fibrositis, flatulence, gingivitis, gonorrhoea, hyperaemia, laryngitis, meningitis, nyctalopia, paraplegia, presbyopia, rheumatics, rheumatism, scarlatina, thrombosis, urethritis.

(11) consumption, haemophilia, indigestion, kwashiorkor, paratyphoid, peritonitis, pharyngitis, psittacosis, septicaemia, tachycardia, tonsillitis.

(12) appendicitis, collywobbles, constipation, encephalitis, haemorrhoids, hyperacidity, incontinence, malnutrition, neurasthenia, parkinsonism, quadriplegia, tuberculosis.

(13) elephantiasis, osteomyelitis, poliomyelitis.

(14) hyperglycaemia.

(15) gastroenteritis, hyperthyroidism, hypochondriasis, schistosomiasis.

(2+ words) angina pectoris, anorexia nervosa, caisson disease, cystic fibrosis, delirium tremens, double pneumonia, glandular fever, hay fever, Hodgkin's disease, housemaid's knee, river blindness, scarlet fever, sleeping sickness, St Vitus's dance, tennis elbow, water on the brain, water on the knee, yellow fever.

DISEASES AFFECTING ANIMALS

(3) BSE, gid, haw, pip.

(4) gape, scab, wind.

(5) bloat, hoove, husks, mange, vives, worms.

(6) cowpox, garget, heaves, rabies, spavin, splint, thrush, warble.

(7) anthrax, footrot, fur-ball, hoofrot, murrain, scrapie.

(8) blackleg, fowl-pest, glanders, staggers, sway-back.   *list continued over*

(9) distemper, strangles.

(10) blackwater, rinderpest, swine-fever.

(11) brucellosis, myxomatosis, psittacosis.

(2+ words) blue tongue, bovine spongiform encephalopathy, feline enteritis, foot and mouth, mad cow disease.

disfigure I *v* (3) mar; (4) scar; (5) spoil; (6) damage, deface, deform; (7) blemish, distort; (8) mutilate; II *cryptic* ANAGRAM CUE.

disgrace I *n & v* (5) shame, stain, taint; (9) discredit, dishonour; II *n* (6) infamy; (7) scandal; (8) ignominy; (9) discredit, disfavour, disrepute; (11) humiliation; III *v* (5) abase, sully; (6) debase, defame, defile, demean; (9) humiliate; (10) stigmatise (*or* stigmatize).

disgraceful *adj* (8) dreadful, shameful, shocking, unworthy; (9) appalling, degrading; (10) scandalous; (12) disreputable; (13) dishonourable.

disguise I *v & n* (4) mask, veil; (5) cloak, cover; (6) screen, shroud; (10) camouflage; II *v* (4) hide; (7) conceal, deceive, falsify; (9) dissemble; III *n* (5) front; (6) façade; (7) costume; (8) pretence; (9) semblance; (10) masquerade; (11) concealment; IV *cryptic* 1 ANAGRAM CUE; 2 HIDDEN WORD CUE.

disgust I *n* (6) nausea; (8) aversion, distaste, loathing; (9) repulsion, revulsion; (10) abhorrence, repugnance; (11) detestation; II *v* (5) repel; (6) offend, revolt, sicken; (7) outrage; (8) nauseate; (2+ words) put off, turn one's stomach.

disgusting *adj* (4) foul, vile; (5) nasty; (6) odious; (7) obscene; (8) horrible; (9) offensive, repellent, repugnant, repulsive, revolting, sickening; (10) abominable, detestable, nauseating; (11) distasteful; (12) unappetising (*or* unappetizing); (13) objectionable; (14) stomach-turning.

dish I *n* 1 (4) bowl; (5) plate; 2 (6) beauty; (7) stunner; II *v* 1 **dish out** (4) dole, give, hand, mete; (7) inflict; (8) allocate; (10) distribute; 2 **dish up** (5) ladle, offer, serve, scoop, spoon; (7) present.

DISHES ON THE MENU

(3) dip, pie, poi.

(4) flan, hash, loaf, mash, oleo, olio, pâté, soup, stew, taco.

(5) broth, curry, gumbo, kabob, kebab, pasta, pasty, patty, pilau, pizza, purée, roast, sauce, sushi.

(6) bisque, borsch, canapé, fondue, haggis, hotpot, omelet, paella, panada, pastry, potage, quiche, ragout, tamale.

(7) burrito, chowder, compote, fritter, goulash, lasagne, pottage, pudding, ramekin, rarebit, ravioli, risotto, rissole, soufflé, tempura, terrine, tostada.

(8) bouillon, consommé, crudités, fishcake, hotchpot, julienne, kedgeree, marinara, moussaka, omelette, ossobuco, pemmican, quenelle, sandwich, sukiyaki, teriyaki, yakitori.

(9) antipasto, casserole, cassoulet, colcannon, croquette, croustade, enchilada, fricassee, galantine, hamburger, humble-pie, jambalaya, macédoine, schnitzel, succotash, tabbouleh, vol-au-vent.

(10) beefburger, blanquette, chaudfroid, florentine, hodgepodge, hotchpotch, jardinière, salmagundi, stroganoff.

(11) chimichanga, olla-podrida, ratatouille.

(13) bouillabaisse, chateaubriand.

(2+ words) chow mein, chop suey, dim sum, pot roast, toad in the hole.

---

dishonest *adj* (3) sly; (5) false, lying, shady; (6) crafty, sneaky; (7) crooked, dubious; (8) cheating, guileful, two-faced; (9) deceitful, deceiving, deceptive, insincere, swindling, underhand; (10) fraudulent, misleading, unreliable, untruthful; (11) duplicitous; treacherous; (12) disreputable, hypocritical, unprincipled; (13) double-dealing, untrustworthy.

dishonour *see* **disgrace**.

dismiss *v* 1 (4) drop, fire, sack; (7) release; (9) discharge; (2+ words) lay off, let go, make redundant; 2 (5) spurn; (6) reject, shelve; (7) discard; (8) discount; (9) disregard.

display I *v* (4) show; (5) prove; (6) expose, flaunt, parade, reveal; (7) exhibit, explain, present, testify; (8) disclose, flourish indicate, manifest; (10) illustrate; (11) demonstrate; (2 words) show off, show forth; II *n* (4) show; (6) parade; (7) showing; (8) exposure; (9) spectacle; (10) exhibition, exposition, expression, revelation; (12) illustration, presentation; (13) manifestation.

distracted I *adj* 1 (7) faraway; (8) dreaming; (9) wandering; (10) abstracted; (11) inattentive, preoccupied; (2+ words) miles away, not with it; 2 *see* **confused**, **distraught**; II *cryptic* ANAGRAM CUE.

distraught I *adj* (5) upset; (7) anxious, frantic; (8) agitated; (10) distracted, distressed, hysterical; (11) overwrought; (2 words) beside oneself, het up, worked up; II *cryptic* ANAGRAM CUE.

distribute *v* (4) deal, dole, give, hand, mete; (5) allot, share; (6) assign, bestow, divide; (9) apportion (2 words) deal out, dole out, give out, hand out, mete out, share out.

district *n* (4) area, ward; (5) shire, state, tract; (6) **canton**, **county**, parish, region, sector; (7) quarter; (8) division; (9) territory.

Dives *Bible* the rich man in the parable of Dives and Lazarus (Luke 16).

divide *v* 1 (5) allot, share, split; (6) assign, cleave; (9) apportion; (10) distribute (2 words) deal out, dole out, give out, hand out, mete out, share out; 2 (4) part; (5) loose, sever; (6) detach, remove; (8) alienate, disunite, estrange, separate, uncouple, unfasten; (9) disengage, segregate; (10) disconnect, dissociate; 3 (4) sort; (8) classify.

divine I *adj* 1 (4) holy; (6) sacred; (7) angelic, godlike; (8) heavenly; (9) celestial,

spiritual; (10) superhuman; (12) supernatural; **2** (6) gifted, lovely (8) glorious,
heavenly, talented; (9) beautiful, delicious,
excellent, wonderful; (10) delightful; **II** *n*
(6) bishop, priest; (9) churchman, clergy-
man; **III** *v* **1** (5) guess, (7) foresee, predict;
(9) ascertain, determine, establish *see also*
discover; **IV** *cryptic* the letters DD (doctor
of divinity).

division *n* **1** (4) area, unit; (6) branch,
domain, league, region, sector, sphere; (7)
section, segment; (8) district; (10) department; (11) subdivision; **2** (7) sharing; (9)
allotment; (12) distribution; (13) appor-
tionment; **3** (5) split; (8) conflict, disunity;
(12) disagreement, estrangement.

do **I** *v* **1** (3) act, end, fix; (4) make; (5)
enact; (6) create, effect, finish, fulfil; (7)
achieve, execute, present, realise (*or* realize); (8) complete, conclude; (9) implement, undertake; (10) accomplish; (2+
words) carry off, carry out, deal with,
look after; work at, work on; **2** (3) con; (4)
have; (5) cheat, cozen, trick; (6) diddle;
(7) defraud, swindle; **3** (4) char; (5) clean;
4 *also* **do in** *see* **kill**; **II** *n* **1** (5) party, treat;
(9) festivity; (11) celebration; (13) jollifi-
cation; **2** *see* **doh**; **III** *abbrev* ditto.

dock **I** *n* **1** (4) port, quay; (5) basin, berth,
jetty, wharf; (7) harbour; **2** (4) weed; (5)
plant; **II** *v* (3) cut, lop; (6) lessen, reduce;
(7) curtail.

doctor **I** *n* (3) doc; (5) medic; (6) intern;
(7) surgeon; (9) clinician, physician, reg-
istrar; (10) consultant, pill-pusher; (2
words) general practitioner; *see also* **specialist**; **II** *v* (3) fix; (5) alter; (6) change,
dilute, fiddle; (7) falsify, pervert; (10)
adulterate; (12) misrepresent; **III** *cryptic*
any of the combinations of letters making
an abbreviation for a doctor's title: DD,
DR, GP, MB, MD, MO (medical officer)

FAMOUS DOCTORS

Aesculapius *Roman god of medicine*,
Caius *fict.* (Shakespeare) *Merry Wives
of Windsor*, Cameron *fict. Dr Finlay's
senior partner*, Crippen *Edwardian
murderer caught by radio*, Doolittle *fict.*

(Hugh Lofting, film and
musical) *'talks to the animals'*, Faust *or*
Faustus *fict.* (Chr. Marlowe, Goethe)
sold his soul to the devil, Finlay *fict.*
(A. J. Cronin, TV) *Scottish GP in
Tannochbrae*, Grace, W.G. *cricketer*,
Hippocrates *Greek father of medicine,
associated with the Hippocratic oath*,
Jekyll *fict.* (R. L. Stevenson) *changes
into Mr Hyde after drinking potion*,
Johnson, Samuel *author*, *lexico-
grapher*, Livesey *fict.* (R. L.
Stevenson) *in 'Treasure Island'*,
Livingstone, David *explorer in Africa*,
Manette *fict.* (Dickens) *Tale of Two
Cities*, No *fict.* (Ian Fleming) *adversary
of James Bond*, Schweitzer, Albert
*medical missionary, theologian and
organist*, Slop *fict.* (Sterne) *Tristram
Shandy*, Strangelove *fict.* (film
directed by Stanley Kubrick) *lover of
the bomb*, Syn *fict.* (R. Thorndike)
parson and smuggler, Syntax *fict.* (W.
Combe) *travelling parson in satirical
early-19th-century novels*, Watson *fict.*
(Conan Doyle) *companion to Sherlock
Holmes*, Who *fict.* (TV) *timelord and
fighter of Daleks, Cybermen etc.*

---

dog **I** *n* & *fig* (3) cur, pup, toy; (4) mutt;
(5) bitch, hound, pooch, puppy, whelp;
(6) bowwow, canine, gundog, lapdog,
ratter; (7) mongrel; **II** *v* (4) tail; (5) harry,
hound, haunt, stalk, track, trail, worry;
(6) follow, plague, shadow; (7) trouble.

BREEDS OF DOG

(3) pom, pug, pye.

(4) chow; peke, skye.

(5) boxer, cairn, corgi, dingo, spitz.

(6) Afghan, basset, beagle, borzoi,
cocker, collie, poodle, saluki, scotty,
setter, yorkie.

(7) bulldog, griffon, lurcher, maltese,
mastiff, pointer, samoyed, spaniel,
terrier, whippet.

(8) Airedale, alsatian, blenheim,
chow-chow, elkhound, foxhound,
keeshond, labrador, malemute,

list continued ovr

WORDSWORTH CROSSWORD COMPANION ◇ **89**

papillon, pekinese, pinscher, sealyham, springer.

(9) boarhound, chihuahua, dachshund, dalmatian, dobermann, greyhound, pekingese, retriever, ridgeback, schnauzer, wolfhound.

(10) bedlington, bloodhound, pomeranian, rottweiler, schipperke.

(12) Newfoundland.

(13) Affenpinscher.

(2 words) (6) pug dog, pye dog; (9) great Dane, lhasa apso, red setter, St Bernard; (11) Afghan hound, bull terrier, Jack Russell; (12) Border collie; cairn terrier; (13) cocker spaniel, Dandie Dinmont; (14) clumber spaniel, Irish wolfhound; (15) golden retriever.

(3 words) King Charles spaniel, Pyrenean mountain dog, West Highland terrier.

FAMOUS DOGS

(3) Jip (*David Copperfield*, Dickens).

(4) Asta (*Thin Man*), Dash (Queen Victoria), Nana (*Peter Pan*), Toto (*Wizard of Oz*).

(5) Argus (Ulysses), Flush (*Barretts of Wimpole Street*), Laika (first dog in space), Pluto (Disney), Timmy (*Famous Five*).

(6) Lassie (films), Nipper (HMV), Snoopy (*Peanuts*).

(7) Diamond (Sir Isaac Newton).

(8) Bullseye (*Oliver Twist*, Dickens), Cerberus (*Gk myth*).

(9) Rin-Tin-Tin (TV).

(3 words) Mick the Miller (racing greyhound).

---

doh *n* (4) note; (5) tonic.

domestic I *adj* (3) pet; (4) home, tame; (6) family, inland, native; (8) internal; (9) household (10) indigenous; (12) domesticated, house-trained; **II** *n* (4) char, help, maid; (5) daily; (7) servant; (9) charwoman; (2 words) au pair.

dominant *adj* (4) main; (5) chief; (6) ruling; (7) primary; (8) foremost, superior; (9) assertive, governing, principal; (10) commanding, pre-eminent, prevailing; (11) controlling, influential, predominant.

dominate *v* (4) lead, rule; (6) direct, govern; (7) command, control, prevail; (8) overbear, overlook, overrule; (11) predominate.

Don *n* 1 Spanish nobleman; 2 river in N England; 3 **(the) Don** Don Bradman (Australian cricketer); 4 **the Dons** (or **dons**) *hist.* the Spanish; *football* Aberdeen; Wimbledon.

don I *n* (5) tutor; (6) fellow; (7) teacher; *see also* **Don**; **II** *v* (6) assume; (2 words) put on *etc*.

Don Juan *fict.* the archetypal woman-chaser, seducer, and general libertine who invites the statue of the father of one of his (attempted) conquests, whom he has killed in a duel, to dinner. The statue arrives at the feast, tries to persuade Don Juan to repent and, when he refuses, drags him off to hell. Don Juan is the hero of plays by Tirso de Molina, **Molière** and, less directly **G. B. Shaw** (*Man and Superman*), an opera by Mozart and da Ponte (*Don Giovanni*) and a long poem, only loosely connected with the original story, by Byron. *See also* **lover**.

dope *n* 1 *see* **drug**; 2 *see* **fool**; 3 (3) gen; (4) info; (5) facts; (7) details, low-down; (11) **information**.

double I *adj* (4) dual, twin; (6) paired; (7) twofold; (9) duplicate; **II** *n* 1 (4) copy, pair, twin; (5) clone, image; (6) ringer; (7) replica; (9) duplicate, lookalike; (12) doppelganger; (2 words) dead ringer, dead spit, spitting image; 2 (8) stuntman; (10) understudy; **III** *v* 1 (6) repeat; (7) enlarge; (8) multiply; 2 (4) fold, loop, turn; 3 (3) run; (4) race; **IV doubles** *cryptic* letters SS.

doublet I *n* (5) tunic; (6) jacket, jerkin; (*often* doublet and hose); **II** *cryptic* letters TT.

doubleton I *n* (4) pair; (6) couple (*of cards*); II *cryptic* letters CC (Roman numerals for 200 – double ton).

doubt I *n & v* (4) fear; (5) query; (8) distrust, mistrust, question; II *n* (7) dilemma; (8) quandary; (9) misgiving, suspicion; (10) hesitation, indecision, misgivings, perplexity, scepticism; (11) incredulity, reservation, uncertainty; (12) apprehension, reservations; III *v* (7) suspect; (10) disbelieve.

doubtful *adj* (4) moot; (5) vague; (6) unsure; (7) dubious, suspect, unclear; (8) hesitant, unlikely; (9) debatable, sceptical, uncertain, undecided, unsettled; (10) disputable, improbable, irresolute, suspicious; (11) contentious, contestable, problematic; (12) questionable; (13) controversial, problematical; (2+ words) at issue, in dispute, open to question;

drain I *n* (4) pipe, tube; (5) ditch, sewer; (6) trench; (7) conduit; II *v* 1 (4) leak, milk, ooze; (5) bleed, empty; (8) evacuate; (2 words) draw off, flow out; 2 (3) sap; (4) tire; (7) consume, exhaust; 3 *see* **drink**.

drama *see* **play**, **theatre**.

dramatist *see* **playwright**.

draw I *v* 1 (3) map, pen; (5) paint, trace; (6) depict, design, pencil, sketch; (7) outline, portray; (8) **describe**; (9) delineate; (10) illustrate; 2 (3) tow, tug; (4) drag, haul, pull; (6) entice, remove; (7) **attract**, **extract**; (8) persuade; 3 (3) tie; II *n* 1 (3) tie; (9) stalemate; (2 words) dead heat; 2 (4) bait, lure; (6) appeal; (10) attraction; 3 (6) raffle; (7) lottery.

drawing *n* (4) plan; (5) draft; (6) design, sketch; (7) cartoon, diagram, graphic, outline, picture; (9) blueprint.

dress I *n* (3) rig; (4) garb, gear, gown, robe, suit; (5) frock, get-up, habit; (6) outfit; (7) clothes, costume; (8) clothing; II *v* 1 (6) clothe; 2 (4) tend; (5) treat; (7) bandage; 3 (5) align, range; (7) prepare.

dressing *n* 1 (7) donning; (8) clothing, covering; 2 (7) bandage, plaster; 3 (5) sauce; (10) mayonnaise.

drink I *v* (3) lap, sip, sup; (4) gulp, swig, tope; (5) drain, quaff, swill, toast; (6) absorb, guzzle, imbibe, tipple; (7) carouse, indulge, partake, swallow; II *n* 1 (5) booze; (6) liquid, liquor, poison; (7) alcohol; (8) beverage; 2 (3) cup, jar, nip, peg; (4) half, pint, shot; (5) bevvy, glass, snort, toddy; (6) bracer, chaser, noggin, splash; (7) quickie, snifter; (8) aperitif, pick-me-up; (9) sundowner; (2+ words) one for the road, quick one, the other half; III *cryptic* one part of the answer appears inside, is 'swallowed' by, another part, as in: 'Direction to drink mother's ruin makes one a driving force' (6) = engine (direction = ENE east north east).

TYPES OF DRINK

(3) ale, gin, pop, rum, rye, tea.

(4) beer, bock, char, coke, cola, flip, grog, kava, mead, mild, milk, ouzo, port, sake, soda, wine (*see also* **wine**).

(5) cider, cocoa, crush, heavy, hooch, julep, kvass, lager, light, negus, perry, Pimms®, punch, sling, stout, tonic, vodka, water.

(6) arrack, bitter, brandy, cassis, coffee, cognac, egg-nog, gimlet, grappa, kirsch, kummel®, malibu, mescal, nectar, Pernod®, porter, poteen, red-eye, rot-gut, scotch, shandy, sherry, spirit, squash, whisky.

(7) aquavit, bitters, Campari®, Cinzano®, cobbler, collins, cordial, curacao, koumiss, liqueur, madeira, Martini®, mineral, scrumpy, seltzer, sherbet, sidecar, tequila, whiskey.

(8) absinthe, advocaat, ambrosia, anisette, armagnac, calvados, cocktail, Drambuie®, Dubonnet®, gluhwein, highball, hollands, lemonade, schiedam, schnapps, snowball, Tia Maria®, vermouth.

(9) applejack, champagne, Cointreau®, manhattan, orangeade, slivovitz.

(10) buttermilk, chartreuse.

(11) Benedictine®, John Collins, screwdriver.

(12) old-fashioned.

(13) crème de menthe.

driver *n* 1 (8) engineer; (9) chauffeur; 2 (4) club, wood (*golf*).

drop I *v* 1 (3) dip; (4) dive, fall, sink; (5) slope; (6) lessen, plunge, reduce, tumble; (7) descend, plummet; (8) decrease; (2 words) fall off, go down, move down *etc.* 2 (3) cut; (4) jilt, omit, shed; (5) cease; (7) abandon, discard; (11) discontinue; (2 words) give up, throw over; 3 (7) deliver; (2 words) set down; II *n* 1 (3) dab, sip; (4) bead, dash, drip, spot, tear; (5) trace; (6) bubble; (7) droplet, earring, globule, soupcon; 2 (3) dip; (4) fall; (5) abyss, chasm, slope, slump; (7) decline; (8) decrease, downturn; (9) precipice, reduction; (10) falling-off; III *cryptic* omit a particular letter or word, as in: 'Drop the pose in this instance before tourist attraction to get a clearer view' (7) = insight (pose = stance).

drug I *n* (3) fix; (4) pill; (5) upper; (6) downer, emetic, opiate, potion, remedy; (7) anodyne, antacid, placebo, pep-pill, steroid; (8) antidote, narcotic, medicine, sedative; (9) analgesic, stimulant; (10) antibiotic, depressant, medicament, medication, pain-killer; (11) anaesthetic, aphrodisiac; (13) antihistamine, tranquilliser (*or* tranquillizer); (14) hallucinogenic; II *v* (4) dope; (6) inject, sedate; (7) stupefy; (8) medicate; (12) anaesthetise (*or* anaesthetize).

NAMES OF DRUG – MEDICAL

(6) Prozac®, Valium®, Viagra®.

(7) aspirin, codeine, ginseng, insulin, Librium®, menthol, Mogadon®, morphia, quinine, veronal.

(8) caffeine, camomile, diazepam, laudanum, morphine, Nembutal®, sennapod, valerian.

(9) barbitone, cortisone, digitalis, ibuprofen, mepacrine, methadone, pethidine.

(10) belladonna, Benzedrine®, chloroform, penicillin, Terramycin®.

(11) amphetamine, barbiturate, paracetamol, thalidomide.

NAMES OF DRUGS – NARCOTIC

(3) LSD, pot.

(4) coke, dope, hemp, snow, weed.

(5) bhang, crack, dagga, ganja, grass, horse, opium, smack, speed.

(6) heroin.

(7) cocaine, ecstasy, hashish.

(8) cannabis, mescalin, nicotine.

(9) marijuana (*or* marihuana), mescaline.

---

drunk I *adj* (5) tipsy; (7) drunken; (10) inebriated; (11) intoxicated; II *n* (3) sot; (4) lush, soak, wino; (5) dipso, toper; (6) boozer; (8) drunkard; (9) alcoholic, crapulent; (11) dipsomaniac; III *cryptic* ANAGRAM CUE.

SLANG TERMS FOR DRUNK

(4) high; (5) merry, tight; (6) blotto, canned, loaded, pissed, soused, stoned, tiddly; (7) half-cut, legless, pie-eyed, sloshed, smashed, sozzled; (9) paralytic, plastered, well-oiled; (2 words) lit up, tanked up; (3+ words) half seas over, over the limit, three sheets to the wind.

---

dry I *adj* 1 (4) arid, fine; (5) solid, sunny; (6) barren; (7) parched, sterile; (9) waterless; (10) dehydrated, desiccated; 2 (4) dull; (6) **boring**; (7) tedious; 3 (6) **ironic**; (7) cynical, deadpan; 4 (2) TT; (8) teetotal (not permitting the sale of alcohol); 5 (3) sec (not sweet) II *v* (3) air; (4) spin, wipe; (5) drain, parch, towel.

dubious *adj see* **doubtful**.

duck I *n* 1 (3) nil; (4) love, zero; (6) nought; (2 words) no score; 2 *see* **dear** II; II *cryptic* letter O; III *v* (3) bob; (4) dive; (5) dodge; (7) curtsey; IV *lit.* (5) Daffy; (6) Dab-dab, Donald; (2 words) Jemima Puddle-Duck.

TYPES OF DUCK

Aylesbury, canvasback, eider, gadwall, goldeneye, harlequin, mallard, mandarin, merganser, muscovy, pekin, pintado, pochard, scaup, sheldrake, shelduck, shoveller, smee, smew, teal, widgeon, wigeon.

dull *adj* 1 (3) dim; (4) drab, grey; (6) cloudy, gloomy; (8) overcast; 2 (4) flat; (6) **boring**, dreary; (7) tedious; (8) tiresome; (10) monotonous, unexciting; (13) uninteresting; 3 (3) dim; (4) dumb, slow; (5) dense, thick; (6) **stupid**; (8) backward; II *v* (3) dim; (4) fade, numb; (5) blunt; (6) deaden, lessen, subdue; (7) obscure; (8) mitigate, moderate (9) alleviate.

dumb *adj* 1 (4) mute; (6) silent; (10) speechless, tongue-tied; 2 *see* **stupid**.

dupe I *n & v* (4) fool, gull; II *v* (2) do; (3) con, kid; (4) have, hoax; (5) abuse, cheat, trick; (6) betray, delude; (7) beguile, deceive, defraud, ensnare, swindle, twotime; (8) hoodwink; (9) bamboozle; (11) double-cross; (2+ words) have on, pull sb's leg, take for a ride, take in; III *n* (3) mug; (6) sucker, stooge, victim; (2 words) fall guy.

dwarf I *n & adj* (4) mini, runt; (6) midget; (9) miniature; (11) Lilliputian; II *adj* (4) tiny; (5) small; (6) petite, pocket; (7) stunted; (10) diminutive; III *lit.* (8) Alberich, Munchkin; (2 words) Tom Thumb.

THE SEVEN DWARFS

Bashful, Doc, Dopey, Grumpy, Happy, Sleepy, Sneezy.

dye I *n & v* (4) tint, wash; (5) stain, tinge; (6) colour; (7) pigment; II *v* (5) imbue; III *n* (9) colouring.

E

E *abbrev* East, eastern, Ecstasy (drug), European (E-number), Spain (international vehicle registration); key (music), note (music).

e *abbrev* electronic (e-commerce, e-mail), energy.

eager *adj* (3) hot; (4) avid, keen, warm; (5) eager; (6) ardent; (7) devoted, earnest, excited, fervent, willing, zealous; (8) vehement, vigorous; (10) passionate; (12) enthusiastic, wholehearted.

eagle *n* 1 bird of prey; 2 score of two under par in golf.

eaglet *n* young eagle.

ear *n* 1 (3) lug; (6) handle; 2 (4) heed; (6) notice, regard; (9) attention; 3 (*of plant*) (4) head; (5) spike.

PARTS OF THE EAR

(5) anvil, helix, incus, pinna; (6) concha, hammer, stapes; (7) cochlea, eardrum, malleus, ossicle, stirrup; (8) tympanum; (9) labyrinth, vestibule.

---

early I *adj* 1 (5) first; (7) forward, initial, opening; (8) untimely; (9) premature; 2 (7) ancient; (8) primeval; (9) primitive; (11) prehistoric; II *cryptic* use the first letter or letters of a word in the clue, as in: 'Roman manners seen in the east and south after the early morning' (5) = mores.

earn *v* (3) get, net, win; (4) draw, gain, make, reap; (5) gross, merit; (7) acquire, realise (*or* realize).

earnest I *adj* (4) firm, keen; (5) eager, fixed, grave; (6) ardent, intent, solemn; (7) fervent, serious, sincere; (9) heartfelt; II *n* (7) advance; (9) foretaste.

earnings *n pl* (3) pay; (5) gains, wages; (6) income, return, salary; (7) profits, revenue; (8) proceeds; (12) remuneration.

earth I *n* 1 (3) sod; (4) clay, land, loam, soil; (6) ground; 2 (5) globe, world; (6) planet, sphere; II *v* to connect something, especially an electrical device to earth.

east I *n* (6) levant, orient; II *cryptic* abbreviated as E.

easy I *adj* 1 (6) simple; (8) painless; (10) effortless, manageable; (11) undemanding; (13) uncomplicated, unproblematic; (15) straightforward; 2 (5) cushy; (7) well-off; (8) affluent, well-to-do; (10) prosperous; (11) comfortable; 3 *see* **easygoing**; II **easy thing to do** (4) walk; (5) cinch; (6) breeze, doddle; (8) pushover, walkover; (2+ words) child's play, piece of cake.

easy-going *adj* (3) lax; (4) calm; (7) relaxed; (8) amenable, carefree, informal, laid-back, tolerant; (9) indulgent, leisurely; (12) even-tempered.

eat I *v* 1 (4) chew, dine, feed; (5) lunch, munch, scoff; (6) devour; (7) consume, swallow; (9) breakfast; 2 (3) rot, sap; (5) drain, erode; (6) absorb; (7) corrode; (2 words) use up, wear away; II *cryptic* one part of the answer appears inside, is 'swallowed' by, another part, as in: 'Promoter ate small cake, took on a worker, ended in plenty' (8) = abundant (promoter = ad, worker = ant).

eccentric I *adj* (3) odd; (5) dotty, queer, weird; (6) strange; (7) bizarre, erratic, offbeat; (8) abnormal, freakish, peculiar; (10) outlandish; (13) idiosyncratic; (14) unconventional; II *n* (5) crank, freak; (6) oddity; (7) oddball; (9) character; (13) nonconformist; III *cryptic* ANAGRAM CUE.

Echo *Gk myth* a talkative nymph who was condemned by **Hera** to be able to do no more than repeat what others had said to her. Falling in love with the self-absorbed **Narcissus** she pined away until only her (still repeating) voice was left.

echo I *n* (4) copy; (6) repeat; (9) imitation; (10) repetition; (13) reverberation; II *v* (4) copy, ring; (5) mimic; (6) mirror, repeat; (7) reflect, resound; (9) reiterate; (11) reverberate.

eddy l *n* (5) swirl, whirl; (6) vortex; (9) maelstrom, whirlpool; ll *cryptic* ANAGRAM CUE, as in (*Guardian, 1 May 99*): 'Eddy the moron or jocular John?' (10) = throneroom (john = US slang for lavatory).

edge l *n* 1 (3) lip, rim; (4) brim, side; (5) brink, limit, verge; (6) border, fringe, margin; (8) boundary; (9) perimeter, periphery, threshold; 2 (4) zest; (7) rancour; (8) acerbity, keenness; (9) sharpness; (10) bitterness; 3 (4) lead; (9) advantage; (11) superiority; ll *v* 1 (3) hem; (4) trim; (6) border, fringe; 2 (4) ease, inch; (5) creep, sidle.

edict *n* (3) law; (5) order; (6) decree, ruling; (7) command, dictate, mandate, precept, statute; (9) enactment, ordinance; (10) injunction, regulation; (12) proclamation.

editor *cryptic* abbreviated as ED.

Edom *Bible see* **Esau**.

educate *v* (5) coach, drill, guide, teach, train, tutor; (6) inform, school; (7) develop, improve; (8) instruct; (9) cultivate, enlighten.

Edward *cryptic* shortened as Ed, Eddie, Eddy, Ned, Ted.

egg l *n* ovum; ll **eggs** (3) ova, roe; (5) spawn; lll **egg on** (4) spur, urge; (6) exhort, incite; (9) stimulate; lV *cryptic* letter O (duck's egg = duck, zero, nought) – therefore **eggs** OO.

ego *n* 1 the Latin word for I, 2 in Freudian psychology, the conscious part of the mind that is responsible for perceiving and dealing with the outside world; 3 *see* **egoism**.

egoism *n* (4) self; (5) pride; (6) vanity; (11) selfishness, self-serving; (12) self-interest; (13) egocentricity; (15) self-centredness.

egret *n* a wading bird similar to a heron.

eject *v see* **expel**.

elaborate l *adj* 1 (5) fancy, fussy, showy; (6) ornate; (7) complex; (8) detailed, involved; (9) decorated; (10) ornamental; (11) complicated; 2 (5) exact; (6) minute; (7) careful; (8) laboured, thorough; (9) extensive; ll *v* (6) devise, evolve, expand, refine; (7) amplify, develop, enlarge, explain; (9) construct; lll *cryptic* ANAGRAM CUE.

Eldorado *myth* a fabled city or region, somewhere in central South America, abounding in gold.

elect *v* (4) pick; (5) adopt; (6) decide, choose, select; (7) appoint; (9) designate; (2 words) opt for, vote for.

Electra *Gk myth* the daughter of **Agamemnon** and his wife Clytemnestra. To avenge her mother's murder of her father, she joined forces with her brother **Orestes** to kill her and her lover Aegisthus in their turn.

electricity *n* (2) AC, DC; (4) amps; (5) power, volts; (6) charge, static; (7) current.

electrify *v* (4) fire, jolt, stir; (5) amaze, rouse, shock; (6) excite, thrill; (7) animate. astound, stagger; (9) galvanise (*or* galvanize), stimulate; (10) invigorate.

elegant *adj* (4) chic, neat; (5) smart; (6) modish; (7) stylish; (8) delicate, graceful, tasteful; (11) fashionable.

elegy *n* mournful poem.

element l *n* 1 (4) hint, part; (5) trace; (6) factor, member; (7) feature; (9) component; (10) ingredient; (11) constituent; 2 **elements** (6) basics; (9) rudiments; (10) essentials, principles; (11) foundations; 3 **the four elements** air, earth, fire, water; ll *cryptic* refers to a part of a word or clue, as in: 'An element of doubt at first, then the French move fast' (6) = double (*doub* from doubt + le *see* **the**).

CHEMICAL ELEMENTS

(3) tin.

(4) gold, iron, lead, neon, zinc.

(5) argon, boron, ozone, radon, xenon.   *list continued over*

---

(6) barium, carbon, cerium, cobalt, copper, curium, erbium, helium, indium, iodine, nickel, osmium, oxygen, radium, silver, sodium.

(7) arsenic, bismuth, bromine, cadmium, caesium, calcium, fermium, gallium, hafnium, halogen, iridium, krypton, lithium, mercury, niobium, rhenium, rhodium, silicon, sulphur, terbium, thorium, thulium, uranium, wolfram, yttrium.

(8) actinium, antimony, astatine, chlorine, chromium, europium, fluorine, francium, hydrogen, lutetium, nitrogen, nobelium, platinum, polonium, rubidium, samarium, scandium, selenium, tantalum, thallium, titanium, tungsten, vanadium.

(9) aluminium, americium, berkelium, beryllium, deuterium, germanium, lanthanum, magnesium, manganese, neodymium, neptunium, palladium, plutonium, potassium, ruthenium, strontium, tellurium, ytterbium, zirconium.

(10) dysprosium, gadolinium, lanthanide, lawrencium, molybdenum, phosphorus, promethium, technetium.

(11) californium, einsteinium, mendelevium.

(12) praseodymium, protactinium.

elementary *adj* (4) easy; (5) basic, clear, (6) simple; (7) primary; (11) fundamental, rudimentary; (12) introductory; (13) uncomplicated.

elephant *n* 1 (*male* bull, *female* cow, *young* calf, *group* herd) (5) jumbo; (6) Indian; (7) African, mammoth; (9) pachyderm; 2 symbol of the US Democratic Party.

FAMOUS ELEPHANTS

Babar *fict.*, Celeste *fict.* (*Babar's wife*), Dumbo *fict.* (*Disney*), Heffalump *fict.* (*Winnie the Pooh*), Jumbo *hist.* Nellie *fict.* (*song*).

---

elevate *v* (4) lift; (5) boost, edify, exalt, hoist, raise, rouse; (6) uplift; (7) advance, promote, upgrade; (8) heighten.

elevated *adj* (4) high; (5) grand, lofty, noble; (6) raised; (7) exalted, sublime.

Eli *Bible* a judge and high priest of Israel who was the teacher of the prophet **Samuel**.

Elia *lit.* the pseudonym used by Charles Lamb as a writer of essays.

Elias *Bible see* **Elijah**.

Elijah 1 *Bible* a Hebrew prophet, also called Elias or the Tishbite, whose story is told in the First Book of Kings. He was fed by ravens, restored the widow's son to life, confounded the prophets of Baal by calling down fire from heaven to burn a sacrificial offering when they could not, was threatened with death by **Jezebel** and went into hiding, and on his death was taken up into heaven in a chariot of fire; 2 an **oratorio** by Felix Mendelssohn.

eliminate 1 *v* (4) drop, kill, omit; (6) defeat, delete, remove; (7) exclude; (9) eradicate, liquidate; (11) exterminate; (2+ words) do away with, get rid of, take out; 2 *cryptic* remove the words or letters indicated.

Elisha *Bible* a Hebrew prophet, whose story is told in the Second Book of Kings. The chosen successor of **Elijah**, he 'took up [the latter's] mantle' when it fell from the fiery chariot in which he was carried up to heaven.

Elysium *or* **Elysian fields** *Gk myth* the place where the souls of the good go after death – *see* **paradise**.

embarrassed 1 *adj* (3) red; (6) uneasy; (7) abashed, ashamed, awkward; (9) flustered; (10) humiliated; (12) disconcerted; 2 ANAGRAM CUE.

embrace 1 *v & n* (3) hug; (4) hold; (5) clasp; (6) clinch, cuddle; (7) squeeze; 2 *v* (5) cover; (6) accept; (7) include, involve, welcome; (8) comprise; (9) encompass; (11) incorporate; 3 *cryptic* 1 one word is split and another word, letter *etc* is inserted in the middle, as in:

'Rees embraces talkative nymph who goes on and on and on' (8) = reechoes; 2 HIDDEN WORD CUE.

eminence *n* 1 (4) fame, note, rank; (6) honour, renown; (8) prestige; (9) greatness; (10) importance; (11) distinction; 2 *see* hill; 3 **éminence grise** (grey eminence) a power behind the throne, especially Cardinal Richelieu's private secretary, Father Joseph (Père Joseph).

eminent *adj* (5) great; (6) famous; (7) notable; (8) elevated, renowned; (9) prominent, respected, well-known; (10) celebrated; (11) illustrious, outstanding, prestigious; (13) distinguished.

emissary *n* (5) envoy; (6) herald; (7) courier; (9) go-between; (10) ambassador; (14) representative.

emperor *n* 1 (4) czar, khan, shah, tsar; (5) ruler; (6) Caesar, mikado; (8) overlord; (9) sovereign; 2 name of species of **butterfly, moth, penguin**.

ROMAN EMPERORS

(3) Leo.

(4) Geta, Nero, Otho, Zeno.

(5) Carus, Galba, Nerva, Titus.

(6) Decius, Gallus, Jovian, Julian, Philip, Trajan.

(7) Gordian, Gratian, Hadrian, Maximus, Tacitus.

(8) Arcadius, Augustus, Aurelian, Balbinus, Caligula, Claudius, Commodus, Domitian, Tiberius, Valerian.

(9) Caracalla, Hostilian, Procopius, Vespasian, Vitellius.

(10) Diocletian.

(11) Constantine.

OTHER EMPERORS

Alexander (*Macedon, Russia*), Hirohito (*Japan*), Atahualpa (*Inca*), Ivan the Terrible (*Russia*), Barbarossa, Frederick (*Holy Roman*), Kublai Khan (*Mongol*), Bokassa (*Central African Empire*),

Montezuma (*Aztec*), Charlemagne (*Holy Roman*), Napoleon (*France*), Charles V (*Holy Roman*), Nicholas (*Russia*), Darius (*Persia*), Peter the Great (*Russia*), Franz Josef (*Austria*), Pharaoh (*Egypt*), Genghis Khan (*Mongol*), Ptolemy (*Egypt*), Haile Selassie (*Ethiopia*), Xerxes (*Persia*).

empress *n* (7) czarina, tsarina.

FAMOUS EMPRESSES

Anna (*Russia*), Josephine (*France*), Catherine (*Russia*), Maria Theresa (*Austria*), Ci-Xi (*China*), Marie Louise (*France*), Cleopatra (*Egypt*), Tzu Hsi *see* Ci-Xi, Elizabeth (*Russia*), Victoria (*Britain*), Eugenie (*France*), Irene (*Byzantine Empire*).

employ *v* (3) use; (4) hire; (5) apply; (6) engage; (7) recruit, utilise (*or* utilize); (10) commission; (2 words) take on.

empty I *adj* 1 (4) void; (5) blank, clear; (6) devoid, hollow, vacant; (8) deserted, desolate, unfilled; (10) unoccupied; (11) uninhabited; 2 (4) idle, vain; (5) inane; (6) futile; (7) trivial, useless, vacuous; (9) senseless, worthless; II *v* (4) void; (5) clear, drain; (6) vacate; (7) exhaust; (8) evacuate; III *cryptic* 1 omit the central letter or letters from a word in the clue, as in: 'Empty tank, push car back in along rough road' = track; 2 insert an O in a word, as in: 'Empty box and do a comic strip' = cartoon (carton + O).

end I *n & v* (4) ruin, stop; (5) close, limit; (6) climax, finish; II *n* 1 (3) tip; (4) edge; (5) death; (6) ending, finale; (8) boundary, terminus; (9) cessation; extremity; (10) completion, conclusion, dénouement, resolution; (11) culmination, termination; 2 (4) butt, stub; (5) scrap; (7) remnant; (8) left-over; (9) remainder; 3 (3) aim; (4) goal; (6) design, object; (7) purpose; (9) intention, objective; III *v* (5) cease; (8) conclude; (9) terminate; (2 words) wind up; *see also* destroy; IV *cryptic* 1 use the last letter of a word (often hidden in another word in the clue) as in:

'Townsend' = N, S (or NS); **2 ends** use the first and last letters of a word, as in: 'butt ends' = B and T.

endless I *adj* (7) eternal; (8) circular, constant, infinite; (9) boundless, continual, perpetual, unlimited; (10) continuous, monotonous; (11) everlasting, measureless; (12) interminable; II *also* **endlessly** *cryptic* omit the last letter (or sometimes the first letter) from a word in the clue, as in: 'Mortify endlessly and remain virtuous' (6) = chaste (mortify = chasten) or 'Endlessly bore and strike pay dirt' (3) = ore.

endorse *v* (4) back, sign; (6) affirm, ratify; (7) approve, confirm; (8) sanction; (9) authorise (*or* authorize), recommend.

endure *v* I (4) hold, last, live; (6) remain; (7) persist, survive; **2** (4) bear, face; (5) allow, brave, stand, stick; (6) permit, suffer; (7) stomach, sustain, undergo, weather; (8) tolerate; (9) withstand; (10) experience; (2+ words) go through, put up with.

energy I *n* (3) vim, zip; (4) zest; (5) drive, force, power; (6) vigour; (8) strength, vivacity; (9) intensity; II *cryptic* letter E (abbreviation) or ERG (unit of energy).

engineer I *n* (6) driver, sapper; II *v* (3) fix; (6) manage; (7) arrange; (8) contrive, organise (*or* organize); (9) manoeuvre; III *cryptic* I abbreviated as Eng; **2 engineers** abbreviated as RE (Royal Engineers).

English *cryptic* abbreviated as E.

enigmatic I *adj see* **mysterious**; II *cryptic* ANAGRAM CUE.

enjoyment *n* I (3) fun, joy; (4) zest; (6) relish; (7) delight; (8) pleasure; (9) amusement, diversion, happiness; (13) gratification; **2** (3) use; (7) benefit; (9) advantage; (10) possession.

enlarge *v* (5) swell, widen; (6) dilate, expand; (7) amplify, augment, broaden, develop, inflate, magnify, stretch; (8) heighten, increase, lengthen; (9) elaborate, expatiate; (2 words) blow up.

entangle I *v* (4) trap; (5) catch, ravel, snare; (6) enmesh, entrap, muddle, tangle; (7) confuse, embroil, ensnare, involve; (9) implicate; II **entangle** *or* **entangled** *cryptic* I ANAGRAM CUE; **2** place the letters of one word around another, as in: 'I'm entangled with Henry and there are storms ahead' (4) = hail (Hal - nickname for Henry).

enter I *v* I (4) join; (5) board, enrol; (6) embark, enlist, insert; (8) commence; (9) introduce, penetrate; **2** (3) log; (5) lodge, write; (6) record; (8) inscribe, register; II *cryptic* a word or letter is to be inserted into another word, as in: 'I enter score with disastrous results' (5) = ruins (score = runs).

enterprise *n* I (4) plan; (7) project, venture; (9) adventure, endeavour, operation, programme; (10) initiative; (11) undertaking; **2** (5) drive; (6) energy; (8) boldness, resource; (10) get-up-and-go; **3** (5) firm; (7) company; (8) business; (13) establishment.

entertain *v* I (5) amuse, cheer; (6) divert, please; (7) delight; **2** (7) harbour, imagine, receive; (8) conceive, consider; (11) contemplate, countenance.

entertainer

TYPES OF ENTERTAINER

(4) star.

(5) actor, clown, comic, mimer, mimic.

(6) artist, busker, dancer, jester, mummer, player, singer, stooge.

(7) acrobat, actress, artiste, buffoon, compère, juggler, showman, stand-up, starlet, tumbler.

(8) comedian, conjuror, magician, minstrel, showgirl, stripper, thespian, virtuoso, vocalist.

(9) anchorman, ballerina, celebrity, fire-eater, hypnotist, performer, presenter, puppeteer, tap-dancer.

(10) bandleader, comedienne, knockabout, mind-reader.

(11) accompanist, belly-dancer, broadcaster, dancing-girl, illusionist.

list continued over

---

(12) escapologist, impersonator, knife-thrower.

(13) contortionist, impressionist, ventriloquist.

(2 words) disc jockey, song-and-dance man, striptease artist, tightrope walker, trapeze artist.

entertainment *n* (3) fun; (5) sport; (8) pleasure; (9) amusement, diversion, enjoyment; (10) recreation; (11) distraction.

TYPES OF ENTERTAINMENT

(4) fête, play, show.

(5) cards, dance, disco, opera, radio, revue, rodeo, video.

(6) casino, cinema, circus.

(7) cabaret, cartoon, concert, dancing, karaoke, musical, pageant, recital, theatre, variety.

(8) barbecue, carnival, clubbing, festival, gymkhana, waxworks.

(9) fireworks, night-club, pantomime, spectacle.

(10) striptease.

(2+ words) magic show, music hall, Punch and Judy, puppet show.

---

enthusiasm *n* **1** (4) zeal; (6) ardour; (7) fervour, passion; (8) keenness; (9) eagerness, vehemence; **2** (5) craze, hobby, mania, thing.

enthusiast *n* (3) fan; (4) buff; (5) fiend, freak, lover; (7) admirer, devotee, fanatic, fancier; (9) supporter.

enthusiastic *adj* (3) hot; (4) avid, keen, warm; (5) eager; (6) ardent; (7) devoted, earnest, excited, fervent, willing, zealous; (8) vehement, vigorous; (10) passionate; (12) wholehearted.

entwine *or* **entwined** *cryptic* **1** ANAGRAM CUE; **2** place the letters of one word around another – *see* **entangle**.

epoch *n see* **era**.

equal **I** *adj & n* (4) like, twin; (10) equivalent; **II** *adj* **1** (4) even, same; (5) alike; (9) identical; (12) commensurate; (13) corresponding; **2** *see* **fair 1**; **II** *n*

(4) peer; (6) fellow; (11) counterpart; **III** *v* (5) match, tally; (6) equate; (7) balance, emulate; (8) coincide, parallel; (10) correspond.

era *n* **1** (3) age, day; (4) aeon, date, days, time; (5) epoch, stage; (6) period; (7) century; **2** for geological eras *see* **geology**.

erica *n* **1** (5) heath; (7) heather; **2** (4) girl.

Erinyes *Gk myth* the **Furies**.

Eris *Gk myth* the goddess of discord who, because she was not invited to the wedding of Peleus and Thetis, threw a golden apple inscribed with the words 'for the fairest' among the assembled gods and goddesses, thus leading to the Judgement of **Paris** and ultimately to the Trojan War.

Eros *Gk myth* the god of love, son of **Aphrodite**, equivalent of **Cupid**.

error *n* (4) flaw, slip; (5) gaffe, lapse; (6) cock-up, slip-up; (7) blunder, fallacy, mistake; (8) misprint, solecism; (9) oversight; (14) miscalculation; (15) misapprehension; (2 words) faux pas.

Esau *Bible* elder twin brother of Jacob, who according to Genesis was 'a hairy man' and who sold his birthright to Jacob for 'a mess of pottage'. Also known as **Edom**.

essay I *n* **1** (5) paper; (6) review; (7) article; (10) assignment; (11) composition; (12) dissertation; **II** *n & v* (3) try; (7) attempt.

essayist *lit*.

FAMOUS ESSAY WRITERS

Addison, Joseph *18th cent., co-founder of and main contributor to The Spectator.* Elia, *pen name of Charles Lamb.* Lamb, Charles *19th cent., wrote for the London Magazine under the pseudonym Elia.*

Montaigne, Michel de *16th-cent. sceptical philosophical essays.*

Orwell, George *20th-cent. essays on political and literary subjects.*

Steele, Sir Richard *18th cent., founder of The Tatler and co-founder of The Spectator.*

---

essential I *adj* (3) key; (4) main; (5) basic, vital; (7) crucial; (8) inherent; (9) important, intrinsic, necessary, principal; requisite; (11) fundamental; (13) indispensable; **II** *n* (4) must; (9) necessity; (11) requirement; (12) prerequisite.

establish *v* 1 (4) form; (5) found, plant, start; (6) create, settle; (7) install; (8) ensconce, entrench; (9) institute; (10) inaugurate; (2 words) set up; 2 (5) prove; (6) ratify, verify; (7) certify, confirm; (11) demonstrate; (12) substantiate.

establishment *n* 1 (8) creation, founding; (9) formation; (11) institution; (12) installation; 2 (4) firm; (7) company, concern; (8) business; (9) institute; (11) institution; (10) enterprise; (12) organisation (*or* organization); 3 **the establishment** the authorities, the powers that be, the ruling class(es), the system.

estimate I *v* (5) gauge, guess, value; (6) assess, reckon; (7) compute; (8) evaluate; (9) calculate; **II** *n* (5) guess; (9) reckoning; (10) assessment, evaluation; (11) calculation, guesstimate.

eternal *adj* (7) endless, lasting, undying; (8) constant, enduring, immortal, infinite, timeless, unending; (9) ceaseless, continual, limitless; (10) continuous, unchanging; (11) everlasting, never-ending; (12) imperishable, interminable.

Eumenides *Gk myth* 'the kindly ones', a euphemistic name for the **Furies**.

Euridyce *Gk myth* the wife of **Orpheus** whom he tried to rescue from the **Underworld**.

Europa *Gk myth* a princess of Tyre whom **Zeus** came to in the form of a bull and who became the mother of **Minos**.

Eve *Bible* the first woman, created by God, according to Genesis, from the rib of Adam, the first man, to be 'an help meet' for him. Succumbing to the serpent's temptation, Eve ate of the fruit of the tree of knowledge of good and evil, and persuaded Adam to do the same, leading to the Fall of Man and their expulsion from the Garden of Eden.

even *adj* 1 (4) flat; (5) flush, level, plane; (6) smooth, steady; (7) regular, uniform; (8) constant, parallel; (9) unvarying; (10) horizontal; 2 (4) same; (5) alike, equal; (8) balanced, matching; (10) fifty-fifty; (11) symmetrical; (3 words) neck and neck, side by side.

ex I *prefix see* **former**; **II** *prep* 1 direct from (ex factory); 2 excluding (ex dividend); **III** *n* former husband/wife/partner *etc.*

exact I *adj* 1 (4) true; (5) right; (6) strict; (7) correct, precise; (8) accurate, detailed, explicit, faithful, flawless, unerring; (9) faultless; (10) blow-by-blow; (11) word-perfect; 2 (7) careful, orderly; (8) rigorous; (10) methodical, meticulous, particular, scrupulous; (11) painstaking; **II** *v* (5) force, wrest, wring; (6) compel, demand, extort, impose; (7) command, extract, require.

exaggerate *v* (6) overdo; (7) magnify, stretch; (8) overblow; (9) embellish, embroider, emphasise (*or* emphasize), overstate; (13) overemphasise (*or* overemphasize).

exam *n* (4) GCSE, oral, quiz, test, viva.

examination *n* 1 *see* exam; 2 (4) scan; (5) check, study, trial; (6) review, search, survey; (7) enquiry (*or* inquiry), perusal; (8) analysis, once-over, scrutiny; (9) appraisal; (10) inspection; (11) exploration, inquisition, observation; (13) interrogation, investigation.

examine *v* (3) try, vet; (4) quiz, pore, scan, sift, test; (5) assay, audit, check, grill, probe, study; (6) review, survey; (7) analyse, explore, inspect, observe; (8) appraise, consider, question; (10) scrutinise (*or* scrutinize); (11) interrogate, investigate.

excellent *adj* (4) good, rare; (5) great; (6) choice, select, superb, worthy; (8) splendid, superior; (9) admirable, exemplary, first-rate, wonderful; (10) first-class, marvellous, phenomenal, remarkable, surpassing; (10) prodigious, unequalled; (11) exceptional, outstanding, superlative; (13) distinguished.

exceptional *adj* 1 *see* **excellent**; 2 (3) odd; (7) strange; (8) abnormal, uncommon; (9) anomalous, irregular; (13) extraordinary.

excerpt I *n* (4) clip; (5) quote; (7) cutting, extract, passage; (8) abstract; (9) quotation, selection; II *cryptic* 1 HIDDEN WORD CUE; 2 omit a letter or letters from one of the words in the clue.

excessive *adj* (5) steep, undue; (7) extreme; (10) exorbitant, immoderate, inordinate; (11) extravagant, superfluous, unnecessary; (12) unreasonable; (16) disproportionate.

exchange I *v & n* (4) swap; (5) trade; (6) barter, change, switch; (11) interchange; II *n* 1 (7) dealing, traffic; (11) replacement; (12) substitution; 2 (4) chat, talk; (8) dialogue; (10) discussion; (12) conversation; 3 (11) switchboard; 4 (2 words) **stock exchange**; III *cryptic* ANAGRAM CUE.

excite *v* (4) fire, jolt, stir; (5) amaze, rouse, shock; (6) excite, thrill; (7) animate, astound, stagger; (9) galvanise (*or* galvanize), stimulate; (10) invigorate.

excited I *adj* (3) hot; (4) high, keen, wild; (5) eager, moved; (6) ardent, elated, roused; (7) aroused, stirred; (8) thrilled, vehement, vigorous; (10) passionate; (12) enthusiastic, wholehearted; II *cryptic* ANAGRAM CUE.

excitement *n* (3) ado; (4) buzz, fuss, kick; (5) fever, tizzy; (6) flurry, furore, thrill, tumult; (7) elation, passion; (9) agitation, animation, enthusiasm; (12) exhilaration, intoxication.

exciting *adj* (7) rousing; (8) stirring; (9) thrilling; (10) nail-biting; (11) enthralling, sensational; (12) cliff-hanging, electrifying, exhilarating, intoxicating.

exclude I *v* (3) ban, bar; (4) omit; (5) debar, eject, evict, expel; (6) forbid, refuse, reject; (7) prevent; (8) disallow, preclude; (9) blacklist, eliminate, ostracise (*or* ostracize) proscribe; (13) excommunicate; (2 words) keep out, leave out, rule out; II *cryptic* omit a word, letter or letters.

exclusive *adj* 1 (4) chic, posh; (5) (6) choice, classy, closed, narrow, select; (7) cliquey, elegant; (8) clannish, snobbish; (9) selective; (11) fashionable; 2 (4) only, sole; (5) whole, total; (6) single, unique; 3 (12) incompatible; (13) contradictory; (14) irreconcilable.

excuse I *v* (4) free; (5) spare; (6) acquit, exempt, pardon; (7) absolve, condone, explain, forgive, justify, release; (8) mitigate, overlook; (9) discharge, exonerate, vindicate; II *n* (4) plea; (5) alibi, shift; (6) cop-out, reason; (7) apology, defence, grounds, pretext; (11) exoneration, explanation.

execute *v* 1 (2) do; (4) make; (5) enact; (6) create, effect, finish, fulfil; (7) achieve, realise (*or* realize); (8) complete, dispatch; (9) discharge, implement, undertake; (10) accomplish; (2 words) carry out, deal with, look after; 2 (3) gas; (4) hang, **kill**; (5) shoot; (6) behead; (10) decapitate, guillotine; (11) electrocute; (3 words) put to death.

exercise I *n* 1 (2) PE, PT; (5) drill; (7) workout; (8) activity, aerobics, exertion, practice, training; 2 (4) task, test; (6) lesson; (10) assignment; (3) use; (9) discharge, operation; (11) utilisation (*or* utilization); II *v* 1 (5) drill, train; (8) practise; (2 words) keep fit, pump iron, work out; 2 (3) use; (5) apply, exert, wield; (6) employ; (7) utilise (*or* utilise); 3 (3) vex; (5) annoy, upset, worry; (7) afflict, agitate, disturb, trouble; III *cryptic* the letters PE or PT.

exhaust I *v* (3) sap, tax; (4) tire: (5) drain, empty, spend, waste, weary; (6) finish, strain, weaken; (7) consume, deplete, fatigue; (8) bankrupt, squander, overwork; (9) dissipate; (10) impoverish; II *n* (4) pipe; (6) outlet; (8) manifold.

exhibit *v see* **display**, **show**.

exit I *v* (2) go; (4) quit; (5) leave, split; (6) decamp, depart, escape, remove, retire, vanish; (8) withdraw; (9) disappear; (2+ words) absent oneself, go away, move away, take off, take one's leave; II *n* (4) door, gate, vent; (5) going; (6) exodus;

(7) doorway, gateway, retreat; (8) farewell; (9) departure; (10) retirement; (11) leave-taking.

exotic I *adj* (5) alien; (7) bizarre, curious, foreign, unusual; (8) imported; (9) different; (10) introduced, outlandish, unfamiliar; (3) extraordinary; II *cryptic* ANAGRAM CUE.

expand *v* (5) swell, widen; (6) dilate; (7) amplify, augment, broaden, develop, enlarge, inflate, stretch; (8) increase; (9) elaborate, expatiate.

expect *v* (4) want, wish; (5) await, guess, think, trust; (6) assume, demand, reckon; (7) believe, foresee, imagine, predict, presume, project, require, suppose, surmise; (8) envisage, envision, forecast; (10) anticipate; (11) contemplate; (2+ words) bank on, bargain on, count on, hope for, look for, look forward to, rely on.

expel *v* (3) ban, bar; (4) oust, void; (5) debar, eject, evict, exile; (6) banish, deport, reject; (7) exclude; (8) evacuate; (9) discharge.

expert I *n & adj* (3) ace, pro; (5) adept; (8) virtuoso; (10) specialist; (12) professional; II *n* (7) maestro; (9) authority; (11) connoisseur; (2 words) dab hand; III *adj* (4) able, deft; (6) adroit; (7) capable, skilful, skilled; (8) masterly; (9) masterful, practised, qualified; (10) proficient; (13) knowledgeable.

explain *v* (5) solve; (6) define, excuse; (7) clarify, expound, justify, resolve, unravel, warrant; (8) describe, simplify, untangle; (9) elucidate, explicate, interpret, translate; (11) rationalise (*or* rationalize); (2 words) account for, make clear, spell out.

explicit *adj* (4) open; (5) clear, exact, frank, plain; (6) direct, stated; (7) express; (8) absolute, declared, distinct, positive, specific; (9) outspoken; (10) unreserved; (11) categorical, unambiguous.

explore *v* (5) probe, scout; (6) search, survey, travel; (7) examine, inspect; (8) prospect, research; (11) investigate, reconnoitre.

explorer *n* (5) scout; (9) traveller; (10) discoverer; (12) investigator.

**FAMOUS EXPLORERS
BY LAND OR AIR**

Amundsen, Roald (*Norwegian – South Pole*)

Burke, Robert (*Irish – central Australia south to north with Wills*)

Burton, Sir Richard (*British – East Africa*)

Byrd, Richard (*US – North Pole*)

Fuchs, Sir Vivian (*British – Antarctic*)

Hillary, Sir Edmund (*NZ – ascent of Mt Everest*)

Hunt, Sir John (*British – Mt Everest*)

Livingstone, David (*British – central Africa - Victoria Falls*)

Nansen, Fridtjof (*Norwegian – Arctic – ship 'Fram'*)

Park, Mungo (*British – West Africa – River Niger*)

Peary, Robert (*US – North Pole*)

Polo, Marco (*Venetian – route to China*)

Scott, Sir Robert (*British – South Pole – ship 'Discovery'*)

Shackleton, Sir Ernest (*British – Antarctic – ship 'Endurance'*)

Speke, John Hanning (*British – East Africa – Lake Victoria*)

Wills, William (*British – central Australia south to north with Burke*).

FAMOUS EXPLORERS BY SEA

Baffin, William (*English – northern Canada – NW Passage*)

Bering, Vitus (*Danish – North Pacific*)

Cabot, John (*English/Italian – Newfoundland – ship 'Matthew'*)

Cartier, Jacques (*French – Canada, St Lawrence River*)

Columbus, Christopher (*Italian/ Spanish – America – ships 'Santa Maria', 'Nina', 'Pinta'*)

Cook, Capt. James (*British – Australia – ship 'Endeavour'*)

Cousteau, Jacques (*French – underwater*)

da Gama, Vasco (*Portuguese – via Cape of Good Hope to India*)

Dias (*or* Diaz), Bartolomeu (*Portuguese – around Cape of Good Hope*)

list continued over

Drake, Sir Francis (*English – around the world – ship 'Golden Hind' or 'Pelican'*)
Hudson, Henry (*English – North America, Hudson Bay and River*)
Magellan, Ferdinand (*Portuguese – around the world – ship 'Trinidad'*)
Vespucci, Amerigo (*Italian – South American coast*)

explosive *adj* (5) tense; (6) touchy; (7) fraught; (8) unstable, volatile; (9) dangerous, hazardous.

TYPES OF EXPLOSIVE

(3) TNT; (6) napalm, Semtex; (7) cordite, lyddite; (8) dynamite; (9) gelignite, gunpowder; (14) nitroglycerine; (15) trinitrotoluene.

expose *v* (4) show; (6) flaunt, reveal, unmask; (7) exhibit, explain, present; (8) disclose, indicate, manifest; (10) illustrate; (11) demonstrate; (2 words) show off, show forth, testify to.

exposed *adj* (4) **bare,** nude, open; (5) bleak, empty, naked, windy; (8) desolate; (9) vulnerable, uncovered, windswept; (11) unprotected, unsheltered; (2 words) at risk, in danger, in peril, on display, on show, on view.

express I *v* (3) say; (4) show, tell; (5) speak, state, utter, voice; (5) assert, convey, denote, depict, embody, reveal; (7) declare, signify; (8) announce, disclose, indicate, intimate; (9) designate, formulate, pronounce, represent, verbalise (*or* verbalize); (10) articulate; (11) communicate; (2 words) make known, put across; II *adj* 1 (4) **fast;** (5) quick, rapid; (6) speedy; (9) high-speed; 2 *see* **deliberate;** *see* **explicit;** III *n* (3) TGV; (5) **train.**

expression *n* 1 (3) air; (4) **face,** look, mien; (6) aspect; 2 (4) tone; (7) diction; (8) delivery; (10) intonation; (11) enunciation; 3 (5) idiom; (6) phrase, saying; 4 (9) assertion, statement, utterance; (10) indication; (11) declaration; (12) announcement; (13) verbalisation (*or* verbalization).

extra I *adj* (3) new; (4) more; (5) added, other, spare; (6) excess; (7) further, surplus; (8) left-over; (9) ancillary, redundant; (10) additional; (13) supernumerary, supplementary; II *adv* (9) unusually; (10) especially; (12) particularly; (13) exceptionally; III *n* 1 (5) bonus; (7) adjunct; (8) addition; (9) extension; (10) supplement; 2 *cricket* (3) bye; (4) wide; (2 words) leg bye, no ball; 3 *film* (2 words) bit part, bit player, spear carrier; (**extras**) crowd; IV *cryptic* letters PS or X.

extract I *n* (4) clip; (7) cutting, excerpt, passage; (8) abstract; (9) quotation, selection; II *v* (3) get; (4) cull, draw, milk; (5) exact, glean, wrest, wring; (6) choose, derive, distil, gather, obtain, remove, select; (8) withdraw; III *cryptic* 1 HIDDEN WORD CUE; 2 omit a letter or letters from one of the words in the clue.

extra large I *adj* (7) outsize; II *cryptic* the letters OS (outsize), X (extra) or XL (extra large).

extraordinary *adj* (4) rare; (6) unique; (7) notable; (7) amazing, bizarre, special, strange, unusual; (8) peculiar; (10) marvellous, noteworthy, remarkable, surprising.

extreme I *adj* 1 (4) last; (5) acute, final, great, outer, utter; (6) utmost; (7) endmost, highest, intense, maximum, serious; (8) farthest, furthest, greatest, terminal, ultimate; (9) outermost; (10) exorbitant, immoderate, inordinate; (11) exceptional, extravagant; (12) unreasonable; (13) extraordinary; (16) disproportionate; 2 (5) harsh, rigid, stern, strict; (6) severe; (7) drastic, radical; (9) fanatical; (14) uncompromising; II *n* (3) end, top; (4) edge, peak; (5) limit; (6) climax; (7) maximum; (8) pinnacle; (9) extremity; III *cryptic* **extreme** use the first *or* last letter or **extremes** use the first *and* last letter of a word in the clue, as in: 'Knob outsize in the extremes of bliss' = boss (b . . . s; outsize = OS).

extremely I *adv* (4) unco, very; (6) highly; (7) greatly; (13) exceptionally; II *cryptic* use the first and last letter of a word in the clue, as in: 'Englishman loses it and gets extremely angry at asinine racket' = bray (Englishman = Brit (minus it) plus a....y).

extreme sport *n* a sport involving a high degree of physical risk, through taking place in a dangerous environment or involving stunts on a moving board or vehicle. Extreme sports include: BMX, canyoning, in-line skating, snowboarding, street luge, wakeboarding, and white-water rafting.

eye I *n* **1** (3) orb; (6) peeper; **II** *v* (3) spy; (4) look, quiz, pore, scan; (5) stare, study, watch; (6) assess, regard, review, survey; (7) examine, inspect, observe; (8) appraise, consider; (10) scrutinise (*or* scrutinize); (11) contemplate.

PARTS OF THE EYE

(4) ball, iris, lens, rods; (5) orbit, pupil, white; (6) cornea, retina; (9) sclerotic.

CONDITIONS AFFECTING THE EYE

(4) cast, stye; (6) iritis, myopia (myopic), myosin, myosis (myotic), squint; (8) cataract, glaucoma, trachoma; (9) blindness, nystagmus; (10) strabismus; (11) astigmatism; (14) conjunctivitis.

---

eye-catching *adj* (8) striking, stunning; (9) prominent; (10) attractive, noticeable; (11) conspicuous.

eyesore *n* (6) blight, horror; (7) blemish; (9) carbuncle; (11) monstrosity; (3 words) blot on the landscape.

Ezekiel *Bible* Old Testament prophet and book of the Old Testament.

Ezra *Bible* Old Testament prophet and book of the Old Testament.

F

F *abbrev* Fahrenheit, farad, fellow, fine (on pencils), fluorine, France (international vehicle registration); key (music), note (music).

f *abbrev* fathom, female, feminine, folio, following, forte (music).

fab *see* **fabulous**.

fable *n* (3) lie; (4) myth, tale, yarn; (5) story; (6) legend; (7) fiction; (8) allegory; (9) invention; (11) fabrication; (2+ words) tall story, old wives' tale.

fabric *n* 1 (5) cloth, stuff; (7) textile; (8) material; 2 (6) make-up; (9) framework, structure; (12) construction.

TYPES OF FABRIC

(3) fur, kid, net, PVC, rep, tat.

(4) buff, calf, cire, coir, down, drab, duck, ecru, felt, lace, lamé, lawn, rack, silk, vair, wool.

(5) arras, baize, braid, chino, crape, crash, crepe, denim, drill, flock, floss, gauze, khaki, linen, lisle, moire, nylon, orris, pique, plaid, plush, rayon, sable, satin, scrim, serge, suede, terry, toile, tulle, tweed, twill, voile.

(6) alpaca, angora, beaver, boucle, burlap, caddis, calico, camlet, canvas, chintz, cloque, cotton, crepon, crewel, dacron, damask, dimity, dowlas, dralon, duffel, durrie, ermine, fablon, frieze, jersey, kersey, lining, linsey, madras, merino, mohair, muslin, poplin, russet, sateen, shoddy, tartan, tissue, velour, velvet.

(7) batiste, bombast, brocade, buckram, bunting, cambric, catskin, chamois, chiffon, cowhide, drugget, flannel, fustian, gingham, grogram, hessian, holland, karakul, leather, mechlin, miniver, nankeen, netting,

oilskin, organza, paisley, plastic, sacking, taffeta, ticking, tiffany, veiling, wadding, worsted.

(8) buckskin, cashmere, chenille, corduroy, cretonne, damassin, diamanté, dungaree, gossamer, homespun, jacquard, moleskin, moquette, nainsook, oilcloth, organdie, paduasoy, quilting, rickrack, shagreen, shantung, terylene, whipcord.

(9) astrakhan, bombazine, courtelle, crimplene, crinoline, gaberdine, georgette, grosgrain, huckaback, lamb's-wool, petersham, polyamide, polyester, polythene, sackcloth, satinette, tarpaulin, towelling, velveteen.

(10) candlewick, mackintosh, needlecord, polycotton, seersucker, winceyette.

(11) cheesecloth, flannelette, leatherette, stockinette.

(12) crepe-de-chine.

(2 words) American cloth, chantilly lace, cavalry twill, shot silk, viscose rayon.

---

fabricate 1 *v* 1 (4) make; (5) build, erect; (6) create, devise; (8) assemble; (9) construct; (11) manufacture; 2 (4) fake; (5) forge; (6) invent; (7) concoct, falsify; (2 words) cook up, make up, trump up; 11 **fabricate** *or* **fabricated** *cryptic* ANAGRAM CUE.

fabulous *adj* 1 (5) brill, great, super; (6) superb; (7) amazing, immense; (8) terrific; (9) brilliant, fantastic, wonderful; (10) incredible, marvellous, phenomenal; (12) unbelievable; 2 (6) fabled; (8) mythical; (9) legendary; (10) fictitious.

FABULOUS CREATURES

(3) elf, fay, imp, lar, roc.

(4) bogy, boyg, faun, jinn, ogre, peri, pixy, puck, yeti.

(5) bogle, demon, devil, djinn, drake, dryad, dwarf, fairy, genie, ghost, ghoul, giant, gnome, harpy, houri, jinni, lamia, naiad, nymph, oread, pixie, satyr, siren, snark, spook, sylph, troll, zombi.

(6) boojum, bunyip, daemon, dragon, dybbuk, goblin, kelpie, kobold, kraken, merman, nereid, ogress, sphinx, undine, wivern, wyvern, zombie.

(7) banshee, brownie, bugaboo, centaur, chimera, griffin, griffon, gryphon, incubus, lakshmi, mermaid, phantom, sandman, spectre, unicorn, vampire, warlock.

(8) basilisk, behemoth, giantess, isengrim, phantasm, succubus, sylphide, werewolf.

(9) bottle-imp, cacodemon, hamadryad, hobgoblin, leviathan, manticore.

(10) cockatrice, hippogriff, leprechaun, salamander.

(11) hippocampus, poltergeist.

(12) bandersnatch, doppelgänger, hippocentaur.

(15) flibbertigibbet.

face I *n* 1 (3) mug, pan; (4) dial; (5) clock, front; (6) façade, visage; (7) outside; (8) features; (11) countenance, physiognomy; 2 *see* **typeface**; II *v* (4) defy, meet; (5) beard, brave; (6) oppose, tackle; (8) confront; (9) encounter.

factor *n* 1 (4) item, fact, part; (5) cause; (6) aspect, detail; (9) component, influence; (10) ingredient; (12) circumstance; 2 (5) agent.

fade *v* (4) fail, fall, sink, wane; (5) decay; (6) bleach, lessen, reduce, wither, worsen; (7) crumble, dwindle, shrivel; (8) decrease; (10) degenerate; (11) deteriorate.

fail *v* (4) flop; (5) flunk; (6) plough; (7) misfire; (8) miscarry; (2 words) break down, conk out, fall through, go awry, go wrong, pack up.

faint I *adj* 1 (3) dim, low; (4) dull, hazy, pale, weak; (5) faded, light, vague; (6) feeble, hushed, slight; (7) muffled, subdued; (10) indistinct; 2 (5) dizzy, giddy, woozy; (11) light-headed; II *v* (5) swoon; (8) collapse; (2 words) black out, flake out, keel over, pass out.

fair I *adj* 1 (4) just; (5) right, square; (6) honest, lawful, proper; (8) unbiased; (9) equitable, impartial, objective; (10) even-handed, honourable, legitimate; (13) disinterested; 2 (2) OK; (4) so-so; (7) average; (8) adequate, middling, moderate, passable; (9) tolerable; (10) acceptable, reasonable; (12) satisfactory; 3 (5) blond, light; (6) blonde, lovely; (9) beautiful; 4 (3) dry; (4) fine; (5) sunny; (6) bright; II *n* (4) expo, fete, show; (6) bazaar, market; (7) funfair; (10) exposition.

fairy *n* (3) elf, fay; (4) peri, pixy, puck; (5) bogle, dwarf, gnome, pixie, sylph; (6) sprite; (7) brownie.

FAIRIES FROM A MIDSUMMER NIGHT'S DREAM

Cobweb, Moth, Mustardseed, Oberon (king), Peasblossom, Puck (Robin Goodfellow), Titania (queen).

---

faithful *adj* 1 (4) true; (5) loyal; (6) trusty; (7) devoted, staunch; (8) constant, reliable; (9) steadfast; (10) dependable; 2 (5) exact; (6) strict; (7) precise; (8) accurate.

fake I *n & adj* (4) hoax, sham; (6) phoney; (7) replica; (9) imitation; (11) counterfeit; (12) reproduction; II *adj* (5) bogus, false; (6) forged, pseudo; (9) simulated; (10) artificial; III *n* (4) copy; (7) forgery; (8) impostor; (9) charlatan; IV *v* (5) feign, forge; (6) affect; (7) falsify, pretend; (8) simulate; V *cryptic* ANAGRAM CUE.

fall I *v & n* 1 (3) dip; (4) dive, drop; (6) plunge, tumble; (8) collapse, nosedive; 2 *see* **decrease**; II *v* (4) sink, trip; (5) pitch, slope; (6) lessen, plunge, topple, tumble; (7) descend, plummet; (8) collapse, nosedive; (2 words) go down, keel over, move down; **III** *n* **1** (7) cropper, descent; **2** (5) slump; (6) defeat; (8) downfall; (9) overthrow, surrender; (12) capitulation; **3** autumn (in US); **4** *see* **waterfall**; **5 Fall (of Man)** *Christianity* Adam and Eve's original sin, described in Genesis, of disobeying God by eating the fruit of the tree of knowledge of good and evil.

false I *adj* **1** (4) **fake**, mock, sham; (5) bogus; (8) illusive; (10) artificial; **2** (3) sly; (5) lying, shady; (6) crafty, sneaky; (7) crooked, dubious; (8) cheating, guileful, two-faced; (9) deceitful, deceiving, deceptive, insincere, swindling, underhand; (10) fraudulent, misleading, unreliable, untruthful; (11) duplicitous; treacherous; (12) disreputable, hypocritical, unprincipled; **3** (5) wrong; (9) erroneous, **incorrect**; (10) fallacious; **II** *cryptic* ANAGRAM CUE.

familiar I *adj* **1** (6) common; (7) routine; (8) everyday, ordinary; (9) well-known; (12) recognisable (*or* recognizable); **2** (4) free; (5) close; (7) relaxed; (8) informal, intimate; (10) acquainted; **3 familiar with** (2 words) abreast of, aware of, cognisant (*or* cognizant) of, conversant with, knowledgeable about; **II** an animal - strictly speaking, a demon in the form of an animal – supposed to advise a witch or warlock and assist in the working of magic spells.

family *n* (3) kin; (4) clan, folk, line, race; (5) birth, blood, house, stock, tribe; (7) kindred, kinsmen, lineage; (8) ancestry, pedigree; (9) forebears, relations, relatives; (10) extraction; *see also* **children** *under* **child** *and* **relation**.

famine *n* (4) lack, need, want; (6) dearth; (7) absence, paucity, poverty; (8) scarcity, shortage, sparsity; (10) deficiency, inadequacy, scantiness, sparseness; (13) insufficiency.

famous *adj* (5) great, noted; (7) eminent, notable; (8) elevated, renowned; (9) prominent, respected, well-known; (10) celebrated; (11) illustrious, outstanding, prestigious; (13) distinguished.

famous five *fict.* **1** *Enid Blyton* Anne, Dick, George, Julian, Timmy (the dog); **2** *Frank Richards (Greyfriars)* Johnnie Bull, Bob Cherry, Frank Nugent, Hurree Jamset Ram Singh, Harry Wharton.

fan I *n* **1** (4) vane; (9) extractor; (10) ventilator; **2** (4) buff; (5) fiend, freak, lover; (7) admirer, devotee, fanatic, fancier; (9) supporter; (10) enthusiast; **II** *v* **1** (3) air; (4) cool, stir, waft, wave; **2** (6) arouse, excite, incite, kindle; (7) provoke; (9) stimulate.

fancy I *adj* (6) ornate; (9) decorated, elaborate, fantastic; **II** *n* (3) yen; (4) idea, urge, whim; (5) dream, image; (6) desire, liking, notion; (7) fantasy, thought; (8) fondness; (9) hankering; (11) imagination; **III** *v* **1** (5) guess, think; (6) reckon; (7) believe, imagine, suppose; (8) conceive; (10) conjecture; **2** (4) like, want; (6) desire, favour, prefer; (2 words) go for, take to; **IV** *cryptic* ANAGRAM CUE.

fantastic *adj* **1** (5) great; (6) superb; (7) amazing, immense; (8) fabulous, terrific; (9) brilliant, wonderful; (10) incredible, marvellous, phenomenal; (12) unbelievable; **2** (6) fabled; (8) mythical; (9) legendary; (10) fictitious.

fantasy *n* (4) myth; (5) dream, fancy, story; (6) legend, mirage, vision; (7) reverie; (8) daydream, delusion, illusion; (9) invention, unreality; (10) apparition; (11) fabrication; (13) hallucination; (2 words) pipe dream, science fiction.

fashion I *n & v* (3) cut, fit; (4) form; (5) model, mould, shape, style; (6) design; **II** *n* **1** (3) way; (4) mode; (6) manner, method; **2** (3) fad, line, look, rage; (5) craze, trend, vogue; (6) latest; **III** *v* (5) adapt, alter; (6) create; (9) construct; **IV** *cryptic* ANAGRAM CUE.

fashionable *adj* (2) in; (4) chic, neat; (5) smart; (6) latest, modish, trendy; (7) current, elegant, popular, stylish; (2+ words) à la mode, all the rage, in vogue, up to the minute.

fast I *adj* **1** (5) brisk, fleet, hasty, nippy, quick, rapid, swift; (6) flying, speedy; (7) hurried; **2** (3) set; (4) firm; (5) fixed, stuck;

(6) secure; (8) immobile; (9) immovable; II *adv* 1 (5) apace; (6) presto; (7) briskly, quickly, rapidly, swiftly; (8) speedily; (2+ words) like a flash, like a shot; III *v* (4) diet; (6) starve; (7) abstain.

FASTS

(4) Lent; (6) Friday; (7) Ramadan; (2 words) Ember Day.

---

fasten *v see* **fix** I 1.

fastener *or* **fastening** *n* (3) eye, pin, tie, zip; (4) belt, bolt, bond, clip, hook, glue, lace, loop, nail; (5) catch, clasp, rivet, screw; (6) anchor, button, cement, popper, staple, Velcro®.

fat I *adj* 1 (5) obese, plump, podgy, round, stout, thick, tubby; (6) chubby, fleshy, portly, rotund; (7) paunchy; (9) corpulent; (10) overweight; 2 (4) oily; (6) greasy; 3 (5) large; (8) generous, handsome, sizeable; (12) considerable; II *n* (4) flab; (6) grease; (7) blubber.

fatal *adj* (6) deadly, lethal, mortal; (7) killing; (8) terminal; (9) incurable; (10) calamitous, disastrous; (12) catastrophic.

fate *n* (3) end, lot; (4) doom, ruin; (5) death, stars; (7) destiny, fortune; (9) horoscope.

Fates I *Gk myth* three goddesses who measured out and determined the span of individual human lives. Their names were **Clotho**, who presided over birth and drew the thread of life from her distaff, **Lachesis**, who spun the thread and determined its length, and **Atropos** who cut the thread with her shears. In ancient Greece they were also called the Moirai, while the Roman name for them was the Parcae; II *Norse Myth see* **Norns**.

father I *n* 1 (2) pa; (3) dad, pop; (4) papa, sire; (5) daddy, pater; (6) guvnor; (8) ancestor; (10) progenitor; (2 words) old man; 2 (6) author; (7) creator, founder, pioneer; (8) inventor; (9) architect; (10) originator; 3 (5) abbot, padre; (6) priest; II *v* (4) sire; (5) beget; (6) create; (7) produce; (9) originate, procreate; III *cryptic* abbreviated as Fr; frequently also indicates the letters PA.

fatherless *cryptic* omit the letters PA, FR or those making up any other word for father from a word in the clue, as in: 'First success for fatherless pauper – jolly well done!' (5) = super.

fault I *n* (3) bug; (4) flaw, lack, spot; (5) blame, error, taint; (6) defect; (7) absence, blemish, failing, frailty, mistake; (8) weakness; (10) deficiency, inadequacy; (11) shortcoming; (14) responsibility; II *v* (5) blame; (9) criticise (*or* criticize).

faun *Rom. myth* a mythical creature with the upper body of a man and the lower body of a goat, equivalent to a Greek satyr.

favour I *n* 1 (4) boon; (7) service; (8) courtesy, kindness; (2 words) good turn; 2 (6) esteem; (7) support; (8) approval, goodwill, sympathy; (10) partiality, preference; II *v* (4) back, like; (6) choose, prefer; (7) approve, promote, support; (8) champion; (9) encourage.

fawn I *n* 1 young deer; 2 beige colour; II *v see* **flatter**.

fear *n* (4) funk; (5) alarm, dread, panic; (6) fright, phobia, qualms, terror; (7) anxiety; (8) distress; (9) agitation, cowardice; (10) foreboding, misgivings; (11) trepidation; (12) apprehension.

fearful *adj* 1 *see* **afraid**; 2 (5) awful; (6) grisly; (7) ghastly, hideous; (8) dreadful, shocking, **terrible**.

February *n* the second month, the month of purification for Romans, its name comes the Latin *februo* I purify.

fellow I *n* 1 (3) boy, man; (4) chap, cove, gent; (5) bloke; 2 (3) don; (5) tutor; (6) member; (7) teacher; II *cryptic* abbreviated as F or sometimes represented by the letters HE.

female *adj & n* (3) she; (4) girl; (5) woman.

FEMALE ANIMALS

(3) doe, cow, ewe, hen, pen, sow.

(4) duck, gill, hind, mare.

(5) bitch, brach, goose, jenny, nanny, queen, reeve, vixen.

---

feminine I *adj* (6) female; (7) girlish, womanly; II *cryptic* abbreviated as F or FEM.

field I *n* **1** (3) lea; (6) meadow; (7) paddock, pasture; **2** (5) pitch; (6) ground; **3** (4) area, line; (5) forte, realm; (6) branch, domain, region, sector, sphere; (7) concern, section; (8) division, province; (10) speciality; (14) responsibility; **4** (4) pack; (5) bunch; (7) runners; (8) entrants; (9) opponents; (10) contenders; (11) competitors; II *v* (4) stop; (5) catch; (9) intercept; (2 words) deal with.

fielder, fieldsman

FIELDERS AND FIELDING POSITIONS IN CRICKET

cover, cover point, fine leg, forward short leg, gully, leg slip, long leg, long off, long on, long stop, mid on, mid off, midwicket, point, silly mid off, silly mid on, silly point, slip (first, second etc), square leg.

---

fiend *n* **1** (5) demon, devil; (7) monster; **2** (3) fan; (4) buff; (5) fiend, freak, lover; (7) admirer, devotee, fanatic, fancier; (9) supporter; (10) enthusiast.

fifth *cryptic* the fifth letter of a word in the clue, *e.g.* Mahler's Fifth = E.

fifty *cryptic* Roman numeral L.

fight I *n & v* (3) row, war; (4) duel; (5) brawl, clash, scrap; (6) battle, combat, tussle; (7) crusade, dispute, quarrel, scuffle, wrangle; (8) campaign, conflict, skirmish, squabble, struggle; (9) encounter; II *n* **1** (4) bout, fray; (5) match, set-to; (6) action; (8) argument; (10) free-for-all; **2** (5) drive; (8) firmness, tenacity; (9) willpower; (10) resolution; (13) determination; III *v* (3) box; (5) fence; (6) bicker, oppose, resist; (7) grapple, wrestle.

figure I *n* **1** (3) sum; (4) cost; (5) digit, price; (6) amount, number; (7) numeral; **2** (4) body, form; (5) build, shape; (7) outline; (8) physique; (10) silhouette; **3** (5) image; (6) emblem, sketch; (7) diagram, drawing, pattern, picture; (12) illustration; (14) representation; **4** (6) person;

(9) celebrity, character, dignitary; (11) personality; II *v* **1** (5) guess, judge, think; (6) reckon; (7) compute; (8) estimate; (9) calculate; (2 words) work out; **2** (6) appear; (7) feature.

film I *n* **1** (5) layer; (7) coating; (8) membrane; **2** (4) reel; (5) flick, movie, video, weepy; (6) B-movie, weepie; (7) picture, western; (8) thriller; (9) docudrama; (11) documentary; (2 words) costume drama, film noir, motion picture; II *v* (5) shoot, video; (6) record; (10) photograph; III *cryptic* one of the letters denoting (or formerly denoting) categories of film and the types of audience allowed to watch them, *e.g.* A, AA, PG, U, X.

final I *adj* (4) last; (5) dying, omega; (6) latest; (7) closing; (8) eventual, terminal, ultimate; (9) finishing; (10) concluding, conclusive; II *cryptic* use the last letter of the word indicated, as in: 'Drive to create Arsenal's first and final score' = goal.

find I *v* (3) see, spy; (4) espy, note, spot; (5) sight, trace; (6) detect, expose, locate, notice, reveal, unmask; (7) discern, observe, uncover, unearth; (8) discover, identify, perceive, retrieve; (9) ascertain, recognise (*or* recognize); (11) distinguish; II *n* (9) discovery; (10) trouvaille.

finish I *n & v* (3) end; (4) ruin, stop; (5) close, limit; (6) climax; II *n* (5) death; (6) ending, finale; (8) boundary, terminus; (9) cessation; extremity; (10) completion, conclusion, dénouement, resolution; (11) culmination, termination; III *v* (5) cease; (8) conclude; (9) terminate; (2 words) wind up; *see also* **destroy**.

fire I *n* **1** (5) blaze; (6) flames, hearth; (7) inferno; (13) conflagration; **2** (4) heat, zeal; (6) ardour, warmth; (7) passion; (10) enthusiasm; II *v* **1** (5) shoot; (6) launch; (9) discharge; **2** (4) drop, sack; (7) dismiss, release; (9) discharge; (2+ words) lay off, let go, make redundant; (4) stir; (6) arouse, ignite, incite, kindle; (7) inspire, trigger.

firm I *adj* **1** (3) set; (4) fast, hard; (5) dense, fixed, rigid, solid, stiff, tight; (6)

secure, stable, steady; (7) compact; (8) embedded; (10) unyielding; **2** (4) sure, true; (7) adamant; (8) resolute; (10) determined, unwavering; **II** *n* (7) company; (8) business; (10) enterprise; (11) corporation; (13) establishment; **III** *cryptic* letters CO, or sometimes LTD or PLC.

first **I** *adj* **1** (5) early; (6) eldest, oldest, primal; (7) initial, opening; (8) earliest, original, primeval; (9) primitive; (11) prehistoric, preliminary; (12) introductory; **2** (3) key; (4) head, main; (5) chief, prime; (6) ruling, senior; (7) leading, primary; (8) cardinal; (9) principal, sovereign; **II** *cryptic* **1** use the first letter of the designated word in the clue, as in: 'Peter's first workers wore shorts' = pants (workers = ants) – NB the use of first is often more elliptical, so that 'first base' might mean B, 'first floor' F, the 'first of January' J, and the 'first of the month' M or any of the letters beginning the names of the months; **2** place the designated word, letter or letters in front of something else in order to form the solution, as in: 'At first enticing, but trying in the end' (10) = attempting.

first born *cryptic* B, Cain.

first-class **I** *adj* (3) top; (4) fine; (8) splendid, top-notch; (9) **excellent**, first-rank, first-rate, top-flight; **II** *cryptic* letters AI or C.

first issue *cryptic* I, Cain.

first lady **I** *n* wife of the President of the United States; **II** *cryptic* L, Eve, Pandora.

first person **I** *grammar* I, WE; **II** *cryptic* P, Adam.

fish *v* (5) angle, catch, trawl, troll.

TYPES OF FISH AND CRUSTACEANS

(3) ayu, bib, cod, dab, dar, eel, gar, ged, ide, ray, tai.

(4) bass, blay, butt, carp, chad, char, chub, clam, cusk, dace, dory, drum, goby, hake, hind, huss, kelt, keta, ling, luce, lump, opah, orfe, parr, pike, pout, rudd, ruff, scad, scup, shad, sild, sole, tope, tuna.

---

(5) ablen, angel, bleak, bream, brill, charr, cisco, coley, danio, doree, dorse, elops, elver, fluke, gibel, grunt, guppy, krill, loach, lythe, manta, moray, perch, pogge, porgy, powan, prawn, roach, roker, saury, scrod, sepia, sewen, sewin, shark, skate, skeet, smelt, smolt, smout, snoek, snook, sprat, squid, sudak, tench, torsk, trout, tunny, twait, witch.

(6) alevin, allice, baggit, barbel, beluga, bichir, blenny, bonito, bounce, bowfin, braize, burbot, caplin, cockle, conger, cuttle, darter, dipnoi, doctor, dorado, elleck, finnan, ganoid, goramy, grilse, groper, gunnel, gurnet, kipper, launce, limpet, medusa, milter, minnow, morgay, mullet, mussel, nerite, oyster, plaice, pollan, porgie, poulpe, quahog, red-eye, remora, robalo, salmon, samlet, sardel, sargus, saurel, scampi, sea-bat, sea-bun, sea-cat, sea-cow, sea-dog, sea-eel, sea-egg, sea-fox, sea-hog, sea-orb, sea-owl, sea-pig, sea-rat, sephen, shanny, shiner, shrimp, sucker, tarpon, tautog, tomcod, turbot, twaite, urchin, weever, winkle, wrasse, zander.

(7) abalone, acaleph, actinia, alewife, anchovy, anemone, asterid, bergylt, bivalve, bloater, bummalo, capelin, catfish, cichlid, codfish, codling, crucian, dogfish, echinus, escolar, fiddler, finback, finnock, garfish, garpike, gourami, grouper, grunter, gudgeon, gurnard, gwyniad, haddock, hagfish, halibut, herling, herring, ice fish, lampern, lamprey, lobster, mahseer, mollusc, monodon, mooneye, morrhua, mudfish, oarfish, octopus, ophiura, piddock, pigfish, pin-fish, piranha, pollack, polypus, pomfret, quahaug, quinnat, red-bass, red-drum, red-fish, rhytina, ripsack, ronchil, ronquil, rotchet, sand-dab, sand-eel, sardine, sargina, sawfish, scallop, schelly, scollop, scomber,

list continued over

sea-bass, sea-cock, sea-dace, sea-fish, sea-lily, sea-luce, sea-mink, sea-pert, sea-pike, sea-rose, sea-ruff, sea-slug, sea-wife, sea-wolf, sillago, skipper, skulpin, snapper, sockeye, spur-dog, sterlet, sunfish, torpedo, trepang, tubfish, vendace, vestlet, whip-ray, whiting.

(8) albacore, billfish, bluefish, boarfish, brisling, bummaloe, clupeoid, coalfish, crayfish, dragonet, earshell, escallop, flatfish, flounder, forktail, frogfish, gilt-head, goldfish, grayling, lumpfish, lungfish, mackerel, monkfish, nautilus, pickerel, pilchard, rockfish, sail-fish, salmonet, sandfish, sea-adder, sea-bream, sea-devil, sea-perch, sea-robin, sea-shark, sea-snail, sea-squid, sea-tench, sea-trout, siluroid, skipjack, solaster, sparling, starfish, stingray, sturgeon, thrasher, univalve, zoanthus.

(9) amberjack, angelfish, barracuda, blackfish, bulltrout, devilfish, jellyfish, porbeagle, spearfish, spoonbill, stargazer, stockfish, stonefish, swordfish, whitefish, wobbegong.

(10) angelshark, anglerfish, archerfish, barramundi, butterfish, candlefish, coelacanth, cuttlefish, demoiselle, dragonfish, fingerling, flutemouth, flying-fish, hammerhead, needlefish, paddlefish, parrotfish, periwinkle, sand-dollar, sandhopper, suckerfish.

(11) hippocampus, stickleback,

(2 words) balloon fish, basking shark, blue shark, brown trout, carpet shark, conger eel, dolly varden, electric eel, electric ray, globe fish, guitar fish, miller's thumb, pilot fish, rainbow trout, thresher shark, tiger shark, trigger fish, zebra shark.

fit I *adj* 1 (3) apt; (4) able, meet; (5) ready, right; (6) proper, seemly, suited; (7) capable, correct, fitting; (8) suitable; (11) appropriate; 2 (4) hale, well; (5) sound; (6) strong; (7) healthy; (2+ words) in (good) form; in (good) shape; II *n* (4) bout; (5) burst, spasm, spell; (6) attack; (7) seizure; (8) outbreak, outburst, paroxysm; (9) transport; (10) convulsion; III *v* 1 (2) go; (4) suit; (5) agree, match, tally; (6) belong; (7) conform; (8) dovetail; (9) harmonise (*or* harmonize); (10) correspond; 2 (5) adapt, alter, shape; (6) adjust, change, tailor; (7) fashion; 3 (5) equip; (7) **install**.

five *cryptic* Roman numeral V.

fix I *v* 1 (3) pin, tie; (4) bind, glue, join, nail, root; (5) embed, plant, rivet, stick; (6) anchor, attach, cement, couple, fasten, secure; (7) install; (9) establish; 2 (4) mend; (6) repair; (7) rectify, restore; 3 (6) settle; (7) **arrange**, specify; (8) organise (*or* organize); (9) determine, establish; II *n* (4) bind; (6) plight; (7) dilemma; (8) quandary; (10) difficulty.

flag I *n* 1 (4) jack; (6) banner, ensign; (7) colours, pennant; (8) standard, streamer; 2 (4) iris; 3 (9) flagstone (paving stone); II *v* (3) sag, (4) fade, fail, flop, sink, tire, wilt; (5) abate, droop, faint, slump, weary; (6) falter, lessen; (7) decline.

flat I *adj* 1 (4) even; (5) flush, level, plane, prone; (6) smooth, steady, supine; (7) regular, uniform; (8) constant, parallel; (9) unvarying; (10) horizontal; 2 (4) dull; (6) **boring**; 3 (6) direct; (8) emphatic, straight; (9) downright; (11) categorical, unequivocal, unqualified; 4 (8) deflated; (9) punctured; II *n* (8) basement, tenement; (9) apartment, penthouse.

flatter *v* (4) fawn; (5) court, creep, toady; (6) cajole, humour, praise; (7) adulate, wheedle; (9) brown-nose, sweet-talk; (10) compliment; (2+ words) butter up, curry favour, play up to.

flattery *n* (6) praise; (7) blarney, fawning, flannel; (8) cajolery, toadyism; (9) adulation, servility; (10) sycophancy; (11) compliments.

flaunt *v* (4) show; (5) prove; (6) expose, parade, reveal; (7) display, exhibit; (8) flourish, manifest; (2 words) show off.

flaw *n* (3) bug; (4) spot; (5) error, fault, taint; (6) defect; (7) blemish, failing, frailty, mistake; (8) weakness; (10) deficiency, inadequacy; (11) shortcoming.

fleet I *n* (5) ships; (6) armada; (8) flotilla; (9) task-force; **II** *see* **fast**; **III** *cryptic* letters RN or USN.

flexible I *adj* (5) bendy; (6) pliant; (7) elastic, plastic, pliable; (8) amenable, bendable, stretchy; (9) adaptable, malleable; (10) adjustable; (13) accommodating; **II** *cryptic* ANAGRAM CUE.

flourish I *v* **1** (4) wave; (5) shake, swing, twirl, vaunt, wield; (6) parade; (7) display; (8) brandish; **2** (3) wax; (4) grow; (5) bloom; (6) flower, thrive; (7) blossom, develop, prosper, succeed; (8) increase; **II** *n* (8) ornament; (10) decoration.

flout *v* (4) defy, jeer, mock; (5) break, scoff, scorn; (7) disobey, violate; (9) disregard; (10) disrespect.

flower I *n & v* (3) bud; (5) bloom; (7) blossom; **II** *n* (4) best; (5) elite; (6) choice; **III** *cryptic* river or name of river – *see* **river** – also fountain, tide, spring *etc.*

NAMES OF FLOWERS

(3) may, rue.

(4) arum, flag, flax, iris, lily, musk, pink.

(5) aspic, aster, briar, broom, calla, canna, daisy, dilly, gowan, hosta, lilac, lotus, lupin, ox-eye, oxlip, pansy, peony, phlox, poppy, stock, tulip, viola, yucca, yulan.

(6) azalea, camass, cistus, clover, crocus, cyphel, dahlia, funkia, jasmin, kowhai, mallow, mimosa, moutan, nerine, nuphar, orchid, scilla, shasta, squill, tagete, thrift, violet, yarrow, zinnia.

(7) aconite, althaea, anemone, banksia, begonia, campion, cup-rose, dog-rose, freesia, fuchsia, gentian, gladwyn, godetia, honesty, jasmine, jonquil, kingcup, lobelia, nigella, petunia, picotee, primula, rambler, rampion, seringa, shirley, syringa, tea-rose, vanilla, verbena, vervain.

---

(8) agrimony, amaranth, asphodel, auricula, bluebell, buddleia, camellia, clematis, cyclamen, daffodil, dianthus, dog-brier, foxglove, gardenia, geranium, gillenia, girasole, gloxinia, gold-lily, harebell, hawthorn, hibiscus, hyacinth, japonica, larkspur, lavender, lent-lily, magnolia, marigold, myosotis, noisette, oleander, plumbago, primrose, snowdrop, sweet-pea, tuberose, turnsole, wistaria, wisteria, woodbine.

(9) buttercup, campanula, candytuft, carnation, cineraria, coltsfoot, columbine, dandelion, edelweiss, eglantine, forsythia, gladiolus, goldenrod, hydrangea, lavateria, narcissus, speedwell, sunflower.

(10) cornflower, delphinium, frangipani, gypsophila, marguerite, montbretia, nasturtium, pennyroyal, periwinkle, poinsettia, polyanthus, snapdragon, wallflower.

(11) antirrhinum, forget-me-not, gillyflower, honeysuckle, marshmallow, stephanotis.

(12) rhododendron.

(13) chrysanthemum.

(14) bougainvillaea.

(2+ words) Aaron's rod, busy Lizzie, busy Lizzy, Canterbury bell, Guernsey lily, lady's mantle, love in the mist, morning glory, red hot poker, sweet william.

fluorine *cryptic* abbreviated as F.

fly I *v* **1** (4) soar, wing; (5) glide, hover, pilot; (6) aviate; **2** (2) go; (4) dash, flee, race, rush, tear, zoom; (6) escape; **II** *n* **1** (6) insect; (10) bluebottle; **2** type of **carriage**; **III** (5) aware, smart; (6) shrewd; (7) cunning.

folio *cryptic* abbreviated as F or FO.

follow *v* **1** (4) hunt, tail; (5) chase, track, trail; (6) escort, pursue, shadow; (9) accompany; **2** (7) replace, succeed; (8) supplant; (9) supersede, (2 words) come after; **3** (5) arise, ensue; (6) **result**; (7)

develop; **4** (4) heed, mind, obey; (6) comply; (7) observe; **5** (10) **understand**.

follower I *n* **1** (3) **fan**; (7) fancier; (8) disciple; (9) supporter; **2** (7) pursuer, tracker; II *cryptic* the letter of the alphabet following the one referred or alluded to, as in: 'Urge on Jesus's first follower on a horse' (3) = egg (second letter of 'Jesus' – horse = GG); or in: 'Napoleon's second follower had to dash into skirmish' (5) = brush (B follows A second letter of 'Napoleon').

food *n* (4) diet, eats, fare, grub, menu, nosh; (5) scoff; (6) fodder (7) rations; (8) eatables, victuals; (9) nutriment; (10) provisions; (11) comestibles; *see also* **cheese, dish, meat** *etc*.

fool I *n* **1** (3) ass, mug, nit; (4) clot, dope, dupe, twit; (5) chump, clown, dunce, idiot, ninny, twerp, wally; (6) dimwit, jester, sucker, stooge, victim; (7) fathead, halfwit; (8) imbecile; (9) blockhead; (10) nincompoop, simpleton; **2** a type of crushed fruit pudding. II *v* (2) do; (3) con, kid; (4) dupe, gull, have, hoax; (5) abuse, cheat, trick; (6) betray, delude; (7) beguile, deceive, defraud, swindle, two-time; (8) hoodwink; (9) bamboozle; (11) double-cross; (2+ words) have on, pull somebody's leg, take for a ride, take in.

foot I *n* **1** *see* **base** I **1**; **2** for poetic foot *see* **metre**; II **foot it** (4) **walk**; (5) **dance**; III *cryptic* abbreviated as FT.

football *n*

PLAYERS AND POSITIONS

(4) back; (6) goalie, keeper, winger; (7) forward, striker; (8) fullback, left back, left half, midfield, wingback; (9) right back, right half; (10) centre back, centre half, goalkeeper, inside left, midfielder; (11) inside right, outside left, (12) outside right.

FOOTBALL TEAMS (UK)

Team – Nickname – Ground

Aberdeen – Dons – Pittodrie Park
Arsenal – Gunners – Highbury
Barnet – Bees – Underhill Stadium

Bournemouth – Cherries – Dean Court
Bradford – Bantams – Valley Parade
Brighton & Hove Albion – Seagulls – Goldstone Ground
Bolton Wanderers – Trotters – Reebok Stadium
Bristol City – Reds (Robins) – Ashton Gate
Cardiff City – Bluebirds – Ninian Park
Charlton Athletic – Addicks – The Valley
Chelsea – Blues (Pensioners) – Stamford Bridge
Coventry City – Sky Blues – Highfield Road
Crystal Palace – Palace (Glaziers) – Selhurst Park
Derby County – Rams – Pride Park
Everton – Blues (Toffees) – Goodison Park
Hull City – Tigers – Boothferry Park
Leicester City – Foxes – Filbert Street
Liverpool – Reds – Anfield
Luton Town – Hatters – Kenilworth Road
Manchester United – Red Devils – Old Trafford
Mansfield Town – Stags – Field Mill
Middlesbrough – Boro' – Riverside Stadium
Newcastle United – Magpies – St James's Park
Northampton – Cobblers – Sixfields Stadium
Norwich – Canaries – Carrow Road
Notts County – Magpies – Meadow Lane
Portsmouth – Pompey – Fratton Park
Sheffield United – Blades – Bramall Lane
Sheffield Wednesday – Owls – Hillsborough
Southampton – Saints – The Dell
Torquay – Gulls – Plainmoor
Tottenhan Hotspur – Spurs – White Hart Lane
Watford – Hornets – Vicarage Road
West Ham United – Hammers – Upton Park
Wolverhampton Wanderers – Wolves – Molineux

FOOTBALL TEAMS (EUROPE)

(4) Ajax (Holl.), (AC) Roma (It.).

(5) Lazio (It.), (AC) Milan (It.), Inter (It.), (FC) Porto (Port.), (FC) Malmo (Swed.).

(6) Monaco (Fr.), Napoli (It.).

(7) Benfica (Port.).

(8) Juventus (It.), Valencia (Sp.).

(9) Barcelona (Sp.), Feyenoord (Holl.), Sampdoria (It.).

(10) Gothenburg (Swed.), Olympiakos (Gr.).

(13) Panathinaikos (Gr.).

(2 words) (10) Dynamo Kiev (Ukr.), Inter Milan (It.), Real Madrid (Sp.).

(12) Bayern Munich (Germ.), Moscow Dynamo (Russ.), PSV Eindhoven (Holl.).

(13) Moscow Spartak, Spartak Moscow (Russ.).

(14) Atletico Bilbao (Sp.), Atletico Madrid (Sp.), Paris St Germain (Fr.), Sporting Lisbon (Port.).

(15) Red Star Belgrade (Yug.), Steava Bucharest (Rom.).

(16) Borussia Dortmund (Ger.),

FOOTBALL TEAMS (US)

Home	Name
Atlanta	Falcons
Baltimore	Colts
Buffalo	Bills
Chicago	Bears
Cincinnati	Bengals
Cleveland	Browns
Dallas	Cowboys
Denver	Broncos
Detroit	Lions
Green Bay	Packers
Houston	Oilers
Kansas City	Chiefs
Los Angeles	Raiders
Los Angeles	Rams
Miami	Dolphins
Minnesota	Vikings
New England	Patriots
New Orleans	Saints
New York	Giants
New York	Jets
Philadelphia	Eagles
Pittsburgh	Steelers
St Louis	Cardinals
San Diego	Chargers
San Francisco	49-ers
Seattle	Seahawks
Washington	Redskins

footwear *n see* **shoe**.

forbid *v* (3) ban, bar; (4) deny, veto; (5) block; (6) oppose, outlaw, refuse, reject; (7) inhibit, prevent; (8) disallow, preclude, prohibit; (9) interdict, proscribe; (2 words) rule out, turn down.

force I *n* **1** (5) drive, might, power; (6) effort, impact, stress; (7) impetus; (8) emphasis, strength; (9) intensity; **2** (6) duress; (8) coercion, pressure, violence; (10) compulsion, constraint; **3** (4) army, unit; (5) corps, troop; (8) division; (9) battalion; **II** *v* **1** (4) make; (5) press; (6) coerce, compel, impose, oblige; (7) inflict; (8) bulldoze; (9) constrain, pressgang; (10) pressurise (*or* pressurize); (11) necessitate; **2** (4) cram, push; (5) drive, lever, prise (*or* prize), wrest; (6) propel, thrust, wrench.

forget I *v* (4) omit; (6) ignore; (7) neglect; (8) overlook; (9) disregard; **II** *cryptic* omit a letter, letters, or a word.

forgive *v* (5) remit; (6) acquit, excuse, exempt, pardon; (7) absolve, condone, explain, justify, release; (8) mitigate, overlook; (9) discharge, exculpate, exonerate.

form I *n & v* (4) cast, make; (5) build, frame, model, mould, shape; (6) design, format; (7) outline, pattern; (9) structure; **II** *n* **1** (4) kind; (6) manner, nature; (6) system; **2** (5) paper, sheet; (8) document; (13) questionnaire; **3** (6) health; (9) condition; **4** (4) year; (5) class, grade; **5** (5) bench; **III** *v* (7) compose; (8) comprise; (10) constitute; **IV form of** *cryptic* ANAGRAM CUE.

former I *adj* (2) ex; (3) old; (4) past; (5) first, prior; (6) bygone; (7) ancient, one-time, quondam; (8) previous, sometime; (9) erstwhile; ‖ *cryptic* **1** (5) maker; (7) moulder, potter etc; **2** (5) pupil; (7) student; **3** refers to an older equivalent of a modern word, as in: 'For his own well-being, the former has mixed with the Spanish' (6) = health (hath and el combined).

forte *cryptic* abbreviated as F.

fortify *v* (5) brace, shore; (6) secure, (7) protect; (8) buttress; (9) reinforce; (10) strengthen.

FORTIFICATIONS

(3) dun, sap.

(4) berm, dike, dyke, fort, keep, moat, wall.

(5) fosse, motte, redan, talus, walls.

(6) abatis, bailey, donjon, escarp, gabion, glacis, merlon, trench, turret, vallum.

(7) barrier, bastion, battery, bulwark, citadel, curtain, flanker, foxhole, mirador, outwork, parados, parapet, pill-box, rampart, ravelin, redoubt.

(8) barbette, barbicon, bartisan, casemate, defilade, fortress, martello, parallel, platform, stockade.

(9) barricade, earthwork, fortalice, pontlevis, revetment.

(10) battlement, blockhouse, breastwork, drawbridge, epaulement, portcullis, stronghold.

(11) strongpoint.

(12) counterscarp.

(13) cheval-de-frise, machicolation.

(2 words) martello tower.

---

forward I *adv* (2) on; (5) ahead; (6) onward; ‖ *adj* **1** (4) fore, head; (5) first, front; (7) leading; (8) advanced, foremost; **2** (4) bold, pert; (5) brash, fresh, pushy; (6) brazen, cheeky; (8) impudent; (10) precocious; (11) impertinent; ‖‖ *v* **1** (4) post, send, ship; (8) dispatch; **2** (3) aid; (4) back, help; (5) hurry, speed; (6) assist, foster, hasten; (7) advance, further, promote; (9) encourage; (10) facilitate; ‖V *n* (4) prop; (7) striker.

found *v* **1** (4) form; (5) begin, build, endow, erect, plant, start; (7) install; (8) initiate, organise (*or* organize); (9) establish, institute, originate; (10) inaugurate; (2 words) set up; **2** (4) base, rest; (5) prove; (6) ground, settle; (7) certify, confirm; (9) establish; (11) demonstrate; (12) substantiate; **3** *past tense of* find.

fourth *cryptic* the fourth letter of a word in the clue, *e.g.* Brahms' Fourth = H.

fox I *n* **1** (*male* dog, *female* vixen, *young* cub, *group* skulk, *home* earth) (6) Russel; (7) Reynard; **2** a cunning or sly person; ‖ *v* **1** (4) fool; (5) trick; (6) baffle, outwit; (7) **confuse**; **2** (9) discolour (as paper may acquire brown spots with age).

franc I *n* French unit of currency; ‖ *cryptic* abbreviated as FR.

France *cryptic* abbreviated as F.

frank I *adj* (4) open; (5) blunt, overt, plain; (6) candid, direct; honest; (8) explicit, straight, truthful; (9) downright, outspoken; (10) forthright; ‖ *v* (4) mark; (5) stamp; (6) cancel.

frantic *adj* (5) upset; (7) anxious; (8) agitated; (10) distracted, distraught, distressed, hysterical; (11) overwrought; (2 words) beside oneself, het up, worked up.

freak I *n* **1** (5) crank; (6) mutant, oddity, weirdo; (7) monster, oddball; (9) character, eccentric; (11) monstrosity; (13) nonconformist; **2** *see* **fan**; **3** (4) whim; (5) quirk, twist; (6) oddity, vagary; (7) anomaly, caprice; (9) curiosity; (10) aberration; (11) abnormality; ‖ *adj* (3) odd; (5) fluky, queer; (6) chance; (7) bizarre, strange; (8) aberrant, abnormal, atypical, surprise; (10) fortuitous, unexpected; (11) exceptional; (13) unpredictable.

free I *adj* **1** (5) clear, loose; (7) unbound; (2 words) at large, at liberty; **2** (6) gratis; (2+ words) for nothing, no charge, on the house, without charge; **3** (5) idle; (5) empty, spare; (6) vacant; (9) available; (10) unoccupied; **4** (6) lavish; (7) liberal; (8) **generous**; ‖ *v* **1** (4) save; (5) loose, untie; (6) rescue, unbind; (7) deliver, release, unchain, unleash; (8) liberate, unfasten; (10) emancipate; **2** (3) rid; (5) clear; (6) exempt; (7) relieve; (8) unburden; **III** free *or* freely *cryptic* ANAGRAM CUE.

freedom *n* (5) right; (6) leeway; (7) liberty, licence, release; (8) autonomy, immunity, impunity; (9) exemption, privilege; (11) deliverance; (12) emancipation, independence.

French *cryptic* use a (usually simple) French word as part of the solution, especially 'a French' = UN or UNE and 'the French' = LE, LA, or LES. To take another example: 'Student's absent and French town seems really horrible' (4) = vile (town in French = ville, minus L).

Frenchman *cryptic* letter M (monsieur).

Frenchwoman *cryptic* letters MME (madame) or MLLE (mademoiselle) – the latter also possibly prompted by French girl.

frenzy I *n* **1** (5) mania; (7) turmoil; (8) hysteria; (9) agitation; **2** (3) fit; (4) fury, rage; (5) spasm; (9) transport; (10) convulsion; **II** frenzy *or* frenzied *cryptic* ANAGRAM CUE.

Frey *Norse myth* the god of fertility, crops, who made the sun and moon to shine. The brother of **Freya** and also known as **Freyr**.

Freya *Norse myth* the goddess of love and the night, brother of **Frey**, often identified as a wife of Odin with **Frigga**.

Friday *n* sixth day of the week, named after Frigga, abbreviated as F, FR, or FRI.

friend *n* (3) pal; (4) ally, chum, mate; (5) buddy, china, crony; (6) patron; (7) comrade, partner; (8) intimate; (9) companion, confidant, supporter.

friendly *adj* (4) kind, maty, warm; (5) matey, pally (6) genial, kindly; (7) affable, amiable; (10) supportive; (11) neighbourly, sympathetic.

Frigga *Norse myth* the wife of **Odin** and chief goddess in the Scandinavian pantheon. The goddess of married love,

fertility, the hearth and the home. Friday is named after her.

fright *n* (4) fear, funk; (5) alarm, dread, panic, scare; (6) qualms, terror; (7) anxiety; (8) distress; (9) agitation, cowardice; (10) foreboding, misgivings; (11) trepidation; (12) apprehension.

frighten *v* (5) alarm, daunt, panic, scare; (6) dismay; (7) petrify, startle, terrify, unnerve; (9) terrorise (*or* terrorize); (10) intimidate.

from *cryptic* **1** HIDDEN WORD CUE, as in: 'Took fright from hard reading matter' (5) = dread; **2** ANAGRAM CUE.

fruit *n* (4) crop; (5) issue, yield; (6) result, reward; (7) product, revenue.

TYPES OF FRUIT

(3) fig, haw, hip, nut.

(4) akee, crab, date, doum, gean, kaki, kiwi, lime, pear, plum, sloe, tuna, ugli.

(5) ackee, acorn, apple, berry, gourd, grape, guava, lemon, logan, mango, melon, morel, morus, olive, papaw, peach.

(6) ananas, banana, cherry, citron, codlin, damson, drupel, durian, litchi, loquat, lucama, lychee, mammee, medlar, muscat, orange, papaya, pawpaw, pippin, pisang, pomelo, pumelo, punica, quince, raisin, ramoon, rennet, russet, sharon, tampor, tomato, wampee.

(7) apricot, avocado, bouchet, bullace, coconut, codling, costard, cumquat, currant, genipap, golding, kumquat, leechee, morello, pomeroy, pompion, pumpkin, (rhubarb), rose-hip, ruddock, saffron, satsuma, shallon, sultana, syringa, tangelo, winesap.

(8) bergamot, bilberry, blenheim, bromelia, burgamot, cadillac, clematis, faeberry, fenberrry, japonica, mandarin, marigold, mulberry, muscatel, pearmain, plantain, prunello, shaddock, sweetsop, xylocarp. *list continued over*

---

(9) nectarine, ortanique, persimmon, pineapple, raspberry, tangerine.

(10) blackberry, gooseberry, loganberry, mangosteen, redcurrant, strawberry.

(11) boysenberry.

(12) blackcurrant, whitecurrant.

(2 words) custard apple, sugar apple.

fuel *v* (3) fan; (4) feed, fire; (5) stoke; (6) incite; (7) inflame; (9) encourage.

TYPES OF FUEL

(3) gas, oil.

(4) coal, coke, peat, wood.

(5) avgas, calor®, meths.

(6) benzol, butane, diesel, hexane, octane, oil-gas, petrol.

(7) methane, propane.

(8) gasoline, kerosene, kerosine, methanol, paraffin, triptane.

(9) acetylene, benzoline, petroleum, steam-coal.

(10) anthracite.

(2 words) aviation spirit, bituminous coal, calor gas®, carburetted gas.

funny *adj* 1 *see* **comic**; 2 *see* **odd**.

fur *n* (4) coat, hide, pelt.

TYPES OF FUR

(3) fox.

(4) lamb, lynx, mink, seal.

(5) fitch (polecat), otter, sable.

(6) beaver, ermine, fisher, jaguar, marten, nutria, rabbit.

(7) leopard, miniver, muskrat, opossum, raccoon.

(8) squirrel.

(10) chinchilla.

Furies *Gk myth* three avenging godesses who relentlessly pursued wrongdoers. Their names were **Alecto**, **Megaera** and **Tisiphone**.

furious *adj* (3) mad; (4) wild; (5) angry, livid; (6) fierce, fuming, raging, stormy; (7) enraged, frantic, violent; (8) incensed; (10) infuriated; (3 words) up in arms.

furnish *v* (3) rig; (4) give; (5) equip, grant, stock; (6) afford, supply; (7) present, provide.

furniture *n* (8) fitments, fittings, movables; (9) equipment; (11) furnishings.

PIECES OF FURNITURE

(3) bed, cot, pew.

(4) bunk, crib, desk, form, seat, sofa.

(5) bench, chair, couch, divan, stand, stool, suite, table.

(6) air-bed, box-bed, buffet, bureau, carver, cradle, drawer, locker, lowboy, pouffe, put-u-up, rocker, settee, settle, teapoy, tester, throne, toilet.

(7) armoire, box-seat, bunk-bed, cabinet, camp-bed, charpoy, commode, console, counter, hammock, hassock, leg-rest, lounger, ottoman, sofa-bed, tallboy, truckle, what-not.

(8) armchair, bassinet, bedstead, bookcase, carry-cot, cupboard, fauteuil, hatstand, loo-table, loveseat, recliner, tabouret, wardrobe, water-bed.

(9) camp-stool, coatstand, davenport, deck-chair, easy-chair, footstool, garderobe, hallstand, headboard, palanquin, pier-table, sideboard, side-table, washstand, workbench, worktable.

(10) chiffonier, escritoire, feather-bed, four-poster, music-stool, night-chair, night-stool, piano-stool, secretaire, tea-trolley, truckle-bed, window-seat.

(11) coffee-table, dining-table, dinner-table, reading-desk, swivel-chair, toilet-table, writing-desk.

(12) chaise-longue, chesterfield, console-table, writing-table.

list continued over

(2+ words) bedside table, chest of drawers, cheval mirror, filing cabinet, folding chair, gate-leg(ged) table, occasional table, rocking chair, three-piece suite.

FURNITURE MAKERS

Adam, Chippendale, Hepplewhite, Kent, Sheraton.

---

fury *n* (3) ire; (4) rage; (5) anger, wrath; (6) frenzy; (7) madness, passion; (8) ferocity, violence.

fuss I *n* (3) row; (4) flap, stir, to-do; (5) hoo-ha; (6) bother, bustle, furore, hassle; (7) fluster, palaver, trouble; (9) commotion; (10) excitement; II *v* (4) flap, fret; (5) worry; (6) bother.

fussy *adj* 1 (5) picky; (6) choosy; (7) finicky; (10) fastidious, particular, pernickety, scrupulous; 2 (4) busy; (5) fancy; (6) ornate; (9) cluttered.

G

G *abbrev* German, a grand (1000), key (music), note (music).

g *abbrev* gallon, giga, gram, gravity.

gadget *n* (5) gizmo, thing; (6) device; (7) gimmick; (9) appliance; (11) contrivance.

Gaea *Gk myth* the earth goddess who was the mother of the **Titans, Cyclops** and other giants by **Uranus** – also called **Ge** or **Gaia**.

gag I *v* (4) curb; (5) check; (6) censor, muzzle, stifle; (7) silence; (8) suppress; II *n* (3) pun; (4) jest, joke, quip; (5) crack; (8) one-liner; (9) witticism.

Gaia I *Gk myth see* **Gaea**; II *ecol.* a name given to the earth or the biosphere and all its inhabitants considered as one vast self-regulating organism in accordance with the theories of James Lovelock.

gain I *v* 1 (3) get, net, win; (4) make, reap; (5) clear, earn, gross; (6) obtain, secure; (7) achieve, acquire, realise (*or* realize); 2 (5) reach; (6) arrive; (8) approach, overtake; (2+ words) catch up on, level with; II *n* 1 (6) **income**, profit, return; (7) revenue; (8) earnings, proceeds; 2 (4) rise; (6) growth; (7) advance, headway; (8) increase, progress.

Galahad *fict.* a Knight of the Round Table, the son of Sir **Lancelot**, the purest and noblest of all King Arthur's knights (Tennyson makes him say 'my strength is as the strength of ten because my heart is pure'), the one who was able to sit in the siege perilous and who eventually completed the quest for the **Holy Grail**.

Galatea *Gk myth* 1 a sea nymph in love with the beautiful mortal **Acis** but herself loved by the Cyclops **Polyphemus**. Polyphemus killed Acis and Galatea returned to the sea; 2 the statue carved by **Pygmalion** and brought to life at his request by **Aphrodite**.

gallant I *adj* 1 (4) bold; (5) **brave**; (6) heroic, plucky; (7) defiant, valiant; (8) fearless, intrepid; (9) audacious, dauntless; (10) courageous; (11) adventurous; 2 (6) polite; (10) chivalrous; (11) gentlemanly; II *n* (5) lover; (2 words) lady's man.

gallery *n* 1 *theatre* (4) gods; (7) balcony; 2 (4) show; (10) exhibition.

FAMOUS ART GALLERIES

(4) Fogg (Boston USA), Tate (London, Liverpool, St Ives).

(5) Brera (Milan), Freer (Washington), Pitti (Florence), Prado (Madrid).

(6) Dahlem (Berlin), Louvre (Paris), Uffizi (Florence), Walker (Liverpool).

(7) Academy (Florence), Dulwich (London), Hayward (London).

(8) National (London).

(9) Accademia (Florence), Albertina (*or* Albertine) (Vienna), Ashmolean (Oxford), Cloisters (New York), Courtauld (London), Hermitage (St Petersburg), Tretiakov (Moscow).

(10) Guggenheim (New York), Gulbenkian (Lisbon).

(11) Fitzwilliam (Cambridge), Rijksmuseum (Amsterdam).

(12) Metropolitan (New York).

---

game I *n* 1 (4) play; (5) sport; (7) pastime; (9) amusement; (10) recreation; 2 (5) event, match, round; (6) partie; (7) contest; 3 animals hunted for sport; II *adj* 1 (5) eager; ready; (7) willing; 2 (5) **brave**, (6) plucky; (8) spirited.

GAMES

see also **sport**

(2) go.

(3) gin, loo, nap, nim, pit, tag, taw, tig.

(4) brag, crib, dice, faro, I-spy, keno, ludo, ruff, skat, snap, solo.

(5) bingo, booby, bride, cheat, chess, craps, darts, house, jacks, lotto, ombre, pairs, poker, rummy, whist.

(6) beetle, chemmy, Cluedo®, crambo, donkey, écarté, euchre, fantan, hazard, hearts, piquet, sevens, Tetris®.

(7) auction, bezique, canasta, cassino, conkers, diabolo, forfeit, mah-jong, marbles, pontoon, primero, tombola.

(8) baccarat, charades, checkers, contract, cribbage, dominoes, draughts, freecell, mah-jongg, Monopoly®, napoleon, patience, pinochle, roulette, Scrabble®, Subbuteo®.

(9) bagatelle, blackjack, newmarket, quadrille, solitaire, vingt-et-un.

(10) backgammon, jack-straws, spillikins.

(11) chase-the-ace, tiddlywinks.

(12) blow-football, consequences, housey-housey, knuckle-bones.

(13) blindman's-buff, snip-snap-snorp.

(14) hunt-the-slipper, hunt-the-thimble, shove-halfpenny.

(15) catch-as-catch-can.

(2+ words) auction bridge, chemin de fer, chinese checkers, contract bridge, Donkey Kong®, dumb crambo, gin rummy, knockout whist, musical chairs, old maid, postman's knock, solo whist, three-card brag, three-card monty, Tomb Raider®, Trivial Pursuit®.

GAME ANIMALS AND BIRDS

(4) buck, deer, duck, hare.

(5) quail, snipe.

(6) grouse, rabbit.

(8) pheasant, woodcock.

(9) partridge.

G & S *see* **Gilbert and Sullivan**.

gang *n* (3) lot, mob, set; (4) band, crew, pack, ring, team; (5) crowd, group, squad; (6) circle, clique; (7) coterie.

gangster *n* (4) hood, thug; (5) crook, heavy, rough, tough; (7) hoodlum, mobster, ruffian; (8) criminal; (9) racketeer.

NOTORIOUS GANGSTERS

Al Capone, Bonnie and Clyde, Bonnie Parker (of Bonnie and Clyde), Bugsy Malone *fict.*, Bugsy Siegel, Clyde Barrow (of Bonnie and Clyde), Dutch Schultz, John Dillinger (Public Enemy Number 1), Legs Diamond, Lucky Luciano, Machine-gun Kelly, Pretty Boy Floyd.

Ganymede *Gk myth* a beautiful youth who was seized on by **Zeus** in the form of an eagle and carried away to Mount Olympus, where he became the cup-bearer to the gods.

gaol *see* **prison**.

gap *n* **1** (4) hole, void; (5) blank, break, chink, cleft, crack, space; (6) breach, divide; **2** (4) lull; (5) pause; (8) interval; (9) interlude; (12) intermission, interruption; **3** (4) rift; (9) disparity; (10) difference, divergence.

garble **I** *v* (6) jumble, muddle; (7) scramble; (2 words) mix up; **II** **garble** *or* **garbled** *cryptic* ANAGRAM CUE.

Garibaldi **I** *hist.* a popular leader who played a major role in liberating and unifying Italy. His followers were known as 'red shirts'; **II** a type of **biscuit**.

gas **I** *n* (4) fuel, wind (US); (6) petrol; **II** *v* *see* **chatter**.

GASES

(4) neon.

(5) argon, niton, ozone, radon, sarin, xenon.

(6) butane, ethane, helium, oxygen, thoron.

(7) ammonia, krypton, methane, propane.

(8) chlorine, firedamp, hydrogen, nitrogen, phosgene.

(9) acetylene.

(2 words) carbon dioxide, carbon monoxide, coal gas, laughing gas, marsh gas, mustard gas, natural gas, sewer gas, tear gas.

gate *n* 1 (4) door, exit; (6) access, wicket; (7) barrier, opening, postern; (8) entrance; 2 (5) crowd; (10) attendance, spectators; 3 (4) take; (7) takings; (8) receipts.

gauge I *v* (5) count, guess, value; (6) assess, reckon; (7) compute, measure; (8) estimate, evaluate; (9) calculate; II *n* (4) bore, norm, size; (5) meter, model, width; (7) calibre, pattern; (8) standard; (9) benchmark, criterion, indicator, yardstick.

Ge *see* **Gaea**.

gear *n* 1 (3) cog; 2 (3) kit, rig; (5) stuff, tools; (6) tackle, things; (9) apparatus, equipment; 3 (4) togs; (5) dress, get-up; (6) outfit; (7) clothes; (8) clothing.

Gehenna *Bible* a place of burning or fire – originally a valley where sacrifices were offered to Baal and Moloch, it came to be synonymous with hell.

gem *n* (5) jewel, prize, stone; (8) treasure; (11) masterpiece.

GEMS

(3) jet.

(4) jade, onyx, opal, ruby, sard.

(5) agate, amber, beryl, lapis, pearl, topaz.

(6) garnet, jasper, quartz, scarab, zircon.

(7) crystal, diamond, jacinth, peridot, smaragd.

(8) amethyst, baguette, cabochon, diamante, fire-opal, hyacinth, sapphire, sardonyx.

(9) carbuncle, cornelian, girandole, marcasite, moonstone, solitaire, turquoise.

(10) aquamarine, bloodstone, chalcedony, chrysolite, rhinestone.

(11) chrysoberyl

(2 words) cat's eye, lapis lazuli.

Gemini I *astrol. & astron.* the constellation that is the third sign of the zodiac; also known as the Twins or Dioscuri, the twins in question being Castor and Pollux, the sons of **Zeus** and **Leda**; II *hist.* a two-seater American space capsule or the programme to put capsules of this type into earth orbit.

gen *see* **information**.

general I *adj* (5) broad, usual, vague; (6) common, global; (7) blanket, overall; (8) standard, sweeping; (9) inclusive, prevalent, universal; (10) indefinite, unspecific, widespread; (12) comprehensive; II *n* high-ranking military officer.

FAMOUS GENERALS

(3) Lee (Robert E., US), Ney (Marshal, Fr.).

(4) Foch, (Fr.), Haig, (UK), Slim (UK).

(5) Dayan (Moshe, Israel), Grant (Ulysses S., US), Wolfe (UK).

(6) Custer (US), Gordon (UK), Joffre (Fr.), Patton (US), Rommel (Ger.), Zhukov (Marshal, USSR).

(7) Allenby (UK), Blücher (Ger.), Roberts (Lord, UK), Sherman (US).

(8) Burnside (US), de Gaulle (Fr.), Galtieri (Arg.), Montcalm (Fr.), Pershing (US), Wolseley (UK).

(9) Bonaparte (Fr.), Lafayette (Fr.), Kitchener (UK), Macarthur (US).

(10) Clausewitz (Ger.), Eisenhower (US), Hindenburg (Ger.), Kesselring (Ger.), Ludendorff (Ger.),

list continued over

Montgomery (UK), Wellington (Duke of, UK).

(11) Marlborough (Duke of, UK).

generous *adj* 1 (4) free, kind; (6) giving, lavish; (7) liberal; (9) bountiful, unselfish, unsparing; (10) big-hearted, charitable, free-handed, open-handed; (11) magnanimous; 2 (3) big; (4) full; (5) ample, large.

gentle *adj* (4) calm, easy, kind, mild, slow, soft; (5) light, quiet; (6) kindly, serene, slight, tender; (7) gradual; (8) peaceful, soothing; (13) imperceptible.

geology *n*

GEOLOGICAL ERAS AND PERIODS

Archaean (aeon or era), Archeozoic (era), Azoic (era), Cambrian (period), Carboniferous (period), Cainozoic (era), Cenozoic *or* Cretaceous (period), Devonian (period), Eocene (epoch), Holocene (epoch), Jurassic (period), Mesozoic (era), Miocene (epoch), Mississippian (period), Oligocene (epoch), Palaeocene (epoch), Palaeozoic (era), Pennsylvanian (period), Permian (period), Pleistocene (epoch), Pliocene (epoch), Precambrian (era), Proterozoic (era), Quaternary (period), Silurian (period), Tertiary (period), Triassic (period).

German *cryptic* use a (usually simple) German word as part of the solution, especially 'a German' = EIN or EINE and 'the German' = DER, DIE, or DAS.

Germany *cryptic* abbreviated as D or G.

get *v* I (3) net, win; (4) draw, earn, gain, make, reap; (5) gross; (6) obtain, secure; (7) achieve, acquire, procure, realise (*or* realize), receive; II **get away** (4) flee; (6) escape; III **get by** (4) cope; (6) manage; IV **get on** 1 (6) thrive; (7) advance, prosper, succeed; (8) progress; (2 words) make it, make good; 2 (5) agree; V **get out** (4) emerge, escape; VI **get up** (4) rise.

ghost I *n* 1 (4) soul; (5) shade, spook; (6) spirit, wraith; (7) phantom, spectre; (8) revenant; (10) apparition; (11) poltergeist;

2 *also* **ghost-writer** a professional writer who does most of the writing of a book that appears under the name of somebody else, usually a celebrity; II *v* (5) write.

FAMOUS GHOSTS

Banquo (in Shakespeare's *Macbeth*).
Canterville Ghost (in a story by Oscar Wilde).
Caesar (historically recorded and in Shakespeare's *Julius Caesar*).
Elvira (dead wife in Noël Coward's *Blithe Spirit*).
Ghost of Christmas Past (appearing to Scrooge in Dickens' *A Christmas Carol* and followed by the Ghosts of Christmas Present and Christmas Still to Come).
Hamlet's father (King Hamlet in Shakespeare's *Hamlet*).
Jessel, Miss (the dead governess in *The Turn of the Screw* by Henry James).
Marley, Jacob (also appearing to Scrooge in *A Christmas Carol*).
Phantom of the Opera (in the novel by Gaston Leroux and the musical by Andrew Lloyd-Webber).
Quint, Peter (the dead valet in *The Turn of the Screw*).

giant I *adj* (4) huge, vast; (5) jumbo; (7) immense, mammoth, monster, outsize, titanic; (8) colossal, enormous, gigantic, king-size; II *n* (4) ogre; (5) titan; (7) monster; (8) colossus.

GIANTS

Antaeus (a giant, eventually slain by **Hercules**, who became stronger whenever he touched the ground).
Atlas (one of the **Titans**, made by **Zeus** to support the heavens as a punishment for his rebelliousness).
BFG (the big friendly giant of Roald Dahl).
Brobdingnagians (the sympathetic race of giants in Swift's *Gulliver's Travels*).
Despair (the giant who imprisons Pilgrim in Bunyan's *Pilgrim's Progress*). *list continued over*

Fafner and Fafnold (the giants in Wagner's *Ring Cycle* who build the palace of Valhalla for the gods).

Gargantua and Pantagruel (the giants created by the French medieval author Rabelais).

Gog and Magog (legendary giants taken prisoner by Brute, the first king of Britain, whose statues stand outside the Guildhall in London).

Goliath *see below*.

Orgoglio (a giant in Spenser's *Faerie Queen* who symbolises the power of the Catholic Church).

gift *n* **1** (3) tip; (6) bounty; (7) freebie, present; (8) donation, largesse, offering; **2** (5) flair, knack; (6) genius, talent; (7) ability; (8) aptitude.

gifted *adj* (4) able; (6) bright, clever, expert; (7) capable, skilful, skilled; (8) talented; (9) brilliant; (12) accomplished.

Gilbert and Sullivan

COMIC OPERAS OF GILBERT AND SULLIVAN

Gondoliers, The (*or* The King of Barataria).

Grand Duke, The (*or* The Statutory Duel).

HMS Pinafore (*or* The Lass that Loved a Sailor).

Iolanthe (*or* The Peer and the Peri).

Mikado, The (*or* The Town of Titipu).

Patience (*or* Bunthorne's Bride).

Pirates of Penzance (*or* The Slave of Duty).

Princess Ida (*or* Castle Adamant).

Ruddigore (*or* The Witch's Curse).

Sorcerer, The.

Trial by Jury.

Utopia Limited.

Yeomen of the Guard, The (*or* The Merryman and his Maid).

GILBERT AND SULLIVAN CHARACTERS

Angelina (plaintiff – *Trial*).

Bunthorne (caricature of Oscar Wilde and aesthetes – *Patience*).

Duke of Plaza Toro ('celebrated underrated nobleman' – *Gondoliers*).

Edwin (defendant – *Trial*).

Ko-Ko (Lord High Executioner – *Mikado*).

Little Buttercup (bum-boat woman – *Pinafore*).

Lord Chancellor ('such a susceptible Chancellor' – *Iolanthe*).

Major General ('the very model of a modern major general' – *Pirates*).

Nanki-Poo (disguised as a wandering minstrel – *Mikado*).

Pirate King (*Pirates*).

Point, Jack (sad jester – *Yeomen*).

Pooh-Bah (Lord High Everything Else – *Mikado*).

Porter, Sir Joseph ('ruler of the Queen's navy' – *Pinafore*).

Ruth ('pirate maid of all work' – *Pirates*).

Yum-Yum (delicious heroine – *Mikado*).

gill *n* **1** quarter of a pint – *cryptic* P, I, N, or T; **2** female ferret or polecat.

gin *n* **1** drink; **2** (4) trap; (5) snare.

girl I *n* (3) gal; (4) bird, lass, miss; (5) wench; (6) lassie; **II** *cryptic* frequently the word 'girl' or 'woman' prompts for a girl's name – *see below*.

GIRLS' NAMES

(3) Ada, Amy, Ann, Ava, Bea, Bet, Cyd, Dee, Dot, Ena, Eva, Eve, Fay, Flo, Gay, Ida, Ina, Ivy, Jan, Jen, Joy, Kay, Kim, Kit, Lea, Lee, Liz, Lou, Lyn, Mai, May, Meg, Mia, Nan, Pam, Pat, Ray, Sal, Sue, Una, Val, Viv, Win, Zoe.

(4) Ally, Alma, Alys, Anna, Anne, Babs, Bebe, Bess, Beth, Cass, Cath, Ceri, Cher, Cleo, Cora, Dale, Dana, Dawn, Dora, Edie, Edna, Ella, Elsa, Else, Emma, Emmy, Enid, Esme, Etta, Evie, Faye, Fern, Fifi, Fran, Gaby, Gert, Gigi, Gill, Gina, Gwen, Hope, Ines, Inga, Inge, Iona, Iris, Irma, Isla, Jade, Jane, Jean, Jess, Jill,

list continued over

Joan, Jodi, Joni, Judy, June, Kate, Katy, Kiki, Lara, Leah, Lena, Lily, Lisa, Liza, Lois, Lola, Lucy, Lulu, Lynn, Mary, Maud, Mimi, Mina, Moll, Mona, Myra, Nell, Nina, Noel, Nola, Nora, Olga, Oona, Prue, Rene, Rita, Rosa, Rose, Ruby, Ruth, Sara, Sian, Suky, Susy, Tara, Tess, Thea, Tina, Vera, Zara, Zena, Zola.

(5) Abbie, Adela, Adele, Aggie, Agnes, Ailsa, Alexa, Alice, Anita, Annie, Anona, Aphra, April, Avril, Becky, Bella, Belle, Beryl, Betsy, Bette, Betty, Biddy, Bunny, Bunty, Candy, Carla, Carly, Carol. Casey, Cathy, Celia, Chloe, Chris, Cilla, Cindy, Circe, Cissy, Clair, Clara, Coral, Daisy, Debby, Delia, Della, Diana, Diane, Dilys, Dinah, Donna, Doris, Edith, Effie, Elise, Eliza, Ellen, Ellie, Elsie, Emily, Erica, Ethel, Faith, Fanny, Fiona, Fleur, Flora, Freda, Gemma, Gerda, Ginny, Grace, Greer, Greta, Gussy, Haley, Hazel, Heidi, Helen, Helga, Hilda, Holly, Honor, Ilana, Irene, Isold, Janet, Janie, Jenny, Jilly, Jodie, Joyce, Julia, Julie, Karen Katie, Kelly, Kerry, Kitty, Kylie, Laura, Leigh, Leila, Letty, Liana, Libby, Lilly, Linda, Lindy, Lorna, Lotty, Lucia, Lydia, Lynda, Lynne, Mabel, Madge, Maeve, Magda, Mamie, Mandy, Maria, Marie, Maude, Mavis, Megan, Mercy, Merle, Meryl, Milly, Minna, Mitzi, Moira, Molly, Morag, Nancy, Naomi, Nelly, Nessa, Nesta, Netta, Niobe, Norah, Norma, Olive, Olwen, Pansy, Patsy, Patty, Paula, Pearl, Peggy, Penny, Pippa, Polly, Poppy, Renée, Rhian, Rhoda, Robin, Robyn, Rosie, Sadie, Sally, Sandy, Sarah, Sibyl, Sindy, Sissy, Sonia, Sonja, Stacy, Susan, Susie, Sybil, Tammy, Tania, Tanya, Terry, Tessa, Thora, Tilly, Tracy, Trixy, Trudy, Venus, Vesta, Vicky, Viola, Wanda, Wendy, Wilma, Xenia, Zelda.

(6) Adella, Agatha, Aileen, Alexis, Alicia, Alison, Althea, Alyssa,

Amanda, Amelia, Andrea, Angela, Angiem, Anneka, Anthea, Arleen, Arlene, Astrid, Audrey, Aurora, Averil, Barbie, Beatty, Benita, Bertha, Bessie, Biddie, Billie, Bobbie, Bonita, Bonnie, Brenda, Brigid, Briony, Bryony, Bunnie, Carmel, Carmen, Carole, Carrie, Cecile, Cecily, Cherry, Cicley, Claire, Connie, Daphne, Davina, Deanna, Debbie, Deidre, Denise, Dianne, Dionne, Dorcas, Doreen, Dulcie, Edwina, Eileen, Elaine, Elinor, Eloisa, Eloise, Alvira, Emilia, Asther, Eunice, Evelyn, Fatima, Felice, Flavia, Frieda, Gaynor, Gertie, Ginger, Gladys, Glenda, Gloria, Glynis, Gracie, Gretel, Gudrun, Gussie, Gwenda, Hannah, Hattie, Hayley, Hedwig, Helena, Hester, Hilary, Honora, Ianthe, Imelda, Imogen, Ingrid, Isabel, Isobel, Isolda, Isolde, Jackie, Janice, Jemima, Jennie, Jessie, Joanna, Joanne, Joleen, Jolene, Judith, Juliet, Kirsty, Lalage, Lallie, Lauren, Leonie, Lesley, Lettie, Lilian, Lillie, Linsay, Linsey, Lizzie, Lottie, Louisa, Louise, Lynsey, Maggie, Maisie, Marcia, Margie, Margot, Marina, Marion, Marnie, Marsha, Martha, Mattie, Maxine, Melody, Millie, Minnie, Miriam, Mollie, Monica, Morven, Muriel, Myrtle, Nadine, Nellie, Nessie, Nettie, Nicola, Nicole, Odette, Olivia, Oonagh, Pamela, Pattie, Petula, Phoebe, Portia, Rachel, Ramona, Regina, Renata, Robina, Rosina, Rowena, Roxana, Sabina, Sabine, Salome, Sandie, Sandra, Sappho, Saskia, Selina, Serena, Sharon, Sheena, Sheila, Sherry, Sigrid, Silvia, Simone, Sinead, Sophia, Sophie, Sorcha, Stella, Stevie, Sylvia, Tamara, Tamsin, Teresa, Tessie, Thalia, Thecla, Thelma, Tracey, Trixie, Ulrica, Ursula, Valery, Verity, Violet, Vyvyen, Winnie, Yasmin, Yvette, Yvonne.   *list continued over*

(7) Abigail, Adelina, Adeline, Adriana, Annabel, Annette, Antonia, Ariadne, Augusta, Aurelia, Babette, Barbara, Beatrix, Belinda, Bernice, Bettina, Blanche, Blodwen, Blossom, Bridget, Bronwen, Camilla, Candice, Candida, Carolyn, Cecilia, Celeste, Charity, Chloris, Clarice, Caludia, Clodagh, Colette, Coralie, Corinna, Corinne, Crystal, Cynthia, Deborah, Désirée, Dolores, Dorinda, Dorothy, Eleanor, Elspeth, Estella, Eugenia, Eugenie, Eulalia, Evelina, Eveline, Felicia, Fenella, Florrie, Flossie, Frances, Georgia, Gillian, Gwyneth, Harriet, Heather, Heloise, Horatia, Hypatia, Isadora, Isidora, Jacinta, Jacquie, Janetta, Janette, Jasmine, Jeannie, Jessica, Jillian, Jocelyn, Johanna, Josepha, Juanita, Juliana, Juliane, Justina, Kathryn, Katrina, Katrine, Lavinia, Leonora, Letitia, Lettice, Lillian, Lisbeth, Lisette, Loretta, Lorinda, Lucilla, Lucille, Lucinda, Lucrece, Lynette, Madonna, Margery, Marilyn, Marjory, Marlene, Martina, Matilda, Maureen, Melanie, Melissa, Michele, Mildred, Miranda, Monique, Morgana, Morwena, Myfanwy, Natalia, Natalie, Natasha, Ninette, Octavia, Olympia, Ophelia, Ottilie, Pandora, Paulina, Pauline, Perdita, Phyllis, Queenie, Rebecca, Ricarda, Roberta, Rosalia, Rosalie, Rosanna, Rosetta, Rosheen, Sabrina, Shelley, Shirley, Sidonia, Siobhan, Susanna, Susanne, Suzanne, Sybilla, Tabitha, Tatiana, Theresa, Therese, Tiffany, Vanessa, Venetia, Yolanda, Yolande, Zenobia.

(8) Adelaide, Adrianne, Adrienne, Angelica, Angelina, Angharad, Arabella, Atalanta, Beatrice, Berenice, Beverley, Brigitta, Brigitte, Carlotta, Carolina, Caroline, Catriona, Charlene, Charmian, Chrissie, Chrystal, Clarinda, Clarissa, Clotilda, Consuela, Cordelia, Cornelia, Daniella, Danielle, Dorothea, Drusilla, Eleanora, Emmeline, Euphemia, Faustina, Felicity, Florence, Francine, Georgina, Germaine, Gertrude, Gretchen, Griselda, Hermione, Hortense, Hyacinth, Ingeborg, Isabella, Jacintha, Jeanette, Jennifer, Joceline, Julietta, Katerina, Kathleen, Kimberly, Kirsteen, Laetitia, Lauretta, Lavender, Lorraine, Lucretia, Madeline, Marcelle, Margaret, Marianne, Marietta, Marigold, Marjorie, Michaela, Michelle, Nathalie, Patience, Patricia, Penelope, Philippa, Phyllida, Primrose, Prudence, Prunella, Rhiannon, Rosalind, Rosaline, Rosamond, Rosamund, Roseanna, Rosemary, Samantha, Sapphire, Sheelagh, Susannah, Tallulah, Theodora, Theresia, Veronica, Victoria, Violetta, Virginia, Vivienne, Winifred.

(9) Albertine, Alexandra, Anastasia, Annabella, Annabelle, Cassandra, Catharine, Catherine, Celestine, Charlotte, Charmaine, Christina, Christine, Cleopatra, Clothilda, Clothilde, Columbine, Constance, Desdemona, Elisabeth, Elizabeth, Ernestine, Esmeralda, Francesca, Francoise, Frederica, Gabriella, Gabrielle, Genevieve, Georgette, Georgiana, Geraldine, Guinevere, Gwendolen, Henrietta, Hephzibah, Hildegard, Hortensia, Iphigenia, Jacquelyn, Jacquetta, Jessamine, Josephine, Katharine, Katherine, Kimberley, Madeleine, Margareta, Millicent, Philomena, Priscilla, Stephanie, Thomasina, Valentina.

(10) Antoinette, Bernadette, Christabel, Clementina, Clementine, Ermintrude, Evangelina, Evangeline, Gwendoline, Jacqueline, Margherita, Marguerite, Petronella, Wilhelmina.

(11) Alexandrina.

give l *v* 1 (4) deal, dole, gift, hand, lend, mete; (5) allot, allow, award, endow, grant, share; (6) assign, bestow, commit, confer, devote, donate, impart, supply; (7) entrust, furnish, present, provide; (8) transfer; (9) apportion; (10) contribute, distribute; (2 words) deal out, dole out, hand out, make over mete out, share out; **2** (4) bend, fall, sink; (5) yield; (8) collapse; **II give away** (4) leak, shop; (5) grass; (6) betray, expose, reveal; (7) divulge; (8) disclose; (2 words) let slip; **III give in** (5) yield; (6) submit; (9) surrender; (10) capitulate; **IV give off** (4) emit; (5) exude; (6) exhale; (7) produce; (9) discharge; **V give up 1** *see* **give in**; **2** (4) quit, stop; (5) waive; (7) abandon; (8) renounce; (10) relinquish.

glad *adj* **1** (3) gay; (5) happy, merry; (6) joyful; (7) pleased; (8) cheerful; (9) delighted; **2** (4) keen; (5) eager, ready; (7) willing; (8) disposed, inclined.

glass *n* **1** (3) cup, mug; (4) pony; (5) flute, stein, stoup; (6) bumper, copita, goblet, rummer; (7) tankard; (8) schooner; **2** (6) mirror; **3** (9) barometer; **4 glasses** (4) bins; (5) binns, specs; (7) monocle; (8) bifocals, pince-nez; (9) lorgnette; (10) binoculars, spectacles.

glisten *see* **glitter**.

glitter I *v & n* (5) flash, gleam, glint, shine; (7) glimmer, shimmer, sparkle, twinkle; **II** *v* (7) glisten; (9) coruscate; (11) scintillate; **III** *n* (5) sheen; (6) lustre, tinsel; (8) radiance; (10) brightness, brilliance; (11) coruscation; (13) scintillation.

go I *v* **1** (4) move, pass; (6) travel; (7) advance, journey, proceed; (8) progress; **2** (4) lead; (6) extend, spread, stretch; **3** (5) leave; (6) depart, retire, vanish; (7) retreat; (8) withdraw; **4** (3) fit; (4) suit; (5) agree, match, tally; (6) belong; (7) conform; (8) dovetail; (9) harmonise (*or* harmonize); (10) correspond; **II** *n* **1** (3) pep, zip; (4) life; (5) drive; (6) energy, spirit, vigour; (8) dynamism, vitality; **2** (3) try; (4) bash, shot, stab, turn; (7) attempt.

go back I *v* (6) return, revert; (7) regress; **II** *cryptic* indicates that a word should be written in reverse order to make all or part of the answer, as in: 'Electricity produced when mother goes back to French father' (6) = ampere.

go off *v* **1** (7) explode; (8) detonate; **2** (3) rot; (4) sour, turn; (6) fester; (7) putrefy; (2 words) turn bad.

go on *v* **1** (7) persist; (8) **continue**; (9) persevere; **2** (6) rabbit, witter; (7) chatter.

go without *v* (4) lack, want, need; (6) forego; (2 words) abstain from, dispense with

goat *n* **1** (*male* billy, *female* nanny, *young* kid, *group* herd); **2 the Goat** *see* **Capricorn**.

TYPES OF GOAT

(4) ibex; (5) izard; (6) angora; (7) chamois.

---

go-between *n* (5) agent; (6) broker; (7) contact, liaison; (8) mediator; (9) middleman; (12) intermediary.

god *n* (4) idol; (5) deity; (8) divinity.

GODS

Greek

Aeolus – (winds)
Agathodaemon – (prosperity)
Alastor – (fate)
Apollo – (arts, beauty, healing, music and the sun)
Ares – (war)
Asclepius – (medicine)
Boreas – (north wind)
Cronos *or* Kronos – (early chief god, deposed by Zeus)
Dionysus – (wine and fertility)
Eros – (love)
Hades – (**Underworld**)
Helios – (sun)
Hephaestus – (fire, the forge and craft)
Hermes – (messenger of the gods)
Hymen – (marriage)
Hypnos – (sleep)
Nereus – (the sea, 'the old man of the sea')
Oceanus – (the sea)
Pan – (flocks and herds)
Plutus – (riches)
Poseidon – (chief sea god)

list continued over

Thanatos – (personification of death)

Triton – (sea god who blows through a conch shell)

Uranus – (first chief god deposed by Cronos)

Zephyrus – (west wind)

Zeus – (supreme god)

Roman

Aesculapius – (medicine and healing)

Apollo – (arts, beauty, healing, music, and the sun)

Auster – (south wind, the Sirocco)

Bacchus – (wine and fertility)

Cupid – (love, son of Venus)

Dis – (**Underworld**)

Faunus – (forest and field and prophecy)

Genius – (individual man's attendant spirit)

Iacchus – = Bacchus

Janus – (doorways and beginnings)

Jove – = Jupiter

Jupiter – (supreme god)

Lar(es) – (the household, family and ancestors)

Liber – = Bacchus

Lupercus – = Faunus or Pan

Mars – (war)

Mercury – (messenger of the gods, god of science, commerce, travellers and thieves)

Morpheus – (dreams)

Neptune – (the sea)

Orcus – (**Underworld**)

Penates – (protective gods of the household and storeroom)

Phoebus – (sun)

Pluto – (**Underworld**)

Saturn(us) – (early chief god deposed by Jupiter)

Silvanus – (woods)

Somnus – (sleep)

Terminus – (boundaries)

Vulcan – (fire, the forge, and crafts)

Egyptian

Amun – (chief god)

Anubis – (jackal-headed god of **Underworld**)

Apis – (bull god of war)

Geb – (earth)

Hapi – (the Nile)

Horus – (hawk-headed sun god)

Osiris – (fertility, vegetation, and the dead)

Ptah – (creator god, arts and crafts)

Ra or Re – (sun)

Serapis – (death, **Underworld**)

Set or Seth – (evil, brother and killer of Osiris)

Shu – (air)

Thoth – (baboon-headed god of wisdom)

Indian

Agni – (fire)

Brahma – (creator and chief god)

Ganesha – (elephant-headed god of wisdom)

Hanuman – (monkey god)

Indra – (rain)

Kama – (love)

Krishna – (earth, fertility, and love)

Shiva or Siva – (destroyer)

Vishnu – (preserver)

Yama – (lord of the dead)

Middle Eastern

Anu – (Babylonian chief god)

Ashur – (Assyrian national battle god)

Baal – (Phoenician fertility god)

Bel – = Baal

Dagon – (Philistine chief god)

Marduk – (Babylonian chief god)

Mithras – (Persian chief god and god of sun and light)

Moloch – (Ammonite fire and war god demanding human sacrifices)

Nabu or Nebo – (Babylonian god of wisdom)

Tammuz or Thammuz – (Babylonian fertility god, who died every winter and rose again every spring)

Norse

Aesir – (collective name for the chief gods)

Balder – (sun, the good god)

Bragi – (poetry and eloquence)

Frey or Freyr – (fertility)

list continued over

Heimdal – (watchman, keeper of the
  rainbow bridge)
Loki – (fire and evil or mischief)
Njord *or* Njordhr – (sea and ships)
Odin – (chief god)
Thor – (thunder and war)
Woden – = Odin
Wotan – = Odin

Native American

Inti – (Inca personification of sun)
Huitzilopochtli – (Aztec god of war
  and the sun)
Kon-tiki – (Inca sun god)
Quetzacoatl – (Aztec chief god, a
  feathered serpent)
Tlaloc – (Aztec rain god).

goddess *n* (4) diva, idol, star; (5) deity.

GODDESSES

Greek

Amphitrite – (sea, wife of Poseidon)
Aphrodite – (love and beauty)
Artemis – (hunting and the moon)
Astraea – (justice)
Ate – (vengeance and mischief)
Athene – (wisdom)
Chloris – (flowers)
Cybele – (earth)
Cynthia – = Artemis
Demeter – (crops and harvest)
Enyo – (war)
Eos – (dawn)
Erinyes – (the **Furies**)
Eumenides – (the **Furies**)
Gaea *or* Ge – (earth)
Hebe – (goddess of youth and cup-
  bearer to the gods)
Hecate – (night, the **Underworld** and
  witchcraft)
Hera – (queen of the gods, goddess of
  marriage and women, wife of Zeus)
Hestia – (the hearth and fire)
Hygiea – (health)
Irene – (peace)
Iris – (goddess of the rainbow and
  divine messenger)
Mnemosyne – (memory, mother of
  the Muses)
Moirai – (the **Fates**)

Nemesis – (retribution and vengeance)
Nike – (victory)
Nyx – (night)
Persephone – (**Underworld**)
Rhea – (mother of the gods)
Selene – (moon)
Tyche – (destiny)

Roman

Aurora – (dawn)
Bellona – (war)
Ceres – (crops and harvest)
Diana – (moon and hunting)
Fauna – (country goddess, sister of
  Faunus)
Flora – (flowers)
Fortuna – (fortune, destiny)
Juno – (queen of heaven, goddess of
  marriage and women, and wife of
  Jupiter)
Juventas – (youth)
Libera – = Proserpina
Luna – (moon)
Minerva – (wisdom)
Nox – (night)
Ops – (wife of Saturn)
Parcae – (the **Fates**)
Pax – (peace)
Pomona – (orchards and gardens)
Proserpina – (the **Underworld**, wife of
  Pluto)
Salus – (health)
Tellus *or* Terra – (earth)
Venus – (love and beauty)
Vesta – (fire and the hearth)
Victoria – (victory)

Egyptian

Bast *or* Bubastis – (cat goddess)
Hathor – (love and joy)
Isis – (chief goddess, sister of Osiris)
Ma *or* Maat – (justice)
Nut – (earth mother)
Tefnut – (sea)

Indian

Devi – (chief goddess)
Durga – = Kali
Kali – (destruction, wife of Shiva)
Lakshmi – (beauty and wealth, wife
  of Vishnu)   *list continued over*

Middle Eastern

Astarte – (Phoenician goddess of love)
Ishtar – (Babylonian goddess of love and feritility)
Tiamit – (Babylonian dragon goddess)

Norse

Freya – (god of love and fertility)
Frigg *or* Frigga – (chief goddess and wife of Odin)
Hel – (the **Underworld** and the dead)
Valkyries – (warrior maidens who brought the souls of those slain in battle to Valhalla).

godless *adj* (3) bad; (4) evil; (5) pagan; (6) unholy; (7) heathen, immoral, impious, profane, ungodly; (9) atheistic; (10) irreverent; (11) irreligious.

godly *adj* (4) good, holy, pure; (5) pious; (6) devout; (8) virtuous; (9) religious, righteous; (10) God-fearing.

Goethe *lit.* the most famous of all German poets and dramatists. His most well-known work is *Faust*, a verse play in two parts reworking the medieval story of the scholar Faust or Faustus who sells his soul to the devil in return for twenty-four years of life in which all pleasures and all knowledge are at his command. Besides Faust, the chief characters are the devil Mephistopheles and Faust's innocent lover, Gretchen.

gold *cryptic* letters AU (chemical symbol) or OR (heraldry).

Golden Fleece *Gk myth* the skin of a ram with a golden fleece hung on a sacred oak in **Colchis**, which was the object of the quest of **Jason** and the **Argonauts**.

Golden Gate *geog.* the strait leading into San Francisco Bay spanned by a famous suspension bridge.

Golden Hind *hist.* the ship (originally named the 'Pelican') in which Sir Francis Drake sailed round the world.

golden jubilee *n* a 50th anniversary.

golden rule *n* 'do as you would be done by'.

golf club *n see* club.

golf course *n* (5) links.

> **GOLF COURSES**
>
> (5) Troon; (6) Belfry (the);
> (7) Augusta, Hoylake; (8) Sandwich;
> (9) Muirfield, Prestwick, St Andrews, Turnberry, Wentworth;
> (10) Carnoustie, Gleneagles; (11) Blairgowrie, Sunningdale; (2+ words) Lytham St Annes, Royal Birkdale.

golfer *n*

> **FAMOUS GOLFERS**
>
> Alliss, Peter; Baiocchi, Hugh; Ballesteros, Seve; Cotton, Henry; Faldo, Nick; Hogan, Ben; Jacklin, Tony; Langer, Bernhard; Locke, Bobby; Lyle, Sandy; Nicklaus, Jack; Norman, Greg; Olazabal, Jose; Palmer, Arnold; Player, Gary; Rees, Dai; Snead, Sam; Trevino, Lee; Woods, Tiger; Woosnam, Ian.

Goliath *Bible* a giant Philistine of Gath whose height was 'six cubits and a span' and who challenged a champion of the Israelites to single combat. He was slain by the boy **David** with a single stone to the forehead from his slingshot.

good *adj* **1** (4) able, fine, nice; (5) great, super; (6) expert; (7) capable; (8) adequate, pleasing; (9) competent, efficient, excellent, first-rate; (10) first-class, proficient; (12) satisfactory; **2** (4) holy, kind, pure; (5) godly, moral; (6) honest; (7) upright; (8) generous, obedient, virtuous; (9) admirable, righteous; (10) benevolent, charitable; (11) well-behaved; (12) well-mannered; **3** (5) sound, valid, (7) genuine; (8) thorough.

goodbye *n* (3) bye; (4) ciao, ta-ta, vale; (5) addio, adieu; (6) bye-bye; (7) cheerio, parting; (8) farewell; (11) leave-taking, valediction; (2 words) au revoir, see you, so long.

good man *cryptic* letters ST (saint).

goods *pl n* (5) stock, wares; (7) effects, freight; (8) chattels, property; (11) commodities, merchandise.

goose *n* (*male* gander, *female* goose, *young* gosling, *group* flock, gaggle, skein).

> **TYPES OF GEESE**
>
> (4) bean; (5) anser, brent; (6) Canada; (7) greylag; (8) barnacle, Egyptian; (12) white-fronted.

gorge I *n* (5) abyss, chasm, cleft, gully; (6) canyon, defile, ravine; **II** *v* (4) cram, fill, gulp, sate; (5) stuff; (6) gobble, guzzle; (7) swallow.

Gorgon *Gk myth* one of three monstrous creatures with snakes for hair whose look turned humans to stone. The names of the three Gorgons were **Medusa**, Euryale and Stheno.

Gospel I *n* (4) true; (5) truth; **II** the four Gospels form the first four books of the New Testament and all contain accounts of the life of Jesus Christ. They are known by the names of the saints who are traditionally credited with having written them – **Matthew, Mark, Luke** and **John**.

gossip I *v & n* (4) chat, talk; (7) chatter; (8) chitchat; (12) tittle-tattle; **II** *n* **1** (6) rumour; (7) hearsay, scandal; **2** (7) babbler, tattler; (8) busybody, prattler, telltale; (10) talebearer; (13) scandalmonger; **III** *v* (6) natter; (7) prattle, whisper; (2 words) tell tales.

grab *v* (3) nab; (4) grip, take; (5) catch, seize; (6) clutch, collar, snatch.

graceful *adj* (4) easy; (5) agile, lithe; (6) lissom, smooth, supple; (7) elegant, flowing.

Graces *Gk myth* three daughters of **Zeus** who were believed both to embody beauty and charm and to be able to pass on these qualities to favoured mortals. Their names were Aglaia, Euphrosyne and Thalia.

gracious *adj* **1** (4) kind; (5) sweet; (8) merciful, obliging; (9) courteous, forgiving; (11) considerate; (13) accommodating; **2** (7) elegant, refined; (9) luxurious; (11) comfortable.

grade I *v* (4) mark, rank, rate, sift, sort; (5) brand, class, group, label, range; (6) assess; (7) arrange; (8) classify; (10) categorise (*or* categorize), pigeonhole; **II** *n* (4) rank, rung, step; (5) level, notch, place, stage; (6) degree, status; (8) category; (9) condition.

graduate I *v* **1** (4) pass; (7) qualify; **2** (5) grade; (9) calibrate; **II** *cryptic* the letters BA or MA or any others representing an academic title.

Graeae *Gk myth* three old women who possessed only one eye and one tooth between them and who were consulted by **Perseus**. Their names were Dino, Enyo and Pephredro.

Grail *see* **Holy Grail**.

grand I *adj* (5) great, large, lofty, noble, regal; (6) lordly; (7) stately; (8) imposing, splendid, striking; (9) dignified, grandiose; (10) impressive, monumental; (11) magnificent; **II** *n* (5) piano; **III** *cryptic* the letter K or M meaning thousand.

grant I *v* **1** (4) gift, give, lend, mete; (5) allot, allow, award, endow; (6) assign, bestow, commit, confer, devote, donate, supply; (7) entrust, furnish, present, provide; (9) apportion; (10) contribute, distribute; **2** (5) admit; (7) concede, confess; (11) acknowledge; **II** *n* (5) award; (7) bequest, bursary, subsidy; (9) allowance, endowment; (10) concession; (11) scholarship.

grasp I *n & v* (4) grip, hold; (5) clasp; (6) clutch; **II** *v* **1** (3) nab; (4) grab, take; (5) catch, seize; (6) collar, snatch; **2** (6) follow; (10) comprehend, understand; **III** *n* **1** (5) poser, reach; (7) control; (8) clutches; **2** (9) knowledge; (13) comprehension, understanding.

grass I *n* **1** (4) lawn, turf; (5) green, sward; (7) grazing, herbage, pasture; **2** *slang* (4) nark; (8) informer; **II** *v slang* (6) betray, inform.

> **TYPES OF GRASS**
>
> (3) ers, fog, rye.
>
> (4) aira, alfa, bent, blue, coix, diss, doub, dura, kans, lyme, reed, rusa, tare, teff, tore. *list continued over*

(5) arrow, briza, bunch, couch, cutch, durra, grama, halfa, haulm, medic, melic, oryza, panic, quake, sedge, spear, vetch.

(6) bajree, barcoo, cactus, clover, darnel, fescue, fiorin, lolium, lucern, marram, medick, nardus, pampas, phleum, quitch, redtop, ruppia, twitch, uniola, wawant.

(7) alfalfa, clivers, esparto, eulalia, festuca, foggage, foxtail, lucerne, sacaton, sorghum, squitch, timothy, vetiver, whangee, zizania.

(8) cleavers, dog-grass, dogstail, dog-wheat, eleusine, gynerium, puss-tail.

(9) cocksfoot.

(10) citronella.

(2 words) creeping medic, Job's tears, purple medic.

grave I *n* (3) pit; (4) tomb; (5) cairn; (6) barrow; (7) tumulus; (9) sepulchre; **II** *adj* 1 (4) grim; (5) sober; (6) sedate, solemn; (7) pensive, serious, subdued; (8) reserved; (10) thoughtful; 2 (5) acute, vital; (6) severe, urgent; (7) crucial, weighty; (8) critical; (9) dangerous, important, momentous.

gravity *cryptic* abbreviated as G.

great *adj* 1 (3) big; (4) huge; (5) large; (7) immense; (8) enormous; 2 (5) major; (6) famous; (7) eminent, notable; (8) elevated, renowned; (9) prominent, respected, well-known; (10) celebrated; (11) illustrious, outstanding, prestigious; (13) distinguished; 3 (3) fab; (5) brill, super; (6) superb; (7) amazing; (8) fabulous, terrific; (9) brilliant, fantastic, wonderful; (10) incredible, marvellous, phenomenal; (12) unbelievable.

Great Lakes *geog.* (4) Erie; (5) Huron; (7) Ontario; (8) Michigan, Superior.

greedy *adj* (4) avid; (8) covetous; (9) voracious; (10) gluttonous, insatiable; (11) acquisitive.

Greek alphabet *see* **alphabet**.

green I *colour* (4) jade, sage, moss, nile; (5) apple, beryl, lovat, olive; (7) emerald,

Lincoln; (9) turquoise; (3 words) eau de nil; **II** *adj* 1 (5) leafy; (6) grassy; (7) verdant; 2 (3) new, raw; (5) fresh, naive; (6) unripe; (8) gullible, immature; (9) credulous; (10) unseasoned; (13) inexperienced; (15) unsophisticated; 3 (10) ecological; (11) eco-friendly; (13) environmental; **IV** *n* (4) lawn; (5) sward; (6) common; **V** *cryptic* vert (*heraldry*).

greet *v* (4) hail, meet; (6) accost, salute; (7) address, receive, welcome; (11) acknowledge.

greeting *n* (4) wave; (7) welcome; (10) salutation.

GREETINGS

(2) hi, ho, yo. (3) ave (*Latin*), hey; (4) ahoy, ciao, hail, hiya, hola; (5) aloha, hallo, hello, howdy, hullo.

---

grey I *colour* (4) dove, drab; (8) charcoal, elephant, gunmetal; (10) battleship; **II** *adj* 1 (3) dim; (4) drab, dull; (6) cloudy, gloomy; (8) overcast; 2 (4) flat; (6) **boring**, dreary; (7) tedious; (8) tiresome; (10) monotonous, unexciting; (13) uninteresting.

Greyfriars *fict.* a fictional public school that was the setting for the stories by Frank Richards featuring Billy **Bunter** and his **Famous Five** fellow pupils.

grief *n* (3) woe; (4) pain; (5) agony; (6) misery, regret, sorrow; (7) anguish, remorse, sadness; (8) distress, mourning; (9) dejection, heartache; (10) affliction, desolation, heartbreak; (11) unhappiness.

ground I *n* 1 (3) sod; (4) clay, dirt, land, loam, soil; (5) earth; (2 words) the deck, terra firma; 2 (5) arena, field, pitch; (7) stadium; **3 grounds** (5) cause; (6) **reason**; (13) justification; **II** *v* 1 (4) base; (5) found; (9) establish; 2 (5) coach, train, tutor; (8) instruct; **III** *adj* (6) milled; (7) crushed; (8) powdered; **IV** *cryptic* ANAGRAM CUE.

group I *n* (3) lot, mob, set; (4) band, club, crew, gang, pack, ring, team; (5) batch, bunch, class, clump, crowd, squad; (6) circle, clique; (7) cluster, coterie; (8) category; (9) gathering; **II** *v* (4) sort; (6)

gather; (7) arrange, collect, marshal; (8) assemble, organise (*or* organize); (9) associate.

Grub Street *lit.* the supposed abode of hack writers, or writers of low-grade literature as a group or class.

guard I *v* (4) mind; (5) watch; (6) defend, escort, police, patrol, shield; (7) oversee, protect; (9) safeguard; **II** *n* (6) escort, minder, picket, sentry, warder; (7) lookout; (8) watchman; (9) bodyguard, custodian.

Guinevere *myth* the wife of King Arthur, whose love affair with Sir **Lancelot** led ultimately to the break-up of the **Round Table** and the death of King Arthur.

gules *heraldry* red.

gulf *n* (3) gap; (4) hole, void; (5) abyss, chasm, space; (6) breach, divide.

GULF OF

(4) Aden, Oman, Riga, Suez.

(5) Aqaba, Genoa, Lyons, Sirte.

(6) Alaska, Darien, Guinea, Mexico, Panama, Pecora.

(7) Boothia, Bothnia, Corinth, Finland, Gascony, Taranto, Trieste.

(8) Martaban, Tongking.

(9) Venezuela.

(10) California.

(11) Carpentaria.

---

gun *n* (3) rod; (4) iron; (5) piece; (7) firearm, shooter.

GUNS

(3) gat.

(4) bren, Colt, sten.

(5) Luger, maxim, rifle.

(6) ack-ack, air-gun, Bofors, cannon, Mauser, musket, pistol, pompom, pop-gun, sixgun, Webley.

(7) shotgun, sidearm.

(8) arquebus, basilisk, culverin, howitzer, Oerlikon, repeater, revolver, tommy-gun.

(9) derringer, flintlock, matchlock.

(10) fieldpiece, Lee-Enfield, peacemaker, six-shooter, smoothbore, Winchester.

(11) blunderbuss.

(12) breech-loader, Martini-Henry, mitrailleuse, muzzle-loader.

(13) submachine-gun.

(2 words) Big Bertha, Brown Bess.

---

gunners I *sport* nickname of Arsenal FC; **II** *cryptic* the letters RA (Royal Artillery).

guy I *n* **1** (3) man; (4) chap; (5) bloke; (6) fellow; **2** (4) rope, stay; **II** *v* (4) mock; (8) **ridicule**.

H

H I *abbrev* hard, hospital, hydrogen; II *cryptic for dropping h* ('im, 'eard *etc*) *see* **cockney**.

habit *n* **1** (4) bent, rule, wont; (5) usage; (6) custom; (7) routine; (8) practice; (9) tradition; **2** (9) addiction; (10) dependence; **3** (4) robe; (5) dress, frock; (7) garment.

habitation *see* **home**.

Hades I *Gk myth* the god of the **Underworld** – *see also* **Underworld**; II *n see* **hell**.

half I *adj & n* (4) demi, part, semi; (6) moiety; II *cryptic* **1** use half of the preceding or following word in the answer, so that, for example, 'half-hour' might refer to HO or UR or 'nearly half' to NEA or RLY. As in: 'Half cast get a sudden illumination and lose the plot' (5) = stray (half cast = ST); **2** **not half** omit half of one of the words in the clue when forming the answer, as in: 'On the quiet, is that dog ugly? – not half!' (3) = pug (quiet = piano = P).

half day *cryptic* letters AM or PM.

half-hearted I *adj* (4) cool; (8) lukewarm; (9) apathetic; (14) unenthusiastic; II *cryptic* remove one of a pair of letters in the middle of a word in the clue, as, for example, in: 'Old instrument from farmer's bag removing tail from half-hearted goat' (7) = sackbut (goat = butter minus T and minus final letters).

halt I *v & n* (3) end; (4) rest, stop, wait; (5) break, close, pause; II *n* (8) stoppage; (9) standstill; (11) termination; (12) interruption; III *v* **1** (4) curb, stem; (5) cease, check; (6) arrest, **hinder**; (9) terminate; (11) discontinue; **2** (4) limp; III *adj* (4) lame; (8) crippled.

halting *adj* (7) awkward; (8) hesitant; (9) faltering, stumbling; (10) stammering, stuttering.

Ham *Bible* one of the sons of **Noah**.

ham I *n* **1** meat; **2** thigh; **3** amateur actor; **4** bad actor; II *v* act badly; III *cryptic* anagram of ACT (on the basis of II).

Hamlet *lit.* tragedy by William Shakespeare and the name of the main character. Full title: *The Tragedy of Hamlet, Prince of Denmark*.

Plot outline: The ghost of the recently dead King Hamlet (the hero's father) is seen walking the ramparts of the royal castle of Elsinore by, among others, Horatio, Prince Hamlet's former fellow student at the University of Wittenberg. Prince Hamlet, who has been thrown into a deep depression by his father's death, his mother, Queen Gertrude's, rapid remarriage to his uncle, her first husband's brother, Claudius and Claudius's succession to the throne, is informed by Horatio of the ghost's appearance and decides to confront it. The ghost identifies itself to Hamlet as his father's spirit, informs him that he was murdered by Claudius, and commands him to take revenge on him, but to spare his mother. Hamlet accepts the duty of taking vengeance, but needs both to find an opportunity to carry out the deed and to convince himself that the ghost has spoken the truth and his uncle is indeed a murderer. To buy time, he puts on an 'antic disposition' (pretends to be mad). King Claudius and his elderly and sententious counsellor Polonius attempt to penetrate Hamlet's psychological disguise, the former by getting two other former friends of the prince, Rosencrantz and Guildenstern, to spy on him, the latter by setting up an encounter between Hamlet and his daughter Ophelia, with whom Hamlet is in love. The arrival of a travelling group of actors provides an opportunity for Hamlet to test the ghost's account of the murder.

He persuades the players to re-enact the crime as part of a play performed in front of Claudius. Claudius shows obvious signs of guilt and, immediately afterwards, Hamlet is presented with an opportunity to kill him. He does not take it, because Claudius is apparently praying and Hamlet does not want to kill him and send his soul to heaven. Instead he goes to see his mother to try and persuade her to repent. Polonius, the counsellor, is eavesdropping on the interview. Hamlet speaks to his mother in such a violently angry way that Polonius calls for help, and Hamlet, thinking the eavesdropper to be Claudius, stabs him. The death of Polonius has two consequences. It drives his daughter, Ophelia, to insanity and suicide by drowning. It drives his son, Laertes, to swear vengeance on Hamlet and join forces with Claudius to kill him. Claudius, nothing if not thorough, tries by three means to get rid of Hamlet. First he sends him to England with Rosencrantz and Guildenstern, who are carrying letters instructing the English authorities to put Hamlet to death. Hamlet, however, sees through the plot and turns the tables on his former friends. Then Claudius arranges a friendly fencing match between Laertes and Hamlet in which the former uses a rapier with an unprotected point which is also poisoned. Finally, in case the poisoned rapier does not work, Claudius drops a poisoned ring into a goblet of wine which is to be offered to Hamlet as refreshment during the fencing match. In the event, Laertes stabs Hamlet, but is himself stabbed and killed after an exchange of weapons. Gertrude drinks from the poisoned goblet, and, finally, Hamlet kills Claudius before dying of his wound. The entire Danish royal family is thus wiped out and the crown passes to a Norwegian prince, Fortinbras, whose father had been slain in single combat by the old King Hamlet many years before.

hamper I *n* (6) basket; II *see* hinder.

hand I *n* 1 (3) paw; (4) fist, mitt, palm; 2 (3) man; (6) helper, worker; (7) servant; (8) employee, hireling, labourer; (9) assistant, operative; 3 (3) aid; (4) help; (7) support; (10) assistance; II *v* (4) give, pass; (5) bring, offer, reach; (6) submit; (7) deliver, present.

handicap I *n* (7) penalty; (8) drawback; (9) hindrance; (10) disability, impairment, impediment, limitation; (11) restriction; (12) disadvantage; II *v* (5) limit; (6) burden, hamper, hinder, impede; (7) disable; (8) encumber, restrict.

handle I *v* 1 (4) feel, hold, work; (5) grasp, touch; (6) fondle; 2 (4) work; (5) drive; (6) manage, tackle; (7) control, operate; (2 words) cope with, deal with; II *n* 1 (4) grip, hilt, knob; (5) shaft; stock; (6) holder; 2 (4) name; (5) title (7) moniker (8) monicker.

happy *adj* 1 (3) gay; (4) glad; (5) jolly, merry; (6) joyful, joyous; (7) pleased; (8) cheerful; (9) delighted; 2 (4) keen; (5) eager, ready; (7) willing; (8) disposed, inclined.

harass *v* (3) nag, vex; (4) tire; (5) annoy, harry, worry; (6) badger, bother, chivvy, hassle, molest, pester, plague; (7) disturb, torment; (8) irritate; (9) persecute.

harbour I *n* 1 (4) dock, port, quay; (5) basin, berth, haven, jetty, wharf; (6) marina, refuge; (7) mooring; (9) anchorage; 2 (6) asylum; (7) shelter; (9) sanctuary; II *v* (4) hide; (6) foster, retain; (7) cherish, conceal, nurture, protect, shelter; III *cryptic* 1 place one part of the answer inside another; 2 HIDDEN WORD CUE.

hard I *adj* 1 (4) firm; (5) dense, rigid, solid, stiff, tough; (6) strong; (10) inflexible, unyielding; 2 (6) knotty; (7) complex; (8) baffling, involved; (9) difficult; (11) complicated, problematic; 3 (6) tiring; (7) arduous; (9) laborious, strenuous; (12) backbreaking; 4 (5) cruel, harsh; (6) severe, strict; (7) callous; (8) pitiless, ruthless; (9) merciless, unfeeling; (11) unrelenting; (13) unsympathetic; II *adv* (8) doggedly, intently, steadily; (10) diligently, vigorously; (11) assiduously, strenuously; (13) energetically, industriously; III *cryptic* letter H (abbreviation).

Hardy, Thomas novelist and poet, most of whose novels and poems were set in Wessex, the southwestern counties of England for whose towns and villages Hardy invented names of his own.

NOVELS OF THOMAS HARDY

Desperate Remedies, Far from the Madding Crowd, Jude the Obscure, The Mayor of Casterbridge, A Pair of Blue Eyes, The Return of the Native, Tess of the D'Urbervilles, The Trumpet Major, Under the Greenwood Tree, A View from the Tower, The Woodlanders.

---

hardy *adj* (5) stout, tough; (6) robust, rugged, strong; (7) durable, lasting; (9) resilient.

harm I *n & v* (4) hurt, ruin; (5) abuse, wound, wrong; (6) damage, misuse; II *n* (3) ill; (4) loss; (6) injury; (9) detriment; (10) impairment, misfortune; III *v* (3) mar; (5) spoil (6) injure; (8) ill-treat, maltreat, mistreat; IV *cryptic* ANAGRAM CUE.

harmful *adj* (5) toxic; (7) noxious; (8) damaging; (9) dangerous, hazardous, injurious, poisonous, unhealthy; (10) pernicious; (11) destructive, detrimental, unwholesome.

harmless *adj* (4) safe; (6) gentle; (9) innocuous; (11) inoffensive.

harness I *n* 1 (4) gear, tack; (5) reins; (6) tackle; (9) equipment, fastening; 2 (6) armour; II *v* 1 (3) use; (5) apply; (6) employ; (7) exploit, utilise (*or* utilize); 2 (4) join; (6) **attach**, fasten.

PARTS OF HORSE'S HARNESS

(3) bit; (4) curb, rein; (5) trace; (6) bridle, pelham; (7) snaffle; (8) noseband; (9) hackamore, headstall; (10) martingale.

---

harpy I *Gk myth* a monster with head and body of a woman and the wings and claws of a bird of prey that lived in an atmosphere of filth and foul smells, contaminated everything it came near and tended to swoop down, snatch and carry off food or other things. The harpies were named Aello, Celeno and Ocypete; II *n* (5) shrew; (6) virago; (8) harridan; (9) termagant.

Harry I *name* (3) Hal; (5) Henry; (6) Harold; II **Old Harry** the devil.

harry *v* (3) nag, vex; (5) annoy, worry; (6) badger, bother, chivvy, harass, hassle, pester, plague; (7) torment; (9) persecute.

harsh *adj* 1 (5) rough, sharp; (6) coarse, shrill; (7) grating, jarring, rasping, raucous; (8) guttural, strident; (10) discordant; 2 (4) grim, hard; (5) bleak, cruel; (6) severe, strict; (7) austere, spartan; (9) draconian.

harvest I *n* (4) crop; (5) crops, fruit, yield; (6) fruits, return; (7) produce, product; II *v* (3) mow; (4) pick, reap; (5) amass; (6) gather; (7) collect.

haste *see* **hurry**.

hasten *see* **hurry**.

hat *n see* **headgear**.

hate I *v* (5) abhor; (6) detest, loathe; (7) dislike; (8) execrate; (9) abominate; II *n* (6) enmity, hatred; (7) dislike; (8) aversion, loathing; (9) animosity, hostility; (10) abhorrence, antagonism, execration; (11) detestation.

head I *n* 1 (3) nod; (4) bean, loaf, pate, poll; (5) bonts, skull; (6) napper, noddle, noggin; 2 (4) boss; (5) chief, ruler; (6) leader; (7) captain, manager; (8) director; (9) principal; (14) superintendent; 3 (3) tip, top; (4) apex, peak; (5) crown; (6) summit; 4 (4) cape, ness; (5) point; (10) promontory; II *v* (3) run; (4) lead, rule; (6) direct, govern, manage; (7) command, control, oversee; (9) supervise; (11) superintend; III *adj* (3) key, top; (4) main; (5) chief, prime; (6) ruling, senior; (7) leading, primary; (8) cardinal; (9) principal, sovereign; IV *cryptic* use the first letter of a word (often hidden in another word in the clue) as in: 'Brideshead' = B; *see also* **head off**.

headgear *n*

> **TYPES OF HAT AND HEAD COVERING**
>
> (3) cap, fez.
>
> (4) coif, cowl, helm, hood, kepi, topi.
>
> (5) beret, busby, derby, mitre, shako, snood, tiara, topee, toque.
>
> (6) beaver, boater, bonnet, bowler, castor, cloche, fedora, helmet, mobcap, panama, topper, trilby, turban, wimple.
>
> (7) biretta, homburg, pill-box, stetson, tricorn.
>
> (8) bearskin, nightcap, opera-hat, skullcap, sombrero, tarboosh.
>
> (9) balaclava, billycock, glengarry, sou'-wester, stovepipe.
>
> (11) deerstalker, mortar-board.
>
> (12) cheese-cutter.
>
> (2+ words) pork-pie hat, tam o'shanter, ten-gallon hat.

head off *cryptic* drop the first letter of a word in the clue or the answer, as in: 'Tail bandits and head them off after quarter of an hour at the pass' (4) = hand (tail = remove final letters, quarter of an hour = H (or O, U, or R), main clue = pass).

headquarters *cryptic* letter H, E, A or D – *see* **quarter**.

heap *see* **pile**.

hear *cryptic* often in the form '*we hear*', indicates that the word required in the answer sounds the same as or similar to another suggested by something else in the clue, as in: 'Robert, we hear, has had a short hair cut' (3) = bob.

heard *cryptic* as with **hear**, usually indicates a soundalike, as in: 'Heard the sheep say thank you? - must have been in a state!' (4) = Utah (U = ewe, etc).

hearer I *n* (7) auditor; (8) listener; II **hearers** (8) audience; III *cryptic* often means EAR.

heart I *n* 1 (4) pump; (6) ticker; 2 (3) nub; (4) core, crux; (6) centre, kernel, middle; (7) nucleus; 3 (6) spirit; (7) **courage**; 4 (4) love, pity; (7) emotion, feeling; (9) sentiment; (10) compassion; II *cryptic* 1 refers to the middle letter or letters of a word (often hidden in another word in the clue) as in: 'Braveheart' = A; 2 **at heart** indicates that one word, letter or element is to be placed inside another, as in: 'Simple fellow but with dash enough at heart to become a crime writer' (7) = Simenon (simple Simon and *see* **dash**).

heartless I *adj* (4) cold, hard; (5) cruel, harsh; (6) brutal, unkind; (7) callous, inhuman; (8) pitiless; (9) merciless, unfeeling; II *cryptic* omit the middle letter or letters of a word in the clue, as in: 'Overcome by a heartless beast of a journalist' (6) = bested (journalist = editor = ed).

heaven *n* (3) sky; (4) Sion, Zion; (6) Asgard; (7) elysium, nirvana; (8) empyrean, paradise; (9) afterlife, firmament, hereafter.

heavenly body *n* (3) sun; (4) moon, star; (5) comet; (6) planet; (8) asteroid.

heavy I *adj* 1 (5) bulky, hefty, solid; (7) weighty; (9) ponderous; (10) burdensome; 2 (4) hard; (5) harsh, tough; (6) severe, taxing; (7) arduous; (9) demanding, laborious, strenuous; II *n* (5) tough; (6) minder; (8) gangster.

Hebe *Gk myth* the goddess of youth and cup-bearer to the gods, bringing them the ambrosia that kept them eternally young.

Hecate *Gk myth* the goddess of night, dark places, and witchcraft.

Hector *Gk myth & lit.* the eldest son of King **Priam**, the noblest of the fighting men of Troy and their leader until he was killed by Achilles, who harnessed his body to his chariot and dragged it three times around the walls of the city.

Hecuba *Gk myth & lit.* the wife of King Priam of Troy and mother of nineteen children. Mentioned in Shakespeare's *Hamlet*: 'What's Hecuba to him, or he to Hecuba?'

he has *cryptic* letters HES.

he is *cryptic* letters HES.

held *see* **hold**.

Helen *Gk myth & lit.* the daughter of **Zeus** and **Leda**, reputed the most beautiful of women, who became the wife of King **Menelaus** of Sparta, but was abducted by Paris to Troy, the abduction being the main cause of the Trojan War.

Helicon *geog. & myth* a mountain in central Greece believed to be the home of the nine **Muses**.

Helios *Gk myth* the god of the sun.

helium *cryptic* abbreviated as He.

hell *n* (3) Dis, pit; (5) abyss, Hades; (6) Erebus; (7) Abaddon, Gehenna, inferno; (10) **Underworld**.

Hellespont *geog.* the old name for the **Dardanelles**, named after a character in Greek mythology, Helle, who was supposed to have fallen into the sea while fleeing from her mother Ino on the back of the golden ram which was later sacrificed to provide the **Golden Fleece**. Notable swimmers of the Hellespont are **Leander** and Lord **Byron**.

help I *v* (3) aid; (4) back, ease; (5) serve; (6) assist, foster, hasten; (7) advance, forward, further, promote, succour, support; (8) mitigate; (9) alleviate, encourage; (10) facilitate; II *n* 1 (3) aid; (6) advice, helper; (7) service, support; (8) guidance; (9) assistant; (10) assistance; (11) co-operation; (13) collaboration; 2 (5) grant; (6) relief; (7) benefit, funding, subsidy, welfare; (8) donation; (9) patronage; (11) sponsorship; (12) contribution.

helpful *adj* (4) kind; (6) useful; (7) friendly; (8) obliging; (9) practical; (10) beneficial, supportive; (11) co-operative, neighbourly; (12) advantageous, constructive.

helpless *adj* (4) weak; (6) feeble; (8) forlorn, disabled; (9) dependent, incapable, paralysed, powerless; (10) vulnerable; (11) defenceless, incompetent.

Henry *name* (3) Hal; (5) Harry.

Hephaestus *Gk myth* the god of fire, the forge, and crafts, equivalent of (and *see*) **Vulcan**.

Hera *Gk myth* the sister and wife of Zeus, and queen of the gods – *see also* **Juno** (her Roman equivalent).

Heracles *Gk myth* Greek name for **Hercules**.

herald I *n* (5) envoy; (7) courier; (8) emissary; (9) go-between, harbinger, messenger, precursor; (10) ambassador; (14) representative; II *v* (7) precede, presage; (8) announce, foretell, indicate, proclaim; (9) advertise, broadcast; (10) foreshadow; (2 words) usher in.

heraldry

HERALDIC COLOURS (TINCTURES)

argent – silver, azure – blue, gules – red, purpure – purple, sable – black, tenné – orange or brown or gold, vert – green

---

HERALDIC TERMS

bend (diagonal stripe), couchant (lying down, head up), dexter (right-hand side), dormant (lying down, head down), estoile (star), fess (horizontal stripe), gardant (looking outward), naiant (swimming), passant (walking), rampant (rearing up), regardant (looking over shoulder), saltire (diagonal cross), sinister (left-hand side)

---

herb *n* (5) plant, simple.

HERBS

(3) bay, rue.

(4) balm, dill, mint, sage.

(5) basil, chive, cress, orris, tansy, thyme.

(6) balsam, borage, catnip, fennel, lovage, savory.

(7) caraway, catmint, chervil, oregano, parsley, saffron, vervain.

(8) feverfew, marjoram, rosemary, tarragon, turmeric, valerian.

(9) coriander, fenugreek, spearmint, woundwort.

(10) belladonna, lemon-grass, peppermint.

Hercules *Rom. myth* the son of Zeus and Alcmene, a hero of enormous strength, who having killed his children in a mad fury was made to perform twelve apparently impossible labours, all of which he accomplished with the help of various gods.

Hermes *Gk myth* the Greek equivalent of **Mercury**, the messenger of the gods.

Hero *Gk myth* a priestess who lived on the shores of the Hellespont and whose lover, **Leander**, lived on the other side of the strait and swam across nightly to be with her. When Leander was drowned making the crossing in a storm, Hero threw herself into the sea and drowned in her turn.

hero *n* (4) idol, lead, star; (8) champion; (11) protagonist.

Herod *Bible & hist.* **1 Herod the Great** - the king who, according to St Matthew's gospel, tried to find out from the Wise Men where Jesus was to be born and ordered the massacre of the innocents; **2 Herod Antipas** *or* **Herod the Tetrarch**, the son of Herod the Great, was responsible for the death of **John the Baptist** after his niece (and step-daughter) **Salome** asked for it as a reward for dancing the dance of the seven veils for him.

heroic *adj* (4) bold; (5) brave, noble; (7) gallant, valiant; (8) fearless, intrepid, self-less; (9) dauntless; (10) chivalrous.

Herrick, Robert *lit.* an English 'cavalier' poet of the 17th century, whose most famous poem begins 'Gather ye rosebuds while ye may'.

hesitate *v* (4) wait; (5) delay, demur, doubt, pause, waver; (6) boggle, dither, falter; (7) stammer, stumble, stutter; (9) vacillate; (12) shilly-shally; (2+ words) have second thoughts, hold back, think twice.

hesitation I *n* (5) delay, doubt, pause; (6) doubts, qualms; (8) scruples; (9) faltering, misgiving, stumbling; (10) misgivings, reluctance, stammering, stuttering; (11) vacillation, uncertainty; (12) reservations; (13) unwillingness; II *cryptic* letters ER or UM.

he will *cryptic* abbreviated as HELL.

he would *cryptic* abbreviated as HED.

hide I *v* (4) mask, veil; (5) cloak, cover, stash; (6) screen, shadow, shroud; (7) conceal, eclipse, secrete; (8) disguise; (10) camouflage; II *n* (3) fur; (4) fell, pelt, skin; (7) leather; III HIDDEN WORD CUE.

high *adj* **1** (4) tall; (5) lofty; (7) exalted, soaring; (8) towering; **2** (6) senior; (7) leading; (9) **important**; **3** (6) shrill, treble; (7) soprano; (8) piercing; **4** (5) drunk; (7) drugged.

hill *n* (3) dun, tor; (4) down, drop, fell, heap, knoll, pile, ramp, rise; (5) mound, mount, slope; (6) ascent; (7) descent, hillock, hummock, incline; (8) eminence, gradient; (10) prominence; *see also* **mountain, seven hills of Rome**.

RANGES OF HILLS

(5) Downs, Wolds.

(6) Ochils.

(7) Mendips.

(8) Cheviots, Cuillins, Malverns, Pennines.

(9) Chilterns, Cotswolds, Grampians, Quantocks; (2 words) Drum Hills, Naga Hills (Asia).

(10) Cairngorms; (2 words) Ochil Hills, the Glyders, North Downs, South Downs, Touch Hills.

(11) (2 words) Berwyn Hills, Cleish Hills, Fintry Hills, Lennox Hills, Mendip Hills, Sidlaw Hills.

(12) (2 words) Brendon Hills, Cheviot Hills, Cuillin Hills, Kilsyth Hills, Malvern Hills, Nilgiri Hills (Asia), Peak District, Preseli Hills, Siwalik Hills (Asia).

(13) (2 words) Chiltern Hills, Moorfoot Hills, Pentland Hills.

(14) (2 words) Blackdown Hills, Cleveland Hills.

(15) Kilpatrick Hills, Lammermuir Hills.

hinder *v* (4) curb; (5) check, damp, limit; (6) burden, hamper, impede, retard, thwart; (7) disable; (8) encumber, handicap, obstruct, restrict; (9) frustrate, hamstring.

hindrance *n* (3) bar; (4) snag; (5) hitch; (7) barrier; (8) drawback, handicap, nuisance, obstacle; (10) difficulty, disability, impairment, impediment, limitation; (11) encumbrance, restriction; (12) disadvantage.

hint I *n* **1** (3) tip; (4) clue, sign; (6) tip-off; (7) mention, pointer; (8) allusion, innuendo, reminder; (10) indication, intimation, suggestion; (11) insinuation; **2** (4) dash; (5) tinge, touch, trace; (7) inkling, soupcon; (9) suspicion; **II** *v* (5) imply; (7) suggest; (8) indicate, intimate (9) insinuate.

historian *n*

FAMOUS HISTORIANS

(4) Bede (The Venerable, Eng.), Hall (Edward, Eng.), Hume (David, Brit.), Livy (Roman), Hill (Christopher, Brit).

(5) Acton (Lord, Brit.).

(6) Briggs (Asa, Brit.), Gibbon (Edward, Brit.), Tawney (R. H., Brit), Taylor (A. J. P., Brit.).

(7) Tacitus (Roman), Toynbee (Arnold, Brit.).

(8) Hobsbawm (Eric, Brit), Macaulay (Lord, Brit), Michelet (Jules, French), Wedgwood (C. V., Brit.), Xenophon (Greek).

(9) Clarendon (Lord, Eng.), Trevelyan (George, Brit.).

(10) Thucydides (Greek).

(11) Trevor-Roper (Hugh, Brit.).

---

history *n* **1** (4) past; (8) heritage; (9) antiquity; **2** (6) annals, record; (8) archives; (9) biography, chronicle.

hit I *v* (3) tap; (4) bang, bash, beat, belt, bump, cuff, slap, whop (*or* whap); (5) clout, knock, punch, smack, smash, thump; (6) strike, thrash, wallop; **II** *n* **1** (4) blow, shot; (6) impact, stroke; (9) collision; **2** (7) success, triumph.

hold I *v & n* (4) grip; (5) clasp, grasp; (6) clutch; (7) embrace; **II** *v* **1** (4) bear, seat; (5) carry; (7) contain, enclose, include, support, sustain; (8) comprise, surround; (11) accommodate, incorporate; **2** (6) arrest, detain; (8) imprison; **3** (4) call; (7) conduct, convene; **4** (4) deem; (5) judge, think; (6) reckon; (7) believe; (8) consider, maintain; **III** *n* (4) sway; (5) power; (7) control; (9) dominance, influence; **IV** *also* **held, holds** etc *cryptic* **1** one word is placed around another word, letter or letters, as in: 'Anne is losing heart till she holds party and gets handsome man' (6) = Adonis (*see* **heart**); **2** HIDDEN WORD CUE, as in: 'Barrel held in vicelike grip' (3) = keg.

hold back I *v* **1** (4) curb; (5) check; (6) detain, impede, retain; (7) inhibit, repress; (8) restrict, restrain, suppress; **2** (5) delay; (6) refuse, shrink; (7) refrain; (8) hesitate; **II** *cryptic* **1** one word is placed around another word that is to be written in reverse order, as in: 'Worker, for example, held back by middleman' (5) = agent (worker = ant, for example = e.g.); **2** HIDDEN WORD CUE, the hidden word being shown in reverse order, as in: 'Vehicles held back as Queen's racehorses go by' (4) = cars.

hold up I *v* **1** (5) brace, raise, shore; (7) support, sustain; **2** (4) slow; (5) delay; (6) hinder, impede, retard; **II** *cryptic* works in the same way as **hold back** in *down* clues, as in: 'Child held up to get a bearing – this is what you have to follow' (4) = nose (child = son, bearing = E = east).

hole *n* **1** (3) gap, pit; (4) pore, slot, tear, vent, void; (5) blank, break, chink, cleft, crack, space, split; (6) breach, cavity, eyelet, outlet; (7) fissure, opening, orifice; (8) puncture; **2** (3) den; (5) earth; (6) burrow; **3** (4) flaw; (5) error, fault; (7) mistake.

hollow I *adj* **1** (4) void; (5) empty; (8) unfilled; (10) unoccupied; **2** (4) idle, vain; (5) inane; (6) futile; (7) trivial, useless, vacuous; (9) senseless, worthless; **II** *n* (3) pit; (4) cave, dell, dent; (6) crater, dimple,

valley; (10) depression; (11) indentation; **III** *v* (5) gouge, scoop; (6) groove; (8) excavate.

Holmes, Sherlock *lit.* one of the earliest and most famous of literary detectives, created by Sir Arthur Conan Doyle. Holmes supposedly lived at 221B Baker Street in London and shared his lodgings with Dr John **Watson**, who not only acts as his assistant, but also chronicles his various cases and adventures. Holmes was remarkable for his powers of deduction, being apparently able to envisage most of a person's character and life history from the state of his or her boots or watch case. He was lean and aquiline, wore a deerstalker hat, smoked a large pipe, took cocaine and played the violin. He had a brother, **Mycroft**, who was supposed to be even cleverer than he was, his landlady was Mrs Hudson, he collaborated with Scotland Yard in the shape of Inspectors Lestrade and Gregson, and his chief opponents were Irene Adler ('the Woman'), Col. Sebastian Moran, and Prof. James **Moriarty**. Conan Doyle attempted to kill off his immensely popular hero by having him fall over the Reichenbach Falls while locked in combat with Moriarty, but was forced to bring him back to life again. Famous (but inaccurate) catchphrase: 'Elementary, my dear Watson.'

holy *adj* (4) good, pure; (5) godly; (6) devout, sacred; (7) saintly; (8) hallowed; (10) sanctified; (11) consecrated.

Holy Grail *myth & lit.* the cup used by Jesus Christ at the **Last Supper**, often supposed also to have been used to collect some of his blood at the Crucifixion, and to have been brought to England by **Joseph of Arimathea**. After that its precise whereabouts became a mystery. In Arthurian legend, finding the Holy Grail is the ultimate quest for the Knights of the Round Table. It could only be found by a knight of unblemished honour and purity. It was eventually found by Sir Galahad, Sir Percival and Sir Bors de Ganis.

home I *n* (5) abode, house; (7) habitat; (8) domicile, dwelling; (9) residence; (10) birthplace, habitation, pied-à-terre; (2 words) native country, native town etc; **II at home** *cryptic* IN.

HOMES OF ANIMALS	
Animal	*Home*
Badger	Earth, Set *or* Sett
Beaver	Lodge
Bee	Hive
Bird	Nest
Cattle	Byre, Cowshed
Eagle	Eyrie
Fox	Burrow, Earth
Hare	Form
Heron	Colony
Horse	Stable
Insect eggs	Nidus
Otter	Holt, Lodge
Penguin	Rookery
Pig	Sty
Rabbit	Burrow, Warren
Rook	Rookery
Seal	Rookery
Sparrow	Colony
Squirrel	Dray, Drey
Swan	Colony
Wild beast	Den, Lair

Homer *lit.* the Greek poet credited with the authorship of the two great epics of ancient Greece, the **Iliad** and the **Odyssey**.

honest *adj* 1 (4) fair, just; (5) legal, moral; (7) upright; (8) virtuous; (9) reputable; (10) honourable; (11) trustworthy; 2 (4) open; (5) blunt, frank, plain; (6) candid, direct; (7) sincere; (8) explicit, straight, truthful; (9) downright, outspoken; (10) forthright; (15) straightforward.

honour I *n* 1 (4) fame; (5) glory; (6) credit, esteem, praise, regard, renown, repute; (7) dignity, probity, respect; (9) integrity; (10) admiration, reputation; 2 (5) award, title; (7) peerage; (10) knighthood; (11) recognition; (12) commendation; **II** *v* 1 (6) admire, praise, revere, reward; (7) acclaim, respect; (9) recognise (*or* recognize); (11) acknowledge;

2 (4) keep; (6) fulfil; (7) execute, observe, perform; (9) discharge; **III** *cryptic* a group of letters representing an honourable award or title conferred on somebody, such as: CBE, CH, DBE, MBE, OBE, OM *etc.*

Horace *lit.* Roman poet, especially famous as a writer of odes.

horse I *n* **1** (*male* stallion, *female* mare, *young* colt, foal, filly, *group* herd) (3) bay, cob, nag; (4) Arab, grey, jade, pony, roan; (5) mount, pinto, shire, steed; (6) dapple, Dobbin, geegee; (7) charger, courser, piebald, trotter; (8) chestnut, palomino, skewbald; (9) Percheron; (10) Clydesdale, Lippizaner; (12) thoroughbred; (13) steeplechaser; (2 words) Shetland pony, Suffolk Punch; **2** piece of gymnastic equipment - (4) buck; **3** frame for drying clothes; **4** slang term for heroin; **II** *v* **horse around** (4) lark, play (about); **III** *cryptic* letters GG.

FAMOUS HORSES

Arion – *myth* horse belonging to Neptune and Hercules that spoke with a human voice; *Arkle* – *sport* steeplechaser; *Black Beauty* – *lit.* in book by Anna M. Sewell; *Black Bess* – *hist.* ridden by Dick Turpin; *Black Nell* – *hist.* ridden by Wild Bill Hickock; *Boxer* – *lit.* character in George Orwell's *Animal Farm*; *Bucephalus* – *hist.* the horse tamed and later ridden by Alexander the Great; *Champion* – *TV* the 'wonder horse'; *Clover* – *lit.* character in George Orwell's *Animal Farm*; *Copenhagen* – *hist.* the Duke of Wellington's horse, ridden by him at Waterloo; *Desert Orchid* – *sport* steeplechaser; *Grane* – *myth & lit* Brunnhilda's horse in Wagner's *Ring Cycle*; *Houyhnhm* – *lit.* one of the civilised horses in Swift's *Gulliver's Travels*; *Hercules* – *TV* the horse owned by Steptoe and son; *Incitatus* – *hist.* the horse that the Roman emperor Caligula made a consul; *Lamri* – *myth* King Arthur's horse; *Marengo* – *hist.* ridden by Napoleon at Waterloo; *Marsala* – *hist.* Garibaldi's horse; *Mollie* – *lit.* character in George Orwell's *Animal Farm*; *Pegasus* – *Gk myth* winged horse ridden by Bellerophon and Perseus; *Pi* – *lit.* in book by Enid Bagnold and film; *Red Rum* – *sport* Grand National winner; *Ronald* – *hist.* ridden by Lord Cardigan in the Charge of the Light Brigade; *Rosinante* – *lit.* Don Quixote's horse that was all skin and bone; *Scout* – *TV* Tonto's horse in *The Lone Ranger*; *Shergar* – *sport* kidnapped racehorse; *Silver* – *TV* ridden by the Lone Ranger; *Sleipner* – *myth* Odin's eight-legged horse in Norse myth; *Sorrel* – *hist.* ridden by King William III, tripped over a molehill, throwing off the king who eventually died from the fall; *Trigger* – *TV* ridden by Roy Rogers; *Volonel* – *hist.* ridden by Lord Roberts; *White Surrey* – *hist.* ridden by King Richard III at the battle of Bosworth.

hospital *cryptic* abbreviated as H.

host *n* **1** (8) landlord, publican; (9) innkeeper; **2** (7) compere, linkman; (9) anchorman, presenter; (11) anchorwoman; **3** (4) army, lots, many; (5) array, crowd, horde, swarm; (6) throng.

hostile *adj* (7) warlike; (8) inimical; (10) aggressive, unfriendly; (11) belligerent; (12) antagonistic, unfavourable.

hot *adj* **1** (4) warm; (5) fiery; (6) baking, heated, sultry, torrid; (7) burning; (8) roasting, scalding, sizzling, steaming, tropical; (9) scorching; (10) blistering, sweltering; **2** (5) sharp, spicy; (7) peppery, piquant, pungent; **3** (3) new; (5) fresh; (8) up-to-date; **4** (6) stolen.

house I *n* **1** (4) hall, home, semi; (5) abode, croft, lodge, manor, manse, shack, villa; (6) grange, prefab, shanty; (7) cottage, mansion, rectory; (8) bungalow, detached, domicile, dwelling, vicarage; (9) parsonage, residence; (10) maisonette, pied-à-terre; (12) semi-detached; **2** (5) Lords; (7) Commons; (8) assembly; (10)

Parliament; **3** (4) clan; (5) tribe; (6) family; (7) dynasty; **4** full card in Bingo, Lotto *etc*; **II** *v* (5) board, lodge; (6) billet; (7) quarter, shelter; (11) accommodate; **III** *cryptic* cue for an insertion or hidden word, *see* **hold**.

huge **I** *adj* (3) big; (4) vast; (5) giant, great, jumbo, large; (7) immense, mammoth, monster, outsize, titanic; (8) colossal, enormous, gigantic, king-size; **II** *cryptic* letters OS (outsize), XL (extra large) *etc*.

hum *n & v* **I** (4) buzz, purr; (5) drone, throb, thrum, whirr, whizz; (6) murmur; **2** (4) pong; (5) smell, stink.

humble **I** *adj* **I** (4) meek; (6) modest, polite; (7) servile; (10) submissive; (10) obsequious, unassuming; (11) deferential, subservient sycophantic; **2** (3) low; (4) mean; (5) lowly, plain; (6) simple; (8) ordinary; (13) unpretentious; **II** *v see* **humiliate**.

humiliate *v* (5) abase, crush, lower, shame; (6) demean, humble; (7) chasten, deflate, degrade, mortify; (8) disgrace; (9) discredit, embarrass.

hundred *cryptic* letter C (Roman numeral).

hungry *adj* (4) avid; (5) eager, empty; (6) greedy, hollow; (7) peckish; (8) famished, ravenous, starving.

hurry **I** *v* (3) fly, run; (4) bolt, dart, dash, flit, leap, race, rush, tear; (5) bound, flash, speed (6) bustle, hasten, hustle, sprint; (7) scuttle; **II** *n* (4) rush; (5) haste; (6) flurry; (7) urgency.

hurt **I** *v* **I** (3) cut; (4) burn, maim, harm; (5) wound; (6) bruise, damage, injure, misuse; (7) disable, scratch; **2** (4) pain; (5) upset; (6) grieve, sadden; (7) afflict; (8) distress; **II** *adj* **I** (3) cut; (7) injured, scarred, wounded; **2** (3) sad; (5) upset; (7) annoyed; (8) offended; (9) affronted, aggrieved.

Hyde, Mr *fict.* the evil alter ego of Dr **Jekyll** in the novel by R.L. **Stevenson**.

Hydra *Gk myth* a snake with many heads, that grew two new heads each time one was cut off – eventually killed by **Hercules** as one of his labours.

hydrogen *cryptic* abbreviated as H.

Hymen *Gk myth* the god of marriage.

Hyperion *Gk myth* a **Titan**, one of the sons of Uranus and Gaea.

hypocritical *adj* (5) false; (6) hollow; (8) two-faced; (9) deceitful, insincere, pharisaic; (11) dissembling; (13) double-dealing.

hysterical *adj* **I** (6) raving; (7) berserk, frantic; (8) frenzied, neurotic; **2** (9) hilarious; (10) uproarious; (13) side-splitting.

I

I *abbrev* iodine, island, Italy.

Icarus *Gk myth* the son of **Daedalus**, who escaped with him from Crete, flying away with a pair of wings constructed of feathers and wax. Icarus grew over-confident and flew too near the sun so that the wax in his wings melted and he fell into the sea and was drowned.

ice l *n* 1 (4) pack, rime; (5) brash, frost; (7) glacier; 2 (3) tub; (4) whip; (5) lolly, wafer; (6) cornet; (7) vanilla; (2 words) knickerbocker glory; 3 (8) diamonds; ll *v* 1 (4) cool; (5) chill, frost, glaze; (6) freeze; (11) refrigerate; 2 *slang see* **kill.**

icy *adj* 1 (3) raw; (4) cold (5) chill, polar; (6) arctic, biting, bitter, chilly, frozen, wintry; (7) glacial; (8) freezing; 2 (4) cool; (5) aloof; (7) distant, hostile; (10) un-friendly.

idea *n* (4) clue, plan; (5) hunch, image, sense; (6) notion, scheme, theory, vision; (7) concept, thought; (8) proposal; (9) brainwave, intention; (10) conception, hypothesis, impression, perception; (11) proposition.

ideal l *adj* (4) best; (5) dream, model (7) optimal, optimum, perfect, supreme, utopian; (8) exemplary; ll *n* (4) acme; (5) model; (6) example; (7) epitome, para-gon, pattern; (8) exemplar, standard; (10) perfection.

idiot *n see* **fool** l 1.

idle l *adj* 1 (4) lazy; (6) unused; (7) jobless, work-shy; (8) inactive, indolent; (10) un-occupied; (11) inoperative; 2 (4) vain; (5) empty; (6) casual, futile; (7) trivial; (9) pointless; ll *v* (4) laze, loaf; (5) skive, slack; (6) dawdle, loiter, lounge.

Iliad *lit.* a Greek epic poem by **Homer** that recounts the story of the **Trojan War**, centring on an episode in which **Achilles**, the Greeks' greatest warrior, refuses to fight and remains in his tent until his companion Patroclus is killed. This brings Achilles back into action and leads to his killing of **Hector**, the Trojan champion.

ill *adj* 1 (4) sick; (5) frail, seedy; (6) ailing, infirm, poorly, queasy, unwell; (9) off-colour, unhealthy; (10) indisposed; (2+ words) not oneself, out of sorts, under the weather; 2 (3) bad; (4) evil; (6) unkind; (7) harmful, hostile, ominous, unlucky; (8) sinister; (10) unfriendly; (11) threaten-ing; (12) inauspicious, unfavourable.

illicit *adj* (5) wrong; (7) illegal; (8) crimi-nal, improper, unlawful; (9) forbidden; (10) contraband, unlicensed; (11) clan-destine; (12) illegitimate, unauthorised (*or* unauthorized).

illusion *n* (5) dream, fancy, ghost, story; (6) legend, mirage, vision; (7) fantasy, reverie; (8) daydream, delusion; (9) in-vention, unreality; (10) apparition; (13) hallucination; (2 words) pipe dream.

imaginary *adj* (6) made-up, unreal; (7) pretend; (8) fanciful, illusory, invented; (9) fictional; (10) fictitious; (11) make-believe, non-existent; (12) hypothetical.

imaginative *adj* (8) creative, inspired; (9) ingenious, inventive, visionary; (10) in-novative; (11) resourceful.

imagine *v* (5) fancy, guess, think; (6) assume, create, devise, gather, invent; (7) believe, picture, pretend, suppose; (8) conceive, envisage; (9) fantasise (*or* fanta-size), visualise (*or* visualize); (10) conjecture.

imitate *v* (3) ape; (4) echo; (5) mimic; (6) follow, mirror, parody, parrot, repeat; (7) emulate; (8) simulate; (9) duplicate, reproduce; (10) caricature; (11) imper-sonate; (2 words) send up, take off.

imitation l *n* 1 (6) parody, send-up; (7) mimicry, mockery; (8) travesty; (10) cari-cature, impression; (13) impersonation;

2 (4) copy, fake; (5) clone; (7) forgery, replica; (9) duplicate; (10) simulation; (11) duplication; (12) reproduction; **‖** *adj* (4) fake, mock, sham; (6) ersatz, phoney, pseudo; (7) man-made; (9) simulated, synthetic; (10) artificial.

immoral *adj* (3) bad; (4) evil; (5) wrong; (6) impure, sinful, unholy, wicked; (7) corrupt, impious, profane, obscene, ungodly; (8) depraved, indecent; (9) dissolute, unethical; (10) degenerate, irreverent; (11) irreligious, promiscuous; (12) pornographic, unprincipled, unscrupulous.

immortal ‖ *adj* (7) abiding, ageless, endless, eternal, lasting, undying; (8) enduring, timeless; (9) perpetual; (11) everlasting; **‖** *n see* **god**.

impertinent *adj* (4) bold, pert; (5) brash, fresh, pushy; (6) brazen, cheeky; (7) forward; (8) impudent; (10) precocious.

important *adj* (3) key; (5) grave, major, noted, vital; (6) urgent; (7) crucial, leading, primary, salient, serious; (8) foremost, material, relevant; (9) high-level, momentous, prominent; (10) meaningful; (11) far-reaching, high-ranking, influential, significant; (13) consequential.

impress *v* **1** (4) grab, move, stir; (5) touch; (6) affect, excite, strike; (7) inspire; (9) influence; **2** (4) mark, seal; (5) stamp; (6) indent; (7) engrave, imprint; **3** (5) seize; (7) enforce; (8) shanghai; (9) conscript, press-gang.

impression *n* **1** (4) idea; (5) hunch, sense; (6) belief, effect, impact, notion; (7) feeling; (9) intuition, suspicion; **2** (4) dent, mark; (5) print, stamp; (7) imprint; **3** (6) parody, send-up; (7) take-off; (9) imitation; (13) impersonation.

impressionism *art* late-19th-century movement in painting that aimed to capture the artist's 'impression' of a particular scene at a particular moment in time on canvas.

impressionist *n* (5) mimic; (8) imitator; (12) impersonator.

IMPRESSIONIST PAINTERS
(5) Degas, Manet, Monet;
(6) Boudin, Renoir, Sisley;
(7) Cezanne, Morisot, Pissaro.

---

impudent *see* **impertinent**.

in *cryptic* insert a word, letter or group of letters into another word (*in* often being incorporated into a word in the clue, such as *indeed*, *inlay*, *intake*, *etc*), as in: 'At home in bed? – Heartless, in such a difficult situation' (4) = bind (at home = in; bed heartless = b-d); or: 'Dangerous creature needs an enclosure – insert at once' (7) = serpent.

in charge *cryptic* letters IC (abbreviation), or, occasionally, insert a word or letter into a words meaning 'charge'.

Incitatus *hist.* the horse that the Roman emperor Caligula appointed as a consul.

include ‖ *v* (3) add; (5) cover; (6) insert; (7) contain, embrace, involve, subsume; (8) comprise; (10) comprehend; (11) incorporate; **‖** *cryptic* **1** include a word, letter, or group of letters in another word to get the answer, as in: 'Include a little time during dinner to get out the silver, for example' (5) = metal (a little time = T); **2** HIDDEN WORD CUE.

income *n* (3) pay; (5) gains, wages; (6) return, salary; (7) profits, revenue, takings; (8) dividend, earnings, interest, proceeds, receipts; (12) remuneration.

incomplete ‖ *adj* (4) part; (5) short; (6) broken; (7) lacking, partial; (8) abridged; (9) defective, deficient, imperfect; (10) unfinished; (11) fragmentary; **‖** *cryptic* **incomplete** *or* **incompletely 1** use part of a word in the clue in the answer, as in: 'Thesis incomplete, also lecture – need total image for factual overview' (3, 4, 7) = the full picture; **2** HIDDEN WORD CUE, as in: 'Reference to Jo in Ted's speech incompletely articulated' (7) = jointed.

incorrect ‖ *adj* (3) off, out; (5) false, wrong; (6) faulty, untrue; (7) inexact; (8) improper, mistaken; (9) erroneous, imprecise; (10) fallacious, inaccurate; (12) illegitimate; (13) ungrammatical;

‖ incorrect *or* **incorrectly** *cryptic* ANA-GRAM CUE.

increase ‖ *v* (5) swell, widen; (6) dilate, expand; (7) amplify, augment, broaden, develop, enlarge, inflate, magnify, stretch; (8) heighten, lengthen; (9) elaborate, expatiate; (2 words) blow up; **‖** *n* (6) growth; (11) enlargement.

in debt *see* **debt**.

individual ‖ *adj* (3) own; (6) proper, single, unique; (7) special; (8) discrete, distinct, peculiar, personal, separate, singular, specific; (10) particular; (11) distinctive; (13) idiosyncratic; (14) characteristic; **2** *n* (1) I; (3) ego; (4) soul; (5) being; (6) person; (8) creature.

industry *n* **1** (5) trade; (8) business, commerce; (13) manufacturing; **2** (4) work, toil; (6) effort, labour; (9) diligence; (11) application.

inebriated *see* **drunk**.

inexpensive *see* **cheap**.

inexperienced *adj* (3) new, raw; (5) green, naïve, young; (6) callow; (7) untried; (8) immature, innocent, inexpert; (10) unfamiliar; (12) probationary, unaccustomed, unacquainted; (15) unsophisticated.

inexperienced person ‖ *n* (4) tyro; (7) amateur, learner, trainee; (8) beginner; (9) debutante; (10) apprentice; **‖** *cryptic* letter L.

inform *v* **1** (4) tell, warn; (5) brief; (6) advise, notify; (8) acquaint, instruct; (9) enlighten; (2 words) fill in, tip off; **2** (4) shop; (5) grass; (6) betray; (8) denounce; (11) incriminate.

informal *adj* (4) easy, free; (6) casual; (7) natural, relaxed; (8) friendly; (10) colloquial, unofficial; (13) unpretentious.

information *n* (3) gen; (4) data, dope, news, word; (5) facts; (6) advice, notice; (8) briefing; (9) knowledge; (12) intelligence.

initial ‖ *adj* **1** (5) early, first; (6) eldest, oldest, primal; (7) opening; (8) earliest, original, primeval; (9) primitive; (11) preliminary; (12) introductory; **‖ initial** *or*

initially *cryptic* **1** use the first letter of a word, or the first letters of a number of words, in the clue, as in: 'Harold's initial hesitation creates a bad odour' (3) = hum (*see* **hesitation**); **2** use the word or letters referred to in front of another word to form the answer, as in: 'The Spanish alternative followed by the poet with the composer initially was a state of unwedded bliss' (12) = bachelorhood (composer = Bach, poet = Hood).

in order *see* **order**.

in ruins *see* **ruin, ruined**.

insect

INSECTS
(3) ant, bee, bug, fly, lug, nit.
(4) cleg, flea, frit, gnat, mite, moth, tick, wasp.
(5) aphid, drone, egger, emmet, louse, midge.
(6) bedbug, beetle, botfly, caddis, chafer, chigoe, cicada, earwig, gadfly, hopper, hornet, jigger, locust, mantis, may-bug, mayfly, spider, tsetse.
(7) ant-lion, crocket, firefly, katydid, skipper, termite.
(8) crane-fly, geometer, greenfly, hook-worm, horsefly, inch-worm, ladybird, mealy-bug, mosquito, puss-moth, scorpion.
(9) bumble-bee, butterfly, caddis-fly, centipede, cochineal, cockroach, dragonfly, ichneumon, millipede, shield-bug, tarantula, tsetse-fly, warble-fly.
(10) bluebottle, boll-weevil, cabbage-fly, cheese-mite, cockchafer, demoiselle, fritillary, leaf-cutter, silver-fish, stag-beetle.
(11) caterpillar, grasshopper, greenbottle, lamellicorn, swallow-tail.
(12) water-boatman.
(13) daddy-long-legs.
(2 words) black widow, ichneumon fly, praying mantis.

inside *cryptic* place a word, letter or letters inside another word, as in: 'Trainee placed inside box with weapon to qualify for exclusive Tory organisation?' (7, 4) = Carlton Club (trainee = L).

inspiration *n* **1** (4) muse, spur; (8) stimulus; (9) incentive, influence; (10) motivation; (11) stimulation; **2** (4) idea; (7) insight; (9) brainwave; (10) revelation; (12) illumination.

install I *v* **1** (3) fit, fix, lay, put; (4) site; (5) erect, place; (6) locate; (7) station; (8) position; (9) establish; (2+ words) put in place, put in position, set up; **2** (6) induct, invest, ordain; II *cryptic* **install** *or* **installed** place a word, letter or letters inside another word, as in: 'From message sounds like Poirot's installed himself in Morse's Jag' (8) = circular (Poirot = Hercule … sounds like 'ircul').

instrument *n* (4) dial, tool; (6) device, gadget; (7) utensil; (9) appliance, implement; *see also* **musical instruments**.

interval *n* **1** (3) gap; (4) lull, rest, time, wait; (5) break, pause, space, spell; (7) interim; (8) meantime; (9) entr'acte, interlude, meanwhile; (12) intermission, interruption; **2** *music* (5) fifth, sixth, third; (6) fourth, octave, second; (7) seventh.

invent *v* (5) frame; (6) create, design, devise; (7) concoct, imagine; (8) conceive, contrive, discover; (9) formulate, originate; (2 words) cook up, dream up, make up, think up, trump up.

invention *n* **1** (6) design, device, gadget; (8) creation; (9) discovery; (10) brainchild; **2** (9) ingenuity; (10) creativity; (11) imagination; (13) inventiveness.

inventor *n* (5) maker; (6) author; (7) creator; (8) designer; (10) discoverer, originator.

INVENTORS

(4) Bell (*telephone*), Benz (*car engine*), Biró (*ball-point pen*), Colt (*revolver*), Davy (*miner's lamp*), Holt (*combine harvester*), Howe (*sewing machine*), Hunt (*safety pin*), Land (*Polaroid camera*), Otis (*passenger lift*), Otto (*four-stroke engine*), Tull (*seed drill*), Very (*flare signal*), Watt (*condensing steam engine*), Yale (*cylinder lock*).

(5) Aiken (*digital computer*), Baird (*mechanical television*), Booth (*vacuum cleaner*), Carré (*refrigerator*), Dewar (*vacuum flask*), Gabor (*holograph*), Hyatt (*celluloid*), Magee (*parking meter*), Maxim (*machine-gun*), Morse (*telegraph*), Smith (*ship's propeller*), Volta (*electric battery*).

(6) Bunsen (*bunsen burner*), Cayley (*glider*), Diesel (*diesel engine*), Dunlop (*pneumatic tyre*), Eckert (*phonograph*), Fuller (*solar battery*), Fulton (*torpedo*), Geiger (*geiger counter*), Hughes (*microphone*), Judson (*zip-fastener*), Lenior (*internal-combustion engine*), McAdam (*macadamised road surface*), Pincus (*contraceptive pill*), Sholes (*typewriter*), Singer (*sewing machine*), Sperry (*gyro-compass*), (Fox-)Talbot (*calotype photography*), Wallis (*bouncing bomb*).

(7) Bardeen (*transistor*), Braille (*reading system for the blind*), Daimler (*car-engine pioneer*), Dickson (*terylene*), Gatling (*rapid-fire gun*), Glidden (*barbed wire*), Lumière (*cine cinema*), Mauchly (*electronic computer*), Neilson (*blast furnace*), Parsons (*turbine steamship*), Pearson (*solar battery*), Poulsen (*tape recorder*), Stanley (*electric transformer*), Whitney (*cotton gin*), Whittle (*jet engine*).

(8) Berliner (*gramophone*), Bessemer (*steel converter*), Birdseye (*frozen food process*), Brattain (*transistor*), Brewster (*kaleidoscope*), Bushnell (*submarine*), Crompton (*spinning mule*), Daguerre (*daguerreotype photography*), Foucault

list continued over

(*gyroscope*), Franklin (*lightning conductor*), Gillette (*safety razor*), Goodyear (*vulcanised rubber*), Harrison (*chronometer*), Jacquard (*Jacquard loom*), Mercator (*cylindrical world projection*), Newcomen (*steam engine*), Oughtred (*slide rule*), Plantson (*dental plate*), Shockley (*transistor*), Shrapnel (*shrapnel shell*), Sikorsky (*practical helicopter*), Sturgeon (*electro-magnet*), Waterman (*fountain pen*), Zeppelin (*rigid airship*), Zworykin (*standard television*).

(9) Arkwright (*spinning frame*), Baekeland (*bakelite*), Blanchard (*parachute*), Burroughs (*commercial adding machine*), Cockerell (*hovercraft*), Gutenberg (*printing press*), Macintosh (*waterproof clothing*), Poniatoff (*videotape recorder*), Whinfield (*terylene*).

(10) Fahrenheit (*mercury thermometer*), Farnsworth (*electrical television*), Hargreaves (*spinning jenny*), Harrington (*water closet*), Lanchester (*disc-brake*), Lippershey (*telescope*), Torricelli (*barometer*), Trevithick (*steam carriage*).

(11) Baskerville (*advanced printing type*), Mège-Mouriés (*margarine*), Montgolfier (*hot-air balloon*).

invest I *v* 1 (5) spend; (6) commit, devote; (8) dedicate; 2 (4) vest; (5) endow; (6) bestow, clothe; 3 (7) besiege; (8) surround; II *cryptic* **invest** or **invested** place a word, letter or letters (especially one referring to money) inside another word, as in: 'Invested a pound in a dandy scheme that failed' (4) = flop (pound = L).

investigate *v* (3) vet; (4) quiz, pore, scan, sift, test; (5) assay, audit, check, grill, probe, study; (6) review, survey; (7) analyse, examine, explore, inspect, observe; (8) appraise, consider, question; (10) scrutinise (*or* scrutinize); (2 words) go into, look into.

Io *Gk myth* a priestess of Hera, loved by Zeus, who turned her into a heifer to protect her from Hera's wrath. Hera thereupon sent a gadfly to torment her; it chased her through Europe across the Bosphorus and thence to Egypt, where she regained her human form.

iridium *cryptic* letters IR (chemical symbol).

iron I *adj* (4) hard; (5) metal, rigid; (6) ferric; (7) ferrous; II *v* (5) press; (6) smooth; (7) flatten; III *n* 1 golf club; 2 **irons** (6) chains; (7) fetters (9) handcuffs; IV *cryptic* letters FE (chemical symbol).

irritate *v* (3) irk, rub, vex; (4) itch, rile; (5) anger, annoy, chafe; (6) bother, harass, hassle, needle, nettle; (7) torment; (9) aggravate; (10) exasperate.

Isaac *Bible* the son of **Abraham** (who nearly sacrificed him), husband of **Rebecca** and the father of **Jacob** and **Esau**.

Isaiah *Bible* Old Testament prophet and book of the Old Testament.

island *n* (3) ait; (4) eyot, inch, isle; (5) islet; (6) refuge.

ISLANDS IN THE BRITISH ISLES

(3) Hoy, Man, Rat, Rum.

(4) Aran, Bute, Eigg, Herm, Iona, Jura, Muck, Mull, Rhum, Sark, Skye, Tory, Uist.

(5) Annet, Arran, Barra, Barry, Caldy, Canna, Clare, Eagle, Ensay, Foula, Islay, Lewis, Lundy, Ronay, Tiree, Wight.

(6) Achill, Canvey, Dursey, Fetlar, Jersey, Lambay, Mersea, Oldany, Potton, Puffin, Raasay, Ramsey, Rousay, Sanday, Scarba, Skomer, Staffa, Stroma, Tresco, Walney.

(7) Bardsey, Cramond, Eriskay, Gometra, Hayling, Lismore, Oronsay, Portsea, Rockall, Sheppey, Thorney, Westray, Whalsey.

(8) Alderney, Anglesey, Brownsea, Colonsay, Foulness, Gruinard, Guernsey, Mainland, Mingulay, Portland, Skokholm, Stronsay, Vatersay, Wallasea.

list continued over

(9) Benbecula, Havengore, Inchkeith, Inishmaan, Inishmore, Inishturk.

(11) Lindisfarne.

(2+ words) Calf of Man, Fair Isle, Flat Holm, Holy Island, North Uist, South Uist, Steep Holme, St Kilda.

(not true islands) Isle of Dogs, Isle of Ely, Isle of Purbeck, Isle of Thanet.

BRITISH ISLAND GROUPS

(7) Orkneys; (8) Hebrides, Scillies; (9) Shetlands.

ISLANDS (WORLD)

(6) Baffin, Borneo, Cyprus, Easter, Hawaii, Honshu, Ischia, Ithaca, Lemnos, Lesbos, Midway, Patmos, Penang, Phuket, Rhodes, Robben, Sicily, Skiros, Staten, Tahiti, Taiwan, Tobago, Tuvalu.

(7) Antigua, Barbuda, Bermuda, Celebes, Corsica, Curacao, Formosa, Grenada, Iceland, Jamaica, Madeira, Majorca, Menorca, Mikonos, Minorca, Mykonos, Okinawa, Palmyra, Reunion, Roanoke, Salamis, Sumatra, Vanuatu.

(8) Alcatraz, Anguilla, Barbados, Bathurst, Hokkaido, Kiribati, Krakatoa, Mallorca, Miquelon, Navarino, Pitcairn, Sardinia, Skiathos, Tasmania, Tenerife, Trinidad, Zanzibar.

(9) Ascension, Christmas, Ellesmere, Galveston, Kerguelen, Lanzarote, Manhattan, Mauritius, Nantucket, Santorini, Singapore, Stromboli, Vancouver.

(10) Cephalonia, Guadeloupe, Heligoland, Hispaniola, Madagascar, Martinique, Montserrat, Samothrace.

(11) Guadalcanal, Spitzbergen.

(12) Newfoundland.

(2 words) Belle Isle, Gran Canaria, Hong Kong, Key Largo, Iwo Jima, Long Island, New Guinea, Puerto Rico, Sri Lanka, South Georgia, St Helena, St Kitts, St Lucia.

WORLD ISLAND GROUPS

(6) Azores, Faroes.

(7) Bahamas, Faeroes.

(8) Andamans, Antilles, Canaries, Maldives, Moluccas.

(9) Aleutians, Balearics, Falklands, Galapagos, Polynesia.

(10) Seychelles.

(11) Philippines.

Israel I *Bible* the new name given by God to **Jacob**; **II** *Bible* the Hebrew nation thought of as descendants of Jacob; **III** *Bible* the northern kingdom of the Hebrews formed after the reign of Solomon; *see also* **Judaea**; **IV** *geog.* the modern Jewish state founded in Palestine in 1948.

issue I *n* **1** (5) topic; (6) affair, debate, matter; (7) concern, problem, subject; (8) question; **2** (4) copy; (6) number; (7) edition; (10) instalment; **3** (6) supply; (7) release; (11) publication; (12) announcement, distribution; **4** (3) son; (5) child; (8) children, daughter; **II** *v* **1** (4) emit; (6) supply; (7) provide publish, release; (8) announce; (9) broadcast, circulate; (10) distribute, promulgate; (2 words) give out, hand out, send out; **2** (4) flow, gush, stem; (5) arise; (6) emerge, spring; (7) proceed.

Italian *cryptic* **1** letters IT; **2** use a (usually simple) Italian word as part of the solution, especially 'an Italian' = UN, UNA, UNO and 'the Italian' = IL, LA, LE, LO, or I, or 'with Italian' CON or 'with the Italian' COL, COLLA, COLLO.

Italy *cryptic* abbreviated as I or IT.

Ivy League *educ.* a group of famous and long-established colleges and universities in the NE USA. It comprises Brown, Columbia, Cornell, Dartmouth, Harvard, Pennsylvania, Princeton and Yale.

I will *cryptic* letters ILL.

I would *cryptic* letters ID.

Ixion *Gk myth* a king of the Lapiths punished by Zeus by being bound to an ever-revolving wheel of fire in the **Underworld**.

J

J *abbrev* jack, Japan, joule.

jack *n* **1** (4) card; (5) knave; **2** (2) AB; (3) tar; (6) **sailor**; **3** (4) lift; (5) hoist; **4** target ball in bowls.

Jacob *Bible* the younger of twin sons of **Isaac** and **Rebecca**. Jacob ('a smooth man') persuaded his elder brother **Esau** ('a hairy man') to part with his birthright in return for a 'mess of pottage' and also managed to obtain his blind father's blessing, due to Esau, with his mother's help, by covering his arms and neck with the skin of kids. Jacob went to serve his uncle Laban to find a wife. On the way, he had a dream in which he saw a ladder going up into heaven and angels ascending and descending it. He laboured seven years to obtain Laban's daughter Rachel in marriage, only to be fobbed off with her elder sister Leah on the wedding night. To obtain Rachel, he had to serve another seven years. By God's command his name was changed to Israel. He had twelve sons who were the founders of the twelve tribes of Israel.

Jacobin *hist.* a member of a radical revolutionary club and party at the time of the French Revolution.

Jacobite *hist.* a supporter of King James II of England after his deposition or of later Stuart claimants to the throne, especially James II's son, James Edward (the Old Pretender), and grandson, Charles Edward (the Young Pretender).

jade *n* **1** (3) gem; (5) stone; (8) nephrite; **2** (3) nag; (5) **horse**, screw; **3** (4) minx; (5) hussy.

jaded *adj* (4) dull; (5) bored, tired, weary; (8) fatigued; (9) apathetic.

January (3) Jan; (5) month; the first month, named after Janus.

Janus *Rom. myth* the god of doorways, usually represented with two heads facing both ways.

Japan I *geog. also called* Nippon – island country consisting of islands of Hokkaido, Honshu, Kyushu, Shikoku; II *cryptic* abbreviated as J.

jar I *n* (3) jug, mug, pot, urn; (4) ewer, vase; (5) glass; (7) pitcher; (9) container; II *v* (3) jog; (4) jerk, jolt, rock; (5) annoy, clang, clank, clash, grate, shake, shock; (6) rattle; (7) clatter, vibrate; (8) conflict.

jargon *n* (4) cant; (5) argot, idiom, slang; (8) legalese, parlance; (10) journalese, vernacular; (12) gobbledygook, psychobabble.

Jason *Gk myth* the leader of the **Argonauts** who went to recover the **Golden Fleece**. He accomplished this with the help of **Medea**, whom he later married.

jeer I *v & n* (3) boo; (4) gibe (*or* jibe), hiss, hoot, mock; (5) abuse, scoff, sneer, taunt; (6) insult; II *v* (6) deride, heckle; (7) barrack; (8) ridicule; III *n* (7) catcall.

Jehu *Bible* a king of Israel who was famous for driving his chariot fast and furiously.

Jekyll *fict.* in the novel by R. L. **Stevenson**, a Scottish doctor who by drinking one of his own experimental potions turns into the evil Mr **Hyde**.

jerk I *v & n* (3) jar, jog, tug; (4) jolt, pull, yank; (5) lurch, pluck; (6) bounce, jiggle, twitch, wrench; II *n slang see* **fool**; III *cryptic* ANAGRAM CUE.

jerky *adj* (5) bumpy, jumpy, rough, shaky; (6) fitful, uneven; (7) twitchy; (9) spasmodic; (10) convulsive; (12) disconnected; (13) uncoordinated.

Jeroboam I *Bible* a rival to King **Solomon** and his successor, who became king of Israel but incurred the wrath of God because he 'did sin and . . . made Israel to sin'; II *n see* **bottle**.

Jesse *Bible* the father of King **David** and an ancestor of Jesus Christ. The 'tree of Jesse', represented as a literal tree with Jesse as its root and the Virgin Mary and Jesus as its topmost branch, was a favourite symbol in Christian art.

jest *see* **joke**.

Jesus *rel.* the founder of the Christian religion, recognised by Christians as the Christ, the Saviour and Son of God. He was born in Bethlehem and brought up in Nazareth by his mother Mary and her husband Joseph. His earliest followers were the twelve **apostles**. He was eventually betrayed to the Jewish authorities by one of them, Judas Iscariot. He was executed by crucifixion and, according to the gospel accounts and Christian belief, rose from the dead on the third day.

jewel *see* **gem**.

jewellery *n*

PIECES OF JEWELLERY

(3) orb, pin.

(4) drop, ouch, ring, rope.

(5) bijou, cameo, charm, clasp, crown, tiara.

(6) amulet, anklet, armlet, bangle, bauble, brooch, choker, collet, diadem, fibula, gorget, locket, signet, tiepin, torque.

(7) coronet, eardrop, earring, necklet, pendant, sleeper, spangle, trinket.

(8) baguette, bracelet, cufflink, intaglio, necklace, nosering, pectoral, scarf-pin.

(9) breastpin, guard-ring.

(10) chatelaine.

Jezebel *Bible* a Phoenician princess, the wife of King **Ahab**, and archetype of the wicked woman. She introduced the worship of Baal into Israel, 'slew the prophets of the Lord', encouraged her husband to have Naboth killed so that he could get possession of his vineyard, 'painted her face' and died by being thrown from a window.

Joan I Joan of Arc, St Joan *hist.* French heroine of the latter part of the Hundred Years War. Born in Domrémy, she believed she heard the voices of St Michael, St Catherine and St Margaret telling her to drive the English invaders from France. She was instrumental in raising the siege of Orleans and having Charles VII crowned King in Reims. Captured and sold to the English, she was tried for heresy in Rouen and burnt at the stake in 1432. Also called The Maid of Orleans, La Pucelle. **II** *see* **Darby and Joan**.

Job *Bible* a biblical patriarch and model of patient endurance. The Lord gave Satan permission to try Job's faith, which he did by reducing him to utter misery and poverty. Job withstood the test. The friends who merely added to his distress while ostensibly trying to support him are known as Job's comforters.

job *n* (4) duty, post, role, task, work; (5) chore, place, trade; (6) career, errand, office; (7) calling, project; (8) business, capacity, function, position, vocation; (9) situation; (10) assignment, commission, employment, livelihood, occupation; (11) undertaking; (14) responsibility.

jocular *adj* (5) droll, funny, jolly, merry, witty; (6) jocund, jovial; (7) amusing; (8) humorous; (9) facetious.

John *Bible* **1 St John (the Evangelist)** one of the earliest of Jesus's disciples, brother of James and son of Zebedee, 'the disciple whom **Jesus** loved', traditionally credited with the authorship of the fourth Gospel and the Book of Revelations; **2 John the Baptist** a forerunner of **Jesus** who preached repentance and baptised people, including Jesus himself, in the River Jordan. Later killed by **Herod** at the behest of **Salome**.

john *US slang for* lavatory.

John Bull *lit.* the personification of England, the Englishman or Englishness.

John Doe *US* an average man or citizen, an unidentified male or male corpse.

John Hancock *US* a signature (from the conspicuousness of the signature of John

Hancock, the president of the Continental Congress, on the Declaration of Independence – he was the first to sign it).

John o' Groats *geog.* traditionally the most northerly point in Scotland of the mainland of Great Britain.

Johnson, Dr (Samuel) *lit.* the compiler of the most famous early dictionary of the English language, a poet, essayist, moralist and wit, whose sayings and doings were recorded in great detail by his biographer **Boswell**.

join I *v* 1 (3) tie; (4) abut, knit, link, meet, yoke; (5) marry, merge, unite; (6) attach, cement, couple, fasten, splice; (7) combine, connect; (8) dovetail; 2 (5) enrol, enter; (6) enlist; (8) register; II *n* see **joint** I 1.

joint I *n* 1 (4) link, seam; (5) hinge; (8) junction; (10) connection; 2 *of body* (3) hip; (4) knee; (5) ankle, elbow, wrist; (7) knuckle; (8) shoulder; 3 *carpentry* (5) tenon; (7) mortise; (8) dovetail; 4 *meat* (3) cut, leg, rib; (4) side; (5) baron; (8) shoulder; 5 (4) club, dive; (9) nightclub; 6 (5) reefer; II *adj* (6) common, mutual, shared, united; (8) combined, communal; (9) concerted; (10) collective; (11) amalgamated.

joke I *n & v* (3) gag, pun; (4) jape, jest, lark, quip; II *n* (5) crack, prank, trick; (8) one-liner; III *v* (3) kid; (4) fool; (5) clown, tease; (6) banter.

joker *n* 1 (4) card; (2 words) wild card; 2 (3) wag, wit; (5) clown, comic; (6) jester; (7) buffoon; (8) comedian, humorist.

jolly I *adj* (5) happy, merry; (6) hearty, jovial, lively; (7) festive; (8) cheerful; (9) convivial; II *adv* (4) very; (9) extremely.

Jolly Roger *hist.* the pirate flag, a skull and crossbones.

Jonson, Ben *lit.* poet and dramatist, contemporary and friend of **Shakespeare**, traditionally thought of as the first poet laureate: best-known plays: The Alchemist, Bartholomew Fair, Epicoene (or The Silent Woman), Volpone; best-known poem: To Celia – 'Drink to me only with thine eyes'.

Joseph *Bible* 1 *Old Testament* a younger son of **Jacob** who aroused his brothers' jealousy by being his father's favourite, being given a 'coat of many colours', and by dreaming dreams which indicated that one day all his (older) brothers would bow down to him. Thrown into a pit by his brethren, he was rescued and taken to Egypt where, despite attempts by the wife of Potiphar (an officer of Pharaoh) to brand him as a seducer, he became invaluable to Pharaoh as an interpreter of dreams, especially by predicting that seven 'fat years' would be followed by seven 'lean years', and as the organiser of measures to deal with the seven years of famine. When the famine struck, Jacob was compelled to send his sons into Egypt to buy grain – and who did they have to go cap in hand to but Joseph? 2 *New Testament* **St Joseph** a carpenter of Nazareth, husband of the Virgin Mary, and the 'father' who raised Jesus; 3 **Joseph of Arimathea** a wealthy man who offered his tomb as Jesus's burial place, legendarily supposed to have brought the **Holy Grail** to Britain and founded the abbey of Glastonbury.

Joshua *Bible* successor to Moses as leader of the Israelites, who took the city of Jericho by having his men march seven times around the walls blowing on seven ram's horns, at which the walls fell down.

journalist I *n* (4) hack; (6) editor; (8) reporter; (9) columnist; (10) newscaster; (13) correspondent; II *cryptic* letters ED (abbreviation of editor).

journey I *n & v* (4) tour, trek; (6) voyage, wander; II *n* (6) outing, safari; (9) excursion; (10) expedition; III *v* (2) go; (4) roam, rove; (6) travel; (7) proceed.

Jove *see* **Jupiter**.

Judas I *Bible* **Judas Iscariot** the apostle who betrayed **Jesus** (with a kiss) to the authorities for 30 pieces of silver and subsequently repented and hanged himself; II **Judas Maccabeus** *Bible Apocrypha* Jewish hero and leader who led a revolt resulting in the recovery of Jerusalem from the Syrians and the rededication of the Temple.

judge I *n* 1 (4) beak; (6) umpire; (7) arbiter, justice, referee; (8) assessor; (9) moderator; (10) arbitrator, magistrate; (11) adjudicator; 2 (6) critic, expert; (9) authority; (11) connoisseur; II *v* 1 (3) try; (6) assess, umpire; (7) examine, referee; (8) appraise, moderate; (9) arbitrate, ascertain, determine; (10) adjudicate; 2 (4) deem, doom, find, rate, rule; (5) think; (6) decide, decree, reckon; (7) believe; (8) consider, sentence; 3 (5) gauge, guess; (8) estimate; 4 (7) condemn; (9) criticise (*or* criticize).

judgement *or* **judgment** *n* 1 (4) doom, fate; (5) order; (6) decree, ruling; (7) finding, verdict; (8) decision, sentence; (9) appraisal; (10) assessment, conclusion, punishment; (11) arbitration, retribution; (12) adjudication; 2 (6) wisdom; (10) shrewdness; (11) discernment; (12) intelligence; (14) discrimination.

Judgement of Paris *see* **Paris**².

judicial *adj* (5) legal; (8) forensic.

judicious *adj* (4) wise; (5) sound; (6) astute, shrewd; (7) careful, prudent; (8) cautious, sensible; (10) discerning, reasonable, well-judged; (11) well-advised.

Juggernaut *Hinduism* a Hindu god, an incarnation of Vishnu, whose image is dragged in procession through the streets of Puri, in Orissa, India, on a chariot with huge wheels. Frenzied devotees are formerly supposed to have thrown themselves under the wheels to be crushed to death.

juggernaut *n* (5) artic, lorry, truck.

Julius Caesar I *hist.* Roman soldier, statesman and dictator, member of the first **triumvirate** (ruling junta), conqueror of Gaul and invader of Britain. He quarrelled with the senate and Pompey, a fellow triumvir, crossed the **Rubicon** with his army from Gaul and defeated Pompey in the civil war which followed. Appointed dictator, he planned large-scale public works in Rome but was assassinated by conspirators before most of them could be carried out; II *lit.* tragedy by Shakespeare dealing with the events surrounding Caesar's assassination.

Plot outline: Brutus, a friend of Caesar, is persuaded by Cassius to join a conspiracy against him on the grounds that Caesar is too ambitious and autocratic. Caesar is assassinated and Brutus speaks to the Roman people and appears to have convinced them that the murder of Caesar was politically justified. Always noble and high-minded, Brutus permits Mark Antony, a young friend and associate of Caesar's to address the crowd after him ('Friends, Romans, countrymen, lend me your ears'). Antony whips up the crowd against the conspirators, and Brutus and Cassius are forced to flee Rome. They gather an army, but are defeated by the forces of Antony and Caesar's nephew Octavius and both commit suicide. The play ends with Antony's eulogy of Brutus ('This was the noblest Roman of them all').

July *n* abbreviated as Jul, the seventh month, named after Julius Caesar.

jump I *n* & *v* 1 (3) hop; (4) leap, skip; (5) bound, vault; (6) bounce, frolic, gambol, prance, spring; 2 (4) jerk, jolt; (5) start, wince; (6) flinch, recoil; II *v* 1 (5) clear; (6) hurdle; 2 (4) omit, miss, skip; (5) avoid; (6) bypass, ignore; 3 (4) rise, soar; (6) spiral; (8) escalate, increase; III *n* (4) gate; (5) fence, hedge; (6) hurdle; (8) obstacle.

jumper I *n* (6) jersey; (7) sweater; (8) cardigan, pullover; II *cryptic* (4) buck, flea, frog, para; (6) leaper; (7) bounder; (8) kangaroo; (11) grasshopper, parachutist; (13) steeplechaser.

June *n* 6th month, named after Juno or the Roman clan of Junius.

junk *n* 1 (5) scrap, trash, waste; (6) refuse; (7) garbage, rubbish; 2 Chinese sailing boat.

Juno *Rom. myth* the sister and wife of **Jupiter**, queen of the gods and special protectress of marriage and women, frequently intervening in events in the human world out of jealousy over Jupiter's affairs – Greek equivalent **Hera**.

Jupiter I *Rom. myth* king of the gods, *see also* **Zeus** (his Greek counterpart); **II** the fifth planet from the sun, the largest planet in the solar system with a giant 'red spot'.

just I *adj* 1 (4) fair; (5) right; (6) honest, lawful, proper, square; (8) unbiased; (9) equitable, impartial, objective; (10) even-handed, honourable, legitimate; (13) disinterested; **2** (3) due; (7) fitting, merited, suitable; (8) deserved; **II** *adv* (4) only; (6) barely, hardly, merely, simply; (7) exactly; (8) narrowly; (9) precisely.

justify *v* 1 (6) acquit, defend, excuse, pardon, uphold; (7) absolve, explain, forgive, warrant; (8) mitigate, validate; (9) exonerate, vindicate; (11) rationalise (*or* rationalize); (12) substantiate; **2** arrange text evenly on the page.

juvenile I *adj* (5) young; (7) babyish, puerile; (8) childish, immature, youthful; (9) infantile; (10) adolescent; **II** *n* (5) child, minor, youth; (8) teenager; (9) youngster.

K

K *abbrev* kelvin, kilo, king, potassium; one thousand.

Kaiser *hist.* the title of the former German emperors.

Kali *Hinduism* a Hindu goddess, wife of **Siva**, the goddess of death and destruction.

kangaroo *n* (*male* boomer, *young* joey, *group* mob).

keen I *adj* 1 (4) avid; (5) eager; (6) ardent, fierce; (7) fervent, intense; (8) diligent; (12) · enthusiastic; 2 (5) acute, quick, sharp; (6) astute, shrewd; (9) sensitive; (10) discerning, perceptive; 3 (6) bitter; (8) piercing; (11) penetrating; II *v* (5) mourn; (6) lament.

keep I *v* 1 (4) hold, save; (5) stock, store; (6) retain; (7) reserve; (8) conserve, preserve, withhold; 2 (4) stay; (6) remain; (8) continue; 3 (4) feed, mind, tend; (5) guard, watch; (6) defend; (7) nurture, protect, support, sustain; (8) maintain; (2 words) care for, look after, provide for; 4 (4) mark, obey; (6) fulfil; (7) observe; (9) celebrate; (11) commemorate; II *n* 1 (5) board; (6) living; (7) lodging; (11) maintenance; 2 (5) tower; (6) castle; (7) citadel; (10) stronghold; III **keep** *or* **kept** *cryptic* HIDDEN WORD CUE; as in: 'Part of bridle kept in store in stable' (5) = reins.

Kent I *geog.* English county – 'the garden of England'; II *fict.* **Clark Kent** a mild-mannered, bespectacled reporter for the *Daily Planet*, who periodically changes into **Superman**; III *hist.* **William Kent** English architect and landscape designer.

key I *n* 1 (4) clue, sign; (5) answer; (7) pointer; (8) solution; (9) indicator; 2 (5) index, table; (6) legend; (7) caption; (8) glossary; 3 *music* (5) major, minor, tonic; II *adj* (4) main; (5) basic, chief, major, vital; (7) central, crucial, leading; (9) essential, important, necessary, principal; (11) fundamental; III *cryptic* letter A, B, C, D, E, F, or G (musical keys).

kick I *v* 1 (4) boot, drop, hack, pass, punt; (6) propel, strike; 2 (4) quit, stop; (5) break; (2 words) give up; II *n* (4) buzz; (6) recoil, thrill; (10) excitement.

kid I *n* (3) boy, tot; (4) girl; (5) child; (6) nipper; (9) youngster; II *v* (3) con; (4) dupe, fool, hoax, joke; (5) bluff, tease, trick; (6) delude; (8) hoodwink; (2 words) have on.

kill I *v* 1 (4) cull, slay; (6) murder; (7) butcher, destroy, execute; (8) decimate, massacre; (9) slaughter; (10) annihilate; (11) assassinate, exterminate; 2 (5) quell; (6) deaden, stifle; (8) suppress; II *n* (3) bag; (4) haul.

SLANG TERMS FOR 'KILL'

(3) ice; (5) waste; (9) eliminate, liquidate; (2 words) bump off, do in, knock off, rub out.

---

kilo *cryptic* abbreviated as K.

kind I *adj* (4) good, mild, nice; (6) gentle, humane; (7) helpful; (8) friendly, generous, obliging; (10) benevolent, charitable, thoughtful; (11) considerate, good-natured, sympathetic, warm-hearted; (13) compassionate, tender-hearted, philanthropic; II *n* (4) race, sort, type; (5) brand, breed, class, genre, group, stamp, style; (6) nature, manner; (7) variety; (8) category; (9) character; (11) description; III **kind of** *cryptic* ANAGRAM CUE.

kindness *n* 1 (4) help; (7) charity; (8) goodness, goodwill, humanity; (10) compassion, generosity, gentleness; (11) benevolence; (12) philanthropy; 2 (4) boon; (6) favour; (7) service; (8) courtesy; (2 words) good turn.

king I *n* (3) rex; (5) chief, ruler; (6) prince; (7) monarch, pharaoh; (9) sovereign; *see also* **royalty**; II *cryptic* 1 letter K (symbol for king in chess) or letter R (abbreviation of *Rex*, Latin for 'king'); 2 sometimes used as a reference to the **lion** as king of the beasts or to a creature whose name can be preceded by the word king, for example *cobra, penguin, prawn*; **III the king** Elvis **Presley** or various other entertainers.

BIBLICAL KINGS

(3) Asa, Evi, Hur.

(4) Ahab, Ahaz, Amon, Bera, Elah, Jehu, Omri, Saul.

(5) Balak, Cyrus, David, Eglon, Hadad, Herod, Hiram, Hoham, Hosea, Jabin, Joash, Joram, Judah, Nabat, Nadab, Pekah, Piram, Rezin, Zebar, Zimri.

(6) Baasha, Darius, Hoshea, Japhia, Josiah, Jotham, Lemuel, Sargon, Uzziah, Xerxes.

(7) Ahaziah, Amaziah, Azariah, Jehoash, Jehoram, Menahem, Shallum, Solomon, Tryphon.

(8) Hezekiah, Jehoahaz, Jeroboam, Manasseh, Pekahiah, Rehoboam, Zedekiah.

(9) Jehoiakim, Zechariah.

(10) Artaxerxes, Belshazzar, Jehoiachin, Salmanazar.

(11) Jehoshaphat, Melchizedek, Sennacherib.

(14) Nebuchadnezzar.

KINGS OF ENGLAND

(4) Cnut, Edwy, John, Knut, Offa.

(5) Edgar, Edwin, James (I–II), Henry (I–VIII), Sweyn.

(6) Alfred, Arthur, Canute, Eadred, Eadwig, Edward (I–VIII), George (I–VI), Harold (I–II).

(7) Charles (I–II), Richard (I–III), William (I–IV), Stephen.

(8) Ethelred (I–II).

(9) Aethelred, Athelstan, Ethelwulf.

(10) Aethelwulf.

(2+ words) Alfred the Great, Edmund Ironside, Edward the Confessor, Edward the Martyr, Harold Harefoot, Richard the Lionheart, William the Conqueror, William Rufus.

KINGS OF SCOTLAND

(4) Aedh, Duff.

(5) Colin, David (I–II), Edgar, Eocha, Girac, James (I–VI).

(6) Donald (I–III), Duncan (I–II), Robert (I–III).

(7) Kenneth (I–III), Macbeth, Malcolm (I–IV).

(9) Alexander (I–III), Indolphus.

(11) Constantine (I- III).

(2+ words) Donald Bane, John Balliol, Kenneth MacAlpine, Robert (the) Bruce, William the Lion.

King Lear *lit.* tragedy by William Shakespeare and the name of the main character.

Plot outline: King Lear in old age decides to divide his kingdom between his three married daughters, Goneril, Regan and Cordelia, asking each of them to say how much they love him as a way of determining who gets which part. When his youngest and favourite daughter, Cordelia, refuses to play this game, Lear abruptly banishes her together with his loyal follower Kent who stands up for her. Meanwhile Edmund, the illegitimate son of the Earl of Gloucester, plots to throw suspicion of treachery on his legitimate brother Edgar and succeeds in getting him too banished. Lear, who is generally accompanied by his wise and pathetic Fool and by Kent who has returned in disguise, soon begins to see his mistake and falls out with both Goneril and Regan over the question of how much of the trappings of royalty he is to retain. In a fury, accompanied only by the Fool, he walks out on his daughters and takes to the open heath in the middle of a tremendous storm. Seeking shelter in a hut, Lear happens upon Edgar in the disguise of a mad beggar 'Poor Tom' – the scene between Lear, who is on the verge of mental breakdown, and the supposedly mad Poor Tom is one of the most extraordinary in English literature. Gloucester eventually finds Lear and arranges to have him taken to Dover, where Cordelia has landed with a French army. For doing this, Gloucester is punished by Regan and her husband Cornwall, who tear out his eyes on stage. Turned out of the house to wander blind, he is aided by the very son, Edgar, still disguised as Poor Tom, he had cast off earlier in the play. Lear is reunited with Cordelia, but her forces are defeated by the English forces, and she and Lear are taken off to prison. Edmund, Gloucester's other illegitimate son, has been advancing his position further by making up to both Goneril and Regan. He sends a man to kill Lear and Cordelia in prison. However, Goneril's husband, Albany, a good man, has discovered her affair with Edmund, and begins to take charge. Edgar reappears in a different disguise, challenges Edmund to single combat and kills him. Before he dies, Edmund reveals the threat to Lear and Cordelia, but before Albany can do anything, Lear reappears with the dead Cordelia in his arms. After a searing lament for his dead innocent daughter, Lear himself dies.

Kipling, Rudyard *lit.* poet, novelist, journalist and children's writer, born in India, supporter of Britain's imperial role. His most famous works include:

Poems: *Barrack Room Ballads, Gunga Din, If . . . , Recessional.*

Prose: *Kim, Plain Tales from the Hills, The Light that Failed.*

Children's Books: *Just-So Stories, Puck of Pook's Hill, Stalky & Co., The Jungle Book.*

kit I *n* (3) rig, set; (4) gear; (5) tools; (6) outfit, tackle; (7) baggage, clothes, luggage, effects; (9) apparatus, equipment, trappings; (10) implements; (11) instruments; (13) paraphernalia; II *v* (3) arm, fit, rig; (5) dress, equip; (6) supply; (7) furnish, provide.

knack *n* (4) bent, gift, hang; (5) flair, forte, skill, trick; (6) talent; (7) ability, faculty; (8) aptitude, facility, tendency; (9) expertise; (10) propensity; (11) inclination.

knife I *n* (4) dirk; (5) blade; (6) carver, cutter, dagger; (8) penknife; (11) switchblade; (2 words) flick knife, pocket knife; II *v* (3) cut, rip; (4) stab; (5) slash, wound; (6) pierce.

knight *n for Knights of the Round Table see* **Round Table**.

knighthood *n*

ORDERS OF KNIGHTHOOD

Order of the Bath.
Order of the British Empire.
Order of the Garter.
Order of St Michael and St George.
Order of St Patrick.
Order of the Thistle.
Royal Victorian Order.

---

knit *v* (3) tie; (4) join, link, purl; (5) unite; (6) fasten, stitch; (7) connect; (9) interlace; (10) intertwine, interweave.

knock I *n & v* (3) hit, rap, tap; (4) bang, clip, cuff, slap; (5) thump; II *v* I (5) pound; (6) hammer; **2** (4) slam; (5) slate; (9) **criticise** (*or* criticize); III **knock about 1** (3) hit; (4) beat; (5) abuse; (6) batter; (8) mistreat; (9) mishandle; **2** (4) roam, rove; (6) ramble, travel, wander; **3** (9) associate; (2+ words) go around with, hang about with; IV **knock down** (4) fell, rase (*or* raze); (5) floor, level; (7) destroy; (8) demolish; V **knock off 1** (4) **stop**; (6) finish; (2 words) clock off; **2** (6) deduct; (8) subtract; **3** (5) pinch, **steal**; **4** (4) **kill**.

knot I *n & v* (3) tie; (6) splice; II *v* I (4) bind, join, knit, link; (6) fasten, secure; **2** (5) ravel; (6) tangle; (7) entwine; (8) entangle; III *n* I (4) bond; (10) connection; **2** (5) bunch, clump, group; (7) cluster; **3** type of bird; **4** measurement of speed at sea.

TYPES OF KNOT

(3) bow; (4) bend, loop, reef; (5) hitch; (6) granny; (7) bowline; (10) sheepshank; (2+ words) clove hitch, fisherman's knot, half hitch, granny knot, reef knot, sheet bend, Turk's head.

---

know *v* (3) ken, see; (4) tell; (5) grasp; (7) discern, realise (*or* realize); (8) identify; (9) recognise (*or* recognize); (10) experience, understand; (11) distinguish.

knowledge *n* (3) ken; (5) grasp; (8) learning; (9) awareness, cognition; (10) cognisance (*or* cognizance); (11) familiarity, information; (11) recognition; (12) acquaintance.

knowledgeable *adj* (5) aware; (6) expert; (7) **learned**; (8) educated, familiar, informed; (10) acquainted, conversant.

Krishna *rel.* a Hindu god, an incarnation of Vishnu.

Kronos *Gk myth see* **Cronos**.

Krypton *fict.* Superman's home planet.

krypton *chem.* element with the symbol Kr.

kryptonite *fict.* substance that makes Superman lose his superhuman powers.

L

L *abbrev* lake, large, Latin, learner, Liberal, lira (lire), Luxembourg (international vehicle registration), pound (as in: LSD), 50 (Roman numeral).

l *abbrev* large, left, long.

LA *abbrev* Los Angeles, Louisiana.

la *music* note (sixth note).

label I *n & v* (3) tag; (4) mark; (5) brand, stamp; (6) docket, ticket; (10) stereotype; II *n* (5) badge; (6) marker; (7) sticker; (14) categorisation (*or* categorization), classification, identification; III *v* (3) dub; (4) call; (6) define; (8) classify, identify; (9) designate; (10) categorise (*or* categorize); (12) characterise (*or* characterize).

Labour *cryptic* abbreviated as LAB.

labour I *n & v* (4) work, slog, toil; (5) grind sweat; II *n* I (3) job; (4) task; (5) chore; (6) effort; (8) drudgery, exertion; 2 (4) help; (7) workers; (9) employees, workforce; 3 (4) birth, pains; (11) confinement; (12) contractions; III *v* I (5) slave; (6) drudge, strive; (8) struggle; (9) endeavour; 2 (6) overdo; (8) overwork; (10) exaggerate, overstress; (13) overemphasise (*or* overemphasize).

labyrinth I *n* (4) maze; (7) network; II *Gk myth* the network of passages and tunnels built by **Daedalus** for King **Minos** to house the **Minotaur**.

Lachesis *Gk myth* one of the three **Fates**. She spun out the thread of life and determined its length.

laconic *adj* (4) curt; (5) brief, pithy, short, terse; (7) concise; (8) succinct, taciturn.

lack I *n & v* (4) need, want; (6) desire; II *v* (4) miss; (7) require; III *n* (6) dearth; (7) absence, paucity, poverty; (8) scarcity, shortage, sparsity; (10) deficiency, inadequacy, scantiness, sparseness; (13) insufficiency; IV *cryptic* **lack** *or* **lacking** I remove the word or letter indicated or alluded to, as in: 'Though starting with aplomb, trumpet lacks spirit – something to with the valve?' (6) = Tappet (spirit = rum, and take first letters of 'aplomb'); 2 place NO, UN or a similar negative prefix at the start of the answer, as in: 'Insignificant person lacking substance' (6) = nobody.

Laertes *lit*. I father of **Odysseus**; 2 character in Shakespeare's **Hamlet**.

lah *music* note – *see* **la**.

lake *n* I (4) llyn, loch, mere, pool, tarn; (5) lough; 2 (3) red; (7) crimson.

BRITISH AND IRISH LAKES

(4) Bala, Conn, Derg, Mask, Wast.

(5) Allen, Celyn, Leane, Neagh, Ogwen, Rydal (Water).

(6) Brenig, Corrib, Swilly.

(7) Cwellyn, Derwent (Water), Grafham (Water), Rutland (Water).

(8) Coniston (Water), Crummock (Water), Grasmere, Menteith, Tal-y-lynn.

(9) Ennerdale (Water), Esthwaite, Llangorse, Thirlmere, Ullswater.

(10) Buttermere, Loweswater, Windermere.

see also **loch**.

WORLD LAKES

(3) Tuz, Van.

(4) Chad, Como, Erie, Eyre, Mead, Ohau.

(5) Garda, Gatun, Huron, Kyoga, Nyasa, Tahoe.

(6) Albert, Baikal, Geneva, Kariba, Ladoga, Lugano, Malawi, Nasser, Placid, Rudolf, Texoma, Wanaka, Zurich.

list continued over

(7) Balaton, Bolsena, Chapala, Francis, Ontario, Quesnel.

(8) Attersee, Bodensee, Chiemsee, Flathead, Kentucky, Maggiore, Manitoba, Michigan, Seminole, Superior, Tiberias, Titicaca, Victoria, Wakatipu, Winnipeg.

(9) Champlain, Constance, Maracaibo, Neuchatel, Nicaragua, Trasimeno.

(10) Tanganyika.

(2 words) Great Bear, Great Salt, Great Slave.

lame *adj* (4) halt; (7) limping; (8) crippled, disabled; (11) handicapped; (4) poor, weak; (6) feeble, flimsy; (10) inadequate; (14) unsatisfactory.

Lancelot *lit.* a Knight of the **Round Table**, the husband of Elaine, father of Galahad, and lover of Queen Guinevere.

land I *n* **1** (4) soil; (5) earth; (6) ground, estate; (8) property; **2** (5) state; (6) nation; (7) country; **II** *v* **1** (5) pitch; (6) alight, arrive, settle; (9) disembark; (2 words) come down, touch down; **2** (3) get, net, win; (4) gain; (5) catch; (6) obtain, secure; (7) acquire, capture.

language *n* (5) idiom, lingo; (6) jargon, patois, pidgin, speech, tongue; (7) dialect; (9) discourse; (10) vocabulary; (11) terminology.

WORLD LANGUAGES

(3) Ibo, Ido, Kwa, Twi.

(4) Ainu, Akan, Erse, Igbo, Manx, Norn, Pali, Serb, Thai, Tupi, Urdu, Zulu.

(5) Aztec, Bantu, Carib, Czech, Doric, Dutch, Fante (*or* Fanti), Farsi, Greek, Hindi, Iraqi, Irish, Karen, Khmer, Latin, Malay, Maori, Norse, Oriya, Oscan, Saxon, Scots, Shona, Tamil, Tatar, Ugric, Uzbek, Welsh, Xhosa, Yakut.

(6) Arabic, Basque, Basuto, Berber, Breton, Creole, Danish, French, Gaelic, German, Gothic, Gullah, Hebrew, Herero, Ionian, Kalmyk, Ladino, Magyar, Micmac, Mongol, Pashto, Polish, Pushtu, Romaic, Romany, Shelta, Slovak, Syriac, Telugu, Tswana, Turkic, Ugrian, Yoruba.

(7) Amharic, Aramaic, Avestan, Bengali, Burmese, Catalan, Chinese, Chinook, Choctaw, Cornish, English, Finnish, Flemish, Frisian, Guarani, Iranian, Kalmuck, Kurdish, Lettish, Maltese, Marathu, Nahuatl, Nynorsk, Persian, Punjabi, Quechua, Russian, Semitic, Serbian, Spanish, Swahili, Swedish, Tagalog, Turkish, Yiddish.

(8) Cherokee, Estonian, Gujarati, Japanese, Mandarin, Nepalese, Romanian, Romansch, Sanskrit.

(9) Afrikaans, Bulgarian, Castilian, Esperanto, Franglais, Hungarian, Icelandic, Mongolian, Norwegian, Sinhalese, Ukrainian.

(10) Anglo-Saxon, Hindustani, Portuguese, Serbo-Croat, Vietnamese.

lares *Rom. myth* household gods, usually deified ancestors or heroes – *see also* **penates**.

large I *adj* (3) big; (4) huge, vast, wide; (5) ample, broad, bulky, giant, great, jumbo, roomy; (7) immense, mammoth, monster, outsize; (8) colossal, enormous, generous, gigantic, king-size, sizeable, spacious; (9) extensive; **II** *cryptic* letters L (large), OS (outsize), XL (extra large) *etc.*

last I *adj* (3) end; (5) dying, final; (6) latest, utmost; (7) closing; (8) eventual, terminal, ultimate; (9) finishing; (10) concluding, conclusive; **II** *v* (4) stay; (5) abide; (6) endure, remain; (7) persist, survive; (8) continue; (2 words) carry on, hold out, keep on; **III** *n* **1** **the last** (3) end, zed, zee; (5) omega; **2** cobbler's tool; **IV** *cryptic* **1** use the last letter of the word or words concerned, as in: 'French wine? Used last of it with a hot curry – and ended up in the toilet' (8) = vindaloo (vin = French for wine, 'd' last letter of 'used'); **2** letter Z.

late *adj* **1** (4) slow; (5) tardy; (6) behind; (7) delayed, overdue; (10) unpunctual; **2** (4) dead, past; (6) former; (8) deceased, previous; **3** (5) new; (5) fresh; (6) recent; (7) current.

Latin I *n* a person from a country such as Spain, France, or Italy whose language developed from Latin; **II** *cryptic* **1** abbreviated as L or LAT; **2** use a Latin word, as in: 'This game I play in Latin' (4) = ludo (ludo = Latin for 'I play').

laugh I *v & n* (4) grin, hoot; (5) smile; (6) giggle, guffaw, scream, titter; (7) chortle, chuckle, snigger; **II** *n* (3) fun; (4) joke, lark; **III laugh at** (4) jeer, mock; (5) scoff, scorn; (6) deride; (8) ridicule.

law *n* (3) act; (4) code, rule; (5) axiom, canon, edict, order; (6) decree; (7) statute; (9) ordinance, principle; (10) regulation.

lawful *adj see* **legal**.

lawyer *n* (7) counsel; (8) advocate, attorney; (9) barrister, solicitor.

lay I *v* **1** (3) put, set; (5) place; (6) locate, spread; (7) arrange, deposit, dispose, stretch; (8) position; **2** (7) produce (an egg); **3** (3) bet; (5) stake, wager; **II** *adj* (7) amateur, secular; (13) non-specialist; (15) non-professional; **III** *n* (4) **poem**, song; (6) ballad.

layer I *n* (4) film; (5) level; (7) coating, stratum; (9) thickness; **II** *cryptic* **1** (3) hen; **2** (6) better, punter.

lead¹ I *v* **1** (5) guide, pilot, steer, usher; (6) direct, escort; **2** (4) head, rule; (5) cause; (6) govern; (7) control; (8) persuade; (9) influence; **3** (4) live, pass; (5) spend; (10) experience; **II** *n* **1** (3) van; (4) head; (5) front; (8) vanguard; (9) forefront; **2** (7) example; (8) guidance; (9) direction; **3** (3) tip; (4) clue, hint; (5) guide; (10) indication, suggestion; **4** (4) star; (9) principal.

lead² I (5) metal; **II** *cryptic* letters PB (chemical symbol).

leading *adj* (3) key; (4) head, main; (5) chief, prime; (6) ruling, senior; (7) leading, primary; (8) cardinal; (9) principal, sovereign.

lean I *v* (4) bank, bend, list, tilt; (5) slant, slope; (7) incline; **II** *adj* (4) bony, slim, thin, trim; (5) lanky; (7) fatless.

Leander *Gk myth* the lover of **Hero**, who drowned while swimming the Hellespont to visit her.

Lear *lit.* **1** *see* King Lear; **2** Edward Lear writer of nonsense verses, such as 'The Dong with the Luminous Nose', 'The Jumblies', 'The Owl and the Pussycat', and 'The Pobble who has no Toes'.

learn *v* (4) hear; (6) gather, master; (7) acquire; (8) discover, memorise (*or* memorize); (9) ascertain.

learned *adj* (7) erudite; (8) academic, educated, literate, well-read; (9) scholarly; (12) intellectual, well-informed.

learner I *n* (4) tyro; (7) amateur, scholar, student, trainee; (8) beginner; (9) debutante; (10) apprentice; **II** *cryptic* letter L.

leave I *v* **1** (2) go; (4) exit, quit; (6) decamp, depart, desert, retire; (7) abandon, forsake; (8) withdraw; (2 words) go away, move out, set off, set out; **2** (4) will; (8) bequeath; **II** *n* **1** (7) holiday; (8) furlough, vacation; **2** (7) consent; (8) approval; (10) permission; **III** *cryptic* a word, letter, or letters are to be omitted from part of the clue, as in: 'Boy's leaving from a London airport; his little brother remains behind' (3) = Ted (airport = Stansted).

Leda *Gk myth* the wife of Tyndarus, king of Sparta, whom Zeus came to in the form of a swan. She produced two eggs from which were born the heavenly twins, **Castor** and **Pollux**, **Helen** (of Troy) and **Clytemnestra**.

left *cryptic* letter L.

legal *adj* **1** (5) licit, valid; (6) honest, lawful, proper; (7) allowed; (8) rightful; (10) above-board, legitimate; (11) permissible; (14) constitutional; **2** (8) forensic, judicial.

legislative assembly *n see* **parliament**.

Leo *astrol. & astron.* the constellation that is the fifth sign of the zodiac, also known as the Lion.

lessen *v* (3) cut; (5) lower; (6) **reduce**; (7) lighten; (8) decrease.

lesson *n* **1** (5) class; (6) period; (7) lecture, seminar; (8) tutorial; **2** (5) model; (7) example, warning; (9) deterrent; (11) inspiration; (13) encouragement.

let I *v* **1** (5) allow; (6) permit; (8) sanction; (9) authorise (*or* authorize); **2** (4) rent; (5) lease; **3** (6) hinder; (7) prevent; **II let off** *v* **1** (6) acquit, excuse, exempt, pardon; (7) forgive; **2** (4) emit, fire; (7) explode, release; (8) detonate; (9) discharge.

lethal *adj* (5) fatal; (6) deadly, lethal, mortal; (7) killing; (8) terminal; (9) incurable; (10) calamitous, disastrous; (12) catastrophic.

Lethe *Gk myth* one of the four rivers of the **Underworld**. Drinking the waters of Lethe resulted in instant and total forgetfulness of everything a soul had said or done in life.

letter I *n* **1** (4) line, mail, note, post; (7) epistle, message, missive; (8) dispatch; (13) communication; **2** (4) sign; (6) symbol; (9) character; **II** *cryptic* A, B, C, etc.

level I *adj* (4) even, flat; (5) equal, flush, plane; (6) smooth, stable, steady; (7) regular, uniform; (8) constant; (10) horizontal; **II** *n* **1** (5) floor, layer, plane; (6) storey; (7) stratum; **2** (4) rank; (5) class, grade, stage, value; (6) amount, degree, extent, status; (7) echelon; (8) position, standard, standing; **3** (6) height; (8) altitude; (9) elevation; **III** *v* (4) rase (*or* raze); (5) plane; (6) smooth; (7) flatten; (8) **demolish**.

levy I *v* (5) exact, raise; (6) charge, demand, enlist, impose; (7) collect; (8) mobilise (*or* mobilize); (9) conscript; **II** *n* **1** (3) tax; (4) duty, toll; (6) charge, tariff; **2** (7) militia.

liberal I *adj* **1** (4) free; (5) ample; (8) abundant, generous; (9) bountiful, plentiful; (10) open-handed; **2** (7) lenient; (8) tolerant; (9) reformist; (11) progressive; **II** *cryptic* letter L or letters LIB.

liberty 1 *n* (5) right; (7) freedom, licence, release; (8) autonomy, immunity, impunity; (9) exemption, privilege; (10)

permission; (11) deliverance; (12) emancipation, independence; **2** (9) impudence; (11) presumption; (12) impertinence.

Libra *astrol. & astron.* the constellation that is the seventh sign of the zodiac, also known as the Scales.

licence *n* **1** (6) permit; (7) charter, warrant; (9) franchise; (11) certificate; (12) dispensation; **2** (5) right; (7) freedom, **liberty**; **3** (6) excess; (7) abandon; (10) debauchery, indulgence; (11) dissipation.

license *v* (5) allow; (6) enable, permit; (7) certify, charter, empower, entitle, warrant; (8) sanction; (9) authorise (*or* authorize), franchise.

lift *v* **1** (4) buoy; (5) boost, exalt, hoist, raise; (7) elevate; **2** (5) relax; (6) cancel, remove, revoke; **3** (4) nick; (5) pinch, **steal**.

light I *adj* **1** (4) fair, pale; (5) blond, faded, faint; (6) blonde, pastel; **2** (3) lit; (6) bright; (7) radiant, shining; (8) luminous; (11) illuminated; **3** (4) airy; (5) nippy; (6) flimsy, nimble, slight; (7) buoyant, unladen; (8) delicate; (10) weightless; **4** (7) amusing, trivial; (8) cheerful, flippant, humorous; (15) inconsequential; **5** (5) short (of); (7) lacking; **II** *n* (3) day, ray; (4) beam, bulb, dawn, glow, lamp; (5) blaze, flame, flash, glare, gleam, glint, match, shine, spark, torch; (6) beacon, candle; (7) lantern, sunrise; (8) radiance; (10) brightness, brilliance, chandelier; (12) illumination; **III** *v* (4) fire; (6) ignite, kindle; **2** (8) illumine; (10) illuminate.

like I *v* (4) love; (5) adore, enjoy, fancy; (6) esteem, favour, prefer, relish; (7) cherish; **II** *adj & prep.* (2) as; (4) akin, same; (5) alike, equal; (7) similar; (9) identical; (10) equivalent.

limit I *v* (4) curb; (5) bound, check; (6) define, hinder, ration; (7) confine, control; (8) restrain, restrict; (9) demarcate; **II** *n* (3) end, rim; (4) brim, edge, line; (5) brink, verge; (6) border, bounds, utmost; (7) ceiling, extreme, maximum, minimum; (8) boundary, frontier, terminus; (9) perimeter, threshold.

line I *n* **1** (3) bar; (4) band, dash, mark, rule; (5) score, strip; (6) crease, furrow, groove, streak, stripe; (7) scratch, wrinkle; **2** (3) row; (4) file, rank; (5) chain, queue; (6) column, series, string; (8) sequence; (10) procession; (11) progression; **3** (4) cord, rope; (5) cable; **4** (4) race; (5) breed, stock; (6) family; (7) descent, lineage; (8) ancestry, pedigree; **5** (3) **job**; (5) field; (7) calling, pursuit; (8) business; **6** (4) path; (5) route, track; (6) avenue, course, **method**, policy, scheme, system; (8) approach, ideology; (9) procedure; **7** (5) **limit** (II); **8** *see* **railway**; II *v* (3) pad; (4) fill; (5) cover; (9) reinforce; III **line, lined** *or* **lining** *cryptic* insert a word, letter or group of letters into another word, as in: 'Miraculous creation made of depleted mica lined with silver' (5) = magic (silver = Ag (chemical symbol)).

liner I *n* (4) boat; (7) steamer; *see also* **ship**; II *cryptic* **1** (3) pen; (4) poet; (5) actor, ruler; (6) artist, drawer, pencil, writer; (11) draughtsman; **2** insert word *etc*, as at **line**, as in: 'Remove lid with metal liner – it's clean as a whistle inside!' (8) = pristine (metal = tin).

lion *n* **1** (*male* lion, *female* lioness, *young* cub, *group* pride); **2 the Lion** *see* **Leo**; **3** (4) hero, star; (9) **celebrity**.

liqueur *n see also* **drink**.

TYPES OF LIQUEUR

(6) cassis, kummel.

(7) curacao.

(8) absinthe, advocaat, anisette, Calvados, Drambuie®, Tia Maria®.

(9) Cointreau®.

(10) chartreuse.

(11) Benedictine®.

(2+ words) cherry brandy, crème de cacao, crème de menthe, Grand Marnier®, sloe gin.

---

lira I *n* (*pl* **lire**) Italian unit of currency; II *cryptic* letter L (abbreviation).

list I *n & v* **1** (3) log; (4) book; (5) index, table; record; (8) register, schedule; (9) catalogue; **2** (4) heel, lean, tilt; (5) slant, slope; (7) incline; II *n* (4) roll; (6) series; (9) directory, inventory; III *v* (5) enter; (7) itemise (*or* itemize); (9) enumerate.

little I *adj* (3) wee; (4) mini, tiny (5) brief, dwarf, scant, short, small, teeny; (6) meagre, minute, paltry, petite, scanty, sparse, teensy; (8) trifling; (9) miniature, minuscule; (10) diminutive, negligible; (11) microscopic; (13) infinitesimal, insignificant; II *n* (3) bit, dab, tad; (4) dash, drop, hint, spot; (5) grain, pinch, speck, touch; (7) soupçon; (10) suggestion; III *cryptic* use a shortened form or an abbreviation of a word or name in the answer, as in: 'Scratch meal from a little potato with luck' (7) = potluck.

little boy *cryptic* use shortened form of boy's name, as in: 'Little boy finds the clue – but the answer isn't a horse' (6) = donkey.

little girl *cryptic* use shortened form of girl's name, as in: 'Bar little girl from her instrument' (5) = banjo.

little man *cryptic see* **little boy**.

little woman *cryptic see* **little girl**.

Little Women *lit.* novel by Louisa M. Alcott, main characters: Amy, Beth, Jo, Meg (and Laurie).

lively *adj* **1** (4) busy, spry; (5) agile, alert, brisk, nifty, perky, quick; (6) active, chirpy; (8) animated, bustling, spirited, vigorous; (9) energetic, sprightly, vivacious; **2** (5) vivid; (6) bright; (8) eventful, exciting; (9) colourful; (11) stimulating.

lizard *n*

TYPES OF LIZARD

(5) agama, anole, gecko, skink;

(6) iguana; (7) axolotl, monitor;

(8) basilisk; (9) chameleon;

(10) salamander; (2 words) Gila monster, Komodo dragon.

---

loch *n see also* **lake**.

LOCHS

(3) Awe, Eil, Ewe, Ken, Lee, Tay.

(4) Alsh, Buie, Earn, Fyne, Gare, Gorm, Hope, Lyon, Mhor, More, Ness, Shin.

(5) Broom, Duich, Etive, Fitty, Garry, Glass, Hourn, Leven, Lochy, Loyal, Loyne, Lussa, Maree, Morar, Muick, Naver, Orrin, Quien, Sheil, Sween, Treig, Tuath.

(6) Arkaig, Assynt, Calder, Ericht, Laggan, Linnhe, Lomond, Ossian, Quoich, Sunart, Tummel, Watten.

(7) Cluanie, Eishort, Eriboll, Fannich, Katrine, Melfort, Mochrum, Rannoch, Snizort, Striven.

(8) Langavat, Scridian, Seaforth, Stenness, Torridon.

(9) Kirbister, Ochiltree, Vennachar.

(10) Mullardoch.

(11) Glascarnoch.

(15) Clatteringshaws.

lock *n* 1 (4) bolt, hasp; (5) latch; (7) padlock; 2 (4) hair; (5) tress.

log I *n & v* (4) book, list; (5) table; (6) record; (7) account; (8) register, schedule; (9) catalogue; II *n* 1 (5) diary; (7) journal; 2 (5) block, chunk; (6) billet.

Loki *Norse myth* the god of fire and mischief or evil.

lone *adj* 1 (3) one; (4) only, sole, solo; (6) single; (8) separate, solitary; 2 *see* **lonely**.

lonely *adj* (5) alone; (6) remote; (8) deserted, desolate, forsaken, isolated, lonesome, solitary, abandoned; (10) friendless; (11) uninhabited; (12) unfrequented.

long I *adj* (5) large; (7) lengthy; (8) extended; (9) extensive, prolonged, sustained; (10) protracted; (12) interminable; II *v* (4) itch, lust, pine, want; (5) crave, yearn; (6) desire, hanker, hunger, thirst.

Longfellow, Henry Wadsworth *lit.* American poet. His most famous poems include: *Evangeline, Excelsior, Hiawatha, The Village Blacksmith* and *The Wreck of the Hesperus*.

look I *v & n* (4) gaze, peek, peep, scan, view; (5) stare; (6) glance, regard; (7) glimpse; II *v* (3) con, see; (5) study, watch; (6) survey; (7) examine, inspect; (8) consider; (10) scrutinise (*or* scrutinize); (11) contemplate, investigate; III *n* (3) air; (4) mien; (6) aspect; (7) bearing; (10) appearance, expression.

look after *v* (4) mind, tend; (5) guard; (7) protect; (9) supervise; (2+ words) attend to, care for, keep an eye on, minister to, take care of, watch over.

look back *cryptic* often used to suggest that a word should be written in reverse order to make all or part of the answer, as in: 'Worthless object little Melanie looked back on' (5) = lemon.

lord *see* **noble**.

lose I *v* (4) miss; (5) waste; (6) mislay; (7) forfeit; (8) misplace, squander; (9) dissipate; II *cryptic* **lose** *or* **losing** *or* **lost** omit the word, letter or letters indicated or alluded to, as in: 'Barman loses arm in bar' (3) = ban *or*: 'Student lost his head and got a well-paid job' = earner (student = learner).

Lot *Bible* the nephew of **Abraham**. He and his family were the only ones spared in the destruction of **Sodom**, being instructed by God to leave the city without looking back. Lot's wife disobeyed the instruction, looked back, and was turned into a pillar of salt.

lot *n* 1 *or* **lots** *see* **many**; 2 (3) set; (5) batch, quota; (6) number; (10) assortment, collection; 3 (4) draw, fate; (5) straw.

Lothario *fict.* **(a gay) Lothario** a cheerful libertine and seducer, originally a character in the play *The Fair Penitent* by Nicholas Rowe.

loud I *adj* 1 (5) noisy; (6) shrill; (7) blaring, booming; (9) clamorous, deafening; (10) resounding, thundering, vociferous; (12) ear-splitting; 2 (5) brash, gaudy, showy; (6) flashy, garish; (7) glaring; (12) ostentatious; II *cryptic* letter F or letters FF (musical abbreviations).

lough *n see* **lake**.

lour *see* **lower 2**.

love I *v* (4) dote, like; (5) adore, enjoy, fancy; (6) desire, esteem, favour, prefer, relish; (7) cherish, idolise (*or* idolize), worship; (8) treasure; **II** *n* **1** (3) sex; (4) eros; (5) amour; (6) ardour, liking, warmth; (7) passion, romance; (8) devotion, fondness; (9) adoration, affection; (10) attachment; (11) amorousness; **2** *tennis* (3) nil; (4) duck, zero; (5) zilch; (6) nought; **III** *cryptic* letter O (on basis of tennis sense).

lovely *adj* (4) fine; (5) sweet; (6) pretty; (7) lovable, winsome; (8) adorable, charming, fetching, loveable, pleasant, pleasing; (9) beautiful, enjoyable, exquisite; (10) attractive, delightful, enchanting, entrancing.

lover *n* (6) suitor; (7) admirer, beloved; (8) follower, mistress; (9) inamorata, inamorato, boyfriend; (10) girlfriend, ladykiller, sweetheart; (2+ words) bit on the side, fancy man, fancy woman, ladies' (*or* lady's) man, toy boy.

MALE LOVERS

see also separate entries

Casanova, Don Juan, Lothario, Romeo.

PAIRS OF LOVERS

Abelard and Heloise, Nelson and Lady (Emma) Hamilton, Antony and Cleopatra, Pyramus and Thisbe, Darby and Joan, Romeo and Juliet, Henry II and Fair Rosamond, Tristan and Isolde, Leander and Hero, Napoleon and Josephine.

---

low I *adj* **1** (5) short, small, squat; (6) sunken; (7) stunted; **2** (4) base, mean, rude; (6) abject, coarse, humble, vulgar; (8) degraded; **3** (4) bass, deep; **4** (3) sad; (4) down; (9) **depressed**; **II** *v* (3) moo; (6) bellow; **III** *n* (7) cyclone; (10) depression.

lower I *v* **1** (4) drop; (6) debase, lessen, reduce; (7) degrade; (8) decrease, diminish; **2** (4) loom, lour; (5) frown; (6) menace; (8) threaten; **II** *adj* (6) lesser, nether; (8) inferior; **III** *cryptic* (2) ox; (3) cow.

loyal *adj* (4) true; (6) trusty; (7) devoted, staunch; (8) constant, faithful, reliable; (9) steadfast; (10) dependable.

LSD *abbrev* **1** pounds, shillings, and pence – pre-decimal British money; **2** a hallucinogenic drug – lysergic acid diethylamide.

Lucifer *rel.* a name applied to the morning star (the planet Venus when seen at dawn), but also to **Satan**, especially in so far as he was one of the brightest angels before he rebelled against God and was thrown down from heaven.

lucifer *n* a match.

luck *n* (4) fate; (5) fluke; (6) chance; (7) destiny, fortune; (8) accident, fortuity.

lucky *adj* (5) happy; (6) timely; (9) fortunate; (10) auspicious, favourable, prosperous; (12) providential.

ludicrous *adj* (5) crazy, funny, silly; (6) absurd, stupid; (7) comical, foolish; (8) derisory, farcical; (9) hilarious, laughable; (10) outrageous, ridiculous; (11) nonsensical; (12) preposterous.

lug I *n see* **ear**; **II** *v see* **carry, pull**.

Luke *Bible* **St Luke** traditionally credited with the authorship of the third Gospel and the Acts of the Apostles, a companion of St Paul, patron saint of artists and doctors, being mentioned in the Bible as practising both professions.

Luxembourg *cryptic* abbreviated as L.

M

M *abbrev* Majesty, Malta (international vehicle registration), Mark (German currency), Master, Monday, Monsieur, Motorway, 1000 (Roman numeral).

m *abbrev* male, married, masculine, meridiem (Latin = noon), metre, mile, million, minute, month.

MA *abbrev* Massachusetts, Master of Arts, Morocco (international vehicle registration).

Macbeth *hist. & lit.* an 11th-century king of Scotland and hero of a tragedy by Shakespeare often referred to by actors as 'the Scottish play' because it is believed to be unlucky to mention or quote from *Macbeth* during the production of another play.

Plot outline: Three witches, 'the weird sisters', encounter Macbeth and his friend Banquo on a 'blasted heath' as they return from victory in battle against rebels against the saintly Scottish king Duncan. The witches make three prophecies concerning Macbeth – the first two soon turn out to be true, the third is that he will be 'king hereafter'. They also prophesy that though Banquo will not be king himself, his descendants will be kings. Macbeth writes to his wife about the prophecies and she at once decides that the way to make him king is to murder Duncan. When he returns to her, she bullies and cajoles the wavering Macbeth into action. When Duncan arrives at their castle in Inverness, Macbeth, though troubled by his conscience and a vision of an 'airborne dagger', commits the murder with the active assistance of Lady Macbeth. Duncan's two sons, Malcolm and Donalbane, fear that they will be the next victims and flee, leaving Macbeth to be crowned king.

The second half of the play deals with the retribution that finally catches up with Macbeth. To secure his position and that of his family he hires murderers to kill Banquo and his son Fleance. Fleance escapes, Banquo is killed but Macbeth sees his ghost at a banquet and decides to consult the witches again. They tell him three more things – to beware Macduff, that 'no man of woman born' shall ever harm him, and that he will never be defeated until 'Birnam Wood to high Dunsinane Hill shall come'. Macduff, the thane of Fife and no supporter of Macbeth, has already fled to England where he joins Duncan's elder son Malcolm in an expedition against Scotland. Lady Macbeth's conscience, meanwhile, has become increasingly troubled. She reveals this while walking in her sleep trying to wash blood off her hands ('out, damned spot'). She finally commits suicide. Macbeth has succeeded in killing his own conscience and awaits the invading force with cynical bravado. Malcolm orders his men to cut down forest branches and use them as a screen as they advance, thus making the wood appear to move. Seeing the prophecy fulfilled, Macbeth abandons hope and caution. He meets Macduff in single combat. Macduff announces that he was 'from his mother's womb untimely ripped', defeats and kills Macbeth and the play ends with the rightful heir Malcolm being acclaimed as Scotland's new king.

machine *n* **1** (4) tool; (5) robot; (6) device, engine; (9) apparatus, appliance automaton, mechanism; **2** (3) car; (5) plane; (8) aircraft; (9) motorbike; (10) motorcycle.

TYPES OF MACHINE

(3) fan, gin.

(4) grab, jack, lift, mill, mule, pump, till.

(5) adder, baler, borer, churn, crane, drier, dryer, hoist, jenny, lathe, lever, mixer, motor, mower, press, punch, telex, video, winch, Xerox®.

(6) binder, blower, bowser, copier, cutter, digger, dredge, dynamo, harrow, jogger, linter, mangle, milker, mincer, packer, peeler, picker, plough, pulper, ram-jet, reaper, scales, seeder, shears, washer, winder.

(7) automat, balance, capstan, crusher, cyclone, dredger, ejector, exciter, printer, riveter, spinner, stapler, starter, steamer, tumbler, turbine, wringer.

(8) computer, conveyor, elevator, espresso, feed-pump, foot-pump, hand-loom, hand-mill, heat-pump, jig-borer, pulp-mill, pulsator, purifier, recorder, shredder, teletype, turbo-jet, vibrator, windmill.

(9) dispenser, escalator, excavator, extractor, generator, hand-press, harvester, headphone, incubator, lawnmower, macerator, photostat, polygraph, power-loom, projector, radiogram, separator, sigmatron, simulator, spin-drier, stone-mill, sugar-mill, telephone, tomograph, totaliser (*or* totalizer), treadmill, water-mill, water-pump, wine-press.

(10) beam-engine, calculator, centrifuge, coal-cutter, coffee-mill, compressor, cyclostyle, Dictaphone®, dishwasher, drop-hammer, dumb-waiter, duplicator, exsiccator, galvaniser (*or* galvanizer), gramophone, guillotine, mimeograph, motor-mower, passimeter, phonograph, pile-driver, power-lathe, power-press, servo-motor, steam-crane, steam-navvy, steriliser (*or* sterilizer), tilt-hammer, travelator, travolator, trip-hammer, typewriter, vacuum-pump, ventilator, water-wheel.

(11) comptometer, epidiascope, grass-cutter, letter-press, nickelodeon, paper-cutter, paper-feeder, pasteuriser (*or* pasteurizer), paternoster, photocopier, steam-digger, steam-hammer, steam-shovel, stirrup-pump, teleprinter, totalisator (*or* totalizatior), tumble-drier, weighbridge.

(12) decompressor.

(2+ words) block and tackle, cash register, concrete mixer, conveyor belt, donkey engine, extractor fan, fruit machine, iron lung, jacquard loom, printing press, record player, spinning jenny, tape recorder, vacuum cleaner, video recorder.

mad *adj* 1 (4) wild; (5) crazy; (6) absurd, insane; (7) frantic, idiotic, lunatic; (8) demented, deranged; (9) psychotic; (10) irrational, unbalanced; 2 (5) **angry**, cross; (7) annoyed, furious; 3 (6) hectic; (7) chaotic; (8) confused.

SLANG TERMS FOR MAD

(4) bats, nuts; (5) dotty, loony, loopy, nutty; (6) mental, screwy; (7) barking, bonkers; (2+ words) mad as a hatter, mad as a March hare, not all there, off one's chump, off one's head, out of one's mind.

madman *see* **mad person**.

madness *n* (5) mania; (6) idiocy, lunacy; (8) dementia, insanity; (9) craziness, psychosis.

mad person *n* (5) idiot, loony; (6) maniac, nutter; (7) lunatic, nutcase; (8) headcase; (9) psychotic; (10) psychopath.

Maecenas *hist. & lit.* Roman statesman and famous patron of the arts (especially literature). He was a great supporter and benefactor of **Horace** and **Virgil**.

magazine *n* 1 (3) mag; (5) paper; (6) weekly; (7) fanzine, journal, monthly; (9) quarterly; (10) periodical; 2 (5) depot, store; (7) arsenal.

MAGAZINE TITLES

(3) Mad (magazine); (4) Lady (the), Life, Time; (5) Hello, Punch, Woman; (6) Lancet (the), Loaded, Tatler (the); (7) Playboy; (9) Spectator (the); (10) Gramophone (the); (12) Cosmopolitan; (2+ words) History Today, New Musical Express, New Scientist, New Statesman (the), New Yorker (the), Private Eye, Woman's Own, Woman's Weekly.

Magi *Bible* the Three Wise Men from the east who came to find the infant Jesus. Their names were Balthazar, Caspar and Melchior.

magician *n* (5) witch; (6) wizard; (7) warlock; (8) conjurer, sorcerer; (9) enchanter; (11) illusionist, necromancer, thaumaturge.

magnificent *adj* (4) fine; (5) grand, great, noble, regal; (6) superb; (7) stately; (8) glorious, gorgeous, imposing, splendid; (9) brilliant, excellent, sumptuous, **wonderful**; (10) impressive.

magnify **1** *v* (6) deepen, dilate, expand; (7) amplify, augment, broaden, develop, enhance, enlarge, greaten, inflate, stretch; (8) heighten, increase, lengthen; (9) elaborate, expatiate; (2 words) blow up; **2** (8) overplay; (9) dramatise (*or* dramatize), overstate; (10) exaggerate.

Maia **1** *Gk myth* the eldest of the **Pleiades**, daughter of Atlas and mother of Hermes by Zeus; *Rom. myth* an earth goddess, also associated with the Greek Maia, whose festivals fell in May and after whom the month is named.

maid *n* **1** (6) skivvy, tweeny; (7) servant; (8) domestic; **2** *see* **maiden** **1** **1**.

maiden **1** *n* **1** (4) girl, lass, miss; (6) damsel, virgin; (8) spinster; **2** an over in cricket in which no runs are scored; **3** a horse that has never won a race; **II** *adj* first (as in: maiden flight, maiden voyage); **III** *cryptic* **1** letter O (= zero with reference to a maiden over); **2** a reference to first, *e.g.* first word or letter.

Maid Marian *lit.* the lover of **Robin Hood**.

Maid of Kent *hist.* Elizabeth Barton, a Catholic opponent of the English Reformation, who, like Joan of Arc, claimed to be inspired. After denouncing Henry VIII's marriage to Anne Boleyn, she was hanged in 1534.

Maid of Orleans *hist. see* **Joan (of Arc)**.

main **I** *adj* (3) key; (5) basic, chief, first, major, prime, vital; (7) central, crucial, leading, supreme; (8) cardinal, critical; (9) essential, important, paramount, principal; (11) fundamental; **II** *n* **1** (4) duct, line, pipe; (5) cable; (7) conduit; **2** **the main** (3) sea; (5) ocean.

maintain *v* **1** (4) keep;(7) sustain; (8) continue; **2** (6) repair; (7) finance, support; (8) conserve, preserve; (2+ words) care for keep up, look after, take care of; **3** (4) hold; (5) claim; (6) affirm, assert, declare, insist; (7) believe, contend.

majestic *adj* (5) grand, lofty, noble, regal, royal; (7) splendid, stately; (8) imposing; (9) dignified; (10) impressive, monumental; (11) magnificent.

major **I** *adj* (3) key; (4) main; (5) basic, chief, vital; (7) central, crucial, leading, notable; (9) essential, important, necessary, principal; (11) fundamental; **II** *n see* **rank**; **III** *music* (3) key; (5) scale.

make **I** *v* **1** (5) build, erect, mould, shape; (6) create, devise; (8) assemble; (9) construct, fabricate; (11) manufacture; (2 words) put together; **2** (5) force, press; (6) coerce, compel, impose, oblige; (7) inflict; (8) bulldoze; (9) constrain, pressgang; (10) pressurise (*or* pressurize); (11) necessitate; **II** *n* (4) mark, sort, type; (5) brand, model; (6) marque; (7) variety; **III** *cryptic* ANAGRAM CUE.

make off *v* **1** (2) go; (3) fly; (4) bolt, flee, quit; (5) leave, split; (6) decamp, escape, vanish; (7) migrate, retreat; (8) withdraw; (9) disappear; (2+ words) beat a retreat, clear off, go away, run away, take off; **2** **make off with** (5) elope, steal; (6) kidnap.

---

make out *v* **1** (3) **see**; (7) discern; (10) **understand**; (11) distinguish, **2** (4) fare; (7) succeed; (8) progress; **3** *slang* have sex.

make up I *v* **1** (6) create, devise, invent; (7) compose, concoct, imagine; (9) fabricate; **2** (4) form; (8) comprise; (10) constitute; **3** (6) settle; (9) reconcile; **4** **make up for** (5) amend, atone; (10) compensate, recompense.

make-up *n* **1** (5) paint; (7) compact; (8) cosmetic, warpaint; (9) cosmetics; (11) greasepaint; **2** (4) form; (6) fabric; (9) structure; (11) composition; (12) constitution, construction. *For types of make-up see* **cosmetic**.

male *adj & n* (2) he; (3) boy, man.

MALE ANIMALS

(3) cob, dog, ram, tom, tup.

(4) boar, bull, buck, cock, hart, jack, stag.

(5) billy, drake, hound.

(6) gander.

(8) stallion.

---

man I *n* **1** (3) boy; (4) chap, cove, gent, male; (5) bloke; (6) fellow; **2** (7) mankind; (8) humanity; (9) humankind; **3** (4) hand; (5) valet; (6) worker; (7) servant, soldier; (8) employee; **II** *v* (4) crew, fill; (5) staff; (6) occupy.

manage *v* **1** (3) run; (6) direct, handle, tackle; (7) control, oversee; (8) organise (*or* organize); (9) supervise; (10) administer; (11) superintend; **2** (4) cope, fare; (7) survive; (2 words) get by, get along, get on, make do.

manager *n* (4) boss, head; (5) chief; (8) director, overseer; (9) executive; (10) supervisor; (13) administrator; (14) superintendent.

manner *n* **1** (3) way; (4) form; (5) means, style; (6) method; (7) fashion, process; (9) procedure; **2** (3) air; (4) look, mien; (7) bearing, conduct; (9) demeanour; **3** **manners** (8) breeding, courtesy; (9) etiquette; (10) politeness.

manoeuvre I *n & v* (4) move, plan, plot; (5) dodge; (6) scheme, wangle; **II** *n* (4)

ploy, ruse; (5) trick; (6) gambit, tactic; (8) exercise; (9) stratagem; (11) machination; **III** *v* (5) drive, steer; (6) handle, manage; (8) contrive; (10) manipulate; **IV** *cryptic* ANAGRAM CUE.

manufacture I *v* **1** (4) **make**; (5) build; (7) produce; (8) assemble; (9) construct; (11) mass-produce; **2** (6) invent; (7) concoct; (9) fabricate; **II** *n* (6) making; (8) assembly; (10) production; (12) construction.

many *adj* (4) lots; (5) heaps, loads, piles; (7) umpteen; (8) hundreds, manifold, millions, numerous; (9) countless, thousands; (2 words) a hundred *etc*, a load, a lot *etc*.

March *n* abbreviated as Mar, the third month, named after **Mars**.

march I *n & v* (4) file, hike, jomp, pace, slog, step, trek, walk; (5) stalk, tramp; (6) parade, trudge; (7) protest; (8) footslog; **II** *n* **1** (4) demo; (13) demonstration; **2** (7) advance; (8) progress; (11) development; **3** (6) border, fringe, margin; (8) boundary.

margin *n* **1** (3) rim; (4) brim, edge; (5) bound, brink, limit, verge; (6) border; (7) selvage; (8) selvedge; **2** (4) play, room; (5) extra, scope, space; (6) leeway; (8) latitude; (9) allowance; **3** (6) profit.

marine I *adj see* **maritime**; **2** (5) jolly; (11) leatherneck; **II** *cryptic* letters RM.

maritime *adj* (3) sea; (5) naval; (6) marine; (7) coastal, oceanic, seaside; (8) littoral, nautical; (9) seafaring.

Mark *Bible* **St Mark** an early Christian saint, traditionally credited with the authorship of the second Gospel.

mark I *n & v* **1** (4) blot, dent, scar, spot; (5) stain; (6) blotch, bruise, smudge; (7) blemish, scratch; **2** (4) tick; (5) grade; **II** *n* **1** (4) sign; (5) badge, token, stamp; (6) emblem, symbol; (8) evidence; (9) indicator; (10) indication; **2** (3) aim; (4) goal; (6) target; (9) objective; **III** *v* **1** (6) assess; (7) correct; (8) evaluate; **2** (4) heed, mind, note; (6) listen, regard, notice; (7) observe; **IV** *fin.* modern currency unit in Germany and an amount of money (13 shillings and 4 pence – 66⅔p) but not a coin in medieval England and Scotland.

Mark Antony *hist. & lit.* Roman General and friend and supporter of Julius Caesar. One of the triumvirs, the three rulers of Rome after Caesar's death, he was in: charge of the eastern half of the Roman Empire. He became the lover of Cleopatra the Queen of Egypt, quarrelled with Octavius Caesar, another of the triumvirs, was defeated by him at the battle of Actium and committed suicide. He appears as a leading character in Shakespeare's plays **Julius Caesar** and **Antony and Cleopatra**.

market I *n* (4) fair, mart, souk; (6) bazaar; (8) exchange; **II** *v* (4) hawk, sell; (5) trade; (6) barter, peddle, retail.

FAMOUS LONDON MARKETS

Billingsgate (fish), Camden (Lock) (general – trendy gear), Covent Garden (fruit and vegetables), Nine Elms (fruit and vegetables – the new Covent Garden), Petticoat Lane (general), Portobello Road (general, *esp.* second-hand good and antiques), Smithfield (meat).

---

marriage *n* (5) hymen, union; (7) wedding, wedlock; (8) alliance, nuptials; (9) matrimony.

marry *v* (3) wed; (4) join, knit, link, mate, pair; (5) hitch, match, unite; (6) splice; (2+ words) get wed, get hitched, get spliced, take the plunge, tie the knot.

Mars I *Rom myth* god of war, lover of Venus; **II** the fourth planet from the sun, the 'red planet'.

marsupial *n* animal that carries its young in a pouch.

MARSUPIALS

(5) koala; (6) glider, wombat; (7) opossum, wallaby; (8) kangaroo; (9) bandicoot, phalanger, thylacine; (2 words) Tasmanian devil, Tasmanian wolf.

Martial *lit.* Roman poet, known mainly as a composer of satirical epigrams.

martial *adj* (7) warlike; (8) military; (9) soldierly; (11) belligerent.

martial art *n*

MARTIAL ARTS

(4) judo; (5) kendo, wushu; (6) aikido, karate; (7) ju-jitsu; (2 words) kung fu, tae kwon do, tai chi.

Marx I Karl Marx *hist.* German philosopher whose writings, *esp. Capital* (das Kapital) and *The Communist Manifesto*, written with Friedrich Engels, form the basis of Communist thought; **II Marx Brothers** *film* stars of several highly successful comic films in the 1930s, including *Duck Soup, A Day at the Races*, and *A Night at the Opera*. Their names were: Chico, Groucho, Gummo, Harpo, and Zeppo.

mask I *n & v* (4) veil; (5) cloak, cover; (6) screen, shield, veneer; (8) disguise; (10) camouflage; **II** *n* (4) show; (5) front, guise, visor; (6) façade; (9) semblance.

master I *n* **1** (4) boss, head, lord, tuan; (5) chief, owner, ruler, sahib; (7) captain, skipper; (8) employer, governor, overseer; (9) commander; (10) controller; **2** (3) ace; (6) **expert**; (7) maestro; **3** (4) guide; (5) tutor; (7) **teacher**; (10) instructor; **II** *v* **1** (5) grasp, learn; (7) acquire; **2** (6) defeat, subdue; (7) control; (8) dominate, overcome; **III** *cryptic* letters MA or any other combination used for a master's degree.

match I *v* (2) go; (3) fit; (4) join, link, mate, suit, team; (5) agree, equal, marry, tally; (6) accord, belong, relate; (7) compare, conform; (8) dovetail; (9) harmonise (*or* harmonize); (10) correspond; **II** *n* **1** (4) bout, game, test; (7) contest; (8) friendly; **2** (5) vesta; (7) lucifer; **3** (8) **marriage**.

mate I *n* **1** (3) pal; (4) chum; (5) china; (6) **friend**; **2** (4) wife; (6) spouse; (7) husband, partner; **3** (6) helper; (9) assistant, associate, colleague; **4** ship's officer; **5** winning move in chess; **II** *v* (4) join, pair, team; (5) breed, match; (6) couple; (8) copulate.

material I *n* (5) cloth, stuff; (6) fabric; (7) textile; *for types of textiles see* **fabric**;

II *adj* (3) key; (5) major, vital; (7) crucial, primary, salient, serious; (8) relevant; (9) important; (10) meaningful; (11) far-reaching, significant; (13) consequential.

Matthew *Bible* **St Matthew** traditionally credited with the authorship of the first Gospel, he was a tax gatherer before being called by Jesus and becoming one of the twelve apostles.

May *n* the fifth month, named after the goddess Maia.

meal *n* (3) tea; (4) bite; (5) feast, lunch, snack; (6) brunch, buffet, dinner, picnic, repast, spread, supper, tiffin, tuck-in; (7) banquet, blow-out; (8) barbecue, luncheon, take-away; (9) breakfast, elevenses.

mean¹ *adj* **1** (4) near; (5) tight; (6) stingy; (7) miserly, selfish; (9) niggardly; (11) tight-fisted; (12) parsimonious; (13) penny-pinching; **2** (5) cruel, nasty; (6) unkind; (9) malicious; **3** (4) base, poor; (5) lowly; (6) humble, shabby; (8) wretched.

mean² *v* **1** (5) imply; (6) denote; (7) signify, suggest; (8) indicate; (9) symbolise (*or* symbolize); **2** (4) bode; (5) augur; (6) entail, intend; (7) portend; (8) forebode, foretell; (10) foreshadow.

mean³ *n & adj* (3) mid; (6) median, medium, middle; (7) average, halfway; (10) compromise.

means *n* **1** (3) way; (4) mode; (6) agency, medium, method; (7) channel, process, vehicle; (8) facility; (9) mechanism, procedure; **2** (5) funds, money; (6) income, riches, wealth; (9) resources; (11) wherewithal.

measure **I** *v* (5) count, gauge, judge, value, weigh; (6) assess, survey; (7) compute; (8) evaluate, quantify; **II** *n* **1** (4) size; (5) range, scope; (6) amount, degree, extent; (8) quantity; (9) magnitude; (10) proportion; **2** (3) rod; (4) rule, tape; (5) gauge, meter, ruler, scale; (8) standard; (9) criterion, yardstick; **3** (3) act, law; (4) bill, step; (5) means; (6) action, method, policy; (11) legislation; **4** *see* **dance**; **5** poetic rhythm *or* **metre**; **III** *cryptic* the

letters making up an abbreviation of a standard unit of measurement, *e.g.* CC, CM, FT, IN, LB, MM, OZ.

MEASURES OF AREA

(3) are; (4) acre, rood; (7) hectare; (2 words) square inch/foot/ mile *etc.*

MEASURES OF CAPACITY

(3) tot, tun; (4) butt, dram, gill, peck, pint; (5) litre, quart; (6) barrel, bushel, firkin, gallon; (8) hogshead.

MEASURES OF LENGTH

(3) ell, rod; (4) foot, inch, mile, nail, pole, yard; (5) cable, chain, metre, perch; (6) fathom, league; (7) furlong, (9) kilometre; (10) centimetre, millimetre.

MEASURES OF WEIGHT

(3) ton; (4) dram, gram, kilo; (5) grain, ounce, pound, stone, tonne; (6) drachm; (7) quarter, scruple; (8) kilogram; (13) hundredweight.

METRICAL MEASURES

The words for metrical measures are formed by adding standard prefixes to the name of the standard unit. The prefixes are milli- (1/1000), centi- (1/100), deci- (1/10), UNIT, deca- (x 10), hecto- (x 100), kilo- (x 1000).

---

meat *n* (4) body, core, pith; (5) flesh; (7) essence; (9) substance.

TYPES OF MEAT

(3) ham; (4) beef, duck, hare, lamb, paté, pork, veal; (5) bacon, goose, heart, liver, mince, offal, tripe; (6) brains, burger, faggot, gammon, grouse, kidney, mutton, oxtail, rabbit, tongue, turkey; (7) chicken, rissole, sausage, venison; (8) pheasant; (9) hamburger; (10) beefburger, sweetbread.

CUTS OF MEAT

(3) leg, rib; (4) chop, hand, hock, neck, loin, rump, shin, wing; (5) chine, flank, scrag, steak; (6) breast, cutlet, fillet, saddle; (7) brisket, knuckle, sirloin, topside; (8) escalope, shoulder, spare-rib; (10) silverside.

---

medal *n* (4) gong; (5) award, badge; (8) insignia.

MEDALS

CGM (Conspicuous Gallantry Medal), DFC (Distinguished Flying Cross), DFM (Distinguished Flying Medal), DSM (Distinguished Service Medal), DSO (Distinguished Service Order), GC (George Cross), GM (George Medal), MC (Military Cross), MM (Military Medal), VC (Victoria Cross), Congressional Medal of Honour; Iron Cross, Legion of Honour, Purple Heart.

Medea *Gk myth* the daughter of Aetes, King of Colchis, and a sorceress, who assisted **Jason** in his quest for the **Golden Fleece**, and later returned to Greece with him as his wife. When Jason was unfaithful to her, she killed their two sons to revenge herself on him.

media *see also* **medium**.

THE MEDIA

(2) TV; (5) press, radio, video; (10) newspapers, television.

---

medicine *n* (4) cure, drug, pill; (5) drops, purge, tonic; (6) emetic, gargle, lotion, potion, remedy, tablet; (7) antacid, capsule, draught, linctus, panacea, placebo; (8) laxative, ointment; (9) analgesic; (10) antibiotic, medicament, medication, painkiller; (11) suppository; (12) prescription.

mediocre *adj* (4) poor, so-so, weak; (6) medium; (7) average; (8) inferior, middling, ordinary; (10) second-rate, uninspired; (11) commonplace, indifferent; (12) run-of-the-mill; (13) insignificant, unexceptional; (15) undistinguished.

medium I *adj* (4) fair, mean; (6) medial, median, middle, midway; (7) average; (8) moderate; (12) intermediate; II *n* I (3) way; (4) form, mode; (5) means; (6) agency, method; (7) channel, process, vehicle; (10) instrument; 2 (7) psychic; (11) clairvoyant; (12) spiritualist; *see also* **media**.

Medusa *Gk myth* chief of the **Gorgons**. She was slain by **Perseus** who cut off her head and fixed it in the centre of Athene's shield.

meet *v* I (4) find; (9) encounter; (2 words) bump into, chance (up)on, come across, come (up)on, happen (up)on, run into; 2 (4) join; (5) touch; (6) gather; (7) collect, connect, convene; (8) assemble, converge; (9) intersect; (10) congregate; 3 (3) pay; (5) equal, match; (6) answer, fulfil, settle; (7) satisfy; (9) discharge; 4 (4) face; (7) undergo; (10) experience.

meeting *n* (4) date; (5) event, forum, rally, tryst; (7) session; (8) assembly, conclave, junction; (9) encounter, gathering; (10) conference, confluence, convention, rendezvous, tournament; (11) appointment, assignation, convergence; (12) congregation, intersection; (13) confrontation.

Megaera *Gk myth* 'the jealous one', one of the three **Furies**.

Melpomene *Gk myth* the muse of tragedy, see **Muses**.

Menelaus *Gk myth & lit*. a king of Sparta, the husband of **Helen** of Troy and brother of **Agamemnon**.

Mephistopheles *lit*. the name of the devil in the legend of **Faust**.

merchandise *n* (5) cargo, goods, stock, wares; (7) produce; (8) products; (11) commodities.

merchant *n* (6) broker, dealer, seller, trader, vendor; (8) retailer; (10) shopkeeper, trafficker, wholesaler.

Merchant of Venice *lit*. play by Shakespeare.

Plot outline: An improvident young Venetian, Bassanio, asks his older friend

Antonio (the merchant of Venice of the title) to finance his attempt to woo and win a wealthy heiress called Portia. Antonio agrees, but lacking ready money has to borrow from a Jewish money-lender, Shylock, whom he makes no secret of despising. Shylock proposes an arrangement in which the only security Antonio has to offer is 'a pound of flesh', to be cut off if he defaults on the loan. Despite Bassanio's misgivings, Antonio agrees to the deal, confident that his ships will come home in time. Bassanio goes to Belmont, Portia's home, and wins her hand in marriage in a contest that involves making a correct choice of one of three caskets (of gold, silver and lead – the lead casket being the correct choice). His celebrations are interrupted by news that Antonio's ships have apparently been lost at sea and that Shylock, enraged by his daughter Jessica's eloping with a Christian and carrying off a large quantity of money and jewels, is demanding his pound of flesh. Bassanio returns to Venice, quickly followed by Portia who disguises herself as a lawyer and appears at Antonio's trial. After pleading in vain for mercy ('The quality of mercy is not strained'), she tells Shylock that he is legally entitled to take his pound of flesh, but may not shed one drop of Antonio's blood in so doing. Shylock then finds himself at the mercy of the law and is heavily fined and forced to become a Christian. Bassanio offers to reward the disguised Portia for saving his friend. All she will accept is a ring that she herself gave him on their betrothal and he swore not to part with. The play ends back at Belmont with much banter over the sorting out of the business of the ring.

Mercury I *Rom. myth* the messenger of the gods, Greek equivalent, **Hermes**; **II** *astron.* the planet closest to the sun; **III mercury** *n* a metal also known as quicksilver, symbol Hg.

merry *adj* **1** (4) glad; (5) happy, jolly; (6) jovial, joyful; (7) festive; (8) cheerful, mirthful; (9) convivial; **2** *see* **drunk**.

Merry Men *see* **Robin Hood**.

mess I *n & v* (6) jumble, muddle, tangle; (7) clutter; (8) disorder; **II** *n* **1** (3) tip; (4) dirt, dump, hole; (5) chaos, filth; (7) squalor; (8) disarray, shambles; (9) confusion; (10) untidiness; (15) disorganisation (*or* disorganization); **2** (3) fix; (7) trouble; (10) difficulty; (11) predicament; **III** *v* (6) meddle, tamper; (8) dishevel; (9) interfere; (10) disarrange; **IV mess** *or* **in a mess** *cryptic* ANAGRAM CUE.

message *n* **1** (4) memo, note; (5) cable; (6) letter, report; (7) missive; (8) bulletin, dispatch, telegram; (10) communiqué, memorandum; (13) communication; **2** (4) idea; (5) moral, point, theme; (6) lesson; (7) meaning.

messenger *n* (5) envoy; (6) herald; (7) courier; (8) emissary; (9) go-between, harbinger, precursor; (10) ambassador; (14) representative.

metal *n*

METALS

(3) tin (Sn).

(4) gold (Au), iron (Fe), lead (Pb), zinc (Zn).

(5) cupro- (Cu), ferro- (Fe), plumb (Pb).

(6) barium (Ba), chrome (Cr), cobalt (Co), copper (Cu), nickel (Ni), osmium (Os), radium (Ra), silver (Ag), sodium (Na).

(7) argento (Ag), bismuth (Bi), cadmium (Cd), calcium (Ca), gallium (Ga), iridium (Ir), lithium (Li), mercury (Hg), thorium (Th), uranium (U), wolfram (W).

(8) antimony (Sb), chromium (Cr), platinum (Pt), thallium (Tl), titanium (Ti), tungsten (W), vanadium (V).

(9) aluminium (Al), beryllium (Al), magnesium (Mg), manganese (Mn), palladium (Pd), potassium (K), strontium (Sr), ytterbium (Yb), zirconium (Zr).

(10) molybdenum (Mo), phosphorus (P).

---

method *n* (3) way; (4) mode, plan; (5) means, order; (6) agency, avenue, course, medium, policy, scheme, system; (7) channel, process; (8) approach, ideology, planning; (9) mechanism, procedure, technique; (12) organisation (*or* organization).

Methuselah I *Bible* the oldest man mentioned in the Bible, the grandfather of **Noah**, said to have lived 969 years; II *see* **bottle**.

metre *n* 1 unit of length abbreviated as M; 2 a rhythmic pattern in poetry.

METRICAL UNITS (FEET) IN POETRY

(4) iamb; (6) dactyl, iambic, iambus; (7) anapest, spondee, trochee; (8) choriamb, dactylic, spondaic, tribrach, trochaic; (10) amphibrach, choriambic, choriambus, tribrachic; (12) amphibrachic.

METRES

(9) hexameter; (10) heptameter, pentameter, tetrameter; (11) alexandrine.

---

mid I *adj see* **middle**; II *cryptic* use the middle letter or letters of the word involved (often combined in a longer word, so that, *e.g.* 'midday' might = a, 'midstream' = re).

Midas *Gk myth* a king of Phrygia, who was granted his wish by the gods that everything he touched should turn to gold. Since this included his food, he asked for the gift to be taken back again. It was removed when he bathed in the river Pactolus, which ever after ran over sands containing gold.

middle I *n* (4) core, mean; (5) heart, midst, waist; (6) centre; (8) midpoint; (2 words) bull's eye; II *adj* (4) mean; (6) median; (7) average, central, halfway; (12) intermediate.

Milne, A. A. *fict.* creator of Winnie the Pooh.

MILNE CHARACTERS

(3) Roo; (4) Pooh; (5) Alice, Kanga; (6) Eeyore, Piglet, Tigger; (9) Heffalump; (2 words) Christopher Robin.

---

mind I *n* 1 (4) soul, wits; (5) brain, sense; (6) brains, memory, reason; (8) thinking, thoughts; (9) attention, intellect, mentality; (11) remembrance; (12) intelligence, recollection; (13) concentration, understanding; 2 (4) view; (6) belief; (7) opinion; (8) attitude, judgment; (9) judgement; II *v* 1 (4) tend; (5) guard; (7) protect; (2+ words) care for, look after, take care of, watch over; 2 (4) heed, mark, note; (6) follow, listen, regard, notice; (7) observe; 3 (4) fuss; (5) worry; (6) object.

mine I *n* 1 (3) pit; (4) seam, vein; (5) shaft; (6) quarry, tunnel; (7) deposit, gallery; (8) colliery; 2 (4) fund; (5) hoard, stock, store; (6) source, supply, wealth; (7) reserve; (8) treasury; 3 (6) weapon; (9) explosive; II *v* (3) dig; (6) quarry, tunnel; (7) extract; (8) excavate.

mineral *n* (4) soda; (5) drink, mixer, tonic.

MINERALS

(3) jet, ore.

(4) clay, coal, coke, lime, marl, mica, peat, salt, spar, talc.

(5) borax, boron (B), emery.

(6) albite, barite, baryte, carbon (C), galena, garnet, gypsum, iolite, pumice, pyrite, quartz, silica, spinel.

(7) arsenic (As), asphalt, azurite, bauxite, bitumen, calcite, jacinth, lignite, olivine, perlite, pyrites, realgar, silicon, tripoli, uralite, zeolite.

(8) antimony (Sb), asbestos, calamine, chromite, cinnabar, corundum, cryolite, dolomite, feldspar, fluorite, graphite, lazurite, obsidian, plumbago, pyrozene, siderite, silicate, tinstone.

list continued over

---

(9) alabaster, anhydrite, brimstone, fluorspar, ironstone, limestone, lodestone, malachite, marcasite, saltpetre, wulfenite.

(10) aventurine, chalcedony, hornblende, meerschaum, phosphorus (P), sphalerite.

(11) molybdenite, pitchblende, vesuvianite.

(2 words) fool's gold, iron pyrites.

Minerva *Rom. myth* the goddess of wisdom, equivalent to Greek **Athene**.

minor I *adj* (5) light, small, petty; (6) junior, lesser, little, slight; (7) trivial, younger; (8) inferior, trifling; (9) secondary; (10) negligible, subsidiary; (11) subordinate; (13) insignificant; (14) inconsiderable; II *n* (4) ward; (5) child; (6) infant; III *music* (3) key; (5) scale; IV *cryptic* use an abbreviation or shortened form of the word.

Minos *Gk myth* a king of Crete, and celebrated lawgiver. He employed **Daedalus** to build the labyrinth for the **Minotaur**. After death he became a judge of souls in the **Underworld**.

Minotaur *Gk myth* a monster with the head of a bull and body of a man, born to **Pasiphae**, the wife of **Minos**, who built the labyrinth to house him. An annual tribute of young men and women was sent from Greece to be sacrificed to him, until he was killed by **Theseus** with the help of **Ariadne**.

minute I *n see* **moment**; II *adj* (3) wee; (4) mini, tiny (5) brief, dwarf, small, teeny; (6) little, meagre, paltry, petite, scanty, sparse, teensy; (9) miniature, minuscule; (10) diminutive, negligible; (11) microscopic; (13) infinitesimal.

miserable *adj* **1** (3) low, sad; (4) blue, down, glum; (6) dismal, gloomy, gutted, morose; (7) forlorn, joyless, unhappy; (8) dejected, downcast, wretched; (9) depressed; (10) despondent, distressed, melancholy; (11) crestfallen, downhearted, heartbroken; (12) disheartened; **2** (4) grey; (5) bleak; (6) dismal, dreary, gloomy,

shabby, sombre; (7) squalid; (8) mournful; (9) cheerless; (12) impoverished; **3** (4) mean; (6) meagre, measly, paltry; (7) pitiful; (8) derisory, pathetic; (9) niggardly; (10) despicable; (12) contemptible.

misery *n* **1** (3) woe; (4) pain; (5) agony, grief; (6) sorrow; (7) anguish, sadness; (8) distress, mourning; (9) dejection, heartache; (10) affliction, desolation, heartbreak; (11) unhappiness; **2** (4) want; (7) poverty; (8) hardship; (9) privation; (11) deprivation; **3** (5) Jonah; (7) killjoy; (8) Jeremiah; (10) spoilsport; (11) partypooper.

miss I *v* **1** (4) drop, omit, skip; (5) avoid, dodge, evade, forgo; (6) bypass, escape, ignore; (7) exclude; (8) overlook; (2 words) leave out, let go; **2** (4) long, pine, need, want, wish; (5) mourn; (6) lament, regret; II *n* (5) error; (7) blunder, failure, mistake; (8) omission; (9) oversight.

missile *n* (4) dart, shot; (5) arrow, shaft; (6) rocket; (10) projectile.

GUIDED MISSILES

(3) Sam; (4) ICBM, MIRV, Skud; (6) Cruise, Exocet, Rapier; (7) Polaris, Trident; (8) Pershing; (9) Minuteman.

---

mistake I *n* (4) boob, flaw, slip; (5) error, gaffe, lapse; (6) cock-up, howler, slip-up; (7) blunder, clanger, fallacy; (8) misprint, solecism; (9) oversight; (10) inaccuracy; (14) miscalculation; (15) misapprehension; (2 words) faux pas; II *v* (7) confuse; (8) misjudge; (12) miscalculate; (13) misunderstand (2 words) mix up.

mistaken I *adj* (3) off, out; (5) false, wrong; (6) faulty, untrue; (7) inexact; (8) improper; (9) erroneous, imprecise, incorrect; (10) fallacious, inaccurate; (12) illegitimate; (13) ungrammatical; II **mistaken** *or* **mistakenly** *cryptic* ANAGRAM CUE.

mistreat *v see* **misuse**.

misunderstanding *n* **1** (5) error, mix-up; (7) mistake; (10) misreading; (13) misconception; (15) misapprehension, misconstruction; **2** (4) rift; (6) breach;

(7) discord, dispute; (8) argument, conflict; (10) difference; (12) disagreement.

misuse l *v & n* (4) harm, hurt; (5) abuse, waste; ll *v* (5) wrong; (6) ill-use, molest; (7) corrupt, distort, exploit, pervert; (8) ill-treat, misapply, maltreat, mistreat, squander; (14) misappropriate; lll *cryptic* ANAGRAM CUE.

mix l *v* 1 (4) fuse, join, meld; (5) blend, merge, unite; (6) garble, jumble, mingle, muddle; (7) combine, confuse; (8) compound, confound, scramble; (10) amalgamate, homogenise (*or* homogenize), synthesise (*or* synthesize); 2 (6) hobnob; (7) consort; (9) associate, socialise (*or* socialize); (10) fraternise (*or* fraternize); ll *n see* **mixture**; lll *cryptic* ANAGRAM CUE.

mixed l *adj* 1 (4) co-ed; (6) hybrid, motley, sundry, unisex, varied; (7) diverse, mingled, various; (8) assorted, compound; (9) composite, crossbred; 2 (9) equivocal, uncertain; (10) ambivalent; (11) conflicting; ll *cryptic* ANAGRAM CUE.

mixture *n* (3) mix; (4) brew; (5) alloy, blend, cross, union; (6) fusion, hybrid, jumble, medley; (7) amalgam, mélange; (8) compound; (9) composite, potpourri, synthesis; (10) assortment, concoction, hotchpotch, miscellany; (11) combination; (12) amalgamation.

Mnemosyne *Gk myth* goddess of memory, mother of the Muses.

Moby Dick *lit.* novel by Herman Melville describing the fanatical hunt for Moby Dick, the great white whale, by Captain Ahab and his ship the *Pequod*. The narrator of the story is called Ishmael.

mock l *v & n* (3) boo; (4) gibe, hiss, hoot, jeer; (5) abuse, scoff, sneer, taunt; (6) insult; (7) catcall; ll *v* (6) deride, heckle; (7) barrack; (8) ridicule; lll *adj* (4) **fake**, sham; (5) false; (9) imitation; (10) artificial.

mockery *n* 1 (5) scorn; (7) disdain, sarcasm; (8) contempt, derision, ridicule, scoffing; 2 (4) sham; (6) parody, satire; (8) travesty; (10) caricature.

model l *n* 1 (4) copy, norm, type; (5) ideal; (6) design, master, matrix, mockup, puppet; (7) example, pattern, replica; (8) exemplar, maquette, standard, template; (9) blueprint, prototype; (14) representation; (2 words) lay figure; 2 (5) power; (6) sitter; (7) subject; (9) mannequin; ll *adj* (5) ideal; (7) perfect, typical; (9) exemplary; lll *v* (4) cast, form, plan; (5) carve, mould, shape; (6) create, design, sculpt; (7) fashion.

moderate l *adj* 1 (4) calm, cool, mild; (8) sensible; (10) reasonable, restrained; 2 (4) fair; (6) medium, modest; (7) average; (8) mediocre, ordinary; (15) middle-of-the-road; ll *v* (4) calm, curb, ease, tame; (5) abate, allay, check; (6) lessen, reduce, soften, subdue; (7) control, subside; (8) decrease, mitigate; (9) alleviate, softpedal; (2 words) play down, tone down, water down.

modern *adj* (3) new; (5) fresh, novel; (6) latest, recent; (7) current, go-ahead, present; (8) advanced, up-to-date; (10) avant-garde, newfangled, present-day; (11) fashionable; (12) contemporary; (13) state-of-the-art, up-to-the-minute.

modest *adj* 1 (3) coy, shy; (5) quiet; (6) chaste, humble; (7) bashful; (8) reserved, retiring; (9) diffident; (10) unassuming; (12) self-effacing; 2 (5) small; (7) limited; (8) moderate; (10) restricted; (13) unexceptional; (14) unpretentious.

Mohammed *rel.* the founder and Prophet of Islam.

moment *n* 1 (2) mo; (3) sec; (4) tick; (5) jiffy, trice; (6) minute, second; (7) instant; 2 (6) import, weight; (7) gravity; (10) importance; (12) significance.

momentary *adj* (5) brief, short; (7) passing; (8) fleeting; (9) ephemeral, temporary, transient; (10) transitory.

momentous *adj* (5) major, vital; (7) crucial, fateful, serious, weighty; (8) critical, decisive, historic; (9) important; (11) epoch-making, significant; (12) earthshaking.

Moirai *Gk myth see* **Fates**.

Molière *lit.* generally recognised as France's greatest comic dramatist. His plays include: *L'Avare* (the Miser), *Le Bourgeois gentilhomme*, *L'Ecole des femmes* (The School for Wives), *Le Malade Imaginaire* (The Imaginary Invalid), *Le Misanthrope* and *Tartuffe*.

monarch *n* (4) czar, **king**, tsar; (5) **queen**, ruler; (6) prince; (7) emperor, empress; (9) sovereign.

money *n* (4) cash, coin, pelf; (5) lucre, funds; (6) riches, wealth; (7) capital; *see also* **coin, currency**.

SLANG TERMS FOR MONEY

(3) tin; (4) dosh, loot; (5) brass, bread, dough, ready, rhino; (6) moolah; (7) readies, shekels; (11) spondulicks, wherewithal.

---

monitor I *n* (3) VDU; (6) screen; (7) display, scanner; (8) overseer, recorder, watchdog; (10) supervisor; (11) invigilator; II *v* (4) plot, scan; (5) check, trace, track, watch; (6) follow, record; (7) oversee; (9) eavesdrop, supervise.

monk *n* (5) abbot, friar, prior; (6) hermit; (7) brother, recluse; (8) monastic; (9) anchorite.

MONASTIC ORDERS

Augustinian, Benedictine, Buddhist, Carthusian, Cistercian, Trappist.

---

monkey I *n* **1** (3) ape; (6) simian; (7) primate; **2** (3) imp; (4) brat. II *v* (4) fool, mess, play; (6) fiddle, meddle, tamper, tinker; (9) interfere.

SPECIES OF MONKEY (*see also* **ape**)

(3) sai.

(4) douc, mona, saki, titi, zati.

(5) cebus, drill, indri, lemur, loris, magot, potto.

(6) aye-aye, baboon, chacma, coaita, colugo, grivet, guenon, howler, langur, indris, rhesus, tee-tee, vervet.

(7) barbary (ape), colobus, guereza, hanuman, macaque, sapajou, tamarin, tarsier.

---

(8) bushbaby, capuchin, entellus, hylobate, kinkajou, mandrill, marmoset, talapoin, wanderoo.

---

moon I *n* (9) satellite; II *v* (4) idle, loaf, mope; (5) brood, dream, mooch; (8) daydream; (9) fantasise (*or* fantasize).

MOONS OF THE PLANETS

Mars – (6) Deimos, Phobos.
Jupiter – (2) Io; (4) Leda; (5) Carme, Elara, Metis, Thebe; (6) Ananke, Europa, Sinope; (7) Himalia; (8) Adrastea, Amalthea, Callisto, Ganymede, Lysithea, Pasiphae.
Saturn – (3) Pan; (4) Rhea; (5) Atlas, Dione, Janus, Mimas, Titan; (6) Helene, Phoebe, Tethys; (7) Calypso, Iapetus, Pandora, Telesto; (8) Hyperion; (9) Enceladus; (10) Epimetheus, Prometheus.
Uranus – (4) Puck; (5) Ariel; (6) Bianca, Juliet, Oberon, Portia; (7) Belinda, Miranda, Ophelia, Titania, Umbriel; (8) Cordelia, Cressida, Rosalind; (9) Desdemona.
Neptune – (5) Naiad; (6) Nereid, Triton; (7) Despina, Galatea, Larissa, Proteus.
Pluto – (6) Charon.

Moriarty, Professor James, *lit.* the 'Napoleon of crime' and chief antagonist of Sherlock **Holmes**. Killed, supposedly with Holmes, by falling over the Reichenbach Falls in Switzerland.

Morse I *lit. TV* Oxford-based detective, erudite and lover of classical music, assisted by more down-to-earth Sgt Lewis, created by Colin Dexter and played by John Thaw; II *hist.* **Samuel Morse** invented the electric telegraph and the Morse Code of dots and dashes to send messages by.

Moses *Bible* great leader and lawgiver of the Jewish people and, traditionally, the author of the first five books of the Old Testament. Moses was born, according to the Book of Exodus, when the Jews were in Egypt, oppressed by the Pharaoh, who ordered all boy children to be killed at birth. Moses' mother hid him in the bul-rushes where he was found by Pharaoh's daughter who raised him as her son. When Moses was grown up God appeared to him in the burning bush and com-manded him to lead the Jewish people out of Egypt into a land 'flowing with milk and honey'. Moses attempted to persuade Pharaoh to let the Jews go peacefully, but he refused, until the seventh of seven **plagues** of Egypt had been visited on him and his people. Moses and the Jews then set out into the wilderness, pursued by Pharaoh and his chariots. Moses was able to part the waters of the Red Sea so that the Jews could cross it, but when Pharaoh and his soldiers attempted to follow the waters rolled back and overwhelmed them. Moses then led his people through the wilderness for forty years, receiving the Ten Commandments from God on Mount Sinai, orders to build the Ark of the Covenant, and the basic tenets of traditional Jewish law. Moses was not permitted by God to enter the Promised Land, but he was able to see it from the top of Mount Pisgah before his death.

mostly *cryptic* ANAGRAM CUE, but with some letters omitted, as in: 'There are fenlands mostly in this part of Belgium' (8) = Flanders.

mother I *n* (2) ma; (3) dam, mum; (4) mama; (5) mater, mummy; (11) progenitrix; (2 words) old lady, old woman; **II** *v* (4) baby, bear, rear; (5) nurse, spoil; (6) pamper; (7) cherish, nurture; (11) mollycoddle; **III** *cryptic* frequently indicates the letters MA.

motherless *cryptic* omit the letters MA or those making up any other word for mother from a word in the clue, as in: 'Motherless expert takes direction and still ends up at rear' = stern (expert = master, direction = N [north]).

motorway *cryptic* letter M or letters MI or MIV.

mould I *n & v* (4) cast, form, make; (5) build, shape, stamp; (6) design; (7) pat-tern; **II** *v* (5) carve, forge, model; (6)

create, sculpt; (7) fashion; **III** *n* 1 (3) die; (6) matrix; (8) template; 2 (3) rot; (5) decay; (6) blight, fungus, mildew.

mount I *v* 1 (4) grow, rise, soar; (5) climb; (6) ascend; (8) increase; (10) accumulate; (2 words) get on, go up; 2 (4) hang; (5) frame; (7) display; 3 (5) stage; (7) produce; (2 words) put on; **II** *n* 1 *see* **mountain**; 2 (5) horse, steed; 3 (4) base, card; (5) frame; (7) backing.

mountain *n* 1 (3) alp, tor; (4) crag, hill, peak; (5) mount; (8) eminence; (9) elev-ation; 2 (4) heap, mass, pile; (5) stack; (7) backlog.

MOUNTAINS

(3) Elk, Ida, Kea.

(4) Azul, Cook, Dore, Ebal, Etna, Fuji, Jaya, Joma, Meru, Ossa, Rigi, Roan, Rosa, Viso.

(5) Adams, Asahi, Athos, Baker, Binga, Blanc, Cenis, Cinto, Corno, Cowan, Dendi, Djaja, Eiger, Elgon, Gughe, Hayes, Hekla, Huila, Kamet, Lenin, Logan, Lyell, Marcy, Misti, Monch, Overo, Pelee, Perdu, Sinai, Tabor.

(6) Ararat, Bogong, Carmel, Duarte, Elbert, Elbrus, Elbruz, Erebus, Hermon, Hotaka, Kailas, Lelija, Makalu, Musala, Muztag, Ortles, Pissis, Powell, Rungwe, Sajama, Sangay, Tasman, Tolima, Wilson, Yeguas, Zirkel.

(7) Bernina, Bolivar, Brocken, Everest, Foraker, Harvard, Hoffman, Illampu, Jezerce, Kerinci, Lookout, Markham, Ohakune, Olympus, Pelvoux, Peteroa, Pollino, Rainier, Roraima, Sanford, Simplon, Thabana, Timarum, Toubkal, Townend, Triglav, Whitney; (2 words) Dykh Tau, San Jose, St Elias.

(8) Adamello, Columbia, Cotopaxi, Demavend, Durmitor, Fujiyama, Illimani, Jungfrau, Kinabalu, Krakatoa, Licoreia, McKinley, Mitchell, Mulhacén, Murallón, Olivares, Rushmore, Sarameti,

list continued over

Smólikas, Snöhetta, Sokhondo, Tarawera, Vesuvius, Victoria, Wrangell; (2 words) Anai Mudi, Mauna Kea, Mont Blanc, Mont Dore, St Helens.

(9) Aconcagua, Annapurna, Blackburn, Breithorn, Communism, Dachstein, Huascarán, Karakoram, Karisimbe, Koh-I-Mazar, Klinovaec, Kosciusko, Lafayette, Maladetta, Marmolada, Muztagata, Parnassus, Pelatsoeu, Pietrosul, Rakaposhi, Stromboli, Tocorpuri, Tongariro, Tupungato, Zugspitze; (2+ Words) Adam's Peak, Borah Peak, Büyük Agri, Emi Koussi, Gran Sasso, King's Peak, Long's Peak, Mont Cenis, Monte Rosa, Monte Viso, Mont Perdu, Nanda Devi, Pic du Midi, Pike's Peak, Ras Dashan, Sugar Loaf.

(10) Chimborazo, Dhaulagiri, Diablarets, Kuh-E-Taftan, Matterhorn, Mercedario, Washington, Wetterhorn, Wildspitze; (2+ words) Dent Du Midi, Gongga Shan, Grand Teton, Grassy Knob, Gray's Peaks, La Malinche, Minja Konka, Monte Cinto, Monte Corno, Robson Peak, Spruce Knob, Tabun Bogdo.

(11) Assiniboine, Drachenfels, Fairweather, Hochstetter, Kilimanjaro, Kirkpatrick, Loolmalasin, Schreckhorn; (2 words) Garnett Peak, Gora Belukha, Munku Sardyk, Namcha Barwa, Nanga Parbat, Vatna Jökull, Wheeler Peak.

(12) Citlaltepetl, Galdhöpiggen, Llullaillaco, Popocatepetl, Tinguiririca; (2+ words) Godwin Austen, Gran Paradiso, Monte Pollino.

(13) Kangchenjunga; (2+ words) Gross Glockner, Jabal Alchdhar, Mount of Olives, Ojos Del Salado, Table Mountain.

(14) Finsteraarhorn, Mont Aux Sources.

(15) Pidurutalalgala; (2 words) Champagne Castle.

MOUNTAIN RANGES

(4) Alps, Harz, Jura.

(5) Altai, Andes, Atlas (Mountains), Ghats, Urals.

(6) (Mountains of) Mourne, Taunus, Taurus, Vosges.

(7) Balkans, Rockies, Sierras.

(8) Cascades, Caucasus, Pennines, Pyrenees,

(9) Apennines, Catskills, Dolomites, Grampians, Himalayas, Yablonovy.

(10) Cairngorms, Erzgebirge.

(11) Adirondacks, Cantabrians, Carpathians, Drakensberg.

(12) Appalachians.

(2+ words) Blue Ridge Mountains, Hindu Kush, Sierra Madre. Tien Shan.

move I *v* **1** (2) go; (4) stir; (5) budge, shift; (6) depart, switch; (7) advance, proceed, migrate, retreat; (8) progress, relocate; **2** (5) touch; (6) affect, excite; (7) agitate, impress; **3** (4) urge; (5) drive; (6) impel, incite, induce, prompt; (7) inspire; (8) motivate, persuade; (9) stimulate; **4** (7) propose; (8) advocate; (9) recommend; II *n* (3) act; (4) ploy, step; (6) action, device; (7) measure; (9) manoeuvre, stratagem; III **move** *or* **moving** *cryptic* ANAGRAM CUE.

much I *adj* (4) lots; (5) ample, heaps, piles; (7) copious; (8) abundant; (11) substantial; (12) considerable; II *adv* (5) often; (6) plenty; (7) greatly; (10) frequently.

muse I *n* (11) inspiration; II *v* (5) think; (6) ponder; (7) reflect.

THE NINE MUSES

Calliope (epic poetry), Clio (history), Erato (love songs), Euterpe (lyric poetry), Melpomene (tragedy), Polyhymnia (singing), Terpsichore (dancing), Thalia (comedy), Urania (astronomy).

music *for* **musical instruments, musical terms and symbols** *and* **musical works** *see below – see also entries at* **composer, musician, note,** *and* **voice**.

musical *adj* (5) sweet; (6) dulcet; (7) lyrical, tuneful, melodic; (9) melodious; (10) harmonious.

in St Louis, Singin' in the Rain, The Sound of Music, The Vagabond King.

(15+) Jesus Christ Superstar, Joseph and his Amazing Technicolour Dreamcoat, Phantom of the Opera.

FAMOUS MUSICALS

(4) Cats, Fame, Gigi, Hair, Mame.

(5) Annie, Evita, Gypsy, Tommy.

(6) Grease, Jeeves, Kismet, Oliver, Xanadu; (2 words) The Wiz, Top Hat.

(7) Cabaret, Camelot, Rosalie, Scrooge; (2 words) GI Blues, Pal Joey.

(8) Carousel, Godspell, Oklahoma, Showboat; (2 words) Mamma Mia.

(9) Brigadoon, Evergreen; (2 words) Rose Marie.

(10) (2+ words) Blue Hawaii, Hello Dolly, Kiss Me Kate, Lady Be Good, My Fair Lady.

(11) (2+ words) A Chorus Line, Call Me Madam, Carmen Jones, Chu Chin Chow, High Society, Mary Poppins, Me And My Girl, No, No Nanette, The King and I, The Music Man.

(12) (2+ words) Anything Goes, April in Paris, Easter Parade, Guys and Dolls, Love Me Tender, Song of Norway, South Pacific, Sweet Charity, The Boy Friend, Viva Las Vegas.

(13) (2+ words) Blood Brothers, Daddy Long Legs, Half a Sixpence, Jailhouse Rock, Les Misérables, Silk Stockings, Summer Holiday, The Desert Song, The Pajama Game, The Wizard of Oz.

(14) (2+ words) Broadway Melody, Finian's Rainbow, Flower Drum Song, Follow the Fleet, Paint Your Wagon, The Gay Divorcee.

(15) (2+ words) Annie Get Your Gun, Flying Down to Rio, Meet Me

MUSICAL INSTRUMENTS

(4) bell, drum, fife, gong, harp, horn, lute, lyre, oboe, pipe, tuba, viol.

(5) banjo, bones, bugle, cello, flute, gamba, grand, kazoo, organ, piano, pipes, rebec, regal, shawm, sitar, tabor, vibes, viola.

(6) cornet, cymbal, fiddle, guitar, spinet, spoons, syrinx, tam-tam, tom-tom, violin, zither.

(7) baryton, bassoon, bombard, celesta, celeste, cembalo, cithara, cittern, clarion, gamelan, maracas, marimba, ocarina, pianola, piccolo, sackbut, saxhorn, serpent, tambour, theorbo, timbrel, timpani, trumpet, ukelele, ukulele, whistle.

(8) bagpipes, bouzouki, clappers, clarinet, dulcimer, handbell, jew's-harp, mandolin, melodeon, oliphant, post-horn, psaltery, recorder, triangle, trombone, virginal, waldhorn.

(9) accordion, alpenhorn, balalaika, castanets, euphonium, flageolet, harmonica, harmonium, krummhorn, nose-flute, saxophone, snare-drum, washboard, xylophone; (2 words) brass drum.

(10) clavichord, concertina, didgeridoo, double-bass, flügelhorn, fortepiano, hurdy-gurdy, kettle-drum, mouth-organ, ophicleide, pianoforte, sousaphone, tambourine; (2 words) basset horn, cor anglais, French horn, grand piano.

(11) barrel-organ, harpsichord, violoncello, wobble-board; (2 words) aeolian harp.

(12) glockenspiel; (2+ words) theatre organ, viola da gamba.

MUSICAL TERMS AND SYMBOLS

(1) f (forte – loudly), p (piano – softly)

(2) ff (fortissimo – very loudly), fz (sforzando – with sudden emphasis), mf (mezzo forte – quite loudly), mp (mezzo piano – quite softly), pp (pianissimo – very softly).

(3) bis (repeat), rit (ritardando – slowing down)

(4) flat, meno (less).

(5) forte (f – loudly), largo (slowly), lento (slowly), mezzo (moderately), mosso (rapidly), piano (p – quietly), sharp, tacet (is silent).

(6) adagio (slowly), da capo (repeat), legato (smoothly), presto (very fast), rubato (in flexible tempo), vivace (briskly).

(7) agitato (agitatedly), allegro (quite fast), amoroso (lovingly), andante (quite slowly), animato (animatedly), con brio (with spirit), natural, tremolo (with a shake), vibrato (decorative fluctuation in pitch).

(8) a capella (unaccompanied singing), arpeggio (split chord), maestoso (majestically), ritenuto (held back), staccato (jerkily).

(9) adagietto (slowly), cantabile (in a singing tone), crescendo (getting louder), glissando (sliding run), obbligato (obligatory accompaniment), pizzicato (with plucked strings), sforzando (sf – with sudden emphasis), sostenuto (sustained).

(10) allegretto (quite lively), diminuendo (getting softer), fortissimo (ff – very loudly), pianissimo (pp – very softly).

(11) decrescendo (getting softer), prestissimo (very fast), rallentando (slowing down).

MUSICAL WORKS

(3) air, duo, rag.

(4) aria, coda, duet, lied, mass, song, trio.

(5) canon, dumka, étude, fugue, gigue, march, motet, nonet, octet, opera, polka, rondo, round, suite, waltz.

(6) anthem, bolero, chorus, medley, minuet, septet, sextet, sonata.

(7) arietta, cadenza, cantata, chorale, fanfare, gavotte, lullaby, mazurka, partita, quartet, quintet, scherzo, toccata.

(8) canticle, cavatina, chaconne, concerto, fantasia, madrigal, nocturne, operetta, oratorio, overture, rhapsody, ricercar, serenade, sonatina, symphony; (2 words) tone poem.

(9) allemande, bagatelle, barcarole, cantilena, capriccio, cassation, impromptu, pastorale, polonaise.

musician *n* (6) bugler, busker, oboist, player; (7) bassist, cellist, drummer, fiddler, flautist, harpist, pianist; (8) bandsman, organist; (9) performer, guitarist, timpanist, trumpeter, violinist; (10) bassoonist, trombonist; (11) accompanist, saxophonist; (12) clarinettist; (15) instrumentalist; *see also* **singer**.

mutual *adj* (5) joint; (6) common, shared, united; (8) combined, communal; (9) concerted; (10) collective, reciprocal; (11) amalgamated; (13) complementary.

Mycroft Holmes *lit.* Sherlock Holmes's elder and supposedly even cleverer brother. He made occasional appearances in the Holmes stories, was a civil servant and was usually to be found at the Diogenes Club.

mysterious *adj* (5) weird; (6) hidden, (7) curious, furtive, obscure, strange; (8) baffling, puzzling; (9) enigmatic, secretive; (10) mystifying, perplexing; (12) inexplicable, unfathomable.

myth *n* (3) lie; (4) tale, yarn; (5) fable, story; (6) legend; (7) fiction; (8) allegory; (9) invention; (11) fabrication; (2+ words) tall story, old wives' tale.

N

N *abbrev* knight (in chess), name, national, new, nitrogen, north, northern, Norway (international vehicle registration), noun.

nag I *v* (5) scold, worry; (6) badger, berate, bother, harass, niggle, pester, plague; (7) henpeck, upbraid; II *n* (5) horse; (6) geegee.

naïve *adj* (6) simple; (7) artless; (8) gullible, innocent, trusting, wide-eyed; (9) credulous, guileless, ingenuous; (12) unsuspecting; (15) unsophisticated.

naked *adj* 1 (4) bare, nude; (7) denuded, exposed; (8) starkers, stripped; (9) unclothed, uncovered, undressed; (2+ words) in the altogether, in one's birthday suit; 2 (4) open; (5) overt, stark; (7) blatant; (8) flagrant; (9) unadorned; (11) unconcealed, undisguised, unqualified.

name I *n* 1 (5) style, title; (6) handle; (7) moniker; (8) cognomen; (9) sobriquet; (11) appellation, designation; 2 (4) fame, note; (6) esteem, honour, renown, repute; (8) standing; (9) character; (10) reputation; (11) distinction; II *v* 1 (3) dub; (4) call, term; (5) label, style; (7) baptise (*or* baptize), entitle; (8) christen; (9) designate; 2 (4) cite; (6) choose, select; (7) appoint; (8) nominate.

Napoleon *hist.* 1 Napoleon Bonaparte *also known as* Boney, the Corsican Tyrant, the Little Corporal. Born in Corsica, Napoleon rose to prominence in the wars following the French Revolution. Seemingly invincible after a series of victories, he was appointed Consul and later crowned himself Emperor. His first wife was Josephine Beauharnais, his second Marie Louise of Austria. The tide turned against him after a disastrous attack on Russia in 1812. He was deposed in 1814 and exiled to the island of Elba. Returning from exile in 1815, he was finally defeated at Waterloo and exiled again, this time to the remote island of St Helena, where he

died. Napoleon's most famous battles include: Austerlitz, Borodino, Jena, Leipzig, Marengo, Wagram, Waterloo; 2 Napoleon III, nephew of Napoleon I, Emperor of the French, responsible for the rebuilding of Paris under Baron Haussmann, deposed after the French defeat in the Franco-Prussian war.

Narcissus *Gk myth* a handsome youth, loved unrequitedly by Echo, who fell in love with his own reflection seen in a pool and pined away, eventually being turned into a flower.

narrow I *adj* 1 (4) fine, slim, thin; (7) cramped; (8) confined, tapering; (11) constricted; 2 (5) petty; (7) bigoted, insular, limited; (8) dogmatic; (9) exclusive, illiberal, parochial; (10) intolerant, prejudiced; (11) small-minded; (13) circumscribed, unenlightened; II *v* (6) reduce; (7) tighten; (8) contract; (9) constrict.

narrow-minded *adj see* **narrow** I 2.

nasty *adj* 1 (3) bad; (4) foul, mean, ugly, vile; (5) dirty; (6) filthy; (7) obscene, vicious; (8) horrible, spiteful; (9) malicious, offensive, repellent, repugnant, repulsive; (10) malevolent, unpleasant; (13) objectionable; 2 (5) grave; (7) **serious**.

naughty *adj* 1 (3) bad; (7) wayward; (11) disobedient, misbehaving, mischievous; 2 (4) blue; (5) bawdy; (6) risqué, smutty; (7) obscene; (8) indecent.

navigate *v* (4) sail; (5) chart, drive, guide, pilot, steer; (6) cruise, direct, voyage; (7) captain, skipper.

navigator *n see* **sailor** *and* EXPLORERS BY SEA *at* **explorer**.

near I *adj* 1 (2) by; (5) close; (6) nearby; (8) adjacent; (9) adjoining, alongside; (12) neighbouring; 2 (4) nigh; (6) coming; (8) imminent, (9) impending; (11) approaching; 3 (4) mean; (5) tight; (6) stingy; II *v* (8) **approach**.

nearly I *adv* (5) about; (6) almost; (8) well-nigh; (9) virtually; (11) practically; (13) approximately; II *cryptic* omit a letter or letters from a word in the clue, as in: 'My hat! It's nearly a show-stopper!' (6) = topper.

neat *adj* 1 (4) tidy, trim; (5) clean, smart; (6) spruce; (9) shipshape; 2 (4) deft; (5) handy; (6) adroit, clever, expert; (7) compact, skilful; (10) convenient; 3 (4) pure; (8) straight; (9) undiluted.

Nebuchadnezzar I *Bible* the mighty king of Babylon, who rebuilt the city, besides being a conqueror who captured and destroyed Jerusalem and led the Jews into the Babylonian captivity. According to the Bible, his dreams were interpreted by Daniel, he threw Shadrach, Meshach and Abednego into the burning fiery furnace, and when 'the kingdom was departed from him' he 'did eat grass as oxen, and his body was wet with the dew of heaven, till his hairs were grown like eagles' feathers, and his nails like birds'claws'; II *see* **bottle**.

necessary *adj* (5) vital; (6) needed; (7) certain, needful; (9) essential, mandatory; (10) compulsory, inevitable, obligatory; (11) inescapable, unavoidable; (13) indispensable.

need I *n & v* (4) lack, want; (6) desire; II *v* (5) crave; (6) demand; (7) require; (11) necessitate; III *n* (6) dearth; (7) absence, paucity, poverty; (8) scarcity, shortage, sparsity; (10) deficiency, inadequacy, scantiness, sparseness; (13) insufficiency.

needy *adj* (4) poor; (8) badly-off, deprived; (9) destitute, penniless; (12) impoverished; (13) disadvantaged; (15) poverty-stricken, underprivileged.

neglect I *n* (4) omit; (5) scorn, shirk, skimp, spurn; (6) forget, ignore, rebuff, slight; (7) abandon, disdain; (8) overlook; II *v* (4) ruin; (5) decay; (9) disregard, disrepair, slackness; (10) negligence; (11) inattention, dereliction; (12) carelessness, heedlessness, indifference; (13) forgetfulness.

Nemesis *Gk myth* the goddess of retribution.

neon *cryptic* abbreviated as NE.

Neptune *Rom. myth* god of the sea, usually depicted riding a dolphin or horse and carrying a trident, brother of **Jupiter** and **Pluto** and the equivalent of the Greek **Poseidon**.

Nero *hist.* Roman Emperor, the last of the Caesars, a byword for cruelty because of his persecution of the Christians and murder of several members of his family, and for vanity, debauchery and artistic pretentiousness. He is said to have set fire to the city of Rome so that he could admire the spectacle and to have played the fiddle to enhance the aesthetic quality of the experience.

nerve *n* (5) cheek, pluck; (6) spirit; (7) bravery, courage, resolve; (8) audacity, boldness, chutzpah; (9) impudence, insolence; (10) effrontery, resolution.

nervous *adj* (4) edgy; (5) jumpy, nervy, shaky, tense; (6) uneasy; (7) fearful, fidgety, jittery, worried; (8) agitated; (9) flustered; (12) apprehensive.

never-ending I *adj* (7) abiding, ageless, endless, eternal, lasting, non-stop, un dying; (8) enduring, timeless, unbroken; (9) continual, permanent, perpetual, unceasing; (10) continuous, persistent, relentless; (11) everlasting, unremitting; (12) interminable; (13) uninterrupted; II *cryptic* omit the last letter or letters from a word in the clue, as in: 'Short computer buff discovers colleague when he joins never-ending party' (7) = partner (part(y) + ner(d)).

new I *adj* 1 (4) mint; (5) fresh, novel; (6) latest, modern, recent, unused, virgin; (7) changed, current, topical; (8) brand-new, original, up-to-date; (9) different; (10) innovative, newfangled; (13) unprecedented, up-to-the-minute; 2 (5) alien; (7) strange, unknown; (8) unversed; (10) unfamiliar; (12) unaccustomed, unacquainted; (13) inexperienced; II **new** *or* **newly** *cryptic* ANAGRAM CUE.

news *n* 1 (3) gen; (4) info, word; (6) latest; (7) low-down, tidings (11) information; (12) intelligence; 2 (5) story; (6) report;

(7) account, release; (8) bulletin, dispatch; (9) statement; (10) communiqué.

newspaper *n* (3) rag; (5) daily, sheet, weekly; (7) journal, tabloid; (10) broadsheet.

New Testament I *for books of the New Testament see* **Bible**; II *cryptic* abbreviated as NT.

nick I *n & v* (3) cut; (4) chip, dent, mark, scar; (5) notch, score, snick; (6) groove; (7) scratch; II *v* **1** (5) pinch, **steal**; **2** (6) **arrest**, detain; III *n* (4) gaol, jail; (6) prison; (2 words) cop shop, police station.

nickel I *n* **1** metal and element; **2** US coin worth five cents; II *cryptic* abbreviated as NI.

Nimrod I *Bible* 'a mighty hunter' descended from Noah, mentioned in Genesis; II *mil.* a military aircraft; III *music* one of the Enigma Variations by Elgar.

nine *Gk myth & lit.* **the nine** = the **muses**.

Niobe *Gk myth* a daughter of **Tantalus** who boasted that she had more children than Leto, who had only two, the gods Apollo and Artemis. They, however, killed all Niobe's children, leaving her to weep continuously until she was turned to stone.

nip I *v & n* (4) bite, clip, grip, snip; (5) catch, pinch, tweak; (6) nibble; (7) squeeze; II *v* (2) go; (3) pop; (4) dash.

nippy *adj* **1** (4) spry; (5) agile, brisk, quick; (6) lively, nimble; (12) manoeuvrable; **2** (4) cold, cool; (5) chill, fresh, parky; (6) chilly.

nitrogen *cryptic* abbreviated as N.

no *cryptic* **1** omit the letter, letters or word referred to, so that 'no left' means omit the letter L, 'no right', omit the letter R, *etc*; **2** the word required is the opposite of the one preceded by 'no', as in: 'He's no child' (5) = adult.

Noah *Bible* According to Genesis, God warned Noah that he was about to destroy the whole human race on account of its wickedness by sending a great flood to cover the earth and instructed Noah to build an ark of gopher wood large enough to carry two of every kind of living thing. It rained for forty days, and the flood remained for one hundred and fifty days. The ark finally came to rest on the top of Mount Ararat. Noah sent out first a raven and then a dove. When it was sent out a second time the dove returned with an olive leaf (or branch) as a sign that the flood was over. The rainbow was to be a sign of God's covenant with Noah that there would never be another flood. Noah had three sons, Ham, Shem and Japhet(h). He is also said to have planted a vineyard and to have been drunk with the wine that he made.

noble I *adj* **1** (6) gentle, titled; (8) highborn; (9) patrician; (11) blue-blooded; (12) aristocratic; **2** (6) worthy; (8) elevated, generous, virtuous; (10) chivalrous, high-minded, honourable, principled; (11) gentlemanly, magnanimous, magnificent; **3** (4) fine; (5) grand, great; (7) stately; (8) imposing, majestic, splendid; II *n* (3) nob; (4) lady, lord, peer; (7) grandee, peeress; (9) magnifico, patrician; (10) aristocrat.

NOBLE TITLES

(3) Aga (Turkish), Beg (Turkish), Bey (Turkish), Dom (Portuguese), Don (Spanish).

(4) Dame, Doña (Spanish), Duke, Earl, Graf (German).

(5) Baron, Begum (Indian), Boyar (Russian), Comte (France), Conte (Italy), Count, Laird, Mirza (Persian), Nawab (Indian), Pasha (Turkish), Thane (ancient Scottish).

(6) Daimyo (Japanese), Gräfin (German), Junker (German), Knight, Shogun (Japanese).

(7) Baronet, Dowager, Duchess, Elector (German), Hidalga (Spanish), Hidalgo (Spanish), Khedive (Egypt), Marquis (France), Paladin (Frankish).

(8) Archduke, Atheling (Anglo-Saxon), Baroness, Comtesse (France),

list continued over

Contessa (Italy), Countess, Marchesa (Italy), Marchese (Italy), Margrave (Germany), Marquess, Marquise (France), Viscount.

(9) Electress (Germany); Landgrave (Germany) Palsgrave (Germany), Waldgrave (Germany).

(10) Rhinegrave (Germany).

(11) Archduchess, Landgravine (Germany), Marchioness, Palsgravine (Germany), Viscountess, Waldgravine (Germany).

noisy *adj* I (4) loud; (5) vocal; (9) clamorous; (10) boisterous, tumultuous, vociferous; II **noisy** *or* **noisily** *cryptic* letter F or letters FF ('loud' in musical terminology).

nonsense *n* (3) rot; (4) bosh; (5) trash; (6) drivel; (7) garbage, rubbish, twaddle; (8) claptrap, cobblers; (9) gibberish; (10) balderdash; (12) gobbledygook; (2 words) double Dutch.

no-one *cryptic* omit letter I or A from word in clue – see **one**.

no quarter *cryptic* omit letter N, E, S or W from word in clue.

normal *adj* 1 (5) usual; (6) common; (7) average, general, regular, routine, typical; (8) ordinary, standard; (12) conventional; 2 (4) sane; (8) rational; (10) reasonable.

Norn *lang.* a version of the Norse language formerly spoken in the Orkneys and Shetlands.

Norns *Norse myth* three virgin goddesses who sat at the foot of the world ash tree and spun the web of fate. Their names were Urd (*or* Urdar), Skuld and Verdandi.

north *cryptic* abbreviated as N.

note I *n* 1 (4) line, memo; (5) draft; (6) letter, minute, record, remark; (7) comment, jotting, outline; (8) reminder; (10) annotation, memorandum; 2 (4) heed; (6) notice, regard; (9) attention, awareness; (11) observation; (13) consideration; 3 (4) fame; (6) renown; (8) eminence; (11)

distinction; 4 (4) bill; (8) banknote *see* **currency**; 5 *music see below*; II *v* (3) see; (4) mark; (6) detect, notice, record, remark; (7) observe; (8) perceive, register; III *cryptic* any letter from A–G corresponding to a note in the scale or DO(H), RAY *or* RE, ME *or* MI, FA(H), SO(H), LA(H) *or* TE *or* TI.

NOTES IN MUSIC

(5) breve, minim; (6) quaver; (8) crotchet; (9) semibreve; (10) semiquaver.

---

noted I *adj* (5) great; (7) eminent, notable; (8) elevated, renowned; (9) prominent, respected, well-known; (10) celebrated; (11) illustrious, outstanding, prestigious; (13) distinguished; II *cryptic* insert or add a letter or letters referring to a musical note (*see above*) as in: 'Noted medical man takes speed in cathedral city – but not overmuch' (10) = moderately (MO = D + ELY).

notice I *n* 1 (4) bill, sign; (6) advert, poster; (12) announcement; (13) advertisement; 2 (4) heed; (6) notice, regard; (9) attention, awareness; (11) observation; (13) consideration; 3 (7) warning; (12) notification; 4 (4) crit; (6) review; (9) criticism; II *v* (3) see; (4) mark, note, spot; (6) detect, record, remark; (7) discern, observe; (8) perceive, register; (11) distinguish.

notify *v* (4) tell, warn; (5) alert; (6) advise, inform; (7) declare; (8) acquaint, announce.

novel I *adj* (3) new; (7) unusual; (8) original, uncommon; (11) imaginative; II *adj* (4) book, tale; (5) story; (9) narrative.

novelist *lit*

SOME FAMOUS NOVELISTS

Amis (Kingsley, UK) Lucky Jim, The Old Devils.

Amis (Martin, UK) London Fields, Time's Arrow.

Austen (Jane, UK) *see separate entry*.

Balzac (Honoré de, Fr.) 'The Human Comedy' (series), Cousin Bette, Le Père Goriot. *list continued over*

Bellow (Saul, US) Herzog, Humboldt's Gift, Mr Sammler's Planet.

Bennet (Arnold, UK) Anna of the Five Towns, Clayhanger.

Borges (Jorge Luis, Argentina) Labyrinth.

Brontë (Ann, Charlotte, Emily, UK) *see separate entry.*

Cervantes (Miguel de, Span.) Don Quixote.

Conrad (Joseph, UK) Heart of Darkness, Lord Jim, Nostromo.

Cooper (Fenimore, US) The Last of the Mohicans.

Dickens (Charles, UK) *see separate entry.*

Drabble (Margaret, UK) The Millstone, Jerusalem the Golden.

Eliot (George, UK) Middlemarch, The Mill on the Floss.

Dostoyevsky (Fyodor, Russ.) Crime and Punishment, The Idiot, The Brothers Karamazov.

Fielding (Henry, UK) Joseph Andrews, Tom Jones.

Fitzgerald (Scott, US) Tender is the Night, The Great Gatsby.

Flaubert (Gustave, Fr,) Madame Bovary.

Grass (Günter, Ger.) The Tin Drum.

Greene (Graham, UK) Brighton Rock, The End of the Affair, The Power and the Glory.

Hardy (Thomas, UK) *see separate entry.*

Hawthorne (Nathaniel, US) The Scarlet Letter.

Hemingway (Ernest, US) Farewell to Arms, For Whom the Bell Tolls, The Old Man and the Sea.

Huxley (Aldous, UK) Brave New World.

James (Henry US/UK) Portrait of a Lady, The Wings of a Dove.

Joyce (James, Ire.) Dubliners, Finnegans Wake, Ulysses.

Kafka (Franz, A./Cz.) The Trial.

Laclos (Choderlos de, Fr.) Dangerous Liaisons.

Lawrence (D.H., UK) Sons and Lovers, The Rainbow, Women in Love, Lady Chatterley's Lover.

Mann (Thomas, Ger.) Buddenbrooks, The Magic Mountain.

Marquez (Gabriel Garcia, Colombia) One Hundred Years of Solitude.

Melville (Herman, US) Moby Dick, Billy Budd.

Orwell (George, UK) 1984, Animal Farm.

Powell (Anthony, UK) Dance to the Music of Time (series).

Proust (Marcel, Fr.) Remembrance of Things Past (series).

Richardson (Samuel, UK) Pamela, Clarissa.

Stendhal (Fr.) The Red and the Black, The Charterhouse of Parma.

Thackeray (William Makepeace, UK) Vanity Fair.

Tolstoy (Leo, Russ.) Anna Karenina, War and Peace.

Trollope (Anthony, UK) Barchester novels, Palliser novels.

Turgenev (Ivan, Russ.) Fathers and Sons.

Waugh (Evelyn, UK) Brideshead Revisited, Decline and Fall.

Wells (H.G., UK) The War of the Worlds, Kipps.

Woolf (Virginia, UK) To The Lighthouse, Mrs Dalloway.

Zola (Émile, Fr.) Germinal, Thérèse Raquin.

nude *adj see* **naked** 1.

number I *n* 1 (4) unit; (5) digit; (6) figure; (7) integer, numeral; (8) fraction; 2 (3) sum; (5) total; (6) amount; (8) quantity; (9) aggregate; 3 (4) copy; (5) issue; (6) volume; (7) edition; II *v* (5) count, total; (6) reckon; (7) compute; (9) calculate, enumerate; III *cryptic* letters NO or any letter corresponding to a **Roman numeral**.

nurse I *n* (3) SRN; (4) amah, ayah; (6) matron, sister; (7) midwife; II *v* 1 (4) tend; (5) treat; 2 (4) feed; (6) suckle; (10) breastfeed; 3 (6) foster; (7) cherish, harbour, nurture, promote; (9) encourage.

nut *n* **1** (8) fastener; **2** (4) **head**; **3** (3) **fan**; (10) enthusiast.

TYPES OF NUT

(3) cob; (5) acorn, hazel, pecan;
(6) almond, brazil, cashew, cobnut,
peanut, walnut; (7) coconut, filbert;
(8) hazelnut; (9) pistachio; (2 words)
beech nut, ground nut, monkey nut.

---

nymph *myth* (5) dryad, naiad, oread; (6) nereid; (9) hamadryad.

O

O *abbrev.* Ocean, Ohio, Old, Oxygen.

oath *n* 1 (3) vow; (4) word; (6) pledge; (7) promise; (9) assurance; 2 (5) curse; (9) blasphemy, expletive, obscenity, profanity; (11) imprecation; 3 (4) blow, damn, drat; (5) blast; (6) bother *etc.*

obey *v* (4) heed, keep; (6) adhere, comply, follow, fulfil, submit; (7) conform, execute, perform; (9) discharge; (2 words) abide by, defer to.

object I *n* 1 (4) item; (5) thing; (6) entity; (7) article; 2 (3) aim, end; (4) butt, goal; (5) point; (6) motive, reason, target; (7) purpose; (9) intention, objective; **II** *v* (6) oppose; (7) dislike, protest; (8) complain; (10) disapprove.

objective I *adj* (4) fair, just; (7) neutral; (8) detached, unbiased; (9) equitable, impartial; (10) even-handed, open-minded; (12) unprejudiced; (13) dispassionate; **II** *n see* **object I** 2.

obligation *n* (4) bond, duty, onus; (6) charge; (8) contract; (9) liability; (14) responsibility.

obligatory *adj* (7) binding; (8) enforced; (9) essential, mandatory, necessary, statutory; (10) compulsory.

oblige *v* 1 (4) make; (5) force; (6) coerce, compel; (7) require; (9) constrain; (11) necessitate; 2 (4) help; (5) serve; (6) assist, please; (7) gratify; (11) accommodate.

obliging *adj* (4) kind; (5) civil; (7) helpful, willing; (8) friendly; (9) agreeable; (11) considerate, co-operative; (13) accommodating.

observe *v* (3) eye, see, spy; (4) look, quiz, pore, scan; (5) stare, study, watch; (6) assess, regard, review, survey; (7) examine, inspect; (8) appraise, consider; (10) scrutinise (*or* scrutinize); (11) contemplate.

obsess *v* (4) grip, rule; (5) haunt; (7) possess; (8) dominate; (9) preoccupy; (10) monopolise (*or* monopolize).

obsession *n* (5) mania; (6) fetish, hang-up; (7) complex; (8) fixation; (10) compulsion, enthusiasm; (11) infatuation.

obstinate *adj* (4) fast, firm; (6) dogged, wilful; (7) stubborn; (9) immovable, pigheaded; (10) determined, headstrong, inflexible, persistent, unyielding, intractable; (12) intransigent.

obstruct *v* (3) bar; (4) clog, slow, stop; (5) block, choke, stall; (6) hinder, impede, retard, thwart; (7) inhibit, prevent; (8) restrict; (9) interfere, interrupt.

obtain *v* 1 (4) get, win; (4) earn, gain; (6) attain, secure; (7) achieve, procure; 2 (5) exist, reign, stand; (7) prevail.

obvious *adj* (4) open; (5) clear, plain; (6) patent; (7) evident, glaring, visible; (8) apparent, distinct, flagrant, manifest; (10) noticeable, pronounced, undeniable; (11) conspicuous, perceptible, transparent, unconcealed; (12) recognisable (*or* recognizable), unmistakable.

occasion I *n* 1 (4) time; (5) event, party; (6) affair; (8) function, incident, instance; (9) happening; (10) occurrence; (11) celebration; 2 (5) cause; (6) excuse, reason; (7) grounds; **II** *v* (5) **cause**; (6) prompt; (7) provoke.

occasional *adj* (3) odd; (4) rare; (8) periodic, sporadic; (9) irregular; (10) infrequent, incidental; (12) intermittent.

ocean *n* (6) Arctic, Indian; (7) Pacific; (8) Atlantic; (9) Antarctic.

October *n* (3) Oct; (5) month. In the Roman calendar, October was the eighth month (*octo* Latin for eight).

odd I *adj* 1 (3) rum; (5) dotty, fluky, funny, queer, weird; (6) chance; (7) bizarre, erratic, offbeat, strange, unusual;

(8) aberrant, abnormal, atypical, freakish, peculiar; (9) eccentric; (10) fortuitous, outlandish, unexpected; (11) exceptional; (13) idiosyncratic, unpredictable; (14) unconventional; **2** (4) over; (5) extra; (6) casual, uneven; (7) surplus; (8) left-over, unpaired; (9) remaining, unmatched; (10) additional; (11) unconnected; **|| odd** *or* **oddly** *cryptic* ANAGRAM CUE.

oddity *n* (4) whim; (5) quirk, twist; (6) vagary; (7) anomaly, caprice; (9) curiosity; (10) aberration; (11) abnormality; (12) eccentricity.

Odin *Norse myth* the chief god in Norse mythology, one-eyed because he gave one eye to drink at the fountain of Mimir and become all-wise. He was god of war, wisdom, poetry, agriculture and the dead. He rode an eight-legged horse called Sleipnir, but is often depicted as a wanderer with a hat, staff and eye patch.

Odysseus *Gk myth* the king of Ithaca, usually represented as the most cunning of the Greeks besieging Troy and the one who devised the scheme of the wooden horse. His wanderings on the journey home from Troy are the subject of Homer's Odyssey – also known as **Ulysses**.

Oedipus *Gk myth & lit.* Oedipus was born the son of Laius and Jocasta, the king and queen of Thebes. It was prophesied that he would kill his father and marry his mother, so he was exposed and left to die on a mountainside. He was found and raised by shepherds and, when he grew up, unknowingly killed his father and then, after solving the riddle of the **Sphinx**, returned to Thebes as a hero and married the queen, his mother. When the truth of his parentage was revealed, Oedipus tore out his eyes and Jocasta killed herself. Oedipus is the hero of one of the best-known Greek tragedies by Sophocles.

off | ** *adv* (3) out; (4) away, from; (5) apart, aside, loose; (8) detached, separate; **|| adj 1 (3) bad; (4) sour; (5) stale; (6) mouldy, rancid, spoilt, turned; **2** (9) cancelled, postponed; **||| ** *cryptic* **1** ANAGRAM CUE;

2 omit the letter, letters or word referred to as in: 'Removes beefsteak after cooking as the meat was off' (5) = takes (omit 'beef' – cooking = ANAGRAM CUE).

offence *n* **1** (3) sin; (4) foul; (5) **crime**, wrong; (6) felony; (7) affront, misdeed; (8) trespass; (9) violation; (10) wrongdoing; (12) infringement, misdemeanour; (13) transgression; **2** (4) hurt; (5) pique; (7) disgust, outrage, umbrage; (9) annoyance; (10) resentment; (11) displeasure, indignation.

offend *v* **1** (4) hurt, snub; (5) annoy, repel, upset, wound, wrong; (6) injure, insult; (7) affront, disgust, outrage; (9) displease; **2** (3) err, sin; (10) transgress.

offensive | ** *adj* **1 (4) rude; (7) abusive; (8) insolent; (9) insulting; (11) impertinent; **2** (3) bad; (4) foul, vile; (5) nasty; (6) filthy, odious; (7) obscene, vicious; (8) horrible; (9) loathsome, obnoxious, repellent, repugnant, repulsive, revolting; (10) abominable, disgusting, nauseating, unpleasant; (12) disagreeable; (13) objectionable; **|| ** *n* (4) raid; (6) attack; (7) assault; (8) campaign, invasion; (9) onslaught.

office *n* **1** (6) branch, bureau; (8) division, workroom; (10) department; **2** (4) duty, post, role, task; (7) service; (8) function, position; (9) situation; (10) employment, occupation; (14) responsibility.

officer *n* **1** *see* **rank**; **2** (5) chair; (7) bailiff; (8) chairman; (9) constable, secretary, treasurer; *see also* **official ||**.

**official | ** *adj* (6) proper; (8) licensed; (9) authentic; (10) accredited, authorised (*or* authorized), legitimate; (2 words) bona fide; **|| ** *n* (5) agent; (7) officer; (9) executive; (10) bureaucrat; (11) functionary.

offspring *see* **young** *and* **child**.

old *adj* **1** (4) aged, grey; (6) senile; (7) ancient, antique, elderly, worn-out; (8) decrepit, obsolete; (9) out-of-date; (10) antiquated; **2** (2) ex; (4) past; (6) former; (7) earlier, one-time, quondam; (8) original, previous; **3** (8) hallowed; (11) traditional; (12) long-standing.

SLANG EXPRESSIONS FOR OLD

getting on, long in the tooth, no spring chicken, one foot in the grave, over the hill, past it, past one's sell-by date.

old boy *cryptic* abbreviated as OB.

old-fashioned *adj* (5) dated, passé; (7) archaic; (8) obsolete, outdated, outmoded; (9) out-of-date; (10) antiquated; (11) obsolescent.

old girl *cryptic* abbreviated as OG.

Old Testament I *for books of the Old Testament see* **Bible**; II *cryptic* abbreviated as OT.

Olympus *Gk myth & geog.* a mountain in Greece thought in ancient times to be the home of the gods.

omen *n* (4) sign; (6) augury; (7) portent, warning; (10) foreboding, indication; (11) premonition.

ominous *adj* (7) fateful, warning; (8) menacing, sinister; (10) foreboding, portentous; (11) threatening, unpromising; (12) inauspicious.

omit I *v* (3) cut; (4) drop, edit, miss, skip; (6) forget; (7) neglect; (8) overlook; (9) eliminate; (2 words) edit out, leave out, miss out; II *cryptic* leave out the letter, letters, or word referred to (often cryptically), as in: 'Doctor omitted to write' (3) = doc (omit TO + R = right/write).

on board *cryptic* insert letters or a word between the letters SS (abbreviation of 'steamship'), as in: 'Remains on board just a second' (6) = sticks (second = tick).

one I *adj* (4) lone, only, sole, unit; (6) single; (8) solitary; (10) individual; II *cryptic* insert or add letter I, letter A, or letters AN, as in: 'Drink one with the French' (3) = ale (*see* French).

op *abbrev* opus.

open I *v* **1** (4) undo; (5) clear, unbar, untie; (6) expose, extend, uncork, unfold, unfurl, unlock, unseal, unwrap; (7) uncover; **2** (5) begin, start; (6) launch; (8) commence, initiate; (10) inaugurate; II *adj* **1** (4) ajar; (6) gaping; (7) exposed, lidless;

(8) unclosed, unlocked; (9) uncovered; **2** (5) clear, exact, frank, plain; (6) direct, honest, stated; (7) express; (8) absolute, declared, distinct, explicit, positive, specific; (9) outspoken; (10) unreserved; (11) categorical, unambiguous; **3** (5) overt; (7) **obvious**; (8) flagrant; (11) undisguised; **4** (4) moot; (9) debatable, undecided; (10) unresolved.

opener *cryptic* the first letter of the relevant word, so that *e.g.* ' tin opener' = T.

opening I *n* **1** (3) gap; (4) hole, pore, slot, tear, vent, void; (5) blank, break, chink, cleft, crack, space, split; (6) breach, eyelet, outlet; (7) fissure, orifice; (8) puncture; **2** (4) dawn; (5) birth, onset, start; (6) launch; (8) premiere; (9) inception; (12) inauguration; **3** (5) break; (6) chance; (7) vacancy; (8) occasion; (11) opportunity; II *adj* (5) early, first (7) initial; (8) starting; (9) inaugural; (12) introductory; III *cryptic* refers to the first letter of a word in the clue, as in: ' To get machine through wide opening needs measurement' (5) = winch.

operate *v* (2) go; (3) act, run, use; (4) work; (6) , direct, handle, manage; (7) control; (8) function.

operation *n* **1** (3) use; (6) action; (7) control, running, working; (8) handling; (10) management; (12) manipulation; **2** (4) task; (6) affair, effort; (7) process; (8) business, exercise; (9) manoeuvre, procedure; (10) enterprise; (11) transaction, undertaking.

opinion *n* (4) idea, mind, view; (6) belief, stance, theory; (8) attitude, judgment, position; (9) judgement, sentiment; (10) impression; (2+ words) point of view, way of thinking.

opponent *n* (3) foe; (4) anti; (5) enemy, rival; (8) objector; (9) adversary; (10) antagonist, challenger, competitor, contestant, opposition.

opportune *adj* (5) lucky; (6) proper, timely; (8) suitable; (9) fortunate.

opportunity *n* (4) hour; (5) break; (6) chance, moment; (7) opening.

oppose *v* (4) defy, face; (5) fight; (6) attack, combat, resist, thwart; (7) contest, counter, prevent; (9) withstand.

opposite I *adj* (6) facing, unlike; (8) fronting; (9) different; (11) contrasting; (12) antithetical; (13) contradictory; (14) irreconcilable; II *n* (7) antonym, inverse, reverse; (8) contrary, contrast; (10) antithesis; (13) contradiction.

oppress *v* 1 (5) abuse, crush; (6) subdue; (7) trample; (8) maltreat, suppress; (9) overpower, overwhelm, persecute, subjugate, terrorise (or terrorize), tyrannise (or tyrannize); 2 (5) worry; (6) burden, sadden; (7) afflict, depress, trouble.

optimistic *adj* (7) buoyant, hopeful; (8) cheerful, positive, sanguine; (9) confident, expectant; (10) idealistic.

opus *n* a work, *esp.* a numbered work by a composer – *see* **work**.

oracle *hist.* a sacred site where, according to the ancients, the gods would speak to and advise mortals often through the mouth of a priest or priestess. The best-known oracles were at Delphi (Apollo's oracle) and Dodona (Zeus).

oral I *adj* (4) said; (5) vocal; (6) spoken, verbal; (9) unwritten; II *n* (4) exam, viva; (2 words) viva voce.

oratorio *music* large-scale dramatic (but not staged) musical work for orchestra, choir and soloists.

FAMOUS ORATORIOS

Bach: *The Christmas Oratorio, The St John Passion, The St Matthew Passion.*
Elgar: *The Apostles, The Dream of Gerontius, The Kingdom.*
Handel: *Israel in Egypt, Judas Maccabeus, Messiah, Saul, Solomon.*
Haydn: *The Creation, The Seasons.*
Mendelssohn: *Elijah, St Paul.*
Tippett: *A Child of our Time.*
Walton: *Belshazzar's Feast.*

Orcus *Rom. myth* the Roman name for **Hades**, the **Underworld**.

order I *n & v* (6) charge, decree, demand; (7) command, mandate, request; (10)

commission; (11) requisition, reservation; II *n* 1 (5) edict; (6) diktat; (7) booking, precept; (9) direction, directive; (10) injunction; (11) instruction; 2 (4) plan; (5) array; (6) layout, line-up, method, system; (8) grouping, sequence; (9) formation, structure; (10) succession; (11) arrangement, disposition; (12) organisation (*or* organization); 3 (4) calm; (5) peace; (7) decorum, harmony; (8) neatness, tidiness; (10) discipline; 4 (4) kind, sort, type; (5) class; (6) family; (9) hierarchy; 5 (8) sorority; (9) community; (10) fraternity, sisterhood; (11) brotherhood; III *v* 1 (3) bid; (4) book; (6) compel, direct, enjoin; (7) require, reserve; (8) instruct; 2 (4) sort; (5) group; (7) arrange, dispose, marshal; (8) classify, organise (*or* organize); (9) catalogue; IV **order** *or* **ordered** *cryptic* ANAGRAM CUE.

ordinary *adj* (5) plain, usual; (6) common, simple, normal; (7) average, general, regular, routine, typical; (8) everyday, familiar, habitual, mediocre, standard; (9) customary; (12) conventional, run-of-the-mill, unremarkable; (14) common- or-garden; (15) undistinguished.

Orestes *Gk myth* son of **Agamemnon** and Clytemnestra and brother of **Electra**, who killed his mother in revenge for her killing of his father and was pursued for this by the **Furies**.

organisation (*or* **organization**) I *n* 1 (4) club, firm; (5) group, union; (7) company, society; (8) business; (10) federation; (11) association, corporation, institution; (13) establishment; 2 (5) array, order, set-up; (6) layout, line-up, method, system; (7) pattern; (8) grouping, sequence; (9) formation, structure; (10) succession; (11) arrangement; II *cryptic* ANAGRAM CUE.

organise (*or* **organize**) I *v* 1 (4) sort; (5) group; (7) arrange, dispose, marshal; (8) classify; (9) catalogue; 2 (4) plan; (5) found; (7) prepare, provide; (9) establish; (2 words) set up; II **organise** *or* **organised** *cryptic* ANAGRAM CUE.

origin *n* (4) base; (5) basis, cause, fount,

start; (6) source, spring; (7) descent; (8) ancestry, pedigree; (9) beginning, parentage; (10) derivation, extraction, foundation, provenance, wellspring.

original I *adj* **1** (5) first, prime; (6) primal; (7) initial; primary; (8) earliest; **2** (3) new; (4) mint; (5) fresh, novel; (6) modern, unused, virgin; (8) brand-new, pristine; **3** (8) creative; (10) innovative; (11) imaginative; II *n* (6) master; (7) pattern, (8) paradigm; (9) archetype, prototype; III *cryptic* **1** use the first letter of the word referred to, so that *e.g.* 'original idea' = I; **2** ANAGRAM CUE.

ornament I *n* (5) frill; (6) bauble; (7) trinket; (8) trimming; (9) accessory, adornment; (10) decoration; (13) embellishment; II *v* (4) deck, gild, trim; (5) adorn; (7) garnish; (8) decorate; (9) embellish.

Orpheus *Gk myth* a legendary musician (he played the lyre, though Shakespeare speaks of 'Orpheus with his lute') whose wife Eurydice died. He loved her so much that he followed her down into the **Underworld**, charmed Dis (or Pluto) with his playing, and was allowed to take her back on condition that he did not turn round and look at her until they were back on earth. He could not, however, resist looking back and lost her again. His grief at this second loss so enraged the women of Thrace that in a Bacchanalian frenzy they tore him to pieces.

Osiris *Egyptian myth* god of death, he was killed by his jealous brother Set and his body hacked to pieces. His wife Isis searched for and found all the pieces and he was brought back to life.

Othello *lit.* the 'Moor of Venice', hero of a tragedy by Shakespeare.
Plot outline: Othello is a black soldier who has served the Republic of Venice with great distinction. At the beginning of the play he has eloped with and married Desdemona, the daughter of a senator, against her father's wishes, and also incurred the enmity of his 'ancient' (or

ensign) Iago, who both suspects Othello of cuckolding him and resents the fact that Cassio has been made lieutenant over his head. Othello is ordered to Cyprus to take charge of the defence of the island against a threatened Turkish invasion. While there, Iago hatches a plot to make Othello suspect Desdemona of infidelity with Cassio. Circumstances conspire to lend a certain credence to Iago's story and Othello begins to suspect his wife, indeed feels that his suspicions have been confirmed when a handkerchief he had given to Desdemona is seen being used by Cassio – Iago arranged this with the unwitting help of his wife and Desdemona's waiting gentlewoman Emilia. Othello's jealousy completely overpowers him at this – he murders Desdemona by smothering her with a pillow. When the truth comes out, largely through Emilia, he attempts to kill Iago and finally kills himself.

out I *adj* **1** (4) away, gone; (6) abroad, absent; (8) outdoors; **2** (4) over; (5) ended; (9) exhausted; (12) extinguished; (2 words) used up; **3** (6) public; (7) exposed; (8) revealed; (9) available, disclosed, published; **4** (8) excluded; (9) forbidden; (10) disallowed; (12) unacceptable; **5** (11) unconscious; **6** (5) wrong; (10) inaccurate; **7** *cricket* (3) lbw; (6) bowled, caught; (7) stumped; II *cryptic* **1** ANAGRAM CUE, as in: 'Eats out with king – food provided by the baron' (5) = steak; **2** the letters of a word forming part of the answer are placed outside (at either end of) another word, as in: 'Awfully hot, relations out, strips off' (9) = unclothes (awfully = ANAGRAM CUE, relations = uncles); **3** omit a letter, letters, or word, as in: 'When run out, an opener is often shaken' (4) = fist (opener = first, run = R).

outfit *n* **1** (3) rig; (4) garb, gear, suit, togs; (5) get-up; (7) clothes, costume; (8) ensemble; **2** (4) crew, firm, gang, team, unit; (5) group, set-up; (7) company; (12) organisation (*or* organization).

outlaw I *n* (6) bandit, robber; (7) brigand; (8) criminal, fugitive, marauder; (9) desperado; (10) highwayman; **II** *v* (3) ban, bar; (5) debar, exile; (6) banish, forbid; (7) embargo, exclude; (8) prohibit; (10) disqualify.

out of *cryptic* **1** HIDDEN WORD CUE, as in: 'Quickly ran out of share deposit slips' (5) = hared; **2** the letters of a word forming part of the answer are placed outside (at either end of) another word, as in: 'Roman goddess out of New Testament? Recent mistranslation nearly explains it' (7) = centres (goddess = Ceres).

outright **I** *adj* (4) open; (5) clear, total, utter; (8) absolute, complete, thorough; (9) out-and-out; (10) undisputed; (11) unqualified; (14) unquestionable; **II** *adv* (6) openly; (7) clearly, totally, utterly; (8) honestly; (10) absolutely, completely, thoroughly; **III** *cryptic* omit letter R or letters RT.

outside *cryptic* the letters of a word forming part of the answer are placed outside (at either end of) another word, as in: 'Guarantee Irishman's outside before eleven' (6) = patent (before eleven = ten).

outsider *cryptic* either first or last letter of a word or (**outsiders**) both.

outsize *cryptic* letters OS or XL.

outstanding **I** *adj* **1** (4) fine, good, rare; (5) great; (6) signal, superb; (8) splendid, superior; (9) admirable, excellent, exemplary, first-rate, wonderful; (10) first-class, marvellous, phenomenal, remarkable, surpassing; (10) unequalled, prodigious; (11) conspicuous, exceptional, superlative; (13) distinguished; **2** (3) due; (5) owing; (6) unpaid; (7) overdue; (9) unsettled; **II** *cryptic* as at **outside**.

outwardly **I** *adv* (7) visibly; (9) seemingly; (10) apparently, externally; (13) superficially; **II** **outwardly** *or* **outward** *cryptic* the letters of a word forming part of the answer are placed outside (at either end of) another word, as in: 'Despite outward sign of age, the old boy is still hale and hearty' (6) = robust (old boy abbreviated as OB).

over **I** *adv* **1** (5) above; (6) beyond; **2** (4)

done, past; (6) closed, ended; (8) finished; **3** (4) left; (5) extra, spare; (7) surplus; (9) remaining; **II** *n* set of six balls bowled in succession in cricket; **III** *cryptic in down clues* place letters or word in front of another word to form the answer (NB *over* may be incorporated in a longer word), as in: 'Weep over complete absence of information relating to very cold substance' (7) = cryogen (absence of information = zero (= O) gen).

overflow **I** *v & n* (5) flood, spill; (9) overspill; **II** *v* (4) soak; (5) swamp; (6) deluge; (8) inundate, submerge; **III** *n* (7) surplus; (10) inundation.

overhaul **I** *v* **1** (4) mend; (5) renew; (6) repair; (7) inspect, restore, service; (8) renovate; (11) recondition; **2** *see* **overtake**; **II** *cryptic* ANAGRAM CUE.

overlook *v* **1** (4) miss, omit; (6) excuse, ignore, pardon; (7) condone, forgive, neglect; (9) disregard; (2+ words) let pass, let ride, pass over, turn a blind eye, wink at; **2** (4) face; (7) command; (2 words) front on.

override *see* **overrule**.

overrule *v* (5) quash; (6) cancel, reject, repeal, revoke; (7) rescind, reverse; (8) override, overturn; (10) invalidate; (11) countermand.

oversight *n* (5) error, lapse; (6) slip-up; (7) blunder, mistake; (8) omission.

overtake *v* (4) pass; (5) catch; (8) outstrip, overhaul; (2+ words) catch up, draw level.

overthrow **I** *v* (4) oust; (5) upset; (6) defeat, depose, subdue, topple, unseat; (7) abolish, conquer; (8) dethrone, displace, overcome; **II** *n* (3) end; (4) fall, rout, ruin; (7) undoing; (8) downfall; (10) deposition; (11) destruction.

own **I** *v* **1** (4) have, hold, keep; (5) enjoy; (6) retain; (7) possess; **2** (5) admit; (7) confess; (11) acknowledge; **II** *adj* proper; (8) personal; (10) individual; (11) independent.

oxygen *cryptic* abbreviated as O.

P

P *abbrev* parking, pawn, phosphorus, Portugal (international vehicle registration).

p *abbrev* page, penny (*or* pence), piano (music).

pace I *n & v* (4) step, walk; (5) tread; (6) stride; (8) progress; II *n* (4) rate; (5) speed, tempo; (6) motion; (8) velocity; III *v* (5) march, tramp; (6) patrol.

pack I *n* 1 (3) bag, box; (4) load; (6) bundle, burden, carton, kitbag, packet, parcel; (7) package; (8) backpack, knapsack, rucksack; 2 (3) lot, mob, set; (4) band, gang, herd; (5) batch, bunch, crowd, group, troop; (10) collection; II *v* (3) ram; (4) cram, fill, load; (5) crowd, press, stuff; (6) charge, throng; (7) compact; (8) compress.

page I *n* 1 (4) leaf, side; (5) folio, recto, sheet, verso; 2 (6) squire; (7) bellboy, bellhop; (9) attendant; II *v* (4) call; (6) summon.

paint I *n & v* (3) dye; (5) stain; (6) colour; (7) pigment; II *v* (4) coat, daub; (5) cover; (6) depict; (7) picture, portray; (9) represent.

TYPES OF PAINT

(3) oil; (4) matt, oils; (5) glaze, gloss;
(6) enamel, pastel, primer; (7) acrylic, gouache, lacquer, varnish;
(8) eggshell, emulsion; (9) distemper, undercoat, whitewash;
(11) watercolour.

---

painter I *n* 1 (5) fauve; (6) artist, cubist; (7) dadaist; (8) futurist; (9) decorator, mannerist; (10) surrealist; (11) miniaturist, portraitist; (13) expressionist, impressionist; 2 (4) line; (7) mooring; II *cryptic* letters RA (royal academician).

FAMOUS PAINTERS

(3) Cox (David, UK), Dix (Otto, Ger.), Dou (Gerard, NL), Fry (Roger, UK).

(4) Bell (Robert Anning, UK), Bone (Muirhead, UK), Cuyp (Albert, NL), Dali (Salvador, Sp.), Doré (Gustave, Fr.), Dufy (Raoul, Fr.), Etty (William UK), Gill (Eric, UK), Goya (Francisco, Sp.), Gris (Juan, Sp.), Hals (Frans, NL), Hunt (William Holman, UK), John (Augustus *and* Gwen, UK), Kent (William, UK), Klee (Paul, Switz.), Lely (Peter, UK), Maes (Nicolaes, NL), Marc (Franz, Ger.), Miró (Joan, Sp.), Nash (Paul, UK), Opie (John, UK), Reni (Guido, It.), West (Benjamin, US/UK).

(5) Bacon (Francis, Ire./UK), Blake (William, UK), Bosch (Hieronymus, NL), Bouts (Dirk, NL), Brown (Ford Madox, UK), Corot (Camille, Fr.), Crome (John, UK), Danby (Francis, Ire.), David (Jacques Louis Fr.), Degas (Edgar, Fr.), Dürer (Albrecht, Ger.), Ernst (Max, Ger.), Frith (William, UK), Grosz (George, Ger.), Hooch (Pieter de, NL), Klimt (Gustav, A.), Léger (Fernand, Fr.), Lewis (Wyndham, UK), Lippi (Fra Filippo, It.), Lowry (L.S., UK), Manet (Edouard, Fr.), Mengs (Anton, Ger.), Monet (Claude, Fr.), Moses (Grandma, US) Munch (Edvard, Nor.), Nolde (Emil, Ger.), Orpen (William, Ire.), Redon (Odilon, Fr.), Rossi (Giovanni, It.), Scott (Peter, UK), Spear (Ruskin, UK), Steen (Jan, NL), Watts (George Frederick, UK).

(6) Boudin (Eugène, Fr.), Braque (Georges, Fr.), Buffet (Bernard, Fr.), Cooper (Samuel, UK), Copley (John, US), Cosway (Richard, UK),

list continued over

Cotman (John Sell, UK), Duccio (It.), Fuseli (Henry, Switz./UK), Giotto (It.), Girtin (Thomas, UK), Greuze (Jean-Baptiste, Fr.), Guardi (Francesco, It.), Haydon (Benjamin Robert, UK), Ingres (Jean, Fr.), Knight (Laura, UK), Laszlo (Philip, Hung.), Mabuse (Jan, NL), Matsys (Quentin, NL), Millet (Jean, Fr.), Morris (William, UK), Palmer (Samuel, UK), Renoir (Pierre, Fr.), Rivera (Diego, Mex.), Romney (George, UK), Rubens (Peter-Paul, NL), Seurat (Georges, Fr.), Sisley (Alfred, UK), Stubbs (George, UK), Tenier (David, NL), Titian (It.), Turner (J.W.M., UK), Verrio (Antonio, It.), Warhol (Andy, US).

(7) Apelles (Anc. Gk), Audubon (John, US), Bellini (Gentile *and* Giovanni, It.), Bonnard (Pierre, Fr.), Cézanne (Paul, Fr.), Chagall (Marc, Russ./Fr.), Chardin (Jean-Baptiste, Fr.), Cimabue (It.), Courbet (Gustave, Fr.), Daumier (Honoré, Fr.), Da Vinci (Leonardo, It.), De Hooch (Pieter, NL), El Greco (Gk/Sp.), Gauguin (Paul, Fr.), Hobbema (Meindert, NL), Hockney (David, UK), Hogarth (William, UK), Hokusai (Jap.), Holbein (Hans Ger./ UK), Hoppner (John, UK), Kneller (Godfrey, UK), Lancret (Nicolas, Fr.), Lorrain (Claude, Fr), Matisse (Henri, Fr.), Memlinc *or* Memling (Hans, NL), Millais (John, UK), Morisot (berthe, Fr.), Murillo (Bartolome, Sp.), Picasso (Pablo, Sp.), Pollock (Jackson, US), Raeburn (Henry, UK), Raphael (It.), Rouault (Georges, Fr.), Sargent (John Singer, US/UK), Sickert (Walter, UK), Soutine (Chaim, Fr.), Spencer (Stanley, UK), Tiepolo (Giovanni, It.), Uccello (Paolo, It.), Van Dyck (Anthony, NL/UK), Van Eyck (Jan, NL), Van Gogh (Vincent, NL), Vermeer (Jan, NL), Watteau (Antoine, Fr.), Wootton (Frank, UK).

(8) Angelico (Fra, It.), Annigoni (Pietro, It.), Beckmann (max, Ger.),

Breughel (Jan *and* Pieter, NL), Bronzino (It.), Brueghel (Jan *and* Pieter, NL), Carracci (Annibale, It.), Del Sarto (Andrea, It.), Hilliard (Nicholas, UK), Jordaens (Jakob, NL), Kirchner (Ludwig, Ger.), Kollwitz (Käthe, Ger.), Landseer (Edwin, UK), Lawrence (Thomas, UK), Leonardo (It.), Magritte (René, Belg.), Mantegna (Andrea, It.), Masaccio (Tommaso, It.), Mondrian (Piet, NL), Munnings (Alfred, UK), Perugino (Pietro, It.), Pissarro (Camille, Fr.), Reynolds (Joshua, UK), Rossetti (Dante Gabriel, UK), Rousseau (Henri 'Douanier', Fr.), Ruysdael (Jakob, NL), Veronese (Paolo, It.), Vlaminck (Maurice, Fr.), Whistler (James, US).

(9) Beardsley (Aubrey, UK), Canaletto (Giovanni, It.), Constable (John, UK), Correggio (Antonio, It.), De Chirico (Giorgio, Gk/It.), Delacroix (Eugène, Fr.), Feininger (Lyonel, US), Fragonard (Jean, Fr.), Giorgione (Giorgio, It.), Greenaway (Kate, UK), Grünewald (Matthias, Ger.), Honthorst (Gerrit, NL), Kandinsky (Vassili, Russ.), Kokoschka (Oscar, A.) Nicholson (Ben, UK), Rembrandt (NL), Velasquez *or* Velazquez (Diego, Sp.), Verrochio (Andrea, It.).

(10) Alma-Tadema (Lawrence, NL/ UK), Botticelli (It.), Burne-Jones (Edward, UK), Caravaggio (Michelangelo, It.), Holman Hunt (William, UK), Modigliani (Amedeo, It.), Rowlandson (Thomas, UK), Sutherland (Graham, UK), Tintoretto (Jacopo, It.).

(11) Della Robbia (Luca, It.), Gentileschi (Orazio, It.), Ghirlandaio (Domenico, It.).

(12) Fantin-Latour (Henri, It.), Gainsborough (Thomas, UK), Lichtenstein (Roy, US), Michelangelo (It.).

(15) Toulouse-Lautrec (Henri de, Fr.).

painting *n* (3) oil; (5) mural; (6) canvas, fresco; (8) portrait; (9) landscape, miniature; (11) watercolour; (2 words) still life.

pair I *n* (3) duo, two; (5) brace, twins; (6) couple; (7) twosome; **II** *v* (3) wed; (4) join, mate, team; (5) marry, match; (7) bracket; **III** *cryptic* letters OO (from score of nought in both innings in cricket).

pale I *adj* **1** (3) wan; (4) ashy, waxy; (5) ashen, faded, light, livid, white; (6) sallow; (7) anaemic; (8) bleached; (9) bloodless; (10) colourless; **2** (3) dim; (4) weak; (5) faint; (6) feeble; **II** *v* (4) fade; (6) blanch, bleach.

Pallas *see* **Athene**.

Pan *Gk myth* the god of pastures, forests, flocks and herds, represented as part man, part goat.

pan I *n* (3) pot; (4) dish; (6) vessel; (8) saucepan; **II** *v* (5) slate; (9) criticise (*or* criticize).

Pandora *Gk myth* the first woman, given a box by the gods (in revenge for the theft of fire by **Prometheus**) containing all human ills. When she opened the box, all the evils that afflict the world flew out, but hope was left in the bottom.

paper I *n* **1** (4) bank; (4) bond; (5) atlas, crown, folio; (6) quarto, vellum; (8) foolscap; **2** *see* **newspaper**; **3** (5) essay; (6) report; (7) article, lecture; (8) treatise; (12) dissertation; **II** *v* (5) cover; (8) decorate; (9) wallpaper.

paradise *n* (4) Eden; (6) heaven, utopia; (7) Elysium; (8) Valhalla; (9) Shangri-La.

parasite *n* (7) sponger; (8) hanger-on; (9) scrounger; (11) bloodsucker.

ANIMAL AND PLANT PARASITES

(4) flea, tick; (5) leech, louse;
(6) dodder; (8) tapeworm;
(9) ichneumon, mistletoe.

Parcae *Rom. myth see* **Fates**.

Paris¹ I *geog.* the capital of France; **II** *cryptic* **from/of/in Paris**, **Parisian** *etc*, use a French word (*see* **French**), as in: 'Lady from Paris receives English title' (4) = dame.

Paris² *Gk myth* a son of King **Priam** of Troy and Queen Hecuba, who dreamt she was giving birth to a firebrand, so that he was exposed on Mount Ida and left to die. Found and raised by shepherds as a shepherd, he was chosen by the three goddesses **Hera, Athene** and **Aphrodite** to award the **apple of discord** to the most beautiful of them (the **judgement of Paris**). Each tried to bribe him, Hera with infinite power, Athene with infinite wisdom, Aphrodite with the most beautiful woman in the world. Paris awarded the apple to Aphrodite, who in return helped him to elope with **Helen**, the wife of **Menelaus**, king of Sparta. Menelaus gathered together the other Greek princes in an attempt to get his wife back and they made war on Troy. Paris was noted as an archer during the conflict; he killed **Achilles** with an arrow in the heel. He was killed when the Greeks eventually overran Troy.

Parisian *see* **Paris¹ II**.

parliament *n* (4) diet; (7) council; (8) assembly.

NATIONAL PARLIAMENTS

Single Chamber – Lower House – Upper House

Australia – House of Representatives – Senate.

Austria – Nationalrat – Bundesrat.

Canada – House of Commons – Senate.

China – National People's Congress.

Denmark – Folketing.

Finland – Eduskunta.

France – National Assembly – Senate.

Germany – Bundestag – Bundesrat.

Iceland – Althing.

India – Lok Sabha – Rajya Sabha.

Iran – Majlis.

Ireland – Dáil – Seanad.

Isle of Man – House of Keys.

Israel – Knesset.

Italy – Chamber of Deputies – Senate.

list continued over

Japan – Diet.
Netherlands Staaten-Generaal (States General).
Norway – Storting.
Poland – Sejm.
Portugal – Cortes.
Russia – Duma.
Spain – Cortes.
Sweden – Riksdag.
Turkey – Porte.
USA – Congress House of Representatives – Senate.

Parnassus *geog. & Gk myth* a mountain in Greece with twin peaks, one peak being sacred to **Apollo** and the **Muses**, the other to **Dionysus**. Parnassus is sometimes used to mean the arts in general, especially poetry and music.

part l *n* **1** (3) bit; (4) some; (5) piece, scrap, share, spare; (7) element, portion, section, segment; (8) division, fraction, fragment; (9) component; (11) constituent; **2** (4) role; (9) character; ll *n* **1** (4) tear; (5) break, sever, share, split; (6) detach; (8) separate; (10) disconnect; **2** (2) go; (5) leave; (6) depart; (7) diverge; (8) disperse; lll *cryptic* **1** HIDDEN WORD CUE, as in: 'Firewatcher once part of Stone Roses or string band?' (4) = Nero; **2 parts, parted** *or* **in parts** one word in the answer 'splits' another word, or is split and surrounds it, as in: 'Bridge in parts, ancient Greek needs skill to repair it' (7) = Spartan (bridge = span); **3** ANAGRAM CUE.

partial l *adj* **1** (4) part; (5) short; (6) broken; (7) lacking; (8) abridged; (9) defective, deficient, imperfect; (10) incomplete, unfinished; (11) fragmentary; **2** (6) biased, unfair, unjust; (8) one-sided, partisan; (10) prejudiced; **3** (4) fond, keen; ll *cryptic* **partial** *or* **partially** *see* part lll.

particular *adj* **1** (6) single; (7) special; (8) distinct, peculiar, specific; **2** (6) marked; (7) notable, unusual; (8) especial; (10) pronounced; (11) exceptional; **3** (5) fussy, picky; (6) choosy; (7) finicky; (10) fastidious, pernickety, scrupulous.

partly *cryptic see* **part lll.**

partner *n* (4) ally, mate, wife; (5) lover; (6) helper, spouse; (7) consort, husband; (8) sidekick; (9) associate, colleague; (10) accomplice; (11) confederate; (12) collaborator.

party l *n* **1** (2) do; (4) rave; (6) at-home, rave-up, social; (7) knees-up, reunion, shindig; (8) function; (9) festivity, gathering; (11) celebration, get-together; **2** (4) band, gang, side; (5) group; (7) faction; (8) alliance, grouping; (11) association; **3** (6) person; (8) litigant; (9) defendant, plaintiff; (10) individual; ll *cryptic* a letter or group of letters making up an abbreviation of the name of a political party, *e.g.* C, CON, DEM, L, LAB, LIB, REP.

Pasiphae *Gk myth* wife of **Minos**, who conceived a passion for a white bull sent by **Poseidon**, mated with it and bore the **Minotaur**.

pass l *v* **1** (2) go; (3) run; (4) flow, move, roll; (7) proceed; **2** (5) cross, outdo; (6) exceed; (7) surpass; (8) overtake, outstrip; **3** (4) give, hand, will; (8) bequeath, transfer; **4** (7) qualify, succeed; (8) graduate; (2 words) get through; **5** (5) adopt, enact; (6) permit; (7) approve; (8) sanction; (9) authorise (*or* authorize); **6** (4) fill; (5) spend; (6) elapse, occupy, vanish; (9) disappear; (2 words) while away; ll *n* **1** (3) col, gap; (5) gorge; (6) defile; **2** (6) permit, ticket; (7) licence, warrant; (13) authorisation (*or* authorization); **3** (5) state; (9) condition; (11) predicament.

passage *n* **1** (4) hall, lane, path; (5) aisle, alley, route; (8) corridor; **2** (6) voyage; (7) journey; (8) crossing; **3** (4) text; (7) excerpt; (8) abstract; (9) quotation, paragraph, selection.

passion *n* **1** (4) heat, love, lust, zeal; (6) ardour, desire, warmth; (7) craving, emotion, feeling, fervour; (8) devotion, fondness, keenness; (9) adoration, eagerness, intensity, vehemence; (10) enthusiasm; (11) infatuation; **2** (5) craze, hobby, mania, thing.

passionate *adj* (3) hot; (4) avid, keen, warm, wild; (5) eager, fiery; (6) ardent, loving, stormy; (7) devoted, earnest, excited, fervent, intense, willing, zealous; (8) vehement, vigorous; (9) emotional, excitable, impetuous; (10) hot-blooded; (11) tempestuous; (12) enthusiastic, wholehearted.

patron saint *n*

PATRON SAINT OF
Accountants – St Matthew
Actors – St Genesius
Animals – St Francis of Assisi
Archers – St Sebastian
Artists – St Luke
Athletes – St Sebastian
Bakers – St Elizabeth of Hungary, St Nicholas
Bellfounders – St Agatha
Blacksmiths – St Dunstan
Booksellers – St John of God
Brewers – St Augustine
Bricklayers – St Stephen
Carpenters – St Joseph
Children – St Nicholas
Comedians – St Vitus
Cooks – St Lawrence
Czech Rep. – St Wenceslas
Dentists – St Apollonia
Doctors – St Luke, St Pantaleon
England – St George
Farmers – St George
Firemen – St Florian
France – St Denis (Denys), St Joan
Gardeners – St Dorothea
Grocers – St Michael
Housewives – St Anne
Hunters – St Hubert
Innkeepers – St Amand
Ireland – St Patrick
Jewellers – St Eloi
Librarians – St Jerome
Music & musicians – St Cecilia
Scotland – St Andrew
Shoemakers – St Crispin, St Crispinian
Travellers – St Christopher
Wales – St David
Wine growers – St Vincent
Workers – St Joseph

pattern *n* **1** (5) guide, model, mould; (6) matrix; (7) example, templet; (8) standard, template; **2** (5) motif; (6) design, figure; (8) ornament; (10) decoration.

Paul *Bible* **St Paul**, the apostle to the Gentiles. Originally known as Saul of Tarsus and a persecutor of Christians, he was, according to the Acts of the Apostles, converted by a vision on the road to Damascus that temporarily blinded him. After three days he recovered his sight and was baptised. Thereafter he became Christianity's leading missionary, along with St Peter, to the Roman empire. He expounded Christian doctrine in a series of letters (epistles) to the infant churches of Asia Minor. He was eventually martyred in Rome.

THE EPISTLES OF ST PAUL
(5) Titus; (6) Romans; (7) Hebrews, Timothy; (8) Philemon;
(9) Ephesians, Galatians;
(10) Colossians; (11) Corinthians, Philippians; (13) Thessalonians.

pause *n* (3) gap; (4) lull, rest, time, wait; (5) break, space, spell; (7) interim; (8) interval, meantime; (9) entr'acte, interlude; (12) intermission, interruption.

pay I *v* **1** (5) clear, remit; (6) reward, settle; (9) discharge, reimburse; (10) recompense, remunerate; **2** (6) profit; (7) benefit; **3** (5) atone; (6) suffer; (10) compensate; (2 words) make amends; **II** *n* (3) fee; (5) wages; (6) income, salary; (7) stipend; (8) earnings; (10) honorarium; (12) remuneration; (13) reimbursement.

payment *n* (3) fee; (4) fare, hire, toll; (6) outlay; (7) advance, deposit, expense, premium; (8) donation; (9) discharge; (10) instalment, remittance, settlement; (11) expenditure; (12) contribution, remuneration.

peaceful *adj* (4) calm; (5) quiet, still; (6) gentle, placid, serene; (7) pacific, restful; (8) relaxing, tranquil; (9) unruffled; (10) untroubled; (11) undisturbed.

peak I *n* (3) tip, top; (4) apex, crag, horn; (5) crest, point; (6) climax, summit, zenith; (8) mountain, pinnacle; **II** *v* (6) climax; (9) culminate.

peculiar *adj* 1 (3) odd; (4) rare; (5) funny, queer, weird; (6) unique; (7) amazing, bizarre, erratic, notable, offbeat, special, strange, unusual; (8) aberrant, abnormal, atypical, freakish, singular; (9) eccentric, remarkable; (10) marvellous, noteworthy, surprising; (13) extraordinary; 2 (3) own; (6) proper, single; (7) special; (8) discrete, distinct, personal, separate, specific; (10) individual, particular; (11) distinctive; (13) idiosyncratic; (14) characteristic.

peer¹ *v* (3) pry; (4) gaze, look, peek, peep; (6) squint; (7) glimpse.

peer² *n* 1 *see* **noble**; 2 (5) equal; (6) fellow; (10) equivalent; (11) counterpart; (12) contemporary.

Pegasus *Gk myth* a winged horse ridden by **Bellerophon**.

pen I *n* 1 (4) biro; (5) quill; (6) marker, writer; (9) ballpoint; 2 (3) sty; (4) cage, coop, fold; (5) hutch, stall; (9) enclosure; 3 a female swan; 4 short for penitentiary; **II** *v* 1 (5) draft, write; (7) compose; (8) scribble; 2 (4) cage; (5) fence; (7) confine, enclose; (8) imprison; (2 words) coop up, hem in, shut up.

Penelope *Gk myth & lit.* the faithful wife of **Odysseus**, who was besieged by suitors when her husband failed to return from Troy. She promised to give them an answer as soon as she had completed the shroud she was weaving for her father-in-law, but whatever she wove during the day she unwove during the following night.

penny *cryptic* abbreviated as D or P.

perceive *v* 1 (3) see; (4) feel, hear, spot, view; (5) sense; (6) detect, notice, remark; (7) discern, glimpse, observe; (9) apprehend, recognise (*or* recognize); (11) distinguish; 2 (5) grasp, learn; (6) deduce, gather; (7) realise (*or* realize); (8) conclude; (10) appreciate, understand.

perfect I *adj* 1 (4) pure; (5) ideal, model; (8) flawless, spotless, ultimate; (9) exemplary, faultless, matchless; (10) immaculate, impeccable; (12) incomparable; 2 (5) sheer, total, utter; (6) entire; (8) absolute, complete; (10) consummate; **II** *v* (6) finish, polish, refine; (8) complete, finalise (*or* finalize); (10) consummate.

perform *v* 1 (2) do; (3) run; (4) work; (6) effect, fulfil; (7) achieve, execute, operate; (8) function; (9) discharge; (10) accomplish; (2 words) bring about, bring off, carry out, pull off; 2 (3) act; (4) play, sing; (5) dance; (6) appear; (9) entertain, represent.

performance *n* 1 (3) gig; (4) play, show; (7) concert, recital; (9) rendition; (10) appearance, production; (12) presentation; (13) entertainment; 2 (9) discharge, execution; (10) fulfilment; (11) achievement; (14) accomplishment, implementation; 3 (5) value, yield; (6) return; (7) success; (10) efficiency; (12) productivity; (13) effectiveness, profitability.

period *n* 1 (3) age, day, era; (4) date, hour, span, term, time, year; (5) cycle, phase, stage; (6) decade; (7) century, lustrum; (8) interval; (10) generation, millennium; (12) quinquennium; 2 (5) class; (6) lesson; (7) session.

periodic *adj* (4) rare; (6) annual, weekly, yearly; (7) monthly, regular; (8) repeated, seasonal, sporadic; (9) recurrent, recurring; (10) occasional; (11) fortnightly.

periodical I *adj see* **periodic**; **II** *n see* **magazine**.

permanent *adj* (5) fixed; (6) stable; (7) durable, eternal, lasting; (8) constant, enduring, lifelong; (9) perennial, perpetual, steadfast; (10) unchanging; (11) everlasting, long-lasting, unalterable; (12) imperishable; (14) indestructible.

perpetual *adj* (7) abiding, ageless, endless, eternal, lasting, non-stop, undying; (8) enduring, timeless, unbroken; (9) continual, permanent, unceasing; (10) persistent, relentless; (11) everlasting, never-ending, unremitting; (12) interminable; (13) uninterrupted.

Persephone *Gk myth* daughter of **Demeter**, the goddess of nature, crops, fruit and vegetation, who was carried off by **Dis** to be queen of the **Underworld**. Demeter was distraught at her loss and as a result ceased to ensure that the crops would grow. To safeguard the survival of humanity, the gods sent Hermes down to the **Underworld** to fetch Persephone back. She was allowed to return to the upper world, but only for part of the year. The period when she is in the **Underworld** and Demeter grieves is winter – Roman equivalent **Proserpina**.

Perseus *Gk myth* son of **Zeus** and **Danae**, who, with the help of **Athene**, slew the gorgon **Medusa** and rescued **Andromeda** from a sea monster.

Phaeton *Gk myth* the son of Helios the sun god, who longed to drive his father's chariot drawing the sun across the sky. Helios eventually allowed him to, but Phaeton was unable to control the horses of the sun, who took it too close to the earth. To stop the whole world being turned into a desert, Zeus struck Phaeton down with a thunderbolt.

phantom *n* (5) ghost; (6) spirit, mirage, vision; (7) figment, spectre; (8) illusion; (10) apparition; (13) hallucination.

philosopher *n* (7) thinker; (8) moralist, theorist; (9) Platonist, schoolman; (13) metaphysician.

FAMOUS PHILOSOPHERS

(4) Ayer (UK), Cato (Rom.), Hume (UK), Kant (Ger.), Mill (UK), Vico (It.), Zeno (Gk).

(5) Hegel (Ger.), Locke (UK), Plato (Gk).

(6) Fichte (Ger.), Pascal (Fr.), Hobbes (UK), Popper (UK), Sartre (Fr.), Seneca (Rom.), Thales (Gk).

(7) Aquinas (St Thomas, It.), Bentham (UK), Diderot (Fr.), Erasmus (NL), Russell (UK), Spinoza (It.).

(8) Diogenes (Gk), Epicurus (Gk),

Leibnitz (Ger.), Socrates (Gk), Voltaire (Fr.).

(9) Aristotle (Gk), Descartes (Fr.), Epictetus (Gk), Nietzsche (Ger.).

(10) Democritus (Gk), Heraclitus (Gk), Xenocrates (Gk).

(12) Schopenhauer (Ger.), Wittgenstein (A).

---

phosphorus *cryptic* abbreviated as P.

piece I *n* (3) bit; (4) bite, lump, part, some; (5) chunk, scrap, share, slice, spare; (6) morsel; (7) element, portion, section, segment; (8) division, fraction, fragment; (9) component; II HIDDEN WORD CUE *see* **part**.

Pilate *Bible* Roman governor of Judaea and Samaria at the time of the trial and crucifixion of Jesus. Jesus was sent to Pilate because the Jewish authorities were unable to condemn a prisoner to death. According to the Gospel accounts, Pilate offered to release one prisoner to the Jewish people, as was the custom at the Passover, but the mob shouted for Barabbas not Jesus. Pilate is also said by St Matthew to have washed his hands symbolically before handing Jesus over for execution.

pile I *n & v* (4) heap, mass; (5) hoard, mound, stack; (9) stockpile; II *n* 1 (3) ton; (4) tons; (5) heaps; (8) mountain; (12) accumulation; 2 (6) castle, palace; (8) building; 3 (3) nap; (4) shag; (5) plush; 4 (4) pier, post; III *v* 1 (5) amass; (6) gather; (7) collect; (10) accumulate; 2 (4) pack, rush; (5) crowd, flock, flood; (6) charge, stream.

pillar *n* (4) mast, pier, pile, post, prop; (5) shaft; (6) column; (7) support, upright; (8) mainstay; (3 words) tower of strength.

pinch I *n & v* (3) nip; (4) grip; (5) grasp, press, tweak; (7) squeeze; II *v* 1 (4) nick; (5) filch, **steal**; 2 (6) **arrest**; III *n* (3) bit, jot; (4) dash, mite; (5) speck; (7) soupçon.

pious *adj* (2) pi; (5) godly; (6) devout; (7) dutiful, saintly; (8) faithful, reverent; (9) religious, righteous; (13) sanctimonious.

Pisces *astrol. & astron.* the constellation that is the twelfth sign of the zodiac, also known as the Fishes.

pity I *n* (4) ruth; (5) mercy; (6) regret, sorrow; (8) sympathy; (10) compassion; (13) commiseration; **II** *v* (10) sympathise (*or* sympathize); (11) commiserate.

place I *n* **1** (4) area, city, site, spot, town; (5) point, venue; (6) locale, region; (7) country, village; (8) district, locality, location; (13) neighbourhood; **2** (4) **home**; (5) house; (9) residence; **3** (4) post; (8) position; **II** *v* (3) lay, put, set; (4) rest; (5) lodge, plant, stand; (6) locate, settle, spread; (7) arrange, deposit, dispose, stretch; (8) position.

plague I *n* **1** (7) disease; (8) epidemic; (9) infection; (10) pestilence; (11) infestation; **2** (5) curse, trial; (7) scourge; (8) nuisance; (9) annoyance; (10) affliction; **II** *v* (3) vex; (5) annoy, haunt, hound; (6) bother, harass, pester; (7) afflict, bedevil, torment, torture, trouble; (9) persecute.

THE TEN PLAGUES OF EGYPT

(1) water turned to blood; (2) frogs; (3) lice; (4) flies; (5) murrain (a disease that caused all the Egyptians' cattle to die); (6) boils; (7) hail; (8) locusts; (9) thick darkness; (10) death of the first-born.

---

plain I *adj* **1** (5) basic; (6) modest, simple; (7) uniform; (8) ordinary; (9) unadorned; (10) uncoloured; (11) undecorated, unelaborate, unpatterned; **2** (5) clear; (6) patent; (7) evident, obvious, visible; (8) apparent; (12) unmistakable; **3** (4) open; (5) blunt, frank; (6) candid, honest, direct; (8) truthful; (9) outspoken; (15) straightforward; **4** (4) ugly; (6) homely; (12) unattractive; **II** *n* (6) pampas, steppe, tundra; (7) lowland, prairie; (9) grassland, tableland.

plan I *n & v* (4) plot; (5) draft; (6) design, scheme; (7) outline, project, venture; (8) schedule; **II** *n* **1** (4) idea; (6) tactic; (8) proposal, scenario, strategy; (9) operation, programme; (10) enterprise, initiative; (11) proposition, undertaking; **2** (3) map;

(5) chart; (6) layout, sketch; (7) diagram, drawing; (9) blueprint; **III** *v* (5) frame; (6) devise, intend, invent; (7) arrange, prepare, propose; (8) contrive, organise (*or* organize); (9) formulate; **IV** *cryptic* ANAGRAM CUE.

plane I *n* **1** *see* **aircraft**; **2** (4) tool; **3** (4) area; (5) level; (7) surface; **II** *v & adj* (5) level, smooth.

planet *n*

THE PLANETS

(4) Mars; (5) Earth, Pluto, Venus; (6) Saturn, Uranus; (7) Jupiter, Mercury, Neptune.

---

plant I *n* **1** (4) alga, bulb, bush, crop, fern, herb, reed, tree, vine, weed; (5) grass, shrub; (6) annual, cactus, cereal, flower, hybrid, lichen; (7) climber, sapling; (8) cultivar, seedling; (9) evergreen, succulent, vegetable; **2** (4) mill, shop, yard; (5) works; (7) factory, foundry; (8) workshop; **3** (4) gear; (5) tools; (9) equipment, machinery; **II** *v* **1** (3) fix, put, set, sow; (4) bury, root; (5) embed, found, lodge, place; (6) insert, settle; (9) establish; **2** conceal something on somebody's person or property in order to incriminate them.

PLANT SPECIES

(*see also* **flower**)

(3) box, ers, fog, hop, ivy, rye, udo.

(4) aira, alfa, anil, arum, bene, bent, blue, coca, coix, diss, dock, doob, dura, fern, flag, gill, hebe, hemp, iris, kans, kava, ling, lyme, moss, reed, rhea, rusa, rush, sego, sunn, tare, teff, tore, tutu, weld, whin, woad, wort, yarr.

(5) abaca, anise, arold, bhang, bohea, brier, briza, broom, bugle, bunch, caper, carex, chive, couch, cutch, durra, dwale, erica, furze, gorse, guaco, halfa, haulm, kemps, liana, lupin, melic, naiad, orach, oryza, oshac, panax, panic, rhyne, sedge, sisal, spear, sumac, thorn, vetch, viola.   *list continued over*

---

(6) alsike, arnica, arrach, arundo, bajree, barley, bedder, bejuco, betony, biblus, blinks, bocage, borage, briony, bryony, burnet, cactus, cassia, cereus, cicely, cicuta, cissus, citrus, cockle, coffee, comfry, conium, cotton, cowage, croton, cummin, darnel, desmid, dodder, fescue, filago, fimble, fiorin, frutex, fungus, garlic, gervas, ginger, gnetum, gromel, hedera, hypnum, iberis, kalmia, knawel, kousso, lolium, lupine, madder, mallow, marram, matico, medick, myrtle, nardus, nettle, orache, orchil, orpine, ox-heel, paigle, pampas, pepper, phleum, privet, protea, pteris, quitch, radish, ramson, redtop, riccia, ruppia, sabine, sesame, sesban, seseli, smilax, spurge, sumach, thrift, twitch, uniola, urtica, viscum.

(7) acantha, aconite, ale-hoop, alfalfa, all-good, allseed, alyssum, amellus, ash-wort, atropin, awl-wort, blawort, bog-bean, bog-rush, bracken, bramble, bugloss, bug-wort, bulrush, burdock, calumba, campion, caraway, cardoon, carluus, cassave, catmint, clivers, comfrey, coneine, cowbane, cowslip, cudweed, dionaea, dittany, dogwood, elf-wood, esparto, eulelia, festuca, foggage, foxtail, genista, ginseng, hogweed, heather, hedeoma, hemlock, henbane, jasmine, lucerne, malacca, milfoil, mugwort, mustard, navette, oregano, osmunda, pop-weed, ragwort, rhubarb, saffron, sea-pink, skirret, sorghum, spignel, squitch, thistle, timothy, vetiver, wagwant, whangee, zizania.

(8) absinthe, acanthus, agrimony, angelica, banewort, bedstraw, berberry, bindweed, camomile, cannabis, capsicum, cleavers, cowberry, demerara, dog-grass, dog-wheat, eleusine, flax-wort, gynerium, mandrake, plantain, pondweed, puffball, puss-tail, star-wort, turmeric, valerian, veronica, virginia, wormwood, xanthium.

(9) arrowroot, artemisia, baldmoney, blueberry, chickweed, coriander, cranberry, crosswort, dandelion, forsythia, horehound, horsetail, liverwort, marijuana, monkshood, raspberry, sagebrush, spearmint, speedwell, stinkweed.

(10) belladonna, blackberry, blackthorn, chokeberry, cinquefoil, gooseberry, loganberry, peppermint, tumbleweed; (2 words) lady's thumb.

(11) gillyflower, huckleberry, wintergreen; (2 words) pussy willow.

platform *n* **1** (4) dais; (5) stage, stand; (6) podium; (7) rostrum; **2** (6) **policy**; (9) manifesto, programme.

platinum *cryptic* abbreviated as PT.

play I *v* **1** (4) romp; (5) caper, sport; (6) frolic, gambol; (2 words) amuse oneself, enjoy oneself, have fun; **2** (2) do; (3) act; (5) stage; (7) perform, portray, present; (9) represent; **II** *n* **1** (3) fun; (4) game; (5) sport; (7) pastime; (9) amusement, diversion, enjoyment; (10) recreation; **2** (4) show; (5) drama, farce; (6) comedy; (7) tragedy; (9) melodrama; (10) production; (11) performance, tragicomedy; **3** (4) give, room; (5) space; (6) leeway; (8) latitude, movement; (11) flexibility.

player *n* **1** *see* **musician**; **2** (5) actor; (6) mummer; (7) artiste; (8) thespian; **3** (9) cricketer, sportsman; (10) competitor, contestant, footballer; (11) participant, sportswoman.

playwright *n* (9) dramatist; (12) scriptwriter.

FAMOUS PLAYWRIGHTS

(3) Fry (Christopher, UK), Gay (John, UK), Kyd (Thomas, UK).

(4) Behn (Aphra, UK), Bolt (Robert, UK), Ford (John, UK), Gems (Pam, UK), Gray (Simon, UK), Hall (Willis, UK), Hare (David, UK), Shaw (George Bernard, Ire./UK), Vega (Lope de, Sp.).

list continued over

(5) Albee (Edward, US), Arden (John, UK), Behan (Brendan, Ire.), Frayn (Michael, UK), Friel (Brian, Ire.), Genet (Jean, Fr.), Gogol (Nikolai, Russ.), Havel (Vaclav, Cz.), Ibsen (Henrik, Norw.), Mamet (David, US), Odets (Clifford, US), Orton (Joe, UK), Synge (John, Ire.), Wilde (Oscar, Ire./UK).

(6) Barrie (J.M., UK), Brecht (Berthold, Ger.), Coward (Noël, UK), Frisch (Max, Switz.), Fugard (Athol, SA), Goethe (J.W. von, Ger.), Jonson (Ben, UK), Miller (Arthur, US), O'Casey (Sean, Ire.), Pinero (Arthur Wing, UK), Pinter (Harold, UK), Racine (Jean, Fr.), Seneca (Rom.), Wesker (Arnold, UK), Wilder (Thornton, US).

(7) Anouilh (Jean, Fr.), Beckett (Samuel, Ire./Fr.), Büchner (Georg, Ger.), Chekhov (Anton, Russ.), Cocteau (Jean, Fr.), Feydeau (Georges, Fr.), Goldoni (Carlo, It.), Hampton (Christopher, UK), Hellman (Lillian, US), Ionesco (Eugène, Rum./Fr.), Marlowe (Christopher, UK), Molière (Fr.), Osborne (John, UK), Plautus (Rom.), Rostand (Edmond, Fr.), Shaffer (Peter *and* Anthony, UK), Shepard (Sam, US), Terence (Rom.), Travers (Ben, UK), Webster (John, UK), Whiting (John, UK).

(8) Beaumont (Francis, UK), Calderon (Pedro, Sp.), Congreve (William, UK), Farquhar (George, Ire.), Marivaux (Pierre, Fr.), Menander (Gk), Mortimer (John, UK), Rattigan (Terence, UK), Schiller (Friedrich, Ger.), Sheridan (Richard Brinsley, Ire./UK), Stoppard (Tom, UK/Cz.), Vanbrugh (John, UK), Williams (Tennessee, US).

(9) Aeschylus (Gk), Ayckbourn (Alan, UK), Bleasdale (Alan, UK), Corneille (Pierre, Fr.), Churchill (Caryl, UK), Euripides (Gk), Goldsmith (Oliver, UK), Hauptmann

(Gerhard, Ger.), Middleton (Thomas, UK), Sophocles (Gk), Wycherley (William, UK).

(10) Dürrenmatt (Friedrich, Switz.), Pirandello (Luigi, It.), Schnitzler (Arthur, A.), Strindberg (August, Swe.), Waterhouse (Keith, UK).

(11) Grillparzer (Franz, A.), Shakespeare (William, Eng.).

(12) Aristophanes (Gk), Beaumarchais (Pierre, Fr.).

please *v* 1 (5) amuse, charm, cheer; (6) humour; (7) content, delight, gladden, gratify, indulge, satisfy; (9) captivate, fascinate; 2 (4) like, want, will; (6) choose, desire, prefer.

Pleiades I *Gk myth* the seven daughters of Atlas; II *astron.* a cluster of six or seven visible stars in the constellation of **Taurus**.

plot I *n & v* (4) plan; (5) cabal; (6) design, scheme; (8) intrigue; II *n* 1 (9) stratagem; (10) conspiracy; (11) machination; 2 (5) story, theme; (6) thread; (7) outline, subject; (8) scenario; (9) narrative; 3 (3) bed, lot; (4) area, lawn; (5) patch, tract; (6) garden, parcel; (9) allotment; III *v* 1 (6) devise; (8) conspire; 2 (4) scan; (5) check, trace, track, watch; (6) record; (7) oversee.

Pluto *Rom myth* the god of the **Underworld** and the dead, Greek equivalent **Dis** or **Hades**.

Plutus *Gk myth* the god of riches.

poem *n* (3) lay, ode; (4) epic, song; (5) elegy, haiku, idyll, lines, rhyme, tanka; (6) aubade, ballad, sonnet; (8) clerihew, limerick, madrigal; (9) roundelay.

poet *n* (4) bard; (9) rhymester, versifier.

POETS

(3) Poe (Edgar Allan, US), Pye (Henry, UK)

(4) Gray (Thomas, UK), Gunn (Thom, UK/US), Hill (Geoffrey, UK), Hood (Thomas, UK),

list continued over

Hugo (Victor, Fr.), Hunt (Leigh, UK), Lear (Edward, UK), Li-Po (Ch.), Muir (Edwin, UK), Ovid (Rom.), Owen (Wilfred, UK), Pope (Alexander, UK), Rowe (Nicholas, UK), Sadi (Pers.), Tate (Nahum, UK), Wain (John, UK).

(5) Auden (W. H., UK), Blake (William, UK), Burns (Robert, Scot.), Byron (Lord George Gordon, UK), Clare (John, UK), Crane (Hart, US), Dante (Alighieri, It.), David (*Bible*), Donne (John, UK), Eliot (T. S., US/UK), Frost (Robert, US), Gosse (Edmund, UK), Gower (John, UK), Hardy (Thomas, UK), Heine (Heinrich, Ger.), Homer (Gk), Keats (John, UK), Keyes (Sidney, UK), Lorca (Federico García, Sp.), Lucan (Rom.), Moore (Marianne, US), Noyes (Alfred, UK), Perse (St Jean, Fr.), Plath (Sylvia, US), Pound (Ezra, US), Rilke (Rainer Maria, A), Scott (Sir Walter, UK), Smith (Stevie, UK), Tasso (Torquato, It.), Watts (Isaac, UK), Yeats (W.B., Ire.).

(6) Austin (Alfred, UK), Binyon (Robert, UK), Bishop (Elizabeth, US), Brooke (Rupert, UK), Cowper (William, UK), Crabbe (George, UK), Dobson (Henry, UK), Dowson (Ernest, UK), Dryden (John, UK), Eusden (Laurence, UK), Fuller (Roy, UK), Goethe (J.W. von, Ger.), Graves (Robert, UK), Hesiod (Gk), Horace (Rom.), Hughes (Ted, UK), Jonson (Ben, UK), Landor (Walter Savage, UK), Larkin (Philip, UK), Lowell (Amy *and* Robert, US), Milton (John, UK), Musset (Alfred de, Fr.), Pindar (Gk), Sappho (Gk), Sidney (Sir Philip, UK), Thomas (Dylan, UK), Virgil (Rom.).

(7) Addison (Joseph, UK), Ariosto (Ludovico, It.), Bentley (Edmund Clerihew, UK), Blunden (Edmund, UK), Bridges (Robert, UK), Chaucer, Geoffrey, Eng.), Collins (William, UK), Douglas (Keith, UK), Flecker

(James Elroy, UK), Herbert (George, UK), Herrick (Robert, UK), Hopkins (Gerard Manley, UK), Housman (A.E., UK), Johnson (Lionel, UK), Khayyam (Omar, Pers.), Kipling (Rudyard, UK), Martial (Rom.), Marvell (Andrew, UK), McGough (Roger, UK), Newbolt (Sir Henry, UK), Pushkin (Alexander, Russ.), Rimbaud (Arthur, Fr.), Sassoon (Siegfried, UK), Shelley (Percy Bysshe, UK), Sitwell (Dame Edith, UK), Skelton (John, UK), Southey (Robert, UK), Stevens (Wallace, UK), Wharton (Thomas, UK), Whitman (Walt, US).

(8) Berryman (John, US), Betjeman (John, UK), Browning (Robert, UK), Catullus (Rom.), cummings (e.e., US), Davenant (Sir William, UK), Day Lewis (Cecil, UK), de la Mare (Walter, UK), Ginsberg (Allen, US), Lawrence (D.H., UK), Mallarmé (Stéphane, Fr.), Petrarch (Francesco, It.), Philemon (Gk), Rossetti (Dante Gabriel *and* Christina, UK), Tennyson (Alfred Lord, UK), Verlaine (Paul, Fr.), Williams (William Carlos, US).

(9) Coleridge (Samuel Taylor, UK), Dickinson (Emily, US), Goldsmith (Oliver, UK), Masefield (John, UK), Swinburne (Algernon Charles, UK).

(10) Baudelaire (Charles, Fr.), Chesterton (G.K., UK), Fitzgerald (Edward, UK), Longfellow (Henry Wadsworth, US).

(11) Shakespeare (William, Eng.), Yevtushenko (Yevgeny, Russ.).

point l *n* 1 (3) dot, tip; (4) apex, site, spot; (5) place; (8) location, position; (9) situation; 2 (4) time; (5) stage; (6) moment; (7) instant; (8) juncture; 3 (3) aim; (5) **object**; (9) intention, objective; 4 (4) core, crux, gist, pith; (5) drift; (6) thrust; (7) essence, meaning; (12) significance; 5 (4) item; (5) topic; (7) subject; (10) particular; ll *v* (3) aim; (4) show; (5) level, train; (6) direct; (8) indicate; (9) designate; lll *cryptic* letter N,

E, S, or W (or any combination representing a compass point).

pointless I *adj* (6) futile; (11) meaningless; II *cryptic* 1 blunt *or* nil, zero, no score etc; 2 remove letter N, E, S, or W etc (*see* **point**) from the word or words referred to, as in: 'Pointless pencil changed for fastener, (4) = clip (changed = ANAGRAM CUE).

poison I *n* (4) bane; (5) venom, toxin; (6) blight; (9) contagion; defoliant, fungicide, herbicide, pesticide; (11) insecticide; (13) contamination; II *v* (4) kill; (5) taint; (6) infect, murder; (7) corrupt, envenom, pervert, pollute.

TYPES OF POISON

(3) DDT.

(6) curare, phenol.

(7) aconite, arsenic, cyanide, hemlock, henbane.

(8) antimony, atropine, chlorine, nicotine, ptomaine.

(9) digitalis, wolfsbane.

(10) belladonna, strychnine.

---

pole I *n* (3) bar, rod; (4) mast, post, spar; (5) shaft, staff, stake, stick; II *cryptic* letter N or S (referring to the north or south pole).

police I *n* (2 words) the Bill, the cops, the Feds, the filth, the force, the fuzz; II *cryptic* letters CID or FBI.

policeman *or* **police officer** *n* (2) PC; (3) WPC; (6) lawman; (7) officer; (8) sergeant; (9) constable, detective, inspector; (14) superintendent.

SLANG TERMS FOR A POLICE OFFICER

(3) cop, pig; (4) dick, plod; (5) bobby; (6) copper, peeler, rozzer.

Pollux *Gk myth* one of the heavenly twins, brother of **Castor** (*see also* **Gemini**).

Polyphemus *Gk myth* a one-eyed giant (**Cyclops**), who took **Odysseus** and his men prisoner and was blinded by them as they made their escape.

Pompey I *Rom hist.* a Roman soldier and statesman, a member of the first **triumvirate**, the rival of Julius Caesar who eventually defeated him in a civil war; II *UK* Portsmouth.

Pontius Pilate *see* **Pilate**.

Pooh, Winnie the Pooh, Pooh Bear *see* **Milne**.

pool I *n* 1 (4) lake, mere, pond, tarn; (6) puddle; 2 (3) pot; (4) bank, fund; (5) kitty; (7) jackpot, reserve; II *v* (5) merge; (7) combine; (10) amalgamate.

poor I *adj* 1 (5) broke, needy, skint, stony; (8) badly-off, bankrupt, deprived; (9) destitute, penniless; (12) impoverished; (13) disadvantaged; (15) poverty-stricken, underprivileged; (2 words) hard up; 2 (3) bad; (4) weak; (5) sorry; (6) faulty, feeble; (7) average; (8) inferior, mediocre, pathetic; (9) third-rate, worthless; (10) second-rate, uninspired; (11) substandard; (14) unsatisfactory; (15) undistinguished; 3 (6) meagre, scanty, skimpy, sparse; (7) lacking; (9) deficient; (12) insufficient; 4 (7) unhappy, un–lucky; (8) luckless; (9) miserable; (11) unfortunate; II *cryptic* ANAGRAM CUE.

poorly I *adj* (3) ill; (4) sick; (6) unwell; (10) indisposed; II *cryptic* ANAGRAM CUE.

pop *n* I *n & v* (4) bang, snap; (5) burst, crack; II *n* 1 (9) explosion; 2 (2) pa; (3) dad; (6) **father**; 3 (4) fizz, soda; (8) lemonade; 4 (4) rock; (5) music.

POP GROUPS

(3) ABC, A-Ha, Dio, ELO, Fox, Gun, Jam, Mud, PhD, Sky, UFO, Wah!, Who (the), XTC, Yes.

(4) Abba, AC/DC, Band (the), Beat, Bros, Cars (the), Chic, Cult, Cure (the), Devo, Firm, Free, Herd, INXS, Jets, Linx, Move, News, Nice, Opus, Pips, Ruts, Slik, Styx, Tams, Them, Toto, Toys, T-Rex, Trio, Wham!

(5) Alarm, Avons, Bread, Byrds, Cameo, Clash (the), Cream, Darts, Doors, Exile, Faces, Falco, Focus, Goons, Hello, Japan, Kenny,

list continued over

Kinks (the), Mojos, O'Jays, Pilot, Queen, Racey, Rufus, Saxon, Skids, Slade, Space, Steam, Sweet, Truth, Tymes, Wings, Yazoo; (2 words) Mr Big, ZZ Top.

(6) Angels, Berlin, Comets (the), Damned, Dollar, Eagles, Equals, Europe, Family, Fureys, Gillan, Motors (the), Nolans (the), Pearls, Pigbag, Pogues, Police (the), Raydio, Rumour, Sailor, Smiths (the), Smokie, Sparks, Trans-x, Tweets, Vapors, Vipers, Visage; (2 words) Boney M, Go West, Mai Tai, Our Kid, Red Box, UK Subs.

(7) Amazulu, America, Animals (the), Archies, Arrival, Bangles, Bauhaus, Beatles (the), Blondie, Buggles, Casuals, Chicago, Dakotas, Delrons, Doolies, Dynasty, Erasure, Genesis, Goodies (the), Hollies (the), Jesters, Luvvers, Madness, Marbles, Marcels, Merseys, Moments, Monkees (the), Monsoon, Odyssey, Osmonds (the), Ottawan, Outlaws, Peppers, Piglets, Pinkies, Pirates, Rainbow, Ramones, Ramrods, Rattles, Redbone, Redding, Regents, Replays, Santana, Seekers (the), Shadows (the), Sherbet, Squeeze, Strawbs, Tavares, Tonight, Traffic, Trammps, Turtles, Wailers (the), Weavers, Whistle, Wizzards, Wombles (the), Wurzels, Zodiacs, Zombies; (2 words) Bee Gees (the), Bon Jovi, Box Tops, Gap Band, It Bites, Sad Café, SOS Band.

(8) Allisons, All-Stars, Banshees, Chiffons, Chi-lites, Coasters, Crickets, Crystals, Diamonds, Dreamers, Drifters (the), Fentones, Floaters, Fortunes, Fourmost, Hawkwind, Heatwave, Honeybus, Hotshots, Jacksons (the), Miracles, Mixtures, Mudlarks, Nazareth, Newbeats, Olympics, Peddlers, Pharaohs, Pioneers, Piranhas, Platters, Pussycat, Ronettes, Scaffold, Shakatak, Shalamar, Specials (the), Spinners, Supremes (the), Surfaris, Survivor, Tornados, Tourists,

Ultravox, Ventures, Whispers; (2 words) Big Three, Blue Mink, Crew Cuts, Five Star, Four Aces, Four Tops, Ink Spots, Lipps Inc, Meat Loaf, New Order, New World, Soft Cell, Talk Talk, Tight Fit, Union Gap, Van Halen.

(9) Bachelors, Badfinger, Bluebells, Bluetones, Bluenotes, Buzzcocks, Crusaders, Cufflinks, Dubliners, Easybeats, Foreigner, Greyhound, Kraftwerk, Landscape, Marillion, Marmalade, Mr Minster, Motorhead, Poni-tails, Scorpions, Searchers, Shirelles, Shondells, Spotnicks, Teenagers, Tremeloes, Upsetters, Vandellas, Yardbirds; (2+ words) Beach Boys, Black Lace, Bow Wow Wow, Bucks Fizz, Dixie Cups, Four Preps, Hot Butter, Ivy League, Loose Ends, Los Bravos, Mel And Kim, Men At Work, Migil Five, Paper Lace, Pink Floyd, Real Thing, Rose Royce, Roxy Music, Simply Red, Status Quo, Steely Dan, Stray Cats, Thin Lizzy, Yellow Dog.

(10) Bananarama, Blancmange, Blockheads, Caravelles, Carpenters, Checkmates, Chordettes, Commodores, Communards, Eurythmics, Highwaymen, Honeycombs, Hurricanes, Kajagoogoo, Lambrettas, Pacemakers, Pretenders (the), Sandpipers, Shangri-las, Stargazers, Stranglers (the), Stylistics, Supertramp, Undertones, Wavelength, Whitesnake; (2+ words) Amen Corner, Art Of Noise, Bad Manners, Belle Stars, Big Country, Bob and Earl, Canned Heat, Chicory Tip, Deep Purple, Def Leppard, Duran Duran, Iron Maiden, Jan and Dean, Jethro Tull, Kalin Twins, Liquid Gold, Matt Bianco, Moody Blues, Mötley Crüe, Mungo Jerry, New Edition, New Seekers, Racing Cars, Ram Jam Band, Sam and Dave, Sex Pistols, Small Faces, Teddy Bears, Third World, Tom Tom Club, Vanity Fare.   *list continued over*

(11) Big Brothers, Foundations, Hilltoppers, Imagination, Jordanaires, Lindisfarne, Marvelettes, Merseybeats, Mindbenders, Modernaires, Overlanders, Steppenwolf, Temptations; (2+ words) Big Roll Band, Bronski Beat, Chas and Dave, China Crisis, Culture Club, Dead Or Alive, Depeche Mode, Dire Straits, Fatback Band, Four Pennies, Four Seasons, Fun Boy Three, Generation X, Glitter Band, Human League, Jackson Five, Judas Priest, Kaye Sisters, Killing Joke, Manfred Mann, Ohio Express, Orange Juice, Pet Shop Boys, Piltdown Men, Playboy Band, Poppy Family, Procol Harum, Quantum Jump, Simple Minds, T Connection, White Plains.

(12) Crypt-kickers, Dreamweavers, Housemartins (the), Showstoppers, Springfields; (2+ words) Black Sabbath, Bob and Marcia, Boomtown Rats, Boystown Gang, Cockney Rebel, Fiddlers Dram, First Edition, Fleetwood Mac, Flowerpot Men, Four Freshmen, Grateful Dead, Guys and Dolls, Hot Chocolate, Kingston Trio, Medicine Head, Midnight Star, Miki And Griff, Modern Lovers, Musical Youth, Paul and Paula, Peters and Lee, Plastic Penny, Power Station, Pretty Things, Secret Affair, Shocking Blue, Sister Sledge, Sonny and Cher, Steeleye Span, St Louis Union, Style Council, Sunshine Band, Talking Heads, The Young Ones, Three Degrees, Vernons Girls, Weather Girls, Young Rascals.

(13) Heartbreakers, Showaddywaddy; (2+ words) Altered Images, Atomic Rooster, Barron Knights, Brook Brothers, Dave Clark Five, Deep River Boys, Fat Larry's Band, Flying Lizards, Flying Pickets, Isley Brothers, Lovin' Spoonful, Magic Lanterns, Mills Brothers, Modern Romance, Modern Talking, Mott the Hoople, Ollie and Gerry, Picketty Witch, REO Speedwagon, Rockin' Berries, Rolling Stones, Spandau Ballet, Stealers Wheel, Tears For Fears, Thompson Twins, Three Dog Night, Twisted Sister, Village People, Zager and Evans.

(14) Adam and the Ants, Althea and Donna, Andrews Sisters, Bay City Rollers, Doobie Brothers, Dorsey Brothers, Everly Brothers, Fifth Dimension, Gibson Brothers, Godley and Creme, Haysi Fantayzee, Herman's Hermits, John Barry Seven, Jon and Vangelis, Kool and the Gang, McGuire Sisters, Nashville Teens, Peaches and Herb, Peter and Gordon, Plastic Ono Band, Pointer Sisters, Public Image Ltd, Renée and Renato, Rocksteady Crew, Rooftop Singers, Scritti Politti, Shaky and Bonnie, Sweet Sensation, Swing Out Sister, Walker Brothers.

(15) Bellamy Brothers, Beverly Sisters, Big Ben Banjo Band, Classic Nouveaux, Delta Rhythm Boys, Detroit Emeralds, Detroit Spinners, McGuinness Flint, Middle of the Road, Partridge Family, Psychedelic Furs, Temperance Seven, Unit Four Plus Two, Womack and Womack.

pope *n* (7) pontiff; (2 words) Holy Father.

NAMES OF POPES

(3) Leo.

(4) John, Paul, Pius.

(5) Caius, Conon, Donus, Felix, Linus, Peter, Urban.

(6) Adrian, Agatho, Eugene, Fabian, Hilary, Julius, Landus, Lucius, Marcus, Martin, Sixtus, Victor.

(7) Anterus, Clement, Damasus, Gregory, Hyginus, Marinus, Paschal, Pontian, Romanus, Sergius, Soterus, Stephen, Zachary, Zosimus.

list continued over

(8) Agapetus, Anicetus, Benedict, Boniface, Eusebius, Formosus, Gelasius, Honorius, Innocent, John-Paul, Liberius, Nicholas, Pelagius, Siricius, Theodore, Vigilius, Vitalian.

(9) Adeodatus, Alexander, Anacletus, Dionysius, Eutychian, Evaristus, Hormisdas, Marcellus, Miltiades, Severinus, Silverius, Sissinius, Sylvester, Symmachus, Valentine.

(10) Anastasius, Sabinianus, Simplicius, Zephyrinus.

(11) Constantine, Eleutherius, Marcellinus, Telesphorus.

port *n* **1** (4) dock; (7) harbour; **2** (4) left; (8) larboard; **3** (4) gate; (6) socket, window; (7) opening; **4** (4) wine.

PORTS

(4) Acre, Aden, Bari, Cork, Hull, Kiel, Kobe, Oban, Oran, Riga, Suez, Tyre.

(5) Accra, Basra, Beira, Brest, Cadiz, Dover, Eilat, Genoa, Goole, Haifa, Jaffa, Lagos, Malmo, Osaka, Ostia, Perth, Poole, Pusan, Rabat, Sidon, Tunis, Vaasa, Yalta.

(6) Abadan, Albany, Ancona, Barrow, Belize, Bergen, Bombay, Bootle, Boston, Bremen, Calais, Canton, Danzig, Darwin, Dieppe, Dublin, Durban, Gdansk, Havana, Jarrow, Jeddah, Kuwait, London, Luanda, Lübeck, Madras, Muscat, Naples, Narvik, Odense, Odessa, Ostend, Panama, Recife, St Malo, Sydney, Tobruk, Toulon, Whitby.

(7) Aalborg, Abidjan, Ajaccio, Antwerp, Bangkok, Belfast, Bristol, Chatham, Colombo, Conakry, Corunna, Dunedin, Dunkirk, Geelong, Grimsby, Hamburg, Harwich, Karachi, Leghorn, Le Havre, Livorno, Mombasa, Newport, New York, Palermo, Piraeus, Rangoon, Roscoff, Rostock, Swansea, Tallinn, Trieste, Tripoli.

(8) Bordeaux, Boulogne, Brindisi, Brisbane, Calcutta, Cape Town, Djibouti, Haiphong, Helsinki, Holyhead, Hong Kong, Honolulu, Istanbul, Kingston, Limassol, Murmansk, Nagasaki, Newhaven, Port Said, Rosslare, Shanghai, Valencia, Valletta, Yarmouth, Yokohama.

(9) Algeciras, Archangel, Baltimore, Barcelona, Fremantle, Liverpool, Lowestoft, Newcastle, Peterhead, St Nazaire, Santander, Sheerness, Stavanger, Stockholm, Trondheim, Vancouver, Zeebrugge.

(10) Alexandria, Casablanca, Charleston, Copenhagen, Folkestone, Gothenburg, Hartlepool, Marseilles, Montevideo, Portsmouth, Sunderland, Wellington, Wollongong.

(11) Southampton, Trincomalee.

(12) Kristiansund, San Francisco, Thessaloniki.

Poseidon *Gk myth* god of the sea, brother of **Zeus** and **Hades**, husband of **Amphitrite**, Roman equivalent **Neptune**.

position I *n* **1** (4) site, spot; (5) **place**; (8) location; (9) situation; **2** (3) job; (4) duty, post, rank, role; (5) grade, level; (6) office, status; (8) function, standing; (10) occupation; **3** (4) pose; (6) stance; (7) posture; **4** (4) view; (7) **opinion**, outlook **II** *v* (3) lay, put, set; (4) rest; (5) lodge, place, plant, stand; (6) deploy, locate, settle, spread; (7) arrange, deposit, dispose, station, stretch.

potato *n* (4) mash, spud; (6) murphy, pratie; (2 words) King Edward, Maris Piper.

Potter *lit.* **Beatrix Potter**

TALES & BOOKS BY BEATRIX POTTER

A Fierce Bad Rabbit, Appley Dapply's Nursery Rhymes, Benjamin Bunny, Cecily Parsley's Nursery Rhymes, Ginger and Pickles, Jemima Puddle-Duck, Johnny Town-Mouse, Little Pig Robinson, Miss Moppet, Mr Jeremy Fisher, Mrs Tiggy-Winkle, Mrs Tittlemouse, Mr Tod, Peter Rabbit, Pigling Bland, Samuel Whiskers, Squirrel Nutkin, The Flopsy Bunnies, The Pie and the Patty Pan, The Tailor of Gloucester, Timmy Tiptoes, Tom Kitten, Two Bad Mice.

Other characters

Cats – Mitten, Moppet, Simpkin, Tabitha Twitchet, *Farmer* – Mr McGregor, *Owl* – Old Brown, *Rabbits* – Benjamin Bunny, Cottontail, Flopsy, Mopsy, Peter.

pound I *n* **1** (4) coin, quid; (9) sovereign; **2** (3) pen; (4) yard; (6) corral; (9) enclosure; **II** *v* **1** (4) bang, beat, drum, thud; (5) pulse, throb, thump; (6) batter, hammer, strike; **2** (4) mash; (5) crush, grind; (6) powder; (9) pulverise (*or* pulverize); **III** *cryptic* letter L or letters LB.

precious *adj* **1** (4) dear, fine, rare; (6) costly; (8) valuable; (9) expensive, priceless; **2** (5) loved; (6) adored, prized; (7) beloved, darling; (9) treasured; **3** (8) affected.

precious stone *see* gem.

precise *adj* **1** (4) true, very; (5) clear, exact, right; (6) strict; (7) correct; (8) accurate, detailed, explicit, faithful, flawless, specific, unerring; (9) faultless; (10) blow-by-blow; (11) unambiguous, unequivocal; **2** (7) careful, orderly; (8) rigorous; (10) methodical, meticulous, particular, scrupulous; (11) painstaking, punctilious.

prepare I *v* **1** (4) plan; (5) adapt, equip; (6) adjust; (7) arrange; (8) organise (*or* organize); (2+ words) get ready, make ready, pave the way; **2** (4) cram, swot; (5) coach, study, train, tutor; (2 words) warm up; **3** (3) fix; (4) make; (6) devise, invent; (7) compose, concoct; (8) assemble; (9) construct; **II** *cryptic* **prepare** *or* **prepared** ANAGRAM CUE.

present I *v* **1** (4) give, hand; (5) award, grant, offer; (6) bestow, confer, donate, extend, submit, tender; (7) entrust; (2 words) hold out; **2** (4) host, show; (5) mount, stage; (6) depict; (7) compère, display, exhibit, portray; (9) introduce, represent; **II** *n* (3) tip; (4) gift; (5) grant; (7) prezzie; (8) donation, largesse, offering; (9) endowment; (11) benefaction; **III** *adj* **1** (4) here, near; (5) there; (9) attending, available; (2 words) at hand, to hand; **2** (7) current; (8) existing; (12) contemporary.

president *n*

PRESIDENTS OF THE US

(4) Bush (George *and* George W.), Ford (Gerald), Polk (James K.), Taft (William Howard).

(5) Adams (John & John Quincey), Grant (Ulysses S.), Hayes (Rutherford B.), Nixon (Richard M.), Tyler (John).

(6) Arthur (Chester A.), Carter (Jimmy), Hoover (Herbert C.), Monroe (James), Pierce (Franklin), Reagan (Ronald), Taylor (Zachary), Truman (Harry S.), Wilson (Woodrow).

(7) Clinton (Bill – William J.), Harding (Warren Gamaliel), Jackson (Andrew), Johnson (Lyndon B.), Kennedy (John F.), Lincoln (Abraham), Madison (John).

(8) Buchanan (James), Coolidge (Calvin), Fillmore (Millard), Garfield (James A.), Harrison (Benjamin), McKinley (William), Van Buren (Martin).

(9) Cleveland (Grover), Jefferson (Thomas), Roosevelt (Franklin Delano & Theodore).

(10) Eisenhower (Dwight D.), Washington (George).

previous *adj* **1** (2) ex; (3) old; (4) past; (5) prior; (6) former; (7) earlier, one-time, quondam; (8) original, sometime; (9) erstwhile, preceding; **2** (5) early; (9) premature.

priest *see* **religious**.

prime minister

PRIME MINISTERS OF GREAT BRITAIN

(4) Bute (Lord/ Earl of), Eden (Sir Anthony), Grey (Earl), Peel (Sir Robert), Pitt (William).

(5) Blair (Tony), Derby (Earl of), Heath (Edward), Major (John), North (Lord).

(6) Attlee (Clement), Pelham (Henry), Wilson (Harold).

(7) Asquith (Herbert Henry), Baldwin (Stanley), Balfour (Arthur), Canning (George), Chatham (Earl of), Grafton (Duke of), Russell (Lord John), Walpole (Sir Robert).

(8) Aberdeen (Earl of), Bonar Law (Andrew), Disraeli (Benjamin), Goderich (Viscount), Perceval (Spencer), Portland (Duke of), Rosebery (Earl of), Thatcher (Margaret).

(9) Addington (Henry), Callaghan (James), Churchill (Winston Spencer), Gladstone (William Ewart), Grenville (George), Liverpool (Earl of), Macdonald (James Ramsay), Macmillan (Harold), Melbourne (Lord/Viscount), Newcastle (Duke of), Salisbury (Marquess of), Shelburne (Earl of).

(10) Devonshire (Duke of), Palmerston (Viscount), Rockingham (Marquess of), Wellington (Duke of), Wilmington (Earl of).

(11) Chamberlain (Neville), Douglas-Hume (Sir Alec), Lloyd George (David).

---

principal **I** *adj* (3) key; (4) head, main; (5) chief, first, prime; (6) ruling, senior; (7) highest, leading, primary, supreme; (8)

cardinal, dominant, foremost; (9) essential, sovereign; **II** *n* **1** (4) boss, head; (5) chief; (8) director; (2 words) head teacher; **2** leading actor.

principle *n* **1** (3) law; (4) rule; (5) axiom, canon, creed, dogma, maxim, tenet, truth; (6) dictum; (7) formula, precept; (8) doctrine, standard; (9) criterion, essential; (11) proposition; **2** (6) ethics, honour, morals, virtue; (7) decency; (8) morality; (9) integrity, rectitude.

prior **I** *adj see* **previous**; **II** *n* head of religious community.

prison *n* (4) cage, cell, gaol, jail; (6) lock-up; (12) penitentiary.

SLANG TERMS FOR PRISON

(3) can, jug, pen; (4) brig, nick, quod, stir; (5) clink; (6) chokey, cooler, inside; (7) jankers, slammer; (8) porridge; (10) glasshouse.

FAMOUS PRISONS

Alcatraz (US), Barlinnie (UK), Bastille (The, Fr.), Bridewell (UK), Brixton (UK), Broadmoor (UK), Dartmoor (UK), Devil's Island (Fr.), Durham (UK), Fleet (The, UK), Holloway (UK), Marshalsea (UK), Maze (The, UK), Newgate (UK), Parkhurst (UK), Pentonville (UK), Scrubs (The, UK), Sing Sing (US), Strangeways (UK), Winchester (UK), Wormwood Scrubs (UK).

---

private **I** *adj* **1** (3) own; (7) special; (8) personal, separate; (9) exclusive; (10) individual; **2** (6) secret; (8) hush-hush; (10) classified, restricted; (12) confidential; **3** (5) quiet; (6) hidden; (7) retired; (8) isolated, secluded, solitary; **II** *n* (2) GI; (5) tommy; (6) ranker; (7) soldier.

process **I** *n* **1** (4) step; (5) stage; (6) method, system; (9) operation, procedure, technique, treatment; **2** (6) **course**, growth; (9) evolution; (11) development; **II** *v* (5) alter, treat; (6) refine; (7) prepare; (9) transform; **III** *cryptic* **process** *or* **processed** ANAGRAM CUE.

produce I *v* **1** (4) make; (5) cause; (6) prompt, supply; (7) furnish, provide, provoke, secrete; (8) generate, occasion; (9) construct, fabricate; (11) manufacture; **2** (4) show; (5) mount, offer, stage; (7) exhibit, present; (2 words) bring forth, bring out, put on, put forth; II *n* (4) crop; (5) fruit, yield; (6) output; (7) harvest, **product**; (10) vegetables; III *cryptic* ANAGRAM CUE.

product I *n* **1** (5) fruit, goods, yield; (6) return; (7) spin-off; (8) artefact; (9) commodity, invention; (11) merchandise; **2** (6) **result**, upshot; (7) outcome; II *cryptic* ANAGRAM CUE.

profit I *n & v* (4) gain; (5) avail; (7) benefit; II *n* (5) yield; (6) return; (7) revenue, surplus, takings; (8) earnings, interest, proceeds, receipts, winnings; (9) advantage; (2 words) bottom line.

Prometheus *Gk myth* a **Titan** who stole fire from the gods to give to mortals and, as a punishment, was chained to a rock by the gods so that an eagle could feed off his liver.

prominent *adj* **1** (5) great; (6) famous; (7) eminent, notable; (8) elevated, renowned; (9) respected, well-known; (10) celebrated; (11) illustrious, outstanding, prestigious; (13) distinguished; **2** (6) raised; (7) jutting; (10) projecting, protruding; (11) conspicuous, protuberant.

property *n* **1** (4) land; (5) house; (6) estate; (8) building; (2 words) real estate; **2** (5) goods, means; (6) assets, wealth; (7) effects; (8) chattels; (10) belongings; (11) possessions; **3** (4) mark; (5) trait; (7) feature, quality; (9) attribute; (11) peculiarity; (12) idiosyncrasy; (14) characteristic.

prophecy *n* (6) augury; (8) forecast; (9) prognosis; (10) divination, prediction.

prophesy *v* (5) augur; (7) foresee, predict; (8) forecast, foretell.

prophet *n* (4) seer; (5) augur; (6) oracle; (10) soothsayer; (11) clairvoyant.

OLD TESTAMENT PROPHETS

(4) Amos, Ezra, Joel.

(5) Jonah, Micah, Hosea, Nahum.

(6) Daniel, Elijah, Elisha, Haggai, Isaiah, Joseph, Samuel.

(7) Ezekiel, Malachi, Obadiah.

(8) Habakkuk, Jeremiah.

(9) Zechariah, Zephaniah.

Proserpina *or* **Proserpine** *Rom. myth* equivalent of **Persephone**.

protest I *v* (5) argue; (6) object; (7) complain; (8) disagree; (10) disapprove; (11) demonstrate; II *n* (5) march; (6) outcry; (7) dissent; (9) complaint, objection; (10) opposition; (11) disapproval.

proud *adj* **1** (4) smug, vain; (5) cocky; (6) snooty; (7) haughty, stuck-up; (8) arrogant, boastful, snobbish; (9) big-headed, conceited; (11) egotistical, overbearing, toffee-nosed; (12) supercilious; **2** (4) glad; (7) pleased; (8) honoured; (9) delighted, gratified; **3** (5) grand, noble; (8) glorious, **splendid**; **4** (6) raised; (9) **prominent**.

proverb *n* (3) saw; (5) adage, maxim; (6) byword, dictum, saying; (7) precept; (8) aphorism.

provide I *v* **1** (3) add; (4) give, lend; (5) bring, cater, equip, grant, stock, yield; (6) afford, extend, outfit, supply; (7) furnish, present; (10) contribute; **2** (5) state; (7) require, specify; (9) stipulate; II **provide for 1** (4) keep; (7) support; (8) maintain; **2** (2+ words) allow for, prepare for, take precautions against.

province *n* **1** (4) area, zone; (5) region, sector; (8) district, division; **2** (4) line; (5) forte, realm; (6) branch, domain, sphere; (7) concern, section; (10) department, speciality; (14) responsibility.

PROVINCES OF CANADA

Alberta (AL), British Columbia (BC), Manitoba (MAN), New Brunswick (NB), Newfoundland (NF), North West Territories (NWT), Nova Scotia (NS), Ontario (ONT), Prince Edward Island (PEI), Quebec (Q), Saskatchewan (SAS), The Yukon (YUK).

prudent *adj* (4) wise; (5) sound; (7) careful; (8) cautious, sensible; (9) judicious; (10) reasonable, well-judged; (11) well-advised.

public I *adj* **1** (5) civic; (6) common; (7) general; (8) national; (9) universal; (10) collective; **2** (4) open; (5) known, overt; (9) published; (10) recognised (*or* recognized); (12) unrestricted; **II** *n* **1** (6) masses, nation, people; (7) country, society; (8) citizens; (9) citizenry; (9) community; (10) population; **2** (4) fans; (7) patrons; (8) audience.

PUBLIC SCHOOLS

(4) Eton; (5) Rugby, Stowe; (6) Harrow, Oakham, Oundle, Radley, Repton; (7) Alleyn's, Bedales, Clifton, Dulwich, Lancing, Malvern; (8) Ardingly, Bluecoat, Downside, Gresham's, Oswestry; (9) Blundell's, Cranleigh, Millfield, Sherborne, Tonbridge, Uppingham; (10) Ampleforth, Haileybury, Shrewsbury, Stonyhurst, Winchester; (11) Gordonstoun, Marlborough, Westminster; (12) Charterhouse, Haberdashers'.

pull I *n & v* (3) tow, tug; (4) drag, draw, haul, jerk, lure, yank; **II** *v* (5) tempt; (6) allure, entice; (7) attract, extract.

punctuation *n*

PUNCTUATION MARKS

(4) dash, star, stop; (5) colon, comma; (6) hyphen; (7) bracket; (8) brackets; (9) semicolon; (11) parentheses, parenthesis; (2 words) full stop, exclamation mark, inverted comma, question mark, quotation mark.

put *v* (3) fit, fix, lay, set; (4) rest; (5) lodge, place, plant, plonk, stand; (6) deploy, locate, settle, spread; (7) arrange, deposit, dispose, station, stretch; (8) position.

puzzle I *v* **1** (3) fox; (5) floor, stump; (6) baffle; (7) confuse, flummox, mystify, nonplus, perplex; (8) bewilder, confound; **2** (5) **think**; (6) ponder; (8) consider; **II** *n* (5) poser; (6) enigma; (7) mystery, paradox; (8) question; (9) conundrum, crossword; (11) brainteaser.

Pygmalion *Gk myth* a king of Cyprus who sculpted an ivory statue of his ideal woman and fell in love with his own handiwork. Aphrodite granted his prayer and the statue was brought to life as Galatea.

Pythias *Gk myth see* **Damon and Pythias**.

Q

Q *abbrev* Quebec, queen, question.

quail I *v* (5) cower, shake; (6) blench, cringe, falter, flinch, recoil, shrink; (7) shudder; (2 words) shy away; II *n* type of bird.

quaint *adj* (3) odd, old; (4) cute, twee; (7) bizarre, curious, strange; (8) charming, fanciful, old-world; (9) whimsical; (10) antiquated, olde-worlde.

quake *v* (4) rock, sway; (5) heave, shake; (6) shiver, wobble; (7) shudder, tremble, vibrate; (8) convulse.

qualification *n* 1 (2) BA, MA; (3) BSc, MSc; (4) GCSE, GNVQ; (6) A-level, O-level; (7) diploma; (11) certificate; 2 (5) **skill**; (7) ability; (8) training; (10) competence; 3 (5) rider; (6) caveat; (7) proviso; (9) condition, exception, provision; (10) limitation; (11) restriction, stipulation; (12) modification.

qualify *v* 1 (4) pass (8) graduate; 2 (3) fit; (5) equip; (6) permit; (7) empower, entitle; (9) authorise (*or* authorize); 3 (5) limit; (6) lessen, reduce, modify, soften, temper; (8) mitigate, moderate, restrain, restrict.

quality *n* 1 (4) rank; (5) class, grade, merit, value; (6) degree, status; (7) calibre; (8) standard; (10) excellence; (11) , pre-eminence, superiority; 2 (5) trait; (6) aspect; (7) feature; (8) property; (9) attribute; (14) characteristic.

quarrel I *n & v* (3) row; (4) feud, spat, tiff; (5) brawl, clash, fight, scrap; (7) dispute, quibble, wrangle; (8) conflict, squabble; II *n* (4) rift, tiff; (6) breach, schism; (7) discord, rupture; (8) argument, vendetta; (9) complaint, grievance; (10) difference, dissension; (11) controversy; (12) disagreement; (16) misunderstanding; III *v* 1 (5) argue; (6) bicker; (7) contend; (8) disagree; 2 (5) fault; (6) criticise (*or* criticize); (2+ words) find fault with; IV *cryptic* ANAGRAM CUE.

quarry I *n* 1 (4) goal, kill, prey; (5) prize; (6) object, target, victim; 2 (4) mine; (8) diggings; (10) excavation; II *v* (3) dig; (4) mine; (8) excavate.

quarter I *n* 1 (4) coin; (6) fourth; (7) measure; (8) fraction; 2 (4) area, side, part, zone; (6) region; (8) district; (9) direction; (13) neighbourhood; 3 **quarters** (4) digs; (5) rooms; (6) billet; (7) lodging; (8) barracks, dwelling, lodgings; (9) residence; (13) accommodation; 4 (5) mercy; II *v* (5) house, lodge; (6) billet; (11) accommodate; (2 words) put up; III *cryptic* 1 letter N, E, S, W or any letters indicating a compass direction; 2 a single letter from a four-letter word, so that 'quarter of an hour' might = H, O U, or R.

quarter day *n* 1 in England, Wales and Ireland: Lady Day (Mar. 25), Midsummer's Day (June 24), Michaelmas Day (Sept. 29), Christmas Day (Dec. 25); 2 in Scotland: Candlemas (Feb. 2), Whitsun (May 15), Lammas Day (Aug. 1), Martinmas Day (Nov. 11).

quash *v* 1 (4) void; (5) annul; (6) cancel, revoke; (7) nullify, rescind, reverse; (8) overrule; (10) invalidate; 2 (5) crush, quell; (6) defeat, subdue; (8) suppress; (9) overthrow.

quay *n* (4) dock, mole, pier; (5) berth, jetty, wharf; (7) harbour.

queen *n* (5) **ruler**; (7) consort, empress, monarch.

SOME FAMOUS QUEENS

Biblical: Candace, Hephzibah, Jezebel, Michal, Vasht.

Egyptian: Cleopatra, Nefertiti.

English, British: Alexandra, Anne, Bess (Elizabeth I), Boadicea (Boudicca), Catherine, Charlotte, Eleanor, Elizabeth, Jane (Grey, Seymour), Mary, Matilda, Victoria.

French: Marie Antoinette.

---

queer *adj* 1 (3) odd; (5) dotty, fluky, funny, weird; (7) bizarre, erratic, offbeat, strange, unusual; (8) aberrant, abnormal, atypical, freakish, peculiar; (9) eccentric; (10) fortuitous, outlandish, unexpected; (11) exceptional; (13) idiosyncratic; (14) unconventional; 2 (4) sick; (5) dizzy, giddy; (6) queasy, unwell; 3 (3) gay; (10) homosexual.

quell *v* 1 (5) crush, quash; (6) defeat, squash, subdue; (7) conquer; (8) overcome, suppress; (9) overthrow; 2 (4) calm, hush; (5) allay, quiet; (6) pacify, soothe, stifle; (8) mitigate, moderate; (9) alleviate; (10) extinguish.

question l *n & v* (5) doubt, query; (6) debate; (7) dispute; ll *n* 1 (7) enquiry (*or* inquiry); 2 (5) issue, point, topic; (6) matter; (7) subject; 3 (7) dilemma, problem; (10) difficulty; (11) controversy, uncertainty; lll *v* (3) ask; (4) pump, quiz; (5) grill, probe; (7) debrief, enquire (*or* inquire), examine; (9) interview; (11) interrogate; (12) cross-examine.

questionable *adj* 1 (4) iffy; (5) fishy, shady; (7) dubious, suspect; (8) doubtful; (10) suspicious; 2 (4) moot; (8) arguable, unproven; (9) debatable, uncertain; (13) controversial.

queue *n* (4) file, line; (5) train; (6) series, string; (8) sequence, tailback; (9) crocodile; (10) procession, succession.

quick *adj* 1 (4) deft, fast; (5) brief, brisk, fleet, hasty, nippy, rapid, swift; (6) flying, nimble, prompt, speedy, sudden; (7) cursory, hurried, instant; (8) fleeting; (9) immediate, sprightly; (13) instantaneous; 2 (4) keen; (5) alert, smart, sharp; (6) astute, shrewd; (10) perceptive, responsive; (11) intelligent; 3 *old* (5) alive.

quiet l *adj* 1 (3) low; (4) soft; (5) muted, still; (6) gentle, hushed, silent; (7) muffled, subdued; (9) inaudible, noiseless; 2 (4) calm; (6) placid, serene; (8) composed, peaceful, tranquil; (10) untroubled; (11) undisturbed; 3 (3) shy; (8) reserved, reticent, retiring, taciturn; (13) unforthcoming; (15) uncommunicative; ll *n* (4) calm, hush, rest; (5) peace; (6) repose; (7) silence; (8) serenity; (12) tranquillity; lll *v* *see* **quieten**; lV *cryptic* letters P (piano), PP, or SH.

quieten *v* 1 (4) dull, hush, mute; (5) lower; (6) deaden, muffle, soften, stifle; (7) silence; (8) diminish; 2 (4) calm; (5) still; (6) pacify, soothe, subdue; (7) compose.

quit *v* 1 (2) go; (4) exit; (5) leave; (6) decamp, depart, desert, retire; (7) abandon, forsake; (8) withdraw; (2 words) go away, move out; 2 (3) end; (4) stop; (5) cease; (6) resign, retire; (7) abandon; (8) renounce, withdraw; (9) surrender; (10) relinquish; (11) discontinue; (2 words) give up.

quite *adv* 1 (6) fairly, rather; (8) somewhat; (10) moderately, relatively; (13) comparatively; 2 (5) fully; (6) wholly; (7) totally, utterly; (8) entirely; (10) absolutely, completely.

R

R *abbrev* Rand, Réaumur, Regina (Queen), Rex (King), River, Romania (international vehicle registration).

r *abbrev* recto, right, run.

RA *abbrev* Royal Academician, Royal Academy, radium.

rabbit I *n* **1** (*male* buck, *female* doe, *group* warren) (5) bunny; (6) angora; **2** a poor or inexperienced player or performer. a duffer; **II** *n & v* (4) chat, talk, yack; (7) **chatter**.

race I *n* **1** (4) mile; (5) relay; (6) medley, sprint; (7) contest; (8) marathon, scramble; (11) competition; (12) steeplechase; (2+ words) egg and spoon race, grand prix, obstacle race, sack race; **2** (4) clan, kind, line; (5) breed, tribe; (6) nation, people; (7) descent; (8) ancestry; (9) ethnicity; (2 words) ethnic group; **II** *v* (3) fly, run; (4) dart, dash, rush, tear, zoom; (5) hurry, speed; (6) career, gallop, hasten.

racecourse *or* **racetrack** *n*

COURSES FOR HORSES

(3) Ayr.

(4) Bath, Evry (Fr.), Naas (Ire.), York.

(5) Ascot, Epsom, Perth, Ripon.

(6) Bangor, Craven (Ire.), Galway (Ire.), Laurel (US), Ludlow, Redcar, Thirsk.

(7) Aintree, Auteuil (Fr.), Cartmel, Chester, Curragh (The) (Ire.), Lincoln, Newbury, Taunton, Warwick, Windsor.

(8) Beverley, Brighton, Camptown (US), Carlisle, Chepstow, Goodwood, Hereford, Wetherby, Yarmouth.

(9) Catterick, Chantilly (Fr.), Deauville (Fr.), Doncaster, Edinburgh, Leicester,

---

Longchamp (Fr.), Newcastle, Newmarket, Stratford, Uttoxeter, Worcester.

(10) Cheltenham, Folkestone, Huntingdon, Nottingham, Pontefract.

(2 words) Churchill Downs (US), Haydock Park, Kempton Park, Market Rasen, Newton Abbot, Sandown Park.

MOTOR-RACING CIRCUITS

(3) Pau (Fr.), Rio (Braz.), Spa (Belg.).

(5) Imola (It.), Monza (It.).

(6) Le Mans (Fr.), Monaco.

(7) Daytona (US), Detroit (US), Kyalami (SA).

(8) Adelaide (Aus.), Goodwood, Montreal (Can.), Thruxton.

(9) Montlhéry (Fr.), Zandvoort (NL).

(10) Brooklands, Hockenheim (Ger.).

(11) Brand's Hatch, Castle Combe, Nurburgring (Ger.), Silverstone.

(12) Indianapolis (US).

---

racket *n* **1** (3) bat; **2** (3) din, row; (4) fuss; (5) noise; (6) hubbub, uproar; (7) clamour; (9) commotion; (11) pandemonium; **3** (3) con; (4) scam; (5) dodge, fraud, trick; (6) fiddle, scheme; (7) swindle.

radical I *adj* (5) basic, total; (8) complete, sweeping, thorough; (11) far-reaching, fundamental; (13) comprehensive, thoroughgoing; **II** *adj & n* (3) red; (7) leftist; (8) militant; (9) extremist, reformist; (13) revolutionary.

radium *cryptic* abbreviated as RA.

rage I *n* **1** (3) ire; (4) fury; (5) anger, paddy, wrath; (6) frenzy, temper; (7) passion, tantrum; (8) ferocity, violence; **2** (3) fad; (5) craze, thing, vogue; (7)

fashion; **ll** *v* (4) fume, rant, rave; (5) storm; (6) seethe; (7) explode, rampage.

raid **l** *n & v* (4) bust; (5) blitz; (6) attack **ll** *n* (5) foray, onset, swoop; (6) hold-up, inroad, sortie; (7) break-in, robbery; (8) invasion; (9) onslaught; **lll** *v* (4) loot; (5) storm; (6) invade; (7) pillage, plunder, ransack.

rail **l** *n* **1** *see* **railway**; **2** (3) bar, rod; (5) fence; (6) paling; (7) barrier, railing; **3** type of bird; **ll** *v* (4) rage, rant, rave; (5) abuse; (8) complain; (9) criticise (*or* criticize).

railway **l** *n* (4) line; (5) track; (2 words) iron way, permanent way; **ll** *cryptic* letters BR, RLY, or RY.

rain **l** *n & v* (4) spit; (5) storm; (6) shower; (7) drizzle; **ll** *n* (6) deluge, squall; (7) torrent; (8) downpour; (10) cloudburst; (13) precipitation; **lll** *v* (4) pelt, pour, teem; (6) bucket; **lV** *cryptic* insert letters RA into word in clue.

raise **l** *v* **1** (4) jack, lift; (5) hoist; (7) elevate; **2** (5) build, erect; (9) construct; **3** (5) boost; enhance; (7) augment, enhance; (8) escalate, heighten, increase; (9) intensify; (10) strengthen; **4** (3) get; (6) gather, muster, obtain; (7) acquire, collect, recruit; **5** (6) broach; (7) suggest; (9) introduce; **6** (4) grow, rear; (5) breed; (7) develop; (9) cultivate; **ll** *cryptic* **raise**, **raised** *etc* reverse the order of the letters of a word in a down clue, as in: 'East missing when alarm raised – must have fled in short with prizes from lottery' (6) = raffle (alarm = fear – E (east)).

range **l** *n* **1** (4) area, span; (5) ambit, field, gamut, orbit, reach, scale, scope, sweep; (6) domain, extent, sphere, spread; (7) compass; (8) distance, spectrum; **2** (4) line; (5) stock; (6) choice; (7) variety; (9) diversity, selection; (10) assortment; **3** (4) land; (7) grazing, prairie; **ll** *v* **1** (4) roam; (6) wander; (7) explore; **2** (5) reach; (6) extend, spread; (7) stretch; **3** (4) **vary**; (6) change; **4** (4) rank; (5) align, order; (6) deploy; (7) arrange; (8) classify; (9) catalogue.

rank **l** *n & v* (4) file, line, sort; (5) class, grade, group, order, range; **ll** *n* (3) row;

(4) type; (5) caste, level, title; (6) estate, status; (7) echelon, station, stratum; (8) division, position, standing; **lll** *v* (4) rate; (7) arrange, marshal; (8) classify; (10) categorise (*or* categorize).

BRITISH ARMY RANKS

Private, Lance Corporal, Corporal, Sergeant, Colour/Staff Sergeant, Warrant Officer, Second Lieutenant, Lieutenant, Captain, Major, Lieutenant Colonel, Colonel, Brigadier, Major General, Lieutenant General, General, Field Marshal.

ROYAL NAVY RANKS

Ordinary Seaman, Able Seaman, Leading Seaman, Petty Officer, Chief Petty Officer, Warrant Officer, Midshipman, Sublieutenant, Lieutenant, Lieutenant Commander, Commander, Captain, Commodore, Rear Admiral, Vice Admiral, Admiral, Admiral of the Fleet.

RAF RANKS

Aircraftman, Senior Aircraftman, Corporal, Sergeant, Chief Technician, Flight Sergeant, Warrant Officer, Pilot Officer, Flying Officer, Flight Lieutenant, Squadron Leader, Wing Commander, Group Captain, Air Commodore, Air Vice Marshal, Air Marshal, Air Chief Marshal, Marshal of the Royal Air Force.

---

rap **l** *n & v* (3) hit, tap; (4) bang, clip, cuff, slap; (5) knock, thump; **ll** *v* **1** (5) pound; (6) hammer; **2** (4) slam; (5) slate; (9) **criticise** (*or* criticize).

rare *adj* **1** (6) scarce, sparse; (7) unusual; (8) uncommon; (10) infrequent; **2** (4) fine; (6) superb; (8) precious; (9) excellent, exquisite, wonderful; (10) remarkable.

rat **l** *n* (3) cad; (4) heel, scab; (5) Judas, swine; (6) rotter; (7) traitor; (8) betrayer, blackleg, renegade, turncoat; **ll** *v* (6) betray, desert; (7) abandon; (2 words) change sides.

rate I *n* **1** (3) mph, (5) ratio, speed, tempo; (8) velocity; (9) frequency, incidence; (10) occurrence, proportion, recurrence; **2** (3) fee, tax; (4) cost, duty, hire, levy, toll; (5) price; (6) charge, tariff; (10) percentage; **3** (4) rank; (5) grade; (6) degree, rating; (8) standard; **II** *v* **1** (4) deem, rank; (5) class, grade, judge; (6) assess, esteem, regard; (8) consider, estimate, evaluate; **2** (5) value; (6) admire; (7) respect.

rating *see* **sailor**.

raw *adj* **1** (5) fresh; (7) natural; (8) uncooked; (9) unrefined, untreated; **2** (3) new; (5) green; (6) callow; (8) immature; (9) untrained; (13) inexperienced; **3** (4) cold; (5) bleak; (6) chilly, biting, bitter; (8) freezing; **4** (4) open, sore; (6) bloody, grazed, tender; (8) bleeding.

reach I *v* (4) make; (5) touch; (6) arrive, attain, extend; (7) contact, stretch; (7) achieve; (2+ words) arrive at, get to, get through to; **II** *n* (5) grasp, range, scope; (6) extent, spread; (7) command, compass; (8) distance; (12) jurisdiction.

read I *v* **1** (3) con; (4) scan, skim; (5) study; (6) peruse; **2** (5) speak; (6) recite; (7) deliver; **3** (6) decode; (8) construe, decipher; (9) interpret; (10) comprehend, understand; **4** (4) show; (7) display; (8) indicate; **II** *cryptic* **read, we read 1** read the words in the clue in a different way, usually by splitting them up differently from the way they are printed. As in: 'Notice is fluid, we read' (5) = water (not ice); **2** HIDDEN WORD CUE.

ready I *adj* **1** (3) fit, set; (4) done, ripe; (6) cooked; (7) waiting; (8) finished, prepared; (9) completed; **2** (4) near; (5) handy; (7) present; (9) available; (10) accessible, convenient; **3** (4) game, keen; (5) alert, eager, quick, sharp; (6) astute, prompt; (7) willing; (9) receptive; (10) perceptive; **II** *v* (7) arrange, prepare; (8) organise (*or* organize); (2 words) get ready, make ready, warm up.

real *adj* (4) sure, true; (5) valid; (6) actual, honest; (7) factual, genuine, sincere; (8) existing, material, physical, tangible; (9) authentic, unfeigned, veritable.

reason I *n* **1** (3) aim; (5) basis, cause; (6) excuse, ground, motive; (7) grounds, purpose, warrant; (9) incentive, intention, rationale; (13) justification; **2** (4) mind, wits; (5) brain, logic, sense; (6) wisdom; (8) judgment; (9) intellect, judgement, mentality; (11) rationality; (13) understanding; **II** *v* **1** (5) infer, think; (6) deduce; (8) conclude; **2** (4) urge; (5) argue; (6) debate; (7) discuss; (8) persuade.

reasonable *adj* **1** (4) calm, cool, sane, wise; (5) sound; (6) viable; (7) logical; (8) amenable, credible, moderate, possible, rational, sensible; (9) plausible, practical, tractable; (10) restrained; **2** (4) fair; (6) medium, modest; (7) average; (8) ordinary, mediocre; (9) tolerable; (10) acceptable; (11) inexpensive; (12) satisfactory.

recede I *v* (3) ebb; (4) sink, wane; (6) lessen, retire, return; (7) decline, dwindle, retreat, subside; (8) decrease, diminish, withdraw; **II recede, receding** *cryptic* reverse the order of the letters in a word or part of a word in the clue or in the answer, as in: 'Rearrange passage as tide receding' (4) = edit.

record I *n & v* **1** (3) log; (4) file, list, memo, note; (6) minute, report; (7) account; (8) document, register; (9) chronicle; **2** (4) tape; (5) video; (9) videotape; **II** *n* **1** (2) CD, EP, LP; (4) disc; (5) album; (6) single; (9) recording; **2** (5) diary, entry; (6) annals, memoir; (7) archive, dossier, journal; **3** (2) CV; (6) career; (10) background; **4** best performance; **III** *v* **1** (5) enter, write; (8) inscribe; **2** (4) show; (7) express; (8) indicate; **IV** *cryptic* letters EP or LP.

red I *adj & n* **1** (4) pink, ruby; (5) gules; (6) auburn, carrot, cherry, ginger, Titian; (7) crimson, scarlet; (9) vermilion; **2** (6) commie, leftie; (7) leftist, Marxist, radical; (9) Bolshevik, communist, socialist; (13) revolutionary; **II** *adj* (4) rosy, sore; (5) ruddy; (7) flushed; (8) blushing, inflamed; (9) bloodshot; (11) embarrassed.

reel I *n* **1** (4) coil; (5) spool; **2** (5) dance; **II** *v* (4) rock, roll, sway; (5) lurch, pitch, twirl, whirl; (6) gyrate, totter, wobble; (7) revolve, stagger; **III** *cryptic* ANAGRAM CUE.

refer **I** *v* **1** (4) cite; (5) quote; (6) allude; (7) mention; (2 words) bring up, touch on; **2** (7) concern; (2 words) apply to, relate to, pertain to; **3** (7) consult; (2 words) look up, resort to; **4** (4) pass, send; (8) transfer; (9) recommend; **II** *cryptic* reverse the order of a word in the clue or answer.

reference *n* **1** (6) remark; (7) comment, mention; (8) allusion, citation; (9) quotation; **2** (9) character; (11) endorsement, testimonial; (14) recommendation.

reference book *n* (3) ABC; (7) almanac; (8) handbook; (9) companion, thesaurus; (10) dictionary; (11) concordance; (13) encyclopaedia.

FAMOUS REFERENCE BOOKS

Almanach de Gotha (genealogy and statistics)
Baedeker (travel guide)
Bradshaw (railway timetables)
Britannica (encyclopaedia)
Burke's Peerage (British aristocracy)
Chambers (dictionary and encyclopaedia)
Collins (dictionary)
Crockford (register of clergy)
Debrett (British aristocracy)
Encarta (encyclopaedia on CD for computers)
Jane's (ships, *esp.* naval vessels, and aircraft)
Lloyds Register (shipping)
Nautical Almanac (nautical tables)
OED (Oxford English Dictionary)
Old Moore's Almanac (annual statistics and predictions)
Roget (thesaurus)
Stud Book (racehorses)
Whitaker's Almanack (general information and statistics)
Who's Who (famous people)
Wisden (cricket).

---

reflect **I** *v* **1** (4) echo, show; (6) mirror, reveal; (7) display, exhibit, express, imitate; (8) indicate; (9) reproduce; (11)

demonstrate; **2** (4) mull, muse; (5) think; (6) ponder; (8) consider; (10) deliberate; **II** **reflect, reflected, reflection** *etc* reverse the order of the letters in a word in the clue, as in: 'Melancholy reflection on the German headland' (7) = sadness (the German = das).

reform **I** *v* (4) cure, mend; (5) amend, purge; (6) better, change, repair; (7) correct, improve, rebuild, rectify, remodel, restore; (10) ameliorate, regenerate, reorganise (*or* reorganize); (12) rehabilitate; (13) revolutionise (*or* revolutionize); **II** *n* (6) change; (7) shake-up; (9) amendment; (11) improvement; (14) rehabilitation; **III** **reform, reformed, reformation** *etc* *cryptic* ANAGRAM CUE.

refrain **I** *v* (4) stop; (5) avoid, cease; (6) desist, forego; (7) abstain; (8) renounce; **II** *n* (6) burden, chorus, repeat.

refuse **I** *v* (4) deny, shun; (5) spurn; (6) rebuff, reject; (7) decline; (8) withhold; (2 words) turn down; **II** *n* (4) junk; (5) trash; (6) litter; (7) garbage, rubbish.

regal *adj see* **royal**.

regard **I** *v* **1** (4) deem, rate, view; (5) class, judge, think; (6) esteem; (7) believe, imagine, suppose; (8) consider, estimate, evaluate; **2** (6) relate; (7) concern, involve; **II** *n* **1** (4) care, heed; (6) notice; (7) concern; (9) attention; (13) consideration; **2** (6) esteem; (7) respect; (9) deference; (10) admiration; **3** (4) gaze, look.

region *n* (4) area, zone; (5) field, realm; (6) domain, sector, sphere; (7) country, terrain; (8) district, province; *see also* **county**.

REGIONS OF SCOTLAND

Border, Central, Dumfries and Galloway, Fife, Grampian, Highland, Lothian, Orkney, Shetland, Strathclyde, Tayside, Western Isles.

---

register **I** *n & v* (3) log; (4) file, list, memo, note; (6) minute, record; (8) document; (9) catalogue, chronicle; **II** *n* (5) index; (6) ledger; (8) schedule; **III** *v* **1**

(5) enrol; (6) enlist; (2 words) check in, sign on, sign up; **2** (4) show; (6) betray, reveal; (7) display, exhibit, express; (8) indicate, manifest.

regret I *n* (5) grief, shame; (6) sorrow; (7) remorse; (10) contrition, repentance; II *v* (3) rue; (5) mourn; (6) grieve, lament, repent; (7) deplore.

Rehoboam I *Bible* son of **Solomon** and his successor as king of Israel, a harsh ruler; II *n see* **bottle**.

reject I *n* **1** (4) deny, veto; (5) spurn; (6) rebuff, refuse; (7) decline, despise, exclude; **2** (5) scrap; (7) discard; (8) jettison; II *n* (6) second; (7) cast-off, discard, failure; III *cryptic* omit a letter, letters or word, as in: 'Stone rejected from the scheme but rocks retained' (6) = strata (scheme = stratagem) .

relation I *n* **1** (3) tie; (4) bond, link; (5) ratio; (8) parallel; (10) connection, proportion, similarity; (11) affiliation, correlation; (12) relationship; (14) correspondence; **2** (7) kinship, kinsman; (8) relative; (9) kinswoman; **3** (4) tale; (5) story; (7) account, recital, telling; (9) narration, narrative; II **relations 1** (3) kin; (4) kith; (6) family; **2** (3) sex; (5) terms; (6) affair; (7) contact, liaison, rapport, romance; (8) dealings, intimacy; (10) friendship; (11) interaction, intercourse; (14) communications.

ONE'S FAMILY RELATIONS

(3) son; (4) aunt, wife; (5) in-law, uncle; (6) cousin, father, mother, sister; (7) brother, husband, sibling; (8) daughter, grandson; (11) grandfather, grandmother; (13) granddaughter.

---

relationship *n* **1** *see* **relation** I **1**; **2** *see* **relation** II **2**.

relative I *adj* **1** (10) respective; (11) comparative; (12) proportional; (13) proportionate; **2** *see* **relevant**; II *n see* **relation** TABLE.

relevant *adj* (3) apt; (6) proper; (7) fitting, germane, related; (8) apposite, material, suitable; (9) pertinent; (10) admissible, applicable; (11) appropriate, significant.

religion *n* (5) faith, piety; (7) worship; (12) denomination.

RELIGIONS

(3) Zen; (5) Islam; (6) Taoism, Voodoo; (7) Baha'ism, Jainism, Judaism, Lamaism, Sikhism; (8) Buddhism, Druidism, Hinduism; (9) Calvinism, Methodism, Mormonism, Quakerism, Shintoism; (11) Anglicanism, Catholicism, Lutheranism; (12) Christianity, Confucianism; (13) Protestantism; (14) Evangelicalism, Zoroastrianism; (15) Presbyterianism; (17) Congregationalism.

---

religious *adj* **1** (4) holy; (6) divine, sacred; (9) spiritual; (10) devotional, scriptural; **2** (2) pi; (5) godly, pious; (6) devout; (8) reverent; **3** (7) careful; (9) attentive; (10) meticulous; (11) painstaking; (13) conscientious; *see also* **clergy**.

remedy I *v* (3) fix; (4) cure, ease, heal, help, mend; (5) solve, treat; (6) repair; (7) correct, rectify, redress, relieve; (10) counteract; II *n* (4) cure; (6) answer; (7) panacea, therapy; (8) antidote, medicine, solution; (9) treatment; (10) corrective; (14) countermeasure; III *cryptic* ANAGRAM CUE.

remove I *v* **1** (4) move; (5) carry, shift; 6 convey; (8) relocate, transfer; (9) transport; **2** (4) doff, shed; (5) strip; (6) detach; (7) extract; (8) abstract, amputate, subtract; (2 words) take away, take off; **3** (4) oust; (5) eject, erase, purge; (6) delete, efface; (7) abolish, discard, dismiss, expunge; (9) discharge, eliminate; (2+ words) get rid of, strike out, throw out; II *cryptic* omit the letter, letters or word referred to, as in: 'Remove member from camper and reorganise with caution' (4) = care (member = MP).

Remus *Rom. myth see* **Romulus and Remus**.

reorder *cryptic* ANAGRAM CUE.

repair I *n & v* (4) darn, mend, weld; (5) patch; (7) service; (8) overhaul; II *v* I (5) amend, renew; (7) inspect, rectify, redress, restore; (8) renovate; (11) recondition; (2 words) make good, patch up; **2** (2) go; (6) retire; (7) proceed; (2+ words) make one's way; III *cryptic* ANAGRAM CUE.

repeat I *v & n* (4) echo; (5) rerun; (6) rehash, replay; II *v* (4) redo; (6) parrot, reshow, retell; (7) restate; (9) duplicate, reiterate, reproduce; (12) recapitulate; III *n* (3) bis; (6) encore; (10) repetition; IV **repeat, repeated, repeatedly** *cryptic* use an element in the clue or answer twice as in: ' Confess repeatedly in US prison' (4, 4) = Sing Sing.

repel I *v* I (5) check, parry; (6) rebuff, refuse, reject, resist; (7) repulse; (2 words) drive back, ward off; **2** (6) revolt, sicken; (7) disgust; (8) nauseate; II **repel, repelled, repellent** *cryptic* reverse the order of the letters in a word in the clue or answer.

repellent I *adj see* **repulsive**; II *cryptic see* **repel**.

report I *n* I (5) story; (6) gossip, rumour; (7) account, article, hearsay, message; (8) relation; (9) narrative, statement; (10) communiqué; (11) description; (12) announcement; (13) communication; **2** (4) bang, shot; (5) crack; (9) explosion; II *v* (3) say; (4) tell; (5) relay; (6) relate; (7) declare, publish; (8) announce, describe, proclaim; (11) communicate.

reptile *n see also* **dinosaur, lizard, snake**.

REPTILES

(5) gecko, skink, snake; (6) lizard, turtle; (7) monitor; (8) dinosaur, terrapin, tortoise; (9) alligator, crocodile.

Republican *n* I *cryptic* abbreviated as Rep.; II the symbol of the US Republican Party is a donkey.

repulsive *adj* (3) bad; (4) foul, mean, ugly, vile; (5) dirty, nasty; (6) filthy, odious; (7) obscene, vicious; (8) horrible; (9) loathsome, obnoxious, offensive,

repellent, repugnant, revolting; (10) abominable, disgusting, nauseating, unpleasant; (12) disagreeable; (13) objectionable;

reputation *n* (4) fame, name, note; (6) esteem, honour, renown, repute; (7) stature; (8) standing; (9) celebrity, character, notoriety; (11) distinction.

require *v* I (4) lack, want; (5) crave; (6) demand, desire; **2** (4) make; (5) force; (6) coerce, compel; (7) require; (9) constrain; (11) necessitate.

resolve I *v* (5) solve; (7) answer, decide, settle; (7) analyse; (8) conclude; (9) determine; (2 words) sort out, work out; II *n* (4) grit, guts; (8) tenacity; (9) willpower; (10) commitment, dedication, resolution; (11) persistence; (13) determination; III *cryptic* ANAGRAM CUE.

rest I *n & v* (3) nap; (4) doze, halt, stop; (5) break, sleep; (6) repose, snooze; II *n* I (4) lees; (5) dregs; (6) others; (7) balance, residue; (9) remainder; **2** (7) leisure; (10) relaxation; **3** (4) lull; (5) space, spell; (6) recess, siesta; (7) holiday, respite; (8) breather, interval, vacation; (9) entr'acte, interlude; (12) intermission, interruption; **4** (4) base, prop; (5) stand; (7) support; II *v* I (4) laze; (5) relax; (6) lounge; (7) recline; **2** (4) lean; (5) stand.

restrict *v* (4) curb; (5) bound, check, limit; (6) define, hinder, ration, reduce; (7) confine, control, delimit; (8) restrain; (9) demarcate.

result I *n* (5) fruit, issue; (6) effect, sequel, upshot; (7) outcome, product; (8) reaction; (10) end-product; (11) consequence; (12) repercussion; II *v* (4) flow, stem; (5) arise, ensue; (6) derive, emerge, follow, spring; (7) develop, proceed.

retire I *v* (5) leave; (6) depart, recede; (7) retreat, scratch; (8) withdraw; (2 words) go to bed; II **retire, retired, retiring** *cryptic* reverse the order of the letters of a word in the clue or answer, as in: 'NUS old boy retiring to take job on board' (5) = bosun (old boy = OB).

retort I *n & v* (4) quip; (5) reply; (6) answer; (7) counter, riposte; II *n* (8) response; (9) rejoinder; III *cryptic* reverse order of letters, *see* **retire, return**.

retreat I *v* (4) back; (6) **retire**; (8) withdraw; II *cryptic* reverse the order of the letters in a word or words in the clue or answer, as in: 'The French advance guard retreating was a thing to gaze at' (5) = navel (advance guard = van).

return I *v* 1 (6) revert; (7) regress; (8) reappear; (9) backtrack; (2 words) come back, go back; 2 (5) repay; (6) refund; (7) deliver, replace, requite, restore; (9) redeliver, reimburse; (10) recompense; (2 words) give back, hand back, pay back, put back; II *n* 1 (8) comeback; (9) reversion; (10) homecoming, recurrence; (12) reappearance; 2 (9) refunding, repayment; (11) replacement, restoration; 3 (5) yield; (6) profit; (7) revenue, takings; (8) earnings, interest, proceeds, receipts, winnings; III *cryptic* reverse the order of the letters in a word in the clue to make all or part of the answer, as in: 'Obtain the gold by first returning firearm' (6) = nugget *or*: 'Wanderer returns as ancient Greek's best and truest friend' (5) = Damon.

reveal I *v* (4) leak, show, tell; (6) betray, expose, unmask, unveil; (7) display, divulge, publish, uncover; (8) announce, disclose, discover; II *cryptic* HIDDEN WORD CUE.

reverse I *v* 1 (4) back; (7) retreat; (9) backtrack; 2 (5) alter, upset; (6) change, invert; (7) reorder; (9) transpose; 3 (5) quash; (6) cancel, reject, repeal, revoke; (7) rescind, retract; (8) override, overrule, overturn; (9) overthrow; (10) invalidate; (11) countermand; II *n* 1 (4) back, rear; (7) inverse; (8) contrary, converse, opposite; (10) antithesis; 2 (5) U-turn; (8) reversal; (9) turnabout; (10) turnaround; 3 (4) blow; (5) check, delay; (6) defeat, mishap; (7) failure, problem, setback; (9) adversity; (10) misfortune; III **reverse, reversal, reversing** *etc cryptic* reverse the order of the letters in a word in the clue to make all or part of the answer, as in: 'Vehicle reversed into motorist's best friend' (3) = RAC.

revise I *v* 1 (4) edit; (5) alter, amend; (6) change, modify, recast, review, revamp, reword, update; (7) correct; (10) reconsider; 2 (4) cram, swot; (5) learn, study; II **revise, revision** *etc cryptic* ANAGRAM CUE.

revolutionary I *adj & n* (3) red; (5) rebel; (7) leftist; (8) militant; (9) anarchist, insurgent, reformist; II *adj* (3) new; (5) novel; (7) drastic, radical; (10) avant-garde, innovative; III *cryptic* reverse the order of the letters in a word in the clue or answer, as in: 'Pistol carried by revolutionary Marxist lookalike?' (9) = derringer (Marxist = red).

rewrite I *see* **revise**; II *cryptic* 1 ANAGRAM CUE; 2 reverse order of letters.

rich *adj* 1 (5) flush; (6) loaded; (7) moneyed, opulent, rolling, wealthy, well-off; (8) affluent, well-to-do; (10) prosperous, well-heeled; 2 (6) costly, lavish, ornate; (8) gorgeous, precious, splendid, valuable; 3 (4) full (of), high (in), lush; (5) ample; (7) copious, fertile, profuse; (8) abundant, fruitful, prolific; (9) plentiful; (10) productive; 4 (5) fatty, heavy, juicy, spicy; (6) creamy; (10) full-bodied; 5 (4) deep, warm; (5) vivid; (6) bright, mellow; (7) intense, vibrant; (8) sonorous.

ridicule I *n* (5) chaff, irony, scorn; (6) banter, satire; (7) mockery, teasing; (8) derision, laughter; II *v* (3) rag, rib; (4) mock; (5) chaff, scorn; (6) deride, parody; (7) lampoon; (8) satirise (*or* satirize); (9) burlesque; (10) caricature.

ridiculous *adj* (5) funny, silly; (6) absurd, stupid; (7) comical, foolish; (8) derisory, farcical; (9) hilarious, laughable, ludicrous; (10) outrageous; (11) nonsensical; (12) preposterous.

rift *n* (6) breach; (7) discord, dispute; (8) argument, conflict; (10) difference; (12) disagreement.

right I *adj* 1 (4) real, true; (5) exact; (7) correct, precise; (8) accurate; 2 (3) fit; (4) fair, good, just; (5) moral; (6) honest, lawful, proper, seemly; (7) ethical, fitting; (8) becoming, suitable; (9) desirable, equitable; (10) honourable; (11) appropriate; **ll** *n* **1** (3) due; (5) claim, power; (9) authority, privilege; (11) prerogative; **2** (6) equity, honour; (7) justice; (8) fairness, legality, morality; **lll** *cryptic* letter R or letters RT.

right away I *adv* (3) now; (8) promptly; (9) forthwith, instantly; (11) immediately; (2+ words) at once, on the spot, without delay; **ll** *cryptic* omit letters R or RT from a word in the clue or the answer: 'Say thank you to the sailor right away' (2) = ta, *or*: 'Wakes up and changes trousers right away' (6) = rouses.

ring I *n & v* **1** (4) peal, toll; (5) chime, clang, clink; (6) jingle, tinkle; **2** (4) buzz, call; (5) phone; (9) telephone; **ll ring, rings, ringed** *cryptic* **1** insert letter O (or **rings** letters OO) to obtain the answer; **2** *also* **ringing** place the letters of one word around those of another, as in: 'Sunburnt Ted is ringing his girl' (6) = tanned.

rise I *v* (4) grow, soar; (5) climb, mount; (6) ascend, spiral; (8) escalate, increase; (9) intensify; **ll** *n* **1** (6) upturn; (7) upsurge; (8) progress; (9) increment; **2** (4) hill; (5) slope; (6) ascent; (7) incline; **lll** *cryptic* reverse the order of the letters of a word in a down clue, *see* **raise**.

river *n* (4) beck, burn; (5) brook, creek, flood; (6) stream; (7) rivulet; (8) waterway; (9) tributary; (11) watercourse.

RIVERS

(2) Aa (Fr.), Ii (Fin.), Ob (Russ.), Po (It.).

(3) Aar (Switz.), Ain (Fr.), Aln (UK), Axe (UK), Ayr (UK), Bug (Ukr., Pol.), Cam (UK), Dee (UK), Don (Russ., UK), Ems (Ger.), Esk (UK), Exe (UK), Fal (UK), Hay (Aus., Can.), Ili (Russ.), Inn (Ger.), Lea (UK), Lee (UK, Ire.), Lek (NL), Lot (Fr.), Lyn (UK), Mur (A.), Moy (Ire.), Nar (UK), Oka (Russ.), Red (US), Rib (UK), Roe (UK), Rye (UK), Taf (UK), Taw (UK), Tay

(UK), Ure (UK), Usk (UK), Var (Fr.), Wey (UK), Wye (UK), Yeo (UK).

(4) Adda (It.), Adur (UK), Aire (UK), Amur (Russ.), Arno (It.), Arun (UK), Aube (Fr.), Aude (Fr.), Avon (UK), Back (Can.), Bann (Ire.), Bush (UK), Char (UK), Cher (Fr.), Chew (UK), Coln (UK), Cree (UK), Dart (UK), Doon (UK), Dove (UK), Earn (UK), Ebro (Sp.), Eden (UK), Elbe (Ger.), Eure (Fr.), Gila (US), Glen (UK), Hull (UK), Isar (Ger.), Isis (Thames, UK), Juba (Somalia), Lune (UK), Maas (NL), Main (Ger.), Meon (UK), Mole (UK), Nene (UK), Nidd (UK), Nile (Afr.), Oder (Pol.), Ohio (US), Oise (Fr.), Orne (Fr.), Ouse (UK), Oxus (Asia), Peel (Aus, US), Plym (UK), Ruhr (Ger.), Saar (Ger.), Spey (UK), Swan (Aus.), Tavy (UK), Tawe (UK), Tees (UK), Test (UK), Tyne (UK), Ural (Russ.), Vaal (SA), Waal (NL), Wear (UK), Wyre (UK), Yare (UK).

(5) Adige (It.), Adour (Fr.), Aeron (UK), Aisne (Fr.), Allan (UK), Aller (Ger., Sp.), Annan (UK), Benue (Nig.), Bovey (UK), Boyne (Ire.), Camel (UK), Clare (Ire.), Clwyd (UK), Clyde (UK), Colne (UK), Congo (Afr.), Conwy (UK), Deben (UK), Dnepr (Russ.), Doubs (Fr.), Douro (Port.), Dovey (UK), Dvina (Russ.), Ellen (UK), Fleet (UK), Forth (UK), Fowey (UK), Frome (Aus., UK), Garry (UK), Indus (Ind., Pak.), Inver (UK), Isère (Fr.), Jumna (Ind.), Jurua (Braz.), Lagan (UK), Loire (Fr.), Marne (Fr.), Meuse (Fr.), Miami (US), Minho (Sp., Port.), Mosel (Ger.), Nairn (UK), Neath (UK), Niger (Afr.), Orchy (UK), Otter (UK), Peace (Can., US), Pearl (Ch., US), Pecos (US), Plate (Arg.), Purus (Braz.), Rhine (Ger.), Rhône (Fr.), Saône (Fr.), Seine (Fr.), Snake (US), Somme (Fr.), Spree (Ger.), Stour (UK), Swale (UK),

list continued over

Tagus (Sp., Port.), Tamar (UK),
Teign (UK), Tiber (It.), Trent (UK),
Tweed (UK), Volga (Russ.), Volta
(Ghana), Weser (Ger.), Xingu
(Braz.), Yarra (Aus.), Yonne (Fr.),
Yukon (Can., US), Zaïre (Afr.).

(6) Amazon (Braz.), Angara (Russ.),
Barrow (Ire.), Bio-Bio (Chile),
Bourne (UK), Brenta (It.), Calder
(UK), Danube (Eur.), Dnestr (Ukr.),
Escaut (Fr., Belg.), Fraser (Can.),
Gambia (The Gambia), Ganges
(Ind.), Grande (Mex., US) Granta
(UK), Hudson (US), Humber (UK),
Itchen (UK), Kennet (UK), Japura
(Braz.), Jordan (Israel), Kolyma
(Russ.), Liffey (Ire.), Medway (UK),
Mekong (Vietnam), Mersey (UK),
Mohawk (US), Moldau (Cz.), Moskva
(Russ.), Murray (Aus.), Neckar (Ger.),
Neisse (Ger., Pol.), Nelson (Can.),
Orange (SA), Orwell (UK), Ottawa
(Can.), Parana (Braz.), Parrot (UK),
Pripet (Russ.), Ribble (UK), Sambre
(Fr.), Sarthe (Fr.), Severn (UK),
Swanee (US), Tanana (US), Teviot
(UK), Thames (UK), Tigris (Iraq),
Tugela (SA), Tummel (UK), Ussuri
(Ch., Russ.), Wabash (US), Weaver
(UK), Yarrow (UK), Yellow (Ch.).

(7) Alabama (US), Darling (Aus.),
Derwent (UK), Deveron (UK),
Dnieper (Russ.), Durance (Fr.),
Garonne (Fr.), Dironde (Fr.),
Huang-Ho (Ch.), Limpopo (SA,
Mozambique), Madeira (Braz.),
Meander (Turkey), Moselle (Fr.,
Ger.), Orinoco (Venezuela), Potomac
(US), Roanoke (US), Scheldt (Belg.),
Shannon (Ire.), Trinity (US),
Uruguay (Uruguay), Vistula (Pol.),
Waveney (UK), Welland (UK),
Yangtse (Ch.), Yenisei (Russ.),
Zambezi (Zimbabwe, Mozambique).

(8) Amu-Darya (Russ.), Araguaya
(Braz.), Arkansas (US), Cherwell
(UK), Colorado (US), Columbia
(US), Demerara (Guyana), Dordogne
(Fr.), Evenlode (UK), Findhorn

(UK), Illinois (US), Missouri (US),
Paraguay (Arg.), Putumayo
(Ecuador), Rio Bravo (Mex.),
Savannah (US), Suwannee (US),
Torridge (UK), Tunguska (Russ.),
Windrush (UK).

(9) Churchill (Can.), Essequibo
(Guyana), Euphrates (Iraq), Indigirka
(Russ.), Irrawaddy (Myanmar/
Burma), Mackenzie (Can.),
Macquarie (Aus.), Pilcomayo (Arg.,
Paraguay), Rio Grande (Mex.),
Roosevelt (US), Tennessee (US),
Tocantins (Braz.).

(10) Blackwater (Ire., UK),
Changjiang (Ch.), Hackensack (US),
Hawkesbury (Aus.), Parramatta
(Aus.), Sacramento (US),
Shenandoah (US), St Lawrence
(Can.).

(11) Brahmaputra (Ind.), Mississippi
(US), Shatt-al-Arab (Iraq),
Yellowstone (US).

(12) Guadalquivir (Sp.),
Murrumbidgee (Aus.), Rappahannock
(US), Saskatchewan (Can.).

road I *n* (3) way; (4) drag, lane, pike; (5) route, track; (6) avenue, bypass, street; (7) highway; (8) crescent, motorway; (9) boulevard; (12) thoroughfare; II *cryptic* letters AVE, MI, MIV, RD, ST.

Robin Hood *myth* English folk hero, usually presented as a nobleman, Robin of Locksley, who fell foul of Prince John while Richard the Lionheart was away on a crusade, was outlawed, and went to live in Sherwood Forest in Nottinghamshire where he robbed the rich to help the poor and evaded the clutches of the Sheriff of Nottingham, Guy of Gisborne, and Prince John himself. He was an expert archer, gathered a band of 'merry men' to help him in his exploits, and loved Maid Marian.

ROBIN HOOD'S MERRY MEN
Alan-a-Dale, Friar Tuck, George-a Green, Little John, Much the Miller's Son, Will Scarlet.

rock¹ I *v* (3) tip; (4) roll, sway, tilt, toss; (5) dance, pitch, shake, swing; (6) wobble; II *n* (3) pop; (5) music.

rock² *n* (3) gem; (4) crag; (5) stone; (7) boulder, diamond.

TYPES OF ROCK

(3) jet, ore.

(4) coal, grit, lava, marl, spar, talc, tufa.

(5) chalk, flint, scree, shale, slate.

(6) basalt, clunch, gabbro, gneiss, gravel, marble, oolite, pumice, schist.

(7) breccia, granite, moraine.

(8) dolomite, feldspar, laterite, obsidian, porphyry.

(9) alabaster, ironstone, limestone, sandstone.

---

rodent *n*

RODENTS

(3) rat.

(4) cavy, cony, vole.

(5) coypu, hyrax, mouse.

(6) agouti, beaver, dassie, gerbil, gopher, jerboa, marmot, murine, nutria.

(7) hamster, lemming, meerkat, muskrat.

(8) capybara, chipmunk, dormouse, hedgehog, musquash, squirrel.

(9) bandicoot, desert-rat, groundhog, guinea-pig, porcupine, water-vole, woodchuck.

(10) fieldmouse.

Romeo and Juliet *lit.* tragedy by Shakespeare.

Plot outline: Two families in the Italian city of Verona, the Montagues and the Capulets, are involved in a long-running feud. Romeo, the son of the head of the Montague clan, gatecrashes a ball given by the Capulets with some of his friends, meets and falls in love with Juliet, the daughter of the head of the Montague clan. After the ball, Romeo climbs the wall into the Capulets' garden and speaks to Juliet who appears on the balcony of her bedroom ('O Romeo, Romeo, wherefore art thou Romeo?'). They confirm their love and Juliet arranges to send Romeo a message by her nurse the following day. By then, Romeo has arranged for them to be secretly married by Friar Lawrence, who hopes, through this marriage, to reconcile the feud between the two families. The brawling in the streets of Verona, however, continues. Romeo's witty friend Mercutio picks a fight with Juliet's cousin Tybalt. Romeo, newly married and peaceably minded, attempts to stop the fight, but Mercutio is killed through his ill-timed intervention. Romeo then kills Tybalt in another fight and knows that he will have to flee the city to escape justice. There is time for one night of love for the couple, then Romeo leaves for Mantua. Meanwhile the Capulets have made plans for Juliet to marry another suitor, the Count Paris. In order to avoid having to marry Paris or reveal her marriage to Romeo, Juliet agrees to a desperate plan by Friar Lawrence and swallows a potion that leads everyone to suppose that she is dead. The plan is that when she awakes from her drugged sleep, Romeo will take her away from the tomb where she is laid. But the messenger whom Friar Lawrence sends to acquaint Romeo of the plan does not reach him. Romeo returns believing Juliet to be dead and takes poison in her tomb. Juliet awakes, finds Romeo dead, and stabs herself with his dagger. The families are finally reconciled in grief.

Romulus and Remus *Rom. myth* sons of Mars and a vestal virgin, who were exposed at birth and suckled by a she-wolf. They are the legendary founders of Rome, though they quarrelled over the plans for the city and Romulus killed Remus.

room *n* (5) scope, space; (6) leeway, margin; (8) latitude.

TYPES OF ROOM

(3) den, loo.

(4) hall, loft.

(5) attic, diner, foyer, porch, salon, study.

(6) cellar, larder, lounge, office, pantry, studio, toilet.

(7) bedroom, boudoir, box-room, chamber, dinette, kitchen, landing, laundry, library, nursery, parlour.

(8) anteroom, basement, bathroom, lavatory, playroom, scullery, workroom, workshop.

(9) classroom, mezzanine, music-room.

(10) living-room

(2 words) front room, guest room, reception room *etc.*

---

rough I *adj* 1 (5) bumpy, lumpy; (6) coarse, jagged, rugged, shaggy, uneven; (7) bristly; (9) irregular; 2 (4) hard; (5) cruel, harsh, tough; (6) brutal, severe; (7) violent; 3 (4) wild; (6) choppy, stormy; (8) agitated; (9) turbulent; (11) tempestuous; 4 (4) rude; (5) crude, hasty, vague; (6) simple; (7) cursory, general, inexact; (11) approximate; II **rough** *or* **roughly** *cryptic* ANAGRAM CUE.

round I *adj* (5) plump, stout; (6) curved, rotund; (8) circular; (9) spherical; (10) continuous, ring-shaped; II *n* 1 (3) orb; (4) ball, disc, ring; (6) circle, sphere; 2 (3) lap; (4) beat, path; (5) orbit, route; (7) circuit, routine; 3 (4) bout, game, turn; (5) treat (6) period, series; (7) session; 4 (5) shell; (6) bullet; (9) cartridge; III *cryptic* 1 insert letter O in answer; 2 place the letters of one word around those of another, as in: 'Getting himself round a ballet step, the sergeant major has a convulsion' (5) = spasm.

roundabout I *adj* (7) devious, evasive, oblique, winding; (8) indirect, tortuous; (10) circuitous; II *cryptic* 1 reverse the order of the letters in a word in the clue or answer; 2 place the letters of one word around those of another; 3 ANAGRAM CUE; 4 letter C or CA (= circa).

Roundhead I *hist* supporter of the Parliament in the English Civil War; II *cryptic* place letter O before part of the answer.

Round Table *lit.*

KNIGHTS OF THE ROUND TABLE

Sir – (3) Kay; (4) Bors (de Ganis); (6) Gareth, Gawain, Modred; (7) Galahad, Gawaine, Geraint, Mordred, Pelleas; (8) Bedevere, Lancelot, Percival, Tristram.

---

rouse *v* 1 (4) call, stir, wake; (6) awaken; 2 (5) anger, start; (6) excite, incite, prompt; (7) agitate, inflame, provoke; (9) galvanise (*or* galvanize), instigate, stimulate; (2 words) whip up.

routine I *n* 1 (5) habit, usage; (6) custom, method; (7) formula, pattern, system; (8) practice; 2 (3) act, set; (5) piece; (9) programme; (11) performance; II *adj* (5) usual; (6) normal; (7) humdrum, typical; (8) everyday, habitual, ordinary, standard; (9) customary; (12) conventional.

row *n* 1 (4) bank, file, line, rank, tier; (5) queue; (6) column, series, string; (8) sequence; 2 (4) spat, tiff; (5) brawl, fight; (6) fracas; (7) dispute; (8) argument, squabble; 3 (3) din; (6) racket, rumpus, uproar; (9) commotion; (11) disturbance.

royal I *adj* (5) regal; (6) kingly; (7) queenly; (8) majestic, princely, **splendid**; (9) sovereign; II *n* member of royal family – *see* ROYAL TITLES.

ROYAL DYNASTIES, HOUSES OR FAMILIES

Austria – Hapsburg

Bavaria – Wittelsbach

Belgium – Coburg

Britain – Plantagenet, Tudor, Stuart, Hanover, Windsor

China – Hwan, Tang, Ming, Manchu

Denmark – Oldenburg

France – Capet, Valois, Bourbon

Germany – Hohenzollern

Greece – Schleswig-Holstein

Italy – Savoy

Monaco – Grimaldi

Morocco – Alaouite   *list continued over*

Netherlands – Orange
Poland – Jagellon
Portugal – Braganza
Romania – Hohenzollern
Russia – Romanoff
Spain – Hapsburg, Bourbon
Sweden – Vasa, Bernadotte.

ROYAL TITLES

(3) Rex.

(4) Czar, Khan, King, Raja, Rana, Rani, Shah, Tsar.

(5) Queen, Rajah, Ranee.

(6) Kaiser, Mikado, Prince, Regent, Regina, Sultan.

(7) Consort, Czarina, Dauphin, Emperor, Empress, Infanta, Infante, monarch, Pharaoh, Tsarina.

(8) Dauphine, Maharaja, Maharani, Padishah, Princess, Tsaritsa.

(9) Maharajah, Maharanee.

(10) Tsarevitch.

(11) Crown prince, Queen-mother.

(12) Queen-consort, Queen-regnant.

(13) Prince-consort, Princess Royal.

rub *v* (4) buff, wipe; (5) chafe, grate, knead, pinch, scour, scrub. shine; (6) abrade, caress, polish, scrape, stroke; (7) massage.

rubbish I *n* **1** (4) junk; (5) scrap, trash, waste; (6) litter, refuse; (7) garbage; **2** (3) rot; (6) drivel; (7) twaddle; (8) claptrap, cobblers, nonsense; (10) balderdash; (12) gobbledygook; **II** *v* (4) slam; (5) slate, trash; (7) dismiss; (8) pooh-pooh; (9) criticise (*or* criticize), denigrate, disparage.

rude *adj* **1** (4) curt; (5) sharp, short; (6) abrupt, cheeky, (7) abusive, brusque, ill-bred, uncivil, uncouth; (8) impolite, insolent; (9) insulting; offensive; (11) ill-mannered, impertinent; (12) discourteous; (13) disrespectful; **2** (5) crude, rough; (9) unrefined, untutored; (11) uncivilised (*or* uncivilized); (15) unsophisticated; **3** (5) dirty, gross; (6) coarse, smutty, vulgar; (7) naughty.

ruin I *n* **1** (5) shell, wreck; (6) debris; (7) remains; **2** (4) fall; (7) failure; (8) downfall; (9) dishonour, overthrow, ruination; (10) bankruptcy, insolvency; **3** (5) decay, havoc; (8) collapse, wreckage; (9) breakdown, disrepair; (11) destruction, devastation; **II** *v* (3) mar; (4) raze; (5) botch, break, smash, spoil, wreck; (7) destroy; (8) bankrupt, demolish; (9) devastate, overthrow, overwhelm; **III ruin, ruined,** *or* **in ruins** *cryptic* ANAGRAM CUE.

rule I *n* **1** (3) law; (5) axiom, canon, maxim, order, tenet; (6) decree; (7) formula, precept, statute; (8) standard; (9) criterion; guideline, ordinance, principle; (10) regulation; **2** (4) sway; (5) reign; (6) regime; (7) command, control, mastery; (9) authority; (10) governance, government, suzerainty; (11) sovereignty; **II** *v* **1** (4) lead; (5) guide, reign; (6) govern; (7) control; (8) regulate; (10) administer; **2** (4) find; (5) judge; (6) decide, decree; (7) resolve; (9) determine, pronounce.

ruler *n* (4) head, lord; (5) chief; (6) leader; (7) monarch; (8) governor, overlord, suzerain; (9) sovereign; *see also* ROYAL TITLES at **royal** and NOBLE TITLES at **noble**.

run I *v* **1** (3) jog; (4) bolt, dart, dash, flow, gush, lope, move, pour, race, rush, tear; (5) glide, hurry, scoot, slide, speed; (6) double, sprint, streak, stream; (7) scamper, scuttle; **2** (4) head, lead; (6) direct, manage; (7) control, oversee; (8) organise (*or* organize); (9) supervise; (11) superintend; **3** (4) work; (7) operate; (8) function; **4** (5) stand; (7) compete; (9) challenge; **II** *cryptic* letter R or (**runs**) RS (from cricket).

rural *adj* (6) rustic, sylvan; (7) bucolic, country; (8) agrarian, pastoral; (12) agricultural.

rush I *v* **1** (4) bolt, dart, dash, flow, gush, lope, pour, race, rush, tear; (5) glide, hurry, scoot, speed; (6) double, career, hasten, hustle, sprint, streak, stream; (7) scamper, scuttle; (8) stampede; **2** (6) attack, charge; (7) assault; **II** *n* **1** (4) reed; (5) plant; **2** *film* (4) clip; (5) scene.

Ruth *Bible* a book of the Old Testament that tells the story of Ruth, the Moabite, who married a man from Judaea and, when her husband died, returned there with her mother-in-law, Naomi. Gleaning in the cornfields of her adopted home, she came to the attention of Boaz, who married her. She bore him a son who was an ancestor of King David.

S

S *abbrev* society, soprano, south, sulphur, Sunday, Sweden (international vehicle registration).

s *abbrev* second, shilling (solidus).

sack I *v* (3) axe; (4) fire; (7) dismiss; (9) discharge; (2 words) lay off, make redundant; **II the sack** (9) dismissal; (2 words) the axe, the boot, the chop, the elbow, the push, one's cards, one's notice.

sad I *adj* **1** (3) low; (4) blue, down, glum; (5) moody, upset; (6) bereft, dismal, gloomy, gutted, morose; (7) forlorn, tearful, unhappy; (8) dejected, downcast, wretched; (9) depressed, miserable, sorrowful; (10) despondent, distressed, melancholy; (11) crestfallen, downhearted; (12) disheartened, heavyhearted; **2** (5) grave, sorry; (6) moving, tragic; (7) painful, serious; (8) grievous, poignant, touching; (9) upsetting; (10) deplorable, lamentable; (11) distressing, regrettable, unfortunate; (12) heartrending; **II sad** *or* **sadly** *cryptic* ANAGRAM CUE.

safe I *adj* **1** (6) immune, intact, secure, unhurt; (8) unharmed; (9) protected, undamaged, uninjured, unscathed; **2** (8) harmless; non-toxic, (9) innocuous; **3** (4) sure; (5) sound, tried; (6) proven, tested; (7) certain; (8) reliable; (10) dependable; (11) trustworthy; **4** (7) prudent; (8) cautious; (12) conservative; **II** *n* (5) peter; (9) strongbox; (10) strongroom.

Sagittarius *astrol. & astron.* the constellation that is the ninth sign of the zodiac, also known as the Archer.

said I *v see* say; **II** *cryptic* indicates that one word sounds like another, as in: 'The said malefactor then carried out an attack' (4, 2) = fell on.

sail I *n* (5) sheet; (6) canvas; **II** *v* (5) pilot, steer; (6) cruise, travel, voyage; (7) captain, skipper; (8) navigate.

TYPES OF SAIL

(3) jib, lug; (5) genoa, royal; (6) bonnet, course, driver, lateen, mizzen, yankee; (7) skysail, spanker, topsail; (8) mainsail, staysail; (9) spinnaker; (10) topgallant.

---

sailing ship *n*

VESSELS WITH SAILS

(3) cat, hoy.

(4) bark, brig, dhow, dory, junk, pink, prau, proa, scow, yawl.

(5) coble, ketch, skiff, sloop, smack, xebec, yacht, zebec.

(6) barque, caique, carvel, dinghy, dogger, hooker, lugger, tartan, wherry, zebeck.

(7) caravel, carrack, clipper, felucca, frigate, galleon, pinnace, shallop.

(8) corvette, galleass, indiaman, longship, man-of-war, schooner.

(9) catamaran, outrigger.

(10) barkentine, brigantine, windjammer.

(11) barquentine.

(12) quare-rigger.

---

sailor I *n* (3) tar; (4) jack; (6) rating, seaman; (7) mariner, matelot; (8) deckhand; **II** *cryptic* letters AB, RN, or TAR.

FAMOUS SAILORS

(4) Ahab (Capt., *fict.*), Byng (John, UK admiral), Cook (Capt. James, UK explorer), Dias (Bartolomeu, Port. explorer), Howe (Richard, UK admiral), Spee (Maximilian von, Ger. admiral), Togo (Heihachiro, Jap. admiral).

(5) Anson (George, UK admiral and circumnavigator), Blake (Robert, UK admiral), Bligh (Capt. William, UK martinet), Blyth (Chay, UK

list continued over

---

yachtsman), Cabot (John, explorer),
Drake (Francis, UK explorer),
Hawke (Edward, UK admiral),
Rooke (George, UK admiral),
Tromp (Maarten, NL admiral).

(6) Baffin (William, UK explorer),
Beatty (David, UK admiral), Benbow
(William, UK admiral), Bering
(Vitus, Danish explorer), Crusoe
(Robinson, *fict.*), Fisher (John, UK
admiral), Jervis (John, UK admiral),
Nelson (Horatio, UK admiral),
Nimitz (Chester, US admiral),
Rodney (George, UK admiral),
Ruyter (Michiel de, NL admiral),
Scheer (Reinhard, Ger. admiral),
Sinbad (*fict.*); (2 words) da Gama
(Vasco, Port. explorer).

(7) Canaris (Wilhelm, Ger. admiral),
Decatur (Stephen, US admiral),
Hawkins (John, UK adventurer),
Doenitz (Karl, Ger. admiral), Tirpitz
(Alfred, Ger. admiral).

(8) Boscawen (Edward, UK admiral),
Columbus (Christopher, explorer),
Jellicoe (John, UK admiral),
Magellan (Ferdinand, Port. explorer),
Yamamoto (Isoroku, Jap. admiral).

(9) Frobisher (Martin, UK explorer),
Grenville (Richard, Capt. of the
Revenge).

(10) Chichester (Francis, UK
yachtsman), Villeneuve (Pierre, Fr.
admiral).

(11) Collingwood (Cuthbert, UK
admiral), Mountbatten (Louis, UK
admiral).

saint *cryptic* abbreviated as ST.

salary *n* (3) pay; (5) gains, wages;
(6) income, return; (7) profits, revenue,
stipend; (8) earnings, proceeds; (10)
emoluments; (12) remuneration.

salutation *n see* **greeting**.

Samson *Bible* a hero of Israel, endowed
with enormous strength, the source of
which was in his hair, which he never cut.
He slew a thousand of the Philistines
with the jawbone of an ass, but his downfall was his love for a woman called
Delilah. Urged by the Philistines to elicit
the secret of Samson's strength, Delilah
succeeded at the fourth attempt. The
Philistines shaved his hair, blinded him,
and put him to grind corn in the mill.
However, at a great feast in Gaza in
which the blind Samson was put on show,
he pulled down the main pillars of the
house, killing the assembled Philistines
and himself.

Samuel *Bible* a judge and prophet who
was called by the Lord in the house of Eli,
anointed **Saul** as king and later also
anointed David to be Saul's successor.

Sandhurst *cryptic* letters RMA (Royal
Military Academy).

sapper *cryptic* letters RE (Royal Engineers).

Satan *rel.* a Hebrew word meaning 'adversary' or 'enemy', applied to the devil
or the chief among the spirits of evil.
Satan is a main character in Milton's
Paradise Lost.

satisfactory *adj* (2) OK; (4) fine, good,
so-so; (7) correct, welcome; (8) adequate,
passable, pleasant, suitable; (9) tolerable;
(10) acceptable, admissible, gratifying.

satisfy *v* **1** (4) sate; (5) slake; (6) please, (7)
content, delight, gratify, indulge, satiate;
2 (4) fill, meet; (5) serve; (6) answer, fulfil,
settle; (7) suffice; (9) discharge.

Saturday *n* seventh day of the week,
named after Saturn, abbreviated as S, SA,
or SAT.

Saturn *Rom. myth* chief among the
Titans, son of Uranus. He devoured
all his children apart from **Jupiter,**
Neptune and **Pluto,** by whom his rule
was overthrown – equivalent of the
Greek god Cronos.

sauce *n* **1** (5) gravy, juice; (6) relish;
(7) ketchup; **2** (5) cheek, nerve; (9)
impudence; (12) impertinence.

TYPES OF SAUCE

(2) HP®; (3) soy; (4) mint; (5) satay;
(6) hoisin, mornay, tomato;
(7) parsley, tabasco, tartare; (8)
béchamel; (9) béarnaise, Worcester®;
(10) chaudfroid, mayonnaise; (11)
hollandaise, horseradish, vinaigrette.

Saul *Bible* **1** the first king of Israel, the father of Jonathan and an initial protector of **David**. But Saul became jealous of David's success in battle and his popularity ('Saul hath slain his thousands and David his ten thousands'), conspired against him and sought to kill him. Saul fought a civil war with David and a war against the Philistines. Eventually, hard pressed on all sides, Saul consulted the witch of Endor, who conjured up the spirit of **Samuel**, who prophesied Saul's doom. Defeated in battle the next day by the Philistines, Saul fell upon his sword. **2 Saul of Tarsus** the original name of St **Paul**.

save *v* **1** (4) free; (6) redeem, rescue; (7) deliver, reclaim, recover, salvage; (8) liberate, preserve; **2** (4) hold, keep; (5) stash, stock, store; (6) retain; (7) collect, reserve; (8) conserve, withhold; (9) economise (*or* economize); **3** (5) guard, spare; (6) screen, shield; (7) protect; (9) safeguard.

saw I *n* **1** (4) tool; (6) jigsaw; (7) bandsaw, fretsaw, hacksaw; (2 words) circular saw, tenon saw; **2** *see* **saying; II** *v* **1** (3) cut, rip; (4) hack; **2** *see* **see.**

say I *v* **1** (4) tell; (5) claim, imply, reply, speak, state, utter, voice; (6) affirm, allege, answer, assert, convey, impart, recite, remark, repeat, report, reveal; (7) comment, deliver, divulge, exclaim, express, mention, observe, suggest; (8) announce, disclose, indicate, intimate, maintain, vocalise (*or* vocalize); (9) ejaculate, enunciate, pronounce, verbalise (*or* verbalize); (10) articulate; **2** (4) mean; (7) portend, signify; **3** (5) judge; (6) decide; **II** *cryptic* indicates that one word sounds the same as another, *see* **said.**

saying *n* (3) saw; (5) adage, axiom, maxim, motto, quote; (6) dictum, remark; (7) precept, proverb; (8) aphorism; (9) quotation.

scale I *n* **1** (4) area, span; (5) range, reach, scope, sweep; (6) domain, extent, sphere, spread; (7) compass; **2** (3) fur; (4) scab; (5) crust, flake, plate, scurf; (7) deposit; **3** (5) ratio; (6) series; (7) ranking; (8) sequence, standard; (9) hierarchy, yardstick; (10) graduation, proportion; (11) progression; **4** (5) major, minor; (8) diatonic; **II** *v* (4) shin; (5) climb, mount; (6) ascend; (7) clamber; (8) surmount; **III** *cryptic* any letter from A to G, corresponding to one of the musical scales.

Scales *see* **Libra.**

scan I *v* (3) con; (4) skim; (5) study, sweep; (6) glance, peruse, screen, search, survey; **II** *n* (5) check, probe; (8) scrutiny; (9) screening; (11) examination.

scene *n* **1** (4) view; (5) sight, vista; (7) outlook; (8) panorama, prospect; (9) landscape, spectacle; **2** (4) area, site, spot; (5) place; (6) milieu; (8) locality, location; (10) background; **3** (4) clip, part, shot; (7) episode; (8) division, incident; **4** (3) row; (4) fuss, to-do; (5) drama; (9) commotion; (11) performance.

scent I *n* **1** (5) odour, smell, whiff; (7) perfume; (9) fragrance; **2** (5) spoor, track, trail; **II** *v* (5) sense; (6) detect; (7) discern, suspect; (8) perceive.

scheme I *n* & *v* (4) plan, plot; (5) cabal; (6) design; (8) intrigue; **II** *n* (6) agenda; (7) project; (8) proposal, schedule; (9) programme, stratagem; (10) conspiracy; (11) machination; **III** *v* (8) conspire, contrive; (9) machinate.

school I *n* (7) academy, college; (9) institute; **II** *v* (5) coach, prime, teach, train, tutor, verse; (7) educate, prepare; (8) instruct; (10) discipline; *see also* **public school.**

scoff I *v* **1** (4) gibe, jeer, mock; (5) laugh, scorn, sneer, taunt; (6) deride; (8) ridicule; (9) disparage; **2** (3) eat; (4) wolf; (6) devour, gobble, guzzle; **II** *n* (4) food, grub, meal.

scold I *v* (3) nag; (4) rail; (5) blame, chide; (7) censure, lecture, upbraid; (8) admonish, reproach; (9) castigate, reprimand; **II** *n* (5) shrew; (6) virago; (8) spitfire; (9) termagant.

score I *n & v* (4) mark, nick; (5) graze, notch, slash; (6) scrape; (7) scratch; **II** *n* **1** (3) sum; (4) runs; (5) tally, total; (6) points, result; **2** (6) twenty (also *cryptic* XX); **3** (5) music, notes.

Scorpio *or* **Scorpion** *astrol. & astron.* the constellation that is the eighth sign of the zodiac.

scramble I *v* **1** (4) dash, push, race, rush; (5) climb, crawl, hurry, scale; (6) jostle; (7) clamber; (8) scrabble, struggle; **2** (3) mix; (4) stir; (6) garble; (7) confuse; **3** (2 words) take off; **II** *cryptic* ANAGRAM CUE.

scrap I *n & v* (3) row; (5) brawl, **fight**; (7) quarrel, scuffle, wrangle; (8) squabble; **II** *n* **1** (3) bit, jot, rag; (4) atom, bite, iota, hint; (5) crumb, piece, shred, trace; (6) morsel; (7) inkling, oddment, remnant, residue, snippet, vestige; (8) fragment; (9) remainder; **2** (4) junk; (5) waste; (6) refuse; (7) rubbish; (9) leftovers; **3** (6) battle, dust-up; (7) contest, dispute; (8) **argument**; (9) scrimmage; (12) disagreement; **III** *v* (3) axe; (4) drop, dump, junk, shed; (5) ditch; (7) abandon, discard; (2+ words) get rid of, throw away.

scratch I *n & v* (3) cut; (4) mark, nick; (5) graze, notch, score, slash; (6) scrape; **II** *v* **1** (4) etch; (6) incise; (7) engrave; **2** (5) erase, scrub; (6) cancel, delete; **3** (8) withdraw.

scream *n & v* (3) cry; (4) bawl, howl, roar, wail, yell; (5) shout; (6) shriek, squeal; (7) screech.

screen I *n & v* (4) mask, veil; (5) cover, guard, shade; (6) shield, shroud; (7) shelter; **II** *n* (4) grid, mesh; (6) awning, canopy; (7) divider, reredos; (9) partition; **III** *v* **1** (7) conceal, protect; **2** (3) vet; (4) sift, sort, test; (5) grade, sieve; (6) filter; (7) examine; **3** (4) show; (7) present; (9) broadcast.

sculptor *n* (6) artist, carver; (8) modeller.

FAMOUS SCULPTORS

(3) Arp (Hans, Fr.); (4) Caro (Anthony, UK), Gill (Eric, UK); (5) Moore (Henry, UK), Rodin (Auguste, Fr.); (6) Calder (Alexander, US), Canova (Antonio, It.), Houdon (Jean, Fr.); (7) Bernini (Giovanni, It.), Epstein (Jacob, UK), Phidias (Gk); (8) Brancusi (Constantine, Rom.), Ghiberti (Lorenzo, It.), Hepworth (Barbara, UK); (9) Donatello (It.); (10) Giacometti (Alberto, Switz.), Praxiteles (Gk); (12) Michelangelo (Michelangelo Buonarroti, It.).

---

sea *n* (4) deep, main; (5) briny, ocean.

SEAS

(3) Red.

(4) Aral, Azov, Dead, Java, Kara, Sulu.

(5) Banda, Black, Ceram, Coral, Crete, Irish, Japan, North, Timor, White.

(6) Aegean, Baltic, Bering, Celtic, Flores, Ionian, Laptev, Tasman, Wadden.

(7) Andaman, Arabian, Arafura, Barents, Caspian, Celebes, Galilee, Marmara, Molucca, Okhotsk, Solomon.

(8) Adriatic, Amundsen, Beaufort, Bismarck, Hebrides, Ligurian, Sargasso.

(9) Caribbean, Norwegian; (2 words) East China.

(10) Tyrrhenian; (2 words) South China.

(12) (2 words) East Siberian.

(13) Mediterranean.

---

seal¹ *n* (*male* bull, *female* cow, *young* pup, *group* herd, pod, rookery) (6) walrus; (7) sealion.

seal²I *n* (5) stamp; (6) signet; (8) insignia; (9) assurance, guarantee; (10) imprimatur; (14) authentication; **II** *v* (4) cork, plug, shut, stop; (5) close; (7) stopper; (10) waterproof.

seaman *see* **sailor**.

season I *n* (4) fall, span, time; (5) phase, spell; (6) autumn, period, spring, summer, winter; II *v* 1 (4) salt; (5) spice; (7) flavour; 2 (3) age; (5) inure, ripen, train; (6) harden, mature; (7) prepare, toughen; (11) acclimatise (*or* acclimatize).

seat I *n* 1 (3) pew; (4) sofa; (5) bench, chair, couch, divan, stool; (6) carver, pouffe, settee, settle, throne; (7) beanbag; (8) armchair, recliner; (12) chaise-longue, chesterfield; 2 (6) bottom; (8) backside, buttocks; 3 (4) site; (6) centre; (8) location; 4 (5) abode, house, manor; (7) mansion; (9) residence; II *v* 1 (4) hold; (7) contain; (11) accommodate; 2 (3) fit, fix, set; (5) place; (6) locate, settle; (7) install.

second *n* 1 (2) mo; (3) sec; (4) tick; (5) flash, jiffy, trice; (6) minute, moment; (7) instant; 2 (6) backer, helper; (9) assistant; II *adj* (4) next; (5) extra, lower, other; (6) double, lesser; (7) further; (8) inferior; (9) alternate, duplicate; (10) additional; (11) subordinate; III *v* (4) back, help; (6) assist; (7) approve, endorse, further, promote, support; IV *cryptic* 1 letter S or letters SEC; 2 use the second letter of the word referred to, so that, *e.g.*, 'second of April' might = P and 'second hand' or 'second mate' might = A.

secret I *adj* 1 (4) dark; (6) arcane, covert, hidden, occult, untold; (7) cryptic, obscure, private, unknown, unnamed; (8) hush-hush, nameless, secluded; (9) incognito, recondite; (10) classified, mysterious, restricted, undercover, unrevealed; (11) undisclosed; (12) confidential; 2 *see* **secretive**; II *n* (3) key; (4) code; (6) enigma; (7) mystery; (10) confidence.

secretive *adj* (4) deep; (5) cagey, close, quiet; (7) furtive; (8) reserved, reticent; (9) withdrawn; (11) tight-lipped; (13) unforthcoming; (15) uncommunicative.

secure I *adj* 1 (4) safe; (6) immune, intact, unhurt; (8) unharmed; (9) protected, undamaged, uninjured, unscathed; 2 (4) fast, firm, sure; (5) fixed, solid, tight; (6) stable, steady; (8) reliable; (10) dependable; 3 (7) assured; (9) confident; II *v* 1 (4) bind, join, knit, knot, lash, link, lock, shut; (5) close, latch; (6) attach, fasten; 2 (3) get, win; (4) earn, gain; (6) attain, obtain; (7) achieve, procure.

see *v* 1 (3) spy; (4) espy, find, note, spot; (5) sight, trace; (6) detect, expose, locate, notice, remark; (7) discern, glimpse, observe; (8) discover, identify, perceive; (9) ascertain, recognise (*or* recognize); (11) distinguish; 2 (5) grasp; (6) deduce, follow, gather; (7) realise (*or* realize); (8) conclude; (10) appreciate, understand; 3 (4) date, meet; (5) visit; (7) consult, receive; (9) interview.

seed *n* 1 (3) pip; (5) grain, semen, sperm, stone; (6) kernel; (7) nucleus; 2 (5) start; (6) origin, source; (9) beginning; 3 (7) progeny; (9) offspring; (11) descendants.

seize *v* 1 (4) grab, grip; (5) grasp; 2 (4) take; (5) steal, usurp; (7) capture, impound; (10) commandeer, confiscate; (11) appropriate, requisition.

select I *v* (4) pick; (5) adopt, elect; (6) decide, choose; (7) appoint; (9) designate; (2 words) decide on, opt for, vote for; II *adj* (3) top; (4) rare; (5) elite, prime; (6) choice; (7) special; (8) superior; (9) exclusive, first-rate; (10) first-class, handpicked.

send *v* 1 (4) mail, post; (5) remit; (7) consign, forward; (8) dispatch, transmit; (9) broadcast; 2 (4) cast, emit, fire, hurl; (5) fling, force, throw; (6) direct, launch, propel; (7) project.

sense I *n* 1 (5) sight, smell, taste, touch; (7) faculty, hearing; 2 (4) mind, wits; (6) brains, reason, wisdom; (9) awareness, judgement; (12) appreciation, intelligence; (13) consciousness, understanding; 3 (4) gist; (5) point; (7) meaning; (9) substance; (10) definition; (11) implication; (12) significance; II *v* (4) feel; (5) grasp; (6) detect, intuit, notice; (7) realise (*or* realize), suspect; (8) perceive; (10) appreciate, comprehend, understand.

sensible *adj* 1 (4) wise; (5) aware, canny, sound; (6) astute, clever, shrewd; (7) prudent; (8) rational; (9) advisable, judicious;

(11) intelligent; 2 (4) calm, cool, mild, sane; (8) moderate; (9) practical; (10) reasonable, restrained; (11) down-to-earth, level-headed; 3 *see* **sensitive** 1.

sensitive *adj* 1 (5) aware; (7) mindful; (9) conscious; (10) discerning, perceptive, sensitised (*or* sensitized); (12) appreciative; 2 (6) touchy; (9) irritable; (10) vulnerable; (11) thin-skinned; (13) temperamental; 3 (4) fine; (5) exact; (7) precise; (8) delicate.

September *n* (4) Sept; (5) month. In the Roman calendar, October was the seventh month (*septem* Latin for seven).

series *n* (3) row, run, set; (5) chain, cycle, order, train; (8) sequence; (10) succession; (11) progression.

serious *adj* 1 (4) grim; (5) grave, sober; (6) sedate, solemn; (7) earnest, pensive, sincere, subdued; (8) reserved; (10) thoughtful; 2 (5) acute, vital; (6) severe, urgent; (7) crucial, weighty; (8) critical, profound; (9) dangerous, important, momentous.

servant *n* (3) gyp, man; (4) cook, maid; (5) nanny, scout, valet; (6) batman, butler, lackey, menial, skivvy, tweeny; (7) flunkey, footman, steward; (8) factotum, retainer; (9) attendant.

service I *n* 1 (4) boon, help; (6) favour; (7) benefit, utility; (10) assistance; 2 (5) check; (6) repair; (8) overhaul; (11) maintenance; 3 (4) rite; (8) ceremony; (9) sacrament; 4 (2) RN; (3) RAF, USN; (4) army, navy, USAF; (2 words) air force; II *v* (5) check; (6) repair; (8) maintain, overhaul.

CHURCH SERVICES

(4) mass; (5) lauds, nones; (6) matins; (7) baptism, mattins, vespers; (8) compline, evensong; (9) communion, eucharist.

---

set I *v* 1 (3) fit, fix, lay, put; (4) park, site; (5) erect, lodge, place, stick; (6) locate; (7) deposit, install, station; (8) position; (9) establish; (2+ words) put in place, put in position; 2 (3) gel; (4) clot; (6) harden; (7) congeal, stiffen, thicken; (8) solidify; 3 (6) adjust, assign, ordain; (8) regulate; (9) prescribe; (11) synchronise (*or* synchronize); 4 (3) dip; (4) sink, wane; II *n* 1 (3) lot, mob; (4) band, club, crew, gang, pack, ring, team; (5) batch, bunch, class, crowd, group; (6) circle, clique; (7) cluster, coterie; 2 (3) kit; (5) batch, class; (6) clutch, series, outfit; (8) category, sequence; (10) collection; 3 (2) TV; (5) radio; (8) receiver; (10) television; III *adj* 1 (4) fast, firm, hard; (5) dense, fixed, rigid, solid, stiff; 2 (5) ready; (8) prepared; 3 (5) stock, usual; (7) regular, routine; (8) standard; (9) customary; 4 (6) agreed; (8) assigned, ordained; (9) appointed; (10) prescribed.

setback I *n* (4) blow; (5) check, delay; (6) defeat, mishap; (7) failure, problem, reverse; (9) adversity; (10) misfortune; II **set back** *or* **setback** *cryptic* reverse the order of the letters in a word in the clue or answer, as in: 'Somewhere in the distance, beyond Australia, the aviators suffer a setback' (4) = afar.

set off I *v* 1 (2) go; (5) begin, leave, start; (6) depart; 2 (4) foil; (7) display, enhance; (10) complement; 3 (5) light; (6) ignite; (7) explode, trigger, unleash; (8) detonate; II *cryptic* ANAGRAM CUE, especially an anagram of SET.

set out I *v* 1 (2) go; (5) begin, leave, start; (6) depart; 2 (4) show; (7) display, exhibit, explain, present; (8) describe; II *cryptic* ANAGRAM CUE, especially an anagram of SET.

setter *cryptic* letters I or ME (referring to the setter of the puzzle).

settle *v* 1 (3) fix; (5) solve; (6) answer, decide; (7) resolve; (8) conclude; (9) determine, establish; (2 words) sort out, work out; 2 (4) drop, fall, land, sink; (5) perch; (6) alight; (7) subside; 3 (8) colonise (*or* colonize).

seven ages *lit.* the seven ages of man, according to Jaques in Shakespeare's *As You Like It* are:

(1) **the infant** 'mewling and puking in his mother's arms'.

(2) **the schoolboy** 'with his satchel and shining morning face, creeping like a snail unwillingly to school'.

(3) **the lover** 'sighing like a furnace, with a woeful ballad made to his mistress' eyebrow'.

(4) **the soldier** 'full of strange oaths and bearded like the pard, jealous in honour, sudden and quick in quarrel, seeking the bubble reputation even in the cannon's mouth'.

(5) **the justice** 'in fair round belly with good capon lined, with eyes severe and beard of formal cut, full of wise saws and modern instances'.

(6) **the lean and slippered pantaloon** 'with spectacles on nose and pouch on side, his youthful hose, well saved, a world too wide for his shrunk shank, and his big manly voice turning again towards childish treble pipes'.

(7) **second childishness** 'sans eyes, sans teeth, sans taste, sans everything'.

seven deadly sins *see* sin.

seven hills of Rome *geog. & hist.* Aventine; Caelian; Capitoline; Esquiline; Palatine; Quirinal; Viminal.

seven seas *geog.* Antarctic, Arctic, Indian, North Atlantic, North Pacific, South Atlantic, South Pacific (oceans).

seven wonders of the world *hist.* the Colossus of Rhodes; the Hanging Gardens of Babylon; the Mausoleum of Helicarnassus; the Pharos of Alexandria; the Pyramids of Egypt; the Statue of Zeus (Jupiter) at Olympus; the Temple of Diana at Ephesus.

severe *adj* 1 (4) hard; (5) tough; (6) taxing, tiring; (7) arduous; (9) demanding, difficult, gruelling, strenuous, stressful; (10) exhausting; 2 (4) grim; (5) cruel, harsh, rigid, stern; (6) strict; (8) pitiless; (9) merciless, unbending; (10) inflexible, relentless; 3 (5) acute; (6) fierce; (7) extreme, intense, violent; 4 (5) plain; (6) simple; (7) ascetic, austere; (9) unadorned.

shade l *n & v* (5) blind; (6) canopy, screen, shield; shroud; ll *n* 1 (5) gloom; (6) shadow; (7) umbrage; (8) darkness, penumbra; 2 (3) hue; (4) tint, tone; (6) colour; (7) pigment; 3 (4) dash, hint; (5) touch, trace; (6) nuance; (9) suspicion; (10) suggestion; 4 (5) ghost; (6) spirit, wraith; (7) phantom, spectre; lll *v* (3) dim; (5) cloud; (6) darken; (7) obscure.

shadow l *n* 1 *see* shade ll 1, 3 *and* 4; 2 (5) image, shape; (7) outline; (9) semblance; (10) reflection, silhouette; ll *v* (3) dog; (5) stalk, track, trail, watch; (6) follow.

shake *v* 1 (3) wag; (4) jerk, jolt, rock, sway; (5) quake; (6) rattle, shiver, totter, wobble; (7) shudder, tremble, vibrate; (8) convulse; (9) oscillate; 2 (5) shock, upset; (7) agitate, disturb, unnerve; (8) distress, unsettle; (10) discompose, disconcert.

Shakespeare, William *lit.* English dramatist and poet, born and died in Stratford upon Avon, married to Anne Hathaway, children Judith, Susanna and Hamnet. Also known as The Bard, the Bard of Avon.

SHAKESPEARE PLAYS

All's Well That Ends Well

(comedy – *abbrev All's Well*)

Main characters: Helena, a physician's daughter; Countess of Rousillon; Bertram, her son; King of France; Lafeu, a lord; Paroles, a boastful soldier; Diana, a young Florentine woman.

Setting: France, Italy.

Plot: The King of France is seriously ill. Using skills learnt from her father, Helena succeeds in curing him. As a reward, the King offers her any of the young bachelors at his court as a husband. Helena chooses Bertram, the son of her patroness and friend, the Countess of Rousillon, whom she already loves. Bertram, however, objects to a marriage that he considers beneath him. Though he goes through the ceremony at the King's express command, he refuses to consummate the marriage and takes himself off to the wars in Italy, saying that he will never acknowledge her as his wife until she can 'get the ring upon [his] finger that never shall come off' and bear him a child. In Italy, Bertram woos a widow's daughter called Diana. Helena, having followed him there, arranges for Diana to agree to let Bertram come to her bed and takes her place there, thus fulfilling the conditions and being able to claim him back at the end of the play.

Antony and Cleopatra
(tragedy – *abbrev Ant & Cleo*)

Main characters: Mark Antony, member of the ruling triumvirate of Rome; Cleopatra, Queen of Egypt; Octavius Caesar, Aemilius Lepidus, the other triumvirs; Enobarbus, a friend and follower of Antony; Charmian and Iras, women attending Cleopatra.

Setting: Rome and Egypt.

Plot: see entry at **Antony and Cleopatra**

As You Like It (comedy – *abbrev AYLI*)

Main characters: Duke Senior, the rightful ruler living in exile; Duke Frederick, his usurping brother; Rosalind, Duke Senior's daughter; Celia, Duke Frederick's daughter; Orlando, younger son of Sir Rowland de Bois; Oliver, his elder brother; Touchstone, a jester; Corin, an old shepherd; Silvius, a young shepherd; Phoebe, a shepherdess; Audrey, a goatherd.

Setting: court and the Forest of Arden.

Plot: see entry at **As You Like It**.

Comedy of Errors, The
(comedy – *abbrev Com Err*)

Main characters: Aegeon, a merchant of Syracuse; Antipholus of Ephesus and Antipholus of Syracuse, his twin sons; Dromio of Ephesus and Dromio of Syracuse, their twin servants; Adriana, Antipholus of Ephesus's wife; Luciana, her sister; Aemilia, an abbess, revealed as Aegeon's wife.

Setting: Ephesus.

Plot: Aegeon and his wife and their twin baby sons and their twin servants were separated in a shipwreck. Aegeon raised one son and one servant in Syracuse, and, at the beginning of the play, has been arrested in Syracuse while seeking that same young man who had some years before gone off to try to find his missing brother. His brother is in fact living a somewhat tempestuous married life in Ephesus. The main action of the play revolves around the confusion caused when the two pairs of identical twins are mistaken for each other.

Coriolanus (tragedy – *abbrev Corio*)

Main characters: Caius Marcus Coriolanus, a Roman aristocrat and soldier; Volumnia, his mother; Virgilia, his wife; Menenius Agrippa, an elderly Roman aristocrat; Sicinius Velutus, Junius Brutus, tribunes of the people; Tullus Aufidius, the leader of the Volscians.

Setting: Rome.

Plot: *Coriolanus* is set in the early days of the Roman republic against the background of the tension between the ruling class and the common people. When the play begins Caius Marcus is leading an expedition against the Volscians. He rallies the troops when they retreat and almost single-handedly takes the town of Corioli, thus earning the surname Coriolanus. When he returns to Rome in triumph, the aristocratic party are keen to capitalise on his military successes and make him consul. Tradition demands that Coriolanus should stand in the forum and solicit the votes of the people, whose support is required if he is to attain supreme political office. This goes totally against his aristocratic nature. He seems at first to have obtained the necessary amount of popular support, but the tribunes, fearing the loss of their own power if Coriolanus becomes consul, stir up the people against him. Coriolanus cannot pretend any longer and frankly expresses his contempt for the people and the political process. At this the people drive him out of the city. Coriolanus goes to Antium and joins forces with his old enemies the Volscians and their leader Tullus Aufidius. He leads a Volscian army in a successful campaign and has the city of Rome at his mercy. His mother and his wife come out to beg him not to seize the city. The inflexible Coriolanus is, for once, moved to pity and spares Rome, knowing that in doing so he is betraying the Volscians. When he returns to Antium, he is assassinated.

Cymbeline (romance – *abbrev Cymb*)
Main characters: Cymbeline, King of Britain; his Queen; Imogen, his daughter; Guiderius and Arviragus, his sons (living under the names of Polydore and Cadwal), Cloten, the Queen's son; Posthumus Leonatus, Imogen's husband; Iachimo, an Italian gentleman; Belisarius, a nobleman.
Setting: Britain and Italy.
Plot: Imogen has married against her father's will and her husband, Posthumus, has been banished to Italy. There he encounters a gentleman, Iachimo, who boasts that he can get his way with any woman. Posthumus wagers on his wife's fidelity, but, by a trick, Iachimo gets evidence that suggests he has seduced Imogen. Posthumus, enraged, decides to have Imogen killed and sends her a letter telling her he is at Milford Haven, meaning to have his servant Pisanio kill her on the way there. Pisanio cannot do the deed. Imogen disguises herself as a boy to make her escape and, wandering in Wales, encounters her two brothers, Guiderius and Arviragus, stolen by a nobleman, Belisarius, when he was banished. Meanwhile Cloten, the Queen's lumpish son, who has unsuccessfully wooed Imogen, decides to follow her, disguised as Posthumus. He too happens upon Guiderius, challenges him to a fight, is killed and has his head chopped off. Imogen takes a drug given her by the Queen and is thought to be dead. The brothers lay her body alongside Cloten's and when Imogen recovers from the effects of the drug, she believes that the headless body beside her is her husband's. It takes the whole of the fifth act to unravel all the complications and eventually achieve a happy ending.

Hamlet, Prince of Denmark (tragedy)
Main characters: Hamlet; Claudius, King of Denmark (his uncle); Gertude (Hamlet's mother and Claudius's wife); Polonius, a royal counsellor; Ophelia (Polonius's daughter); Laertes (his son); Horatio (Hamlet's friend); the ghost of Hamlet's father.
Setting: The castle of Elsinore.
Plot: see entry at **Hamlet**.

Henry IV Part 1
(history – *abbrev Hen IV 1*)
Main characters: King Henry IV; Prince Hal (his son); Earl of Northumberland; Earl of Worcester (his brother); Hotspur (Henry Percy, Northumberland's son); Owen Glendower; Sir John Falstaff (Prince Hal's boon companion); Bardolph; Peto; Poins (associates of Falstaff and Hal); Mistress Quickly (landlady of the Boar's Head tavern).
Setting: court, the Boar's Head, Kent, Shrewsbury.
Plot: The action of this play follows on historically from that of **Richard II**. Henry IV, as king, is troubled not only by hostile incursions from Scotland in Wales, but by a guilty conscience because of the way he usurped the throne and by the loose behaviour of his son who spends more time with Falstaff and other low-life companions than at court. A dispute over prisoners taken in battle provokes the Percys (Hotspur, Northumberland, Worcester), who originally helped Henry to the throne, to rebel. Prince Hal, meanwhile, is persuaded to take part in a robbery on Gadshill. He and his closest companion Poins, however, rob the robbers and, in a memorable scene at the Boar's Head tavern enjoy listening to Falstaff's completely fabricated and exaggerated account of the incident. When news of the rebellion reaches him, Hal returns to court and makes his peace with his father. The royal and rebel forces meet at Shrewsbury and the battle concludes with a single combat between Hal and Hotspur in which Hal is victorious. During the battle in which he first

pretends to be dead and then to have killed Hotspur, Falstaff delivers his famous speech on 'honour' ('What is honour? – a word').

Henry IV Part 2
(history – *abbrev Hen IV 2*)
Main characters: King Henry; Prince Hal; Prince John of Lancaster; Falstaff and companions; Mistress Quickly; Doll Tearsheet; Justice Shallow; Justice Silence.
Setting: court, Yorkshire, Gloucestershire.
Plot: King Henry is still beset by rebellion and domestic trouble with his son. The rebellion in this play is only a pale reflection of its predecessor and is dealt with by the King's younger son, Prince John, by means of a cold-hearted trick. Falstaff, on a recruiting drive in Gloucestershire, encounters a friend of his youth, Justice Shallow, and plans to make as much money out of him as he can. When news of Henry IV's death arrives, Falstaff rushes to London expecting to gain power, influence and wealth when Hal ascends the throne. But Hal has again been reconciled with his father and on ascending the throne turns over a new leaf, states his intention to become a model king and rejects Falstaff.

Henry V (history – *abbrev Hen V*)
Main characters: King Henry V; King Charles VI of France; The Dauphin (his son); Princess Catherine (his daughter); Captains Gower, Fluellen, Macmorris and Jamy (of Henry's army); Pistol; Nym; Bardolph (former companions of Falstaff); Chorus.
Setting: the English court, northern France, Agincourt.
Plot: The action of this play follows on roughly from that of Henry IV Part 2. To avoid the troubles suffered by his father, Henry decides to lead his potentially rebellious nobles into a foreign war. He asserts a rather tenuous claim to the French throne, lands in France and besieges Harfleur ('Once more unto the breach, dear friends'). When Harfleur is taken, Henry's army is confronted by a much larger force of French troops. On the evening before the battle, Henry goes among his troops in disguise to gauge their morale. On the day, the English are victorious against the odds. To seal the peace between England and France, Henry marries the French king's daughter Catherine, whose attempts to learn English provide most of the light relief in the play. A notable feature of *Henry V* is Shakespeare's use of a Chorus (a single actor) to provide a linking narrative ('O for a muse of fire . . . !').

Henry VI Part 1
(history – *abbrev Hen VI 1*)
Main characters: King Henry VI; his uncle, Humphrey, Duke of Gloucester; Richard, Duke of York; Lord Talbot; Earl of Suffolk; Earl of Somerset; Margaret of Anjou; Joan La Pucelle.
Setting: England and France.
Plot: The play begins with mourning on the death of Henry V, whose infant son now mounts the throne as Henry VI. The play deals with the gradual deterioration of the English position in France, despite the efforts of the fierce Lord Talbot, as the French rally behind Joan of Arc. It also shows the origins of the Wars of the Roses in the intrigues and quarrels of various noble factions, symbolised by a scene in a garden in which the Duke of York and his supporters pluck and wear white roses, and those of the Earls of Somerset and Suffolk pluck red. The play ends with the deaths of Joan and Talbot and with Suffolk wooing Margaret of Anjou to be Henry's queen and his own means to power.

Henry VI Part 2
(history – *abbrev Hen VI 2*)
Main characters: King Henry VI; Margaret, his queen; Humphrey, Duke of Gloucester, his uncle; Richard, Duke of York; Duke of Suffolk; Jack Cade.
Setting: England.
Plot: The second part of Henry VI deals with the early years of the Wars of the Roses. The English nobles are enraged against the Queen's favourite, Suffolk,

for giving away large areas of territory in France. Suffolk and the Queen plot to disgrace the Duke of Gloucester, who still rules as Lord Protector. The fall and murder of Gloucester, however, merely opens the way for the Duke of York to make his bid for the throne – first by secretly sponsoring Jack Cade's rebellion, then by open war against the royal family. The play ends with York victorious at the Battle of St Albans and apparently poised to take the throne.

Henry VI Part 3

(history – *abbrev Hen VI 3*)

Main characters: King Henry VI; Margaret, his queen; Edward, Prince of Wales; Richard, Duke of York; Edward, Earl of March, Richard, Duke of Gloucester, George, Duke of Clarence, and the Earl of Rutland, his sons; Lord Clifford, a supporter of the king; Earl of Warwick, a Yorkist who changes sides.

Setting: England.

Plot: This play deals with the later stages of the Wars of the Roses and the eventual triumph of the House of York, but only after the Duke of York and his youngest son, Rutland, have been killed by Clifford, and the going over to the Lancastrian side of both the Earl of Warwick and George, Duke of Clarence, has given King Henry and his warlike queen, Margaret, the chance to re-establish themselves on the throne. But before the final battle Clarence rejoins his brothers. Warwick is killed and Edward Prince of Wales is stabbed in turn by the three sons of York. When King Henry is murdered in the tower by Richard, Duke of Gloucester, Edward of York is free to mount the throne as Edward IV. This play is particularly notable for the development of the character of Richard, Duke of Gloucester, in a series of long soliloquies, into the gleeful villain so well-known from the last play in the series, **Richard III**.

Henry VIII (history – *abbrev Hen VIII*)

Main characters: King Henry VIII; Queen Katherine of Aragon; Anne Boleyn; Duke of Buckingham; Cardinal Wolsey; Archbishop Thomas Cranmer.

Setting: London and Kimbolton.

Plot: The play deals with a small section of Henry VIII's reign, covering the fall and execution of the Duke of Buckingham, engineered by Cardinal Wolsey, the decline and fall of Wolsey himself when he refuses to go along with the King's plans to divorce Queen Katherine, Katherine's own dignified defence of her position and her eventual death. It ends on a more up-beat note with the birth of the future Queen Elizabeth and a long prophetic paean of praise for the achievements of her reign spoken by Cranmer at her baptism.

Julius Caesar (tragedy – *abbrev JC*)

Main characters: Julius Caesar; Calpurnia (his wife); Brutus (a friend of Caesar's who joins the conspiracy against him); Cassius (the main conspirator); Casca (the conspirator who stabs Caesar first); Mark Antony (a friend of Caesar's); Octavius (Caesar's nephew); Portia (Brutus's wife).

Setting: Rome, Philippi.

Plot: see entry at **Julius Caesar**.

King John (history – *abbrev K John*)

Main characters: King John; Queen Eleanor (his mother); King Philip of France; Arthur, Duke of Brittany (John's young nephew and a rival claimant to the throne); Constance (his mother); Bastard (Philip Falconbridge, an illegitimate son of King Richard Coeur-de-lion).

Setting: England, France.

Plot: The action mainly concerns King John's going to war in France to counter French support for Arthur, the rival claimant for the English throne. England and France make peace, an expedient truce before the town of Angiers, but then fight a battle in which John captures Arthur and orders his servant, Hubert, to kill him. Hubert spares Arthur's life, but the boy is killed trying to escape. Some of John's nobles rebel on hearing of Arthur's death and join the French party, but when John himself dies, poisoned by a monk, they unite behind his son Henry.

The most striking part in the play is that of the Bastard, who is both a satirical commentator on events and a spokesman for English patriotism.

King Lear (tragedy, *abbrev Lear*)
Main characters: King Lear; Goneril, Regan, Cordelia (his daughters); Earl of Gloucester; Edgar (his legitimate son); Edmund (his illegitimate son); Earl of Kent (Lear's faithful follower); The Fool; Duke of Albany (Goneril's husband); Duke of Cornwall (Regan's husband).
Setting: various castles, the open heath, the cliffs of Dover.
Plot: *see entry at* **Lear**.

Love's Labours Lost
(comedy – *abbrev LLL*)
Main characters: King of Navarre; Biron, Longueville, Dumaine, the King's companions; Princess of France; Rosaline, Catherine, Maria, her ladies; Boyet, the Princess's attendant; Don Armado, a Spanish braggart; Costard, a country bumpkin.
Setting: the court of Navarre in southern France.
Plot: The King of Navarre and his companions (despite the misgivings of Biron) solemnly vow to live a life of study and monastic strictness for three years, especially resolving to abjure the company of women. The arrival of the Princess of France, on an embassy from the king her father, accompanied by three ladies, puts an immediate obstacle in the way of this plan. In fact, the four students fall for the four ladies and, after trying to catch each other out, resolve with equal solemnity to abandon their studies and woo the four ladies – which they do, disguised as four Russians for a masque. But the ladies also disguise themselves and make fools of them. The play is about to end with the four couples getting together, when news is brought of the death of the princess's father. The play ends on a semi-sombre note with the ladies ordering the men to show the seriousness of their intentions by waiting a year and a day before seeing them again.

Macbeth (tragedy)
Main characters: Macbeth; Lady Macbeth; Duncan (King of Scotland); Malcolm and Donalbain (his sons); Banquo (a lord and friend of Macbeth); Fleance (his son); Macduff (a lord, an opponent of Macbeth); Lady Macduff; the Three Witches.
Setting: Scotland, especially Macbeth's castle of Dunsinane.
Plot: *see entry at* **Macbeth**.

Measure for Measure
(dark comedy – *abbrev M for M*)
Main characters: Duke of Vienna; Angelo (his deputy); Isabella (a novice in a convent); Claudio (her brother); Mariana (previously engaged to Angelo); Mistress Overdone (a bawd); Pompey (her servant).
Setting: Vienna.
Plot: The Duke of Vienna suddenly announces that he is leaving the city and puts Angelo, a man of stern moral principles, in his place. Angelo adopts a policy of zero tolerance and strictly enforces all the laws which have previously been ignored, as a result of which Claudio is sentenced to death for lechery for getting his fiancée with child. Isabella goes to Angelo to plead for his life. Angelo, against all his previous character, falls in love with her and offers to save his life if she will sleep with him. Isabella refuses, and continues to refuse when Claudio begs her to save him. The Duke, who, instead of leaving the city, has remained disguised as a friar, attempts to sort out the situation by persuading Mariana, Angelo's former fiancée, to stand in for Isabella. But despite apparently having his way with Isabella, Angelo still treacherously orders Claudio's execution and demands to see his head. It takes further manoeuvring by the Duke to stave off disaster. Finally, the Duke stages a ceremonial return and a show trial for Angelo, in which the latter is finally revealed as a villain. His only punishment is to marry Mariana, however, while the Duke marries Isabella.

Merchant of Venice, The
(comedy – *abbrev Merchant*)
Main characters: Antonio, a merchant of
Venice; Bassanio, his friend; Shylock, a
Jewish moneylender; Portia, an heiress;
Nerissa, Portia's waiting gentlewoman;
Graziano, Salerio, Solanio, Lorenzo,
Venetian gentlemen; Jessica, Shylock's
daughter.
Setting: Venice, Belmont.
Plot: see entry at **Merchant of Venice**.

Merry Wives of Windsor, The
(comedy – *M Wives*)
Main characters: Mistress Page, Mistress
Ford, the merry wives; Master Page,
Master Ford, their husbands; Anne Page,
the Pages' daughter; Sir John Falstaff;
Bardolph, Pistol, Nym, his companions;
Dr Caius, a French doctor; Sir Hugh
Evans, a Welsh parson; Slender, a foolish
young man; Fenton, an eligible young
man.
Setting: Windsor and the surrounding
country.
Plot: *The Merry Wives* is a spin-off from
the two parts of *Henry IV*, traditionally
thought to have been written at the
request of Elizabeth I, who wished to see
'Falstaff in love'. Two love plots entwine.
In one, Falstaff attempts to seduce the
two virtuous but good-humoured wives
of the title, but ends up as the victim of
various tricks they play on him. In the
other, three suitors attempt to win the
hand of 'sweet Anne Page'. In a final
scene in Windsor Forest, Falstaff, thinking he is going to a love tryst, is pinched
and tormented by the local children disguised as fairies, while the three suitors
each run away with a supposed Anne
Page, but only Fenton, her actual sweetheart, gets to marry her.

Midsummer Night's Dream, A
(comedy – *abbrev MND*)
Main characters: Hermia and Lysander,
Helena and Demetrius (lovers); Oberon
(fairy king); Titania (fairy queen); Puck
(mischievous fairy servant to Oberon);
the Mechanicals: Nick Bottom (weaver),
Peter Quince (carpenter), Francis Flute

(bellows-mender), Tom Snout (tinker),
Snug (joiner), Robin Starveling (tailor);
Duke Theseus and Queen Hippolyta.
Setting: Athens and 'a wood near the
town'.
Plot: see entry at **Midsummer Night's
Dream**.

Much Ado about Nothing
(comedy – *abbrev Much Ado*)
Main characters: Beatrice and Benedict
(enemies who become lovers); Hero
(Beatrice's cousin, daughter of Leonato);
Leonato (governor of Messina); Don
Pedro (Prince of Aragon); Don John (his
villainous bastard brother); Claudio (a
friend of Don Pedro and Benedict);
Dogberry and Verges (comic watchmen).
Setting: Messina in Italy.
Plot: In the ostensible main plot, Claudio
woos and wins Hero with the help of Don
Pedro, but, deceived by Don John into
thinking her unchaste, rejects her at the
altar. It is given out that Hero has died of
grief and shame, but when the plot is
discovered and Claudio repents, she is
'brought back to life' and marries him.

In the better-known subplot, Beatrice
and Benedict, who are constantly making
witty remarks at each other's expense, are
tricked by their friends into thinking that
each in reality is loved by the other. As a
result they do fall for each other and
marry.

Othello (tragedy)
Main characters: Othello (a Moor in the
service of the state of Venice); Desdemona
(his wife); Iago (his 'ancient'); Emilia
(Iago's wife); Cassio (Othello's lieutenant);
Roderigo (a Venetian gentleman in love
with Desdemona).
Setting: Venice and Cyprus.
Plot: see entry at **Othello**.

Pericles, Prince of Tyre
(romance – *abbrev Peric*)
Main characters: Pericles, Prince of Tyre;
Thaisa, his wife; Marina, his daughter;
Gower, prologue and chorus; Antiochus,
King of Antioch; Simonides, King of
Pentapolis; Cleon, governor of Tarsus;
Dionyza, Cleon's wife.

Setting: Antioch, Pentapolis, Tarsus.

Plot: *Pericles* begins with the hero seeking the daughter of the King of Antioch as a wife, only to discover, by solving the riddle set for all her suitors, that she is incestuously involved with her father. Escaping from Antioch, he enters another love contest and wins the hand of Thaisa, the daughter of the King of Pentapolis. As they are on their way home by sea, his wife apparently dies in childbirth and her body is thrown overboard in a casket. Pericles gives his new-born daughter to Cleon, the governor of Tarsus, to raise. As the girl, Marina, grows up, she proves to be much more beautiful and accomplished than Cleon's own daughter. Cleon's jealous wife arranges to have her killed, but she escapes this fate only to be captured by pirates and eventually sold into a brothel. Her innate goodness enables her to survive there unscathed until, in a very moving recognition scene, her father finds her and is reunited with her – and, ~~in the very last scene~~, with his wife.

Richard II (history – *abbrev Rich II*)

Main characters: King Richard II; John of Gaunt, Duke of Lancaster, and Edmund, Duke of York (his uncles); Henry Bolingbroke (John of Gaunt's son); Earl of Northumberland (a supporter of Bolingbroke); Bushy, Bagot, Green (favourites of King Richard); Thomas Mowbray, Duke of Norfolk.

Setting: England, the Welsh coast, Westminster Hall, Pomfret Castle.

Plot: Richard II is a profligate king who has difficulty controlling his noblemen. He banishes his cousin, Henry Bolingbroke, and when Bolingbroke's father, John of Gaunt, dies, seizes his lands. Bolingbroke returns from exile, ostensibly only to recover his own lands and rights, but, gathering support from the nobility, especially the Earl of Northumberland and the rest of the Percy family, raises his sights to aim at the throne. The frequently self-dramatising Richard is compelled to abdicate in a scene in which he invites Bolingbroke to seize the crown, literally. Bolingbroke is crowned as Henry IV and Richard imprisoned in Pomfret Castle, where he is finally murdered on the new king's orders, though Henry afterwards rejects the murderer.

The play is notable for many fine poetic speeches, especially John of Gaunt's speech on England ('this sceptred isle') and Richard's despairing: 'For God's sake let us sit upon the ground and tell sad stories of the death of kings.'

Richard III (history – *abbrev Rich III*)

Main characters: King Richard III (Duke of Gloucester at start of play); King Edward IV, George Duke of Clarence, his brothers; Duchess of York, their mother; Queen Elizabeth, wife of Edward IV; Queen Margaret, widow of Henry VI; Lady Anne, widow of the former Prince of Wales and later Richard's wife; Lord Hastings; Duke of Buckingham.

Setting: Westminster and Bosworth.

Plot: The most famous speech in the play is Richard's opening soliloquy ('Now is the winter of our discontent made glorious summer by this son of York') describing the peace following the Wars of the Roses and his own unfitness for peacetime activities. He continues his progress towards the throne (first announced in *Henry VI Part III*) by having his brother Clarence killed (drowned in a butt of malmsey wine), and then, when King Edward dies, by having his sons imprisoned in the Tower and murdered. Richard also disposes of two noblemen, Lord Hastings and the Duke of Buckingham, who had previously supported him. Once he is crowned, however, a new threat appears in the person of Henry Tudor, a Lancastrian claimant. On the night before the battle of Bosworth, Richard is visited by the ghosts of the people he has killed. In the ensuing battle ('A horse! A horse! My kingdom for a horse!') Richard fights bravely but is killed and Henry Tudor becomes king with a promise to unite the Houses of York and Lancaster.

Romeo and Juliet
(tragedy – *abbrev R & J*)
Main characters: Romeo, heir of the House of Montague; Juliet, daughter of the head of the House of Capulet; Tybalt, Juliet's cousin; Benvolio, Mercutio, friends of Romeo; Friar Lawrence; Juliet's nurse; Old Capulet; Lady Capulet.
Setting: Verona.
Plot: see entry for **Romeo and Juliet**.

Taming of the Shrew, The
(comedy – *abbrev Shrew*)
Main characters: Petruchio, a gentleman of Verona; Baptista Minola, a gentleman of Padua; Katherina, his elder, bad-tempered, daughter; Bianca, his younger daughter; Grumio, Petruchio's servant.
Setting: Padua.
Plot: Baptista Minola has two daughters, the younger of whom is meek and mild and much sought after as a marriage prospect, but she cannot be married before her elder sister, whose shrewish temper and violent, refractory behaviour puts all suitors off. Enter Petruchio, a gentleman of Verona, who comes to 'wive it wealthily in Padua'. He marries Katherina and tames her not by violence, but by a combination of firmness and perversity that brings her to the point where, at the end of the play, she wins a contest in wifely obedience against her sister.

Tempest, The
Main characters: Prospero, deposed Duke of Milan; Miranda, his daughter; Ariel, an airy spirit attending Prospero; Caliban, a savage and deformed creature forced into Prospero's service; Antonio, Prospero's brother, the usurping Duke of Milan; Alonso, King of Naples; Ferdinand, his son; Sebastian, Alonso's brother; Gonzalo, an honest Neapolitan lord.
Setting: an island in the Mediterranean, where Prospero and Miranda were washed up.
Plot: see entry at **Tempest**.

Timon of Athens
(tragedy – *abbrev Timon*)
Main characters: Timon, a rich Athenian; Alcibiades, an Athenian soldier; Apemantus, a cynical philosopher; Flavius, Timon's faithful steward.
Setting: Athens and a cave in the woods near Athens.
Plot: Timon begins the play as a rich and overly generous man. When he falls on hard times and his creditors call in their debts, none of his fair-weather friends will help him. After inviting them all to a mock banquet with empty dishes, Timon mocks and curses them before taking to the woods and living in a cave as a misanthropic hermit. Here he digs up a crock of gold. Once word of this spreads to Athens, he is again visited. He again gives away his gold, but this time cynically cursing all his visitors and humankind in general. Timon is not killed, he dies offstage and has himself buried on the seashore where the tide washes over his grave.

Titus Andronicus
(tragedy – *abbrev Titus*)
Main characters: Titus Andronicus, a Roman general; Lavinia, his daughter; Tamora, Queen of the Goths; Saturninus, Roman emperor, her husband; Aaron, a Moor, her lover; Chiron and Demetrius, her sons.
Setting: Rome.
Plot: *Titus Andronicus* is perhaps Shakespeare's earliest and probably his bloodiest tragedy. It is marked by a series of revenge killings. Tamora, the Queen of the Goths, defeated in battle by Titus, is brought to Rome, where her eldest son is killed as a sacrifice to appease the families of the Romans slain in battle. Tamora takes her revenge by ordering her sons to rape and mutilate Titus's daughter Lavinia (a famous stage direction reads, *Enter . . . Lavinia, her hands cut off and her tongue cut out and ravished*). In revenge Titus kills Tamora's two younger sons and serves their heads to their mother baked in a pie, before stabbing her, and being stabbed by her husband Saturninus. Saturninus is in turn killed by Lucius, Titus's son, who becomes the next Roman emperor.

Troilus and Cressida
(tragicomedy – *abbrev Tr & Cres*)
Main characters: Troilus, a Trojan prince; Cressida, daughter of Calchas, a priest who has joined the Greeks; Pandarus, her uncle; Agamemnon, Menelaus, Achilles, Ajax, Patroclus, Ulysses, Nestor (Greeks); Hector, Paris (Trojan princes); Helen of Troy; Thersites, a scurrilous Greek.
Setting: Troy
Plot: Troilus, Trojan prince and son of King Priam, is in love with Cressida, but she at first responds very coolly to his overtures. Meanwhile the Greeks are becoming weary and undisciplined as the war drags on – in particular, their chief hero Achilles is refusing to fight. The wily Ulysses evolves a complex plan to get Achilles back into the fray, while at the same time, back in Troy, Troilus enlists the help of Pandarus's uncle to help him win her. Though Troilus has one night of love with Cressida, she is then forced to leave Troy to join her father with the Greeks in an exchange of prisoners, vowing fidelity to Troilus as she goes. Once on the Greek side, however, she takes another lover/protector in Diomedes. Troilus witnesses her infidelity. The play ends in battle, with Troilus seeking to be revenged on Diomedes and Achilles, finally roused to action by the death of his friend, Patroclus, rejoining the battle and killing the great Trojan hero in a cowardly fashion.

Twelfth Night
(comedy – *abbrev T Night*)
Main characters: Orsino, Duke of Illyria; Viola, a shipwrecked lady; Sebastian, her brother; Olivia, an Illyrian lady; Malvolio, her steward; Maria, her waiting gentlewoman; Feste, her jester; Sir Toby Belch, her cousin; Sir Andrew Aguecheek, Sir Toby's companion.
Setting: Illyria.
Plot: *see entry for* **Twelfth Night**.

Two Gentlemen of Verona, The
(comedy – *abbrev Two Gents*)
Main characters: Valentine and Proteus, two gentlemen of Verona; Silvia, daughter of the Duke of Milan; Julia, Proteus's sweetheart; Lance, Proteus's servant; Speed, Valentine's servant; Crab (Lance's dog).
Setting: Milan.
Plot: Valentine leaves Verona to see the world, beginning with Milan, leaving his friend Proteus behind. Proteus is soon sent after him by his father, leaving his beloved Julia behind. Julia, however, disguises herself as a boy and follows. On his arrival in Milan, Valentine falls in love with the Duke's daughter Silvia. No sooner has Proteus joined him than he falls in love with Silvia too, forgetting Julia. Proteus betrays Valentine's plan to elope with Silvia to her father, who banishes Valentine. Julia arrives in Milan just in time to hear Proteus serenading Silvia ('Who is Silvia? What is she?'). She disguises herself as a boy and becomes Proteus's page. Silvia attempts to rejoin Valentine, but is waylaid by Proteus, who threatens to rape her. Valentine rescues her, but when Proteus repents, forgives him and offers him Silvia. At this Julia faints and then reveals herself – at this the couples are at last properly paired off.

Winter's Tale, The
(romance – *abbrev W Tale*)
Main characters: Leontes, King of Sicily; Hermione, his wife; Perdita, his daughter; Polixenes, King of Bohemia; Florizel, his son; Antigonus, a Sicilian lord; Paulina, his wife; Old Shepherd, Perdita's foster father; Autolycus, a pedlar and rogue.
Setting: Sicily and Bohemia.
Plot: Leontes suddenly and unaccountably suspects his pregnant wife, Hermione, of infidelity with his boyhood friend Polixenes, King of Bohemia. When her baby daughter is born, Leontes orders Antigonus to leave it to die in the wilderness. Leontes then puts Hermione on trial, but she is pronounced innocent by the Delphic oracle. Leontes does not accept the oracle, until news is brought of the death of his son and the arrival of this news seems to kill Hermione too. Leontes

then belatedly sees the error of his ways and repents. Meanwhile Antigonus has arrived with the baby girl on the coast of Bohemia. There he leaves the baby and is himself killed (the famous stage direction reads, '*Exit, pursued by a bear*'), but Perdita is found and taken home by an old shepherd and his son. Many years elapse and the next scene shows Perdita as a young woman presiding over a spring festival and being wooed by a disguised Florizel, the son of Polixenes. Polixenes rules out any suggestion of marriage, so the young couple decide to escape to Sicily. The scene is then set for a reunion and reconciliation, which culminates in the unveiling of a statue of the supposedly long-dead Hermione. When unveiled, the statue proves to be Hermione herself, who has been lovingly tended by her friend Paulina, and now 'comes back to life' to be reunited with her husband and her daughter.

SHAKESPEARE CHARACTERS

(*see above for abbreviations*)

(3) Nym (*Hen V, M Wives*), Say (Lord, *Hen VI 2*), Sly (Christopher, *Shrew*).

(4) Adam (*AYLI*), Ajax (*Tr. & Cres.*), Anne (Lady, *Rich III*), Bona (*Hen VI 3*), Cade (Jack, *Hen VI 2*), Cato (*JC*), Davy (*Hen VI 2*), Dick (*Hen VI 2*), Dion (*W Tale*), Dull (*LLL*), Eros (*Ant & Cle*), Fang (*Hen IV 2*), Ford (*M Wives*), Grey (*Hen V, Rich III*), Hero (*Much Ado*), Hume (*Hen VI 2*), Iago (*Othello*), Iden (*Hen VI 2*), Iras (*Ant & Cleo*), Jamy (*Hen V*), John (*K John, Rom & Jul, Hen IV 1&2*), Juno (*Tempest*), Lear (*Lear*), Lena (*JC*), Luce (*Com Err*), Lucy (*Hen VI 1*), Moth (*LLL, MND*), Page (*M Wives*), Peto (Hen *IV* 1 & 2), Puck (*MND*), Ross (*Macbeth, Rich III*), Snug (*MND*), Vaux (*Hen VIII, Hen VI 2*), Wart (*Hen IV 2*).

(5) Aaron (*Titus*), Alice (*Hen V*), Angus (*Macbeth*), Ariel (*Tempest*), Bagot (*Rich II*), Bates (*Hen V*), Belch (Sir Toby, *T Night*), Bevis (*Hen VI 2*),

Bigot (*K John*), Blunt (Sir Walter, Hen *IV 1*), Boult (*Peric*), Boyet (*LLL*), Bushy (*Rich II*), Butts (*Hen VIII*), Caius (*Titus, M Wives*),Casca (*JC*), Celia (*AYLI*), Ceres (*Tempest*), Cinna (*JC*), Cleon (*Peric*), Corin (*AYLI*), Court (*Hen V*), Cupid (*Timon*), Curan (*Lear*), Curio (*T Night*), Denny (*Hen VIII*), Diana (*All's Well, Peric*), Edgar (*Lear*), Egeus (*MND*), Elbow (*M for M*), Evans (Sir Hugh, *M Wives*), Exton (Sir Piers, *Rich II*), Feste (*T Night*), Flute (*MND*), Froth (*M for M*), Gobbo (*Merchant*), Goffe (*Hen VI 2*), Gower (*Hen IV 2, Henry V, Peric*), Green (*Rich II*), Helen (*Cymb, Tr & Cres*), Henry (*K John, Hen V, Hen VI 3, Hen IV 1 & 2, Hen VIII, Rich III*), Julia (*Two Gents*), Lafeu (*All's Well*), Lewis (*Henry V, K John*), Louis (*Hen VI 3*), Lovel (*Rich III*), Lucio (*M for M*), Maria (*LLL, T Night*), Melun (*K John*), Menas (*Ant & Cleo*), Mopsa (*W Tale*), Osric (*Hamlet*), Paris (Rom *& Jul, Tr & Cres*), Percy (*Hen IV 1 & 2, Rich II*), Peter (*Hen VI 2, K John, M for M, Rom & Jul*), Phebe (*AYLI*), Philo (*Ant & Cleo*), Pinch (*Com Err*), Poins (*Hen IV 1 & 2*), Priam (*Tr & Cres*), Regan (*Lear*), Robin (*M Wives*), Romeo (*Rom & Jul*), Rugby (*M Wives*), Smith (*Hen VI 2*), Snare (*Hen IV 2*), Snout (*MND*), Speed (*Two Gents*), Timon (*Timon*), Titus (*Timon*), Tubal (*Merchant*), Varro (*JC*), Viola (*T Night*).

(6) Adrian (*Corio*), Aegeon (*Com Err*), Aeneas (*Tr & Cres*), Alexas (*Ant & Cleo*), Alonso (*Tempest*), Amiens (*AYLI*), Angelo (*Com Err, M for M*), Antony (*Ant & Cleo*), Arthur (*K John*), Audrey (*AYLI*), Banquo (*Macbeth*), Basset (*Hen VI 1*), Bianca (*Othello, Shrew*), Blanch (*K John*), Blount (*Rich III*), Bottom (*MND*), Brutus (*JC, Corio*), Bullen (*Hen VIII*), Caesar (*Ant & Cleo, JC*), Caphis (*Timon*), Cassio (*Othello*),

list continued over

Chiron (*Titus*), Cicero (*JC*), Cimber (*JC*), Clitus (*JC*), Cloten (*Cymb*), Cobweb (*MND*), Curtis (*Shrew*), Dennis (*AYLI*), Dorcas (*W Tale*), Dromio (*Com Err*), Dumain (*LLL*), Duncan (*Macbeth*), Edmund (*Hen VI 3, Lear*), Edward (*Hen VI 2 & 3, Rich III*), Elinor (*K John*), Emilia (*Othello, W Tale*), Fabian (*T Night*), Feeble (*Henry IV 2*), Fenton (*M Wives*), Gallus (*Ant & Cleo*), George (*Hen VI 3, Rich III*), Gremio (*Shrew*), Grumio (*Shrew*), Gurney (*K John*), Hamlet (*Hamlet*), Hecate (*Macbeth*), Hector (*Tr & Cres*), Helena (*All's Well, MND*), Hermia (*MND*), Horner (*Hen VI 2*), Hubert (*K John*), Imogen (*Cymb*), Isabel (*Hen V*), Jaques (*AYLI*), Juliet (*M for M, Rom & Jul*), Launce (*Two Gents*), Le Beau (*AYLI*), Lennox (*Macbeth*), Lovell (*Hen VIII,*), Lucius (*JC, Timon, Cymb, Titus*), Marina (*Peric*), Minola (*Shrew*), Morton (*Hen IV 2, Rich III*), Mouldy (*Hen IV 2*), Mutius (*Titus*), Nestor (*Tr & Cres*), Oliver (*AYLI*), Olivia (*T Night*), Orsino (*T Night*), Oswald (*Lear*), Pistol (*Hen IV 2, Hen V, M Wives*), Pompey (*M for M*), Portia (*JC, Merchant*), Quince (Peter, *MND*), Rivers (Lord, *Rich III, Hen VI 3*), Rumour (*Hen IV 2*), Sandys (*Hen VIII*), Scales (*Hen VI 2*), Scarus (*Ant & Cleo*), Scroop (*Hen IV 1 & 2, Rich II, Hen V*), Seyton (*Macbeth*), Shadow (*Hen IV 2*), Silius (*Ant & Cleo*), Silvia (*Two Gents*), Simcox (*Hen VI 2*), Simple (*M Wives*), Siward (*Macbeth*), Strato (*JC*), Talbot (*Hen VI 1*), Tamora (*Titus*), Taurus (*Ant & Cleo*), Thaisa (*Peric*), Thomas (*Hen IV 2, M for M*), Thurio (*Two Gents*), Tranio (*Shrew*), Tybalt (*Rom & Jul*), Tyrrel (*Rich III*), Ursula (*Much Ado*), Verges (*Much Ado*), Vernon (*Hen IV 1, Hen VI 1*), Wolsey (*Hen VIII*).

(7) Abraham (*Rom & Jul*), Adriana (*Com Err*), Aemilia (*Com Err*), Agrippa (*Ant & Cleo, Corio*), Alarbus (*Titus*), Amazons (*Timon*), Antenor (*Tr & Cres*), Antonio (*Merchant, Much Ado,*

Tempest, T Night, Two Gents), Berowne (*LLL*), Bertram (*All's Well*), Brandon (*Hen VIII, Rich II*), Calchas (*Tr & Cres*), Caliban (*Tempest*), Camillo (*W Tale*), Capulet (*Rom & Jul*), Cassius (*JC*), Catesby (*Rich III*), Cerimon (*Peric*), Charles (*AYLI, Hen VI 1, Hen V*), Claudio (*M for M, Much Ado*), Conrade (*Much Ado*), Costard (*LLL*), Cranmer (*Hen VIII*), Dionyza (*Peric*), Don John (*Much Ado*), Douglas (Earl of, *Hen IV 1*), Eleanor (*Hen VI 2*), Escalus (*M for M, Rom & Jul*), Escanes (*Peric*), Flavius (*JC, Timon*), Fleance (*Macbeth*), Francis (*Hen IV 1, Much Ado*), Goneril (*Lear*), Gonzalo (*Tempest*), Gregory (*Rom & Jul*), Helenus (*Tr & Cres*), Herbert (*Rich III*), Holland (*Hen VI 2*), Horatio (*Hamlet*), Hotspur (*Hen IV 1*), Iachimo (*Cymb*), Jessica (*Merchant*), Laertes (*Hamlet*), Lartius (*Corio*), Lavache (*All's Well*), Lavinia (*Titus*), Leonato (*Much Ado*), Leonine (*Peric*), Leontes (*W Tale*), Lepidus (*Ant & Cleo, JC*), Lord Say (*Hen VI 2*), Lorenzo (*Merchant*), Lucetta (*Two Gents*), Luciana (*Com Err*), Lymoges (*K John*), Macbeth (*Macbeth*), Macduff (*Macbeth*), Malcolm (*Macbeth*), Marcade (*LLL*), Marcius (*Corio*), Mardian (*Ant & Cleo*), Mariana (*All's Well, M for M*), Martext (Sir Oliver, *AYLI*), Martius (*Titus*), Messala (*JC*), Michael (*Hen VI 2, Hen IV 1*), Miranda (*Tempest*), Montano (*Othello*), Montjoy (*Hen V*), Mowbray (*Hen IV 2, Rich II*), Nerissa (*Merchant*), Nicanor (*Corio*), Octavia (*Rom & Jul*), Ophelia (*Hamlet*), Orlando (*AYLI*), Othello (*Othello*), Paulina (*W Tale*), Perdita (*W Tale*), Phyrnia (*Timon*), Pisanio (*Cymb*), Proteus (*Two Gents*), Provost (*M for M*), Publius (*JC, Titus*), Quickly (Mistress, *Hen IV 1 & 2, M Wives*), Quintus (*Titus*), Richard (*Hen VI 2 & 3, Rich II, Rich III*), Salerio (*Merchant*), Sampson (*Rom & Jul*), Shallow (*M Wives, Hen I 2*), Shylock (*Merchant*),

list continued over

Silence (*Hen IV 2*), Silvius (*AYLI*), Slender (*M Wives*), Solanio (*Merchant*), Solinus (*Com Err*), Stanley (*Hen VI 3, Rich III, Hen VI 2*), Theseus (*MND*), Thyreus (*Ant & Cleo*), Titania (*MND*), Travers (*Henry IV 2*), Tressel (*Rich III*), Troilus (*Tr & Cres*), Ulysses (*Tr & Cres*), Urswick (*Rich III*), Valeria (*Corio*), Varrius (*Ant & Cleo*), Vaughan (*Rich III*), Velutus (*Corio*), William (*AYLI*), Witches (*Macbeth*).

(8) Abhorson (*M for M*), Achilles (*Tr & Cres*), Aemilius (*Titus*), Antonius (*JC*), Aufidius (*Corio*), Bardolph (*Hen IV 1, Hen V, M Wives, Hen VI*), Bassanio (*Merchant*), Beatrice (*Much Ado*), Beaufort (*Hen VI 2 & 3, Hen VI 1*), Belarius (*Cymb*), Benedick (*Much Ado*), Benvolio (*Rom & Jul*), Berkeley (*Rich II, Rich III*), Bernardo (*Hamlet*), Borachio (*Much Ado*), Bullcalf (*Hen IV 2*), Campeius (*Hen VIII*), Canidius (*Ant & Cleo*), Capucius (*Hen VIII*), Charmian (*Ant & Cleo*), Claudius (*Hamlet, JC*), Clifford (*Hen VI 2 & 3*), Colville (*Hen IV 2*), Cominius (*Corio*), Cordelia (*Lear*), Cressida (*Tr & Cres*), Cromwell (*Hen VIII*), Dercetas (*Ant & Cleo*), Diomedes (*Ant & Cleo*), Dogberry (*Much Ado*), Don Pedro (*Much Ado*), Eglamour (*Two Gents*), Falstaff (Sir John, *M Wives, Hen IV 1 & 2*), Fastolfe (*Hen VI 1*), Florizel (*W Tale*), Fluellen (*Hen V*), Gadshill (*Hen IV 1*), Gardiner (*Hen VIII*), Gargrave (*Hen VI 1*), Gertrude (*Hamlet*), Grandpre (*Hen V*), Gratiano (*Merchant, Othello*), Griffith (*Hen VIII*), Harcourt (*Hen IV 2*), Hastings (*Hen IV 2, Hen VI 3, Rich III*), Hermione (*W Tale*), Humphrey (*Henry IV 2*), Isabella (*M for M*), Jack Cade (*Hen VI 2*), John Hume (*Hen VI 2*), Jourdain (*Hen VI 2*), King John (*K John*), King Lear (*Lear*), Lady Anne (*Rich III*), Lady Grey (*Hen VI 3*), Lawrence (Friar, *Rom & Jul*), Leonardo (*Merchant*), Leonatus (*Cymb*), Ligarius (*JC*),

Lodovico (*Othello*), Luciento (*Shrew*), Lucilius (*JC, Timon*), Lucullus (*Timon*), Lysander (*MND*), Maecenas (*Ant & Cleo*), Malvolio (*T Night*), Margaret (*Much Ado, Rich III, Hen VI 1, 2 & 3*), Marullus (*JC*), Menelaus (*Tr & Cres*), Menteith (*Macbeth*), Mercutio (*Rom & Jul*), Montague (*Rom & Jul*), Mortimer (*Hen IV 1, Hen VI 1, Hen VI 3*), Overdone (Mistress, *M for M*), Pandarus (*Tr & Cres*), Pandulph (*K John*), Panthino (*Two Gents*), Parolles (*All's Well*), Patience (*Hen VIII*), Pericles (*Peric*), Philario (*Cymb*), Philemon (*Peric*), Philotus (*Timon*), Pindarus (*JC*), Polonius (*Hamlet*), Pompeius (*Ant & Cleo*), Prospero (*Tempest*), Rambures (*Hen V*), Ratcliff (*Rich III*), Reignier (*Hen VI 1*), Reynaldo (*Hamlet*), Roderigo (*Othello*), Rosalind (*AYLI*), Rosaline (*LLL*), Seleucus (*Ant & Cleo*), Stafford (*Hen VI 3, Hen VI 2*), Stephano (*Merchant, Tempest*), Thaliard (*Peric*), Timandra (*Timon*), Titinius (*JC*), Trinculo (*Tempest*), Violenta (*All's Well*), Virgilia (*Corio*), Volumnia (*Corio*), Whitmore (*Hen VI 2*), Williams (*Hen V*).

(9) Agamemnon (*Tr & Cres*), Aguecheek (Sir Andrew, *T Night*), Alexander (*Tr & Cres*), Antigonus (*W Tale*), Antiochus (*Peric*), Apemantus (*Timon*), Arviragus (*Cymb*), Autolycus (*W Tale*), Balthasar (*Merchant, Much Ado, Rom & Jul*), Balthazar (*Com Err*), Bassianus (*Titus*), Biondello (*Shrew*), Brabantio (*Othello*), Caithness (*Macbeth*), Calpurnia (JC), Cassandra (*Tr & Cres*), Chatillon (*K John*), Cleomenes (*W Tale*), Cleopatra (*Ant & Cleo*), Constance (*K John*), Cornelius (*Cymb, Hamlet*), Cymbeline (*Cymb*), Dardanius (*JC*), Deiphobus (*Tr & Cres*), Demetrius (*Ant & Cleo, MND, Titus*), Desdemona (*Othello*), Dolabella (*Ant & Cleo*), Donalbain (*Macbeth*), Elizabeth (*Rich III*),

list continued over

Enobarbus (*Ant & Cleo*), Erpingham (*Hen V*), Ferdinand (*LLL, Tempest*), Fitzwater (*Rich II*), Flaminius (*Timon*), Francisca (*M for M*), Francisco (*Hamlet, Tempest*), Frederick (*AYLI*), Glansdale (*Hen VI 1*), Glendower (*Hen IV 1*), Guiderius (*Cymb*), Guildford (*Hen VIII*), Helicanus (*Peric*), Hippolyta (*MND*), Hortensio (*Shrew*), Katharine (*LLL, Hen VIII*), Katherina (*Shrew*), Katherine (*Hen V*), Lychorida (*Peric*), Macmorris (*Hen V*), Mamillius (*W Tale*), Marcellus (*Hamlet*), Nathaniel (*LLL*), Patroclus (*Tr & Cres*), Petruchio (*Shrew*), Polixenes (*W Tale*), Sebastian (*Tempest, T Night*), Servilius (*Timon*), Simonides (*Peric*), Southwell (*Hen VI 2*), Tearsheet (*Doll, Hen IV 2*), Thersites (*Tr & Cres*), Trebonius (*JC*), Valentine (*Titus, T Night, Two Gents*), Ventidius (*Ant & Cleo, Timon*), Vincentio (*M for M, Shrew*), Voltemand (*Hamlet*), Volumnius (*JC*), Woodville (*Hen VI 1*).

(10) Alcibiades (*Timon*), Andromache (*Tr & Cres*), Andronicus (*Titus*), Antipholus (*Com Err*), Archidamus (*W Tale*), Barnardine (*M for M*), Brakenbury (*Rich III*), Coriolanus (*Corio*), Euphronius (*Ant & Cleo*), Fortinbras (*Hamlet*), Holofernes (*LLL*), Jaquenetta (*LLL*), Longaville (*LLL*), Lysimachus (*Peric*), Margarelon (*Tr & Cres*), Menecrates (*Ant & Cleo*), Montgomery (*Hen VI 3*), Proculeius (*Ant & Cleo*), Saturninus (*Titus*), Sempronius (*Timon, Titus*), Somerville (*Hen VI 3*), Starveling (*MND*), Touchstone (*AYLI*), Willoughby (*Rich II*).

(11) Abergavenny (*Henry VIII*), Artemidorus (*JC*), Bolingbroke (*Rich II*), Mustardseed (*MND*), Philostrate (*MND*), Rosencrantz (*Hamlet*).

(12) Guildenstern (*Hamlet*), Peaseblossom (*MND*).

(13) Faulconbridge (*K John*).

sham I *n & adj* (4) fake, hoax; (6) phoney; (7) replica; (9) imitation; (11) counterfeit; (12) reproduction; **II** *adj* (5) bogus, false; (6) forged, pseudo; (9) simulated; (10) artificial; **III** *n* (4) copy; (7) forgery; (8) impostor; (9) charlatan; **IV** *v* (5) feign, forge; (6) affect; (7) falsify, pretend; (8) simulate; **V** *cryptic* ANAGRAM CUE.

shape I *n & v* (4) cast, form; (5) build, frame, model, mould; (6) format; (7) fashion, outline, pattern, profile; **II** *n* 1 (6) figure; (8) physique; (10) silhouette; 2 (4) trim; (5) state; (6) fettle, health; (9) condition; **III** *v* (5) adapt, carve, forge; (6) create, devise, sculpt; (7) develop, prepare.

SHAPES

(4) cone, cube, kite, oval; (5) helix, prism, rhomb, torus; (6) circle, cuboid, oblong, sphere, square; (7) decagon, diamond, ellipse, hexagon, lozenge, nonagon, octagon, polygon, pyramid, rhombus; (8) crescent, cylinder, heptagon, pentagon, quadrant, triangle; (9) rectangle, trapezium; (13) parallelogram, quadrilateral.

---

share I *v* (4) deal, dole, give, mete; (5) allot, split; (6) assign, divide; (9) apportion; (10) distribute, (2 words) deal out, dole out, give out, hand out, mete out; **II** *n* (3) cut, due, lot; (4) part; (5) quota; (6) ration; (7) portion; (9) allowance; (12) contribution.

sharp *adj* 1 (4) keen; (5) edged, spiky; (6) barbed, jagged; (7) cutting, pointed; (8) piercing, stabbing; 2 (4) acid, sour, tart; (7) acerbic, piquant, pungent; 3 (4) curt; (5) gruff, harsh; (6) abrupt, biting, severe, sudden; (7) violent; (8) incisive, sardonic, scathing; (9) sarcastic; 4 (3) fly, sly; (5) alert, aware; (6) artful, astute, clever, crafty, shrewd; (7) cunning; (9) observant; (10) discerning, perceptive.

shatter I *v* (3) mar; (4) ruin; (5) break, burst, crack, crush, smash, split, spoil, upset, wreck; (6) shiver; (7) destroy; (8) demolish, splinter; (9) devastate, overwhelm; **II** **shatter** *or* **shattered** ANAGRAM CUE.

Shaw, George Bernard *lit.* Irish dramatist, pamphleteer and socialist, often known as GBS.

PLAYS BY SHAW

Androcles and the Lion, The Apple Cart, Arms and the Man, Back to Methuselah, Caesar and Cleopatra, Candida, Captain Brassbound's Conversion, The Devil's Disciple, The Doctor's Dilemma, Getting Married, Heartbreak House, John Bull's Other Island, Major Barbara, Man and Superman, Misalliance, Mrs Warren's Profession, Pygmalion, Saint Joan, Too True to be Good, Widowers' Houses, You Never Can Tell.

---

shear *v* (3) cut; (4) clip, snap; (5) break, shave, strip.

sheer *adj* **1** (5) steep; (6) abrupt; (8) vertical; (11) precipitous; (13) perpendicular; **2** (4) mere, pure; (5) total, utter; (6) simple; (8) absolute, complete; (9) downright, out-and-out, undiluted; (11) unmitigated, unqualified; (13) unadulterated; **3** (4) fine; (5) filmy, gauzy, light; (6) flimsy; (8) gossamer; (10) see-through; (11) translucent, transparent; (13) insubstantial.

shellfish *n* (7) mollusc; (10) crustacean.

TYPES OF SHELLFISH

(4) clam, crab; (5) ormer, prawn, whelk; (6) cockle, mussel, oyster, scampi, shrimp, winkle; (7) abalone, lobster, scallop; (8) barnacle, crawfish, crayfish, nautilus; (9) langouste; (11) langoustine.

---

shelter **I** *n & v* (4) hide, roof; (5) cover, guard, shade; (6) screen; (7) harbour; **II** *n* (5) haven; (6) asylum, refuge, safety; (7) defence, lodging, retreat; (9) sanctuary; (10) protection; **III** *v* (6) defend, shield; (7) protect.

shield **I** *n & v* (4) hide; (5) cover, guard; (6) screen; **II** *n* (5) targe; (6) target; (7) buckler, bulwark, defence, rampart; (9) safeguard; (10) escutcheon; **III** *v* (6) defend; (7) protect, shelter.

shift **I** *n & v* (4) move; (6) change, switch; (8) transfer; **II** *v* (4) vary; (5) alter, budge; (6) remove; (8) displace, dislodge, relocate; (10) reposition; **II** *n* **1** (10) alteration; (12) modification; (13) rearrangement, transposition; **2** (4) gang, turn; (5) spell, watch; (6) period; **3** (5) dodge, trick; (9) expedient, stratagem; **4** (4) sark; (5) shirt; (7) chemise; **IV** *cryptic* ANAGRAM CUE.

shine **I** *v & n* (4) glow; (5) flash, glare, gleam, glint; (7) glimmer, glitter, shimmer, sparkle, twinkle; **II** *v* **1** (4) beam; (7) glisten, glister; **2** (3) rub; (4) buff; (6) polish; **3** (5) excel; **III** *n* (5) gloss, light, sheen; (6) lustre; (8) radiance.

ship **I** *n* (4) boat; (5) craft; (6) vessel; **II** *v* (4) send; (6) embark (7) consign, freight; (9) transport.

TYPES OF SHIP

see also **boat, sailing ship**

(3) ark, cat, hoy, MTB, sub, tug.

(4) bark, boat, brig, dhow, dory, duck, junk.

(5) ferry, liner, sloop, smack, U-boat.

(6) barque, bireme, caique, carvel, galley, lugger, tanker, tender.

(7) caravel, carrack, carrier, clipper, coaster, collier, cruiser, dredger, drifter, frigate, galleon, lighter, monitor, pinnace, steamer, trawler, trireme, tug-boat, vedette.

(8) corvette, flagship, galleass, indiaman, ironclad, longship, mailboat, man-of-war, schooner.

(9) amphibian, destroyer, freighter, hydrofoil, lightship, minelayer, privateer, steamship, submarine, troopship.

(10) barkentine, battleship, brigantine, hydroplane, ice-breaker, packet-boat, windjammer.

(11) barquentine, bulk-carrier, dreadnought, mine-sweeper, motor-vessel, supertanker, torpedo-boat.

(2+ words) aircraft carrier, motor torpedo boat.

---

shipment *n* (4) load; (5) batch; (6) parcel; (7) freight; (8) carriage, delivery, dispatch; (9) transport; (10) conveyance; (11) consignment.

shocking *adj* (5) awful, scary; (7) fearful; (8) alarming, dreadful, gruesome, horrible, horrific; (9) appalling, frightful; (10) horrifying, petrifying; (11) hair-raising; (13) blood-curdling, spine-chilling.

shoe *n* (3) dap; (4) boot, clog, mule, pump; (6) brogue, galosh, loafer, oxford, patten, sandal; (7) slipper, sneaker, trainer; (8) flipflop, footwear, mocassin, platform, plimsoll, stiletto; (9) slingback; (10) espadrille.

shoot l *v* 1 (3) aim; (4) emit, fire, hurl; (5) blast, fling, throw; (6) direct; (9) discharge; 2 (3) hit; (4) kill; (5) wound; 3 (4) bolt, dart, **rush**; 4 (4) film; (10) photograph; ll *n* (3) bud; (4) slip, twig; (5) scion, sprig; (6) branch, sprout, sucker.

shop l *n* (5) store; (6) bazaar, market, outlet; (8) boutique, emporium; (11) hypermarket, supermarket; ll *v* 1 (3) buy; (8) purchase; 2 (5) grass; (6) betray.

short *adj* 1 (3) low, wee; (4) mini, tiny (5) brief, dwarf, scant, small, squat, teeny; (7) compact, stunted; (10) diminutive; 2 (5) brief; (7) passing; (8) fleeting; (9) ephemeral, momentary, temporary, transient; (10) transitory; 3 (5) pithy, terse; (7) concise; (8) abridged, succinct; (9) curtailed; (10) compressed; 4 (4) curt, rude; (5) gruff, sharp; (6) abrupt, snappy; (7) brusque, uncivil; (8) impolite; (12) discourteous; 5 (6) scarce, sparse; (7) lacking; (9) deficient; (10) inadequate; (12) insufficient.

shortage *n* (4) lack; (6) dearth; (7) absence, paucity, poverty; (8) scarcity, shortage, sparsity; (10) deficiency, inadequacy, scantiness, sparseness; (13) insufficiency.

shot *n* (3) cut, pot; (4) pull, putt; (5) drive; (6) glance, stroke, volley.

TYPES OF SHOT

(4) ball, slug; (5) grape, shell; (6) bullet; (8) birdshot, buckshot, canister, caseshot, duckshot; (9) cartridge; (10) cannonball.

---

shout *n & v* (3) cry; (4) bawl, call, hail, howl, roar, yell; (5) cheer; (6) bellow, scream, shriek.

show l *v* 1 (5) prove, teach; (6) expose, flaunt, parade, reveal, unmask, unveil; (7) display, exhibit, explain, present, testify, uncover; (8) disclose, discover, flourish, indicate, instruct, manifest; (9) exemplify, represent; (10) illustrate; (11) demonstrate; 2 (4) lead; (5) guide, usher; (6) escort; (7) conduct; ll *n* 1 (4) fair, play; (6) parade; (7) display, musical; (9) amusement, spectacle; (10), exposition; (11) performance; (13) entertainment; 2 (8) exposure; (10) expression, revelation; (12) illustration, presentation; (13) manifestation; 3 (3) air; (5) front; (6) façade; (8) illusion, pretence; (9) semblance; (10) appearance; 4 (4) pose; (7) bravado, panache, swagger; (11) affectation; lll *cryptic* HIDDEN WORD CUE.

shrub *n* (4) bush; (5) plant.

TYPES OF SHRUB

(3) box, ivy.

(4) hebe.

(5) broom, elder, gorse, holly, lilac.

(6) azalea, daphne, laurel, mallow, mimosa, myrtle, privet.

(7) bramble, dogwood, fuchsia, heather, jasmine, spiraea, syringa, weigela.

(8) berberis, buddleia, camellia, clematis, euonymus, gardenia, japonica, laburnum, lavender, magnolia, rosemary, viburnum.

(9) firethorn, forsythia, hydrangea.

(10) blackberry, periwinkle.

(11) cotoneaster, honeysuckle.

---

sick *adj* 1 (3) ill; (5) frail, seedy; (6) ailing, infirm, poorly, queasy, unwell; (8)

nauseous; (9) off-colour, unhealthy; (10) indisposed; (2+ words) not oneself, out of sorts, under the weather; 2 (6) morbid; (7) macabre.

side I n 1 (4) bank, edge, face, hand, wing; (5) facet, flank, limit, shore, verge; (6) border, fringe, margin; 2 (4) leaf, page; (5) folio, recto, sheet, verso; 3 (4) camp, team; (5) cause, squad; (6) eleven, line-up; (7) faction, fifteen; 4 (4) view; (5) angle, slant; (6) aspect; (9) viewpoint; (10) standpoint; **II** *cryptic* 1 letters II, XI, or XV, or L or R; 2 use the beginning or end (or the first or last letter) of a word in the clue, as in: 'Place of execution by stream on far side of city' (6) = Tyburn (far side of 'city' = TY).

sight I n 1 (6) seeing, vision; (8) eyesight; 2 (4) show, view; (5) scene; (7) display; (9) spectacle; **II** *v see* **see**.

sign I n 1 (4) logo, mark, plus, tick; (5) arrow, badge, cross, minus, token; (6) emblem, signal, symbol; (8) insignia, reminder; 2 (4) clue, hint; (5) scrap, shred, trace, whiff; (7) glimmer, remnant, residue; (8) evidence; (9) suspicion; (10) indication; 3 (4) omen; (6) augury; (7) portent; 4 (5) board; (6) notice, poster; (7) pointer; **II** *v* (7) endorse, initial; (9) autograph; **III** *see* **zodiac**.

signal I n & v (3) cue, nod; (4) mark, sign, wave; (5) morse; (7) gesture; (9) semaphore, telegraph; **II** n 1 (9) indicator; 2 (5) alarm, alert, flare, light; (6) beacon, rocket; **III** *v* (6) beckon, motion; (8) indicate; (11) communicate; **IV** *adj* (7) notable; (10) remarkable; (11) outstanding.

significant *adj* (5) major, vital; (7) crucial, fateful, serious, weighty; (8) critical, decisive, historic; (9) important, momentous; (11) epoch-making; (12) earth-shaking.

silence I n (3) mum; (4) calm, hush, rest; (5) peace, quiet; (6) repose; (8) dumbness, serenity; (9) stillness; (11) taciturnity; (12) tranquillity; **II** *v* 1 (4) dull, hush, mute; (6) deaden, muffle, soften, stifle; (7) quieten; (8) diminish; 2 (3) gag; (6) muzzle; (8) suppress; **III** *cryptic* letters P, PP or SH.

silent *adj* 1 (4) soft; (5) muted, quiet, still; (6) gentle, hushed; (7) muffled, subdued; (9) inaudible, noiseless; 2 (4) calm; (6) placid, serene; (8) composed, peaceful, tranquil; (10) untroubled; (11) undisturbed; 3 (3) shy; (8) reserved, reticent, retiring, taciturn; (13) unforthcoming; (15) uncommunicative; 4 (5) tacit; (8) unspoken; (10) understood.

silicon *cryptic* abbreviated as SI.

silly *adj* (3) mad; (4) bats, daft, nuts, wild; (5) barmy, crazy, dotty, inane, loopy, nutty, potty; (6) absurd, crazed, insane, mental, screwy, simple, stupid, unwise; (7) barking, bonkers, foolish, idiotic, lunatic; (9) fanatical, imprudent, ludicrous, senseless; (10) infatuated, ridiculous; (11) impractical, unrealistic; (12) enthusiastic; (13) irresponsible.

silver *cryptic* abbreviated as AG – also ARGENT (heraldry).

simple I *adj* 1 (4) easy; (5) basic, clear; (7) primary; (8) painless; (10) effortless, elementary, manageable; (11) fundamental, rudimentary, undemanding; (12) introductory; (13) uncomplicated, unproblematic; (15) straightforward; 2 (5) lowly, plain; (6) humble; (8) ordinary; (9) unadorned; 3 (7) artless, natural; (9) guileless, ingenuous; (10) unaffected; (13) unpretentious; (15) unsophisticated; 4 (5) silly; (6) stupid; (7) foolish, idiotic; (8) backward; **II** n (4) herb.

sin I n (5) abuse, crime, error, fault, lapse; (6) injury; (7) misdeed, offence; (8) iniquity, trespass; **II** *v* (3) err; (4) fall; (5) stray; (6) offend; (8) trespass; (10) transgress.

THE SEVEN DEADLY SINS

anger, avarice, envy, gluttony, lechery, pride, sloth.

---

sing *v* (3) hum; (4) pipe; (5) chant, chirp, croon, trill; (6) warble.

singer n (4) alto, bass, diva; (5) tenor; (6) cantor, treble; (7) soloist, soprano; (8) baritone, castrato, choirboy, minstrel, songster, vocalist; (9) balladeer, chorister, choirgirl, contralto, precentor; (10) troubadour.

SOME FAMOUS SINGERS
Classical

(4) Lind (Jenny – the Swedish nightingale).

(5) Baker (Janet), Evans (Geraint), Gedda (Nicolai), Gigli (Beniamino), Gobbi (Tito), Lanza (Mario), Patti (Adelina), Pears (Peter).

(6) Callas (Maria), Caruso (Enrico), Tauber (Richard).

(7) Caballé (Montserrat), Domingo (Placido), Ferrier (Kathleen), Hammond (Joan), Lehmann (Lotte), Robeson (Paul), Tebaldi (Renate), Wallace (Ian).

(8) Björling (Jussi), Carreras (José), Flagstad (Kirsten), Te Kanawa (Kiri).

(9) Brannigan (Owen), Chaliapin (Fedor), McCormack (John), Pavarotti (Luciano).

(10) Sutherland (Joan).

(11) Schwarzkopf (Elizabeth).

Popular

(3) Day (Doris), Lee (Peggy), Ray (Johnnie), Vee (Bobby).

(4) Baez (Joan), Bono, Bush (Kate), Cher, Cole (Nat King), Como (Perry), Dion (Celine), Dury (Ian), Eddy (Duane), Fame (Georgie), Gaye (Marvin), Ives (Burl), Keel (Howard), King (BB, Ben E), Lynn (Vera), Piaf (Edith), Ross (Diana), Shaw (Sandie).

(5) Allen (Chesney), Autry (Gene), Berry (Chuck), Black (Cilla), Boone (Pat), Bowie (David), Brown (James), Clark (Petula), Darin (Bobby), Davis (Sammy), Dylan (Bob), Faith (Adam), Harry (Debbie), Holly (Buddy), Laine (Frankie), Lloyd (Marie), Moyet (Alison), Ocean (Billy), Paige (Elaine), Simon (Paul), Sting, Tormé (Mel).

(6) Bassey (Shirley), Burdon (Eric), Coward (Noel), Crosby (Bing), Denver (John), Fields (Gracie), Formby (George), Geldof (Bob), Gentry (Bobbie), Jagger (Mick),

Jolson (Al), Joplin (Janis), Lennon (John), Marley (Bob), Martin (Dean), Mathis (Johnny), Parton (Dolly), Reeves (Jim), Sedaka (Neil), Steele (Tommy), Tilley (Vesta), Trenet (Charles), Wonder (Stevie).

(7) Andrews (Julie), Bennett (Tony), Diamond (Neil), Hendrix (Jimi), Holiday (Billie), Jackson (Michael), Madonna, Mercury (Freddie), Minogue (Kylie), Presley (Elvis), Robeson (Paul), Shapiro (Helen), Sinatra (Frank), Stewart (Rod), Vaughan (Frankie), Warwick (Dionne), Wynette (Tammy).

(8) Aznavour (Charles), Bygraves (Max), Costello (Elvis), Dietrich (Marlene), Flanagan (Bud), Flanders (Michael), Franklin (Aretha), Harrison (George), Iglesias (Julio), Mitchell (Joni), Williams (Andy).

(9) Armstrong (Louis), Belafonte (Harry), Chevalier (Maurice), Garfunkel (Art), McCartney (Paul), Streisand (Barbra).

(10) Fitzgerald (Ella).

(11) Armatrading (Joan), Springfield (Dusty), Springsteen (Bruce).

sink *v* **1** (3) dip, ebb, sag, set; (4) dive, drop, fall, sink; (5) droop, slope, slump; (6) plunge, tumble; (7) descend, plummet; (8) collapse; (2 words) go down, move down *etc*. **2** (5) drown; (6) engulf; (7) immerse; (8) submerge; **3** (4) slip, wane; (5) decay, slide; (6) lessen, weaken, worsen; (7) decline, dwindle, retreat, subside; (8) decrease; (11) deteriorate.

situation *n* **1** (4) case; (5) state; (9) condition; (13) circumstances; **2** (4) seat, site, spot; (5) place; (7) setting; (8) location, position; **3** (3) job; (4) post; (5) place; (6) office; (7) posting; (8) position; (11) appointment.

sled *n see* **sledge**.

sledge *n* (3) bob; (4) luge, sled; (6) sleigh, troika; (7) bobsled, kibitka; (8) toboggan; (9) bobsleigh.

sleep I *n & v* (3) kip, nap; (4) doze, rest; (6) repose, siesta, snooze; (7) slumber; **II** *n* (7) shuteye; (11) hibernation; (2 words) forty winks; **III** *v* (9) hibernate; (2 words) drop off, nod off.

sleigh *n see* **sledge**.

slender *adj see* **slim** I.

slight I *adj see* **slim, small**; **II** *n & v* (4) slur, snub; (6) insult, rebuff; (7) affront, disdain; **III** *v* (6) ignore, offend; (7) neglect; (9) disparage, disregard; (12) cold-shoulder.

slim I *adj* 1 (4) lean, thin, trim; (5) lanky, spare; (6) narrow, skinny, slight, svelte; (7) slender; (8) graceful; 2 (4) poor; (5) faint, small; (6) flimsy, meagre, remote, scanty, slight; (7) tenuous; (10) inadequate; (12) insufficient; **II** *v* (4) diet; (6) reduce; (2 words) lose weight.

slip I *v* 1 (4) fall, skid, trip; (5) glide, slide; (7) slither, stumble; 2 (5) creep, slink, sneak, steal; 3 (4) drop, fall, sink; (6) worsen (7) decline; **II** *n* 1 (5) error, fault, gaffe, lapse; (6) cock-up, slip-up; (7) blunder, fallacy, mistake; (8) misprint, solecism; (9) oversight; (14) miscalculation; (15) misapprehension; (2 words) faux pas; 2 (9) petticoat; (10) underskirt; 3 (4) chit, form; (5) piece, strip; (6) coupon; (7) voucher; (11) certificate.

small *adj* (3) wee; (4) mini, tiny (5) brief, dwarf, scant, short, teeny; (6) humble, little, meagre, minute, paltry, petite, scanty, sparse, teensy; (8) trifling; (9) miniature, minuscule; (10) diminutive, negligible; (11) microscopic; (13) infinitesimal, insignificant.

smart I *adj* 1 (4) chic, neat; (5) natty; (6) modish, spruce; (7) elegant, stylish; (8) tasteful; (11) fashionable; 2 (5) sharp; (6) bright, **clever**; 3 (4) posh; (6) luxury; (8) upmarket; (9) expensive; **II** *v* (4) burn, hurt; (5) prick, sting; (6) tingle, twinge.

smash *v* (4) rase (*or* raze), ruin, snap, undo; (5) break, crack, crush, level, split, spoil, waste, wreck; (6) deface, impair, injure, ravage; (7) destroy, shatter, torpedo; (8) decimate, demolish, mutilate,

sabotage; (9) devastate, dismantle, eliminate, eradicate; (10) extinguish; (12) incapacitate.

smile *v & n* (4) beam, grin, hoot, leer; (5) laugh, smirk; (6) giggle, guffaw, scream, simper, titter; (7) chortle, chuckle, snigger.

smooth I *adj* 1 (4) even, flat; (5) flush, level, plane, shiny, silky, sleek, slick; (6) glassy, glossy; (8) polished; (10) horizontal; 2 (4) calm; (6) stable, steady; (7) flowing, regular, uniform; (8) constant; 3 (4) glib; (5) suave; (6) smarmy; (9) plausible; (10) persuasive; **II** *v* (4) file, iron, roll, sand; (5) level, plane, press; (6) polish; (7) flatten.

snake I *n* (7) serpent; **II** *v* (4) **wind**; (7) meander.

SNAKES

(3) asp, boa; (5) adder, cobra, krait, mamba, viper; (6) python; (7) rattler; (8) anaconda, moccasin, pit-viper; (9) boomslang, king-cobra, puff-adder, ring-snake, sand-snake; (10) bushmaster, copperhead, coral-snake, fer-de-lance, grass-snake, watersnake; (11) constrictor, cottonmouth, garter-snake, rattlesnake.

---

snare I *n & v* (3) net; (4) trap; (5) catch, trick; **II** *n* (3) gin; (4) ruse, wile; (5) noose; (6) danger, hazard; (7) pitfall; (9) stratagem; **III** *v* (4) dupe, take; (6) enmesh; (7) deceive; (8) entangle.

sodium *cryptic* abbreviated as NA.

soft *adj* 1 (4) easy; (5) downy, furry, silky; (6) marshy, spongy, tender; (7) elastic, plastic, pliable, squashy; (8) flexible, yielding; 2 (3) dim, low; (4) pale; (5) faint, light, muted, quiet; (7) hushed, pastel; (7) subdued; (8) delicate; 3 (4) kind; (6) gentle, loving; (7) lenient, liberal, patient; (9) easy-going, forgiving, indulgent; (10) charitable, forbearing, permissive; 4 (4) weak; (6) feeble; (7) wimpish; (8) cowardly; (9) spineless; (10) indecisive, irresolute, namby-pamby; (11) ineffectual, ineffective.

soil I *n* **1** (3) sod; (4) clay, dirt, dust, land, loam; (5) earth, humus; (6) ground, region; (7) country; II *v* (4) foul, spot; (5) dirty, muddy, stain, sully; (6) smirch, smudge; (7) begrime, pollute, tarnish; (8) besmirch.

soldier I *n* (2) GI; (3) NCO; (5) cadet, guard, tommy; (6) gunner, hussar, lancer, marine, sapper; (7) fighter, officer, private, redcoat, regular, squaddy, terrier, trooper, warrior; (8) commando, doughboy, fusilier, rifleman, squaddie; (9) centurion, guardsman, legionary, mercenary; (11) infantryman, paratrooper, Territorial; *see also* **rank**; II *cryptic* any abbreviation for a military rank, *e.g.* BRIG, CAPT, GEN, GI, PTE *etc.*

Solomon *Bible* son of King David (and Bathsheba) and the successor of David as King of Israel, noted for his wisdom and for the number of his wives and concubines, and for his building of the Temple in Jerusalem.

solve *v* (5) crack; (6) answer, settle; (7) clarify, explain, expound, resolve, unravel; (8) decipher, simplify, untangle; (9) elucidate, explicate; (2 words) account for, clear up, figure out, spell out, work out.

song *n* (3) air, lay; (4) aria, glee, Lied, tune; (5) catch, ditty; (6) shanty; (7) chanson.

sorry *adj* **1** (5) upset; (6) guilty; (7) ashamed; (8) contrite, penitent; (9) regretful, repentant; (10) apologetic, remorseful; (11) embarrassed; **2** (3) bad; (4) poor, weak; (6) dismal, feeble; (8) inferior, mediocre, pathetic; (9) third-rate, worthless; (10) second-rate, uninspired; (11) incompetent, ineffective, substandard; (14) unsatisfactory; **3** (3) sad; (5) moved; (9) concerned; (11) sympathetic.

sort I *n & v* (4) rank; (5) class, grade, group, order; II *n* (3) ilk; (4) form, kind, type; (5) brand, breed, genre, stamp, style; (6) nature, strain; (7) species, variety; (8) category; (11) description; II *v* (4) file, sift; (6) divide, screen; (7) arrange (8) classify, organise (*or* organize); (9) catalogue; (10) categorise (*or* categorize).

sound I *n* (3) din, row; (4) note, tone; (5) noise; (6) racket, timbre; (9) resonance; II *adj* **1** (3) fit; (4) firm, hale, well; (5) solid, whole; (6) intact, robust, unhurt; (7) healthy; (8) unbroken; (9) uninjured; **2** (4) true; (5) right, valid; (7) correct, logical; (8) rational, reliable, sensible; III *v* **1** (4) beat, blow, echo, peal, play, ring, toll; (5) chime; (7) resound; (8) resonate; **2** (4) test; (5) plumb, probe; (6) fathom; (7) measure.

soup I *n* (4) stew; (5) broth, stock; (6) potage; (7) chowder; (8) bouillon, consommé; II *cryptic* ANAGRAM CUE.

sour *adj* **1** (4) acid, sour, tart; (5) acrid, sharp; (8) vinegary; **2** (7) acerbic, cynical; (8) sardonic; (9) jaundiced, rancorous, resentful; (12) acrimonious;

south *cryptic* abbreviated as S.

spare I *adj* **1** (4) free; (5) extra, other; (6) excess, unused; (10) additional, substitute, unoccupied; (11) replacement, superfluous; **2** (4) bony, lean, slim, thin; (5) gaunt, lanky; (6) skinny, slight; (7) scraggy, scrawny, slender; II *v* **1** (4) give; (5) allow, grant; (6) afford; **2** (4) free; (6) pardon; (7) release; (8) reprieve.

sparse *adj* (4) rare; (5) scant; (6) meagre, scanty, scarce, skimpy, sparse; (9) scattered; (12) insufficient.

speak *v* (3) say; (4) tell; (5) state, utter, voice; (6) reveal; (7) declaim, deliver, express, lecture; (8) announce, vocalise (*or* vocalize); (9) enunciate, pronounce, verbalise (*or* verbalize); (10) articulate.

special *adj* **1** (3) own; (6) proper, single, unique; (8) distinct, peculiar, personal, separate, singular, specific; (10) individual, particular; (11) distinctive; (13) idiosyncratic; (14) characteristic; **2** (6) marked; (7) notable, unusual; (8) especial; (10) pronounced; (11) exceptional.

specialist I *n & adj* (3) pro; (5) adept; (6) expert, master; (8) virtuoso; (12) professional; II *n* (7) maestro; (9) authority; (10) consultant; (11) connoisseur; (2 words) dab hand.

speed I *n* **1** (3) mph; (4) rate; (5) tempo; (8) velocity; (9) frequency, incidence; II *v*

(4) bolt, dart, dash, race, rush, tear; (5) hurry, scoot; (6) double, sprint, streak.

Sphinx I *Gk myth* a winged monster with a woman's head and lion's body that devoured anyone who could not answer its riddle (what goes on four legs in the morning, two legs at noon, and three legs in the evening? = man). When **Oedipus** answered the riddle, it killed itself; **II** *geog.* a statue of a similar monster in Egypt, esp. one near the Pyramids.

spice I *n* (4) zest; (9) condiment; (10) flavouring; **II** *v* (6) season; (7) flavour.

TYPES OF SPICE

see also **herb**

(4) mace; (5) chili, clove, cumin, curry; (6) chilli, garlic, ginger, nutmeg, pepper; (7) aniseed, caraway, cayenne, mustard, oregano, paprika, pimento, saffron; (8) allspice, cardamom (*or* cardamum), cinnamon, tarragon, turmeric; (9) coriander.

---

spin I *n & v* (4) reel, roll, turn; (5) swirl, twirl, twist, wheel, whirl; (6) circle, spiral; (9) pirouette; **II** *v* (5) pivot; (6) gyrate, rotate; **III** *n* **1** (8) gyration, rotation; (10) revolution; **2** (4) daze; (6) bustle, flurry, hubbub, tumult, uproar; (9) commotion, confusion; **IV** *cryptic* ANAGRAM CUE.

spirit *n* **1** (4) mind, soul; (6) psyche; **2** (5) bogey, ghost, shade, spook; (6) kobold, wraith; (7) phantom, spectre; (8) revenant; (10) apparition; *see also* **fabulous creatures**; **3** (2) go; (3) pep, vim; (4) elan; (5) nerve, pluck, verve; (6) mettle, vigour; (7) bravery, courage, resolve; (8) audacity, boldness, chutzpah, vivacity; (9) animation; (10) enthusiasm, resolution; **4** (4) mood; (6) humour, manner, morale, temper; (7) outlook; (8) attitude; **5** (5) drink; (7) alcohol.

SPIRITS

(3) gin, rum, rye; (4) ouzo, raki, saki; (5) vodka; (6) arrack, brandy, cognac, grappa, scotch, whisky; (7) aquavit, bourbon, whiskey; (8) schnapps; (9) slivovitz.

---

splendid *adj* (4) fine, good, rare; (5) grand, great, noble, regal; (6) superb; (7) stately; (8) glorious, gorgeous, imposing; (9) admirable, brilliant, excellent, exemplary, first-rate, sumptuous, **wonderful**; (10) first-class, impressive, marvellous, prodigious, remarkable; (11) exceptional, magnificent, superlative; (13) distinguished.

split I *n & v* (3) rip; (4) gash, hole, slit, tear; (5) break, crack; (6) divide; (7) rupture; **II** *v* **1** (4) part, rend; (5) burst, halve; (6) bisect, cleave, shiver; (7) divorce; (8) disunite, separate, splinter; (9) partition; **2** (3) fly, run; (5) leave; **III** *n* **1** (3) gap; (4) rift; (5) cleft; (6) breach; (7) crevice; **2** (6) schism; (7) discord; (8) disunion, division; (10) dissension.

spoil I *v* **1** (3) mar; (4) ruin; (5) abase, lower, stain, taint; (6) debase, defile, demean, reduce; (7) corrupt, degrade, devalue, pollute; (8) disgrace; (9) dishonour; (10) adulterate; (11) contaminate; **2** (6) coddle, cosset, pamper; (7) indulge; (11) mollycoddle, overindulge; **II** *n* **1** (4) slag; (5) waste; **2** **spoils** (4) haul, loot, swag; (5) booty; (7) plunder; (8) pickings; **III** **spoil** *or* **spoilt** *cryptic* ANAGRAM CUE.

sport I *n* (4) game, play; (7) pastime; (8) exercise; (10) recreation; **II** *v* **1** (6) frolic, gambol; **2** (4) show, wear; (7) display.

TYPES OF SPORT

(4) golf, polo, pool.

(5) bowls, fives, rugby.

(6) boules, boxing, diving, hockey, pelota, racing, riding, rowing, shinty, skiing, soccer, squash, tennis.

(7) archery, bowling, cricket, croquet, curling, cycling, fencing, fishing, hunting, hurling, jogging, netball, rackets, running, sailing, skating, snooker, surfing, walking.

(8) baseball, climbing, football, handball, hardball, lacrosse, ping-pong, rounders, shooting, sledging, softball, speedway, swimming, trotting, yachting.

list continued over

---

(9) athletics, badminton, billiards, bobsleigh, pot-holing, sky-diving, wrestling.

(10) basketball, gymnastics, volleyball.

(11) hang-gliding, show-jumping, table-tennis, tobogganing, waterskiing, windsurfing.

(12) cross-country, orienteering, snowboarding, trampolining.

(13) skateboarding, weightlifting.

(14) mountaineering.

spot I *n & v* (3) dot; (4) blot, mark; (5) fleck, stain; (6) blotch, smudge; (7) blemish, speckle; II *n* 1 (3) zit; (4) rash; (6) pimple; (8) eruption; (9) blackhead; 2 (4) area, site; (5) place, point, scene; (6) locale, region; (8) district, locality, location; (13) neighbourhood; 3 (4) dash, drop; (6) little, splash; III *v* (3) see, spy; (4) espy; (6) detect, notice, remark; (7) discern, glimpse, observe; (8) perceive; (9) apprehend, recognise (*or* recognize); (11) distinguish.

spring I *n & v* (4) jump, leap; (5) bound, vault; II *n* (5) fount; (6) source; (8) fountain; (9) reservoir; III *v* (4) flow, stem; (5) arise, ensue; (6) derive, emerge, follow, result; (7) develop, proceed.

stage I *n* 1 (4) dais, (8) platform, scaffold; 2 (5) drama; (6) boards; (7) theatre; 3 (3) lap, leg; (4) step; (5) level, phase; (6) period; (8) division; II *v* (2) do; (4) give, show; (5) mount; (7) arrange, perform, produce; (8) engineer, organise (*or* organize); (2 words) put on.

stain I *n & v* 1 (4) mark, spot; (5) taint; (7) blemish, tarnish; (8) disgrace; (9) dishonour; 2 (3) dye; (5) paint; (6) colour; (7) pigment, varnish; II *v* (5) abase, lower; (6) debase, defile, demean, reduce (7) corrupt, degrade, devalue, pollute; (10) adulterate; (11) contaminate.

stake I *n & v* (3) bet, lay; (4) ante, risk; (5) wager; II *n* (4) pole, post, spit; (5) spike, stick; (6) paling, picket.

stand I *v* 1 (4) rise; (2 words) get up; 2 (3) put, set; 3 (4) bear, face; (5) abide, allow, place, stick; (6) endure, permit, suffer; (7) stomach, sustain, undergo, weather; (8) tolerate; (9) withstand; (10) experience; (2+ words) go through, put up with; II *n* (4) base; (5) frame; (6) plinth; (7) support; (8) pedestal.

standard I *n* 1 (3) par; (4) norm, rule, type; (5) grade, level, model; (7) average, example, measure, pattern, quality; (8) exemplar; (9) benchmark, criterion, guideline, yardstick; (10) touchstone; 2 (4) flag; (6) banner, ensign, pennon; (7) pennant; II *adj* (5) stock, usual; (6) normal; (7) average, routine, typical; (8) orthodox; (14) characteristic, representative.

star *n* 1 *astron.* (3) sun; (4) nova; (6) nebula, pulsar, quasar; (9) supernova; *see also* **constellation**; 2 (3) VIP; (4) lead; (9) celebrity, principal; 3 (8) asterisk.

start I *v* 1 (4) form, open; (5) begin, build, cause, endow, found, plant; (6) create, launch, prompt; (7) trigger; (8) activate, commence, initiate, occasion, organise (*or* organize); (9) establish, institute, introduce, originate; (10) inaugurate; (2 words) set up; 2 (5) leave; (6) depart; 3 (4) jerk, jump; (6) flinch, recoil; II *n* (3) off; (4) dawn; (5) birth, break, onset; (6) launch, origin, outset; (7) opening; (9) beginning, inception; (10) foundation; (11) institution; (12) commencement, inauguration.

starter I *n* 1 (6) course, entrée; (9) appetiser (*or* appetizer); 2 (6) opener; (8) beginner; II *cryptic* use the first letter of the word in question, as in: 'Fish starter mixed with peeled potatoes for dessert?' (6) = afters (potatoes = 'taters (peeled = minus 't')).

state I *n* 1 (4) case, form; (5) shape; (8) position; (9) condition, situation; (13) circumstances; 2 (4) land; (6) nation; (7) kingdom; (8) province, republic; (9) territory; (10) government; 3 (4) flap; (5) panic, tizzy; II *v* (3) say; (4) aver; (5) claim; (6) affirm, assert, reveal; (7) confirm, declare, profess, specify, testify, witness;

(8) announce, maintain, proclaim; (9) broadcast, pronounce; **III** *cryptic* use the letters making up an abbreviation (*esp.* a Zip code abbreviation) of one of the states of the USA in the answer, as in: 'Southern state found in the Channel Islands?' (4) = Sark.

STATES OF THE US

State, Abbrev, Zip code, Capital
Alabama, ALA, AL, Montgomery
Alaska, ALAS, AK, Juneau
Arizona, ARIZ, AZ, Phoenix
Arkansas, ARK, AR, Little Rock
California, CALIF, CA, Sacramento
Colorado, COLO, CO, Denver
Connecticut, CONN, CT, Hartford
Delaware, DEL, DE, Dover
District of Columbia, DC,
  Washington
Florida, FLA, FL, Tallahassee
Georgia, GA, Atlanta
Hawaii, HI, Honolulu
Idaho, IDA, ID, Boise
Illinois, ILL, IL, Springfield
Indiana, IND, IN, Indianapolis
Iowa, IA, Des Moines
Kansas, KANS, KS, Topeka
Kentucky, KY, Frankfort
Louisiana, LA, Baton Rouge
Maine, ME, Augusta
Maryland, MD, Annapolis
Massachusetts, MASS, MA, Boston
Michigan, MICH, MI, Lansing
Minnesota, MINN, MN, St Paul
Mississippi, MISS, MS, Jackson
Missouri, MO, Jefferson City
Montana, MONT, MT, Helena
Nebraska, NEBR, NE, Lincoln
Nevada, NEV, NV, Carson City
New Hampshire, NH, Concord
New Jersey, NJ, Trenton
New Mexico, N MEX, NM, Santa Fe
New York, NY, Albany
North Carolina, NC, Raleigh
North Dakota, N DAK, ND, Bismarck
Ohio, O, OH, Columbus
Oklahoma, O*Lear*A, OK, Oklahoma
  City
Oregon, OREG, OR, Salem

Pennsylvania, PENN, PA, Harrisburg
Rhode Island, RI, Providence
South Carolina, SC, Columbia
South Dakota, S DAK, SD, Pierre
Tennessee, TENN, TN, Nashville
Texas, TEX, TX, Austin
Utah, UT, Salt Lake City
Vermont, VT, Montpelier
Virginia, VA, Richmond
Washington, WASH, WA, Olympia
West Virginia, WVA, WV, Charleston
Wisconsin, WISC, WI, Madison
Wyoming, WYO, WY, Cheyenne

stay I *v* **1** (4) last, stop; (5) abide, dwell; (6) endure, linger, remain, reside, settle; (7) persist, sojourn; **2** (4) halt; (7) suspend; (8) postpone; **II** *n* **1** (5) visit; (7) holiday; **2** (7) **support**; **3** (4) rope.

steal *v* **1** (4) lift, nick, take, whip; (5) pinch, poach, swipe; (6) burgle, pilfer, pirate, remove, thieve; (7) purloin, snaffle; (8) embezzle, half-inch, liberate; (11) appropriate; **2** (4) slip; (5) creep, glide, slink; sneak; (6) tiptoe.

stealthy *adj* (3) sly; (5) quiet; (6) covert, secret, sneaky; (7) furtive; (10) low-profile; (11) clandestine, unobtrusive; (13) surreptitious, inconspicuous.

stern I *adj* (4) grim, hard; (5) harsh, rigid, stark, tough; (6) severe, strict; (8) rigorous; (9) stringent; (10) forbidding, relentless; (13) authoritarian; **II** *n* (3) end; (4) back, rear, rump, tail.

stew I *n* **1** (4) dish; (5) daube; (6) hotpot, ragout; (9) fricassee; **2** (4) fuss; (5) tizzy, worry; (6) bother; (7) anxiety; **II** *v* (4) boil; (6) braise, simmer; (9) casserole; **III** *cryptic* ANAGRAM CUE.

stick I *n* (3) bar, rod; (4) cane, mast, pole, spar, twig, wand, yard; (5) baton, birch, staff, stake; (6) branch, paling; **II** *v* **1** (3) fix, gum, pin; (4) bond, fuse, glue, join, weld; (5) cling, unite; (6) adhere, attach, cement, cleave, fasten, secure; **2** (4) push, stab; (6) pierce, thrust; **3** (6) linger, remain; (7) persist; **4** (4) bear; (5) stand; (8) tolerate.

still I *adj* 1 (4) calm; (5) quiet; (6) gentle, placid, serene; (7) pacific, restful; (8) peaceful, relaxing, tranquil; (9) unruffled; (10) untroubled; (11) undisturbed; 2 (5) inert; (8) immobile, inactive, stagnant; (10) motionless, stationary; II *adv* (3) yet; (4) ever; (11) nonetheless; (12) nevertheless; (15) notwithstanding; III *v* (4) calm; (5) quell; (6) pacify, settle, soothe, subdue; (7) appease, quieten, silence.

stop I *v* 1 (3) end; (4) halt, quit; (5) cease; (6) desist, finish; (8) conclude; (9) terminate; (2 words) call off, give up, pack in, refrain from; 2 (3) ban, bar; (4) foil, veto; (5) block; (6) forbid, oppose, outlaw, refuse, reject, stifle, thwart; (7) exclude, prevent; (8) disallow, preclude, prohibit; (9) interdict, proscribe; 3 (4) plug, seal; (5) close; (7) staunch; (8) obstruct; 4 (4) stay; (6) remain; II *n* 1 (4) halt, rest; (5) break, pause; (9) cessation, standstill; 2 (7) station; (8) terminus; (11) destination; 3 (5) colon, comma, point; (9) semicolon; (2 words) punctuation mark.

storey *n* (4) deck, tier; (5) floor, level, stage.

storm I *n* 1 (4) gale, wind; (6) deluge, squall; (7) tempest, thunder, tornado, typhoon; (8) blizzard, downpour; (9) hurricane; (10) cloudburst; 2 (3) row; (4) stir; (6) furore, outcry, rumpus, uproar; (8) outburst; (9) commotion; II *v* 1 (4) blow, pelt, pour, teem; (6) bucket; (7) thunder; 2 (4) rush; (6) attack, charge; (7) assault; 3 (4) fume, rage, roar.

stormy *adj* 1 (4) wild; (5) gusty, rough, windy; (6) raging; (7) squally, violent; (8) blustery, thundery; (11) tempestuous; 2 (6) heated; (7) intense; (9) turbulent; (10) passionate, tumultuous.

story *n* 1 (4) myth, saga, tale, yarn; (5) fable; (6) legend, report, rumour; (7) account; (8) anecdote; (9) narrative; 2 (3) fib, lie; (7) untruth; (9) falsehood; (11) fabrication.

strange *adj* 1 (3) odd, rum; (5) dotty, eerie, fluky, funny, queer, weird; (6) chance, creepy, spooky; (7) bizarre, erratic, offbeat, uncanny, unusual; (8) aberrant, abnormal, atypical, freakish, peculiar; (9) eccentric; (10) fortuitous, outlandish, unexpected; (11) exceptional; (13) idiosyncratic, unpredictable; (14) unconventional; 2 (3) new; (4) dark; (5) alien; (6) hidden, secret, untold; (7) foreign, obscure, unnamed; (8) nameless; (9) incognito, uncharted; (10) mysterious, unexplored, unfamiliar; (12) undiscovered, unidentified.

strain I *v & n* (4) pull, rick; (5) twist; (6) sprain, wrench; II *v* 1 (3) tax; (7) overtax, stretch; 2 (4) toil; (6) labour; (8) struggle; 3 (4) sift; (5) sieve; (6) filter, purify, screen; III *n* 1 (6) burden, effort, stress; (7) fatigue; (8) exertion, pressure; (9) weariness; 2 (3) air; (4) song, tune; (5) music.

stray I *v* (3) err; (4) roam, rove, veer, wind; (5) drift, range, stray; (6) depart, ramble; (7) deviate, diverge; II *adj* 1 (4) lost; (7) roaming; (8) homeless; (9) abandoned, wandering; 2 (6) casual, chance, random; (10) accidental; III **stray, strayed, straying** *cryptic* ANAGRAM CUE.

street I *n* (3) way; (4) drag, lane, road; (6) avenue; (7) highway; (8) crescent; (9) boulevard; (12) thoroughfare; II *cryptic* letters ST.

strength *n* 1 (5) brawn, force, might, power, sinew; (6) energy, muscle, vigour; (7) stamina; (8) firmness; (9) toughness; (10) resilience, robustness; 2 (7) potency; (8) violence; (9) intensity; (13) concentration, effectiveness; 3 (5) asset, forte; (9) advantage.

strengthen *v* 1 (5) brace, shore, steel; (6) harden, secure; (7) bolster, fortify, protect, support, toughen; (8) buttress; (9) reinforce; (11) consolidate; 2 (7) confirm; (8) increase; (9) intensify; (11) corroborate; (12) substantiate.

strike *v* 1 (3) hit; (4) bash, beat, flog, lick, wham; (5) knock, pound, thump, whack; (6) batter, hammer, lather, thrash, wallop; 2 (5) touch; (6) affect; (7) impress; 3 (4) find; (5) reach; (8) discover; 4 (7) protest; (2+ words) down tools, take (industrial) action, walk out.

stroke I *v* (3) pat, pet, rub; (5) touch; (6) caress, fondle; II *n* (3) cut, hit, pot; (4) blow, chip, hook, loft, pull, putt, slog; (5) drive, knock, slice, sweep, swipe; (6) glance, volley; (8) approach.

strong *adj* 1 (5) beefy, burly, hardy, lusty, rigid, solid, stout, tough; (6) brawny, mighty, potent, robust, sinewy, sturdy; (7) durable; (8) muscular, powerful; (9) heavy-duty, resilient, resistant, strapping; (11) hard-wearing; 2 (3) hot; (4) deep, keen; (5) sharp, spicy, vivid; (7) intense, piquant, pungent; (9) undiluted; (12) concentrated; 3 (6) cogent; (7) telling, weighty; (8) forceful; (9) effective; (10) compelling, convincing, persuasive.

student I *n* 1 (4) grad; (7) scholar; (9) undergrad; 2 (4) tyro; (7) learner, trainee; (8) beginner; (9) debutante; (10) apprentice; II *cryptic* letter L.

study I *v* (3) con; (4) cram, read, scan, skim, swot; (5) learn; (6) peruse, revise, survey; (7) examine; (8) research; (10) scrutinise (*or* scrutinize); II *n* 1 (3) den; (6) office; (7) sanctum; 2 (6) review; (7) inquiry; (8) homework, research, revision, scrutiny; (11) examination, preparation.

stupid *adj* (3) dim, **mad**; (4) daft, dull, dumb, rash, slow; (5) barmy, crazy, dense, inane, silly, thick; (6) absurd, crazed, insane, simple, unwise; (7) foolish, idiotic, lunatic, puerile; (9) ludicrous, senseless; (10) half-witted, ridiculous; (11) nonsensical; (12) enthusiastic; (13) irresponsible.

style I *n* 1 (3) way; (4) form, mode; (5) means, trend, vogue; (6) manner, method; (7) fashion, process; (8) approach; (9) procedure, technique; 2 (4) chic; (5) flair, taste; (6) polish; (7) panache; (8) elegance, urbanity; (9) smartness; (10) refinement; (14) sophistication; 3 (4) tone; (7) wording; (8) phrasing; (10) expression; 4 (4) name; (5) title; (6) handle; (7) moniker; (8) cognomen; (9) sobriquet; (11) appellation, designation; II *v* 1 (3) cut, fit; (5) shape; (6) tailor; (7) fashion; 2 (3) dub; (4) call, name, term; (7) address.

stylish *adj* (4) chic, neat; (5) smart; (6) modish; (7) elegant; (8) tasteful; (11) fashionable.

Styx *Gk myth* the principal river of the **Underworld**, the 'river of hate', supposed to circle the infernal regions nine times.

subject I *n* 1 (4) case; (5) issue, point, theme, topic; (6) affair, debate, matter; (7) concern, problem; (8) business, question; 2 (5) field; (8) province; (10) discipline; 3 (6) vassal; (7) citizen; (8) national; II *v* 1 (6) expose, submit; (2 words) put through; 2 (6) subdue; (9) subjugate.

submit *v* 1 (3) bow; (5) yield; (9) surrender; (10) capitulate; (2 words) give in, knuckle under; 2 (5) offer, table; (6) tender; (7) present, propose, suggest; (2 words) put forward.

subsidy *n* (3) aid; (5) grant; (6) relief; (7) benefit, funding, hand-out; (8) donation; (9) patronage; (11) sponsorship; (12) contribution.

subtract *v* (5) debit; (6) deduct, remove; (8) withdraw; (2 words) take away, take off.

suit I *n* 1 (3) rig; (4) garb, gear, togs; (5) get-up; (6) outfit; (7) clothes, costume; (8) ensemble, two-piece; (10) three-piece; 2 (5) clubs; (6) hearts, spades; (8) diamonds; 3 (5) claim; (6) action; (7) lawsuit; II *v* 1 (3) fit; (6) become, please; (7) gratify, satisfy; 2 (5) agree, befit, match, tally; (9) harmonise (*or* harmonize).

suitable *adj* (3) apt; (5) right; (6) proper, seemly, spot-on, timely; (7) fitting, germane, related; (8) apposite, becoming, material, relevant; (9) opportune, pertinent; (10) admissible, applicable, convenient, seasonable; (11) appropriate.

sulphur *cryptic* abbreviated as S.

Superman *fict.* character in comics and films, originally from the planet **Krypton**, possessing superhuman abilities on earth where he lived as mild-mannered Clark Kent, a reporter on the *Daily Planet* in Metropolis and would-be boyfriend of Lois Lane.

supervise *v* (3) run; (6) direct, handle, manage, tackle; (7) control, oversee; (8) organise (*or* organize); (10) administer; (11) superintend.

supervisor *n* (4) boss, head; (5) chief, tutor; (7) foreman, manager; (8) director, overseer; (9) executive; (13) administrator; (14) superintendent.

supply I *v* (4) fill, give; (5) endow, equip, stock, yield; (6) outfit; (7) furnish, produce, provide; (10) contribute; II *n* (4) fund; (5) hoard, stock, store; (6) amount, source; (7) reserve; (8) quantity; (9) provision, reservoir, stockpile; III *cryptic* 1 ANAGRAM CUE; 2 HIDDEN WORD CUE.

support I *n & v* (3) aid; (4) help, prop; (5) brace, shore; (7) bolster, finance; (8) buttress; II *v* 1 (4) back; (5) serve; (6) assist, foster, hasten, second; (7) advance, forward, further, promote, sponsor, sustain; (8) advocate, champion; (9) encourage, reinforce, subsidise (*or* subsidize); (10) facilitate, strengthen; 2 (6) verify; (7) confirm; (11) corroborate; (12) authenticate, substantiate; III *n* (3) aid, bra; (4) help; (6) backup, crutch, pillar, relief; (7) backing, loyalty, service; (8) guidance; (9) patronage; (10) allegiance, assistance; (11) co-operation; (13) collaboration.

suppose *v* (5) fancy, guess, think; (6) assume, gather; (7) believe, imagine, pretend; (8) conceive, envisage; (9) fantasise (*or* fantasize), visualise (*or* visualize); (10) conjecture.

sure *adj* (3) set; (4) firm; (5) clear, fixed; (7) assured, certain, decided, settled; (8) clear-cut, definite, explicit, positive, specific; (10) determined, guaranteed.

suspect I *v* 1 (4) feel; (5) fancy, guess, sense, think; (6) reckon; (7) suppose; 2 (5) doubt; (8) distrust, mistrust; II *adj* (4) iffy; (5) dodgy, fishy; (7) dubious; (8) doubtful; (9) debatable; (10) suspicious, unreliable; (12) questionable.

suspicion *n* 1 (5) doubt; (8) distrust, mistrust; (9) misgiving; 2 (3) bit, jot; (4) hint, iota, sign; (5) scrap, shred, touch, trace, whiff; (7) glimmer, inkling, remnant, residue, vestige; (8) evidence; (10) indication.

sway I *v* 1 (4) bend, lean, rock, roll; (5) shake, swing; (6) quiver; (7) incline; (8) fluctuate, oscillate; 2 (6) affect, induce; (8) convince, persuade; (9) influence; II *n* (4) rule; (7) control.

Sweden *cryptic* abbreviated as S or SWE.

sweet I *adj* 1 (6) sugary, syrupy; 2 (4) soft; (6) dulcet, lovely, mellow; (8) aromatic, fragrant, luscious, pleasant; (9) delicious, melodious; (10) attractive, delightful, euphonious, harmonious; 3 (4) kind, nice; (6) tender; (7) lovable, winsome; (8) charming, likeable, loveable, generous; (9) appealing; (11) considerate; (12) affectionate; II *n* 1 (6) afters; (7) dessert, pudding; 2 (4) rock; (5) candy, fudge, jelly; (6) humbug, nougat, toffee; (7) caramel, fondant, gumdrop, praline, truffle; (8) lollipop, marzipan, pastille; (9) chocolate, liquorice.

sword *n* (3) fox; (4) épée, foil; (5) blade, sabre, sharp; (6) rapier; (7) cutlass; (8) falchion, scimitar.

system *v* (3) way; (4) mode, plan, rule; (5) logic, order, set-up, usage; (6) manner, method, scheme; (7) fashion, process; (8) approach, practice; (9) procedure, structure, technique; (11) arrangement; (12) organisation (*or* organization).

T

T *abbrev* tenor, Thailand (international vehicle registration), time, tritium.

t *abbrev* ton, tonne, troy (weight).

table I *n* (4) desk, slab; (5) bench, board; (7) counter, worktop; **2** (4) list; (5) chart, index; (6) record; (7) diagram; (8) register, schedule; (9) inventory, programme; II *v* (6) submit; (7) propose, suggest; (2 words) put forward.

taboo I *n* (3) ban; (5) curse; (8) anathema; (11) prohibition, restriction; (12) interdiction; II *adj* (6) banned; (9) forbidden; (10) prohibited, proscribed; (12) unacceptable; (13) unmentionable.

tackle I *n* **1** (3) rig; (4) gear; (5) tools; (6) outfit; (9) apparatus, equipment; (13) paraphernalia; **2** (5) block; (9) challenge; (12) interception; II *v* (4) grab, stop; (5) block, grasp, seize; (6) pinion; (7) grapple; (9) intercept; **2** (4) face; (5) begin; (6) handle; (7) attempt; (9) undertake; (2+ words) deal with, face up to, take on, take up.

tail I *n* (3) end; (4) back, rear, rump; (6) behind; II *v* **1** (3) dog; (5) stalk, track, trail; (6) follow, pursue, shadow; **2** (4) dock; III *cryptic* remove the last letter or last letters of a word, as in: 'Ox tailed round bend to lair in London suburb' (7) = Neasden (ox = neat, bend = S).

take I *v* **1** (4) grab, hold; (5) catch, filch, seize, **steal**; (6) remove, snatch; **2** (4) lead; (5) bring, carry, ferry, guide, usher; (6) convey, escort; (7) conduct; (9) transport; **3** (3) get; (4) gain, pick; (5) adopt; (6) accept, assume, choose, derive, obtain, secure, select; (7) acquire, receive; **4** (4) need; (7) require; (2 words) call for; **5** (6) occupy; (7) capture, conquer; **6** (4) bear; (6) endure; (8) tolerate; II **take**, **took**, **taking** *etc cryptic* add an additional element to the first or main part of the answer, usually at the end. As in: 'Mother takes tea on rug' (3) = mat *or*: 'Simple fellow taking heart from popular but non-U instruction gets a pass' (7) = Simplon (simple fellow = Simon, and *see* **heart**).

take aback *see* **aback**.

take back *v* **1** (4) deny; (6) recant; (7) retract; (8) withdraw; **2** (6) regain; (7) reclaim; (9) repossess; **3** (6) return (7) replace, restore.

take down *v* **1** (4) note; (5) write; (6) record; **2** (6) remove; (8) demolish; (9) dismantle; (11) disassemble.

take in *v* **1** (4) dupe, fool; (7) **deceive**; **2** (5) cover, grasp; (6) absorb, digest; (7) include; (10) assimilate, understand; (11) incorporate; **3** (5) house; (7) shelter; (11) accommodate; **4** (3) see; (5) visit.

take off *v* **1** (4) doff, shed; (6) divest, remove; **2** (2) go; (5) **leave**; **3** (5) mimic; (6) parody; (7) imitate; (10) caricature; (2 words) send up; **4** (8) **subtract**.

take on *v* **1** (6) accept, tackle; (9) undertake; **2** (4) hire; (6) employ, engage; (7) recruit; **3** (4) face; (6) oppose; (8) confront; (9) challenge.

tale *n see* **story**.

talent *n* **1** (4) bent, feel, gift; (5) flair, forte, knack, skill; (6) genius; (7) ability, faculty; (8) aptitude, capacity, strength; **2** *hist.* Greek and Roman coin and measure of weight.

talk I *v & n* (4) chat; (6) gossip, natter; (7) chatter; II *v* (6) confer, parley; (7) discuss; (8) converse; (9) negotiate; (11) communicate; III *n* **1** (7) chinwag; (10) discussion; (12) consultation, conversation; **2** (6) sermon, speech; (7) address, lecture, seminar; (9) discourse; **3** (6) rumour; (7) hearsay.

tar *n see* **sailor**.

Tartarus *Gk myth* the lowest region and place of punishment in the classical **Underworld**.

Taurus *astrol. & astron.* the constellation that is the second sign of the zodiac, also known as the Bull.

tax I *n* (3) VAT; (4) duty, levy, PAYE, scot, rate, toll; (5) tithe; (6) charge, excise, tariff; (7) customs; II *v* (3) sap, try; (4) load, tire; (5) drain, weary; (6) burden, strain; (7) exhaust.

taxing *adj* (4) hard; (5) tough; (6) severe, tiring; (7) arduous; (9) demanding, difficult, gruelling, strenuous, stressful; (10) exhausting.

tea *n* (3) cha; (4) brew, char, meal; (5) cuppa.

TYPES OF TEA

(5) Assam, Bohea, China; (6) Ceylon, Congou, Keemun, Oolong; (7) Lapsang, Suchong; (10) Darjeeling; (2 words) Earl Grey, Orange Pekoe, Lapsang-suchong.

---

teach *v* (5) coach, drill, edify, guide, train, tutor, verse; (6) advise, direct, ground, impart, inform, school; (7) educate, lecture; (8) instruct; (9) enlighten, inculcate.

teacher *v* (3) don; (4) guru; (5) coach, guide, tutor; (6) master, mentor; (7) adviser, trainer; (8) director, educator, lecturer, mistress; (9) pedagogue, professor; (10) instructor; (12) schoolmaster; (14) schoolmistress.

team I *n* I (4) side; (5) squad; (6) eleven, line-up; (7) fifteen; **2** (4) band, crew, gang, yoke; (5) group, shift, staff; (7) company; II *v* (4) join, pair; (5) match; (6) couple; (9) co-operate; (11) collaborate; III *cryptic* letters II or XI (eleven).

tear I *n & v* (3) rip; (4) gash, hole, slit; (5) split; (7) rupture; II *v* I (4) rend; (5) sever, shred; (6) mangle; (8) lacerate, mutilate; **2** (3) fly, run; (4) belt, bolt, dart, dash, race, rush; (5) shoot, speed; (6) career, charge, sprint; III *n* (4) rent; (10) laceration.

tease *v* (3) rag, rib, vex; (4) gibe, mock. twit; (5) annoy, chaff, taunt; (6) pester; (7) provoke, torment; (2 words) wind up.

tedious *adj* (4) drab, dull; (5) banal; (6) boring, dreary; (7) humdrum; (8) tiresome; (9) laborious, wearisome; (10) long-winded, monotonous, unexciting; (13) uninteresting.

telephone I *n* (5) phone; (6) blower, mobile; (7) handset, headset; (8) receiver; II *v* (4) buzz, call, dial, ring; (5) phone; (7) contact; (2+ words) give someone a bell/buzz/ring.

tell *v* I (5) order; (6) direct, impart, inform, notify, reveal; (8) acquaint, instruct; (9) authorise (*or* authorize); (11) communicate; **2** (6) relate, report; (7) mention, narrate, recount; (8) announce, describe; **3** (8) identify; (9) recognise (*or* recognize); (11) distinguish; (13) differentiate; **4** (4) shop; (5) grass; (6) betray; (7) confess, divulge; (8) denounce, disclose; (2 words) inform on; **5** (5) drain; (6) affect, change; (7) exhaust; (9) transform; **6** (5) **count**.

tell off *v* (5) chide, scold; (6) berate, rebuke; (7) censure, lecture, reprove, upbraid; (9) reprimand; (2 words) dress down, tick off.

temper I *n* I (3) ire; (4) fury, rage; (5) anger, paddy; (6) passion, tantrum; (9) annoyance; **2** (4) mood; (6) humour; (9) composure; (11) **temperament**; II *v* I (5) allay; (6) lessen, reduce, soften, soothe; (8) mitigate, moderate; **2** (6) harden; (7) toughen; (10) strengthen.

temperament *n* (4) bent; (6) humour, make-up, nature; (8) attitude, tendency; (9) character; (11) disposition, personality; (12) constitution.

temperamental I *adj* I (5) fiery, moody; (6) touchy; (8) neurotic, volatile; (9) emotional, excitable, irritable, mercurial, sensitive; (10) capricious, unreliable; (12) highly-strung; (13) unpredictable; **2** (6) inborn, innate; (7) natural; (8) inherent; (9) ingrained; II *cryptic* ANAGRAM CUE.

Tempest *lit.* **The Tempest** a play by William Shakespeare.

Plot outline: Prospero, the rightful Duke of Milan and a great scholar and magician, was deposed by his brother Antonio with the help of Alonso, King of Naples, and set adrift in an open boat with his infant daughter Miranda. Prospero and Miranda landed on an island where their only companions were Ariel, an ethereal and beneficent spirit, and Caliban, a deformed earthly monster, the offspring of the witch Sycorax who had formerly ruled there. The play begins with a violent storm in which a ship carrying Antonio, Alonso, Alonso's son Ferdinand and various other characters is wrecked. The next scene reveals that Prospero raised the storm and contrived that the people on board the ship reached the island in separate groups. Ferdinand, who lands alone, soon reaches Prospero's cell, sees Miranda and falls in love with her as she with him. The wicked Antonio plots against his former ally Alonso in league with the latter's brother Sebastian. The drunken butler Stefano and the jester Trinculo find Caliban, who urges them to kill Prospero and make themselves kings of the island. Prospero uses Ariel and his magical powers to torment the villains and to prevent them from carrying out their plots, while gradually drawing them all together at his cell. There, a final recognition, rediscovery and reconciliation scene takes place. The characters prepare to sail back to Italy and, in a final act signifying his return to ordinary human life, Prospero releases his servant spirit Ariel and promises to break his magic staff and throw his magic book into the sea.

The most famous speech in *The Tempest*, 'Our revels now are ended' – which contains the lines, 'We are such stuff/ As dreams are made on, and our little life/ Is rounded by a sleep' – occurs at the end of a masque of spirits that Prospero conjures up to celebrate the betrothal of Ferdinand and Miranda and he has to break off hastily to deal with Caliban and his confederates. It is Miranda in this play who speaks the line, 'O brave new world/ That has such people in it', when she sees Alonso and his company for the first time.

tempestuous *adj* **1** (4) wild; (5) gusty, rough, windy; (6) raging, stormy; (7) squally, violent; (8) blustery, thundery; **2** (6) heated; (7) intense; (9) turbulent; (10) passionate, tumultuous.

tempo *n* (4) beat, pace, rate, time; (5) metre, pulse, speed; (6) rhythm.

MUSICAL TEMPI

(5) largo, lento; (6) adagio, comodo, presto, rubato; (7) allegro, andante, animato, morendo; (8) maestoso; (10) allegretto, largamente, stringendo; (11) accelerando, prestissimo, rallentando.

---

temporal *adj* (6) carnal, mortal; (7) earthly, fleshly, profane, secular, worldly; (11) terrestrial.

temporary *adj* (5) brief; (6) acting; (7) interim, passing, stopgap; (8) fleeting; (9) ephemeral, makeshift, momentary, transient; (10) short-lived, transitory; (11) impermanent, provisional.

tempt *v* (4) bait, coax, draw, lure; (6) allure, entice, incite, seduce; (7) attract, provoke; (8) persuade; (9) tantalise (*or* tantalize).

ten *cryptic* letter X or letters IO.

Ten Commandments *Bible*

1 Thou shalt have no other gods before me.
2 Thou shalt not make unto thee any graven image.
3 Thou shalt not take the name of the Lord thy God in vain.
4 Remember the sabbath day, to keep it holy.
5 Honour thy father and thy mother.
6 Thou shalt not kill.
7 Thou shalt not commit adultery.
8 Thou shalt not steal.
9 Thou shalt not bear false witness against thy neighbour.
10 Thou shalt not covet.

tend *v* 1 (4) keep, mind; (5) guard, serve; (6) handle, manage; (7) operate; (8) maintain; (2 words) care for, look after, minister to, watch over; 2 (4) bend, lean, move; (7) incline; (9) gravitate.

tender I *adj* 1 (3) raw; (4) soft, sore, weak; (5) frail; (6) dainty; (7) fragile, painful; (9) sensitive; 2 (4) fond, kind, warm; (6) caring, gentle, humane, loving; (7) amorous; (8) romantic; (11) considerate, sympathetic; (12) affectionate; (13) compassionate; 3 (5) young; (8) immature, youthful; (13) inexperienced; II *v* 1 (4) give; (5) offer; (6) extend, submit; (7) present, proffer, propose; (9) volunteer; 2 (3) bid; (5) apply; III *n* (3) bid; (5) offer; (8) estimate, proposal; (9) quotation; (10) submission.

tense I *adj* 1 (4) edgy; (5) jumpy; (6) uneasy; (7) anxious, fidgety, fraught, jittery, nervous, worried; (8) strained, worrying; (9) stressful; (12) apprehensive; 2 (4) taut; (5) rigid, stiff, tight; (9) stretched; II *n of a verb* (4) past; (6) future; (7) perfect, present; (9) imperfect; (10) continuous, pluperfect.

term I *n* 1 (4) name, word; (5) title; (6) phrase; (7) epithet; (10) expression; (11) designation; 2 (4) span, time; (5) limit, spell; (6) period; (7) stretch; (8) duration, interval; 3 (7) session; (8) semester; II *v* (3) dub, tag; (4) call, name; (5) label, style, title; (7) entitle; (9) designate; III **terms** 1 (7) footing; (8) position, standing; (9) relations; (12) relationship; 2 (10) conditions, provisions; (11) particulars; (12) stipulations; (14) specifications; 3 (3) fee; (4) cost, fees; (5) price, rates; (6) tariff; (7) charges.

Terpsichore *Gk myth* the muse of dancing.

terrible *adj* 1 (3) bad; (4) dire, foul, vile; (5) awful; (6) horrid; (7) fearful, hateful, hideous; (8) dreadful, gruesome, horrible, horrific, shocking; (9) appalling, frightful, obnoxious, offensive, repugnant, repulsive, revolting; (10) disgusting, outrageous, unpleasant; 2 (5) grave; (7) extreme, serious; (9) desperate, harrowing; (11) distressing.

terrific *adj* 1 (3) fab; (5) brill, great, super; (6) superb; (7) amazing, awesome; (8) fabulous, smashing; (9) brilliant, fantastic, wonderful; (10) incredible, marvellous, phenomenal, stupendous, tremendous; (11) magnificent, outstanding, sensational; (12) breathtaking, unbelievable; 2 (3) big; (4) huge; (5) large; (7) immense; (8) enormous, gigantic; 3 (7) extreme, intense; 4 (10) **terrifying**.

terrify *v* (5) alarm, appal, scare, shock; (6) dismay; (7) horrify, petrify; (8) frighten.

terrifying *adj* (5) awful, scary; (7) fearful; (8) alarming, dreadful, gruesome, horrible, horrific, shocking; (9) appalling, frightful; (10) horrifying, petrifying; (11) hair-raising; (13) bloodcurdling, spine-chilling.

territory *n* (4) area, land, zone; (5) state; (6) domain, region, sector; (7) country, terrain; (8) district, preserve, province; (10) dependency.

terror *n* (4) fear; (5) alarm, dread, panic, shock; (6) dismay, horror; (11) trepidation; (13) consternation.

test I *n* 1 (5) check, trial; (6) try-out; (8) analysis; (10) assessment, evaluation, experiment; (11) examination; (13) investigation; 2 = **test match**; II *v* (3) try; (5) check, prove; (6) assess, screen, verify; (7) analyse, examine; (8) evaluate; (11) investigate.

test match *cricket*

TEST MATCH VENUES IN ENGLAND
(4) Oval (the); (5) Lord's; (9) Edgbaston; (10) Headingley; (2 words) Old Trafford, Trent Bridge.

the *cryptic* **French** la, le, les; **German** das, der, die; **Italian** gli, il, la, lo; **the Spanish** el.

theatre *n* 1 (3) rep; (5) drama, stage; (9) playhouse; (10) auditorium; (2 words) show biz; 2 (4) area, zone; (5) arena, field, scene.

FAMOUS THEATRES

Adelphi, Albery, Aldwych, Ambassadors, Apollo, Barbican, Coliseum, Comedy, Cottesloe, Covent Garden, Criterion, Dominion, Drury Lane, Globe, Haymarket, Hippodrome, La Scala (Milan), Lyceum, Lyric, Lyttleton, Mermaid, National (Theatre), Old Vic, Olivier, Palladium, Phoenix, Piccadilly, Pit (Barbican), Prince's, Queen's, Royal Court, Royal Shakespeare, Sadler's Wells, Shaftesbury, Strand, Swan (Stratford), Variety, Victoria, Whitehall, Wyndham's, Young Vic, Yvonne Arnaud.

Theseus *Gk myth* the son of King Aegeus of Athens, who volunteered to be a member of the group of young men and women sent to Crete to be sacrificed to the **Minotaur**. With the help of **Ariadne**, the daughter of King **Minos**, he was able to slay the Minotaur and find his way back out of the labyrinth. When he left Crete he took Ariadne with him, but abandoned her on the island of Naxos.

thick *adj* 1 (3) fat; (4) wide; (5) broad, dense, heavy, solid; (7) clotted, compact, viscous; (9) condensed; (12) concentrated; 2 (6) **stupid**; (7) **foolish**.

thin I *adj* 1 (4) bony, lean, slim, trim; (5) gaunt, lanky, spare; (6) skinny, slight; (7) scraggy, scrawny, slender; (8) anorexic, skeletal; (9) emaciated; (11) underweight; 2 (4) fine; (5) filmy, light, sheer; (6) flimsy, narrow; (8) gossamer; (10) attenuated, see-through; (11) translucent, transparent; (13) insubstantial; 3 (5) runny; (6) watery; (7) diluted; 4 (5) scant; (6) meagre, scanty, scarce, skimpy, sparse; (9) scattered; (12) insufficient; II *v* (4) cull, trim, weed; (6) dilute, rarefy, reduce, weaken; (9) attenuate.

thing I *n* 1 (4) item, tool; (6) entity, device, gadget, object; (7) article; (9) apparatus, implement; (10) instrument; (11) contrivance; 2 (5) point; (6) affair, detail, factor, matter; (7) element, feature; (10)

phenomenon; (12) circumstance; 3 (3) fad; (5) craze; (6) fetish, hang-up, phobia; (8) fixation; (9) obsession; (13) preoccupation; II **things** (4) bits, gear; (5) stuff; (7) clobber, effects; (8) property; (10) belongings.

think *v* 1 (4) muse; (6) ponder, reason; (7) reflect; (8) cogitate, consider, meditate, ruminate; (10) deliberate; (11) contemplate; 2 (4) deem, hold; (5) judge; (6) esteem, reckon, regard; (7) believe; (8) conclude, estimate; 3 (4) plan; (6) expect, intend; (7) imagine, presume, suppose; surmise; (8) conceive, envisage.

think up *v* (4) plan; (6) design, devise, invent; (7) concoct, imagine; (8) conceive, contrive.

Thor *Norse myth* the god of thunder after whom Thursday is named.

thorium *cryptic* abbreviated as TH.

thought *n* 1 (4) idea; (6) notion; (7) concept; (10) conception; 2 (4) heed; (5) study; (6) regard; (8) thinking; (9) attention; (10) cogitation, meditation, reflection, rumination; (12) deliberation; (13) consideration, contemplation; 3 (4) care; (7) concern; (8) kindness; (10) compassion.

thoughtful *adj* 1 (6) dreamy; (7) pensive, serious, wistful; (8) studious; (10) abstracted, reflective; (11) preoccupied; (13) contemplative, introspective; 2 (4) kind; (6) caring; (7) helpful; (9) attentive; (11) considerate.

thousand *cryptic* letter M (Roman numeral) or K.

throw I *v* 1 *v* & *n* (3) lob; (4) bung, cast, hurl, toss; (5) chuck, fling, heave, pitch, sling; (6) launch; II *v* 1 (4) emit, send, shed; (6) direct; (7) diffuse, project, radiate, scatter; 2 (5) floor; (6) baffle; (7) confuse, perplex; (8) astonish, confound; (9) dumbfound; (10) disconcert; 3 (6) unseat; (7) unhorse; (8) unsaddle.

Thursday *n* the fifth day of the week, named after **Thor**.

tie I *v* 1 (4) bind, join, knot, lash, link, moor, rope; (6) attach, fasten, secure, tether; (7) connect; **2** (5) limit; (6) hamper, hinder; (8) restrain, restrict; **II** *n* **1** (4) band, lace, tape; (6) ribbon; (9) fastening; **2** (4) bond, duty, link; (10) commitment, connection, obligation; (12) relationship; **3** (9) hindrance; (10) restraint, limitation; (11) restriction; **4** (4) draw; (9) stalemate; (2 words) dead heat.

tight *adj* **1** (4) snug, taut; (5) close, rigid, stiff, tense; (7) compact, cramped; **2** (4) fast, firm; (5) fixed, proof; (6) sealed, secure; (10) impervious; (11) impermeable; **3** (4) mean, near; (6) stingy; (7) miserly; (9) niggardly; (11) close-fisted, tight-fisted; **4** *see* **drunk**.

time **I** *n* **1** (3) age, day, era; (4) date, hour, span, term; (5) epoch, spell, stage; (6) minute, moment, period, season; (7) session, stretch; (8) duration, interval; **2** (8) instance, occasion; **3** (4) beat; (5) metre, tempo; (6) rhythm; (7) measure; **II** *v* (5) clock, meter; (7) control, measure; (8) regulate, schedule; (9) timetable; **III** *cryptic* letter T (abbreviation).

tin **I** *n* (3) can; (5) metal, money; **II** *cryptic* letters SN (chemical symbol) or, occasionally, letter T.

tip **I** *n* **1** (3) cap, end, nib, top; (4) acme, apex, head, peak; (5) crown, point; (8) pinnacle; (9) extremity; **2** (4) gift; (8) gratuity; **3** (4) clue, hint; (6) advice; (7) pointer, warning; (8) forecast; (10) suggestion; **4** (4) dump, hole; (6) pigsty; **II** *v* (3) cap, top; (5) crown; **2** (4) cant, lean, list, tilt; (5) slant, upset; (6) topple; (7) capsize, incline; (8) overturn; (11) overbalance; **3** (4) dump, pour, (5) empty, spill; (6) unload; **4** (6) reward; **III** **tip off** (4) tell, warn; (6) advise, inform; (7) caution; **IV** *cryptic* use the first or last letter (*or* **tips** the first and last letters) of the relevant word, as in: 'Shaker writer on asparagus tips takes fresh page' (5, 4) = aspen leaf.

Titan *Gk myth* a member of an older generation of gods, the offspring of **Uranus** and **Gaea** (including **Cronos**, **Hyperion** and **Mnemosyne**), who, having overthrown Uranus and made Cronos chief god in his stead, were themselves overthrown by **Zeus** and his generation of gods, against whom they waged war until being cast out into **Tartarus**.

titanium *cryptic* abbreviated as TI.

title **I** *n* **1** (4) name, rank; (5) label, style; (7) epithet; **2** (6) legend; (7) caption, heading; (8) headline; (11) inscription; **3** (5) claim, deeds, right; (9) ownership; (11) entitlement; **II** *v* (3) dub; (4) call, name, term; (5) style; (7) entitle; (9) designate.

token **I** *n* (4) disc, mark, sign; (6) coupon, emblem, symbol; (7) counter, gesture, memento, voucher, warning; (8) evidence, keepsake, reminder, souvenir; (10) indication; (14) representation; **II** *adj* (7) minimal, nominal; (8) cosmetic, symbolic; (11) perfunctory.

tolerable *adj* **1** (8) bearable; (9) endurable; **2** (2) OK; (4) fair, so-so; (8) adequate, passable; (10) acceptable, reasonable; (2 words) all right.

tolerant *adj* (3) lax; (4) soft; (7) lenient, liberal, patient; (9) easy-going, forgiving, indulgent; (10) charitable, forbearing, permissive; (11) broad-minded, sympathetic; (13) long-suffering, understanding.

tolerate *v* **1** (4) bear, take; (5) abide, stand; (6) endure, suffer; (7) stomach, swallow; **2** (5) admit, allow; (6) permit; (7) condone; (11) countenance.

tone **I** *n* **1** (4) note; (5) pitch, sound; (6) timbre; **2** (3) hue; (4) tint; (5) shade; (6) colour; **3** (3) air; (4) feel, mood, vein; (5) style, tenor; (6) effect, manner; (7) quality; (8) attitude; (9) character; **II** *v* (5) blend, match; (9) harmonise (*or* harmonize).

took *cryptic see* **take**.

tool *n* **1** (5) gizmo, means; (6) device, gadget; (7) utensil; (9) apparatus, implement; (10) instrument; (11) contrivance; **2** (4) dupe, pawn; (6) puppet, stooge; (2 words) cat's paw.

TYPES OF TOOL

(3) awl, axe, bit, bob, die, hod, hoe, jig, key, nut, peg, pin, ram, saw, set.

(4) adze, bolt, brad, burr, clip, file, fork, hook, hose, iron, jack, last, lead, mace, maul, nail, pale, pick, plug, prod, rake, rasp, rose, rule, shim, size, slot, spud, stud, tack, trap, vice.

(5) anvil, auger, besom, blade, borer, brace, brand, brush, burin, chuck, clamp, clasp, cleat, clout, corer, dolly, dowel, drill, float, gavel, gouge, jemmy, knife, level, lever, plane, punch, rivet, ruler, scoop, screw, shave, sieve, snips, spade, spike, spoon, stamp, steel, strop, tongs, wedge, wrest.

(6) beetle, bodkin, bow-saw, broach, chaser, chisel, cotter, dibber, dibble, fraise, gimlet, grater, graver, hammer, jigsaw, ladder, mallet, marker, needle, opener, paddle, pestle, pit-saw, pliers, plough, pulley, rammer, reamer, riddle, ripsaw, roller, sander, screen, scribe, scythe, shears, shovel, sickle, spacer, square, staple, stylus, tamper, tracer, trowel, washer, wrench.

(7) backsaw, bandsaw, bolster, bradawl, buzz-saw, chopper, cleaver, clipper, forceps, fretsaw, grapnel, grapple, hacksaw, handsaw, hatchet, hobnail, jointer, mandrel, mattock, nippers, pickaxe, pincers, plunger, poleaxe, scraper, scriber, shackle, spanner, sprayer, stapler, trimmer, T-square, whipsaw, whittle.

(8) billhook, blowlamp, bootlast, chainsaw, corundum, foot-pump, hand-pump, penknife, picklock, saw-horse, scissors, stripper, tenon-saw, tommy-bar, tweezers, windlass.

(9) callipers, centre-bit, corkscrew, grease-gun, handspike, jack-knife, jack-plane, lazy-tongs, pitchfork, sandpaper, secateurs, sharpener, tin-opener, whetstone.

(10) grindstone, guillotine, paintbrush, paper-knife, protractor, spokeshave, turnbuckle.

(11) carborundum, feeler-gauge, glass-cutter, paint-roller, pinking-iron, ploughshare, pruning-hook, sheath-knife.

top I *n* 1 (3) cap, end, nib, tip; (4) acme, apex, head, peak; (5) crest, crown, point; (6) summit, vertex, zenith; (8) pinnacle; (9) extremity; 2 (3) lid; (4) cork; (5) cover; (7) stopper; 3 (3) bra; (5) shirt; (6) blouse, jacket; II *adj* (4) best, head; (5) chief, first; (6) finest; (7) highest, leading, maximum, supreme; (8) foremost, superior; (9) paramount, principal, uppermost; (10) preeminent; III *v* 1 (3) cap, tip; (4) trim; (5) crown; (7) garnish; (8) decorate, surmount; 2 (4) beat, best; (5) excel, outdo; (6) better, exceed; (7) eclipse, surpass; (8) outshine, outstrip; (9) transcend; 3 (4) kill; (6) behead; (10) decapitate; IV *cryptic* omit the first letter of a word, especially in a down clue, as in: 'Run top team on paper' (4) = ream.

topless *cryptic* omit the first letter of a word, especially in a down clue, as in: 'Life-threatening conditions suffered by a hundred topless dancers?' (7) = cancers.

tot I *n* 1 (4) dram; (5) drink, glass; (7) measure; 2 (4) baby; (5) child; (6) infant; (7) toddler; II *v* **tot up** (3) add, sum; (5) count, total.

total I *adj* (4) full; (5) sheer, utter, whole; (6) entire; (7) perfect; (8) absolute, complete, outright, thorough; (9) downright; (10) consummate; (11) unqualified; (13) unconditional; II *n* (3) all, lot, sum; (5) whole; (8) entirety, totality; (9) aggregate; III *v* 1 (3) add, sum; (5) count; (6) reckon; 2 (5) reach; (2 words) amount to, come to; 3 (5) wreck; (7) destroy.

touch I *v & n* (3) hit, pat, tap; (4) feel; (5) brush, graze; (6) caress, strike, stroke; (7) contact; II *v* 1 (6) finger, fondle, handle; 2 (4) abut, meet; (5) reach; (6) adjoin, attain, border; 3 (4) move, stir; (5) upset; (6) affect, regard; (7) concern, disturb; III *n* 1 (3) bit, jot; (4) dash, hint, spot; (5) pinch, speck, tinge, trace; (7) soupçon;

(10) suggestion; **2** (4) form; (5) flair, knack, skill, style; (6) manner, method; (9) technique.

tough I *adj* **1** (5) hardy, rigid, solid; (6) robust, strong, sturdy; (7) durable; (9) resilient, resistant; **2** (5) chewy; (8) leathery; **3** (4) hard; (6) knotty, taxing, thorny; (7) arduous; (8) exacting, puzzling; (9) demanding, difficult, laborious; **4** (5) harsh, stern; (6) severe, strict; (8) resolute; (10) determined, unyielding; (14) uncompromising; II *n* (3) yob; (4) lout, thug; (5) brute, bully, heavy; (7) ruffian; (8) hooligan.

tower I *n* (4) keep, fort; (5) spire; (6) belfry, turret; (7) bastion, citadel, steeple; (10) skyscraper; II *n* (4) loom, rear, rise, soar; (5) mount; (6) ascend.

trace I *n* **1** (4) mark, sign; (5) relic, spoor, token, track, trail; (6) record; (7) remains, remnant, vestige; (8) evidence, footmark; (9) footprint; (10) indication; **2** (3) bit, jot; (4) dash, hint, spot; (5) pinch, speck, tinge, touch; (7) soupçon; (10) suggestion; II *v* **1** (4) find; (5) track; (6) detect; (7) unearth; (8) discover; **2** (3) map; (4) copy, draw; (5) chart; (6) depict, record, sketch; (7) outline; (9) delineate.

track I *n* **1** (4) mark, sign; (5) scent, spoor, token, trace, trail; (8) footmark; (9) footprint; **2** (3) way; (4) lane, path, road; (8) footpath; (9) bridleway; **3** (4) line; (5) orbit, route; (6) course; (9) direction; II *v* (3) dog; (4) hunt, tail; (5) chase, stalk, trail; (6) follow, shadow.

tract *n* **1** (3) lot; (4) area, plot, zone; (6) extent, region; (7) expanse, stretch; (9) territory; **2** (5) essay; (7) booklet; (8) pamphlet; (9) monograph.

trade I *n* **1** (7) dealing, traffic; (8) business, commerce; **2** (3) job; (5) craft, skill; (7) calling; (8) vocation; (10) occupation, profession; II *v* (3) buy; (4) sell, swap; (6) barter, peddle; (7) bargain; (8) exchange.

trade union *see* **union**.

train I *n* **1** (4) file, line; (5) chain; (6) series, string; (8) sequence; (10) procession, succession; **2** (5) court, staff; (7) cortège,

retinue; (9) household; (10) attendants; **3** (3) TGV; (7) express, pullman; II *v* **1** (5) coach, drill, teach, tutor; (6) school; (7) educate, prepare; (8) instruct, practise, rehearse; **2** (3) aim; (5) level, point; (6) direct; III *cryptic see* **railway**.

trainee *cryptic see* **student**.

transfer I *n* & *v* (4) move; (5) shift; (6) change, remove; (9) transplant; II *v* (5) grant; (6) assign, convey; (7) consign, deliver; (8) relocate, transmit; (9) transpose; (2 words) hand over; III *n* (7) removal; (8) delivery, handover; (10) relocation; IV *cryptic* ANAGRAM CUE.

translate I *n* **1** (6) decode, render; (9) interpret; (10) paraphrase; **2** (5) alter; (6) **change**; II *cryptic* **1** reverse the order of the letters or syllables in a word in the clue or answer; **2** ANAGRAM CUE.

trap I *n* & *v* (3) net; (5) snare, trick; (6) ambush; II *n* **1** (3) gin; (4) plot, ruse, wile; (5) noose; (6) danger, hazard; (7) pitfall; (9) stratagem; **2** (3) gob; (5) mouth; III *v* (4) dupe, take; (5) catch; (6) corner, enmesh; (7) deceive, ensnare.

treat I *v* **1** (3) use; (6) handle, manage, regard; (7) process; (2 words) deal with; **2** (4) cure, heal, tend; (5) nurse; (6) attend; (8) minister; **3** (3) buy; (4) give; (5) stand; (6) regale; (7) provide; II *n* (4) gift; (5) round, shout; III *also* **treatment** *cryptic* ANAGRAM CUE.

tree *n* (4) bush; (5) shrub; (7) conifer; (9) evergreen.

TYPES OF TREE

(2) bo, ti.

(3) ash, asp, ban, bay, box, elm, fig, fir, gum, jak, koa, oak, sal, yew.

(4) acer, akee, aloe, bael, coco, cola, dali, date, dhak, doum, gean, holm, ilex, kola, lana, lime, nipa, palm, pear, pine, plum, poon, rata, rose, sago, shea, sorb, teak, teil, titi, toon, upas.

(5) abele, abies, alder, apple, aspen, balsa, beech, birch, boree, bunya, cacao, carob, cedar, ebony, elder, guava, hazel, holly, *list continued over*

iroko, judas, kauri, larch, lemon, lilac, mango, maple, myali, ngaio, olive, osier, papaw, peach, pipal, plane, rohan, rowan, salix, sumac, taxus, tikul, tilia, tuart, withy, yacca, zamia.

(6) acacia, acajou, almond, antiar, areca, bamboo, banana, banyan, baobab, bog-oak, cashew, cassia, cerris, cherry, citrus, deodar, fustic, gingko, ginkgo, gomuti, gopher, jarrah, jujube, jupati, kittul, laurel, linden, litchi, locust, loquat, mallee, medlar, mimosa, obeche, orange, peepul, poplar, quince, rattan, red-bud, red-gum, red-oak, sandal, sapele, spruce, sumach, tupelo, walnut, wattle, willow, yarran.

(7) ailanto, apricot, arbutus, bay-tree, bebeeru, cajuput, camphor, canella, catalpa, champak, coconut, coquito, cypress, durmast, fan-palm, filbert, hickory, holm-oak, juniper, moriche, oil-palm, palmyra, paxiuba, platane, quassia, redwood, robinia, sequoia, seringa, service, talipot, tanghin, wallaba, wax-palm, wych-elm, yew-tree.

(8) basswood, beefwood, blackboy, carnauba, chestnut, cinchona, coolabah, corkwood, crabwood, date-palm, hawthorn, holly oak, hornbeam, ironwood, kingwood, laburnum, magnolia, mahogany, mangrove, mulberry, oleaster, palmetto, pinaster, quandong, rambutan, rosewood, sago-palm, swamp oak, sycamore, tamarack, tamarind, witch-elm.

(9) ailanthus, blackwood, carambola, chinkapin, hackberry, jacaranda, kurrajong, quebracho, satinwood, terebinth.

(10) blackthorn, breadfruit, chinquapin, coromandel, cotton-wood, eucalyptus, hackmatack, quickthorn, sandalwood, yellow-wood, ylang-ylang.

(2 words) copper beech, monkey puzzle, mountain ash, rain tree, Scots pine, turkey oak.

tremble *v* 1 (4) fear; (5) cower, shake; (6) blench, cringe, falter, flinch, recoil, shrink; 2 (4) rock, sway; (5) quake, shake; (6) shiver, wobble; (7) shudder, tremble, vibrate.

tremendous *adj see* **terrific**.

trial *n* 1 *see* **test**; 2 (4) case; (6) action; (7) hearing, lawsuit; (8) tribunal; 3 (6) ordeal, misery; (7) trouble; (8) distress, hardship; (10) affliction.

triangle *n* (5) delta; (7) scalene; (9) isos-celes; (10) right-angled; (11) equilateral.

trick I *n* 1 (4) hoax, joke, ruse, trap, wile; (5) antic, caper, dodge, prank, stunt; (6) device; (7) leg-pull, swindle; (9) decep-tion; (10) subterfuge; 2 (5) knack; (6) secret; (9) technique; **II** *v* (3) con; (4) dupe, fool, hoax; (5) bluff, cheat; (6) delude, diddle, outwit; (7) beguile, deceive, defraud; (8) hoodwink.

tricky *adj* 1 (4) hard; (6) knotty, thorny; (7) awkward; (8) delicate, ticklish; (9) difficult; (11) complicated, problematic; 2 (3) sly; (4) wily; (6) artful, crafty, subtle; (7) devious; (8) scheming, slippery; (9) deceitful.

trim I *v* 1 (3) cut, lop; (4) clip, crop, pare; (5) prune, shave; (6) neaten; 2 (5) dress; (5) adorn; (7) garnish; (8) decorate; (9) embellish; 3 (7) balance, ballast; **II** *adj* 1 (4) neat, tidy; (5) natty, smart; (6) dapper, spruce; (7) orderly; (9) shipshape; 2 (4) slim; (7) slender; (11) streamlined; **III** *n* (5) shape, state; (6) health; (9) condition.

trip I *n* (4) ride, spin, tour; (5) drive, foray, jaunt; (6) outing, voyage; (7) journey; (9) excursion; (10) expedition; **II** *v* 1 (4) fall, slip; (6) totter, tumble; (7) stagger, stumble; 2 (4) skip; (5) dance; (6) gambol, tiptoe.

triumvirate *Rom. hist.* a ruling group of three. The first triumvirate in Roman history consisted of Julius Caesar, Pompey and Crassus, the second of Mark Antony, Octavius Caesar and Marcus Aemilius Lepidus.

trivial *adj* (5) banal, minor, petty, small, trite; (6) paltry; (8) trifling; (9) frivolous;

(10) negligible; (11) unimportant; (13) insignificant; (14) inconsiderable; (15) inconsequential.

trouble I *n & v* (5) upset, worry; (6) bother; (7) torment; (8) distress; (13) inconvenience; II *n* 1 (3) ado, woe; (4) fuss, pain; (5) grief, trial; (7) anxiety, problem; (8) nuisance; (9) adversity, agitation, annoyance, heartache, suffering; (10) affliction, irritation, misfortune; (11) aggravation, tribulation; 2 (4) care; (5) pains; (6) effort; (7) thought; (9) attention; 3 (6) strife, tumult, unrest; (8) conflict, disorder, upheaval; (9) commotion; (11) disturbance; 4 (7) ailment, disease, illness; III *v* (3) vex; (5) annoy; (6) harass, ruffle; (7) afflict, agitate, disturb, perplex; (8) irritate; (10) disconcert; **IV trouble** *or* **troubled** *cryptic* ANAGRAM CUE.

Troy *Gk myth, hist.* a city in Asia Minor (modern Turkey) that, according to Homer and legend, held out against a ten-year siege by the combined forces of the early Greek kingdoms and was eventually captured by the stratagem of the wooden horse. At the time of the siege, Troy was ruled by King **Priam**, whose sons included **Hector**, **Paris** and **Aeneas**. Troy was also known as Ilion or Ilium.

troy *n* a system of weights for measuring precious metals and gems in which the units are pounds, ounces, pennyweights, and grains.

true *adj* 1 (4) real; (5) exact, right, valid; (6) actual, honest; (7) correct, factual, genuine, precise, sincere; (8) accurate; (9) authentic, veracious; (10) legitimate; 2 (4) firm; (5) loyal; (6) trusty; (7) devoted, staunch; (8) constant, faithful; (9) dedicated, steadfast; (11) trustworthy.

try I *n & v* (7) attempt, venture; (9) endeavour; II *v* 1 (4) seek; (6) strive; (9) undertake; 2 (4) test; (5) taste; (6) sample; (7) inspect; (8) appraise; (10) experiment; (11) investigate; 3 (4) hear; (5) judge; (7) arraign; 4 (3) tax; (6) strain, stress; (7) stretch; III *n* 1 (2) go; (4) bash, shot, stab; (5) crack; (6) effort; 2 (5) score; (9) touchdown.

trying *adj* 1 (8) annoying, tiresome; (9) vexatious, wearisome; (10) irritating; (11) aggravating, troublesome; (12) exasperating; 2 (4) hard; (5) **tough**; (9) demanding, difficult.

Tuesday *n* the third day of the week, named after Tiu, Tiw or Tyr, the Anglo-Saxon god of war.

tune I *n* (3) air; (4) song; (5) motif, theme; (6) melody, strain; II *v* (3) set; (6) adjust; (8) regulate; (9) harmonise (*or* harmonize).

turn I *v & n* (4) bend, loop, move, roll, spin, veer; (5) curve, hinge, pivot, shift, swing, twirl, twist, whirl, wheel; (6) corner, swerve, swivel; II *v* 1 (6) invert, gyrate, rotate; (7) reverse; 2 (5) alter; (6) change, modify; (7) convert; 3 (4) fade, sour; (5) spoil; (6) blanch, curdle; (9) discolour; III *n* 1 (5) cycle; (8) gyration, reversal, rotation; (10) revolution; 2 (2) go; (5) spell, stint; (6) chance; (8) occasion; (11) opportunity; 3 (3) act; (7) routine; (9) performer; (11) performance; **IV turn, turns, turning** *etc cryptic* reverse the order of the letters in a word in the clue or answer, as in: 'Not for turning? Holding to contract in this town!' (9) = Tonbridge *or*: 'Turn colour near local fixture' (5) = derby (colour = red).

turn out I *v* 1 (5) eject, evict, expel; (6) banish, deport; 2 (6) unplug; (10) disconnect, extinguish; (2 words) switch off; 3 (5) ensue, occur; (6) happen, result; (9) transpire; 4 (4) make; (7) produce; (11) manufacture; 5 (5) clear, empty; II **turn-out** *n* 1 (3) kit, rig; (4) gear; (5) dress, get-up; (6) outfit; 2 (4) gate; (5) crowd; (8) audience; III *cryptic* ANAGRAM CUE and/or reverse order of letters.

turn over I *v* 1 (5) upend, upset; (6) invert; (7) capsize; 2 (6) ponder; (7) reflect; (11) contemplate; (2 words) mull over, think about; 3 (4) give, hand; (7) deliver; (9) surrender; 4 *slang* (3) rob; (5) cheat; II *cryptic* ANAGRAM CUE and/or reverse order of letters, as in: 'Heathen turning over a new leaf endlessly' (5) = pagan (leaf = pag(e), new = n).

turnover I *n* **1** (3) pie; (4) tart; **2** (5) sales; (8) business; (10) throughput; II *cryptic see* **turn over**, as in: 'Request more volume in apple turnover' (4) = plea (more volume = not *pp* pianissimo, therefore *p*).

turn up I *v* **1** (4) come, show; (6) appear, arrive, attend; **2** (5) raise; (7) amplify; (8) increase; **3** (4) find; (7) unearth; (8) discover; II **turn-up** *n* (4) cuff; (8) surprise; III *cryptic esp. in down clues* ANAGRAM CUE and/or reverse order of letters, as in: 'Sid turns up a month before in distress' (6) = dismay.

Twelfth Night *lit.* comedy by Shakespeare.

Plot outline: Viola, the heroine, is shipwrecked off the coast of Illyria, saved by a sea captain, but believes that her identical twin brother, Sebastian, has been drowned. The Duke of Illyria, Orsino, is rather self-consciously in love ('If music be the food of love, play on') with Olivia, a lady who uses the recent death of her own brother as an excuse to reject all suitors, especially Orsino. Viola disguises herself as a man (taking the name Cesario) in order to serve Orsino and is immediately sent to woo Olivia on his behalf. Taken in by the male disguise, Olivia falls in love with Viola. Viola realises this, but at the same time recognises that she herself is falling in love with Orsino. Meanwhile, the members of Olivia's household, her drunken, ne'er-do-well uncle, Sir Toby Belch, his companion and dupe, Sir Andrew Aguecheek, Olivia's waiting gentlewoman, Maria, and her jester, Feste, hatch a plot to bring her arrogant and strait-laced steward, Malvolio, down a peg or two. By means of a forged letter, they delude Malvolio into thinking that Olivia loves him ('Some are born great, some achieve greatness, and some have greatness thrust upon them'). They incite him to appear before her in yellow stockings and cross-gartered. As a result of his ridiculous behaviour, Malvolio is deemed mad and hustled away to the madhouse. Then, in a further complication, Sebastian, Viola's twin, appears. The twins are several times mistaken for one another, most notably when Olivia marries Sebastian believing him to be Viola/Cesario. After that the complications are quickly resolved, with Orsino marrying Viola and Malvolio being released from the madhouse.

twice *cryptic* use a letter or syllable twice in forming the answer, as in: 'Cuts open twice, six groups revealed' (9) = vivisects.

twin I *n* (4) copy, mate, pair; (5) clone, match; (6) double, fellow; (9) duplicate, lookalike; (11) counterpart; II *adj* (4) dual; (7) twofold; (8) matching, parallel; (9) identical.

twist I *n & v* (3) arc; (4) bend, coil, curl, loop, roll, spin, turn, warp; (5) curve, screw; (6) spiral, tangle, zigzag; (7) wreathe; II *v* **1** (5) twine; (6) swivel, writhe; (7) entwine, wriggle; **2** (5) alter; (6) change; (7) contort, distort, pervert; (8) misquote; (12) misrepresent; **3** (4) rick; (6) sprain, strain; III *n* **1** (10) contortion, distortion; (11) convolution; **2** (8) surprise; (9) turnabout, variation; **3** (5) dance; **4** (7) tobacco; IV **twist, twisting,** *or* **twisted** *cryptic* ANAGRAM CUE.

type *n* (4) form, kind, sort; (5) brand, breed, group, class, genre, stamp; (6) strain; (7) species, variety; (8) category; (11) description; **2** (5) model; (7) pattern; (9) archetype; (10) embodiment; **3** (4) face, font; (5) fount, print; (7) letters; (9) lettering; *see also* **typeface**.

typeface *n* (4) font; (5) fount.

TYPEFACES

(3) gem.

(4) bold, pica, ruby.

(5) agate, canon, doric, elite, pearl, point, roman, ronde, times.

(6) caslon, cicero, futura, gothic, italic, minion, uncial.

(7) antique, brevier, century, cursive, diamond, electra, elzevir, english, fraktur, paragon.

list continued over

---

(8) garamond, sanserif.

(9) bourgeois, brilliant, clarendon, columbian, excelsior, nonpareil.

(11) baskerville.

typical *adj* (5) stock, usual; (6) normal; (7) average, routine; (8) orthodox, standard; (14) characteristic, representative.

tyrannical *adj* (5) harsh; (6) unjust; (8) absolute, despotic, ruthless; (9) arbitrary, illiberal; (10) autocratic, high-handed, oppressive, repressive; (11) dictatorial, domineering, overbearing; (13) authoritarian.

tyrant *n* (5) bully; (6) despot; (8) autocrat, dictator; (9) oppressor; (10) absolutist; (11) slave-driver; (13) authoritarian.

U

U 1 *abbrev.* united, universal, uranium; **II** *adj* acceptable to the upper classes (*esp.* around the 1950s).

ugly 1 *adj* **1** (5) plain; (6) homely; (7) hideous; (8) deformed; (9) misshapen, monstrous, repellent, repulsive, unsightly; (12) unattractive; **2** (4) vile; (6) horrid; (9) offensive; (10) unpleasant; **3** (8) alarming, menacing; (9) dangerous; (11) threatening; **II** *cryptic* ANAGRAM CUE.

ultimate *adj* **1** (4) last; (5) final; (7) closing; (8) terminal; **2** (4) best; (7) extreme, highest, perfect, supreme; (8) greatest; **3** (5) basic; (11) fundamental.

Ulysses *lit.* **1** *myth see* **Odysseus**; **2** novel by James Joyce, mainly charting a day in the life of Mr Leopold Bloom in Dublin in 1904.

un- *cryptic* words beginning with the prefix un- often act as **1** ANAGRAM CUES, as in: 'Go up with laces undone' (5) = scale *or*: 'Unwrap parcel without the Spanish, who complain' (4) = carp; **2** cues to omit certain letters referred to cryptically in the cue, see *e.g.* **unqualified, unsaintly**.

uncanny *adj* (3) odd; (5) eerie, queer, weird; (6) creepy, spooky; (7) bizarre, strange; (9) unearthly; (10) mysterious; (12) supernatural; (13) unaccountable.

uncertain *adj* **1** (6) unsure; (7) dubious; (8) doubtful, hesitant, insecure, wavering; (9) undecided; (10) ambivalent; (11) vacillating; **2** (4) iffy; (5) risky, shaky, vague; (7) erratic, unknown; (8) variable; (9) irregular, unsettled; (10) changeable, indefinite, unreliable, unresolved; (11) unconfirmed; (13) unforeseeable, unpredictable.

unclear *adj* (3) dim; (4) hazy; (5) vague; (7) obscure; (9) ambiguous, equivocal, **uncertain**; (10) indistinct.

uncomfortable *adj* **1** (4) hard; (7) cramped, crowded, painful; (12) disagreeable; **2** (6) uneasy; (7) anxious, awkward,

worried; (8) troubled; (9) disturbed; (11) embarrassed; (13) self-conscious.

uncommon *adj* **1** (4) rare; (6) scarce; (7) **strange**, unusual; (8) abnormal, atypical; (10) infrequent; **2** (5) great; (7) special; (9) wonderful; (10) remarkable.

under 1 *prep* (5) below; (7) beneath; (2 words) less than, lower than; **II** *cryptic in down clues* place letters or word after another word to form the answer (NB *under* may be incorporated in a longer word), as in: 'This officer is the head and has people under him' (8) = tipstaff.

underground 1 *adj* **1** (6) buried, sunken; (12) subterranean; **2** (6) covert, secret; (10) subversive, undercover, unofficial, unorthodox; (11) alternative; **II** *n* (4) tube; (5) metro; (6) subway.

understand *v* **1** (3) get, see; (4) twig; (5) grasp; (6) fathom, follow; (7) discern, realise (*or* realize); (8) perceive; (9) recognise (*or* recognize); (10) appreciate, comprehend; (2 words) cotton on, make out, take in; **2** (4) hear, know; (5) infer, think; (6) assume, deduce; (7) believe, suppose; (8) conclude; **3** (9) empathise (*or* empathize); (10) sympathise (*or* sympathize); (11) commiserate.

understanding 1 *n* **1** (4) idea; (5) grasp, sense; (6) notion, wisdom; (7) insight, opinion; (8) judgment; (9) awareness, intellect, judgement; (10) perception; (11) discernment; (12) appreciation; (13) comprehension; **2** (4) pact; (6) accord; (9) agreement; (11) arrangement; **3** (7) empathy; (8) kindness, sympathy; **II** *adj* (4) kind; (6) loving, tender; (8) tolerant; (9) forgiving; (10) forbearing; (11) considerate, sympathetic; (13) compassionate.

undertake *v* **1** (3) try; (5) begin; (6) accept, assume, tackle; (7) attempt; (9) endeavour; (2 words) embark on, take on; **2** (5) agree; (6) pledge; (7) promise; (8) contract, covenant.

underwear *n* (5) linen; (6) smalls, undies; (8) lingerie.

ITEMS OF UNDERWEAR

(3) bra; (4) hose, slip, vest; (5) combs, pants, shift, socks; (6) briefs, corset, girdle, tights; (7) drawers, panties, spencer; (8) bloomers, camisole, knickers; (9) petticoat; (10) underpants.

Underworld I *myth* the abode of the dead in Greek and Roman mythology, ruled by the god variously called **Dis**, **Hades** or **Pluto**. The main rivers in the **Underworld** were Acheron, Lethe, Phlegethon and Styx; **II** *n* (4) hell; (6) Erebus; (7) Abaddon, Gehenna, inferno; (8) Tartarus.

undo I *v* **1** (4) free, open; (5) loose, untie; (6) loosen, unbind, unlace, unwrap; (7) release; (8) unbuckle, unbutton, unfasten; **2** (3) mar; (4) ruin; (5) annul, quash, spoil, upset, wreck; (6) cancel, offset; (7) destroy, nullify, reverse, subvert; (8) overturn; (9) undermine; (10) invalidate, neutralise (*or* neutralize); **II** *cryptic* ANAGRAM CUE.

unfair *adj* **1** (6) biased, unjust; (7) partial; (8) one-sided; (9) arbitrary; (10) prejudiced; (11) inequitable; **2** (8) improper, wrongful; (9) dishonest, unethical; (12) illegitimate.

unfasten *v see* **undo I 1**.

unfavourable *adj* (3) bad; (4) poor; (7) adverse, hostile, ominous; (8) contrary, negative; (10) unfriendly; (11) unpromising, threatening; (12) discouraging, inauspicious; (15) disadvantageous.

unholy *cryptic* see **unsaintly**.

unimportant *adj* (5) banal, minor, petty, small, trite; (6) paltry; (7) trivial; (8) trifling; (9) frivolous; (10) immaterial, irrelevant, negligible; (13) insignificant; (14) inconsiderable; (15) inconsequential.

union *n* **1** (5) blend; (6) fusion, league, merger; (7) mixture; (8) alliance; (9) coalition, synthesis; (10) federation; (11) association, combination; (12) amalgamation; (13) confederation; **2** (5) unity; (6) accord; (7) harmony; (9) agreement, unanimity; **3** (7) wedding, wedlock; (8) marriage.

(TRADE) UNIONS

APEX (Association of Professional, Executive, Clerical and Computer Staff), ASLEF (Associated Society of Locomotive Engineers and Firemen), AUEW (Amalgamated Association of Engineering Workers), BALPA (British Airline Pilots Association), GMWU (General and Municipal Workers' Union), NASUWT (National Association of Schoolmasters and Union of Women Teachers), NFU (National Farmers' Union), NUJ (National Union of Journalists), NUM (National Union of Mineworkers), NUS (National Union of Students), NUT (National Union of Teachers), RMT (National Union of Rail, Maritime, and Transport Workers), TGWU (Transport and General Workers' Union), UNISON (representing workers in the public sector and the health service).

---

unite *v* (4) ally, fuse, join, link, pool; (5) marry, merge, unify; (6) couple; (7) combine; (8) coalesce, federate; (9) associate, co-operate; (10) amalgamate; (11) collaborate, confederate, consolidate.

university *n* (6) school; (7) college, varsity; (11) polytechnic.

WELL-KNOWN UNIVERSITIES

(*see also* **college**)

(3) CUA (US), MIT (US), UBC (Can.), USC (US).

(4) Bath (UK), City (UK), CUNY (US), Duke (US), Iowa (US), Kent (UK), Open (UK), UCLA (US), Yale (US), York (Can., UK).

(5) Aston (UK), Brown (US), Essex (UK), Keele (UK), Laval (Can.), Leeds (UK), Padua (It.).

list continued over

---

(6) Bangor (UK), Bombay (Ind.), Brunel (UK), Dundee (UK), Durham (UK), Exeter (UK), London (UK), McGill (Can.), Ottawa (Can.), Oxford (UK), Prague (Cz.), Quebec (Can.), Surrey (UK), Sussex (UK), Ulster (UK), Vassar (US), Vienna (A.).

(7) Belfast (UK), Bologna (It.), Cardiff (UK), Cornell (US), Glasgow (UK), Harvard (US), Leipzig (Ger.), Reading (UK), Salford (UK), Swansea (UK), Toronto (Can.), Warwick (UK).

(8) Aberdeen (UK), Berkeley (US), Bradford (UK), Cape Town (SA), Columbia (US), Freiburg (Ger.), Montreal (Can.), Sorbonne (Fr.), Stanford (US), Stirling (UK).

(9) Cambridge (UK), Dalhousie (Can.), Dartmouth (US), Edinburgh (UK), Göttingen (Ger.), Lancaster (UK), Leicester (UK), Liverpool (UK), Newcastle (UK), Princeton (US), Sheffield (UK), (2 words) Notre Dame (Can.), St Andrews (UK).

(10) Birmingham (UK), Buckingham (UK), Heidelberg (Ger.), Manchester (UK), Nottingham (UK).

(11) Aberystwyth (UK), Southampton (UK).

unkind *adj* (4) mean; (5) cruel, harsh, nasty; (7) callous, inhuman; (8) inhumane, spiteful, uncaring; (9) malicious, unfeeling; (10) malevolent, unfriendly; (11) hard-hearted, insensitive, thoughtless; (13) inconsiderate, unsympathetic.

unknown I *adj* (3) new; (4) dark; (5) alien; (6) hidden, secret, untold; (7) foreign, obscure, unnamed; (8) nameless; (9) incognito, uncharted; (10) mysterious, unexplored, unfamiliar; (12) undiscovered, unidentified; **II** *cryptic* letter X or Y (as in: mathematics).

unnatural *adj* **1** (3) odd, rum; (5) eerie, queer, weird; (6) chance, creepy; (7) bizarre, erratic, offbeat, uncanny, unusual; (8) aberrant, abnormal, atypical, freakish, peculiar; (9) irregular, perverted; (10) fortuitous, outlandish; (12) supernatural; (13) extraordinary; **2** (5) false; (6) forced; (7) feigned, stilted; (8) affected, laboured, mannered, strained; (9) insincere; (10) artificial.

unpleasant *adj* (3) bad; (5) nasty; (9) offensive, repulsive; (11) distasteful, unpalatable; (12) disagreeable; (13) objectionable.

unqualified I *adj* **1** (5) unfit; (7) amateur; (9) unskilled, untrained; (11) incompetent; **2** (5) total, utter; (8) absolute, complete, outright; (9) out-and-out; (10) unreserved; (11) unmitigated; (12) whole-hearted; (13) unconditional; **II** *cryptic* omit letters signifying a qualification (BA, MA, *etc*) from a word in the clue or the answer, as in: 'Unqualified member changing for pool' (4) = mere (omit MB and treat as anagram).

unsaintly *or* **unsainted** *cryptic* omit letters ST from a word in the clue or answer.

unsure *adj see* **uncertain**.

untidy I *adj* (5) messy; (6) sloppy; (7) chaotic, jumbled, muddled, scruffy, unkempt; (8) slipshod, slovenly; (9) cluttered; (10) disordered, disorderly, topsy-turvy; (12) disorganised (*or* disorganized), unsystematic; **II** **untidy** *or* **untidily** *cryptic* ANAGRAM CUE.

untie *v see* **undo I 1**.

up *cryptic in down clues* reverse the order of the letters in a word forming part of the clue or answer, as in: 'Stop up to see mother at conference' (7) = Potsdam.

upright I *adj* **1** (5) erect; (8) vertical; (13) perpendicular; **2** (4) good, just; (5) noble; (6) honest; (7) ethical; (8) virtuous; (9) righteous; (10) principled, upstanding; (10) honourable; **II** *cryptic in down clues* letters TR (RT = right, reversed).

upset I *v* **1** (3) vex; (5) annoy, shake, worry; (6) dismay, grieve, harass, ruffle; (7) afflict, agitate, confuse, disturb, fluster, perplex, trouble, unnerve; (8) distress, irritate; (10) disconcert; **2** (3) tip; (5) spill; (6) topple; (7) capsize; (8)

overturn; (2 words) knock over; **II** *adj* (4) hurt; (6) shaken; (7) annoyed, anxious, grieved, worried; (8) agitated, bothered, dismayed, offended, troubled; (9) disturbed, irritated; (10) distressed; (12) disconcerted; **III** *n* **1** (5) shock; (7) shake-up (8) surprise; (9) agitation; (11) disturbance; **2** (3) bug; (7) illness; **IV** *cryptic* ANAGRAM CUE.

Urania *Gk myth* the muse of astronomy.

uranium *cryptic* abbreviated as U.

Uranus I *Gk myth* the first chief god of heaven, husband of Gaea, father of the Titans, who overthrew him; **II** *astron.* the seventh planet from the sun.

urge I *v* (3) beg, egg; (4) goad, move, push, spur; (5) drive, force, impel, press; (6) advise, exhort, incite, induce, prompt; (7) counsel, entreat, implore; (8) advocate, persuade; (9) encourage, instigate, recommend, stimulate; **II** *n* (3) yen; (4) itch, wish; (5) fancy; (6) desire; (7) impulse, longing; (10) compulsion; (11) inclination.

usage *n* **1** *see* use **II 1**, **2** (4) form, rule; (5) habit; (6) custom; (7) routine; (8) practice; (9) etiquette, procedure, tradition; (10) convention.

use I *v* **1** (5) enjoy, wield; (6) employ, handle, manage; (7) exploit, operate; (8) exercise, practise; **2** *also* **use up** (5) spend; (6) expend; (7) consume, exhaust; **II** *n* **1** (5) usage; (8) exercise; (9) enjoyment, operation; (10) employment; (11) appli-cation; **2** (3) aid, end; (4) good, help; (5) avail, point, value, worth; (6) object, profit; (7) benefit, purpose, service; (9) advantage; (10) usefulness.

useful *adj* **1** (5) handy; (7) helpful; (8) fruitful, valuable; (9) effective, practical; (10) beneficial, convenient, productive, profitable, worthwhile; (12) advantageous; **2** (4) able, good; (6) expert; (7) skilful, skilled; (9) practised; (10) proficient; (11) experienced.

useless *adj* **1** (4) idle, vain; (6) futile; (8) hopeless; (9) fruitless, pointless, worthless; (10) unavailing; (12) unproductive; **2** (4) weak; (5) kaput; (6) broken; (9) defective; (10) broken-down; (11) inoperative; (13) unserviceable; **3** (3) bad; (4) poor; (11) incompetent, ineffective, inefficient.

usual *adj* (5) stock; (6) common, normal; (7) average, general, routine, typical; (8) everyday, expected, familiar, habitual, ordinary, orthodox, standard; (9) customary; (10) accustomed; (11) predictable; (14) characteristic, representative.

utter I *v* (3) say; (4) tell; (5) speak, state, voice; (6) reveal; (7) deliver, express; (8) announce, vocalise (*or* vocalize); (9) enunciate, pronounce, verbalise (*or* verbalize); (10) articulate; **II** *adj* (5) sheer, stark; (6) arrant, entire; (8) absolute, complete, outright, thorough; (9) downright, out-and-out; (10) consummate; (11) unmitigated, unqualified; (13) unconditional.

V

V *abbrev* vanadium, volt, 5 (Roman numeral).

v *abbrev* verb, versus, very, vide (Latin = see).

vacant *adj* 1 (4) free, void; (5) empty; (6) unused; (8) unfilled; (9) available; (10) unoccupied; 2 (5) blank, inane; (6) absent; (7) vacuous; (14) expressionless.

vague *adj* (3) dim; (4) hazy; (5) fuzzy, loose, misty; (6) woolly; (7) blurred, obscure, shadowy, unclear; (8) nebulous; (9) ambiguous, equivocal, imprecise, **uncertain**; (10) indefinite, indistinct, unspecific; (11) generalised (*or* generalized).

vain *adj* 1 (5) proud; (7) stuck-up; (8) arrogant; (9) big-headed, conceited; (11) egotistical, pretentious; (13) self-important, self-satisfied; 2 (4) idle; (5) empty; (6) futile; (7) useless; (8) abortive, hopeless; (9) fruitless, pointless, worthless; (10) unavailing; (12) unproductive.

Valhalla *Norse myth* a great hall in heaven to which the souls of heroes slain in battle were taken by the **Valkyries** to feast with **Odin** through eternity.

valid *adj* 1 (5) sound; (6) cogent; (7) correct, logical, telling, weighty; (10) convincing; (11) substantial, well-founded; 2 (5) legal; (6) lawful; (7) binding, genuine; (8) official; (9) authentic; (10) legitimate.

Valkyrie *Norse myth* one of the twelve handmaidens of **Odin** who chose the heroes slain in battle worthy to enter **Valhalla** and conducted them there.

valuable *adj* 1 (4) dear; (6) costly, prized; (8) precious; (9) expensive, treasured; 2 (6) useful; (7) helpful; (8) fruitful; (9) effective, practical; (10) beneficial, convenient, productive, profitable, worthwhile; (12) advantageous.

value l *n* 1 (4) cost; (5) price, worth; 2 (3) use; (4) good; (5) avail, merit, point; (6) profit; (7) benefit, purpose, service, utility; (9) advantage; (10) usefulness; ll *v* 1 (4) rate; (5) price; (6) assess; (8) appraise, estimate, evaluate; 2 (5) prize; (6) esteem; (7) cherish, respect; (8) treasure; (10) appreciate.

vanish *v* (2) go; (3) end; (4) exit, fade, hide, melt; (6) **depart**, expire; (8) disperse, dissolve; (9) disappear, evaporate.

variable *adj* (6) fitful; (7) mutable, varying; (8) flexible, shifting, unstable, unsteady, wavering; (10) changeable, inconstant; (11) fluctuating; (13) unpredictable.

vault l *n & v* (4) jump, leap; (5) bound; (6) spring; ll *v* (5) clear; (6) hurdle; (8) leapfrog; lll *n* 1 (4) arch, roof, span; 2 (4) tomb; (5) crypt; (6) cavern, cellar; (9) mausoleum; 3 (10) depository, repository, strongroom.

vegetable *n* (5) pulse, tuber; (6) greens.

TYPES OF VEGETABLE

(3) cos, dal, oca, pea, soy, udo, yam.

(4) bean, beet, cole, corn, dhal, eddo, kale, kohl, leek, neep, okra, rape, soya, spud, taro.

(5) chard, chive, colza, cress, maize, navew, onion, orach, pease, savoy, swede.

(6) batata, carrot, celery, endive, fennel, frijol, garlic, legume, lentil, marrow, murphy, pepper, potato, pratie, radish, runner, sprout, squash, tomato, turnip.

(7) cabbage, chicory, gherkin, lettuce, parsnip, pumpkin, salsify, seakale, seaweed, shallot, spinach, truffle.

(8) beetroot, borecole, broccoli, brassica, capsicum, celeriac, chickpea, colerape, colewort, cucumber, egg-plant, eschalot, kohlrabi, mushroom, rutabaga, scallion, zucchini.   *list continued over*

---

(9) artichoke, asparagus, aubergine, calabrese, courgette, curly-kale, flageolet, sweetcorn, mange-tout.

(10) butterbean.

(11) cauliflower.

(2 words) broad bean, brussels sprout, French bean, globe artichoke, green pepper, red pepper, runner bean, spring greens, spring onion.

vehicle *n* 1 (6) wheels; (9) transport; (10) conveyance 2 (5) means, organ; (6) agency, medium; (7) channel.

TYPES OF VEHICLE

(3) bus, cab, car, fly, gig, van.

(4) auto, bike, cart, drag, dray, duck, jeep, kart, limo, loco, pram, ship, sled, tank, taxi, tram, trap, wain.

(5) brake, buggy, coach, coupé, crate, cycle, float, lorry, moped, motor, plane, racer, sedan, stage, sulky, tonga, train, truck, wagon.

(6) banger, barrow, berlin, calash, camper, chaise, diesel, fiacre, gharri, go-kart, hansom, hearse, jalopy, jitney, kit-car, landau, litter, ox-cart, pick-up, roller, saloon, sledge, sleigh, surrey, tandem, tanker, tipper, tourer, troika, waggon, weasel.

(7) bicycle, britzka (*or* britska), caravan, cariole, caroche, chariot, dog-cart, droshky, express, fourgon, growler, hackney, handcar, minibus, minicab, minicar, omnibus, pedicab, phaeton, scooter, sidecar, taxicab, tilbury, tractor, trailer, trolley, tumbrel.

(8) aircraft, barouche, brougham, cable-car, carriage, carriole, clarence, curricle, dragster, dustcart, fastback, horse-box, motorbus, motorcar, push-bike, push-cart, rickshaw, roadster, runabout, stanhope, tricycle, unicycle, victoria.

(9) ambulance, amphibian, bath-chair, bubble-car, bulldozer,

cabriolet, dandy-cart, diligence, dormobile, excavator, half-track, hatchback, landaulet, limousine, low-loader, milk-float, motorbike, palanquin, push-chair, sand-yacht, street-car, two-seater, wagonette.

(10) automobile, boneshaker, fire-engine, four-in-hand, four-seater, juggernaut, locomotive, motorcycle, pedal-cycle, post-chaise, shandrydan, snow-mobile, spring-cart, stagecoach, trolley-bus, two-wheeler, velocipede, wheelchair.

(11) caravanette, caterpillar, cattle-truck, delivery-van, four-wheeler, jaunting-car, steamroller, three-in-hand, transporter, wheelbarrow.

(12) double-decker, freightliner, motor-scooter, pantechnicon, perambulator, single-decker, single-seater, three-wheeler.

(13) drophead-coupé, penny-farthing, shooting-brake.

(2 words) baby buggy, beach buggy, estate car, moon buggy, station wagon.

veil *n & v* (4) film, mask; (5) blind, shade, cloak, cover; (6) screen, shield, shroud; (8) disguise.

Venus I *Rom. myth* the goddess of love, wife of **Vulcan**, mother of **Cupid**, lover of **Mars**, born from the foam of the sea near the island of Cyprus and transported in a chariot drawn by doves. Greek equivalent, Aphrodite; II *astron.* the second planet from the sun.

Verdi, **Guiseppe** *music* Italian opera composer.

VERDI OPERAS

Aïda, Falstaff, Il Trovatore (The Troubadour), La Forza del Destino (The Force of Destiny), La Traviata (The Fallen Woman), Macbeth, Nabucco, Otello, Rigoletto, Un Ballo in Maschera (A Masked Ball).

verse *n* (5) poesy, rhyme; (6) poetry, stanza; (8) doggerel.

versed *adj* (6) expert; (7) skilled, trained; (8) familiar, schooled; (9) competent, practised, qualified; (10) acquainted, conversant, proficient; (11) experienced; (12) accomplished; (13) knowledgeable.

version I *n* 1 (4) form, kind, type; (5) model; (6) design; (7) variant; 2 (7) account, reading; (9) portrayal, rendering; (10) adaptation; (11) translation; (14) interpretation; II *cryptic* ANAGRAM CUE.

very I *adv* (5) truly, (6) deeply, highly, really; (7) acutely, awfully, greatly; (8) terribly; (9) extremely, unusually; (10) remarkably; (11) exceedingly, excessively; II *adj* 1 (4) real, same, true; (5) exact; (6) actual; (7) precise; 2 (4) mere, pure; (5) sheer; (6) simple.

vessel *n* 1 *see* ship; 2 (3) cup, pan, pot, urn; (4) bowl, dish, ewer; (5) cruse, glass, stoup; (6) flagon; (9) container.

Vesta *Rom. myth* the virgin goddess of the hearth. Aeneas was supposed to have brought the sacred flame of Vesta from Troy to Rome, where it was tended by six vestal virgins and never allowed to go out in case a national calamity followed.

vesta *n* a match.

vestige *n* (4) hint, sign; (5) scrap, shred, trace, whiff; (7) glimmer, inkling, remnant, residue; (8) evidence; (9) remainder, suspicion; (10) indication.

vestment *n* (4) gown, robe; (7) garment.

CHURCH VESTMENTS

(3) alb; (4) cope; (5) amice, apron, ephod, fanon, mitre, stole, tiara; (6) rochet, (7) biretta, cassock, chimere, orphrey, soutane, tunicle; (8) corporal, dalmatic, scapular, surplice.

---

veto I *n & v* (3) ban, bar; (5) block; (7) embargo; II *n* (7) refusal; (9) rejection; (11) prohibition; III *v* (6) forbid, refuse, reject; (8) disallow, prohibit; (2 words) rule out, turn down.

vex *v* (5) annoy, upset, worry; (6) bother, harass, hassle, pester; (7) disturb, provoke,

torment, trouble; (8) distress, irritate; (9) aggravate; (10) exasperate.

vicious *adj* (4) mean, wild; (5) cruel, nasty; (6) bitter, brutal, savage; (7) violent; (8) spiteful, virulent; (9) barbarous, ferocious, malicious, merciless; (10) relentless, vindictive.

victory *n* (3) win; (7) success, triumph; (8) conquest.

view I *n* 1 (5) scene, sight, vista; (7) outlook; (8) panorama, prospect; (9) landscape; (11) perspective; 2 (6) belief, notion; (7) feeling, opinion; (8) attitude; (9) judgement, sentiment; (10) impression, perception; (13) understanding; 3 (6) sketch, survey; (7) account, picture; (8) portrait; (9) portrayal; (11) description; II *v* 1 (3) see; (4) scan; (5) watch; (7) observe, witness; (2 words) look at; 2 (5) judge; (6) regard; (8) consider.

violent *adj* 1 (4) wild; (5) cruel, harsh, rough; (6) brutal, savage; (7) vicious; (8) forceful, forcible; (10) aggressive; (11) destructive, devastating; (12) bloodthirsty; 2 (5) acute, fiery, sharp; (6) severe, strong; (7) extreme, intense, painful; (8) powerful, vehement; (10) passionate; (12) ungovernable, unrestrained; (14) uncontrollable.

VIP *see* **celebrity**.

Virgil *lit.* Roman epic poet, author of the *Eclogues*, *Georgics* and the *Aeneid*, the story of the founding of Rome by Aeneas, a Trojan who escaped the fall and sack of Troy. Virgil also appears as the guide of **Dante** through hell and purgatory in the first two books of *The Divine Comedy*.

Virgo *astrol. & astron.* the constellation that is the sixth sign of the zodiac, also known as the Virgin.

virtue *n* 1 (5) worth; (6) honour; (7) probity, justice; (8) chastity, goodness, morality; (9) integrity, principle, rectitude; (10) excellence, worthiness; (11) uprightness; (13) righteousness; 2 (5) asset, merit; (7) benefit, quality; (8) strength; (9) advantage.

CARDINAL VIRTUES

fortitude; justice; patience; prudence; temperance.

THEOLOGICAL VIRTUES

faith; hope; charity.

---

virtuous *adj* (4) good; (5) moral; (6) chaste, modest, worthy; (7) upright; (9) blameless, exemplary; (10) honourable; (11) clean-living; (13) incorruptible, unimpeachable; (14) irreproachable.

vision *n* 1 (5) sight; (6) seeing; (8) eyesight; 2 (4) idea; (5) dream, ideal, image; (6) mirage, wraith; (7) fantasy, phantom, spectre; (8) daydream, delusion, illusion; (10) apparition, conception; (13) hallucination; 3 (10) perception; (11) discernment, penetration.

vital *adj* 1 (3) key; (5) basic; (7) crucial; (8) critical, decisive; (9) essential, important, necessary, requisite; (10) imperative; (11) fundamental, life-or-death, significant; (13) indispensable; 2 (6) lively; (7) dynamic, vibrant; (8) spirited, vigorous; (9) energetic, vivacious.

vivid *adj* 1 (6) bright, strong; (7) glowing, intense, vibrant; (8) dazzling; (9) brilliant, colourful; 2 (5) clear, sharp; (7) graphic; (8) distinct, dramatic, lifelike, powerful, striking; (9) memorable, realistic; (10) expressive.

voice I *n* 1 (4) tone; (6) speech; (10) expression, inflection, intonation; 2 (3) say; (4) view, vote; (7) opinion; II *v* (3) air; (5) utter; (7) express; (10) articulate.

volcano *n* mountain with a crater and the capacity to erupt and throw out molten lava and magma.

VOLCANOES

(4) Etna (It.), Fuji (Jap.), Kaba (Indonesia); (5) Hekla (Iceland), Katla (Iceland), Pelee (Martinique); (6) Colima (Mex.), Erebus (Antarctica), Sangay (Ecuador); (7) Surtsey (Iceland), Vulcano (It.); (8) Fujiyama (Jap.), Krakatoa (*or* Krakatau) (Indonesia), Vesuvius (It.); (9) Stromboli (It.); (2+ words) Mount St Helens (US).

---

volt *cryptic* abbreviated as V.

volume I *n* 1 (4) bulk, mass, size; (5) sound; (6) amount; (8) capacity, loudness, quantity; (9) amplitude; 2 (4) book, tome; (5) issue; (11) publication; II *cryptic* 1 abbreviated as VOL; 2 use an abbreviation for a measure of capacity, *e.g.* CC, CL, GAL.

vote I *v* (5) elect; (6) ballot, choose, return; (7) propose, suggest; II *n* (4) poll; (5) cross; (6) ballot; (8) election, suffrage; (9) franchise; (10) referendum; III *cryptic* letter X.

vow I *n & v* (6) pledge; (7) promise; II *n* (5) swear; (6) affirm, devote; (7) profess; (8) dedicate.

vowel *n* A, E, I, O or U.

Vulcan *Rom. myth* the god of fire and metalworking, whose forge was supposed to be beneath volcanoes where he worked with the **Cyclops** making thunderbolts for Jupiter. He was the husband of **Venus**, and father of **Cupid**, and was said to be lame as a result of being thrown out of heaven by Jupiter for taking Juno's part against him. He was also known as Mulciber, and was the equivalent of the Greek Hephaestus.

vulgar *adj* (4) rude; (5) crude, flashy, gaudy; (6) coarse, common, risqué, tawdry; (7) ill-bred, uncouth; (8) impolite, indecent, plebeian; (9) tasteless, unrefined.

W

W *abbrev* tungsten, watt, west.

w *abbrev* wicket, wide, wife, with.

wage I wage *or* **wages** *n* (3) fee, pay; (4) hire; (5) money; (6) reward, salary; (7) payment; (8) earnings; (10) recompense; (12) remuneration; **II** *v* (6) pursue; (7) conduct; (8) practise; (9) undertake; (2 words) carry on, engage in.

wait *v* **1** (4) rest, stay; (5) delay, pause; (6) linger, remain; (8) hesitate; **2** (5) serve; (6) attend; (8) minister.

wake I *v* (4) rise, stir; (5) arise, rouse; (6) arouse, excite; (7) animate; (9) stimulate; **II** *n* **1** (5) vigil, watch; (7) funeral; **2** (4) wash; (5) track, trail, waves; (8) backwash.

walk I *n & v* (4) hike, pace, plod, step, trek; (5) amble, march, tramp; (6) ramble, stride, stroll, trudge, wander; (7) saunter, traipse; (9) promenade; **II** *n* (4) gait, lane, path; (5) alley, route, trail; (6) avenue; (8) pavement; (14) constitutional.

wander I *v* (3) err; (4) roam, rove, veer, wind; (5) drift, range, stray; (6) depart, ramble, swerve; (7) deviate, diverge, meander, saunter; **II wander** *or* **wandering** *cryptic* ANAGRAM CUE.

wanderer *n* (5) gypsy, nomad, rover, stray; (6) ranger; (7) drifter, vagrant, voyager; (8) vagabond; (9) itinerant, traveller.

want I *n & v* (4) lack, need, wish; (5) fancy; (6) demand, desire; **II** *v* (4) miss; (5) covet, crave; (7) require; (2 words) call for, hunger for, long for, pine for, thirst for, yearn for; **III** *n* (6) dearth, misery; (7) poverty; (8) shortage; (10) deficiency, inadequacy; (13) insufficiency; **IV** *cryptic* something must be added to the main part of the answer to complete it, as in: 'Henry wants nothing to make a show of saintliness' (4) = halo.

war *n* (6) battle, combat, enmity, strife; (7) warfare; (8) campaign, conflict, fighting, struggle; (11) hostilities; (12) belligerence.

ward I *n* **1** (4) area, room, unit, zone; (7) quarter; (8) district, division, precinct; **2** (5) minor; (8) protégée; (9) dependant; **II** *v* (5) avert, avoid, block, parry, repel; (6) thwart; (2 words) fend off, stave off, turn aside.

warm *adj* **1** (3) hot; (5) tepid; **2** (4) kind; (6) genial, hearty; (7) affable, cordial; (8) friendly; (9) welcoming; (12) affectionate; **3** (6) ardent; (7) devoted, fervent, intense, zealous; (10) passionate; (12) enthusiastic, wholehearted; **4** (4) rich; (6) mellow.

warship *n* (3) MTB, sub; (5) sloop; (7) cruiser, frigate, monitor; (8) corvette; (9) destroyer, minelayer, submarine; (10) battleship; (11) dreadnought, minesweeper; (2+ words) aircraft carrier, motor torpedo boat.

wash I *v & n* (4) bath; (5) clean, rinse, scrub; (6) douche, shower; (7) shampoo; **II** *v* (5) bathe; (7) cleanse, launder; **III** *n* **1** (7) laundry; **2** (4) wake; (5) trail.

waste I *v* **1** (4) blow; (6) lavish, misuse; (8) misspend, squander; (9) dissipate; (2 words) fritter away, throw away; **2** (5) drain, erode; (6) shrink; (7) consume, exhaust, shrivel; **II** *n* (4) junk; (5) dregs, dross, scrap, slops, trash; (6) debris, litter; (7) garbage, rubbish; (8) effluent; **III** *adj* **1** (5) extra, spare; (6) excess, unused; (7) useless; (8) unwanted; (9) worthless; (11) superfluous; **2** (4) bare, wild; (5) empty; (6) barren, dreary; (8) desolate; (11) uninhabited; (12) uncultivated.

watch I *v* **1** (3) see; (4) scan, view; (6) regard, survey; (7) observe, witness; (2 words) look at; **2** (4) mind, tend; (5) guard, track; (7) monitor, protect; (2+ words) keep an eye on, keep a lookout, pay attention; **II** *n* **1** (6) hunter; (8) repeater; (9) timepiece; (10) half-hunter; **2**

(4) duty; (5) guard, vigil; (7) lookout; (11) observation; (12) surveillance.

watchful *adj* (4) wary; (5) alert, awake, chary; (7) heedful; (8) cautious, vigilant; (9) attentive, observant.

water I *n* (3) sea; (4) lake, pool; (5) ocean, river; (6) stream; **II** *v* **1** (3) wet; (4) soak; (5) flood, spray; (6) dampen, drench; (7) moisten; (8) irrigate, sprinkle; **2** (4) thin; (6) dilute, weaken; **3** (8) salivate.

waterfall *n* (5) chute, force; (6) rapids; (7) cascade; (8) cataract.

FAMOUS WATERFALLS

Angel Falls (Venezuela), Augrabies Falls (SA), Churchill Falls (Can.), Niagara Falls (Can./USA), Stanley Falls (Congo), Victoria Falls (Zimbabwe).

---

wave I *n* **1** (4) foam, surf; (5) surge, swell; (6) billow, comber, ripple, roller; (7) breaker, tsunami; (2 words) white horse; **2** (3) set; (4) curl, hair, perm; (6) marcel; **II** *v* **1** (4) sign; (6) beckon, signal; (7) gesture; (8) indicate; (11) gesticulate; **2** (4) flap, sway, waft; (5) shake, swing; (6) quiver; (7) flutter; (8) brandish, flourish.

way *n* **1** (4) lane, path, road; (5) route, track, trail; (6) avenue, course, street; (7) channel, highway, passage; (9) direction; (12) thoroughfare; **2** (4) mode; (5) means; (6) manner, method, system; (7) fashion; (8) approach; (9) procedure, technique.

wayward I *adj* **1** (6) fickle, unruly, wilful; (8) perverse; (9) obstinate; (10) self-willed; (11) disobedient; (13) undisciplined; **2** (7) erratic; (9) irregular; (10) inaccurate; (13) unpredictable; **II** *cryptic* ANAGRAM CUE.

weak *adj* **1** (3) low; (5) faint, frail; (6) feeble, flimsy, infirm, sickly, slight; (7) exposed, fragile; (8) delicate, helpless, impotent; (9) deficient, powerless; (10) inadequate, vulnerable; (11) defenceless; (12) unconvincing; **2** (4) soft; (8) cowardly; (9) spineless; (10) indecisive, irresolute; (11) ineffectual, ineffective; **3** (4) thin; (5) runny; (6) dilute, watery; (7) insipid; (9) tasteless.

wealth *n* **1** (4) cash; (5) funds, goods, means, money; (6) assets, estate, riches; (7) capital, fortune; (8) opulence, property; (9) affluence, resources, substance; (11) possessions; **2** (5) store; (6) plenty; (9) abundance, profusion.

wealthy *adj* (4) rich; (5) flush; (6) loaded; (7) moneyed, opulent, rolling, well-off; (8) affluent, well-to-do; (10) prosperous, well-heeled.

weapon *n* (3) arm; (7) fire-arm.

TYPES OF WEAPON

(3) axe, bow, gat, gun, rod, SAM.

(4) bill, bolt, bomb, bren, club, Colt, cosh, dart, dirk, épée, foil, ICBM, kris, mace, mine, MIRV, pike, sten, whip.

(5) A-bomb, arrow, baton, blade, bolas, H-bomb, knout, kukri, lance, Luger, Maxim, panga, rifle, sabre, sharp, sling, spear, sword.

(6) air-gun, Bofors, cannon, cudgel, dagger, Mauser, mortar, musket, Napalm, pistol, pompom, pop-gun, rapier, rocket, six-gun, Webley.

(7) assegai, bayonet, bazooka, bombard, caltrop, carbine, cutlass, grenade, halberd, hand-gun, harpoon, hatchet, javelin, longbow, machete, pump-gun, shotgun, sidearm, torpedo, trident, Walther, warhead.

(8) arbalest, arquebus, basilisk, blowpipe, bludgeon, catapult, claymore, crossbow, culverin, falchion, howitzer, land-mine, Oerlikon, partisan, repeater, revolver, scimitar, shrapnel, skean-dhu, stiletto, tomahawk, tommy-gun.

(9) artillery, automatic, battleaxe, booby-trap, boomerang, derringer, flintlock, matchlock, slingshot, truncheon.

(10) broadsword, fieldpiece, flick-knife, incendiary, knobkerrie, Lee-Enfield, machine-gun,

list continued over

---

nightstick, peacemaker, scatter-gun, shillelagh, six-shooter, sword-stick, Winchester. (11) blockbuster, blunderbuss, depth-charge. (12) breech-loader, flame-thrower, fowling-piece, Martini-Henry, mitrailleuse, muzzle-loader. (13) knuckleduster, submachine-gun; (2 words) guided missile.

weather I *n* (7) climate; (10) conditions; **II** *v* **1** (6) harden, season; (7) toughen; **2** (5) stand; (6) endure, resist; (7) survive; (8) overcome, surmount; (9) withstand; (2 words) come through, ride out, rise above.

WEATHER PHENOMENA

(3) dew, fog, ice.

(4) gale, hail, haze, mist, rain, smog, snow, thaw, wind.

(5) cloud, frost, sleet, slush, storm.

(6) breeze, deluge, shower, squall.

(7) cyclone, drizzle, drought, monsoon, tempest, thunder, tornado, typhoon.

(8) blizzard, downpour, heatwave, sunshine.

(9) hurricane, lightning, snowstorm, whirlwind.

---

wed I *v* (4) join; (5) marry, unite; **II** *adj* (5) mated; (6) paired; (7) hitched, married, spliced.

Wednesday *n* fourth day of the week, named after Woden, abbreviated as W or WED.

weigh *v* **1** (5) poise; (6) assess; (7) measure; **2** (6) ponder; (7) examine; (8) consider, evaluate; (2 words) chew over, mull over, reflect on; **3** (6) burden (7) afflict, oppress, trouble.

weight I *n* **1** (4) load, mass, troy; (5) force; (7) gravity, tonnage; (8) poundage; (9) heaviness; (11) avoirdupois; **2** (6) impact, moment; (9) substance; (10) importance; (11) consequence; (12) significance; **II** *v* (4) bias, load; (5) slant; (6) burden; (8) handicap; (9) prejudice, unbalance.

MEASURES OF WEIGHT

(3) ton; (4) dram, gram, kilo, pood; (5) carat, ounce, pound, stone, tonne; (6) drachm, gramme; (7) centner, kiloton, megaton, quarter, quintal, scruple; (8) decagram, decigram, kilogram, nanogram; (9) centigram, hectogram, microgram, milligram; (10) kilogramme; (11) centigramme, hectogramme, milligramme, pennyweight; (13) hundredweight.

---

well I *adj* (3) fit; (4) hale; (5) sound; (6) robust, strong; (7) healthy; **II** *adv* **1** (4) ably; (8) expertly, properly; (9) correctly, skilfully; (11) competently; (12) successfully; (14) satisfactorily; **2** (5) fully; (7) greatly; (9) carefully; (10) completely, thoroughly; **III** *n* (5) fount; (6) source, spring; (8) fountain; (9) reservoir; **IV** *v* (4) brim, flow, gush, pour; (5) flood, spout, spurt.

west I *n* (8) occident; **II** *cryptic* abbreviated as W.

wet I *adj* **1** (4) damp, dank; (5) humid, moist, rainy, soggy; (6) clammy, marshy, soaked, sodden, watery; (7) pouring, soaking, showery, sopping; (8) drenched; **2** (4) soft, **weak**; (6) feeble; (7) wimpish; (10) namby-pamby; **II** *v* (4) damp, soak; (5) flood, spray, steep, water; (6) dampen, drench, splash; (7) moisten; (8) irrigate, saturate, sprinkle.

whip I *n & v* (4) cane, lash; (5) birch, strap; (7) scourge; **II** *n* (3) cat; (6) switch; (10) riding-crop; (13) cat-o'-nine-tails; **III** *v* **1** (4) beat, flog, goad, urge; (6) punish, thrash; (8) chastise; (10) flagellate; **2** (4) jerk, pull, tear; (5) whisk; (6) snatch; **3** (3) fly, run; (4) dart, dash, rush; (5) flash; **4** (5) **steal**.

whirl I *n & v* (4) reel, roll, spin, turn; (5) swirl, twirl, twist, wheel, whisk; (6) circle, spiral; (9) pirouette; **II** *v* (5) pivot; (6) gyrate, rotate; **III** *n* **1** (8) gyration, rotation; (10) revolution; **2** (4) daze; (6) bustle, flurry, hubbub, tumult, uproar; (9) commotion, confusion; **IV** *cryptic* ANAGRAM CUE.

wicked I *adj* (3) bad; (4) foul, evil, vile; (6) sinful; (7) corrupt, harmful, heinous, immoral, ungodly, vicious; (8) shameful, spiteful, terrible; (9) malicious; (10) abominable, degenerate, iniquitous; (11) mischievous; (12) unprincipled; II *cryptic* = with a wick.

wide *adj* (4) full, vast; (5) baggy, broad, loose, roomy; (7) dilated, general, immense; (8) expanded, spacious; (9) extensive; (13) comprehensive.

wife *n* (4) mate; (5) bride; (6) missus, spouse; (7) consort, (8) helpmeet; (2+ words) ball and chain, better half, old dutch, old woman, other half, trouble and strife.

wild I *adj* 1 (5) waste; (6) brutal, rugged, savage; (7) natural, untamed; (8) desolate; (9) barbarous; (11) uncivilised (*or* uncivilized); (12) uncontrolled, uncultivated, ungovernable, unrestrained; (13) uninhabitable; (14) uncontrollable, undomesticated; 2 (5) rough, rowdy; (6) choppy, raging, stormy, unruly, untidy; (7) lawless, riotous, unkempt, violent; (8) blustery; (9) turbulent; (10) boisterous, disordered, disorderly; (11) tempestuous; 3 (3) mad; (4) rash; (5) angry, crazy; (7) foolish, furious, wayward; (8) demented, frenzied, heedless, reckless; (9) foolhardy, irregular; (10) irrational; (11) impractical, unrealistic; (13) impracticable; II **wild** *or* **wildly** *cryptic* ANAGRAM CUE, as in: 'Beast sows wild oats before tea' (5) = stoat.

Wilde, Oscar *lit.* Irish writer and wit whose career ended in scandal after his admission of homosexuality and conviction for immoral practices. Wilde's best-known works include: An Ideal Husband, A Woman of No Importance, Lady Windermere's Fan, Salome, The Ballad of Reading Gaol, The Importance of Being Earnest, The Picture of Dorian Gray.

wind¹ I *v* (4) bend, coil, loop, roll, wrap; (5) curve, twine, twist; (6) ramble, spiral, zigzag; (7) embrace, meander, wreathe; (8) encircle; II *cryptic* ANAGRAM CUE.

wind² *n* (4) blow, gale, gust, puff; (5) blast, storm; (6) breath, breeze, squall; (7) current, draught, tornado; (9) hurricane.

WINDS IN CLASSICAL MYTHOLOGY

N wind – Boreas, Aquilo
NE wind – Kaikas
E wind – Eurus
SE wind – Volturnus
S wind – Notus, Auster
SW wind – Libs, Afer, Africus
W wind – Zephyr(us), Favonius
NW wind – Caurus, Thrascias

WORLD WINDS

(4) bise (Alps), bora (Adriatic), föhn (Alps), helm (Lake District), puna (Peru).

(5) chili (N Afr.), gibli (N Afr.), norte (Mex.), trade (tropics), zonda (Arg.).

(6) ghibli (N Afr.), samoon (Iran), simoom (*or* simoon) (Arabia), solano (Sp.).

(7) chinook (Rockies), etesian (Med.), gregale (Med.), meltemi (Med.), mistral (S France), monsoon (Ind. Ocean), pampero (Andes), sirocco (Med.).

(8) levanter (Med.), scirocco (Med.), williwaw (S Am.).

(9) harmattan (W Afr.), libecchio (Med.).

(10) tramontana (It.).

(12) brickfielder (Aus.).

(2 words) berg wind (SA), Cape doctor (SA), Santa Anna (US), trade wind (tropics).

---

wine *n* (3) red; (4) rosé; (5) blush, white; (2 words) the grape.

WINES

(4) Asti, Hock, Port, Saki.

(5) Anjou, Macon, Médoc, Mosel, Rhine, Tokay.

(6) Barsac, Beaune, Claret, Graves, Merlot, Sherry, Shiraz.

(7) Chablis, Chianti, Cinsaut, Madeira, Marsala, Moselle, Retsina, Rhenish, Vouvray.   *list continued over*

(8) Bordeaux, Burgundy, Cabernet, Frascati, Montilla, Muscadet.

(9) Champagne, Lambrusco, Minervois, Sauternes.

(10) Beaujolais.

(13) Liebfraumilch.

(2+ words) Châteauneuf du Pape, Côte du Rhône, Côte d'Or, Nuits St Georges, Pouilly Fuissé, St Emilion.

wise *adj* 1 (5) aware, canny, sound; (6) astute, clever, shrewd; (7) prudent; (8) rational, sensible; (9) advisable, judicious; (10) reasonable; (11) intelligent; 2 (7) erudite, knowing, learned; (8) informed; (9) sagacious; (11) experienced.

within *cryptic* HIDDEN WORD CUE.

without I *prep* 1 (6) bereft; (7) lacking; 2 (7) outside; II *cryptic* 1 omit the letter or letters referred to from a word, as in: 'Without afternoon tea, cue giver takes flower and goes on march' (9) = protester (cue giver = prompter, afternoon tea = pmt, flower = river = Test); 2 place the letters of one word around those of another, as in: 'Thus without warning converts to Japanese religion' (6) = Shinto.

Wodehouse, P. G. (Pelham Grenville) English comic writer.

WODEHOUSE CREATIONS

Aunt Agatha (Bertie Wooster's demanding and formidable aunt)

Bertie Wooster (well-meaning but ineffectual upper-class twit hero of Wodehouse's most famous novels)

Bingo Little (friend of Bertie Wooster)

Blandings Castle (seat of Lord Emsworth)

Drones Club (Bertie Wooster's club)

Empress of Blandings (Lord Emsworth's favourite pig)

Gussie Fink-Nottle (friend of Bertie Wooster)

Jeeves (Bertie Wooster's omniscient and versatile valet)

Lord Emsworth (elderly pig-fancying aristocrat)

Psmith (a journalist)

Woden *Anglo-Saxon myth* the chief god, equivalent to **Odin**.

woman I *n* (4) girl, lady; (6) female; II *cryptic* use any female forename, *see* **girl**.

wonderful *adj* (3) fab; (5) brill, great, super; (6) superb; (7) amazing, awesome; (8) fabulous, smashing, terrific; (9) brilliant, fantastic; (10) incredible, marvellous, phenomenal, stupendous, tremendous; (11) magnificent, outstanding, sensational; (12) breath-taking, unbelievable.

wood *n* 1 (4) deal, pine; (6) lumber, timber; (8) mahogany; *see also* **tree**; 2 (5) copse, grove; (6) forest; (7) coppice, spinney, thicket; (10) plantation.

word *n* 1 (4) name, term; (7) vocable; 2 (4) chat, talk; (10) discussion; (12) conversation; 3 (4) hint, line, news, note; (6) letter, notice; (7) message; (8) bulletin; (13) communication; 4 (3) vow; (4) oath; (6) pledge; (7) promise.

Wordsworth, William *lit.* English Romantic poet. Wordsworth's best-known works include: Daffodils, Lyrical Ballads, The Excursion, The Immortality Ode (Intimations of Immortality), The Lucy Poems, The Prelude, The Rainbow, Tintern Abbey.

work I *n & v* (4) slog, toil; (5) graft; (6) labour; II *n* 1 (6) effort; (8) drudgery, exertion, industry; 2 (3) job; (4) duty, task; (5) trade; (6) career; (7) calling; (8) business, vocation; (10) employment, livelihood, occupation, profession; 3 (4) book, opus, play; (8) creation; (11) composition; III *v* 1 (5) slave; (6) drudge; 2 (2) go; (3) run, use; (6) handle, manage; control, operate; (8) function; 3 (3) dig; (4) form, till; (5) knead, mould, shape; (7) fashion, process; IV *cryptic* often letters OP = opus.

worker I *n* (4) hand; (7) artisan; (8) employee, labourer; (9) operative; tradesman; (11) proletarian; II *cryptic* letters ANT or BEE.

worth *n* (3) use; (4) cost, good, help; (5) avail, merit, point, price, value; (6) object, profit, virtue; (7) benefit, purpose, service; (9) advantage; (10) excellence, usefulness.

worthless *adj* (3) bad; (4) idle, poor, vain; (5) cheap; (6) futile, paltry, tawdry, trashy; (7) useless; (8) rubbishy, trifling, unusable; (9) fruitless, pointless, value-less; (10) unavailing; (12) unproductive; (14) good-for-nothing.

worthy *adj* **1** (4) good; (6) decent, honest; (7) upright; (8) laudable; (9) admirable, deserving; (10) creditable, honourable; (11) commendable, meritorious; **2** (3) fit; (8) suitable; (11) appropriate.

wreck I *v* (4) ruin; (5) smash; (7) destroy, shatter; (8) demolish; (9) devastate; (2 words) write off; **II** *n* (4) loss, mess, ruin; (7) remains, remnant; (8) shambles; (9) ruination; (11) destruction, devastation; **III** *cryptic* ANAGRAM CUE.

writer *n* **1** (4) hack, poet; (5) clerk; (6) author, scribe; (7) diarist; (8) essayist, novelist; (9) columnist, dramatist, pen-pusher, scribbler, secretary, wordsmith; **II** *cryptic* a pen, *see* pen.

SOME FAMOUS WRITERS

(3) Boz (= Dickens), Eco (Umberto, It.), Fry (Christopher, UK), Gay (John, UK), Kyd (Thomas, UK), Lee (Harper, US/Laurie, UK), Nin (Anaïs, US), Poe (Edgar Allan, US), Pye (Henry, UK).

(4) Abse (Danny, UK), Amis (Kingsley/Martin, UK), Behn (Aphra, UK), Bolt (Robert, UK), Bond (Edward, UK), Buck (Pearl S., US), Dahl (Roald, UK), Ford (John, UK), Gems (Pam, UK), Gide (André, Fr.), Gray (Thomas/Simon, UK), Gunn (Thom, UK/US), Hall (Willis, UK), Hare (David, UK), Hill (Geoffrey, UK), Hood (Thomas, UK), Hope (Anthony, UK), Hugo (Victor, Fr.), Hunt (Leigh, UK), Jong (Erica, US), King (Stephen, US), Lamb (Charles, UK), Lear (Edward, UK), Li-Po (Ch.), Livy (Rom.), Loos (Anita, US), Mann (Heinrich/Thomas, Ger.), Muir (Edwin, UK), Nash (Ogden,

US), Ovid (Rom.), Owen (Wilfred, UK), Pope (Alexander, UK), Puzo (Mario, US), Rhys (Jean, UK), Roth (Philip, US), Rowe (Nicholas, UK), Sadi (Pers.), Saki (= H.H. Munro, UK), Sand (George, Fr.), Shaw (George Bernard, Ire./UK), Snow (C.P., UK), Tate (Nahum, UK), Uris (Leon, US), Vega (Lope de, Sp.), Wain (John, UK), West (Rebecca, UK), Wouk (Herman, US), Zola (Emile, Fr.).

(5) Adams (Richard, UK), Albee (Edward, US), Arden (John, UK), Auden (W. H., UK), Bacon (Francis, UK), Behan (Brendan, Ire.), Blake (William, UK), Bragg (Melvyn, UK), Burns (Robert, Scot.), Byatt (A.S., UK), Byron (Lord George Gordon, UK), Camus (Albert, Fr.), Capek (Carel, Cz.), Clare (John, UK), Crane (Hart, US), Dante (Alighieri, It.), Defoe (Daniel, UK), Donne (John, UK), Dumas (Alexandre, Fr.), Eliot (George, UK/T. S., US/UK), Frayn (Michael, UK), Friel (Brian, Ire.), Frost (Robert, US), Genet (Jean, Fr.), Gogol (Nikolai, Russ.), Gorki (Maxim, Russ.), Gosse (Edmund, UK), Gower (John, UK), Grass (Gunter, Ger.), Haley (Alex, US), Hardy (Thomas, UK), Harte (Bret, US), Havel (Vaclav, Cz.), Heine (Heinrich, Ger.), Hesse (Hermann, Ger.), Homer (Gk), Ibsen (Henrik, Norw.), Innes (Hammond, UK), James (Henry, US/P.D., UK), Johns (Capt. W.E., UK), Kafka (Franz, Cz.), Keats (John, UK), Keyes (Sidney, UK), Lewis (C.S., UK), Lodge (David, UK), Lorca (Federico García, Sp.), Lucan (Rom.), Mamet (David, US), Marsh (Ngaio, NZ), Milne (A.A., UK), Moore (Marianne, US/Thomas, Ire.), Noyes (Alfred, UK), Odets (Clifford, US), O'Hara (John, US), Orczy (Baroness, UK/Hung.), Orton (Joe, UK), Paton (Alan, SA), Peake (Mervyn, UK),

list continued over

Perse (St Jean, Fr.), Plath (Sylvia, US), Pound (Ezra, US), Powys (John Cowper/Llewellyn, T.F., UK), Rilke (Rainer Maria, A.), Sagan (Françoise, Fr.), Scott (Sir Walter, UK), Shute (Neville, Aus.), Smith (Stevie, UK), Synge (John, Ire.), Tasso (Torquato, It.), Twain (Mark, US), Verne (Jules, Fr.), Watts (Isaac, UK), Waugh (Evelyn, UK), Wilde (Oscar, Ire./UK), Wolfe (Thomas/Tom, US), Woolf (Virginia, UK), Yeats (W.B., Ire.).

(6) Alcott (Louisa M., US), Aldiss (Brian, UK), Ambler (Eric, UK), Archer (Jeffrey, UK), Arnold (Matthew, UK), Asimov (Isaac, US), Austen (Jane, UK), Austin (Alfred, UK), Bagley (Desmond, UK), Balzac (Honoré de, Fr.), Barrie (J.M., UK), Belloc (Hilaire, UK), Bellow (Saul, US), Binchy (Maeve, Ire.), Binyon (Laurence, UK), Bishop (Elizabeth, US), Blyton (Enid, UK), Borges (Jorge Luis, Arg.), Borrow (George, UK), Braine (John, UK), Brecht (Berthold, Ger.), Brontë (Anne, Charlotte, Emily, UK), Brooke (Rupert, UK), Buchan (John, UK), Bunyan (John, UK), Butler (Samuel, UK), Capote (Truman, US), Cather (Willa, US), Coward (Noel, UK), Cowper (William, UK), Crabbe (George, UK), Cronin (A.J., UK), Daudet (Alphonse, Fr.), Dowson (Ernest, UK), Dryden (John, UK), Evelyn (John, UK), Fowles (John, UK), Frisch (Max, Switz.), Fugard (Athol, SA), Fuller (Roy, UK), Gibbon (Edward, UK), Goethe (J.W. von, Ger.), Graves (Robert, UK), Greene (Graham, UK), Hailey (Arthur, US), Harris (Joel Chandler, US), Heller (Joseph, US), Hesiod (Gk), Horace (Rom.), Hughes (Ted, UK), Irving (Washington, US), Jerome (Jerome K., UK), Jonson (Ben, UK), Landor (Walter Savage, UK), Larkin (Philip, UK), Lively (Penelope, UK), London (Jack, US), Lowell (Amy/Robert, US), Ludlum

(Robert, US), Mailer (Norman, US), Malory (Thomas, UK), Miller (Arthur, US), Milton (John, UK), Morris (William, UK), Nesbit (E. E., UK), Musset (Alfred de, Fr.), O'Casey (Sean, Ire.), O'Neill (Eugene, US), Orwell (George, UK), Parker (Dorothy, US), Pindar (Gk), Pinero (Arthur Wing, UK), Pinter (Harold, UK), Porter (Katherine Anne, US), Potter (Beatrix, UK), Powell (Anthony, UK), Proust (Marcel, Fr.), Racine (Jean, Fr.), Runyon (Damon, US), Ruskin (John, UK), Sappho (Gk), Sartre (Jean-Paul, Fr.), Seneca (Rom.), Sewell (Anna, UK), Sharpe (Tom, SA/UK), Sidney (Sir Philip, UK), Steele (Richard, Ire.), Sterne (Laurence, UK), Stoker (Bram, UK), Tagore (Rabindrath, Ind.), Thomas (Dylan, UK), Updike (John, US), Virgil (Rom.), Weldon (Faye, UK), Wesker (Arnold, UK), Wilder (Thornton, US).

(7) Ackroyd (Peter, UK), Addison (Joseph, UK), Anouilh (Jean, Fr.), Ariosto (Ludovico, It.), Baldwin (James, US), Beckett (Samuel, Ire./ Fr.), Bentley (Edmund Clerihew, UK), Blunden (Edmund, UK), Boswell (James, UK), Bridges (Robert, UK), Büchner (Georg, Ger.), Burgess (Anthony, UK), Caedmon (early Eng.), Chaucer (Geoffrey, Eng.), Carlyle (Thomas, UK), Carroll (Lewis, UK), Chekhov (Anton, Russ.), Cobbett (William, UK), Cocteau (Jean, Fr.), Coetzee (J. M., SA), Colette (Fr.), Collins (Wilkie/ William, UK), Cookson (Catherine, UK), Deeping (Warwick, UK), Dickens (Charles, UK), Diderot (Denis, Fr.), Douglas (Keith/Norman, UK), Drabble (Margaret, UK), Durrell (Gerald/Lawrence, UK), Emerson (Ralph Waldo, US), Feydeau (Georges, Fr.), Flecker (James Elroy, UK), Fleming (Ian, UK),

list continued over

Forster (E.M., UK), Forsyth (Frederick, UK), Francis (Dick, UK), Gallico (Paul, UK), Gardner (Erle Stanley, US), Gaskell (Mrs Elizabeth, UK), Gilbert (W.S., UK), Goldoni (Carlo, It.), Grahame (Kenneth, UK), Haggard (Rider, UK), Hammett (Dashiell, US), Hampton (Christopher, UK), Hartley (L.P., UK), Hazlitt (William, UK), Hellman (Lillian, US), Herbert (George, UK), Herrick (Robert, UK), Higgins (Jack, UK), Hopkins (Gerard Manley, UK), Housman (A.E., UK), Ionesco (Eugene, Roma./Fr.), Johnson (Lionel/Dr Samuel, UK), Kerouac (Jack, US), Khayyam (Omar, Pers.), Kipling (Rudyard, UK), Le Carré (John, UK), Lessing (Doris, UK), Marlowe (Christopher, UK), Marquez (Gabriel Garcia, Colombia), Marryat (Capt. Frederick, UK), Martial (Rom.), Marvell (Andrew, UK), Maugham (Somerset, UK), McGough (Roger, UK), Mitford (Nancy, UK), Molière (Fr.), Moravia (Alberto, It.), Murdoch (Iris, UK), Nabokov (Vladimir, Russ./US), Naipaul (V. S., UK), Newbolt (Sir Henry, UK), Osborne (John, UK), , Plautus (Rom.), Pushkin (Alexander, Russ.), Pynchon (Thomas, US), Rendell (Ruth, UK), Rimbaud (Arthur, Fr.), Rostand (Edmond, Fr.), Rushdie (Salman, UK), Russell (Bertrand, UK), Saroyan (William, US), , Sassoon (Siegfried, UK)Shaffer (Peter *and* Anthony, UK), Shelley (Percy Bysshe, UK), Shepard (Sam, US), Simenon (Georges, Fr.), Sitwell (Dame Edith, UK), Skelton (John, UK), Southey (Robert, UK), Spender (Stephen, UK), Spenser (Edmund, UK), Stevens (Wallace, UK), Terence (Rom.), Thoreau (Henry, US), Thurber (James, US), Tolkien (J. R. R., UK), Tolstoy (Leo, Russ.), Travers (Ben, UK), Ustinov (Peter, UK), Webster (John, UK), Whiting (John, UK), Whitman (Walt, US), Wyndham (John, UK).

(8) Andersen (Hans Christian, Den.), Beaumont (Francis, UK), Beauvoir (Simone de, Fr.), Berryman (John, US), Betjeman (John, UK), Bradbury (Malcolm, UK/Ray, US), Brookner (Anita, UK), Browning (Robert, UK), Calderon (Pedro, Sp.), Caldwell (Erskine, US), Cartland (Barbara, UK), Catullus (Rom.), Chandler (Raymond, US), Congreve (William, UK), cummings (e. e., US), Davenant (Sir William, UK), Day Lewis (Cecil, UK), Deighton (Len, UK), de la Mare (Walter, UK), Disraeli (Benjamin, UK), Farquhar (George, Ire.), Faulkner (William, US), Flaubert (Gustave, Fr.), Fletcher (John, UK), Ginsberg (Allen, US), Huysmans (J.K., Fr.), Keneally (Thomas, Aus.), Kingsley (Thomas, UK), Koestler (Arthur, UK), Lawrence (D.H., UK), Macaulay (Lord Thomas, UK), Macneice (Louis, UK), Mallarmé (Stéphane, Fr.), Marivaux (Pierre, Fr.), Melville (Herman, US), Menander (Gk), Meredith (George, UK), Michener (James, US), Mortimer (John, UK), Petrarch (Francesco, It.), Philemon (Gk), Rabelais (François, Fr.), Rattigan (Terence, UK), Remarque (Erich Maria, Ger./US), Rossetti (Dante Gabriel *and* Christina, UK), Rousseau (Jean-Jacques, Switz.), Salinger (J. D., US), Schiller (Friedrich, Ger.), Sheridan (Richard Brinsley Ire./UK), Sillitoe (Alan, UK), Smollett (Thomas, UK), Spillane (Mickey, US), Stendhal (Fr.), Stoppard (Tom, Cz./UK), Vanbrugh (John, UK), Tennyson (Alfred, Lord, UK), Trollope (Anthony/Joanna, UK), Turgenev (Ivan, Russ), Verlaine (Paul, Fr.), Voltaire (Fr.), Vonnegut (Kurt, US), Wheatley (Denis, UK), Williams (Tennessee/William Carlos, US), Xenophon (Gk).

list continued over

(9) Aeschylus (Gk), Ainsworth (Harrison, UK), Allingham (Margery, UK), Ayckbourn (Alan, UK), Bleasdale (Alan, UK), Boccaccio (Giovanni, It.), Cervantes (Miguel de, Sp.), Charteris (Leslie, US), Coleridge (Samuel Taylor, UK), Corneille (Pierre, Fr.), Churchill (Caryl, UK), Dickinson (Emily, US), Du Maurier (Daphne/ Gerald, UK), Euripides (Gk), Goldsmith (Oliver, UK), Grossmith (George/Weedon, UK) Hauptmann (Gerhard, Ger.), Hawthorne (Nathaniel, US), Hemingway (Ernest, US), Highsmith (Patricia, US), Isherwood (Christopher, UK/ US), Lampedusa (Giuseppe, It.), Linklater (Eric, UK), Mansfield (Katherine, NZ/UK), Masefield (John, UK), Metalious (Grace, US), Middleton (Thomas, UK), Monsarrat (Nicholas, UK), Montaigne (Michel de, Fr.), Pasternak (Boris, Russ.), Priestley (J.B., UK), Schreiner (Olive, SA), Sophocles (Gk), Steinbeck (John, US), Stevenson (Robert Louis, UK), Swinburne (Algernon Charles, UK), Thackeray (William Makepeace, UK), Wodehouse (P.G., UK), Wycherley (William, UK).

(10) Bainbridge (Beryl, UK), Ballantyne (R.M., UK), Baudelaire (Charles, Fr.), Chesterton (G.K., UK), Dostoevsky (Fyodor, Russ.), Dürrenmatt (Friedrich, Switz.), Fitzgerald (Edward, UK *and* Scott, US), Galsworthy (John, UK), Longfellow (Henry Wadsworth, US), Maupassant (Guy de, Fr.),

Pirandello (Luigi, It.), Richardson (Samuel, UK), Schnitzler (Arthur, A.), Strindberg (August, Swe.), Waterhouse (Keith, UK), Wordsworth (William, UK).

(11) Delderfield (R.F., UK), Grillparzer (Franz, A.), Kazantzakis (Nicos, Gk), Shakespeare (William, UK), Yevtushenko (Yevgeny, Russ.).

(12) Aristophanes (Gk), Beaumarchais (Pierre, Fr.), Bulwer-Lytton (Edward, UK), Saint-Exupéry (Antoine de, Fr.), Solzhenitsyn (Alexander, Russ.).

wrong I *adj* 1 (3) off, out; (4) awry; (5) amiss, false; (6) faulty, untrue; (7) inexact; (8) improper, mistaken; (9) defective, erroneous, imprecise, incorrect; (10) fallacious, inaccurate; (12) illegitimate; (13) ungrammatical; 2 (3) bad; (4) evil; (6) sinful, unfair, unjust, wicked; (7) crooked, illegal, illicit, immoral; (8) criminal, unlawful; (9) dishonest, unethical; (11) blameworthy; 3 (5) inapt; (8) improper, unseemly; (10) unsuitable; (13) inappropriate; II *n* (3) sin; (5) abuse, crime; (6) injury; (7) misdeed, offence; (8) iniquity, trespass; (9) injustice; III *v* (4) harm, hurt; (6) ill-use, injure, malign; (8) ill-treat, maltreat, mistreat; (9) dishonour; IV **wrong** *or* **wrongly** *cryptic* ANAGRAM CUE.

wrongdoer *n* (5) felon; (6) sinner; (7) culprit; (8) criminal, evildoer, offender; (9) miscreant; (10) delinquent, law-breaker, trespasser; (12) transgressor.

wry I *adj* 1 (3) dry; (6) ironic; (7) mocking; (8) sardonic; (9) sarcastic; 2 (4) skew; (6) uneven, warped; (7) crooked, twisted; II *cryptic* ANAGRAM CUE.

X, Y, Z

X *abbrev* kiss, over 18 (film category), unknown quantity, 10 (Roman numeral).

Xerxes *hist.* king of Persia, who invaded Greece, was held back by the Spartans at Thermopylae and was defeated at the sea battle of Salamis.

Y *abbrev* yen, unknown quantity.

yacht *n* (4) boat; (6) dinghy; (7) cruiser; *see also* **sailing boat**.

yarn *n* 1 (4) wool; (5) fibre; (6) strand, thread; 2 (5) fable, story; (8) anecdote.

yellow *adj* 1 (4) gold; (5) blond, lemon; (6) blonde, flaxen; (8) primrose; 2 (6) afraid; (8) cowardly.

yield I *v* 1 (3) pay; (4) bear, earn, give; (6) return, supply; (7) furnish, produce, provide; (8) generate; 2 (4) cede; (5) allow; (6) permit, submit; (7) abandon, consent, succumb; (8) abdicate; (9) acquiesce, surrender; (10) capitulate, relinquish; (2 words) give in, give up, knuckle under; 3 (4) bend, sink; (6) buckle; (2 words) cave in, give way; II *n* (4) crop; (6) output, profit, return; (7) harvest, produce, product, revenue; (8) earnings.

yoke I *v* (3) tie; (4) join, link; (5) hitch, unite; (6) couple; (7) bracket, connect, harness; II *n* (6) burden; (7) bondage, slavery; (10) oppression; (11) subjugation.

young I *adj* (3) new; (4) baby; (5) green; (6) infant, recent; (8) immature, juvenile, youthful; (10) adolescent; II *n* (5) brood, issue; (6) babies, family, litter; (7) progeny; (8) children; (9) offspring.

youngster *n* (3) boy, kid; (4) baby, girl; (5) child, youth; (6) infant; (7) toddler; (8) juvenile, teenager.

youth *n* 1 (3) boy, kid, lad; (8) juvenile, teenager; (9) youngster; (10) adolescent; 2 (10) immaturity; (11) adolescence.

yttrium *cryptic* abbreviated as Y.

Z *abbrev* unknown quantity; the last, the end.

zeal *n* (4) fire, zest; (5) gusto, verve; (6) ardour, warmth; (7) fervour, passion; (8) devotion, keenness; (9) eagerness; (10) dedication, enthusiasm, fanaticism.

zealot *n* (5) bigot; (7) fanatic; (8) militant, partisan; (9) extremist.

zealous *adj* (4) keen; (5) eager; (6) ardent; (7) devoted, earnest, fervent; (9) dedicated; (10) passionate; (11) impassioned.

zero *n* (3) nil; (4) duck, love; (5) zilch; (6) nought; (7) nothing.

zest *n* 1 (4) zeal; (5) gusto; (6) relish; (8) appetite; (9) enjoyment; 2 (4) tang; (5) spice; (6) savour; (8) piquancy; 3 (4) peel.

Zeus *Gk myth* the king of the gods and ruler of Olympus. The son of **Cronos**, whom he overthrew to rule in conjunction with his brothers, **Poseidon**, who ruled the sea, and **Hades**, who ruled the **Underworld**. Zeus was married to his sister **Hera**, but was famous for his affairs with other goddesses and with mortals. In order to mate with mortal women and perform without showing himself in his divine form, he underwent many transformations, the most notable being: a bull for Europa, a cloud for Io, a shower of gold for Danae, a swan for Leda. Roman equivalent: **Jupiter**.

zodiac *n*

SIGNS OF THE ZODIAC

Aries (Ram), Taurus (Bull), Gemini (Twins), Cancer (Crab), Leo (Lion), Virgo (Virgin), Libra (Scales), Scorpio (Scorpion), Sagittarius (Archer), Capricorn (Goat), Aquarius (Water-carrier), Pisces (Fishes).
